PEARSON CUSTOM BUSINESS RESOURCES

Compiled by

BUSA-40049
Cost Accounting

Pearson Learning Solutions

New York   Boston   San Francisco
London   Toronto   Sydney   Tokyo   Singapore   Madrid
Mexico City   Munich   Paris   Cape Town   Hong Kong   Montreal

Senior Vice President, Editorial and Marketing: Patrick F. Boles
Editor: Ana Díaz-Caneja
Development Editor: Abbey Lee Briggs
Operations Manager: Eric M. Kenney
Production Manager: Jennifer Berry
Art Director: Renée Sartell
Cover Designer: Renée Sartell

Cover Art: Courtesy of EyeWire/Getty Images and PhotoDisc/Getty Images. Photodisc, "Globe surrounded by business people on computer monitors," courtesy of Photodisc/Getty Images. Dave Cutler (Artist), "Man Dropping Coins Into Glass Jar," courtesy of David Cutler/Images.com. Dave Cutler (Artist), "Three Coins in Glass Jar," courtesy of David Cutler/Images.com. Dean Turner, "Stock Vector: Global Finance" Courtesy of Dean Turner/iStockphoto. Hal Bergman, "Refinery Silhouette" Courtesy of Hal Bergman/iStockphoto. Dan Barnes, "Cargo Container Ship Aerial View" Courtesy of Dan Barnes/iStockphoto. Franc Podgorsek, "Stock Numbers" Courtesy of Franc Podgorsek/iStockphoto. "Customer in Line at Grocery Store" Courtesy of Digital Vision Photography/Veer Inc. Owaki-Kulla, "Pumping Gas" Courtesy of Flirt Photography/Veer Inc. Lynn Johnson, "Yunnan Province, People's Republic of China" Courtesy of Lynn Johnson/Getty Images, Inc. Thomas Bendy, "Student Typing" Courtesy of Thomas Bendy/iStockphoto.

This special edition published in cooperation with Pearson Learning Solutions.

Printed in the United States of America.

V3NL

Please visit our web site at *www.pearsoncustom.com.*

Attention bookstores: For permission to return any unsold stock, contact us at *pe-uscustomreturns@pearson.com.*

Pearson Learning Solutions, 501 Boylston Street, Suite 900, Boston, MA 02116
A Pearson Education Company
www.pearsoned.com

ISBN 10: 1-256-20549-4
ISBN 13: 978-1-256-20549-4

Contents

Cost-Volume-Profit Analysis

Cost-Volume-Profit Analysis

All managers want to know how profits will change as the units sold of a product or service change.

Home Depot managers, for example, might wonder how many units of a new product must be sold to break even or make a certain amount of profit. Procter & Gamble managers might ask themselves how expanding their business into a particular foreign market would affect costs, selling price, and profits. These questions have a common "what-if" theme. Examining the results of these what-if possibilities and alternatives helps managers make better decisions.

Managers must also decide how to price their products and understand the effect of their pricing decisions on revenues and profits. The following article explains how the Irish rock band U2 recently decided whether it should decrease the prices on some of its tickets during its recent world tour. Does lowering ticket price sound like a wise strategy to you?

How the "The Biggest Rock Show Ever" Turned a Big Profit[1]

When U2 embarked on its recent world tour, *Rolling Stone* magazine called it "the biggest rock show ever." Visiting large stadiums across the United States and Europe, the Irish quartet performed on an imposing 164-foot high stage that resembled a spaceship, complete with a massive video screen and footbridges leading to ringed catwalks.

With an ambitious 48-date trek planned, U2 actually had three separate stages leapfrogging its global itinerary—each one costing nearly $40 million dollars. As a result, the tour's success was dependent not only on each night's concert, but also recouping its tremendous fixed costs—costs that do not change with the number of fans in the audience.

To cover its high fixed costs and make a profit, U2 needed to sell a lot of tickets. To maximize revenue, the tour employed a unique in-the-round stage configuration, which boosted stadium capacity by roughly 20%, and sold tickets for as little as $30, far less than most large outdoor concerts.

The band's plan worked—despite a broader music industry slump and global recession, U2 shattered attendance records in most of the venues it played. By the end of the tour, the band played to over

---

[1] *Source*: Gundersen, Edna. 2009. U2 turns 360 stadium into attendance-shattering sellouts. *USA Today*, October 4. *www.usatoday.com/life/music/news/2009-10-04-u2-stadium-tour_N.htm*

3 million fans, racking up almost $300 million in ticket and merchandise sales and turning a profit. As you read this chapter, you will begin to understand how and why U2 made the decision to lower prices.

Many capital intensive companies, such as US Airways and United Airlines in the airlines industry and Global Crossing and WorldCom in the telecommunications industry, have high fixed costs. They must generate sufficient revenues to cover

Getty Images, Inc.—Liaison

these costs and turn a profit. When revenues declined at these companies during 2001 and 2002 and fixed costs remained high, these companies declared bankruptcy. The methods of CVP analysis described in this chapter help managers minimize such risks.

Essentials of CVP Analysis

Cost-volume-profit (CVP) analysis studies the behavior and relationship among total revenues, total costs, and income as changes occur in the units sold, the selling price, the variable cost per unit, or the fixed costs of a product. Let's consider an example to illustrate CVP analysis.

> Example: Emma Frost is considering selling GMAT Success, a test prep book and software package for the business school admission test, at a college fair in Chicago. Emma knows she can purchase this package from a wholesaler at $120 per package, with the privilege of returning all unsold packages and receiving a full $120 refund per package. She also knows that she must pay $2,000 to the organizers for the booth rental at the fair. She will incur no other costs. She must decide whether she should rent a booth.

Emma, like most managers who face such a situation, works through a series of steps.

1. **Identify the problem and uncertainties.** The decision to rent the booth hinges critically on how Emma resolves two important uncertainties—the price she can charge and the number of packages she can sell at that price. Every decision deals with selecting a course of action. Emma must decide knowing that the outcome of the chosen action is uncertain and will only be known in the future. The more confident Emma is about selling a large number of packages at a good price, the more willing she will be to rent the booth.

2. **Obtain information.** When faced with uncertainty, managers obtain information that might help them understand the uncertainties better. For example, Emma gathers information about the type of individuals likely to attend the fair and other test-prep packages that might be sold at the fair. She also gathers data on her past experiences selling GMAT Success at fairs very much like the Chicago fair.

3. **Make predictions about the future.** Using all the information available to them, managers make predictions. Emma predicts that she can charge a price of $200 for GMAT Success. At that price she is reasonably confident that she will be able to sell at least 30 packages and possibly as many as 60. In making these predictions, Emma like most managers, must be realistic and exercise careful judgment. If her predictions are excessively optimistic, Emma will rent the booth when she should not. If they are unduly pessimistic, Emma will not rent the booth when she should.

Emma's predictions rest on the belief that her experience at the Chicago fair will be similar to her experience at the Boston fair four months earlier. Yet, Emma is uncertain about several aspects of her prediction. Is the comparison between Boston and Chicago appropriate? Have conditions and circumstances changed over the last four months? Are there any biases creeping into her thinking? She is keen on selling at the Chicago fair because sales in the last couple of months have been lower than expected. Is this experience making her predictions overly optimistic? Has she ignored some of the competitive risks? Will the other test prep vendors at the fair reduce their prices?

Emma reviews her thinking. She retests her assumptions. She also explores these questions with John Mills, a close friend, who has extensive experience selling test-prep packages like GMAT Success. In the end, she feels quite confident that her predictions are reasonable, accurate, and carefully thought through.

4. **Make decisions by choosing among alternatives.** Emma uses the CVP analysis that follows, and decides to rent the booth at the Chicago fair.

5. **Implement the decision, evaluate performance, and learn.** Thoughtful managers never stop learning. They compare their actual performance to predicted performance to understand why things worked out the way they did and what they might learn. At the end of the Chicago fair, for example, Emma would want to evaluate whether her predictions about price and the number of packages she could sell were correct. Such feedback would be very helpful to Emma as she makes decisions about renting booths at subsequent fairs.

How does Emma use CVP analysis in Step 4 to make her decision? Emma begins by identifying which costs are fixed and which costs are variable and then calculates *contribution margin*.

Contribution Margins

The booth-rental cost of $2,000 is a fixed cost because it will not change no matter how many packages Emma sells. The cost of the package itself is a variable cost because it increases in proportion to the number of packages sold. Emma will incur a cost of $120 for each package that she sells. To get an idea of how operating income will change as a result of selling different quantities of packages, Emma calculates operating income if sales are 5 packages and if sales are 40 packages.

	5 packages sold	40 packages sold
Revenues	$ 1,000 ($200 per package × 5 packages)	$8,000 ($200 per package × 40 packages)
Variable purchase costs	600 ($120 per package × 5 packages)	4,800 ($120 per package × 40 packages)
Fixed costs	2,000	2,000
Operating income	$(1,600)	$1,200

The only numbers that change from selling different quantities of packages are *total revenues* and *total variable costs*. The difference between total revenues and total variable costs is called **contribution margin**. That is,

Contribution margin = Total revenues − Total variable costs

Contribution margin indicates why operating income changes as the number of units sold changes. The contribution margin when Emma sells 5 packages is $400 ($1,000 in total revenues minus $600 in total variable costs); the contribution margin when Emma sells

40 packages is $3,200 ($8,000 in total revenues minus $4,800 in total variable costs). When calculating the contribution margin, be sure to subtract all variable costs. For example, if Emma had variable selling costs because she paid a commission to salespeople for each package they sold at the fair, variable costs would include the cost of each package plus the sales commission.

Contribution margin per unit is a useful tool for calculating contribution margin and operating income. It is defined as,

$$\text{Contribution margin per unit} = \text{Selling price} - \text{Variable cost per unit}$$

In the GMAT Success example, contribution margin per package, or per unit, is $200 - $120 = $80. Contribution margin per unit recognizes the tight coupling of selling price and variable cost per unit. Unlike fixed costs, Emma will only incur the variable cost per unit of $120 when she sells a unit of GMAT Success for $200.

Contribution margin per unit provides a second way to calculate contribution margin:

$$\text{Contribution margin} = \text{Contribution margin per unit} \times \text{Number of units sold}$$

For example, when 40 packages are sold, contribution margin = $80 per unit × 40 units = $3,200.

Even before she gets to the fair, Emma incurs $2,000 in fixed costs. Because the contribution margin per unit is $80, Emma will recover $80 for each package that she sells at the fair. Emma hopes to sell enough packages to fully recover the $2,000 she spent for renting the booth and to then start making a profit.

Exhibit 1 presents contribution margins for different quantities of packages sold. The income statement in Exhibit 1 is called a **contribution income statement** because it groups costs into variable costs and fixed costs to highlight contribution margin. Each additional package sold from 0 to 1 to 5 increases contribution margin by $80 per package, recovering more of the fixed costs and reducing the operating loss. If Emma sells 25 packages, contribution margin equals $2,000 ($80 per package × 25 packages), exactly recovering fixed costs and resulting in $0 operating income. If Emma sells 40 packages, contribution margin increases by another $1,200 ($3,200 - $2,000), all of which becomes operating income. As you look across Exhibit 1 from left to right, you see that the increase in contribution margin exactly equals the increase in operating income (or the decrease in operating loss).

Instead of expressing contribution margin as a dollar amount per unit, we can express it as a percentage called **contribution margin percentage** (or **contribution margin ratio**):

$$\text{Contribution margin percentage (or contribution margin ratio)} = \frac{\text{Contribution margin per unit}}{\text{Selling price}}$$

In our example,

$$\text{Contribution margin percentage} = \frac{\$80}{\$200} = 0.40, \text{ or } 40\%$$

Contribution margin percentage is the contribution margin per dollar of revenue. Emma earns 40% of each dollar of revenue (equal to 40 cents).

	Home	Insert	Page Layout	Formulas	Data	Review	View	
	A	B	C	D	E	F	G	H
1				Number of Packages Sold				
2				0	1	5	25	40
3	Revenues	$ 200	per package	$ 0	$ 200	$ 1,000	$5,000	$8,000
4	Variable costs	$ 120	per package	0	120	600	3,000	4,800
5	Contribution margin	$ 80	per package	0	80	400	2,000	3,200
6	Fixed costs	$2,000		2,000	2,000	2,000	2,000	2,000
7	Operating income			$(2,000)	$(1,920)	$(1,600)	$ 0	$1,200

Exhibit 1

Contribution Income Statement for Different Quantities of GMAT Success Packages Sold

Most companies have multiple products. As we shall see later in this chapter, calculating contribution margin per unit when there are multiple products is more cumbersome. In practice, companies routinely use contribution margin percentage as a handy way to calculate contribution margin for different dollar amounts of revenue:

$$\text{Contribution margin } = \text{ Contribution margin percentage } \times \text{ Revenues (in dollars)}$$

For example, in Exhibit 1, if Emma sells 40 packages, revenues will be $8,000 and contribution margin will equal 40% of $8,000, or $0.40 \times \$8,000 = \$3,200$. Emma earns operating income of $1,200 ($3,200 − Fixed costs, $2,000) by selling 40 packages for $8,000.

Expressing CVP Relationships

How was the Excel spreadsheet in Exhibit 1 constructed? Underlying the Exhibit are some equations that express the CVP relationships. To make good decisions using CVP analysis, we must understand these relationships and the structure of the contribution income statement in Exhibit 1. There are three related ways (we will call them methods) to think more deeply about and model CVP relationships:

1. The equation method
2. The contribution margin method
3. The graph method

The equation method and the contribution margin method are most useful when managers want to determine operating income at few specific levels of sales (for example 5, 15, 25, and 40 units sold). The graph method helps managers visualize the relationship between units sold and operating income over a wide range of quantities of units sold. As we shall see later in the chapter, different methods are useful for different decisions.

Equation Method

Each column in Exhibit 1 is expressed as an equation.

$$\text{Revenues} - \text{Variable costs} - \text{Fixed costs} = \text{Operating income}$$

How are revenues in each column calculated?

$$\text{Revenues} = \text{Selling price } (SP) \times \text{Quantity of units sold } (Q)$$

How are variable costs in each column calculated?

$$\text{Variable costs} = \text{Variable cost per unit } (VCU) \times \text{Quantity of units sold } (Q)$$

So,

$$\left[\left(\begin{matrix} \text{Selling} \\ \text{price} \end{matrix} \times \begin{matrix} \text{Quantity of} \\ \text{units sold} \end{matrix} \right) - \left(\begin{matrix} \text{Variable cost} \\ \text{per unit} \end{matrix} \times \begin{matrix} \text{Quantity of} \\ \text{units sold} \end{matrix} \right) \right] - \begin{matrix} \text{Fixed} \\ \text{costs} \end{matrix} = \begin{matrix} \text{Operating} \\ \text{income} \end{matrix} \qquad \textbf{(Equation 1)}$$

Equation 1 becomes the basis for calculating operating income for different quantities of units sold. For example, if you go to cell F7 in Exhibit 1, the calculation of operating income when Emma sells 5 packages is

$$(\$200 \times 5) - (\$120 \times 5) - \$2,000 = \$1,000 - \$600 - \$2,000 = -\$1,600$$

Contribution Margin Method

Rearranging equation 1,

$$\left[\left(\begin{matrix} \text{Selling} \\ \text{price} \end{matrix} - \begin{matrix} \text{Variable cost} \\ \text{per unit} \end{matrix} \right) \times \left(\begin{matrix} \text{Quantity of} \\ \text{units sold} \end{matrix} \right) \right] - \begin{matrix} \text{Fixed} \\ \text{costs} \end{matrix} = \begin{matrix} \text{Operating} \\ \text{income} \end{matrix}$$

$$\left(\begin{matrix} \text{Contribution margin} \\ \text{per unit} \end{matrix} \times \begin{matrix} \text{Quantity of} \\ \text{units sold} \end{matrix} \right) - \begin{matrix} \text{Fixed} \\ \text{costs} \end{matrix} = \begin{matrix} \text{Operating} \\ \text{income} \end{matrix} \qquad \textbf{(Equation 2)}$$

In our GMAT Success example, contribution margin per unit is $80 ($200 − $120), so when Emma sells 5 packages,

$$\text{Operating income} = (\$80 \times 5) - \$2,000 = -\$1,600$$

Equation 2 expresses the basic idea we described earlier—each unit sold helps Emma recover $80 (in contribution margin) of the $2,000 in fixed costs.

Graph Method

In the graph method, we represent total costs and total revenues graphically. Each is shown as a line on a graph. Exhibit 2 illustrates the graph method for GMAT Success. Because we have assumed that total costs and total revenues behave in a linear fashion, we need only two points to plot the line representing each of them.

1. **Total costs line.** The total costs line is the sum of fixed costs and variable costs. Fixed costs are $2,000 for all quantities of units sold within the relevant range. To plot the total costs line, use as one point the $2,000 fixed costs at zero units sold (point A) because variable costs are $0 when no units are sold. Select a second point by choosing any other convenient output level (say, 40 units sold) and determine the corresponding total costs. Total variable costs at this output level are $4,800 (40 units × $120 per unit). Remember, fixed costs are $2,000 at all quantities of units sold within the relevant range, so total costs at 40 units sold equal $6,800 ($2,000 + $4,800), which is point B in Exhibit 2. The total costs line is the straight line from point A through point B.

2. **Total revenues line.** One convenient starting point is $0 revenues at 0 units sold, which is point C in Exhibit 2. Select a second point by choosing any other convenient output level and determining the corresponding total revenues. At 40 units sold, total revenues are $8,000 ($200 per unit × 40 units), which is point D in Exhibit 2. The total revenues line is the straight line from point C through point D.

Profit or loss at any sales level can be determined by the vertical distance between the two lines at that level in Exhibit 2. For quantities fewer than 25 units sold, total costs exceed total revenues, and the purple area indicates operating losses. For quantities greater than 25 units sold, total revenues exceed total costs, and the blue-green area indicates operating incomes. At 25 units sold, total revenues equal total costs. Emma will break even by selling 25 packages.

◄ **Decision Point**

How can CVP analysis assist managers?

Exhibit 2

Cost-Volume Graph for GMAT Success

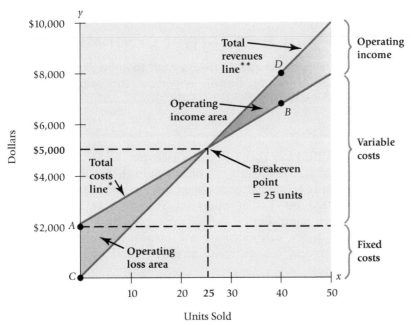

*Slope of the total costs line is the variable cost per unit = $120
**Slope of the total revenues line is the selling price = $200

Cost-Volume-Profit Assumptions

Now that you have seen how CVP analysis works, think about the following assumptions we made during the analysis:

1. Changes in the levels of revenues and costs arise only because of changes in the number of product (or service) units sold. The number of units sold is the only revenue driver and the only cost driver. Just as a cost driver is any factor that affects costs, a **revenue driver** is a variable, such as volume, that causally affects revenues.

2. Total costs can be separated into two components: a fixed component that does not vary with units sold and a variable component that changes with respect to units sold.

3. When represented graphically, the behaviors of total revenues and total costs are linear (meaning they can be represented as a straight line) in relation to units sold within a relevant range (and time period).

4. Selling price, variable cost per unit, and total fixed costs (within a relevant range and time period) are known and constant.

As the CVP assumptions make clear, an important feature of CVP analysis is distinguishing fixed from variable costs. Always keep in mind, however, that whether a cost is variable or fixed depends on the time period for a decision.

The shorter the time horizon, the higher the percentage of total costs considered fixed. For example, suppose an American Airlines plane will depart from its gate in the next hour and currently has 20 seats unsold. A potential passenger arrives with a transferable ticket from a competing airline. The variable costs (such as one more meal) to American of placing one more passenger in an otherwise empty seat is negligible At the time of this decision, with only an hour to go before the flight departs, virtually all costs (such as crew costs and baggage-handling costs) are fixed.

Alternatively, suppose American Airlines must decide whether to keep this flight in its flight schedule. This decision will have a one-year planning horizon. If American Airlines decides to cancel this flight because very few passengers during the last year have taken this flight, many more costs, including crew costs, baggage-handling costs, and airport fees, would be considered variable. That's because over this longer horizon, these costs would not have to be incurred if the flight were no longer operating. Always consider the relevant range, the length of the time horizon, and the specific decision situation when classifying costs as variable or fixed.

Breakeven Point and Target Operating Income

Learning Objective 2

Determine the breakeven point and output level needed to achieve a target operating income

. . . compare contribution margin and fixed costs

Managers and entrepreneurs like Emma always want to know how much they must sell to earn a given amount of income. Equally important, they want to know how much they must sell to avoid a loss.

Breakeven Point

The **breakeven point (BEP)** is that quantity of output sold at which total revenues equal total costs—that is, the quantity of output sold that results in $0 of operating income. We have already seen how to use the graph method to calculate the breakeven point. Recall from Exhibit 1 that operating income was $0 when Emma sold 25 units, the breakeven point. But by understanding the equations underlying the calculations in Exhibit 1, we can calculate the breakeven point directly for GMAT Success rather than trying out different quantities and checking when operating income equals $0.

Recall the equation method (equation 1):

$$\left(\begin{array}{c} \text{Selling} \\ \text{price} \end{array} \times \begin{array}{c} \text{Quantity of} \\ \text{units sold} \end{array} \right) - \left(\begin{array}{c} \text{Variable cost} \\ \text{per unit} \end{array} \times \begin{array}{c} \text{Quantity of} \\ \text{units sold} \end{array} \right) - \begin{array}{c} \text{Fixed} \\ \text{costs} \end{array} = \begin{array}{c} \text{Operating} \\ \text{income} \end{array}$$

Setting operating income equal to $0 and denoting quantity of output units that must be sold by Q,

$$(\$200 \times Q) - (\$120 \times Q) - \$2,000 = \$0$$
$$\$80 \times Q = \$2,000$$
$$Q = \$2,000 \div \$80 \text{ per unit} = 25 \text{ units}$$

If Emma sells fewer than 25 units, she will incur a loss; if she sells 25 units, she will break even; and if she sells more than 25 units, she will make a profit. While this breakeven point is expressed in units, it can also be expressed in revenues: 25 units × $200 selling price = $5,000.

Recall the contribution margin method (equation 2):

$$\left(\begin{array}{c} \text{Contribution} \\ \text{margin per unit} \end{array} \times \begin{array}{c} \text{Quantity of} \\ \text{units sold} \end{array} \right) - \text{Fixed costs} = \text{Operating income}$$

At the breakeven point, operating income is by definition $0 and so,

$$\text{Contribution margin per unit} \times \text{Breakeven number of units} = \text{Fixed cost} \quad \textbf{(Equation 3)}$$

Rearranging equation 3 and entering the data,

$$\begin{array}{c} \text{Breakeven} \\ \text{number of units} \end{array} = \frac{\text{Fixed costs}}{\text{Contribution margin per unit}} = \frac{\$2,000}{\$80 \text{ per unit}} = 25 \text{ units}$$

$$\text{Breakeven revenues} = \text{Breakeven number of units} \times \text{Selling price}$$
$$= 25 \text{ units} \times \$200 \text{ per unit} = \$5,000$$

In practice (because they have multiple products), companies usually calculate breakeven point directly in terms of revenues using contribution margin percentages. Recall that in the GMAT Success example,

$$\begin{array}{c} \text{Contribution margin} \\ \text{percentage} \end{array} = \frac{\text{Contribution margin per unit}}{\text{Selling price}} = \frac{\$80}{\$200} = 0.40, \text{ or } 40\%$$

That is, 40% of each dollar of revenue, or 40 cents, is contribution margin. To break even, contribution margin must equal fixed costs of $2,000. To earn $2,000 of contribution margin, when $1 of revenue earns $0.40 of contribution margin, revenues must equal $2,000 ÷ 0.40 = $5,000.

$$\begin{array}{c} \text{Breakeven} \\ \text{revenues} \end{array} = \frac{\text{Fixed costs}}{\text{Contribution margin \%}} = \frac{\$2,000}{0.40} = \$5,000$$

While the breakeven point tells managers how much they must sell to avoid a loss, managers are equally interested in how they will achieve the operating income targets underlying their strategies and plans. In our example, selling 25 units at a price of $200 assures Emma that she will not lose money if she rents the booth. This news is comforting, but we next describe how Emma determines how much she needs to sell to achieve a targeted amount of operating income.

Target Operating Income

We illustrate target operating income calculations by asking the following question: How many units must Emma sell to earn an operating income of $1,200? One approach is to keep plugging in different quantities into Exhibit 1 and check when operating income equals $1,200. Exhibit 1 shows that operating income is $1,200 when 40 packages are sold. A more convenient approach is to use equation 1.

$$\left[\left(\begin{array}{c} \text{Selling} \\ \text{price} \end{array} \times \begin{array}{c} \text{Quantity of} \\ \text{units sold} \end{array} \right) - \left(\begin{array}{c} \text{Variable cost} \\ \text{per unit} \end{array} \times \begin{array}{c} \text{Quantity of} \\ \text{units sold} \end{array} \right) \right] - \begin{array}{c} \text{Fixed} \\ \text{costs} \end{array} = \begin{array}{c} \text{Operating} \\ \text{income} \end{array} \quad \textbf{(Equation 1)}$$

We denote by Q the unknown quantity of units Emma must sell to earn an operating income of $1,200. Selling price is $200, variable cost per package is $120, fixed costs are

$2,000, and target operating income is $1,200. Substituting these values into equation 1, we have

$$(\$200 \times Q) - (\$120 \times Q) - \$2,000 = \$1,200$$
$$\$80 \times Q = \$2,000 + \$1,200 = \$3,200$$
$$Q = \$3,200 \div \$80 \text{ per unit} = 40 \text{ units}$$

Alternatively, we could use equation 2,

$$\left(\begin{matrix} \text{Contribution margin} \\ \text{per unit} \end{matrix} \times \begin{matrix} \text{Quantity of} \\ \text{units sold} \end{matrix} \right) - \begin{matrix} \text{Fixed} \\ \text{costs} \end{matrix} = \begin{matrix} \text{Operating} \\ \text{income} \end{matrix} \qquad \textbf{(Equation 2)}$$

Given a target operating income ($1,200 in this case), we can rearrange terms to get equation 4.

$$\begin{matrix} \text{Quantity of units} \\ \text{required to be sold} \end{matrix} = \frac{\text{Fixed costs} + \text{Target operating income}}{\text{Contribution margin per unit}} \qquad \textbf{(Equation 4)}$$

$$\begin{matrix} \text{Quantity of units} \\ \text{required to be sold} \end{matrix} = \frac{\$2,000 + \$1,200}{\$80 \text{ per unit}} = 40 \text{ units}$$

Proof:

Revenues, $200 per unit $\times$ 40 units	$8,000
Variable costs, $120 per unit $\times$ 40 units	4,800
Contribution margin, $80 per unit $\times$ 40 units	3,200
Fixed costs	2,000
Operating income	$1,200

The revenues needed to earn an operating income of $1,200 can also be calculated directly by recognizing (1) that $3,200 of contribution margin must be earned (fixed costs of $2,000 plus operating income of $1,200) and (2) that $1 of revenue earns $0.40 (40 cents) of contribution margin. To earn $3,200 of contribution margin, revenues must equal $3,200 ÷ 0.40 = $8,000.

$$\text{Revenues needed to earn operating income of } \$1,200 = \frac{\$2,000 + \$1,200}{0.40} = \frac{\$3,200}{0.40} = \$8,000$$

The graph in Exhibit 2 is very difficult to use to answer the question: How many units must Emma sell to earn an operating income of $1,200? Why? Because it is not easy to determine from the graph the precise point at which the difference between the total revenues line and the total costs line equals $1,200. However, recasting Exhibit 2 in the form of a profit-volume (PV) graph makes it easier to answer this question.

A **PV graph** shows how changes in the quantity of units sold affect operating income. Exhibit 3 is the PV graph for GMAT Success (fixed costs, $2,000; selling price, $200; and variable cost per unit, $120). The PV line can be drawn using two points. One convenient point (M) is the operating loss at 0 units sold, which is equal to the fixed costs of $2,000, shown at –$2,000 on the vertical axis. A second convenient point (N) is the breakeven point, which is 25 units in our example. The PV line is the straight line from point M through point N. To find the number of units Emma must sell to earn an operating income of $1,200, draw a horizontal line parallel to the x-axis corresponding to $1,200 on the vertical axis (that's the y-axis). At the point where this line intersects the PV line, draw a vertical line down to the horizontal axis (that's the x-axis). The vertical line intersects the x-axis at 40 units, indicating that by selling 40 units Emma will earn an operating income of $1,200.

Target Net Income and Income Taxes

Net income is operating income plus nonoperating revenues (such as interest revenue) minus nonoperating costs (such as interest cost) minus income taxes. For simplicity, throughout this chapter we assume nonoperating revenues and nonoperating costs are zero. Thus,

$$\text{Net income} = \text{Operating income} - \text{Income taxes}$$

Until now, we have ignored the effect of income taxes in our CVP analysis. In many companies, the income targets for managers in their strategic plans are expressed in terms of

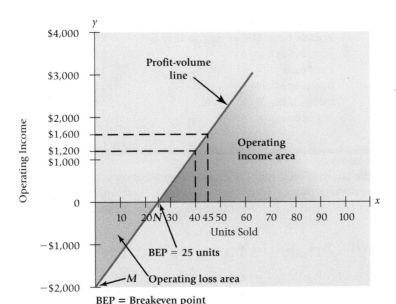

Exhibit 3

Profit-Volume Graph for
GMAT Success

net income. That's because top management wants subordinate managers to take into account the effects their decisions have on operating income after income taxes. Some decisions may not result in large operating incomes, but they may have favorable tax consequences, making them attractive on a net income basis—the measure that drives shareholders' dividends and returns.

To make net income evaluations, CVP calculations for target income must be stated in terms of target net income instead of target operating income. For example, Emma may be interested in knowing the quantity of units she must sell to earn a net income of $960, assuming an income tax rate of 40%.

$$\text{Target net income} = \left(\begin{matrix}\text{Target}\\\text{operating income}\end{matrix}\right) - \left(\begin{matrix}\text{Target}\\\text{operating income}\end{matrix} \times \text{Tax rate}\right)$$

$$\text{Target net income} = (\text{Target operating income}) \times (1 - \text{Tax rate})$$

$$\text{Target operating income} = \frac{\text{Target net income}}{1 - \text{Tax rate}} = \frac{\$960}{1 - 0.40} = \$1,600$$

In other words, to earn a target net income of $960, Emma's target operating income is $1,600.

Proof:

Target operating income	$1,600
Tax at 40% (0.40 × $1,600)	640
Target net income	$ 960

The key step is to take the target net income number and convert it into the corresponding target operating income number. We can then use equation 1 for target operating income and substitute numbers from our GMAT Success example.

$$\left[\left(\begin{matrix}\text{Selling}\\\text{price}\end{matrix} \times \begin{matrix}\text{Quantity of}\\\text{units sold}\end{matrix}\right) - \left(\begin{matrix}\text{Variable cost}\\\text{per unit}\end{matrix} \times \begin{matrix}\text{Quantity of}\\\text{units sold}\end{matrix}\right)\right] - \begin{matrix}\text{Fixed}\\\text{costs}\end{matrix} = \begin{matrix}\text{Operating}\\\text{income}\end{matrix} \quad \text{(Equation 1)}$$

$$(\$200 \times Q) - (\$120 \times Q) - \$2,000 = \$1,600$$

$$\$80 \times Q = \$3,600$$

$$Q = \$3,600 \div \$80 \text{ per unit} = 45 \text{ units}$$

Alternatively we can calculate the number of units Emma must sell by using the contribution margin method and equation 4:

$$\begin{matrix}\text{Quantity of units}\\\text{required to be sold}\end{matrix} = \frac{\text{Fixed costs} + \text{Target operating income}}{\text{Contribution margin per unit}} \quad \text{(Equation 4)}$$

$$= \frac{\$2,000 + \$1,600}{\$80 \text{ per unit}} = 45 \text{ units}$$

Proof:

Revenues, $200 per unit × 45 units		$9,000
Variable costs, $120 per unit × 45 units		5,400
Contribution margin		3,600
Fixed costs		2,000
Operating income		1,600
Income taxes, $1,600 × 0.40		640
Net income		$ 960

How can managers incorporate income taxes into CVP analysis?

Emma can also use the PV graph in Exhibit 3. To earn target operating income of $1,600, Emma needs to sell 45 units.

Focusing the analysis on target net income instead of target operating income will not change the breakeven point. That's because, by definition, operating income at the breakeven point is $0, and no income taxes are paid when there is no operating income.

Using CVP Analysis for Decision Making

We have seen how CVP analysis is useful for calculating the units that need to be sold to break even, or to achieve a target operating income or target net income. Managers also use CVP analysis to guide other decisions, many of them strategic decisions. Consider a decision about choosing additional features for an existing product. Different choices can affect selling prices, variable cost per unit, fixed costs, units sold, and operating income. CVP analysis helps managers make product decisions by estimating the expected profitability of these choices.

Strategic decisions invariably entail risk. CVP analysis can be used to evaluate how operating income will be affected if the original predicted data are not achieved—say, if sales are 10% lower than estimated. Evaluating this risk affects other strategic decisions a company might make. For example, if the probability of a decline in sales seems high, a manager may take actions to change the cost structure to have more variable costs and fewer fixed costs. We return to our GMAT Success example to illustrate how CVP analysis can be used for strategic decisions concerning advertising and selling price.

Decision to Advertise

Suppose Emma anticipates selling 40 units at the fair. Exhibit 3 indicates that Emma's operating income will be $1,200. Emma is considering placing an advertisement describing the product and its features in the fair brochure. The advertisement will be a fixed cost of $500. Emma thinks that advertising will increase sales by 10% to 44 packages. Should Emma advertise? The following table presents the CVP analysis.

	40 Packages Sold with No Advertising (1)	44 Packages Sold with Advertising (2)	Difference (3) = (2) − (1)
Revenues ($200 × 40; $200 × 44)	$8,000	$8,800	$ 800
Variable costs ($120 × 40; $120 × 44)	4,800	5,280	480
Contribution margin ($80 × 40; $80 × 44)	3,200	3,520	320
Fixed costs	2,000	2,500	500
Operating income	$1,200	$1,020	$(180)

Operating income will decrease from $1,200 to $1,020, so Emma should not advertise. Note that Emma could focus only on the difference column and come to the same conclusion: If Emma advertises, contribution margin will increase by $320 (revenues, $800 − variable costs, $480), and fixed costs will increase by $500, resulting in a $180 decrease in operating income.

As you become more familiar with CVP analysis, try evaluating decisions based on differences rather than mechanically working through the contribution income statement. Analyzing differences gets to the heart of CVP analysis and sharpens intuition by focusing only on the revenues and costs that will change as a result of a decision.

Learning Objective 4

Explain how managers use CVP analysis in decision making

. . . choose the alternative that maximizes operating income

Decision to Reduce Selling Price

Having decided not to advertise, Emma is contemplating whether to reduce the selling price to $175. At this price, she thinks she will sell 50 units. At this quantity, the test-prep package wholesaler who supplies GMAT Success will sell the packages to Emma for $115 per unit instead of $120. Should Emma reduce the selling price?

Contribution margin from lowering price to $175: ($175 − $115) per unit × 50 units	$3,000
Contribution margin from maintaining price at $200: ($200 − $120) per unit × 40 units	3,200
Change in contribution margin from lowering price	$ (200)

Decreasing the price will reduce contribution margin by $200 and, because the fixed costs of $2,000 will not change, it will also reduce operating income by $200. Emma should not reduce the selling price.

Determining Target Prices

Emma could also ask "At what price can I sell 50 units (purchased at $115 per unit) and continue to earn an operating income of $1,200?" The answer is $179, as the following calculations show.

Target operating income	$1,200
Add fixed costs	2,000
Target contribution margin	$3,200
Divided by number of units sold	÷ 50 units
Target contribution margin per unit	$ 64
Add variable cost per unit	115
Target selling price	$ 179

Proof:		
	Revenues, $179 per unit × 50 units	$8,950
	Variable costs, $115 per unit × 50 units	5,750
	Contribution margin	3,200
	Fixed costs	2,000
	Operating income	$1,200

Emma should also examine the effects of other decisions, such as simultaneously increasing advertising costs and lowering prices. In each case, Emma will compare the changes in contribution margin (through the effects on selling prices, variable costs, and quantities of units sold) to the changes in fixed costs, and she will choose the alternative that provides the highest operating income.

◄ **Decision Point**

How do managers use CVP analysis to make decisions?

Sensitivity Analysis and Margin of Safety

Before choosing strategies and plans about how to implement strategies, managers frequently analyze the sensitivity of their decisions to changes in underlying assumptions. **Sensitivity analysis** is a "what-if" technique that managers use to examine how an outcome will change if the original predicted data are not achieved or if an underlying assumption changes. In the context of CVP analysis, sensitivity analysis answers questions such as, "What will operating income be if the quantity of units sold decreases by 5% from the original prediction?" and "What will operating income be if variable cost per unit increases by 10%?" Sensitivity analysis broadens managers' perspectives to possible outcomes that might occur *before* costs are committed.

Electronic spreadsheets, such as Excel, enable managers to conduct CVP-based sensitivity analyses in a systematic and efficient way. Using spreadsheets, managers can conduct sensitivity analysis to examine the effect and interaction of changes in selling price, variable cost per unit, fixed costs, and target operating income. Exhibit 4 displays a spreadsheet for the GMAT Success example.

Using the spreadsheet, Emma can immediately see how many units she needs to sell to achieve particular operating-income levels, given alternative levels of fixed costs and variable cost per unit that she may face. For example, 32 units must be sold to earn an

Learning Objective 5

Explain how sensitivity analysis helps managers cope with uncertainty

. . . determine the effect on operating income of different assumptions

Exhibit 4

Spreadsheet Analysis
of CVP Relationships
for GMAT Success

| Home | Insert | Page Layout | Formulas | Data | Review | View |

| D5 | ▼ | fx | =($A5+D$3)/(F1-$B5) |

	A	B	C	D	E	F
1			Number of units required to be sold at $200			
2			Selling Price to Earn Target Operating Income of			
3		Variable Costs	$0	$1,200	$1,600	$2,000
4	Fixed Costs	per Unit	(Breakeven point)			
5	$2,000	$100	20	32[a]	36	40
6	$2,000	$120	25	40	45	50
7	$2,000	$150	40	64	72	80
8	$2,400	$100	24	36	40	44
9	$2,400	$120	30	45	50	55
10	$2,400	$150	48	72	80	88
11	$2,800	$100	28	40	44	48
12	$2,800	$120	35	50	55	60
13	$2,800	$150	56	80	88	96
14						
15	[a]Number of units	=	Fixed costs + Target operating income	=	$2,000 + $1,200	= 32
16	required to be sold		Contribution margin per unit		$200 - $100	

operating income of $1,200 if fixed costs are $2,000 and variable cost per unit is $100. Emma can also use Exhibit 4 to determine that she needs to sell 56 units to break even if fixed cost of the booth rental at the Chicago fair is raised to $2,800 and if the variable cost per unit charged by the test-prep package supplier increases to $150. Emma can use information about costs and sensitivity analysis, together with realistic predictions about how much she can sell to decide if she should rent a booth at the fair.

Another aspect of sensitivity analysis is **margin of safety:**

$$\text{Margin of safety} = \text{Budgeted (or actual) revenues} - \text{Breakeven revenues}$$
$$\text{Margin of safety (in units)} = \text{Budgeted (or actual) sales quantity} - \text{Breakeven quantity}$$

The margin of safety answers the "what-if" question: If budgeted revenues are above breakeven and drop, how far can they fall below budget before the breakeven point is reached? Sales might decrease as a result of a competitor introducing a better product, or poorly executed marketing programs, and so on. Assume that Emma has fixed costs of $2,000, a selling price of $200, and variable cost per unit of $120. From Exhibit 1, if Emma sells 40 units, budgeted revenues are $8,000 and budgeted operating income is $1,200. The breakeven point is 25 units or $5,000 in total revenues.

$$\text{Margin of safety} = \frac{\text{Budgeted}}{\text{revenues}} - \frac{\text{Breakeven}}{\text{revenues}} = \$8,000 - \$5,000 = \$3,000$$

$$\frac{\text{Margin of}}{\text{safety (in units)}} = \frac{\text{Budgeted}}{\text{sales (units)}} - \frac{\text{Breakeven}}{\text{sales (units)}} = 40 - 25 = 15 \text{ units}$$

Sometimes margin of safety is expressed as a percentage:

$$\text{Margin of safety percentage} = \frac{\text{Margin of safety in dollars}}{\text{Budgeted (or actual) revenues}}$$

In our example, margin of safety percentage $= \dfrac{\$3,000}{\$8,000} = 37.5\%$

This result means that revenues would have to decrease substantially, by 37.5%, to reach breakeven revenues. The high margin of safety gives Emma confidence that she is unlikely to suffer a loss.

If, however, Emma expects to sell only 30 units, budgeted revenues would be $6,000 ($200 per unit × 30 units) and the margin of safety would equal:

$$\text{Budgeted revenues} - \text{Breakeven revenues} = \$6,000 - \$5,000 = \$1,000$$

$$\frac{\text{Margin of}}{\text{safety percentage}} = \frac{\text{Margin of safety in dollars}}{\text{Budgeted (or actual) revenues}} = \frac{\$1,000}{\$6,000} = 16.67\%$$

The analysis implies that if revenues decrease by more than 16.67%, Emma would suffer a loss. A low margin of safety increases the risk of a loss. If Emma does not have the tolerance for this level of risk, she will prefer not to rent a booth at the fair.

Sensitivity analysis is a simple approach to recognizing **uncertainty**, which is the possibility that an actual amount will deviate from an expected amount. Sensitivity analysis gives managers a good feel for the risks involved. A more comprehensive approach to recognizing uncertainty is to compute expected values using probability distributions. This approach is illustrated in the appendix to this chapter.

Decision Point

What can managers do to cope with uncertainty or changes in underlying assumptions?

Cost Planning and CVP

Managers have the ability to choose the levels of fixed and variable costs in their cost structures. This is a strategic decision. In this section, we describe various factors that managers and management accountants consider as they make this decision.

Learning Objective 6

Use CVP analysis to plan variable and fixed costs

. . . compare risk of losses versus higher returns

Alternative Fixed-Cost/Variable-Cost Structures

CVP-based sensitivity analysis highlights the risks and returns as fixed costs are substituted for variable costs in a company's cost structure. In Exhibit 4, compare line 6 and line 11.

	Fixed Cost	Variable Cost	Number of units required to be sold at $200 selling price to earn target operating income of	
			$0 (Breakeven point)	$2,000
Line 6	$2,000	$120	25	50
Line 11	$2,800	$100	28	48

Compared to line 6, line 11, with higher fixed costs, has more risk of loss (has a higher breakeven point) but requires fewer units to be sold (48 versus 50) to earn operating income of $2,000. CVP analysis can help managers evaluate various fixed-cost/variable-cost structures. We next consider the effects of these choices in more detail. Suppose the Chicago college fair organizers offer Emma three rental alternatives:

Option 1: $2,000 fixed fee

Option 2: $800 fixed fee plus 15% of GMAT Success revenues

Option 3: 25% of GMAT Success revenues with no fixed fee

Emma's variable cost per unit is $120. Emma is interested in how her choice of a rental agreement will affect the income she earns and the risks she faces. Exhibit 5 graphically depicts the profit-volume relationship for each option. The line representing the relationship between units sold and operating income for Option 1 is the same as the line in the PV graph shown in Exhibit 3 (fixed costs of $2,000 and contribution margin per unit of $80). The line representing Option 2 shows fixed costs of $800 and a contribution margin per unit of $50 [selling price, $200, minus variable cost per unit, $120, minus variable rental fees per unit, $30, (0.15 × $200)]. The line representing Option 3 has fixed costs of $0 and a contribution margin per unit of $30 [$200 − $120 − $50 (0.25 × $200)].

Option 3 has the lowest breakeven point (0 units), and Option 1 has the highest breakeven point (25 units). Option 1 has the highest risk of loss if sales are low, but it also has the highest contribution margin per unit ($80) and hence the highest operating income when sales are high (greater than 40 units).

The choice among Options 1, 2, and 3 is a strategic decision that Emma faces. As in most strategic decisions, what she decides now will significantly affect her operating

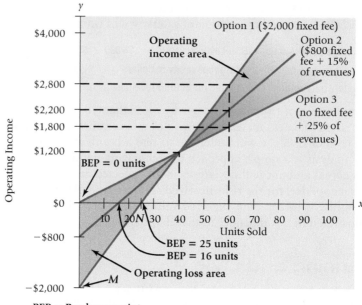

BEP = Breakeven point

income (or loss), depending on the demand for GMAT Success. Faced with this uncertainty, Emma's choice will be influenced by her confidence in the level of demand for GMAT Success and her willingness to risk losses if demand is low. For example, if Emma's tolerance for risk is high, she will choose Option 1 with its high potential rewards. If, however, Emma is averse to taking risk, she will prefer Option 3, where the rewards are smaller if sales are high but where she never suffers a loss if sales are low.

Operating Leverage

The risk-return trade-off across alternative cost structures can be measured as *operating leverage*. **Operating leverage** describes the effects that fixed costs have on changes in operating income as changes occur in units sold and contribution margin. Organizations with a high proportion of fixed costs in their cost structures, as is the case under Option 1, have high operating leverage. The line representing Option 1 in Exhibit 5 is the steepest of the three lines. Small increases in sales lead to large increases in operating income. Small decreases in sales result in relatively large decreases in operating income, leading to a greater risk of operating losses. *At any given level of sales*,

$$\frac{\text{Degree of}}{\text{operating leverage}} = \frac{\text{Contribution margin}}{\text{Operating income}}$$

The following table shows the **degree of operating leverage** at sales of 40 units for the three rental options.

	Option 1	Option 2	Option 3
1. Contribution margin per unit	$ 80	$ 50	$ 30
2. Contribution margin (row 1 × 40 units)	$3,200	$2,000	$1,200
3. Operating income (from Exhibit 5)	$1,200	$1,200	$1,200
4. Degree of operating leverage (row 2 ÷ row 3)	$\frac{\$3,200}{\$1,200} = 2.67$	$\frac{\$2,000}{\$1,200} = 1.67$	$\frac{\$1,200}{\$1,200} = 1.00$

These results indicate that, when sales are 40 units, a percentage change in sales and contribution margin will result in 2.67 times that percentage change in operating income for Option 1, but the same percentage change (1.00) in operating income for Option 3. Consider, for example, a sales increase of 50% from 40 to 60 units. Contribution margin will increase by 50% under each option. Operating income, however, will increase by 2.67 × 50% = 133% from $1,200 to $2,800 in Option 1, but it will increase by only $1.00 \times 50\% = 50\%$ from \$1,200 to \$1,800 in Option 3 (see Exhibit 5). The degree of operating leverage at a given level of sales helps managers calculate the effect of sales fluctuations on operating income.

Keep in mind that, in the presence of fixed costs, the degree of operating leverage is different at different levels of sales. For example, at sales of 60 units, the degree of operating leverage under each of the three options is as follows:

	Option 1	Option 2	Option 3
1. Contribution margin per unit	\$ 80	\$ 50	\$ 30
2. Contribution margin (row 1 × 60 units)	\$4,800	\$3,000	\$1,800
3. Operating income (from Exhibit 5)	\$2,800	\$2,200	\$1,800
4. Degree of operating leverage (row 2 ÷ row 3)	$\frac{\$4,800}{\$2,800} = 1.71$	$\frac{\$3,000}{\$2,200} = 1.36$	$\frac{\$1,800}{\$1,800} = 1.00$

The degree of operating leverage decreases from 2.67 (at sales of 40 units) to 1.71 (at sales of 60 units) under Option 1 and from 1.67 to 1.36 under Option 2. In general, whenever there are fixed costs, the degree of operating leverage decreases as the level of sales increases beyond the breakeven point. If fixed costs are \$0 as in Option 3, contribution margin equals operating income, and the degree of operating leverage equals 1.00 at all sales levels.

But why must managers monitor operating leverage carefully? Again, consider companies such as General Motors, Global Crossing, US Airways, United Airlines, and WorldCom. Their high operating leverage was a major reason for their financial problems. Anticipating high demand for their services, these companies borrowed money to acquire assets, resulting in high fixed costs. As sales declined, these companies suffered losses and could not generate sufficient cash to service their interest and debt, causing them to seek bankruptcy protection. Managers and management accountants should always evaluate how the level of fixed costs and variable costs they choose will affect the risk-return trade-off. See Concepts in Action on the next page for another example of the risks of high fixed costs.

What actions are managers taking to reduce their fixed costs? Many companies are moving their manufacturing facilities from the United States to lower-cost countries, such as Mexico and China. To substitute high fixed costs with lower variable costs, companies are purchasing products from lower-cost suppliers instead of manufacturing products themselves. These actions reduce both costs and operating leverage. More recently, General Electric and Hewlett-Packard began outsourcing service functions, such as post-sales customer service, by shifting their customer call centers to countries, such as India, where costs are lower. These decisions by companies are not without controversy. Some economists argue that outsourcing helps to keep costs, and therefore prices, low and enables U.S. companies to remain globally competitive. Others argue that outsourcing reduces job opportunities in the United States and hurts working-class families.

◄ **Decision Point**

How should managers choose among different variable-cost/ fixed-cost structures?

Effects of Sales Mix on Income

Sales mix is the quantities (or proportion) of various products (or services) that constitute total unit sales of a company. Suppose Emma is now budgeting for a subsequent college fair in New York. She plans to sell two different test-prep packages—GMAT Success and GRE Guarantee—and budgets the following:

Learning Objective 7

Apply CVP analysis to a company producing multiple products

. . . assume sales mix of products remains constant as total units sold changes

	GMAT Success	GRE Guarantee	Total
Expected sales	60	40	100
Revenues, \$200 and \$100 per unit	\$12,000	\$4,000	\$16,000
Variable costs, \$120 and \$70 per unit	7,200	2,800	10,000
Contribution margin, \$80 and \$30 per unit	\$ 4,800	\$1,200	6,000
Fixed costs			4,500
Operating income			\$ 1,500

Concepts in Action — Fixed Costs, Variable Costs, and the Future of Radio

Richard Drew/AP Wide World Photos

Building up too much fixed costs can be hazardous to a company's health. Because fixed costs, unlike variable costs, do not automatically decrease as volume declines, companies with too much fixed costs can lose a considerable amount of money during lean times. Sirius XM, the satellite radio broadcaster, learned this lesson the hard way.

To begin broadcasting in 2001, both Sirius Satellite Radio and XM Satellite Radio—the two companies now comprising Sirius XM—spent billions of dollars on broadcasting licenses, space satellites, and other technology infrastructure. Once operational, the companies also spent billions on other fixed items such as programming and content (including Howard Stern and Major League Baseball), satellite transmission, and R&D. In contrast, variable costs were minimal, consisting mainly of artist-royalty fees and customer service and billing. In effect, this created a business model with a high operating leverage—that is, the companies' cost structure had a very significant proportion of fixed costs. As such, profitability could only be achieved by amassing millions of paid subscribers and selling advertising.

The competitive disadvantage of this highly-leveraged business model was nearly disastrous. Despite amassing more than 14 million subscribers, over the years Sirius and XM rang up $3 billion in debt and tallied cumulative operating losses in excess of $10 billion. Operating leverage, and the threat of bankruptcy, forced the merger of Sirius and XM in 2007, and since then the combined entity has struggled to cut costs, refinance its sizable debt, and reap the profits from over 18 million monthly subscribers.

While satellite radio has struggled under the weight of too much fixed cost, Internet radio had the opposite problem—too much variable costs. But "How?" you ask. Don't variable costs only increase as revenues increase? Yes, but if the revenue earned is less than the variable cost, an increase in revenue can lead to bankruptcy. This is almost what happened to Pandora, the Internet radio service.

Pandora launched in 2005 with only $9.3 million in venture capital. Available free over the Internet, Pandora earned revenue in three ways: advertising on its Web site, subscription fees from users who wanted to opt-out of advertising, and affiliate fees from iTunes and Amazon.com. Pandora had low fixed costs but high variable costs for streaming and performance royalties. Over time, as Pandora's popular service attracted millions of loyal listeners, its costs for performance royalties—set by the Copyright Royalty Board on a per song basis—far exceeded its revenues from advertising and subscriptions. As a result, even though royalty rates were only a fraction of a cent, Pandora lost more and more money each time it played another song!

In 2009, Pandora avoided bankruptcy by renegotiating a lower per-song royalty rate in exchange for at least 25% of its U.S. revenue annually. Further, Pandora began charging its most frequent users a small fee and also started increasing its advertising revenue.

Sources: Birger, Jon. 2009. Mel Karmazian fights to rescue Sirius. *Fortune*, March 16; Clifford, Stephanie. 2007. Pandora's long strange trip. *Inc.*, October 1; Pandora: Royalties kill the web radio star? (A). Harvard Business School Case No. 9-310-026; Satellite radio: An industry case study. Kellogg School of Management, Northwestern University. Case No. 5-206-255; XM satellite radio (A). Harvard Business School Case No. 9-504-009.

What is the breakeven point? In contrast to the single-product (or service) situation, the total number of units that must be sold to break even in a multiproduct company depends on the sales mix—the combination of the number of units of GMAT Success sold and the number of units of GRE Guarantee sold. We assume that the budgeted sales mix (60 units of GMAT Success sold for every 40 units of GRE Guarantee sold, that is, a ratio of 3:2) will not change at different levels of total unit sales. That is, we think of Emma selling a bundle of 3 units of GMAT Success and 2 units of GRE Guarantee. (Note that this does not mean that Emma physically bundles the two products together into one big package.)

Each bundle yields a contribution margin of $300 calculated as follows:

	Number of Units of GMAT Success and GRE Guarantee in Each Bundle	Contribution Margin per Unit for GMAT Success and GRE Guarantee	Contribution Margin of the Bundle
GMAT Success	3	$80	$240
GRE Guarantee	2	30	60
Total			$300

To compute the breakeven point, we calculate the number of bundles Emma needs to sell.

$$\text{Breakeven point in bundles} = \frac{\text{Fixed costs}}{\text{Contribution margin per bundle}} = \frac{\$4,500}{\$300 \text{ per bundle}} = 15 \text{ bundles}$$

Breakeven point in units of GMAT Success and GRE Guarantee is as follows:

GMAT Success: 15 bundles × 3 units of GMAT Success per bundle	45 units
GRE Guarantee: 15 bundles × 2 units of GRE Guarantee per bundle	30 units
Total number of units to break even	75 units

Breakeven point in dollars for GMAT Success and GRE Guarantee is as follows:

GMAT Success: 45 units × $200 per unit	$ 9,000
GRE Guarantee: 30 units × $100 per unit	3,000
Breakeven revenues	$12,000

When there are multiple products, it is often convenient to use contribution margin percentage. Under this approach, Emma first calculates the revenues from selling a bundle of 3 units of GMAT Success and 2 units of GRE Guarantee:

	Number of Units of GMAT Success and GRE Guarantee in Each Bundle	Selling Price for GMAT Success and GRE Guarantee	Revenue of the Bundle
GMAT Success	3	$200	$600
GRE Guarantee	2	100	200
Total			$800

$$\text{Contribution margin percentage for the bundle} = \frac{\text{Contribution margin of the bundle}}{\text{Revenue of the bundle}} = \frac{\$300}{\$800} = 0.375 \text{ or } 37.5\%$$

$$\text{Breakeven revenues} = \frac{\text{Fixed costs}}{\text{Contribution margin \% for the bundle}} = \frac{\$4,500}{0.375} = \$12,000$$

$$\text{Number of bundles required to be sold to break even} = \frac{\text{Breakeven revenues}}{\text{Revenue per bundle}} = \frac{\$12,000}{\$800 \text{ per bundle}} = 15 \text{ bundles}$$

The breakeven point in units and dollars for GMAT Success and GRE Guarantee are as follows:

GMAT Success: 15 bundles × 3 units of GMAT Success per bundle = 45 units × $200 per unit = $9,000

GRE Guarantee: 15 bundles × 2 units of GRE Guarantee per bundle = 30 units × $100 per unit = $3,000

Recall that in all our calculations we have assumed that the budgeted sales mix (3 units of GMAT Success for every 2 units of GRE Guarantee) will not change at different levels of total unit sales.

Of course, there are many different sales mixes (in units) that result in a contribution margin of $4,500 and cause Emma to break even, as the following table shows:

Sales Mix (Units)		Contribution Margin from		
GMAT Success (1)	GRE Guarantee (2)	GMAT Success (3) = $80 × (1)	GRE Guarantee (4) = $30 × (2)	Total Contribution Margin (5) = (3) + (4)
48	22	$3,840	$ 660	$4,500
36	54	2,880	1,620	4,500
30	70	2,400	2,100	4,500

If for example, the sales mix changes to 3 units of GMAT Success for every 7 units of GRE Guarantee, the breakeven point increases from 75 units to 100 units, comprising 30 units of GMAT Success and 70 units of GRE Guarantee. The breakeven quantity increases because the sales mix has shifted toward the lower-contribution-margin product, GRE Guarantee ($30 per unit compared to GMAT Success's $80 per unit). In general, for any given total quantity of units sold, as the sales mix shifts toward units with lower contribution margins (more units of GRE Guarantee compared to GMAT Success), operating income will be lower.

How do companies choose their sales mix? They adjust their mix to respond to demand changes. For example, as gasoline prices increase and customers want smaller cars, auto companies shift their production mix to produce smaller cars.

The multi-product case has two cost drivers, GMAT Success and GRE Guarantee. It shows how CVP and breakeven analysis can be adapted to the case of multiple cost drivers. The key point is that many different combinations of cost drivers can result in a given contribution margin.

Decision Point

How can CVP analysis be applied to a company producing multiple products?

CVP Analysis in Service and Nonprofit Organizations

Thus far, our CVP analysis has focused on a merchandising company. CVP can also be applied to decisions by manufacturing companies like BMW, service companies like Bank of America, and nonprofit organizations like the United Way. To apply CVP analysis in service and nonprofit organizations, we need to focus on measuring their output, which is different from the tangible units sold by manufacturing and merchandising companies. Examples of output measures in various service and nonprofit industries are as follows:

Industry	Measure of Output
Airlines	Passenger miles
Hotels/motels	Room-nights occupied
Hospitals	Patient days
Universities	Student credit-hours

Consider an agency of the Massachusetts Department of Social Welfare with a $900,000 budget appropriation (its revenues) for 2011. This nonprofit agency's purpose is to assist handicapped people seeking employment. On average, the agency supplements each person's income by $5,000 annually. The agency's only other costs are fixed costs of rent and administrative salaries equal to $270,000. The agency manager wants to know how many people could be assisted in 2011. We can use CVP analysis here by setting operating income to $0. Let Q be the number of handicapped people to be assisted:

$$\text{Revenues} - \text{Variable costs} - \text{Fixed costs} = 0$$
$$\$900,000 - \$5,000\,Q - \$270,000 = 0$$
$$\$5,000\,Q = \$900,000 - \$270,000 = \$630,000$$
$$Q = \$630,000 \div \$5,000 \text{ per person} = 126 \text{ people}$$

Suppose the manager is concerned that the total budget appropriation for 2012 will be reduced by 15% to $900,000 × (1 − 0.15) = $765,000. The manager wants to know how many handicapped people could be assisted with this reduced budget. Assume the same amount of monetary assistance per person:

$$\$765,000 - \$5,000\ Q - \$270,000 = 0$$
$$\$5,000Q = \$765,000 - \$270,000 = \$495,000$$
$$Q = \$495,000 \div \$5,000 \text{ per person} = 99 \text{ people}$$

Note the following two characteristics of the CVP relationships in this nonprofit situation:

1. The percentage drop in the number of people assisted, $(126 - 99) \div 126$, or 21.4%, is greater than the 15% reduction in the budget appropriation. It is greater because the $270,000 in fixed costs still must be paid, leaving a proportionately lower budget to assist people. The percentage drop in service exceeds the percentage drop in budget appropriation.

2. Given the reduced budget appropriation (revenues) of $765,000, the manager can adjust operations to stay within this appropriation in one or more of three basic ways: (a) reduce the number of people assisted from the current 126, (b) reduce the variable cost (the extent of assistance per person) from the current $5,000 per person, or (c) reduce the total fixed costs from the current $270,000.

Contribution Margin Versus Gross Margin

In the following equations, we clearly distinguish contribution margin, which provides information for CVP analysis, from gross margin, a measure of competitiveness.

$$\text{Gross margin} = \text{Revenues} - \text{Cost of goods sold}$$
$$\text{Contribution margin} = \text{Revenues} - \text{All variable costs}$$

Gross margin measures how much a company can charge for its products over and above the cost of acquiring or producing them. Companies, such as branded pharmaceuticals, have high gross margins because their products provide unique and distinctive benefits to consumers. Products such as televisions that operate in competitive markets have low gross margins. Contribution margin indicates how much of a company's revenues are available to cover fixed costs. It helps in assessing risk of loss. Risk of loss is low (high) if, when sales are low, contribution margin exceeds (is less than) fixed costs. Gross margin and contribution margin are related but give different insights. For example, a company operating in a competitive market with a low gross margin will have a low risk of loss if its fixed costs are small.

Consider the distinction between gross margin and contribution margin in the context of manufacturing companies. In the manufacturing sector, contribution margin and gross margin differ in two respects: fixed manufacturing costs and variable nonmanufacturing costs. The following example (figures assumed) illustrates this difference:

Contribution Income Statement Emphasizing Contribution Margin (in 000s)			Financial Accounting Income Statement Emphasizing Gross Margin (in 000s)	
Revenues		$1,000	Revenues	$1,000
Variable manufacturing costs	$250		Cost of goods sold (variable manufacturing costs, $250 + fixed manufacturing costs, $160)	410
Variable nonmanufacturing costs	270	520		
Contribution margin		480	Gross margin	590
Fixed manufacturing costs	160		Nonmanufacturing costs	
Fixed nonmanufacturing costs	138	298	(variable, $270 + fixed $138)	408
Operating income		$ 182	Operating income	$ 182

Fixed manufacturing costs of $160,000 are not deducted from revenues when computing contribution margin but are deducted when computing gross margin. Cost of goods sold in a manufacturing company includes all variable manufacturing costs and all fixed manufacturing costs ($250,000 + $160,000). Variable nonmanufacturing costs (such as commissions paid to salespersons) of $270,000 are deducted from revenues when computing contribution margin but are not deducted when computing gross margin.

Like contribution margin, gross margin can be expressed as a total, as an amount per unit, or as a percentage. For example, the **gross margin percentage** is the gross margin divided by revenues—59% ($590 ÷ $1,000) in our manufacturing-sector example.

One reason why gross margin and contribution margin are confused with each other is that the two are identical in the case of merchandising companies. That's because cost of goods sold equals the variable cost of goods purchased (and subsequently sold).

Problem for Self-Study

Wembley Travel Agency specializes in flights between Los Angeles and London. It books passengers on United Airlines at $900 per round-trip ticket. Until last month, United paid Wembley a commission of 10% of the ticket price paid by each passenger. This commission was Wembley's only source of revenues. Wembley's fixed costs are $14,000 per month (for salaries, rent, and so on), and its variable costs are $20 per ticket purchased for a passenger. This $20 includes a $15 per ticket delivery fee paid to Federal Express. (To keep the analysis simple, we assume each round-trip ticket purchased is delivered in a separate package. Thus, the $15 delivery fee applies to each ticket.)

United Airlines has just announced a revised payment schedule for all travel agents. It will now pay travel agents a 10% commission per ticket up to a maximum of $50. Any ticket costing more than $500 generates only a $50 commission, regardless of the ticket price.

Required

1. Under the old 10% commission structure, how many round-trip tickets must Wembley sell each month (a) to break even and (b) to earn an operating income of $7,000?
2. How does United's revised payment schedule affect your answers to (a) and (b) in requirement 1?

Solution

1. Wembley receives a 10% commission on each ticket: 10% × $900 = $90. Thus,

$$\text{Selling price} = \$90 \text{ per ticket}$$
$$\text{Variable cost per unit} = \$20 \text{ per ticket}$$
$$\text{Contribution margin per unit} = \$90 - \$20 = \$70 \text{ per ticket}$$
$$\text{Fixed costs} = \$14,000 \text{ per month}$$

a.
$$\frac{\text{Breakeven number}}{\text{of tickets}} = \frac{\text{Fixed costs}}{\text{Contribution margin per unit}} = \frac{\$14,000}{\$70 \text{ per ticket}} = 200 \text{ tickets}$$

b. When target operating income = $7,000 per month,

$$\frac{\text{Quantity of tickets}}{\text{required to be sold}} = \frac{\text{Fixed costs} + \text{Target operating income}}{\text{Contribution margin per unit}}$$
$$= \frac{\$14,000 + \$7,000}{\$70 \text{ per ticket}} = \frac{\$21,000}{\$70 \text{ per ticket}} = 300 \text{ tickets}$$

2. Under the new system, Wembley would receive only $50 on the $900 ticket. Thus,

$$\text{Selling price} = \$50 \text{ per ticket}$$
$$\text{Variable cost per unit} = \$20 \text{ per ticket}$$
$$\text{Contribution margin per unit} = \$50 - \$20 = \$30 \text{ per ticket}$$
$$\text{Fixed costs} = \$14,000 \text{ per month}$$

a.
$$\frac{\text{Breakeven number}}{\text{of tickets}} = \frac{\$14,000}{\$30 \text{ per ticket}} = 467 \text{ tickets (rounded up)}$$

b. $$\frac{\text{Quantity of tickets}}{\text{required to be sold}} = \frac{\$21,000}{\$30 \text{ per ticket}} = 700 \text{ tickets}$$

The \$50 cap on the commission paid per ticket causes the breakeven point to more than double (from 200 to 467 tickets) and the tickets required to be sold to earn \$7,000 per month to also more than double (from 300 to 700 tickets). As would be expected, travel agents reacted very negatively to the United Airlines announcement to change commission payments. Unfortunately for travel agents, other airlines also changed their commission structure in similar ways.

Decision Points

The following question-and-answer format summarizes the chapter's learning objectives. Each decision presents a key question related to a learning objective. The guidelines are the answer to that question.

Decision	Guidelines
1. How can CVP analysis assist managers?	CVP analysis assists managers in understanding the behavior of a product's or service's total costs, total revenues, and operating income as changes occur in the output level, selling price, variable costs, or fixed costs.
2. How can managers determine the breakeven point or the output needed to achieve a target operating income?	The breakeven point is the quantity of output at which total revenues equal total costs. The three methods for computing the breakeven point and the quantity of output to achieve target operating income are the equation method, the contribution margin method, and the graph method. Each method is merely a restatement of the others. Managers often select the method they find easiest to use in the specific decision situation.
3. How can managers incorporate income taxes into CVP analysis?	Income taxes can be incorporated into CVP analysis by using target net income to calculate the corresponding target operating income. The breakeven point is unaffected by income taxes because no income taxes are paid when operating income equals zero.
4. How do managers use CVP analysis to make decisions?	Managers compare how revenues, costs, and contribution margins change across various alternatives. They then choose the alternative that maximizes operating income.
5. What can managers do to cope with uncertainty or changes in underlying assumptions?	Sensitivity analysis, a "what-if" technique, examines how an outcome will change if the original predicted data are not achieved or if an underlying assumption changes. When making decisions, managers use CVP analysis to compare contribution margins and fixed costs under different assumptions. Managers also calculate the margin of safety equal to budgeted revenues minus breakeven revenues.
6. How should managers choose between different variable-cost/fixed-cost structures?	Choosing the variable-cost/fixed-cost structure is a strategic decision for companies. CVP analysis highlights the risk of losses when revenues are low and the upside profits when revenues are high for different proportions of variable and fixed costs in a company's cost structure.
7. How can CVP analysis be applied to a company producing multiple products?	CVP analysis can be applied to a company producing multiple products by assuming the sales mix of products sold remains constant as the total quantity of units sold changes.

Appendix

Decision Models and Uncertainty

This appendix explores the characteristics of uncertainty, describes an approach managers can use to make decisions in a world of uncertainty, and illustrates the insights gained when uncertainty is recognized in CVP analysis.

Coping with Uncertainty[2]

In the face of uncertainty, managers rely on decision models to help them make the right choices.

Role of a Decision Model

Uncertainty is the possibility that an actual amount will deviate from an expected amount. In the GMAT Success example, Emma might forecast sales at 42 units, but actual sales might turn out to be 30 units or 60 units. A decision model helps managers deal with such uncertainty. It is a formal method for making a choice, commonly involving both quantitative and qualitative analyses. The quantitative analysis usually includes the following steps:

Step 1: Identify a choice criterion. A **choice criterion** is an objective that can be quantified such as maximize income or minimize costs. Managers use the choice criterion to choose the best alternative action. Emma's choice criterion is to maximize expected operating income at the Chicago college fair.

Step 2: Identify the set of alternative actions that can be taken. We use the letter a with subscripts $_1$, $_2$, and $_3$ to distinguish each of Emma's three possible actions:

$$a_1 = \text{Pay \$2,000 fixed fee}$$
$$a_2 = \text{Pay \$800 fixed fee plus 15\% of GMAT Success revenues}$$
$$a_3 = \text{Pay 25\% of GMAT Success revenues with no fixed fee}$$

Step 3: Identify the set of events that can occur. An **event** is a possible relevant occurrence, such as the actual number of GMAT Success packages Emma might sell at the fair. The set of events should be mutually exclusive and collectively exhaustive. Events are mutually exclusive if they cannot occur at the same time. Events are collectively exhaustive if, taken together, they make up the entire set of possible relevant occurrences (no other event can occur). Examples of mutually exclusive and collectively exhaustive events are growth, decline, or no change in industry demand, and increase, decrease, or no change in interest rates. Only one event out of the entire set of mutually exclusive and collectively exhaustive events will actually occur.

Suppose Emma's only uncertainty is the number of units of GMAT Success that she can sell. For simplicity, suppose Emma estimates that sales will be either 30 or 60 units. This set of events is mutually exclusive because clearly sales of 30 units and 60 units cannot both occur at the same time. It is collectively exhaustive because under our assumptions, sales cannot be anything other than 30 or 60 units. We use the letter x with subscripts $_1$ and $_2$ to distinguish the set of mutually exclusive and collectively exhaustive events:

$$x_1 = \text{30 units}$$
$$x_2 = \text{60 units}$$

Step 4: Assign a probability to each event that can occur. A **probability** is the likelihood or chance that an event will occur. The decision model approach to coping with uncertainty assigns probabilities to events. A **probability distribution** describes the likelihood, or the probability, that each of the mutually exclusive and collectively exhaustive set of events will occur. In some cases, there will be much evidence to guide the assignment of probabilities. For example, the probability of obtaining heads in the toss of a coin is 1/2 and that of drawing a particular playing card from a standard, well-shuffled deck is 1/52. In business, the probability of having a specified percentage of defective units may be assigned with great confidence on the basis of production experience with thousands of units. In other cases, there will be little evidence supporting estimated probabilities—for example, expected sales of a new pharmaceutical product next year.

Suppose that Emma, on the basis of past experience, assesses a 60% chance, or a 6/10 probability, that she will sell 30 units and a 40% chance, or a 4/10 probability, that she will sell 60 units. Using P(x) as the notation for the probability of an event, the probabilities are as follows:

$$P(x_1) = 6/10 = 0.60$$
$$P(x_2) = 4/10 = 0.40$$

The sum of these probabilities must equal 1.00 because these events are mutually exclusive and collectively exhaustive.

---

[2] The presentation here draws (in part) from teaching notes prepared by R. Williamson.

Exhibit 6   Decision Table for GMAT Success

	A	B	C	D	E	F	G	H	I
		Home Insert Page Layout Formulas Data Review View							
1	Selling price = $200					Operating Income			
2	Package cost = $120					Under Each Possible Event			
3			Percentage						
4		Fixed	of Fair	Event x_1: Units Sold = 30			Event x_2: Units Sold = 60		
5	Actions	Fee	Revenues	Probability(x_1) = 0.60			Probability(x_2) = 0.40		
6	a_1: Pay $2,000 fixed fee	$2,000	0%	$400[l]			$2,800[m]		
7	a_2: Pay $800 fixed fee plus 15% of revenues	$ 800	15%	$700[n]			$2,200[p]		
8	a_3: Pay 25% of revenues with no fixed fee	$ 0	25%	$900[q]			$1,800[r]		
9									
10	[l]Operating income = ($200 – $120)(30) – $2,000	=	$ 400						
11	[m]Operating income = ($200 – $120)(60) – $2,000	=	$2,800						
12	[n]Operating income = ($200 – $120 – 15% × $200)(30) – $800	=	$ 700						
13	[p]Operating income = ($200 – $120 – 15% × $200)(60) – $800	=	$2,200						
14	[q]Operating income = ($200 – $120 – 25% × $200)(30)	=	$ 900						
15	[r]Operating income = ($200 – $120 – 25% × $200)(60)	=	$1,800						

Step 5:   Identify the set of possible outcomes. Outcomes specify, in terms of the choice criterion, the predicted economic results of the various possible combinations of actions and events. In the GMAT Success example, the outcomes are the six possible operating incomes displayed in the decision table in Exhibit 6. A **decision table** is a summary of the alternative actions, events, outcomes, and probabilities of events.

Distinguish among actions, events, and outcomes. Actions are decision choices available to managers—for example, the particular rental alternatives that Emma can choose. Events are the set of all relevant occurrences that can happen—for example, the different quantities of GMAT Success packages that may be sold at the fair. The outcome is operating income, which depends both on the action the manager selects (rental alternative chosen) and the event that occurs (the quantity of packages sold).

Exhibit 7 presents an overview of relationships among a decision model, the implementation of a chosen action, its outcome, and a subsequent performance evaluation. Thoughtful managers step back and evaluate what happened and learn from their experiences. This learning serves as feedback for adapting the decision model for future actions.

Expected Value

An **expected value** is the weighted average of the outcomes, with the probability of each outcome serving as the weight. When the outcomes are measured in monetary terms, expected value is often called **expected monetary value**. Using information in Exhibit 6, the expected monetary value of each booth-rental alternative denoted by $E(a_1)$, $E(a_2)$, and $E(a_3)$ is as follows:

Pay $2,000 fixed fee: $E(a_1) = (0.60 \times \$400) + (0.40 \times \$2,800) = \$1,360$
Pay $800 fixed fee plus 15% of revenues: $E(a_2) = (0.60 \times \$700) + (0.40 \times \$2,200) = \$1,300$
Pay 25% of revenues with no fixed fee: $E(a_3) = (0.60 \times \$900) + (0.40 \times \$1,800) = \$1,260$

Exhibit 7   A Decision Model and Its Link to Performance Evaluation

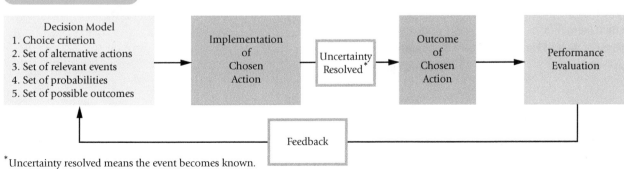

*Uncertainty resolved means the event becomes known.

To maximize expected operating income, Emma should select action a_1—pay the fair organizers a $2,000 fixed fee.

To interpret the expected value of selecting action a_1, imagine that Emma attends many fairs, each with the probability distribution of operating incomes given in Exhibit 6. For a specific fair, Emma will earn operating income of either $400, if she sells 30 units, or $2,800, if she sells 60 units. But if Emma attends 100 fairs, she will expect to earn $400 operating income 60% of the time (at 60 fairs), and $2,800 operating income 40% of the time (at 40 fairs), for a total operating income of $136,000 ($400 × 60 + $2,800 × 40). The expected value of $1,360 is the operating income per fair that Emma will earn when averaged across all fairs ($136,000 ÷ 100). Of course, in many real-world situations, managers must make one-time decisions under uncertainty. Even in these cases, expected value is a useful tool for choosing among alternatives.

Consider the effect of uncertainty on the preferred action choice. If Emma were certain she would sell only 30 units (that is, $P(x_1) = 1$), she would prefer alternative a_3—pay 25% of revenues with no fixed fee. To follow this reasoning, examine Exhibit 6. When 30 units are sold, alternative a_3 yields the maximum operating income of $900. Because fixed costs are $0, booth-rental costs are lower, equal to $1,500 (25% of revenues = 0.25 × $200 per unit × 30 units), when sales are low.

However, if Emma were certain she would sell 60 packages (that is, $P(x_2) = 1$), she would prefer alternative a_1—pay a $2,000 fixed fee. Exhibit 6 indicates that when 60 units are sold, alternative a_1 yields the maximum operating income of $2,800. Rental payments under a_2 and a_3 increase with units sold but are fixed under a_1.

Despite the high probability of selling only 30 units, Emma still prefers to take action a_1, which is to pay a fixed fee of $2,000. That's because the high risk of low operating income (the 60% probability of selling only 30 units) is more than offset by the high return from selling 60 units, which has a 40% probability. If Emma were more averse to risk (measured in our example by the difference between operating incomes when 30 versus 60 units are sold), she might have preferred action a_2 or a_3. For example, action a_2 ensures an operating income of at least $700, greater than the operating income of $400 that she would earn under action a_1 if only 30 units were sold. Of course, choosing a_2 limits the upside potential to $2,200 relative to $2,800 under a_1, if 60 units are sold. If Emma is very concerned about downside risk, however, she may be willing to forgo some upside benefits to protect against a $400 outcome by choosing a_2.[3]

Good Decisions and Good Outcomes

Always distinguish between a good decision and a good outcome. One can exist without the other. Suppose you are offered a one-time-only gamble tossing a coin. You will win $20 if the event is heads, but you will lose $1 if the event is tails. As a decision maker, you proceed through the logical phases: gathering information, assessing outcomes, and making a choice. You accept the bet. Why? Because the expected value is $9.50 [0.5($20) + 0.5(−$1)]. The coin is tossed and the event is tails. You lose. From your viewpoint, this was a good decision but a bad outcome.

A decision can be made only on the basis of information that is available at the time of evaluating and making the decision. By definition, uncertainty rules out guaranteeing that the best outcome will always be obtained. As in our example, it is possible that bad luck will produce bad outcomes even when good decisions have been made. A bad outcome does not mean a bad decision was made. The best protection against a bad outcome is a good decision.

Terms to Learn

This chapter contains definitions of the following important terms:

breakeven point (BEP)	degree of operating leverage	probability
choice criterion	event	probability distribution
contribution income statement	expected monetary value	PV graph
contribution margin	expected value	revenue driver
contribution margin per unit	gross margin percentage	sales mix
contribution margin percentage	margin of safety	sensitivity analysis
contribution margin ratio	net income	uncertainty
cost-volume-profit (CVP) analysis	operating leverage	
decision table	outcomes	

---

[3] For more formal approaches, refer to Moore, J. and L. Weatherford. 2001. *Decision modeling with Microsoft Excel*, 6th ed. Upper Saddle River, NJ: Prentice Hall.

Assignment Material

Note: To underscore the basic CVP relationships, the assignment material ignores income taxes unless stated otherwise.

Questions

3-1 Define cost-volume-profit analysis.

3-2 Describe the assumptions underlying CVP analysis.

3-3 Distinguish between operating income and net income.

3-4 Define contribution margin, contribution margin per unit, and contribution margin percentage.

3-5 Describe three methods that can be used to express CVP relationships.

3-6 Why is it more accurate to describe the subject matter of this chapter as CVP analysis rather than as breakeven analysis?

3-7 "CVP analysis is both simple and simplistic. If you want realistic analysis to underpin your decisions, look beyond CVP analysis." Do you agree? Explain.

3-8 How does an increase in the income tax rate affect the breakeven point?

3-9 Describe sensitivity analysis. How has the advent of the electronic spreadsheet affected the use of sensitivity analysis?

3-10 Give an example of how a manager can decrease variable costs while increasing fixed costs.

3-11 Give an example of how a manager can increase variable costs while decreasing fixed costs.

3-12 What is operating leverage? How is knowing the degree of operating leverage helpful to managers?

3-13 "There is no such thing as a fixed cost. All costs can be 'unfixed' given sufficient time." Do you agree? What is the implication of your answer for CVP analysis?

3-14 How can a company with multiple products compute its breakeven point?

3-15 "In CVP analysis, gross margin is a less-useful concept than contribution margin." Do you agree? Explain briefly.

Exercises

3-16 **CVP computations.** Fill in the blanks for each of the following independent cases.

Case	Revenues	Variable Costs	Fixed Costs	Total Costs	Operating Income	Contribution Margin Percentage
a.		$500		$ 800	$1,200	
b.	$2,000		$300		$ 200	
c.	$1,000	$700		$1,000		
d.	$1,500		$300			40%

3-17 **CVP computations.** Garrett Manufacturing sold 410,000 units of its product for $68 per unit in 2011. Variable cost per unit is $60 and total fixed costs are $1,640,000.

1. Calculate (a) contribution margin and (b) operating income.
2. Garrett's current manufacturing process is labor intensive. Kate Schoenen, Garrett's production manager, has proposed investing in state-of-the-art manufacturing equipment, which will increase the annual fixed costs to $5,330,000. The variable costs are expected to decrease to $54 per unit. Garrett expects to maintain the same sales volume and selling price next year. How would acceptance of Schoenen's proposal affect your answers to (a) and (b) in requirement 1?
3. Should Garrett accept Schoenen's proposal? Explain.

3-18 **CVP analysis, changing revenues and costs.** Sunny Spot Travel Agency specializes in flights between Toronto and Jamaica. It books passengers on Canadian Air. Sunny Spot's fixed costs are $23,500 per month. Canadian Air charges passengers $1,500 per round-trip ticket.

Calculate the number of tickets Sunny Spot must sell each month to (a) break even and (b) make a target operating income of $17,000 per month in each of the following independent cases.

1. Sunny Spot's variable costs are $43 per ticket. Canadian Air pays Sunny Spot 6% commission on ticket price.
2. Sunny Spot's variable costs are $40 per ticket. Canadian Air pays Sunny Spot 6% commission on ticket price.
3. Sunny Spot's variable costs are $40 per ticket. Canadian Air pays $60 fixed commission per ticket to Sunny Spot. Comment on the results.
4. Sunny Spot's variable costs are $40 per ticket. It receives $60 commission per ticket from Canadian Air. It charges its customers a delivery fee of $5 per ticket. Comment on the results.

3-19 CVP exercises. The Super Donut owns and operates six doughnut outlets in and round Kansas City. You are given the following corporate budget data for next year:

Revenues	$10,000,000
Fixed costs	$ 1,800,000
Variable costs	$ 8,000,000

Variable costs change with respect to the number of doughnuts sold.

Required Compute the budgeted operating income for each of the following deviations from the original budget data. (Consider each case independently.)

1. A 10% increase in contribution margin, holding revenues constant
2. A 10% decrease in contribution margin, holding revenues constant
3. A 5% increase in fixed costs
4. A 5% decrease in fixed costs
5. An 8% increase in units sold
6. An 8% decrease in units sold
7. A 10% increase in fixed costs and a 10% increase in units sold
8. A 5% increase in fixed costs and a 5% decrease in variable costs

3-20 CVP exercises. The Doral Company manufactures and sells pens. Currently, 5,000,000 units are sold per year at $0.50 per unit. Fixed costs are $900,000 per year. Variable costs are $0.30 per unit.

Required Consider each case separately:
1a. What is the current annual operating income?
  b. What is the present breakeven point in revenues?

Compute the new operating income for each of the following changes:
2. A $0.04 per unit increase in variable costs
3. A 10% increase in fixed costs and a 10% increase in units sold
4. A 20% decrease in fixed costs, a 20% decrease in selling price, a 10% decrease in variable cost per unit, and a 40% increase in units sold

Compute the new breakeven point in units for each of the following changes:
5. A 10% increase in fixed costs
6. A 10% increase in selling price and a $20,000 increase in fixed costs

3-21 CVP analysis, income taxes. Brooke Motors is a small car dealership. On average, it sells a car for $27,000, which it purchases from the manufacturer for $23,000. Each month, Brooke Motors pays $48,200 in rent and utilities and $68,000 for salespeople's salaries. In addition to their salaries, salespeople are paid a commission of $600 for each car they sell. Brooke Motors also spends $13,000 each month for local advertisements. Its tax rate is 40%.

Required
1. How many cars must Brooke Motors sell each month to break even?
2. Brooke Motors has a target monthly net income of $51,000. What is its target monthly operating income? How many cars must be sold each month to reach the target monthly net income of $51,000?

3-22 CVP analysis, income taxes. The Express Banquet has two restaurants that are open 24-hours a day. Fixed costs for the two restaurants together total $459,000 per year. Service varies from a cup of coffee to full meals. The average sales check per customer is $8.50. The average cost of food and other variable costs for each customer is $3.40. The income tax rate is 30%. Target net income is $107,100.

Required
1. Compute the revenues needed to earn the target net income.
2. How many customers are needed to break even? To earn net income of $107,100?
3. Compute net income if the number of customers is 170,000.

3-23 CVP analysis, sensitivity analysis. Hoot Washington is the newly elected leader of the Republican Party. Media Publishers is negotiating to publish Hoot's Manifesto, a new book that promises to be an instant best-seller. The fixed costs of producing and marketing the book will be $500,000. The variable costs of producing and marketing will be $4.00 per copy sold. These costs are before any payments to Hoot. Hoot negotiates an up-front payment of $3 million, plus a 15% royalty rate on the net sales price of each book. The net sales price is the listed bookstore price of $30, minus the margin paid to the bookstore to sell the book. The normal bookstore margin of 30% of the listed bookstore price is expected to apply.

Required
1. Prepare a PV graph for Media Publishers.
2. How many copies must Media Publishers sell to (a) break even and (b) earn a target operating income of $2 million?
3. Examine the sensitivity of the breakeven point to the following changes:

   a. Decreasing the normal bookstore margin to 20% of the listed bookstore price of $30
   b. Increasing the listed bookstore price to $40 while keeping the bookstore margin at 30%
   c. Comment on the results

3-24 CVP analysis, margin of safety. Suppose Doral Corp.'s breakeven point is revenues of $1,100,000. Fixed costs are $660,000.

1. Compute the contribution margin percentage.
2. Compute the selling price if variable costs are $16 per unit.
3. Suppose 95,000 units are sold. Compute the margin of safety in units and dollars.

3-25 Operating leverage. Color Rugs is holding a two-week carpet sale at Jerry's Club, a local warehouse store. Color Rugs plans to sell carpets for $500 each. The company will purchase the carpets from a local distributor for $350 each, with the privilege of returning any unsold units for a full refund. Jerry's Club has offered Color Rugs two payment alternatives for the use of space.

- Option 1: A fixed payment of $5,000 for the sale period

150 CM

op. income

- Option 2: 10% of total revenues earned during the sale period

Assume Color Rugs will incur no other costs.

1. Calculate the breakeven point in units for (a) option 1 and (b) option 2.
2. At what level of revenues will Color Rugs earn the same operating income under either option?
   a. For what range of unit sales will Color Rugs prefer option 1?
   b. For what range of unit sales will Color Rugs prefer option 2?
3. Calculate the degree of operating leverage at sales of 100 units for the two rental options.
4. Briefly explain and interpret your answer to requirement 3.

3-26 CVP analysis, international cost structure differences. Global Textiles, Inc., is considering three possible countries for the sole manufacturing site of its newest area rug: Singapore, Brazil, and the United States. All area rugs are to be sold to retail outlets in the United States for $250 per unit. These retail outlets add their own markup when selling to final customers. Fixed costs and variable cost per unit (area rug) differ in the three countries.

Country	Sales Price to Retail Outlets	Annual Fixed Costs	Variable Manufacturing Cost per Area Rug	Variable Marketing & Distribution Cost per Area Rug
Singapore	$250.00	$ 9,000,000	$75.00	$25.00
Brazil	250.00	8,400,000	60.00	15.00
United States	250.00	12,400,000	82.50	12.50

1. Compute the breakeven point for Global Textiles, Inc., in each country in (a) units sold and (b) revenues.
2. If Global Textiles, Inc., plans to produce and sell 75,000 rugs in 2011, what is the budgeted operating income for each of the three manufacturing locations? Comment on the results.

3-27 Sales mix, new and upgrade customers. Data 1-2-3 is a top-selling electronic spreadsheet product. Data is about to release version 5.0. It divides its customers into two groups: new customers and upgrade customers (those who previously purchased Data 1-2-3, 4.0 or earlier versions). Although the same physical product is provided to each customer group, sizable differences exist in selling prices and variable marketing costs:

	New Customers		Upgrade Customers	
Selling price		$275		$100
Variable costs				
Manufacturing	$35		$35	
Marketing	65	100	15	50
Contribution margin		$175		$ 50

The fixed costs of Data 1-2-3, 5.0 are $15,000,000. The planned sales mix in units is 60% new customers and 40% upgrade customers.

1. What is the Data 1-2-3, 5.0 breakeven point in units, assuming that the planned 60%:40% sales mix is attained?
2. If the sales mix is attained, what is the operating income when 220,000 total units are sold?
3. Show how the breakeven point in units changes with the following customer mixes:
   a. New 40% and Upgrade 60%
   b. New 80% and Upgrade 20%
   c. Comment on the results

3-28 Sales mix, three products. Bobbie's Bagel Shop sells only coffee and bagels. Bobbie estimates that every time she sells one bagel, she sells four cups of coffee. The budgeted cost information for Bobbie's products for 2011 follows:

	Coffee	Bagels
Selling Price	$2.50	$3.75
Product ingredients	$0.25	$0.50
Hourly sales staff (cost per unit)	$0.50	$1.00
Packaging	$0.50	$0.25
Fixed Costs		
Rent on store and equipment	$5,000	
Marketing and advertising cost	$2,000	

Required

1. How many cups of coffee and how many bagels must Bobbie sell in order to break even assuming the sales mix of four cups of coffee to one bagel, given previously?
2. If the sales mix is four cups of coffee to one bagel, how many units of each product does Bobbie need to sell to earn operating income before tax of $28,000?
3. Assume that Bobbie decides to add the sale of muffins to her product mix. The selling price for muffins is $3.00 and the related variable costs are $0.75. Assuming a sales mix of three cups of coffee to two bagels to one muffin, how many units of each product does Bobbie need to sell in order to break even? Comment on the results.

3-29 CVP, Not for profit. Monroe Classical Music Society is a not-for-profit organization that brings guest artists to the community's greater metropolitan area. The Music Society just bought a small concert hall in the center of town to house its performances. The mortgage payments on the concert hall are expected to be $2,000 per month. The organization pays its guest performers $1,000 per concert and anticipates corresponding ticket sales to be $2,500 per event. The Music Society also incurs costs of approximately $500 per concert for marketing and advertising. The organization pays its artistic director $50,000 per year and expects to receive $40,000 in donations in addition to its ticket sales.

Required

1. If the Monroe Classical Music Society just breaks even, how many concerts does it hold?
2. In addition to the organization's artistic director, the Music Society would like to hire a marketing director for $40,000 per year. What is the breakeven point? The Music Society anticipates that the addition of a marketing director would allow the organization to increase the number of concerts to 60 per year. What is the Music Society's operating income/(loss) if it hires the new marketing director?
3. The Music Society expects to receive a grant that would provide the organization with an additional $20,000 toward the payment of the marketing director's salary. What is the breakeven point if the Music Society hires the marketing director and receives the grant?

3-30 Contribution margin, decision making. Lurvey Men's Clothing's revenues and cost data for 2011 are as follows:

Revenues		$600,000
Cost of goods sold		300,000
Gross margin		300,000
Operating costs:		
Salaries fixed	$170,000	
Sales commissions (10% of sales)	60,000	
Depreciation of equipment and fixtures	20,000	
Store rent ($4,500 per month)	54,000	
Other operating costs	45,000	349,000
Operating income (loss)		$ (49,000)

Mr. Lurvey, the owner of the store, is unhappy with the operating results. An analysis of other operating costs reveals that it includes $30,000 variable costs, which vary with sales volume, and $15,000 (fixed) costs.

Required

1. Compute the contribution margin of Lurvey Men's Clothing.
2. Compute the contribution margin percentage.
3. Mr. Lurvey estimates that he can increase revenues by 15% by incurring additional advertising costs of $13,000. Calculate the impact of the additional advertising costs on operating income.

3-31 Contribution margin, gross margin, and margin of safety. Mirabella Cosmetics manufactures and sells a face cream to small ethnic stores in the greater New York area. It presents the monthly operating income statement shown here to George Lopez, a potential investor in the business. Help Mr. Lopez understand Mirabella's cost structure.

	Home	Insert	Page Layout	Formulas	Data	Review	View
	A	B		C		D	
1		Mirabella Cosmetics					
2		Operating Income Statement, June 2011					
3	Units sold					10,000	
4	Revenues					$100,000	
5	Cost of goods sold						
6	Variable manufacturing costs			$55,000			
7	Fixed manufacturing costs			20,000			
8	Total					75,000	
9	Gross margin					25,000	
10	Operating costs						
11	Variable marketing costs			$ 5,000			
12	Fixed marketing & administration costs			10,000			
13	Total operating costs					15,000	
14	Operating income					$ 10,000	

Required

1. Recast the income statement to emphasize contribution margin.
2. Calculate the contribution margin percentage and breakeven point in units and revenues for June 2011.
3. What is the margin of safety (in units) for June 2011?
4. If sales in June were only 8,000 units and Mirabella's tax rate is 30%, calculate its net income.

3-32 Uncertainty and expected costs. Foodmart Corp, an international retail giant, is considering implementing a new business to business (B2B) information system for processing purchase orders. The current system costs Foodmart $2,500,000 per month and $50 per order. Foodmart has two options, a partially automated B2B and a fully automated B2B system. The partially automated B2B system will have a fixed cost of $10,000,000 per month and a variable cost of $40 per order. The fully automated B2B system has a fixed cost of $20,000,000 per month and $25 per order.

Based on data from the last two years, Foodmart has determined the following distribution on monthly orders:

Monthly Number of Orders	Probability
350,000	0.15
450,000	0.20
550,000	0.35
650,000	0.20
750,000	0.10

Required

1. Prepare a table showing the cost of each plan for each quantity of monthly orders.
2. What is the expected cost of each plan?
3. In addition to the information systems costs, what other factors should Foodmart consider before deciding to implement a new B2B system?

Problems

3-33 CVP analysis, service firm. Lifetime Escapes generates average revenue of $5,000 per person on its five-day package tours to wildlife parks in Kenya. The variable costs per person are as follows:

Airfare	$1,400
Hotel accommodations	1,100
Meals	300
Ground transportation	100
Park tickets and other costs	800
Total	$3,700

Annual fixed costs total $520,000.

1. Calculate the number of package tours that must be sold to break even.
2. Calculate the revenue needed to earn a target operating income of $91,000.
3. If fixed costs increase by $32,000, what decrease in variable cost per person must be achieved to maintain the breakeven point calculated in requirement 1?

3-34 CVP, target operating income, service firm. Snow Leopard Daycare provides daycare for children Mondays through Fridays. Its monthly variable costs per child are as follows:

Lunch and snacks	$150
Educational supplies	60
Other supplies (paper products, toiletries, etc.)	20
Total	$230

Monthly fixed costs consist of the following:

Rent	$2,150
Utilities	200
Insurance	250
Salaries	2,350
Miscellaneous	650
Total	$5,600

Snow Leopard charges each parent $580 per child.

1. Calculate the breakeven point.
2. Snow Leopard's target operating income is $10,500 per month. Compute the number of children who must be enrolled to achieve the target operating income.
3. Snow Leopard lost its lease and had to move to another building. Monthly rent for the new building is $3,150. At the suggestion of parents, Snow Leopard plans to take children on field trips. Monthly costs of the field trips are $1,300. By how much should Snow Leopard increase fees per child to meet the target operating income of $10,500 per month, assuming the same number of children as in requirement 2?

3-35 CVP analysis, margin of safety. (CMA, adapted) Technology Solutions sells a ready-to-use software product for small businesses. The current selling price is $300. Projected operating income for 2011 is $490,000 based on a sales volume of 10,000 units. Variable costs of producing the software are $120 per unit sold plus an additional cost of $5 per unit for shipping and handling. Technology Solutions annual fixed costs are $1,260,000.

1. Calculate Technology Solutions breakeven point and margin of safety in units.
2. Calculate the company's operating income for 2011 if there is a 10% increase in unit sales.
3. For 2012, management expects that the per unit production cost of the software will increase by 30%, but the shipping and handling costs per unit will decrease by 20%. Calculate the sales revenue Technology Solutions must generate for 2012 to maintain the current year's operating income if the selling price remains unchanged, assuming all other data as in the original problem.

3-36 CVP analysis, income taxes. (CMA, adapted) R. A. Ro and Company, a manufacturer of quality handmade walnut bowls, has had a steady growth in sales for the past five years. However, increased competition has led Mr. Ro, the president, to believe that an aggressive marketing campaign will be necessary next year to maintain the company's present growth. To prepare for next year's marketing campaign, the company's controller has prepared and presented Mr. Ro with the following data for the current year, 2011:

Variable cost (per bowl)	
Direct materials	$ 3.25
Direct manufacturing labor	8.00
Variable overhead (manufacturing, marketing, distribution, and customer service)	2.50
Total variable cost per bowl	$ 13.75
Fixed costs	
Manufacturing	$ 25,000
Marketing, distribution, and customer service	110,000
Total fixed costs	$135,000
Selling price	25.00
Expected sales, 20,000 units	$500,000
Income tax rate	40%

Required

1. What is the projected net income for 2011?
2. What is the breakeven point in units for 2011?
3. Mr. Ro has set the revenue target for 2012 at a level of $550,000 (or 22,000 bowls). He believes an additional marketing cost of $11,250 for advertising in 2012, with all other costs remaining constant, will be necessary to attain the revenue target. What is the net income for 2012 if the additional $11,250 is spent and the revenue target is met?
4. What is the breakeven point in revenues for 2012 if the additional $11,250 is spent for advertising?
5. If the additional $11,250 is spent, what are the required 2012 revenues for 2012 net income to equal 2011 net income?
6. At a sales level of 22,000 units, what maximum amount can be spent on advertising if a 2012 net income of $60,000 is desired?

3-37 CVP, sensitivity analysis. The Brown Shoe Company produces its famous shoe, the Divine Loafer that sells for $60 per pair. Operating income for 2011 is as follows:

Sales revenue ($60 per pair)	$300,000
Variable cost ($25 per pair)	125,000
Contribution margin	175,000
Fixed cost	100,000
Operating income	$ 75,000

Brown Shoe Company would like to increase its profitability over the next year by at least 25%. To do so, the company is considering the following options:

Required

1. Replace a portion of its variable labor with an automated machining process. This would result in a 20% decrease in variable cost per unit, but a 15% increase in fixed costs. Sales would remain the same.
2. Spend $30,000 on a new advertising campaign, which would increase sales by 20%.
3. Increase both selling price by $10 per unit and variable costs by $7 per unit by using a higher quality leather material in the production of its shoes. The higher priced shoe would cause demand to drop by approximately 10%.
4. Add a second manufacturing facility which would double Brown's fixed costs, but would increase sales by 60%.

Evaluate each of the alternatives considered by Brown Shoes. Do any of the options meet or exceed Brown's targeted increase in income of 25%? What should Brown do?

3-38 CVP analysis, shoe stores. The WalkRite Shoe Company operates a chain of shoe stores that sell 10 different styles of inexpensive men's shoes with identical unit costs and selling prices. A unit is defined as a pair of shoes. Each store has a store manager who is paid a fixed salary. Individual salespeople receive a fixed salary and a sales commission. WalkRite is considering opening another store that is expected to have the revenue and cost relationships shown here:

	A	B	C	D	E
	Home Insert Page Layout Formulas Data Review View				
1	**Unit Variable Data (per pair of shoes)**			**Annual Fixed Costs**	
2	Selling price	$30.00		Rent	$ 60,000
3	Cost of shoes	$19.50		Salaries	200,000
4	Sales commission	1.50		Advertising	80,000
5	Variable cost per unit	$21.00		Other fixed costs	20,000
6				Total fixed costs	$360,000

Required

Consider each question independently:

1. What is the annual breakeven point in (a) units sold and (b) revenues?
2. If 35,000 units are sold, what will be the store's operating income (loss)?
3. If sales commissions are discontinued and fixed salaries are raised by a total of $81,000, what would be the annual breakeven point in (a) units sold and (b) revenues?
4. Refer to the original data. If, in addition to his fixed salary, the store manager is paid a commission of $0.30 per unit sold, what would be the annual breakeven point in (a) units sold and (b) revenues?
5. Refer to the original data. If, in addition to his fixed salary, the store manager is paid a commission of $0.30 *per unit in excess of the breakeven point*, what would be the store's operating income if 50,000 units were sold?

3-39 CVP analysis, shoe stores (continuation of 3-38). Refer to requirement 3 of Problem 3-38. In this problem, assume the role of the owner of WalkRite.

1. Calculate the number of units sold at which the owner of WalkRite would be indifferent between the original salary-plus-commissions plan for salespeople and the higher fixed-salaries-only plan.
2. As owner, which sales compensation plan would you choose if forecasted annual sales of the new store were at least 55,000 units? What do you think of the motivational aspect of your chosen compensation plan?
3. Suppose the target operating income is $168,000. How many units must be sold to reach the target operating income under (a) the original salary-plus-commissions plan and (b) the higher-fixed-salaries-only plan?
4. You open the new store on January 1, 2011, with the original salary-plus-commission compensation plan in place. Because you expect the cost of the shoes to rise due to inflation, you place a firm bulk order for 50,000 shoes and lock in the $19.50 price per unit. But, toward the end of the year, only 48,000 shoes are sold, and you authorize a markdown of the remaining inventory to $18 per unit. Finally, all units are sold. Salespeople, as usual, get paid a commission of 5% of revenues. What is the annual operating income for the store?

3-40 Alternate cost structures, uncertainty, and sensitivity analysis. Stylewise Printing Company currently leases its only copy machine for $1,000 a month. The company is considering replacing this leasing agreement with a new contract that is entirely commission based. Under the new agreement Stylewise would pay a commission for its printing at a rate of $10 for every 500 pages printed. The company currently charges $0.15 per page to its customers. The paper used in printing costs the company $.03 per page and other variable costs, including hourly labor amount to $.04 per page.

1. What is the company's breakeven point under the current leasing agreement? What is it under the new commission based agreement?
2. For what range of sales levels will Stylewise prefer (a) the fixed lease agreement (b) the commission agreement?
3. Do this question only if you have covered the chapter appendix in your class. Stylewise estimates that the company is equally likely to sell 20,000; 40,000; 60,000; 80,000; or 100,000 pages of print. Using information from the original problem, prepare a table that shows the expected profit at each sales level under the fixed leasing agreement and under the commission based agreement. What is the expected value of each agreement? Which agreement should Stylewise choose?

3-41 CVP, alternative cost structures. PC Planet has just opened its doors. The new retail store sells refurbished computers at a significant discount from market prices. The computers cost PC Planet $100 to purchase and require 10 hours of labor at $15 per hour. Additional variable costs, including wages for sales personnel, are $50 per computer. The newly refurbished computers are resold to customers for $500. Rent on the retail store costs the company $4,000 per month.

1. How many computers does PC Planet have to sell each month to break even?
2. If PC Planet wants to earn $5,000 per month after all expenses, how many computers does the company need to sell?
3. PC Planet can purchase already refurbished computers for $200. This would mean that all labor required to refurbish the computers could be eliminated. What would PC Planet's new breakeven point be if it decided to purchase the computers already refurbished?
4. Instead of paying the monthly rental fee for the retail space, PC Planet has the option of paying its landlord a 20% commission on sales. Assuming the original facts in the problem, at what sales level would PC Planet be indifferent between paying a fixed amount of monthly rent and paying a 20% commission on sales?

3-42 CVP analysis, income taxes, sensitivity. (CMA, adapted) Agro Engine Company manufactures and sells diesel engines for use in small farming equipment. For its 2012 budget, Agro Engine Company estimates the following:

Selling price	$ 3,000
Variable cost per engine	$ 500
Annual fixed costs	$3,000,000
Net income	$1,500,000
Income tax rate	25%

The first quarter income statement, as of March 31, reported that sales were not meeting expectations. During the first quarter, only 300 units had been sold at the current price of $3,000. The income statement showed that variable and fixed costs were as planned, which meant that the 2012 annual net income projection would not be met unless management took action. A management committee was formed and presented the following mutually exclusive alternatives to the president:

a. Reduce the selling price by 20%. The sales organization forecasts that at this significantly reduced price, 2,000 units can be sold during the remainder of the year. Total fixed costs and variable cost per unit will stay as budgeted.

b. Lower variable cost per unit by $50 through the use of less-expensive direct materials. The selling price will also be reduced by $250, and sales of 1,800 units are expected for the remainder of the year.

c. Reduce fixed costs by 20% and lower the selling price by 10%. Variable cost per unit will be unchanged. Sales of 1,700 units are expected for the remainder of the year.

1. If no changes are made to the selling price or cost structure, determine the number of units that Agro Engine Company must sell (a) to break even and (b) to achieve its net income objective. **Required**

2. Determine which alternative Agro Engine should select to achieve its net income objective. Show your calculations.

3-43 Choosing between compensation plans, operating leverage. (CMA, adapted) Marston Corporation manufactures pharmaceutical products that are sold through a network of external sales agents. The agents are paid a commission of 18% of revenues. Marston is considering replacing the sales agents with its own salespeople, who would be paid a commission of 10% of revenues and total salaries of $2,080,000. The income statement for the year ending December 31, 2011, under the two scenarios is shown here.

	Home	Insert	Page Layout	Formulas	Data	Review	View
	A		B	C	D	E	
1			Marston Corporation				
2			Income Statement				
3			For the Year Ended December 31, 2011				
4			Using Sales Agents		Using Own Sales Force		
5	Revenues			$26,000,000		$26,000,000	
6	Cost of goods sold						
7	Variable		$11,700,000		$11,700,000		
8	Fixed		2,870,000	14,570,000	2,870,000	14,570,000	
9	Gross margin			11,430,000		11,430,000	
10	Marketing costs						
11	Commissions		$ 4,680,000		$ 2,600,000		
12	Fixed costs		3,420,000	8,100,000	5,500,000	8,100,000	
13	Operating income			$ 3,330,000		$ 3,330,000	

1. Calculate Marston's 2011 contribution margin percentage, breakeven revenues, and degree of operating leverage under the two scenarios. **Required**

2. Describe the advantages and disadvantages of each type of sales alternative.

3. In 2012, Marston uses its own salespeople, who demand a 15% commission. If all other cost behavior patterns are unchanged, how much revenue must the salespeople generate in order to earn the same operating income as in 2011?

3-44 Sales mix, three products. The Ronowski Company has three product lines of belts—A, B, and C— with contribution margins of $3, $2, and $1, respectively. The president foresees sales of 200,000 units in the coming period, consisting of 20,000 units of A, 100,000 units of B, and 80,000 units of C. The company's fixed costs for the period are $255,000.

1. What is the company's breakeven point in units, assuming that the given sales mix is maintained? **Required**

2. If the sales mix is maintained, what is the total contribution margin when 200,000 units are sold? What is the operating income?

3. What would operating income be if 20,000 units of A, 80,000 units of B, and 100,000 units of C were sold? What is the new breakeven point in units if these relationships persist in the next period?

3-45 Multiproduct CVP and decision making. Pure Water Products produces two types of water filters. One attaches to the faucet and cleans all water that passes through the faucet. The other is a pitcher-cum-filter that only purifies water meant for drinking.

The unit that attaches to the faucet is sold for $80 and has variable costs of $20.
The pitcher-cum-filter sells for $90 and has variable costs of $25.

Pure Water sells two faucet models for every three pitchers sold. Fixed costs equal $945,000.

Required

1. What is the breakeven point in unit sales and dollars for each type of filter at the current sales mix?
2. Pure Water is considering buying new production equipment. The new equipment will increase fixed cost by $181,400 per year and will decrease the variable cost of the faucet and the pitcher units by $5 and $9 respectively. Assuming the same sales mix, how many of each type of filter does Pure Water need to sell to break even?
3. Assuming the same sales mix, at what total sales level would Pure Water be indifferent between using the old equipment and buying the new production equipment? If total sales are expected to be 30,000 units, should Pure Water buy the new production equipment?

3-46 Sales mix, two products. The Stackpole Company retails two products: a standard and a deluxe version of a luggage carrier. The budgeted income statement for next period is as follows:

	Standard Carrier	Deluxe Carrier	Total
Units sold	187,500	62,500	250,000
Revenues at $28 and $50 per unit	$5,250,000	$3,125,000	$8,375,000
Variable costs at $18 and $30 per unit	3,375,000	1,875,000	5,250,000
Contribution margins at $10 and $20 per unit	$1,875,000	$1,250,000	3,125,000
Fixed costs			2,250,000
Operating income			$ 875,000

Required

1. Compute the breakeven point in units, assuming that the planned sales mix is attained.
2. Compute the breakeven point in units (a) if only standard carriers are sold and (b) if only deluxe carriers are sold.
3. Suppose 250,000 units are sold but only 50,000 of them are deluxe. Compute the operating income. Compute the breakeven point in units. Compare your answer with the answer to requirement 1. What is the major lesson of this problem?

3-47 Gross margin and contribution margin. The Museum of America is preparing for its annual appreciation dinner for contributing members. Last year, 525 members attended the dinner. Tickets for the dinner were $24 per attendee. The profit report for last year's dinner follows.

Ticket sales	$12,600
Cost of dinner	15,300
Gross margin	(2,700)
Invitations and paperwork	2,500
Profit (loss)	$(5,200)

This year the dinner committee does not want to lose money on the dinner. To help achieve its goal, the committee analyzed last year's costs. Of the $15,300 cost of the dinner, $9,000 were fixed costs and $6,300 were variable costs. Of the $2,500 cost of invitations and paperwork, $1,975 were fixed and $525 were variable.

Required

1. Prepare last year's profit report using the contribution margin format.
2. The committee is considering expanding this year's dinner invitation list to include volunteer members (in addition to contributing members). If the committee expands the dinner invitation list, it expects attendance to double. Calculate the effect this will have on the profitability of the dinner assuming fixed costs will be the same as last year.

3-48 Ethics, CVP analysis. Allen Corporation produces a molded plastic casing, LX201, for desktop computers. Summary data from its 2011 income statement are as follows:

Revenues	$5,000,000
Variable costs	3,000,000
Fixed costs	2,160,000
Operating income	$ (160,000)

Jane Woodall, Allen's president, is very concerned about Allen Corporation's poor profitability. She asks Max Lemond, production manager, and Lester Bush, controller, to see if there are ways to reduce costs.

After two weeks, Max returns with a proposal to reduce variable costs to 52% of revenues by reducing the costs Allen currently incurs for safe disposal of wasted plastic. Lester is concerned that this would expose the company to potential environmental liabilities. He tells Max, "We would need to estimate some of these potential environmental costs and include them in our analysis." "You can't do that," Max replies. "We are not violating any laws. There is some possibility that we may have to incur environmental costs in the future, but if we bring it up now, this proposal will not go through because our senior management always assumes these costs to be larger than they turn out to be. The market is very tough, and we are in danger of shutting down the company and costing all of us our jobs. The only reason our competitors are making money is because they are doing exactly what I am proposing."

Required

1. Calculate Allen Corporation's breakeven revenues for 2011.
2. Calculate Allen Corporation's breakeven revenues if variable costs are 52% of revenues.
3. Calculate Allen Corporation's operating income for 2011 if variable costs had been 52% of revenues.
4. Given Max Lemond's comments, what should Lester Bush do?

Collaborative Learning Problem

3-49 Deciding where to produce. (CMA, adapted) The Domestic Engines Co. produces the same power generators in two Illinois plants, a new plant in Peoria and an older plant in Moline. The following data are available for the two plants:

	A	B	C	D	E
1			Peoria		Moline
2	Selling price		$150.00		$150.00
3	Variable manufacturing cost per unit	$72.00		$88.00	
4	Fixed manufacturing cost per unit	30.00		15.00	
5	Variable marketing and distribution cost per unit	14.00		14.00	
6	Fixed marketing and distribution cost per unit	19.00		14.50	
7	Total cost per unit		135.00		131.50
8	Operating income per unit		$ 15.00		$ 18.50
9	Production rate per day	400	units	320	units
10	Normal annual capacity usage	240	days	240	days
11	Maximum annual capacity	300	days	300	days

All fixed costs per unit are calculated based on a normal capacity usage consisting of 240 working days. When the number of working days exceeds 240, overtime charges raise the variable manufacturing costs of additional units by $3.00 per unit in Peoria and $8.00 per unit in Moline.

Domestic Engines Co. is expected to produce and sell 192,000 power generators during the coming year. Wanting to take advantage of the higher operating income per unit at Moline, the company's production manager has decided to manufacture 96,000 units at each plant, resulting in a plan in which Moline operates at capacity (320 units per day × 300 days) and Peoria operates at its normal volume (400 units per day × 240 days).

Required

1. Calculate the breakeven point in units for the Peoria plant and for the Moline plant.
2. Calculate the operating income that would result from the production manager's plan to produce 96,000 units at each plant.
3. Determine how the production of 192,000 units should be allocated between the Peoria and Moline plants to maximize operating income for Domestic Engines. Show your calculations.

Job Costing

From Chapter 4 of *Cost Accounting: A Managerial Emphasis*, 14/e. Charles T. Horngren. Srikant M. Datar. Madhav Rajan.

Job Costing

It's fair to say that no one likes to lose money.

Whether a company is a new startup venture providing marketing consulting services or an established manufacturer of custom-built motorcycles, knowing how to job cost—how much it costs to produce an individual product—is critical if a profit is to be generated. As the following article shows, Nexamp, a clean-energy company, knows this all too well.

Job Costing and Nexamp's Next Generation Energy and Carbon Solutions[1]

Making a profit on a project depends on pricing it correctly. At Nexamp, a leading renewable-energy systems provider in Massachusetts, a team of managers and employees is responsible for the costing and pricing of its solar, geothermal, wind, and biomass installation jobs for homeowners and businesses.

For each project, account managers carefully examine and verify job costs as part of a competitive bidding process. Using a computer model developed from previous projects, a company executive double-checks all the numbers, watching for costs that could wreak havoc with the net profit on the job. Projects of a certain size, such as a recent $20 million government stimulus contract to install solar panels, require the approval of a company vice president or other high-ranking officer. This type of approval ensures that Nexamp does not approve jobs that could lose money.

Nexamp holds a weekly project management meeting where managers report on the status of each job approved and scheduled. Once a project is underway, on-site project managers provide weekly reports on the progress of each phase of installation. Nexamp project managers are also responsible for identifying any potential problems with each project and determining any alterations necessary to ensure high quality, on-time delivery within the original project budget.

At Nexamp, job costing includes three key elements: direct costs of a job, indirect costs of a job, and general administrative costs. Direct costs are costs traceable to a specific job such as costs of solar panels, electricity converters, mounting systems, and

---

[1] *Sources*: Conversations with Nexamp management. June 4, 2010. Noblett, Jackie. 2010. Nexamp lands $20M stimulus contract. *Boston Business Journal*, February 5.

subcontractor payments. All materials are purchased through a formal procurement process, which helps Nexamp carefully manage and control material costs. Another key element of direct costs is direct labor. Besides the actual wages paid to employees, direct labor costs include costs of workers' compensation insurance, health insurance, vacations and holidays, sick days, and paid days off.

Indirect costs of a job are allocated to each project. These include cost of supervisory labor, company-owned equipment, construction supplies, and safety equipment. Finally, Nexamp allocates general and administrative costs, such as office rent, utilities, and general insurance to each job.

Just like at Nexamp, managers at Nissan need to know how much it costs to manufacture its new Leaf electric car, and managers at Ernst & Young need to know what it costs to audit Whole Foods, the organic grocer. Knowing the costs and profitability of jobs helps managers pursue their business strategies, develop pricing plans, and meet external reporting requirements. Of course, when making decisions, managers combine cost information with noncost information, such as personal observations of operations, and nonfinancial performance measures, such as quality and customer satisfaction.

Dana Hoff \Getty Images, Inc.—Liaison

Building-Block Concepts of Costing Systems

Before we begin our discussion of costing systems, let's review cost-related terms and introduce the new terms that we will need for our primary discussion.

1. *Cost object*—anything for which a measurement of costs is desired—for example, a product, such as an iMac computer, or a service, such as the cost of repairing an iMac computer.
2. *Direct costs of a cost object*—costs related to a particular cost object that can be traced to that cost object in an economically feasible (cost-effective) way—for example the cost of purchasing the main computer board or the cost of parts used to make an iMac computer.
3. *Indirect costs of a cost object*—costs related to a particular cost object that cannot be traced to that cost object in an economically feasible (cost-effective) way—for example, the costs of supervisors who oversee multiple products, one of which is the iMac, or the rent paid for the repair facility that repairs many different Apple computer products besides the iMac. Indirect costs are allocated to the cost object using a cost-allocation method.

Cost assignment is a general term for assigning costs, whether direct or indirect, to a cost object. *Cost tracing* is a specific term for assigning direct costs; *cost allocation*

41

refs to assigning indirect costs. The relationship among these three concepts can be graphically represented as

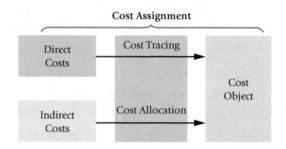

Throughout this chapter, the costs assigned to a cost object, for example, a product such as a Mini Cooper or a service such as an audit of MTV, include both variable costs and costs that are fixed in the short run. Managers cost products and services to guide long-run strategic decisions (for example, what mix of products and services to produce and sell and what prices to charge for them). In the long run, managers want revenues to exceed total costs.

We also need to introduce and explain two more terms before discussing costing systems:

4. **Cost pool.** A **cost pool** is a grouping of individual indirect cost items. Cost pools can range from broad, such as all manufacturing-plant costs, to narrow, such as the costs of operating metal-cutting machines. Cost pools are often organized in conjunction with cost-allocation bases.

5. **Cost-allocation base.** How should a company allocate costs to operate metal-cutting machines among different products? One way to allocate costs is based on the number of machine-hours used to produce different products. The **cost-allocation base** (number of machine-hours) is a systematic way to link an indirect cost or group of indirect costs (operating costs of all metal-cutting machines) to cost objects (different products). For example, if indirect costs of operating metal-cutting machines is $500,000 based on running these machines for 10,000 hours, the cost allocation rate is $500,000 ÷ 10,000 hours = $50 per machine-hour, where machine-hours is the cost allocation base. If a product uses 800 machine-hours, it will be allocated $40,000, $50 per machine-hour × 800 machine-hours. The ideal cost-allocation base is the cost driver of the indirect costs, because there is a cause-and-effect relationship between the cost allocation base and the indirect costs. A cost-allocation base can be either financial (such as direct labor costs) or nonfinancial (such as the number of machine-hours). When the cost object is a job, product, or customer, the cost-allocation base is also called a **cost-application base.**

The concepts represented by these five terms constitute the building blocks that we will use to design the costing systems described in this chapter.

Decision Point ▶

What are the building block concepts of a costing system?

Job-Costing and Process-Costing Systems

Learning Objective 2

Distinguish job costing

... job costing is used to cost a distinct product

from process costing

... process costing is used to cost masses of identical or similar units

Management accountants use two basic types of costing systems to assign costs to products or services:

1. **Job-costing system.** In this system, the cost object is a unit or multiple units of a distinct product or service called a **job.** Each job generally uses different amounts of resources. The product or service is often a single unit, such as a specialized machine made at Hitachi, a construction project managed by Bechtel Corporation, a repair job done at an Audi Service Center, or an advertising campaign produced by Saatchi & Saatchi. Each special machine made by Hitachi is unique and distinct. An advertising campaign for one client at Saatchi and Saatchi is unique and distinct from advertising campaigns for other clients. Job costing is also used by companies such as Ethan Allen

to cost multiple identical units of distinct furniture products. Because the products and services are distinct, job-costing systems accumulate costs separately for each product or service.

2. **Process-costing system**. In this system, the cost object is masses of identical or similar units of a product or service. For example, Citibank provides the same service to all its customers when processing customer deposits. Intel provides the same product (say, a Pentium 4 chip) to each of its customers. All Minute Maid consumers receive the same frozen orange juice product. In each period, process-costing systems divide the total costs of producing an identical or similar product or service by the total number of units produced to obtain a per-unit cost. This per-unit cost is the average unit cost that applies to each of the identical or similar units produced in that period.

Exhibit 1 presents examples of job costing and process costing in the service, merchandising, and manufacturing sectors. These two types of costing systems are best considered as opposite ends of a continuum; in between, one type of system can blur into the other to some degree.

Many companies have costing systems that are neither pure job costing nor pure process costing but have elements of both. Costing systems need to be tailored to the underlying operations. For example, Kellogg Corporation uses job costing to calculate the total cost to manufacture each of its different and distinct types of products—such as Corn Flakes, Crispix, and Froot Loops—and process costing to calculate the per-unit cost of producing each identical box of Corn Flakes. In this chapter, we focus on job-costing systems.

◀ **Decision Point**

How do you distinguish job costing from process costing?

Exhibit 1

Examples of Job Costing and Process Costing in the Service, Merchandising, and Manufacturing Sectors

	Service Sector	Merchandising Sector	Manufacturing Sector
Job Costing Used	• Audit engagements done by Price Waterhouse Coopers • Consulting engagements done by McKinsey & Co. • Advertising-agency campaigns run by Ogilvy & Mather • Individual legal cases argued by Hale & Dorr • Computer-repair jobs done by CompUSA • Movies produced by Universal Studios	• L. L. Bean sending individual items by mail order • Special promotion of new products by Wal-Mart	• Assembly of individual aircrafts at Boeing • Construction of ships at Litton Industries
Process Costing Used	• Bank-check clearing at Bank of America • Postal delivery (standard items) by U.S. Postal Service	• Grain dealing by Arthur Daniel Midlands • Lumber dealing by Weyerhauser	• Oil refining by Shell Oil • Beverage production by PepsiCo

Job Costing: Evaluation and Implementation

We illustrate job costing using the example of Robinson Company, a company that manufactures and installs specialized machinery for the paper-making industry. In early 2011, Robinson receives a request to bid for the manufacturing and installation of a new paper-making machine for the Western Pulp and Paper Company (WPP). Robinson had never made a machine quite like this one, and its managers wonder what to bid for the job. Robinson's management team works through the five-step decision-making process.

1. **Identify the problems and uncertainties.** The decision of whether and how much to bid for the WPP job depends on how management resolves two critical uncertainties: what it will cost to complete the job and the prices that its competitors are likely to bid.

2. **Obtain information.** Robinson's managers first evaluate whether doing the WPP job is consistent with the company's strategy. Do they want to do more of these kinds of jobs? Is this an attractive segment of the market? Will Robinson be able to develop a competitive advantage over its competitors and satisfy customers? Robinson's managers conclude that the WPP job fits well with the company's strategy.

   Robinson's managers study the drawings and engineering specifications provided by WPP and decide on technical details of the machine. They compare the specifications of this machine to similar machines they have made in the past, identify competitors who might bid on the job, and gather information on what these bids might be.

3. **Make predictions about the future.** Robinson's managers estimate the cost of direct materials, direct manufacturing labor, and overhead for the WPP job. They also consider qualitative factors and risk factors and think through any biases they might have. For example, do engineers and employees working on the WPP job have the necessary skills and technical competence? Would they find the experience valuable and challenging? How accurate are the cost estimates, and what is the likelihood of cost overruns? What biases do Robinson's managers have to be careful about? Remember, Robinson has not made a machine quite like this one. Robinson's managers need to be careful not to draw inappropriate analogies and to seek the most relevant information when making their judgments.

4. **Make decisions by choosing among alternatives.** Robinson bids $15,000 for the WPP job. This bid is based on a manufacturing cost estimate of $10,000 and a markup of 50% over manufacturing cost. The $15,000 price takes into account likely bids by competitors, the technical and business risks, and qualitative factors. Robinson's managers are very confident that they have obtained the best possible information in reaching their decision.

5. **Implement the decision, evaluate performance, and learn.** Robinson wins the bid for the WPP job. As Robinson works on the WPP job, it keeps careful track of all the costs it has incurred (which are detailed later in this chapter). Ultimately, Robinson's managers compare the predicted amounts against actual costs to evaluate how well they did on the WPP job.

In its job-costing system, Robinson accumulates costs incurred on a job in different parts of the value chain, such as manufacturing, marketing, and customer service. We focus here on Robinson's manufacturing function (which also includes product installation). To make a machine, Robinson purchases some components from outside suppliers and makes others itself. Each of Robinson's jobs also has a service element: installing a machine at a customer's site, integrating it with the customer's other machines and processes, and ensuring the machine meets customer expectations.

One form of a job-costing system that Robinson can use is actual costing. **Actual costing** is a costing system that traces direct costs to a cost object by using the actual direct-cost rates times the actual quantities of the direct-cost inputs. It allocates indirect costs based on the actual indirect-cost rates times the actual quantities of the cost-allocation bases. The *actual indirect-cost rate* is calculated by dividing actual total indirect costs by the actual total quantity of the cost-allocation base. As its name suggests, actual costing systems calculate the actual costs of jobs. Yet, actual costing systems are not commonly found in practice because actual costs cannot be computed in a *timely* manner. The problem is not with computing direct-cost rates for direct materials and direct manufacturing labor. For example, Robinson records the actual prices paid for materials. As it uses these materials, the prices paid serve as actual direct-cost rates for charging material costs to jobs. As we discuss next, calculating actual indirect-cost rates on a timely basis each week or each month is, however, a problem. Robinson can only calculate actual indirect-cost rates at the end of the fiscal year and Robinson's managers are unwilling to wait that long to learn the costs of various jobs.

Time Period Used to Compute Indirect-Cost Rates

There are two reasons for using longer periods, such as a year, to calculate indirect-cost rates.

1. **The numerator reason (indirect-cost pool).** The shorter the period, the greater the influence of seasonal patterns on the amount of costs. For example, if indirect-cost rates were calculated each month, costs of heating (included in the numerator) would be charged to production only during the winter months. An annual period incorporates the effects of all four seasons into a single, annual indirect-cost rate.

    Levels of total indirect costs are also affected by nonseasonal erratic costs. Examples of nonseasonal erratic costs include costs incurred in a particular month that benefit operations during future months, such as costs of repairs and maintenance of equipment, and costs of vacation and holiday pay. If monthly indirect-cost rates were calculated, jobs done in a month with high, nonseasonal erratic costs would be charged with these costs. Pooling all indirect costs together over the course of a full year and calculating a single annual indirect-cost rate helps smooth some of the erratic bumps in costs associated with shorter periods.

2. **The denominator reason (quantity of the cost-allocation base).** Another reason for longer periods is to avoid spreading monthly fixed indirect costs over fluctuating levels of monthly output and fluctuating quantities of the cost-allocation base. Consider the following example.

Reardon and Pane are tax accountants whose work follows a highly seasonal pattern with very busy months during tax season and less busy months at other times. Assume the following mix of variable indirect costs (such as supplies, food, power, and indirect support labor) that vary with the quantity of the cost-allocation base (direct professional labor-hours) and fixed indirect costs (depreciation and general administrative support) that do not vary with short-run fluctuations in the quantity of the cost-allocation base:

	Indirect Costs			Direct	Allocation Rate per Direct
	Variable	Fixed	Total	Professional Labor-Hours	Professional Labor-Hour
	(1)	(2)	(3)	(4)	(5) = (3) ÷ (4)
High-output month	$40,000	$60,000	$100,000	3,200	$31.25
Low-output month	10,000	60,000	70,000	800	87.50

You can see that variable indirect costs change in proportion to changes in direct professional labor-hours. Therefore, the variable indirect-cost rate is the same in both the high-output months and the low-output months ($40,000 ÷ 3,200 labor-hours = $12.50 per labor-hour; $10,000 ÷ 800 labor-hours = $12.50 per labor-hour). Sometimes overtime payments can cause the variable indirect-cost rate to be higher in high-output months. In such cases, variable indirect costs will be allocated at a higher rate to production in high-output months relative to production in low-output months.

Consider now the fixed costs of $60,000. The fixed costs cause monthly total indirect-cost rates to vary considerably—from $31.25 per hour to $87.50 per hour. Few managers believe that identical jobs done in different months should be allocated indirect-cost charges per hour that differ so significantly ($87.50 ÷ $31.25 = 2.80, or 280%) because of fixed costs. Furthermore, if fees for preparing tax returns are based on costs, fees would be high in low-output months leading to lost business, when in fact management wants to accept more bids to utilize idle capacity. Reardon and Pane chose a specific level of capacity based on a time horizon far beyond a mere month. An average, annualized rate based on the relationship of total annual indirect costs to the total annual level of output smoothes the effect of monthly variations in output levels and is more representative of the total costs and total output that management considered when choosing the level of capacity and, hence, fixed costs. Another denominator reason for using annual overhead rates is that the calculation of monthly indirect-cost rates is affected by the number of Monday-to-Friday workdays in a month. The number of workdays per month varies from 20 to 23 during a year. If separate rates are computed each month, jobs in February would bear a greater share of indirect costs (such as depreciation and property taxes) than jobs in other months, because February has the fewest workdays (and consequently labor-hours) in a month. Many managers believe such results to be an unrepresentative and unreasonable way to assign indirect costs to jobs. An annual period reduces the effect that the number of working days per month has on unit costs.

Decision Point ▶

What is the main challenge in implementing job-costing systems?

Normal Costing

The difficulty of calculating actual indirect-cost rates on a weekly or monthly basis means managers cannot calculate the actual costs of jobs as they are completed. However, managers, including those at Robinson, want a close approximation of the costs of various jobs regularly during the year, not just at the end of the fiscal year. Managers want to know manufacturing costs (and other costs, such as marketing costs) for ongoing uses, including pricing jobs, monitoring and managing costs, evaluating the success of the job, learning about what worked and what didn't, bidding on new jobs, and preparing interim financial statements. Because of the need for immediate access to job costs, few companies wait to allocate overhead costs until year-end when the actual manufacturing overhead is finally known. Instead, a *predetermined* or *budgeted* indirect-cost rate is calculated for each cost pool at the beginning of a fiscal year, and overhead costs are allocated to jobs as work progresses. For the numerator and denominator reasons already described, the **budgeted indirect-cost rate** for each cost pool is computed as follows:

$$\text{Budgeted indirect cost rate} = \frac{\text{Budgeted annual indirect costs}}{\text{Budgeted annual quantity of the cost-allocation base}}$$

Using budgeted indirect-cost rates gives rise to normal costing.

Normal costing is a costing system that (1) traces direct costs to a cost object by using the actual direct-cost rates times the actual quantities of the direct-cost inputs and (2) allocates indirect costs based on the *budgeted* indirect-cost rates times the actual quantities of the cost-allocation bases.

We illustrate normal costing for the Robinson Company example using the following seven steps to assign costs to an individual job. This approach is commonly used by companies in the manufacturing, merchandising, and service sectors.

General Approach to Job Costing

Learning Objective 4

Outline the seven-step approach to normal costing

. . . the seven-step approach is used to compute direct and indirect costs of a job

Step 1: Identify the Job That Is the Chosen Cost Object. The cost object in the Robinson Company example is Job WPP 298, manufacturing a paper-making machine for Western Pulp and Paper (WPP) in 2011. Robinson's managers and management accountants gather information to cost jobs through source documents. A **source document** is an original record (such as a labor time card on which an employee's work hours are recorded) that supports journal entries in an accounting system. The main source document for Job WPP 298 is a job-cost record. A **job-cost record**, also called a **job-cost sheet**, records and accumulates all the costs assigned to a specific job, starting when work begins. Exhibit 2 shows the job-cost record for the paper-making machine ordered by WPP. Follow the various steps in costing Job WPP 298 on the job-cost record in Exhibit 2.

Exhibit 2	Source Documents at Robinson Company: Job-Cost Record

	Home	Insert	Page Layout	Formulas	Data	Review	View	
	A	**B**	**C**	**D**	**E**		
1			JOB-COST RECORD				
2	JOB NO:	WPP 298		CUSTOMER:	Western Pulp and Paper		
3	Date Started:	Feb. 7, 2011		Date Completed	Feb. 28, 2011		
4							
5							
6	DIRECT MATERIALS						
7	Date	Materials		Quantity	Unit	Total	
8	Received	Requisition No.	Part No.	Used	Cost	Costs	
9	Feb. 7, 2011	2011: 198	MB 468-A	8	$14	$ 112	
10	Feb. 7, 2011	2011: 199	TB 267-F	12	63	756	
11						•	
12						•	
13	Total					$ 4,606	
14							
15	DIRECT MANUFACTURING LABOR						
16	Period	Labor Time	Employee	Hours	Hourly	Total	
17	Covered	Record No.	No.	Used	Rate	Costs	
18	Feb. 7-13, 2011	LT 232	551-87-3076	25	$18	$ 450	
19	Feb. 7-13, 2011	LT 247	287-31-4671	5	19	95	
20						•	
21						•	
22	Total					$ 1,579	
23							
24	MANUFACTURING OVERHEAD*						
25		Cost Pool		Allocation Base	Allocation-	Total	
26	Date	Category	Allocation Base	Quantity Used	Base Rate	Costs	
27	Dec. 31, 2011	Manufacturing	Direct Manufacturing	88 hours	$40	$ 3,520	
28			Labor-Hours				
29							
30	Total					$ 3,520	
31	TOTAL MANUFACTURING COST OF JOB					$ 9,705	
32							
33							
34	*The Robinson Company uses a single manufacturing-overhead cost pool. The use of multiple overhead cost pools						
35	would mean multiple entries in the "Manufacturing Overhead" section of the job-cost record.						
36							

Step 2:   Identify the Direct Costs of the Job. Robinson identifies two direct-manufacturing cost categories: direct materials and direct manufacturing labor.

- **Direct materials:** On the basis of the engineering specifications and drawings provided by WPP, a manufacturing engineer orders materials from the storeroom. The order is placed using a basic source document called a **materials-requisition record,** which contains information about the cost of direct materials used on a specific job and in a specific department. Exhibit 3, Panel A, shows a materials-requisition record for the Robinson Company. See how the record specifies the job for which the material is requested (WPP 298), the description of the material (Part Number MB 468-A, metal brackets), the actual quantity (8), the actual unit cost ($14), and the actual total cost ($112). The $112 actual total cost also appears on the job-cost record in Exhibit 2. If we add the cost of all material requisitions, the total actual direct material cost is $4,606, which is shown in the Direct Materials panel of the job-cost record in Exhibit 2.

■ **Direct manufacturing labor:** The accounting for direct manufacturing labor is similar to the accounting described for direct materials. The source document for direct manufacturing labor is a **labor-time sheet**, which contains information about the amount of labor time used for a specific job in a specific department. Exhibit 3, Panel B, shows a typical weekly labor-time sheet for a particular employee (G. L. Cook). Each day Cook records the time spent on individual jobs (in this case WPP 298 and JL 256), as well as the time spent on other tasks, such as maintenance of machines or cleaning, that are not related to a specific job.

The 25 hours that Cook spent on Job WPP 298 appears on the job-cost record in Exhibit 2 at a cost of $450 (25 hours × $18 per hour). Similarly, the job-cost record for Job JL 256 will carry a cost of $216 (12 hours × $18 per hour). The three hours of time spent on maintenance and cleaning at $18 per hour equals $54. This cost is part of indirect manufacturing costs because it is not traceable to any particular job. This indirect cost is included as part of the manufacturing-overhead cost pool allocated to jobs. The total direct manufacturing labor costs of $1,579 for the paper-making machine that appears in the Direct Manufacturing Labor panel of the job-cost record in Exhibit 2 is the sum of all the direct manufacturing labor costs charged to this job by different employees.

All costs other than direct materials and direct manufacturing labor are classified as indirect costs.

Step 3: Select the Cost-Allocation Bases to Use for Allocating Indirect Costs to the Job. Indirect manufacturing costs are costs that are necessary to do a job but that cannot be traced to a specific job. It would be impossible to complete a job without incurring indirect costs such as supervision, manufacturing engineering, utilities, and repairs. Because these costs cannot be traced to a specific job, they must be allocated to all jobs in a systematic way. Different jobs require different quantities of indirect resources. The objective is to allocate the costs of indirect resources in a systematic way to their related jobs.

Companies often use multiple cost-allocation bases to allocate indirect costs because different indirect costs have different cost drivers. For example, some indirect costs such as depreciation and repairs of machines are more closely related to machine-hours. Other indirect costs such as supervision and production support are more closely related to direct manufacturing labor-hours. Robinson, however, chooses direct manufacturing labor-hours as the sole allocation base for linking all indirect manufacturing costs to jobs. That's because, in its labor-intensive environment, Robinson believes that the number of direct manufacturing labor-hours drives the manufacturing overhead resources (such as salaries paid to supervisors, engineers, production support staff, and quality management staff) required by individual jobs. (We will see that, in many manufacturing

Exhibit 3   Source Documents at Robinson Company: Materials Requisition Record and Labor-Time Sheet

PANEL A:

MATERIALS-REQUISITION RECORD				
Materials-Requisition Record No.				2011: 198
Job No. WPP 298		Date:		FEB. 7, 2011
Part No.	Part Description	Quantity	Unit Cost	Total Cost
MB 468-A	Metal Brackets	8	$14	$112
Issued By: B. Clyde		Date:		Feb. 7, 2011
Received By: L. Daley		Date:		Feb. 7, 2011

PANEL B:

LABOR-TIME SHEET								
Labor-Time Record No:		LT 232						
Employee Name: G. L. Cook		Employee No: 551-87-3076						
Employee Classification Code: Grade 3 Machinist								
Hourly Rate: $18								
Week Start: Feb. 7, 2011		Week End: Feb. 13, 2011						
Job. No.	M	T	W	Th	F	S	Su	Total
WPP 298	4	8	3	6	4	0	0	25
JL 256	3	0	4	2	3	0	0	12
Maintenance	1	0	1	0	1	0	0	3
Total	8	8	8	8	8	0	0	40
Supervisor: R. Stuart	Date: Feb. 13, 2011							

environments, we need to broaden the set of cost drivers.) In 2011, Robinson budgets 28,000 direct manufacturing labor-hours.

Step 4: Identify the Indirect Costs Associated with Each Cost-Allocation Base. Because Robinson believes that a single cost-allocation base—direct manufacturing labor-hours—can be used to allocate indirect manufacturing costs to jobs, Robinson creates a single cost pool called manufacturing overhead costs. This pool represents all indirect costs of the Manufacturing Department that are difficult to trace directly to individual jobs. In 2011, budgeted manufacturing overhead costs total $1,120,000.

As we saw in Steps 3 and 4, managers first identify cost-allocation bases and then identify the costs related to each cost-allocation base, not the other way around. They choose this order because managers must first understand the cost driver, the reasons why costs are being incurred (for example, setting up machines, moving materials, or designing jobs), before they can determine the costs associated with each cost driver. Otherwise, there is nothing to guide the creation of cost pools. Of course, Steps 3 and 4 are often done almost simultaneously.

Step 5: Compute the Rate per Unit of Each Cost-Allocation Base Used to Allocate Indirect Costs to the Job. For each cost pool, the budgeted indirect-cost rate is calculated by dividing budgeted total indirect costs in the pool (determined in Step 4) by the budgeted total quantity of the cost-allocation base (determined in Step 3). Robinson calculates the allocation rate for its single manufacturing overhead cost pool as follows:

$$\text{Budgeted manufacturing overhead rate} = \frac{\text{Budgeted manufacturing overhead costs}}{\text{Budgeted total quantity of cost-allocation base}}$$

$$= \frac{\$1,120,000}{28,000 \text{ direct manufacturing labor-hours}}$$

$$= \$40 \text{ per direct manufacturing labor-hour}$$

Step 6: Compute the Indirect Costs Allocated to the Job. The indirect costs of a job are calculated by multiplying the *actual* quantity of each different allocation base (one allocation base for each cost pool) associated with the job by the *budgeted* indirect cost rate of each allocation base (computed in Step 5). Recall that Robinson's managers selected direct manufacturing labor-hours as the only cost-allocation base. Robinson uses 88 direct manufacturing labor-hours on the WPP 298 job. Manufacturing overhead costs allocated to WPP 298 equal $3,520 ($40 per direct manufacturing labor-hour × 88 hours) and appear in the Manufacturing Overhead panel of the WPP 298 job-cost record in Exhibit 2.

Step 7: Compute the Total Cost of the Job by Adding All Direct and Indirect Costs Assigned to the Job. Exhibit 2 shows that the total manufacturing costs of the WPP job are $9,705.

Direct manufacturing costs		
Direct materials	$4,606	
Direct manufacturing labor	1,579	$ 6,185
Manufacturing overhead costs		
($40 per direct manufacturing labor-hour × 88 hours)		3,520
Total manufacturing costs of job WPP 298		$9,705

Recall that Robinson bid a price of $15,000 for the job. At that revenue, the normal-costing system shows a gross margin of $5,295 ($15,000 − $9,705) and a gross-margin percentage of 35.3% ($5,295 ÷ $15,000 = 0.353).

Robinson's manufacturing managers and sales managers can use the gross margin and gross-margin percentage calculations to compare the profitability of different jobs to try to understand the reasons why some jobs show low profitability. Have direct materials been wasted? Was direct manufacturing labor too high? Were there ways to improve the efficiency of these jobs? Were these jobs simply underpriced? Job-cost analysis provides the information needed for judging the performance of manufacturing and sales managers and for making future improvements (see Concepts in Action).

Concepts in Action   Job Costing on Cowboys Stadium

Over the years, fans of the National Football League have identified the Dallas Cowboys as "America's Team." Since 2009, however, the team known for winning five Super Bowls has become just as recognized for its futuristic new home, Cowboys Stadium in Arlington, Texas.

When the Cowboys take the field, understanding each week's game plan is critical for success. But for Manhattan Construction, the company that managed the development of the $1.2 billion Cowboys Stadium project, understanding costs is just as critical for making successful pricing decisions, winning contracts, and ensuring that each project is profitable. Each job is estimated individually because the unique end-products, whether a new stadium or an office building, demand different quantities of Manhattan Construction's resources.

In 2006, the Dallas Cowboys selected Manhattan Construction to lead the construction of its 73,000 seat, 3 million-square-foot stadium. To be completed in three years, the stadium design featured two monumental arches spanning about a quarter-mile in length over the dome, a retractable roof, the largest retractable glass doors in the world (in each end zone), canted glass exterior walls, 325 private suites, and a 600-ton JumboTron hovering 90 feet above the field.

With only 7% of football fans ever setting foot in a professional stadium, "Our main competition is the home media center," Cowboys owner Jerry Jones said in unveiling the stadium design in 2006. "We wanted to offer a real experience that you can't have at home, but to see it with the technology that you do have at home."

Generally speaking, the Cowboys Stadium project had five stages: (1) conceptualization, (2) design and planning, (3) preconstruction, (4) construction, and (5) finalization and delivery. During this 40-month process, Manhattan Construction hired architects and subcontractors, created blueprints, purchased and cleared land, developed the stadium—ranging from excavation to materials testing to construction—built out and finished interiors, and completed last-minute changes before the stadium's grand opening in mid-2009.

While most construction projects have distinct stages, compressed timeframes and scope changes required diligent management by Manhattan Construction. Before the first game was played, Manhattan Construction successfully navigated nearly 3,000 change requests and a constantly evolving budget.

To ensure proper allocation and accounting of resources, Manhattan Construction project managers used a job-costing system. The system first calculated the budgeted cost of more than 500 line items of direct materials and labor costs. It then allocated estimated overhead costs (supervisor salaries, rent, materials handling, and so on) to the job using direct material costs and direct labor-hours as allocation bases. Manhattan Construction's job-costing system allowed managers to track project variances on a weekly basis. Manhattan Construction continually estimated the profitability of the Cowboys Stadium project based on the percentage of work completed, insight gleaned from previous stadium projects, and revenue earned. Managers used the job-costing system to actively manage costs, while the Dallas Cowboys had access to clear, concise, and transparent costing data.

Just like quarterback Tony Romo navigating opposing defenses, Manhattan Construction was able to leverage its job-costing system to ensure the successful construction of a stadium as iconic as the blue star on the Cowboys' helmets.

Sources: Dillon, David. 2009. New Cowboys Stadium has grand design, but discipline isn't compromised *The Dallas Morning News*, June 3. http://www.dallasnews.com/sharedcontent/dws/ent/stories/DN-stadiumarchitecture_03gd.ART.State.Edition2.5125e7c.html; Knudson, Brooke. 2008. Profile: Dallas Cowboys Stadium. *Construction Today*, December 22. http://www.construction-today.com/cms1/content/view/1175/139/1/0/; Lacayo, Richard. 2009. Inside the new Dallas Cowboys stadium. *Time*, September 21. http://www.time.com/time/nation/article/0,8599,1924535,00.html; Penny, Mark, Project Manager, Manhattan Construction Co. 2010. Interview. January 12.

Exhibit 4 is an overview of Robinson Company's job-costing system. This exhibit represents the concepts comprising the five building blocks—cost object, direct costs of a cost object, indirect (overhead) costs of a cost object, indirect-cost pool, and cost-allocation base—of job-costing systems that were first introduced at the beginning of this chapter. Costing-system overviews such as Exhibit 4 are important learning tools. We urge you to sketch one when you need to understand a costing system in manufacturing, merchandising, or service companies. (The symbols in Exhibit 4 are used consistently in the costing-system overviews presented in this book. A triangle always identifies a direct

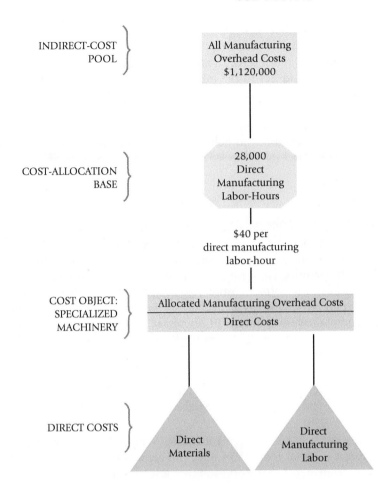

Exhibit 4

Job-Costing Overview for Determining Manufacturing Costs of Jobs at Robinson Company

cost, a rectangle represents the indirect-cost pool, and an octagon describes the cost-allocation base.) Note the parallel between the overview diagram and the cost of the WPP 298 job described in Step 7. Exhibit 4 shows two direct-cost categories (direct materials and direct manufacturing labor) and one indirect-cost category (manufacturing overhead) used to allocate indirect costs. The costs in Step 7 also have three dollar amounts, each corresponding respectively to the two direct-cost and one indirect-cost categories.

Decision Point

How do you implement a normal-costing system?

The Role of Technology

To improve the efficiency of their operations, managers use costing information about products and jobs to control materials, labor, and overhead costs. Modern information technology provides managers with quick and accurate product-cost information, making it easier to manage and control jobs. For example, in many costing systems, source documents exist only in the form of computer records. Bar coding and other forms of online information recording reduce human intervention and improve the accuracy of materials and labor time records for individual jobs.

Consider, for example, direct materials charged to jobs for product-costing purposes. Managers control these costs as materials are purchased and used. Using Electronic Data Interchange (EDI) technology, companies like Robinson order materials from their suppliers by clicking a few keys on a computer keyboard. EDI, an electronic computer link between a company and its suppliers, ensures that the order is transmitted quickly and accurately with minimum paperwork and costs. A bar code scanner records the receipt of incoming materials. The computer matches the receipt with the order, prints out a check to the supplier, and records the material received. When an operator on the production floor transmits a request for materials via a computer terminal, the computer prepares a materials-requisition record, instantly recording the issue of materials in the materials and job-cost records. Each day, the computer sums the materials-requisition records charged to a particular job or manufacturing department. A performance report is then prepared monitoring actual costs of direct materials. Direct material usage can be reported hourly—if the benefits exceed the cost of such frequent reporting.

Similarly, information about direct manufacturing labor is obtained as employees log into computer terminals and key in the job numbers, their employee numbers, and start and end times of their work on different jobs. The computer automatically prints the labor time record and, using hourly rates stored for each employee, calculates the direct manufacturing labor costs of individual jobs. Information technology also provides managers with instantaneous feedback to help control manufacturing overhead costs, jobs in process, jobs completed, and jobs shipped and installed at customer sites.

Actual Costing

Learning Objective 5

Distinguish actual costing

. . . actual costing uses actual indirect-cost rates

from normal costing

. . . normal costing uses budgeted indirect-cost rates

How would the cost of Job WPP 298 change if Robinson had used actual costing rather than normal costing? Both actual costing and normal costing trace direct costs to jobs in the same way because source documents identify the actual quantities and actual rates of direct materials and direct manufacturing labor for a job as the work is being done. The only difference between costing a job with normal costing and actual costing is that normal costing uses *budgeted* indirect-cost rates, whereas actual costing uses *actual* indirect-cost rates calculated annually at the end of the year. Exhibit 5 distinguishes actual costing from normal costing.

The following actual data for 2011 are for Robinson's manufacturing operations:

	Actual
Total manufacturing overhead costs	$1,215,000
Total direct manufacturing labor-hours	27,000

Steps 1 and 2 are exactly as before: Step 1 identifies WPP 298 as the cost object; Step 2 calculates actual direct material costs of $4,606, and actual direct manufacturing labor costs of $1,579. Recall from Step 3 that Robinson uses a single cost-allocation base, direct manufacturing labor-hours, to allocate all manufacturing overhead costs to jobs. The actual quantity of direct manufacturing labor-hours for 2011 is 27,000 hours. In Step 4, Robinson groups all actual indirect manufacturing costs of $1,215,000 into a single manufacturing overhead cost pool. In Step 5, the **actual indirect-cost rate** is calculated by dividing actual total indirect costs in the pool (determined in Step 4) by the actual total quantity of the cost-allocation base (determined in Step 3). Robinson calculates the actual manufacturing overhead rate in 2011 for its single manufacturing overhead cost pool as follows:

$$\begin{aligned} \text{Actual manufacturing overhead rate} &= \frac{\text{Actual annual manufacturing overhead costs}}{\text{Actual annual quantity of the cost-allocation base}} \\ &= \frac{\$1,215,000}{27,000 \text{ direct manufacturing labor-hours}} \\ &= \$45 \text{ per direct manufacturing labor-hour} \end{aligned}$$

In Step 6, under an actual-costing system,

$$\begin{aligned} \text{Manufacturing overhead costs allocated to WPP 298} &= \text{Actual manufacturing overhead rate} \times \text{Actual quantity of direct manufacturing labor-hours} \\ &= \$45 \text{ per direct manuf. labor-hour} \times 88 \text{ direct manufacturing labor-hours} \\ &= \$3,960 \end{aligned}$$

Exhibit 5

Actual Costing and Normal Costing Methods

	Actual Costing	Normal Costing
Direct Costs	*Actual direct-cost rates ×* actual quantities of direct-cost inputs	*Actual direct-cost rates ×* actual quantities of direct-cost inputs
Indirect Costs	*Actual indirect-cost rates ×* actual quantities of cost-allocation bases	*Budgeted indirect-cost rates ×* actual quantities of cost-allocation bases

In Step 7, the cost of the job under actual costing is $10,145, calculated as follows:

Direct manufacturing costs		
Direct materials	$4,606	
Direct manufacturing labor	1,579	$ 6,185
Manufacturing overhead costs		
($45 per direct manufacturing labor-hour × 88 actual		
direct manufacturing labor-hours)		3,960
Total manufacturing costs of job		$10,145

The manufacturing cost of the WPP 298 job is higher by $440 under actual costing ($10,145) than it is under normal costing ($9,705) because the actual indirect-cost rate is $45 per hour, whereas the budgeted indirect-cost rate is $40 per hour. That is, ($45 – $40) × 88 actual direct manufacturing labor-hours = $440.

As we discussed previously, manufacturing costs of a job are available much earlier under a normal-costing system. Consequently, Robinson's manufacturing and sales managers can evaluate the profitability of different jobs, the efficiency with which the jobs are done, and the pricing of different jobs as soon as the jobs are completed, while the experience is still fresh in everyone's mind. Another advantage of normal costing is that corrective actions can be implemented much sooner. At the end of the year, though, costs allocated using normal costing will not, in general, equal actual costs incurred. If material, adjustments will need to be made so that the cost of jobs and the costs in various inventory accounts are based on actual rather that normal costing. We describe these adjustments later in the chapter.

Decision Point

How do you distinguish actual costing from normal costing?

A Normal Job-Costing System in Manufacturing

We now explain how a normal job-costing system operates in manufacturing. Continuing with the Robinson Company example, the following illustration considers events that occurred in February 2011. Before getting into details, study Exhibit 6, which provides a broad framework for understanding the flow of costs in job costing.

The upper part of Exhibit 6 shows the flow of inventoriable costs from the purchase of materials and other manufacturing inputs, to their conversion into work-in-process and finished goods, to the sale of finished goods.

Direct materials used and direct manufacturing labor can be easily traced to jobs. They become part of work-in-process inventory on the balance sheet because direct manufacturing labor transforms direct materials into another asset, work-in-process inventory. Robinson also incurs manufacturing overhead costs (including indirect materials and indirect manufacturing labor) to convert direct materials into work-in-process inventory. The overhead (indirect) costs, however, cannot be easily traced to individual jobs.

Learning Objective 6

Track the flow of costs in a job-costing system

. . . from purchase of materials to sale of finished goods

Exhibit 6   Flow of Costs in Job Costing

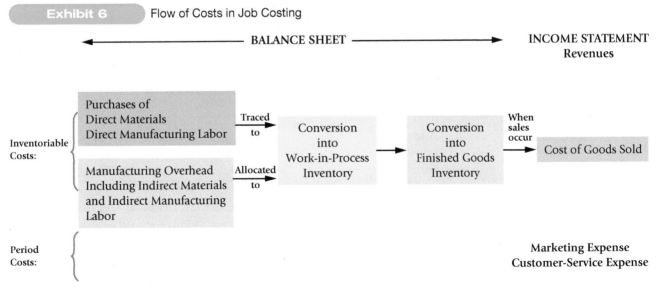

Manufacturing overhead costs, therefore, are first accumulated in a manufacturing overhead account and later allocated to individual jobs. As manufacturing overhead costs are allocated, they become part of work-in-process inventory.

As individual jobs are completed, work-in-process inventory becomes another balance sheet asset, finished goods inventory. Only when finished goods are sold is an expense, cost of goods sold, recognized in the income statement and matched against revenues earned.

The lower part of Exhibit 6 shows the period costs—marketing and customer-service costs. These costs do not create any assets on the balance sheet because they are not incurred to transform materials into a finished product. Instead, they are expensed in the income statement, as they are incurred, to best match revenues.

We next describe the entries made in the general ledger.

General Ledger

You know by this point that a job-costing system has a separate job-cost record for each job. A summary of the job-cost record is typically found in a subsidiary ledger. The general ledger account Work-in-Process Control presents the total of these separate job-cost records pertaining to all unfinished jobs. The job-cost records and Work-in-Process Control account track job costs from when jobs start until they are complete.

Exhibit 7 shows T-account relationships for Robinson Company's general ledger. The general ledger gives a "bird's-eye view" of the costing system. The amounts shown in

Exhibit 7 Manufacturing Job-Costing System Using Normal Costing: Diagram of General Ledger Relationships for February 2011

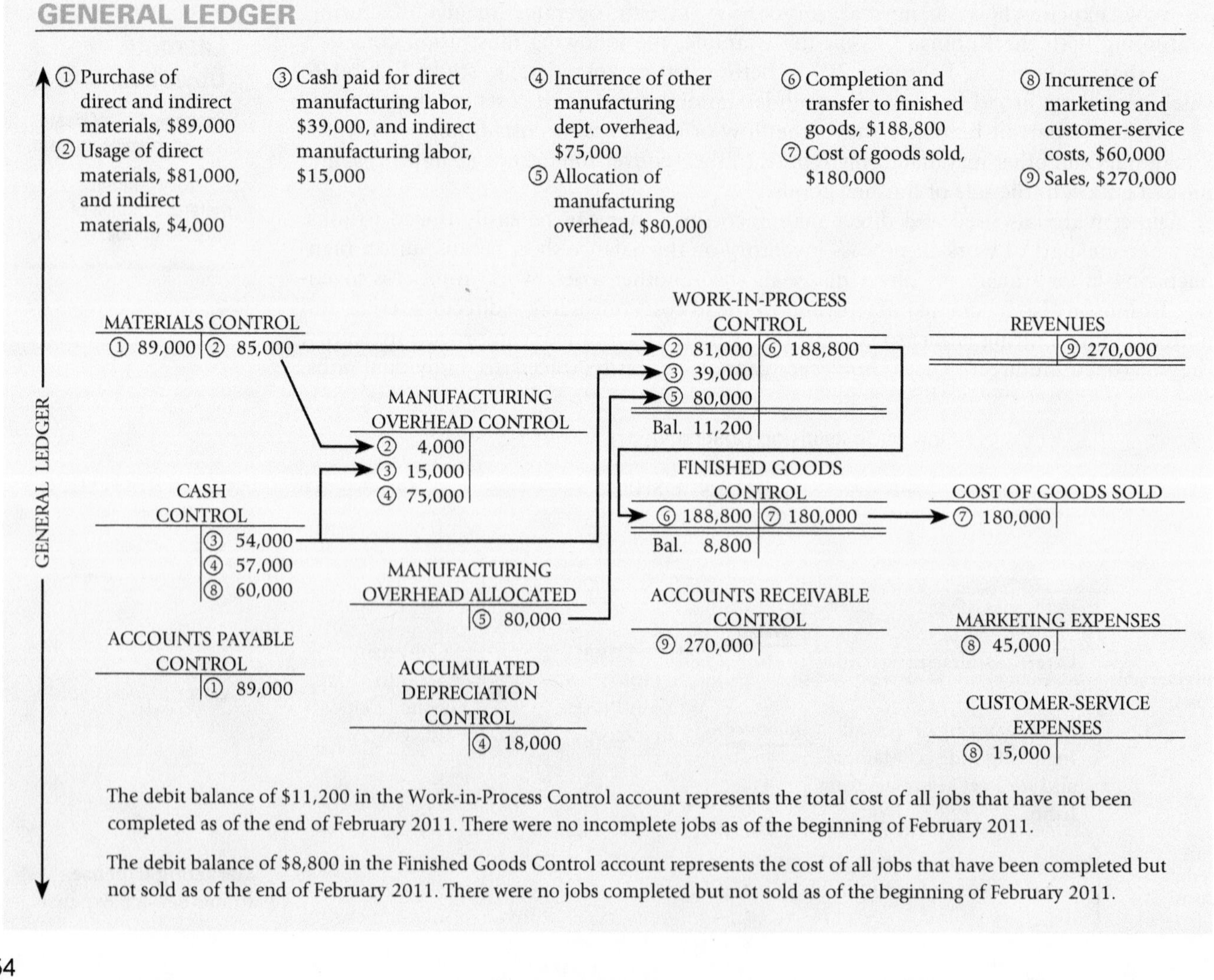

The debit balance of $11,200 in the Work-in-Process Control account represents the total cost of all jobs that have not been completed as of the end of February 2011. There were no incomplete jobs as of the beginning of February 2011.

The debit balance of $8,800 in the Finished Goods Control account represents the cost of all jobs that have been completed but not sold as of the end of February 2011. There were no jobs completed but not sold as of the beginning of February 2011.

Exhibit 7 are based on the transactions and journal entries that follow. As you go through each journal entry, use Exhibit 7 to see how the various entries being made come together. General ledger accounts with "Control" in the titles (for example, Materials Control and Accounts Payable Control) have underlying subsidiary ledgers that contain additional details, such as each type of material in inventory and individual suppliers that Robinson must pay.

Some companies simultaneously make entries in the general ledger and subsidiary ledger accounts. Others, such as Robinson, make entries in the subsidiary ledger when transactions occur and entries in the general ledger less frequently, on a monthly basis.

A general ledger should be viewed as only one of many tools that assist management in planning and control. To control operations, managers rely on not only the source documents used to record amounts in the subsidiary ledgers, but also on nonfinancial information such as the percentage of jobs requiring rework.

Explanations of Transactions

We next look at a summary of Robinson Company's transactions for February 2011 and the corresponding journal entries for those transactions.

1. Purchases of materials (direct and indirect) on credit, $89,000

Materials Control	89,000	
Accounts Payable Control		89,000

2. Usage of direct materials, $81,000, and indirect materials, $4,000

Work-in-Process Control	81,000	
Manufacturing Overhead Control	4,000	
Materials Control		85,000

3. Manufacturing payroll for February: direct labor, $39,000, and indirect labor, $15,000, paid in cash

Work-in-Process Control	39,000	
Manufacturing Overhead Control	15,000	
Cash Control		54,000

4. Other manufacturing overhead costs incurred during February, $75,000, consisting of supervision and engineering salaries, $44,000 (paid in cash); plant utilities, repairs, and insurance, $13,000 (paid in cash); and plant depreciation, $18,000

Manufacturing Overhead Control	75,000	
Cash Control		57,000
Accumulated Depreciation Control		18,000

5. Allocation of manufacturing overhead to jobs, $80,000

Work-in-Process Control	80,000	
Manufacturing Overhead Allocated		80,000

Under normal costing, **manufacturing overhead allocated**—also called **manufacturing overhead applied**—is the amount of manufacturing overhead costs allocated to individual jobs based on the budgeted rate multiplied by actual quantity used of the allocation base. Keep in mind the distinct difference between transactions 4 and 5. In transaction 4, all actual overhead costs incurred throughout the month are added (debited) to the Manufacturing Overhead Control account. These costs are *not* debited to Work-in-Process Control because, unlike direct costs, they cannot be traced to individual jobs. Manufacturing overhead costs are added (debited) to individual jobs and to Work-in-Process Control *only when* manufacturing overhead costs are allocated in Transaction 5. At the time these costs are allocated, Manufacturing Overhead Control is, *in effect*, decreased (credited) via its contra account, Manufacturing Overhead Allocated. Recall that under normal costing, the budgeted manufacturing overhead rate of $40 per direct manufacturing labor-hour is calculated at the beginning of the year on the basis of predictions of annual manufacturing overhead costs and the annual quantity of the cost-allocation base. Almost certainly, the overhead allocated will differ from the actual overhead incurred. In a later section, we discuss what to do with this difference.

6. Completion and transfer of individual jobs to finished goods, $188,800

| Finished Goods Control | 188,800 | |
| Work-in-Process Control | | 188,800 |

7. Cost of goods sold, $180,000

| Cost of Goods Sold | 180,000 | |
| Finished Goods Control | | 180,000 |

8. Marketing costs for February, $45,000, and customer service costs for February, $15,000, paid in cash

Marketing Expenses	45,000	
Customer Service Expenses	15,000	
Cash Control		60,000

9. Sales revenues, all on credit, $270,000

| Accounts Receivable Control | 270,000 | |
| Revenues | | 270,000 |

Subsidiary Ledgers

Exhibits 8 and 9 present subsidiary ledgers that contain the underlying details—the "worm's-eye view" that helps Robinson's managers keep track of the WPP 298 job, as opposed to the "bird's-eye view" of the general ledger. The sum of all entries in

Exhibit 8   Subsidiary Ledger for Materials, Labor, and Manufacturing Department Overhead[1]

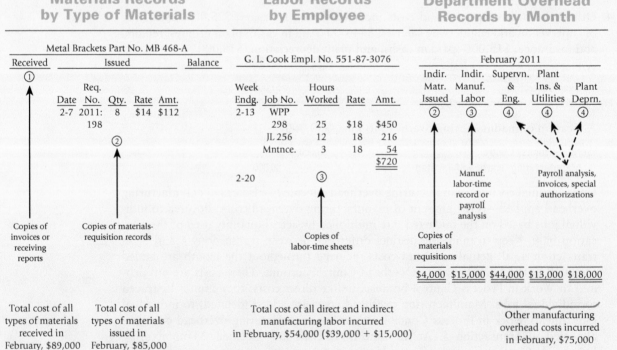

[1]The arrows show how the supporting documentation (for example, copies of materials requisition records) results in the journal entry number shown in circles (for example, journal entry number 2) that corresponds to the entries in Exhibit 7.

| Exhibit 9 | Subsidiary Ledger for Individual Jobs[1] |

PANEL A: Work-in-Process Inventory Records by Jobs

Job No. WPP 298

		In-Process			Completed		Balance	
Date	Direct Materials	Direct Manuf. Labor	Allocated Manuf. Overhead	Total Cost	Date	Total Cost	Date	Total Cost
2-7	$ 112			$ 112				
2-13		$ 450		$ 450				
	•	•	•					
2-28	$4,606	$1,579	$3,520	$9,705	2-28	$9,705	2-28	$0
	②	③	⑤			⑥		

↑ (②) Copies of materials-requisition records

↑ (③) Copies of labor-time sheets

↑ (⑤) Budgeted rate × actual direct manuf. labor-hours

↑ (⑥) Completed job-cost record

Total cost of direct materials issued to all jobs in Feb., $81,000

Total cost of direct manuf. labor used on all jobs in Feb., $39,000

Total manuf. overhead allocated to all jobs in Feb., $80,000

Total cost of all jobs completed and transferred to finished goods in Feb., $188,800

PANEL B: Finished Goods Inventory Records by Job

Job No. WPP 298

Received		Issued		Balance	
Date	Amt.	Date	Amt.	Date	Amt.
2-28	$9,705	2-28	$9,705	2-28	$0
	⑥		⑦		

↑ (⑥) Completed job-cost record

↑ (⑦) Costed sales invoice

Total cost of all jobs transferred to finished goods in Feb., $188,800

Total cost of all jobs sold and invoiced in Feb., $180,000

[1]The arrows show how the supporting documentation (for example, copies of materials requisition records) results in the journal entry number shown in circles (for example, journal entry number 2) that corresponds to the entries in Exhibit 7.

underlying subsidiary ledgers equals the total amount in the corresponding general ledger control accounts.

Material Records by Type of Materials

The subsidiary ledger for materials at Robinson Company—called *Materials Records*—keeps a continuous record of quantity received, quantity issued to jobs, and inventory balances for each type of material. Panel A of Exhibit 8 shows the Materials Record for Metal Brackets (Part No. MB 468-A). In many companies, the source documents supporting the receipt and issue of materials (the material requisition record in Exhibit 3, Panel A) are scanned into a computer. Software programs then automatically update the Materials Records and make all the necessary accounting entries in the subsidiary and general ledgers. The cost of materials received across all types of direct and indirect material records for February 2011 is $89,000 (Exhibit 8, Panel A). The cost of materials issued across all types of direct and indirect material records for February 2011 is $85,000 (Exhibit 8, Panel A).

As direct materials are used, they are recorded as issued in the Materials Records (see Exhibit 8, Panel A, for a record of the Metal Brackets issued for the WPP machine job). Direct materials are also charged to Work-in-Process Inventory Records for Jobs, which are the subsidiary ledger accounts for the Work-in-Process Control account in the general ledger. For example, the metal brackets used in the WPP machine job appear as direct material costs of $112 in the subsidiary ledger under the work-in-process inventory record for WPP 298 (Exhibit 9, Panel A, based on the job-cost record source document in Exhibit 2). The cost of direct materials used across all job-cost records for February 2011 is $81,000 (Exhibit 9, Panel A).

As indirect materials (for example, lubricants) are used, they are charged to the Manufacturing Department overhead records (Exhibit 8, Panel C), which comprise the subsidiary ledger for Manufacturing Overhead Control. The Manufacturing Department overhead records accumulate actual costs in individual overhead categories by each indirect-cost-pool account in the general ledger. Recall that Robinson has only one indirect-cost pool: Manufacturing Overhead. The cost of indirect materials used is not added directly to individual job records. Instead, the cost of these indirect materials is allocated to individual job records as a part of manufacturing overhead.

Labor Records by Employee

Labor records by employee (see Exhibit 8, Panel B for G. L. Cook) are used to trace direct manufacturing labor to individual jobs and to accumulate the indirect manufacturing labor in Manufacturing Department overhead records (Exhibit 8, Panel C). The labor records are based on the labor-time sheet source documents (see Exhibit 3, Panel B). The subsidiary ledger for employee labor records shows the different jobs that G. L. Cook, Employee No. 551-87-3076 worked on and the $720 of wages owed to Cook, for the week ending February 13. The sum of total wages owed to all employees for February 2011 is $54,000. The job-cost record for WPP 298 shows direct manufacturing labor costs of $450 for the time Cook spent on the WPP machine job (Exhibit 9, Panel A). Total direct manufacturing labor costs recorded in all job-cost records (the subsidiary ledger for Work-in-Process Control) for February 2011 is $39,000.

G. L. Cook's employee record shows $54 for maintenance, which is an indirect manufacturing labor cost. The total indirect manufacturing labor costs of $15,000 for February 2011 appear in the Manufacturing Department overhead records in the subsidiary ledger (Exhibit 8, Panel C). These costs, by definition, cannot be traced to an individual job. Instead, they are allocated to individual jobs as a part of manufacturing overhead.

Manufacturing Department Overhead Records by Month

The Manufacturing Department overhead records (see Exhibit 8, Panel C) that make up the subsidiary ledger for Manufacturing Overhead Control show details of different categories of overhead costs such as indirect materials, indirect manufacturing labor, supervision and engineering, plant insurance and utilities, and plant depreciation. The source documents for these entries include invoices (for example, a utility bill) and special schedules (for example, a depreciation schedule) from the responsible accounting officer. Manufacturing department overhead for February 2011 is indirect materials, $4,000; indirect manufacturing labor, $15,000; and other manufacturing overhead, $75,000 (Exhibit 8, Panel C).

Work-in-Process Inventory Records by Jobs

As we have already discussed, the job-cost record for each individual job in the subsidiary ledger is debited by the actual cost of direct materials and direct manufacturing labor used by individual jobs. In Robinson's normal-costing system, the job-cost record for each individual job in the subsidiary ledger is also debited for manufacturing overhead allocated based on the budgeted manufacturing overhead rate times the actual direct manufacturing labor-hours used in that job. For example, the job-cost record for Job WPP 298 (Exhibit 9, Panel A) shows Manufacturing Overhead Allocated of $3,520 (budgeted rate of $40 per labor-hour $\times$ 88 actual direct manufacturing labor-hours used). For the 2,000 actual direct manufacturing labor-hours used for all jobs in February 2011, total manufacturing overhead allocated equals $40 per labor-hour $\times$ 2,000 direct manufacturing labor-hours = $80,000.

Finished Goods Inventory Records by Jobs

Exhibit 9, Panel A, shows that Job WPP 298 was completed at a cost of $9,705. Job WPP 298 also simultaneously appears in the finished goods records of the subsidiary ledger. The total cost of all jobs completed and transferred to finished goods in February 2011 is $188,800 (Exhibit 9, Panels A and B). Exhibit 9, Panel B, indicates that Job WPP 298 was sold and delivered to the customer on February 28, 2011, at which time $9,705 was transferred from finished goods to cost of goods sold. The total cost of all jobs sold and invoiced in February 2011 is $180,000 (Exhibit 9, Panel B).

Revenues		$270,000
Cost of goods sold ($180,000 + $14,000[1])		194,000
Gross margin		76,000
Operating costs		
Marketing costs	$45,000	
Customer-service costs	15,000	
Total operating costs		60,000
Operating income		$ 16,000

[1]Cost of goods sold has been increased by $14,000, the difference between the
Manufacturing overhead control account ($94,000) and the Manufacturing overhead
allocated ($80,000). In a later section of this chapter, we discuss this adjustment, which
represents the amount by which actual manufacturing overhead cost exceeds the manufacturing overhead allocated to jobs during February 2011.

Other Subsidiary Records

Just as in manufacturing payroll, Robinson maintains employee labor records in subsidiary ledgers for marketing and customer service payroll as well as records for different
types of advertising costs (print, television, and radio). An accounts receivable subsidiary
ledger is also used to record the February 2011 amounts due from each customer, including the $15,000 due from the sale of Job WPP 298.

At this point, pause and review the nine entries in this illustration. Exhibit 7 is a handy
summary of all nine general-ledger entries presented in T-account form. Be sure to trace each
journal entry, step-by-step, to T-accounts in the general ledger presented in Exhibit 7.

Exhibit 10 provides Robinson's income statement for February 2011 using information from entries 7, 8, and 9. If desired, the cost of goods sold calculations can be further subdivided and presented in the format of Exhibit 8 in chapter entitled, "An
Introduction to Cost Terms and Purposes."

Nonmanufacturing Costs and Job Costing

Companies use product costs for different purposes. The product costs reported as
inventoriable costs to shareholders may differ from product costs reported for government contracting and may also differ from product costs reported to managers for guiding pricing and product-mix decisions. We emphasize that even though marketing and
customer-service costs are expensed when incurred for financial accounting purposes,
companies often trace or allocate these costs to individual jobs for pricing, product-mix,
and cost-management decisions.

To identify marketing and customer-service costs of individual jobs, Robinson can use
the same approach to job costing described earlier in this chapter in the context of manufacturing. Robinson can trace the direct marketing costs and customer-service costs to
jobs. Assume marketing and customer-service costs have the same cost-allocation base,
revenues, and are included in a single cost pool. Robinson can then calculate a budgeted
indirect-cost rate by dividing budgeted indirect marketing costs plus budgeted indirect
customer-service costs by budgeted revenues. Robinson can use this rate to allocate these
indirect costs to jobs. For example, if this rate were 15% of revenues, Robinson would
allocate $2,250 to Job WPP 298 (0.15 × $15,000, the revenue from the job). By assigning
both manufacturing costs and nonmanufacturing costs to jobs, Robinson can compare all
costs against the revenues that different jobs generate.

Decision Point

How are transactions
recorded in a
manufacturing job-
costing system?

Budgeted Indirect Costs and End-of-Accounting-Year Adjustments

Using budgeted indirect-cost rates and normal costing instead of actual costing has the
advantage that indirect costs can be assigned to individual jobs on an ongoing and
timely basis, rather than only at the end of the fiscal year when actual costs are known.
However, budgeted rates are unlikely to equal actual rates because they are based on

**Learning
Objective** 7

Dispose of under- or
overallocated
manufacturing overhead
costs at the end of the
fiscal year using
alternative methods

. . . for example, writing
off this amount to the
Cost of Goods Sold
account

estimates made up to 12 months before actual costs are incurred. We now consider adjustments that are needed when, at the end of the fiscal year, indirect costs allocated differ from actual indirect costs incurred. Recall that for the numerator and denominator reasons discussed earlier, we do *not* expect actual overhead costs incurred each month to equal overhead costs allocated each month.

Underallocated and Overallocated Direct Costs

Underallocated indirect costs occur when the allocated amount of indirect costs in an accounting period is less than the actual (incurred) amount. **Overallocated indirect costs** occur when the allocated amount of indirect costs in an accounting period is greater than the actual (incurred) amount.

Underallocated (overallocated) indirect costs =
Actual indirect costs incurred − Indirect costs allocated

Underallocated (overallocated) indirect costs are also called **underapplied (overapplied) indirect costs** and **underabsorbed (overabsorbed) indirect costs.**

Consider the manufacturing overhead cost pool at Robinson Company. There are two indirect-cost accounts in the general ledger that have to do with manufacturing overhead:

1. Manufacturing Overhead Control, the record of the actual costs in all the individual overhead categories (such as indirect materials, indirect manufacturing labor, supervision, engineering, utilities, and plant depreciation)
2. Manufacturing Overhead Allocated, the record of the manufacturing overhead allocated to individual jobs on the basis of the budgeted rate multiplied by actual direct manufacturing labor-hours

At the end of the year, the overhead accounts show the following amounts.

Manufacturing Overhead Control		Manufacturing Overhead Allocated	
Bal. Dec. 31, 2011	1,215,000	Bal. Dec. 31, 2011	1,080,000

The $1,080,000 credit balance in Manufacturing Overhead Allocated results from multiplying the 27,000 actual direct manufacturing labor-hours worked on all jobs in 2011 by the budgeted rate of $40 per direct manufacturing labor-hour.

The $135,000 ($1,215,000 – $1,080,000) difference (a net debit) is an underallocated amount because actual manufacturing overhead costs are greater than the allocated amount. This difference arises from two reasons related to the computation of the $40 budgeted hourly rate:

1. **Numerator reason (indirect-cost pool).** Actual manufacturing overhead costs of $1,215,000 are greater than the budgeted amount of $1,120,000.
2. **Denominator reason (quantity of allocation base).** Actual direct manufacturing labor-hours of 27,000 are fewer than the budgeted 28,000 hours.

There are three main approaches to accounting for the $135,000 underallocated manufacturing overhead caused by Robinson underestimating manufacturing overhead costs and overestimating the quantity of the cost-allocation base: (1) adjusted allocation-rate approach, (2) proration approach, and (3) write-off to cost of goods sold approach.

Adjusted Allocation-Rate Approach

The **adjusted allocation-rate approach** restates all overhead entries in the general ledger and subsidiary ledgers using actual cost rates rather than budgeted cost rates. First, the actual manufacturing overhead rate is computed at the end of the fiscal year. Then, the manufacturing overhead costs allocated to every job during the year are recomputed using the actual manufacturing overhead rate (rather than the budgeted manufacturing overhead rate). Finally, end-of-year closing entries are made. The result is that at year-end, every job-cost record and finished goods record—as well as the ending Work-in-Process Control, Finished Goods Control, and Cost of Goods Sold accounts—represent actual manufacturing overhead costs incurred.

The widespread adoption of computerized accounting systems has greatly reduced the cost of using the adjusted allocation-rate approach. In our Robinson example, the actual manufacturing overhead ($1,215,000) exceeds the manufacturing overhead allocated ($1,080,000) by 12.5% [($1,215,000 – $1,080,000) ÷ $1,080,000]. At year-end, Robinson could increase the manufacturing overhead allocated to each job in 2011 by 12.5% using a single software command. The command would adjust both the subsidiary ledgers and the general ledger.

Consider the Western Pulp and Paper machine job, WPP 298. Under normal costing, the manufacturing overhead allocated to the job is $3,520 (the budgeted rate of $40 per direct manufacturing labor-hour × 88 hours). Increasing the manufacturing overhead allocated by 12.5%, or $440 ($3,520 × 0.125), means the adjusted amount of manufacturing overhead allocated to Job WPP 298 equals $3,960 ($3,520 + $440). Note that using actual costing, manufacturing overhead allocated to this job is $3,960 (the actual rate of $45 per direct manufacturing labor-hour × 88 hours). Making this adjustment under normal costing for each job in the subsidiary ledgers ensures that all $1,215,000 of manufacturing overhead is allocated to jobs.

The adjusted allocation-rate approach yields the benefits of both the *timeliness and convenience of normal costing during the year and the allocation of actual manufacturing overhead costs at year-end*. Each individual job-cost record and the end-of-year account balances for inventories and cost of goods sold are adjusted to actual costs. After-the-fact analysis of actual profitability of individual jobs provides managers with accurate and useful insights for future decisions about job pricing, which jobs to emphasize, and ways to manage job costs.

Proration Approach

Proration spreads underallocated overhead or overallocated overhead among ending work-in-process inventory, finished goods inventory, and cost of goods sold. Materials inventory is not included in this proration, because no manufacturing overhead costs have been allocated to it. In our Robinson example, end-of-year proration is made to the ending balances in Work-in-Process Control, Finished Goods Control, and Cost of Goods Sold. Assume the following actual results for Robinson Company in 2011:

	Account	Account Balance (Before Proration)	Allocated Manufacturing Overhead Included in Each Account Balance (Before Proration)
1		A	B	C
2	Work-in-process control	$ 50,000	$ 16,200
3	Finished goods control	75,000	31,320
4	Cost of goods sold	2,375,000	1,032,480
5		$2,500,000	$1,080,000

How should Robinson prorate the underallocated $135,000 of manufacturing overhead at the end of 2011?

Robinson prorates underallocated or overallocated amounts on the basis of the total amount of manufacturing overhead allocated in 2011 (before proration) in the ending balances of Work-in-Process Control, Finished Goods Control, and Cost of Goods Sold. The $135,000 underallocated overhead is prorated over the three affected accounts in proportion to the total amount of manufacturing overhead allocated (before proration) in column 2 of the following table, resulting in the ending balances (after proration) in column 5 at actual costs.

	A	B	C	D	E	F	G
			Allocated Manufacturing Overhead Included in Each	Allocated Manufacturing Overhead Included in Each Account	Proration of $135,000 of Underallocated		Account
10		Account Balance (Before Proration)	Account Balance (Before Proration)	Balance as a Percent of Total	Manufacturing Overhead		Balance (After Proration)
11	**Account**	**(1)**	**(2)**	**(3) = (2) / $1,080,000**	**(4) = (3) x $135,000**		**(5) = (1) + (4)**
12	Work-in-process control	$ 50,000	$ 16,200	1.5%	0.015 x $135,000 =	$ 2,025	$ 52,025
13	Finished goods control	75,000	31,320	2.9%	0.029 x 135,000 =	3,915	78,915
14	Cost of goods sold	2,375,000	1,032,480	95.6%	0.956 x 135,000 =	129,060	2,504,060
15	Total	$2,500,000	$1,080,000	100.0%		$135,000	$2,635,000

Prorating on the basis of the manufacturing overhead allocated (before proration) results in allocating manufacturing overhead based on actual manufacturing overhead costs. Recall that the actual manufacturing overhead ($1,215,000) in 2011 exceeds the manufacturing overhead allocated ($1,080,000) in 2011 by 12.5%. The proration amounts in column 4 can also be derived by multiplying the balances in column 2 by 0.125. For example, the $3,915 proration to Finished Goods is 0.125 × $31,320. Adding these amounts effectively means allocating manufacturing overhead at 112.5% of what had been allocated before. The journal entry to record this proration is as follows:

Work-in-Process Control	2,025	
Finished Goods Control	3,915	
Cost of Goods Sold	129,060	
Manufacturing Overhead Allocated	1,080,000	
Manufacturing Overhead Control		1,215,000

If manufacturing overhead had been overallocated, the Work-in-Process Control, Finished Goods Control, and Cost of Goods Sold accounts would be decreased (credited) instead of increased (debited).

This journal entry closes (brings to zero) the manufacturing overhead-related accounts and restates the 2011 ending balances for Work-in-Process Control, Finished Goods Control, and Cost of Goods Sold to what they would have been if actual manufacturing overhead rates had been used rather than budgeted manufacturing overhead rates. This method reports the same 2011 ending balances in the general ledger as the adjusted allocation-rate approach. However, unlike the adjusted allocation-rate approach, the sum of the amounts shown in the subsidiary ledgers will not match the amounts shown in the general ledger after proration. That's because the amounts in the subsidiary ledgers will still show allocated overhead based on budgeted manufacturing overhead rates. The proration approach only adjusts the general ledger and not the subsidiary ledgers to actual manufacturing overhead rates.

Some companies use the proration approach but base it on the ending balances of Work-in-Process Control, Finished Goods Control, and Cost of Goods Sold before proration (column 1 of the preceding table). The following table shows that prorations based on ending account balances are not the same as the more accurate prorations calculated earlier based on the amount of manufacturing overhead allocated to the accounts because the proportions of manufacturing overhead costs to total costs in these accounts are not the same.

	Account Balance (Before Proration)	Account Balance as a Percent of Total	Proration of $135,000 of Underallocated Manufacturing Overhead		Account Balance (After Proration)
Account	(1)	(2) = (1) / $2,500,000	(3) = (2) x $135,000		(4) = (1) + (3)
Work-in-process control	$ 50,000	2.0%	0.02 x $135,000 =	$ 2,700	$ 52,700
Finished goods control	75,000	3.0%	0.03 x 135,000 =	4,050	79,050
Cost of goods sold	2,375,000	95.0%	0.95 x 135,000 =	128,250	2,503,250
Total	$2,500,000	100.0%		$135,000	$2,635,000

However, proration based on ending balances is frequently justified as being an expedient way of approximating the more accurate results from using manufacturing overhead costs allocated.

Write-Off to Cost of Goods Sold Approach

Under this approach, the total under- or overallocated manufacturing overhead is included in this year's Cost of Goods Sold. For Robinson, the journal entry would be as follows:

Cost of Goods Sold	135,000	
Manufacturing Overhead Allocated	1,080,000	
Manufacturing Overhead Control		1,215,000

Robinson's two Manufacturing Overhead accounts are closed with the difference between them included in cost of goods sold. The Cost of Goods Sold account after the write-off equals $2,510,000, the balance before the write-off of $2,375,000 *plus the underallocated* manufacturing overhead amount of $135,000.

Choice Among Approaches

Which of these three approaches is the best one to use? In making this decision, managers should be guided by the causes for underallocation or overallocation and the purpose of the adjustment. The most common purpose is to state the balance sheet and income statement amounts based on actual rather than budgeted manufacturing overhead rates.

Many management accountants, industrial engineers, and managers argue that to the extent that the under- or overallocated overhead cost measures inefficiency during the period, it should be written off to Cost of Goods Sold instead of being prorated. This line of reasoning argues for applying a combination of the write-off and proration methods. For example, the portion of the underallocated overhead cost that is due to inefficiency (say, because of excessive spending) and that could have been avoided should be written off to Cost of Goods Sold, whereas the portion that is unavoidable should be prorated. Unlike full proration, this approach avoids carrying the costs of inefficiency as part of inventory assets.

Proration should be based on the manufacturing overhead allocated component in the ending balances of Work-in-Process Control, Finished Goods Control, and Cost of Goods Sold. Prorating to each individual job (as in the adjusted allocation-rate approach) is only done if the goal is to develop the most accurate record of individual job costs for profitability analysis purposes.

For balance sheet and income statement reporting purposes, the write-off to Cost of Goods Sold is the simplest approach for dealing with under- or overallocated overhead. If the amount of under- or overallocated overhead is small—in comparison with total operating income or some other measure of materiality—the write-off to Cost of Goods Sold approach yields a good approximation to more accurate, but more complex, approaches. Companies are also becoming increasingly conscious of inventory control, and quantities of inventories are lower than they were in earlier years. As a result, cost of goods sold tends to be higher in relation to the dollar amount of work-in-process and finished goods inventories. Also, the inventory balances of job-costing companies are usually small

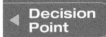

Decision Point

How should managers dispose of under- or overallocated manufacturing overhead costs at the end of the fiscal year?

because goods are often made in response to customer orders. Consequently, as is true in our Robinson example, writing off, instead of prorating, under- or overallocated overhead is unlikely to result in significant distortions in financial statements.

The Robinson Company illustration assumed that a single manufacturing overhead cost pool with direct manufacturing labor-hours as the cost-allocation base was appropriate for allocating all manufacturing overhead costs to jobs. Had Robinson used multiple cost-allocation bases, such as direct manufacturing labor-hours and machine-hours, it would have created two cost pools and calculated two budgeted overhead rates: one based on direct manufacturing labor-hours and the other based on machine-hours to allocate overhead costs to jobs. The general ledger would contain Manufacturing Overhead Control and Manufacturing Overhead Allocated amounts for each cost pool. End-of-year adjustments for under- or overallocated overhead costs would then be made separately for each cost pool.

Variations from Normal Costing: A Service-Sector Example

Learning Objective 8

Apply variations from normal costing

. . . variations from normal costing use budgeted direct-cost rates

Job costing is also very useful in service industries such as accounting and consulting firms, advertising agencies, auto repair shops, and hospitals. In an accounting firm, each audit is a job. The costs of each audit are accumulated in a job-cost record, much like the document used by Robinson Company, based on the seven-step approach described earlier. On the basis of labor-time sheets, direct labor costs of the professional staff—audit partners, audit managers, and audit staff—are traced to individual jobs. Other direct costs, such as travel, out-of-town meals and lodging, phone, fax, and copying, are also traced to jobs. The costs of secretarial support, office staff, rent, and depreciation of furniture and equipment are indirect costs because these costs cannot be traced to jobs in an economically feasible way. Indirect costs are allocated to jobs, for example, using a cost-allocation base such as number of professional labor-hours.

In some service organizations, a variation from normal costing is helpful because actual direct-labor costs—the largest component of total costs—can be difficult to trace to jobs as they are completed. For example, in our audit illustration, the actual direct-labor costs may include bonuses that become known only at the end of the year (a numerator reason). Also, the hours worked each period might vary significantly depending on the number of working days each month and the demand from clients (a denominator reason). In situations like these, a company needing timely information during the progress of an audit (and not wanting to wait until the end of the fiscal year) will use budgeted rates for some direct costs and budgeted rates for indirect costs. All budgeted rates are calculated at the start of the fiscal year. In contrast, normal costing uses actual cost rates for all direct costs and budgeted cost rates only for indirect costs.

The mechanics of using budgeted rates for direct costs are similar to the methods employed when using budgeted rates for indirect costs in normal costing. We illustrate this for Donahue and Associates, a public accounting firm. For 2011, Donahue budgets total direct-labor costs of $14,400,000, total indirect costs of $12,960,000, and total direct (professional) labor-hours of 288,000. In this case,

$$\text{Budgeted direct-labor cost rate} = \frac{\text{Budgeted total direct-labor costs}}{\text{Budgeted total direct-labor hours}}$$
$$= \frac{\$14,400,000}{288,000 \text{ direct labor-hours}} = \$50 \text{ per direct labor-hour}$$

Assuming only one indirect-cost pool and total direct-labor costs as the cost-allocation base,

$$\text{Budgeted indirect cost rate} = \frac{\text{Budgeted total costs in indirect cost pool}}{\text{Budgeted total quantity of cost-allocation base (direct-labor costs)}}$$
$$= \frac{\$12,960,000}{\$14,400,000} = 0.90, \text{ or } 90\% \text{ of direct-labor costs}$$

Suppose that in March 2011, an audit of Hanley Transport, a client of Donahue, uses 800 direct labor-hours. Donahue calculates the direct-labor costs of the Hanley Transport audit by multiplying the budgeted direct-labor cost rate, $50 per direct labor-hour, by

800, the actual quantity of direct labor-hours. The indirect costs allocated to the Hanley Transport audit are determined by multiplying the budgeted indirect-cost rate (90%) by the direct-labor costs assigned to the job ($40,000). Assuming no other direct costs for travel and the like, the cost of the Hanley Transport audit is as follows:

Direct-labor costs, $50 × 800	$40,000
Indirect costs allocated, 90% × $40,000	36,000
Total	$76,000

At the end of the fiscal year, the direct costs traced to jobs using budgeted rates will generally not equal actual direct costs because the actual rate and the budgeted rate are developed at different times using different information. End-of-year adjustments for under- or overallocated direct costs would need to be made in the same way that adjustments are made for under- or overallocated indirect costs.

The Donahue and Associates example illustrates that all costing systems do not exactly match either the actual-costing system or the normal-costing system described earlier in the chapter. As another example, engineering consulting firms often have some actual direct costs (cost of making blueprints or fees paid to outside experts), other direct costs (professional labor costs) assigned to jobs using a budgeted rate, and indirect costs (engineering and office-support costs) allocated to jobs using a budgeted rate. Therefore, users of costing systems should be aware of the different systems that they may encounter.

Decision Point

What are some variations from normal costing?

Problem for Self-Study

You are asked to bring the following incomplete accounts of Endeavor Printing, Inc., up-to-date through January 31, 2012. Consider the data that appear in the T-accounts as well as the following information in items (a) through (j).

Endeavor's normal-costing system has two direct-cost categories (direct material costs and direct manufacturing labor costs) and one indirect-cost pool (manufacturing overhead costs, which are allocated using direct manufacturing labor costs).

Materials Control		Wages Payable Control	
12-31-2011 Bal. 15,000			1-31-2012 Bal. 3,000

Work-in-Process Control		Manufacturing Overhead Control	
		1-31-2012 Bal. 57,000	

Finished Goods Control		Costs of Goods Sold	
12-31-2011 Bal. 20,000			

Additional information follows:

a. Manufacturing overhead is allocated using a budgeted rate that is set every December. Management forecasts next year's manufacturing overhead costs and next year's direct manufacturing labor costs. The budget for 2012 is $600,000 for manufacturing overhead costs and $400,000 for direct manufacturing labor costs.

b. The only job unfinished on January 31, 2012, is No. 419, on which direct manufacturing labor costs are $2,000 (125 direct manufacturing labor-hours) and direct material costs are $8,000.

c. Total direct materials issued to production during January 2012 are $90,000.

d. Cost of goods completed during January is $180,000.

e. Materials inventory as of January 31, 2012, is $20,000.

f. Finished goods inventory as of January 31, 2012, is $15,000.

g. All plant workers earn the same wage rate. Direct manufacturing labor-hours used for January total 2,500 hours. Other labor costs total $10,000.

h. The gross plant payroll paid in January equals $52,000. Ignore withholdings.

i. All "actual" manufacturing overhead incurred during January has already been posted.

j. All materials are direct materials.

Required Calculate the following:

1. Materials purchased during January
2. Cost of Goods Sold during January
3. Direct manufacturing labor costs incurred during January
4. Manufacturing Overhead Allocated during January
5. Balance, Wages Payable Control, December 31, 2011
6. Balance, Work-in-Process Control, January 31, 2012
7. Balance, Work-in-Process Control, December 31, 2011
8. Manufacturing Overhead Underallocated or Overallocated for January 2012

Solution

Amounts from the T-accounts are labeled "(T)."

1. From Materials Control T-account, Materials purchased: $90,000 (c) + $20,000 (e) − $15,000 (T) = $95,000
2. From Finished Goods Control T-account, Cost of Goods Sold: $20,000 (T) + $180,000 (d) − $15,000 (f) = $185,000
3. Direct manufacturing wage rate: $2,000 (b) ÷ 125 direct manufacturing labor-hours (b) = $16 per direct manufacturing labor-hour
   Direct manufacturing labor costs: 2,500 direct manufacturing labor-hours (g) × $16 per hour = $40,000
4. Manufacturing overhead rate: $600,000 (a) ÷ $400,000 (a) = 150%

Manufacturing Overhead Allocated: 150% of $40,000 = 1.50 × $40,000 (see 3) = $60,000

5. From Wages Payable Control T-account, Wages Payable Control, December 31, 2011: $52,000 (h) + $3,000 (T) − $40,000 (see 3) − $10,000 (g) = $5,000
6. Work-in-Process Control, January 31, 2012: $8,000 (b) + $2,000 (b) + 150% of $2,000 (b) = $13,000 (This answer is used in item 7.)
7. From Work-in-Process Control T-account, Work-in-Process Control, December 31, 2011: $180,000 (d) + $13,000 (see 6) − $90,000 (c) − $40,000 (see 3) − $60,000 (see 4) = $3,000
8. Manufacturing overhead overallocated: $60,000 (see 4) − $57,000 (T) = $3,000.

Letters alongside entries in T-accounts correspond to letters in the preceding additional information. Numbers alongside entries in T-accounts correspond to numbers in the preceding requirements.

Materials Control

December 31, 2011, Bal.	(given)	15,000			
	(1)	95,000*		(c)	90,000
January 31, 2012, Bal.	(e)	20,000			

Work-in-Process Control

December 31, 2011, Bal.	(7)	3,000		(d)	180,000
Direct materials	(c)	90,000			
Direct manufacturing labor	(b) (g) (3)	40,000			
Manufacturing overhead allocated	(3) (a) (4)	60,000			
January 31, 2012, Bal.	(b) (6)	13,000			

Finished Goods Control

December 31, 2011, Bal.	(given)	20,000		(2)	185,000
	(d)	180,000			
January 31, 2012, Bal.	(f)	15,000			

*Can be computed only after all other postings in the account have been made.

Wages Payable Control

	(h)	52,000	December 31, 2011, Bal.	(5)	5,000
				(g) (3)	40,000
				(g)	10,000
			January 31, 2012	(given)	3,000

Manufacturing Overhead Control

Total January charges	(given)	57,000	

Manufacturing Overhead Allocated

	(3) (a) (4)	60,000

Cost of Goods Sold

(d) (f) (2)	185,000	

Decision Points

The following question-and-answer format summarizes the chapter's learning objectives. Each decision presents a key question related to a learning objective. The guidelines are the answer to that question.

Decision

Guidelines

1. What are the building-block concepts of a costing system?

The building-block concepts of a costing system are cost object, direct costs of a cost object, indirect costs of a cost object, cost pool, and cost-allocation base. Costing-system overview diagrams represent these concepts in a systematic way. Costing systems aim to report cost numbers that reflect the way chosen cost objects (such as products or services) use the resources of an organization.

2. How do you distinguish job costing from process costing?

Job-costing systems assign costs to distinct units of a product or service. Process-costing systems assign costs to masses of identical or similar units and compute unit costs on an average basis. These two costing systems represent opposite ends of a continuum. The costing systems of many companies combine some elements of both job costing and process costing.

3. What is the main challenge of implementing job-costing systems?

The main challenge of implementing job-costing systems is estimating actual costs of jobs in a timely manner.

4. How do you implement a normal-costing system?

A general seven-step approach to normal costing requires identifying (1) the job, (2) the actual direct costs, (3) the budgeted cost-allocation bases, (4) the budgeted indirect cost pools, (5) the budgeted cost-allocation rates, (6) the allocated indirect costs (budgeted rate times actual quantity), and (7) the total direct and indirect costs of a job.

5. How do you distinguish actual costing from normal costing?

Actual costing and normal costing differ in the type of indirect-cost rates used:

	Actual Costing	Normal Costing
Direct-cost rates	Actual rates	Actual rates
Indirect-cost rates	Actual rates	Budgeted rates

Both systems use actual quantities of inputs for tracing direct costs and actual quantities of the allocation bases for allocating indirect costs.

6. How are transactions recorded in a manufacturing job-costing system?

A job-costing system in manufacturing records the flow of inventoriable costs in the general and subsidiary ledgers for (a) acquisition of materials and other manufacturing inputs, (b) their conversion into work in process, (c) their conversion into finished goods, and (d) the sale of finished goods. The job costing system also expenses period costs, such as marketing costs, as they are incurred.

7. How should managers dispose of under- or over-allocated manufacturing overhead costs at the end of the fiscal year?

The two theoretically correct approaches to disposing of under- or overallocated manufacturing overhead costs at the end of the fiscal year for correctly stating balance sheet and income statement amounts are (1) to adjust the allocation rate and (2) to prorate on the basis of the total amount of the allocated manufacturing overhead cost in the ending balances of Work-in-Process Control, Finished Goods Control, and Cost of Goods Sold. Many companies, however, simply write off amounts of under- or overallocated manufacturing overhead to Cost of Goods Sold when amounts are immaterial.

8. What are some variations from normal costing?

In some variations from normal costing, organizations use budgeted rates to assign direct costs, as well as indirect costs, to jobs.

Terms to Learn

This chapter contains definitions of the following important terms:

actual costing
actual indirect-cost rate
adjusted allocation-rate approach
budgeted indirect-cost rate
cost-allocation base
cost-application base
cost pool
job
job-cost record

job-cost sheet
job-costing system
labor-time sheet
manufacturing overhead allocated
manufacturing overhead applied
materials-requisition record
normal costing

overabsorbed indirect
costsoverallocated indirect costs
overapplied indirect costs
process-costing system
 proration
source document
underabsorbed indirect costs
underallocated indirect costs
underapplied indirect costs

Assignment Material

MyAccountingLab

Questions

4-1 Define cost pool, cost tracing, cost allocation, and cost-allocation base.
4-2 How does a job-costing system differ from a process-costing system?
4-3 Why might an advertising agency use job costing for an advertising campaign by Pepsi, whereas a bank might use process costing to determine the cost of checking account deposits?
4-4 Describe the seven steps in job costing.
4-5 Give examples of two cost objects in companies using job costing?
4-6 Describe three major source documents used in job-costing systems.
4-7 What is the advantage of using computerized source documents to prepare job-cost records?
4-8 Give two reasons why most organizations use an annual period rather than a weekly or monthly period to compute budgeted indirect-cost rates.
4-9 Distinguish between actual costing and normal costing.
4-10 Describe two ways in which a house construction company may use job-cost information.
4-11 Comment on the following statement: "In a normal-costing system, the amounts in the Manufacturing Overhead Control account will always equal the amounts in the Manufacturing Overhead Allocated account."
4-12 Describe three different debit entries to the Work-in-Process Control T-account under normal costing.
4-13 Describe three alternative ways to dispose of under- or overallocated overhead costs.
4-14 When might a company use budgeted costs rather than actual costs to compute direct-labor rates?
4-15 Describe briefly why Electronic Data Interchange (EDI) is helpful to managers.

Exercises

4-16 Job costing, process costing. In each of the following situations, determine whether job costing or process costing would be more appropriate.

a. A CPA firm
b. An oil refinery
c. A custom furniture manufacturer
d. A tire manufacturer
e. A textbook publisher
f. A pharmaceutical company
g. An advertising agency
h. An apparel manufacturing plant
i. A flour mill
j. A paint manufacturer
k. A medical care facility

l. A landscaping company
m. A cola-drink-concentrate producer
n. A movie studio
o. A law firm
p. A commercial aircraft manufacturer
q. A management consulting firm
r. A breakfast-cereal company
s. A catering service
t. A paper mill
u. An auto repair shop

4-17 Actual costing, normal costing, accounting for manufacturing overhead. Destin Products uses a job-costing system with two direct-cost categories (direct materials and direct manufacturing labor) and one manufacturing overhead cost pool. Destin allocates manufacturing overhead costs using direct manufacturing labor costs. Destin provides the following information:

	Budget for 2011	Actual Results for 2011
Direct material costs	$2,000,000	$1,900,000
Direct manufacturing labor costs	1,500,000	1,450,000
Manufacturing overhead costs	2,700,000	2,755,000

1. Compute the actual and budgeted manufacturing overhead rates for 2011.
2. During March, the job-cost record for Job 626 contained the following information:

Direct materials used	$40,000
Direct manufacturing labor costs	$30,000

Compute the cost of Job 626 using (a) actual costing and (b) normal costing.
3. At the end of 2011, compute the under- or overallocated manufacturing overhead under normal costing. Why is there no under- or overallocated overhead under actual costing?

Required

4-18 Job costing, normal and actual costing. Amesbury Construction assembles residential houses. It uses a job-costing system with two direct-cost categories (direct materials and direct labor) and one indirect-cost pool (assembly support). Direct labor-hours is the allocation base for assembly support costs. In December 2010, Amesbury budgets 2011 assembly-support costs to be $8,300,000 and 2011 direct labor-hours to be 166,000.

At the end of 2011, Amesbury is comparing the costs of several jobs that were started and completed in 2011.

	Laguna Model	Mission Model
Construction period	Feb–June 2011	May–Oct 2011
Direct material costs	$106,760	$127,550
Direct labor costs	$ 36,950	$ 41,320
Direct labor-hours	960	1,050

Direct materials and direct labor are paid for on a contract basis. The costs of each are known when direct materials are used or when direct labor-hours are worked. The 2011 actual assembly-support costs were $6,520,000, and the actual direct labor-hours were 163,000.

1. Compute the (a) budgeted indirect-cost rate and (b) actual indirect-cost rate. Why do they differ?
2. What are the job costs of the Laguna Model and the Mission Model using (a) normal costing and (b) actual costing?
3. Why might Amesbury Construction prefer normal costing over actual costing?

Required

4-19 Budgeted manufacturing overhead rate, allocated manufacturing overhead. Gammaro Company uses normal costing. It allocates manufacturing overhead costs using a budgeted rate per machine-hour. The following data are available for 2011:

Budgeted manufacturing overhead costs	$4,200,000
Budgeted machine-hours	175,000
Actual manufacturing overhead costs	$4,050,000
Actual machine-hours	170,000

1. Calculate the budgeted manufacturing overhead rate.
2. Calculate the manufacturing overhead allocated during 2011.
3. Calculate the amount of under- or overallocated manufacturing overhead.

4-20 Job costing, accounting for manufacturing overhead, budgeted rates. The Lynn Company uses a normal job-costing system at its Minneapolis plant. The plant has a machining department and an assembly department. Its job-costing system has two direct-cost categories (direct materials and direct manufacturing labor) and two manufacturing overhead cost pools (the machining department overhead, allocated to jobs based on actual machine-hours, and the assembly department overhead, allocated to jobs based on actual direct manufacturing labor costs). The 2011 budget for the plant is as follows:

	Machining Department	Assembly Department
Manufacturing overhead	$1,800,000	$3,600,000
Direct manufacturing labor costs	$1,400,000	$2,000,000
Direct manufacturing labor-hours	100,000	200,000
Machine-hours	50,000	200,000

Required

1. Present an overview diagram of Lynn's job-costing system. Compute the budgeted manufacturing overhead rate for each department.
2. During February, the job-cost record for Job 494 contained the following:

	Machining Department	Assembly Department
Direct materials used	$45,000	$70,000
Direct manufacturing labor costs	$14,000	$15,000
Direct manufacturing labor-hours	1,000	1,500
Machine-hours	2,000	1,000

Compute the total manufacturing overhead costs allocated to Job 494.
3. At the end of 2011, the actual manufacturing overhead costs were $2,100,000 in machining and $3,700,000 in assembly. Assume that 55,000 actual machine-hours were used in machining and that actual direct manufacturing labor costs in assembly were $2,200,000. Compute the over- or underallocated manufacturing overhead for each department.

4-21 Job costing, consulting firm. Turner & Associates, a consulting firm, has the following condensed budget for 2011:

Revenues		$21,250,000
Total costs:		
Direct costs		
Professional Labor	$ 5,312,500	
Indirect costs		
Client support	13,600,000	18,912,500
Operating income		$ 2,337,500

Turner has a single direct-cost category (professional labor) and a single indirect-cost pool (client support). Indirect costs are allocated to jobs on the basis of professional labor costs.

Required

1. Prepare an overview diagram of the job-costing system. Calculate the 2011 budgeted indirect-cost rate for Turner & Associates.
2. The markup rate for pricing jobs is intended to produce operating income equal to 11% of revenues. Calculate the markup rate as a percentage of professional labor costs.
3. Turner is bidding on a consulting job for Tasty Chicken, a fast-food chain specializing in poultry meats. The budgeted breakdown of professional labor on the job is as follows:

Professional Labor Category	Budgeted Rate per Hour	Budgeted Hours
Director	$198	4
Partner	101	17
Associate	49	42
Assistant	36	153

Calculate the budgeted cost of the Tasty Chicken job. How much will Turner bid for the job if it is to earn its target operating income of 11% of revenues?

4-22 Time period used to compute indirect cost rates. Splash Manufacturing produces outdoor wading and slide pools. The company uses a normal-costing system and allocates manufacturing overhead on the basis of direct manufacturing labor-hours. Most of the company's production and sales occur in the first and second quarters of the year. The company is in danger of losing one of its larger customers, Sotco Wholesale, due to large fluctuations in price. The owner of Splash has requested an analysis of the manufacturing cost per unit in the second and third quarters. You have been provided the following budgeted information for the coming year:

	Quarter			
	1	2	3	4
Pools manufactured and sold	700	500	150	150

It takes 0.5 direct manufacturing labor-hour to make each pool. The actual direct material cost is $7.50 per pool. The actual direct manufacturing labor rate is $16 per hour. The budgeted variable manufacturing overhead rate is $12 per direct manufacturing labor-hour. Budgeted fixed manufacturing overhead costs are $10,500 each quarter.

1. Calculate the total manufacturing cost per unit for the second and third quarter assuming the company allocates manufacturing overhead costs based on the budgeted manufacturing overhead rate determined for each quarter.
2. Calculate the total manufacturing cost per unit for the second and third quarter assuming the company allocates manufacturing overhead costs based on an annual budgeted manufacturing overhead rate.
3. Splash Manufacturing prices its pools at manufacturing cost plus 30%. Why might Sotco Wholesale be seeing large fluctuations in the prices of pools? Which of the methods described in requirements 1 and 2 would you recommend Splash use? Explain.

Required

4-23 Accounting for manufacturing overhead. Consider the following selected cost data for the Pittsburgh Forging Company for 2011.

Budgeted manufacturing overhead costs	$7,500,000
Budgeted machine-hours	250,000
Actual manufacturing overhead costs	$7,300,000
Actual machine-hours	245,000

The company uses normal costing. Its job-costing system has a single manufacturing overhead cost pool. Costs are allocated to jobs using a budgeted machine-hour rate. Any amount of under- or overallocation is written off to Cost of Goods Sold.

1. Compute the budgeted manufacturing overhead rate.
2. Prepare the journal entries to record the allocation of manufacturing overhead.
3. Compute the amount of under- or overallocation of manufacturing overhead. Is the amount material? Prepare a journal entry to dispose of this amount.

Required

4-24 Job costing, journal entries. The University of Chicago Press is wholly owned by the university. It performs the bulk of its work for other university departments, which pay as though the press were an outside business enterprise. The press also publishes and maintains a stock of books for general sale. The press uses normal costing to cost each job. Its job-costing system has two direct-cost categories (direct materials and direct manufacturing labor) and one indirect-cost pool (manufacturing overhead, allocated on the basis of direct manufacturing labor costs).

The following data (in thousands) pertain to 2011:

Direct materials and supplies purchased on credit	$ 800
Direct materials used	710
Indirect materials issued to various production departments	100
Direct manufacturing labor	1,300
Indirect manufacturing labor incurred by various production departments	900
Depreciation on building and manufacturing equipment	400
Miscellaneous manufacturing overhead* incurred by various production departments (ordinarily would be detailed as repairs, photocopying, utilities, etc.)	550
Manufacturing overhead allocated at 160% of direct manufacturing labor costs	?
Cost of goods manufactured	4,120
Revenues	8,000
Cost of goods sold (before adjustment for under- or overallocated manufacturing overhead)	4,020
Inventories, December 31, 2010 (not 2011):	

---

* The term manufacturing overhead is not used uniformly. Other terms that are often encountered in printing companies include job overhead and shop overhead.

Materials Control	100
Work-in-Process Control	60
Finished Goods Control	500

Required
1. Prepare an overview diagram of the job-costing system at the University of Chicago Press.
2. Prepare journal entries to summarize the 2011 transactions. As your final entry, dispose of the year-end under- or overallocated manufacturing overhead as a write-off to Cost of Goods Sold. Number your entries. Explanations for each entry may be omitted.
3. Show posted T-accounts for all inventories, Cost of Goods Sold, Manufacturing Overhead Control, and Manufacturing Overhead Allocated.

4-25 Journal entries, T-accounts, and source documents. Production Company produces gadgets for the coveted small appliance market. The following data reflect activity for the year 2011:

Costs incurred:

Purchases of direct materials (net) on credit	$124,000
Direct manufacturing labor cost	80,000
Indirect labor	54,500
Depreciation, factory equipment	30,000
Depreciation, office equipment	7,000
Maintenance, factory equipment	20,000
Miscellaneous factory overhead	9,500
Rent, factory building	70,000
Advertising expense	90,000
Sales commissions	30,000

Inventories:

	January 1, 2011	December 31, 2011
Direct materials	$ 9,000	$11,000
Work in process	6,000	21,000
Finished goods	69,000	24,000

Production Co. uses a normal costing system and allocates overhead to work in process at a rate of $2.50 per direct manufacturing labor dollar. Indirect materials are insignificant so there is no inventory account for indirect materials.

Required
1. Prepare journal entries to record the transactions for 2011 including an entry to close out over- or underallocated overhead to cost of goods sold. For each journal entry indicate the source document that would be used to authorize each entry. Also note which subsidiary ledger, if any, should be referenced as backup for the entry.
2. Post the journal entries to T-accounts for all of the inventories, Cost of Goods Sold, the Manufacturing Overhead Control Account, and the Manufacturing Overhead Allocated Account.

4-26 Job costing, journal entries. Donnell Transport assembles prestige manufactured homes. Its job costing system has two direct-cost categories (direct materials and direct manufacturing labor) and one indirect-cost pool (manufacturing overhead allocated at a budgeted $30 per machine-hour in 2011). The following data (in millions) pertain to operations for 2011:

Materials Control, beginning balance, January 1, 2011	$ 12
Work-in-Process Control, beginning balance, January 1, 2011	2
Finished Goods Control, beginning balance, January 1, 2011	6
Materials and supplies purchased on credit	150
Direct materials used	145
Indirect materials (supplies) issued to various production departments	10
Direct manufacturing labor	90
Indirect manufacturing labor incurred by various production departments	30
Depreciation on plant and manufacturing equipment	19
Miscellaneous manufacturing overhead incurred (ordinarily would be detailed as repairs, utilities, etc., with a corresponding credit to various liability accounts)	9
Manufacturing overhead allocated, 2,100,000 actual machine-hours	?
Cost of goods manufactured	294
Revenues	400
Cost of goods sold	292

1. Prepare an overview diagram of Donnell Transport's job-costing system.
2. Prepare journal entries. Number your entries. Explanations for each entry may be omitted. Post to T-accounts. What is the ending balance of Work-in-Process Control?
3. Show the journal entry for disposing of under- or overallocated manufacturing overhead directly as a year-end write-off to Cost of Goods Sold. Post the entry to T-accounts.

4-27 Job costing, unit cost, ending work in process. Rafael Company produces pipes for concert-quality organs. Each job is unique. In April 2011, it completed all outstanding orders, and then, in May 2011, it worked on only two jobs, M1 and M2:

	Home Insert Page Layout Formulas Data		
	A	B	C
1	**Rafael Company, May 2011**	**Job M1**	**Job M2**
2	Direct materials	$ 78,000	$ 51,000
3	Direct manufacturing labor	273,000	208,000

Direct manufacturing labor is paid at the rate of $26 per hour. Manufacturing overhead costs are allocated at a budgeted rate of $20 per direct manufacturing labor-hour. Only Job M1 was completed in May.

1. Calculate the total cost for Job M1.
2. 1,100 pipes were produced for Job M1. Calculate the cost per pipe.
3. Prepare the journal entry transferring Job M1 to finished goods.
4. What is the ending balance in the Work-in-Process Control account?

4-28 Job costing; actual, normal, and variation from normal costing. Chico & Partners, a Quebec-based public accounting partnership, specializes in audit services. Its job-costing system has a single direct-cost category (professional labor) and a single indirect-cost pool (audit support, which contains all costs of the Audit Support Department). Audit support costs are allocated to individual jobs using actual professional labor-hours. Chico & Partners employs 10 professionals to perform audit services.

Budgeted and actual amounts for 2011 are as follows:

	Home Insert Page Layout Formulas Data		
	A	B	C
1	**Chico & Partners**		
2	**Budget for 2011**		
3	Professional labor compensation	$990,000	
4	Audit support department costs	$774,000	
5	Professional labor-hours billed to clients	18,000	hours
6			
7	**Actual results for 2011**		
8	Audit support department costs	$735,000	
9	Professional labor-hours billed to clients	17,500	
10	Actual professional labor cost rate	$ 59	per hour

1. Compute the direct-cost rate and the indirect-cost rate per professional labor-hour for 2011 under (a) actual costing, (b) normal costing, and (c) the variation from normal costing that uses budgeted rates for direct costs.
2. Chico's 2011 audit of Pierre & Co. was budgeted to take 150 hours of professional labor time. The actual professional labor time spent on the audit was 160 hours. Compute the cost of the Pierre & Co. audit using (a) actual costing, (b) normal costing, and (c) the variation from normal costing that uses budgeted rates for direct costs. Explain any differences in the job cost.

4-29 Job costing; actual, normal, and variation from normal costing. Braden Brothers, Inc., is an architecture firm specializing in high-rise buildings. Its job-costing system has a single direct-cost category (architectural labor) and a single indirect-cost pool, which contains all costs of supporting the office. Support costs are allocated to individual jobs using architect labor-hours. Braden Brothers employs 15 architects.

Budgeted and actual amounts for 2010 are as follows:

Braden Brothers, Inc.	
Budget for 2010	
Architect labor cost	$2,880,000
Office support costs	$1,728,000
Architect labor-hours billed to clients	32,000 hours
Actual results for 2010	
Office support costs	$1,729,500
Architect labor-hours billed to clients	34,590 hours
Actual architect labor cost rate	$ 92 per hour

Required

1. Compute the direct-cost rate and the indirect-cost rate per architectural labor-hour for 2010 under (a) actual costing, (b) normal costing, and (c) the variation from normal costing that uses budgeted rates for direct costs.
2. Braden Brother's architectural sketches for Champ Tower in Houston was budgeted to take 275 hours of architectural labor time. The actual architectural labor time spent on the job was 250 hours. Compute the cost of the Champ Tower sketches using (a) actual costing, (b) normal costing, and (c) the variation from normal costing that uses budgeted rates for direct costs.

4-30 Proration of overhead. The Ride-On-Wave Company (ROW) produces a line of non-motorized boats. ROW uses a normal-costing system and allocates manufacturing overhead using direct manufacturing labor cost. The following data are for 2011:

Budgeted manufacturing overhead cost	$125,000
Budgeted direct manufacturing labor cost	$250,000
Actual manufacturing overhead cost	$117,000
Actual direct manufacturing labor cost	$228,000

Inventory balances on December 31, 2011, were as follows:

Account	Ending balance	2011 direct manufacturing labor cost in ending balance
Work in process	$ 50,700	$ 20,520
Finished goods	245,050	59,280
Cost of goods sold	549,250	148,200

Required

1. Calculate the manufacturing overhead allocation rate.
2. Compute the amount of under- or overallocated manufacturing overhead.
3. Calculate the ending balances in work in process, finished goods, and cost of goods sold if under- overallocated manufacturing overhead is as follows:
   a. Written off to cost of goods sold
   b. Prorated based on ending balances (before proration) in each of the three accounts
   c. Prorated based on the overhead allocated in 2011 in the ending balances (before proration) in each of the three accounts
4. Which method makes the most sense? Justify your answer.

MyAccountingLab

Problems

4-31 Job costing, accounting for manufacturing overhead, budgeted rates. The Fasano Company uses a job-costing system at its Dover, Delaware, plant. The plant has a machining department and a finishing department. Fasano uses normal costing with two direct-cost categories (direct materials and direct manu- facturing labor) and two manufacturing overhead cost pools (the machining department with machine- hours as the allocation base, and the finishing department with direct manufacturing labor costs as the allocation base). The 2011 budget for the plant is as follows:

	Machining Department	Finishing Department
Manufacturing overhead costs	$10,660,000	$7,372,000
Direct manufacturing labor costs	$ 940,000	$3,800,000
Direct manufacturing labor-hours	36,000	145,000
Machine-hours	205,000	32,000

1. Prepare an overview diagram of Fasano's job-costing system.
2. What is the budgeted manufacturing overhead rate in the machining department? In the finishing department?
3. During the month of January, the job-cost record for Job 431 shows the following:

	Machining Department	Finishing Department
Direct materials used	$15,500	$5,000
Direct manufacturing labor costs	$ 400	$1,1,00
Direct manufacturing labor-hours	50	50
Machine-hours	130	20

Compute the total manufacturing overhead cost allocated to Job 431.
4. Assuming that Job 431 consisted of 400 units of product, what is the cost per unit?
5. Amounts at the end of 2011 are as follows:

	Machining Department	Finishing Department
Manufacturing overhead incurred	$11,070,000	$8,236,000
Direct manufacturing labor costs	$ 1,000,000	$4,400,000
Machine-hours	210,000	31,000

Compute the under- or overallocated manufacturing overhead for each department and for the Dover plant as a whole.
6. Why might Fasano use two different manufacturing overhead cost pools in its job-costing system?

4-32 Service industry, job costing, law firm. Keating & Associates is a law firm specializing in labor relations and employee-related work. It employs 25 professionals (5 partners and 20 associates) who work directly with its clients. The average budgeted total compensation per professional for 2011 is $104,000. Each professional is budgeted to have 1,600 billable hours to clients in 2011. All professionals work for clients to their maximum 1,600 billable hours available. All professional labor costs are included in a single direct-cost category and are traced to jobs on a per-hour basis. All costs of Keating & Associates other than professional labor costs are included in a single indirect-cost pool (legal support) and are allocated to jobs using professional labor-hours as the allocation base. The budgeted level of indirect costs in 2011 is $2,200,000.

1. Prepare an overview diagram of Keating's job-costing system.
2. Compute the 2011 budgeted direct-cost rate per hour of professional labor.
3. Compute the 2011 budgeted indirect-cost rate per hour of professional labor.
4. Keating & Associates is considering bidding on two jobs:
   a. Litigation work for Richardson, Inc., which requires 100 budgeted hours of professional labor
   b. Labor contract work for Punch, Inc., which requires 150 budgeted hours of professional labor
   Prepare a cost estimate for each job.

4-33 Service industry, job costing, two direct- and two indirect-cost categories, law firm (continuation of 4-32). Keating has just completed a review of its job-costing system. This review included a detailed analysis of how past jobs used the firm's resources and interviews with personnel about what factors drive the level of indirect costs. Management concluded that a system with two direct-cost categories (professional partner labor and professional associate labor) and two indirect-cost categories (general support and secretarial support) would yield more accurate job costs. Budgeted information for 2011 related to the two direct-cost categories is as follows:

	Professional Partner Labor	Professional Associate Labor
Number of professionals	5	20
Hours of billable time per professional	1,600 per year	1,600 per year
Total compensation (average per professional)	$200,000	$80,000

Budgeted information for 2011 relating to the two indirect-cost categories is as follows:

	General Support	Secretarial Support
Total costs	$1,800,000	$400,000
Cost-allocation base	Professional labor-hours	Partner labor-hours

1. Compute the 2011 budgeted direct-cost rates for (a) professional partners and (b) professional associates.
2. Compute the 2011 budgeted indirect-cost rates for (a) general support and (b) secretarial support.

3. Compute the budgeted costs for the Richardson and Punch jobs, given the following information:

	Richardson, Inc.	Punch, Inc.
Professional partners	60 hours	30 hours
Professional associates	40 hours	120 hours

4. Comment on the results in requirement 3. Why are the job costs different from those computed in Problem 4-32?

4-34 Proration of overhead. (Z. Iqbal, adapted) The Zaf Radiator Company uses a normal-costing system with a single manufacturing overhead cost pool and machine-hours as the cost-allocation base. The following data are for 2011:

Budgeted manufacturing overhead costs	$4,800,000
Overhead allocation base	Machine-hours
Budgeted machine-hours	80,000
Manufacturing overhead costs incurred	$4,900,000
Actual machine-hours	75,000

Machine-hours data and the ending balances (before proration of under- or overallocated overhead) are as follows:

	Actual Machine-Hours	2011 End-of-Year Balance
Cost of Goods Sold	60,000	$8,000,000
Finished Goods Control	11,000	1,250,000
Work-in-Process Control	4,000	750,000

Required

1. Compute the budgeted manufacturing overhead rate for 2011.
2. Compute the under- or overallocated manufacturing overhead of Zaf Radiator in 2011. Dispose of this amount using the following:
   a. Write-off to Cost of Goods Sold
   b. Proration based on ending balances (before proration) in Work-in-Process Control, Finished Goods Control, and Cost of Goods Sold
   c. Proration based on the overhead allocated in 2011 (before proration) in the ending balances of Work-in-Process Control, Finished Goods Control, and Cost of Goods Sold
3. Which method do you prefer in requirement 2? Explain.

4-35 Normal costing, overhead allocation, working backward. Gibson Manufacturing uses normal costing for its job-costing system, which has two direct-cost categories (direct materials and direct manufacturing labor) and one indirect-cost category (manufacturing overhead). The following information is obtained for 2011:

- Total manufacturing costs, $8,000,000
- Manufacturing overhead allocated, $3,600,000 (allocated at a rate of 200% of direct manufacturing labor costs)
- Work-in-process inventory on January 1, 2011, $320,000
- Cost of finished goods manufactured, $7,920,000

Required

1. Use information in the first two bullet points to calculate (a) direct manufacturing labor costs in 2011 and (b) cost of direct materials used in 2011.
2. Calculate the ending work-in-process inventory on December 31, 2011.

4-36 Proration of overhead with two indirect cost pools. New Rise, Inc., produces porcelain figurines. The production is semi-automated where the figurine is molded almost entirely by operator-less machines and then individually hand-painted. The overhead in the molding department is allocated based on machine-hours and the overhead in the painting department is allocated based on direct manufacturing labor-hours. New Rise, Inc., uses a normal-costing system and reported actual overhead for the month of May of $17,248 and $31,485 for the molding and painting departments, respectively. The company reported the following information related to its inventory accounts and cost of goods sold for the month of May:

	Work in Process	Finished Goods	Cost of Goods Sold
Balance before proration	$27,720	$15,523.20	$115,156.80
Molding Department Overhead Allocated	$ 4,602	$ 957.00	$ 12,489.00
Painting Department Overhead Allocated	$ 2,306	$ 1,897.00	$ 24,982.00

1. Calculate the over- or underallocated overhead for each of the Molding and Painting departments for May. Required

2. Calculate the ending balances in work in process, finished goods, and cost of goods sold if the under- or overallocated overhead amounts in *each* department are as follows:

a. Written off to cost of goods sold

b. Prorated based on the ending balance (before proration) in each of the three accounts

c. Prorated based on the overhead allocated in May (before proration) in the ending balances in each of the three accounts

3. Which method would you choose? Explain.

4-37 General ledger relationships, under- and overallocation. (S. Sridhar, adapted) Needham Company uses normal costing in its job-costing system. Partially completed T-accounts and additional information for Needham for 2011 are as follows:

Direct Materials Control				Work-in-Process Control			Finished Goods Control		
1-1-2011	30,000	380,000		1-1-2011	20,000		1-1-2011	10,000	900,000
	400,000			Dir. manuf.				940,000	
				labor	360,000				

Manufacturing Overhead Control	Manufacturing Overhead Allocated	Cost of Goods Sold
540,000		

Additional information follows:

a. Direct manufacturing labor wage rate was $15 per hour.

b. Manufacturing overhead was allocated at $20 per direct manufacturing labor-hour.

c. During the year, sales revenues were $1,090,000, and marketing and distribution costs were $140,000.

1. What was the amount of direct materials issued to production during 2011? Required

2. What was the amount of manufacturing overhead allocated to jobs during 2011?

3. What was the total cost of jobs completed during 2011?

4. What was the balance of work-in-process inventory on December 31, 2011?

5. What was the cost of goods sold before proration of under- or overallocated overhead?

6. What was the under- or overallocated manufacturing overhead in 2011?

7. Dispose of the under- or overallocated manufacturing overhead using the following:

a. Write-off to Cost of Goods Sold

b. Proration based on ending balances (before proration) in Work-in-Process Control, Finished Goods Control, and Cost of Goods Sold

8. Using each of the approaches in requirement 7, calculate Needham's operating income for 2011.

9. Which approach in requirement 7 do you recommend Needham use? Explain your answer briefly.

4-38 Overview of general ledger relationships. Brady Company uses normal costing in its job-costing system. The company produces custom bikes for toddlers. The beginning balances (December 1) and ending balances (as of December 30) in their inventory accounts are as follows:

	Beginning Balance 12/1	Ending Balance 12/30
Materials Control	$1,200	$ 7,600
Work-in-Process Control	5,800	8,100
Manufacturing Department Overhead Control	—	94,070
Finished Goods Control	3,500	18,500

Additional information follows:

a. Direct materials purchased during December were $65,400.

b. Cost of goods manufactured for December was $225,000.

c. No direct materials were returned to suppliers.

d. No units were started or completed on December 31.

e. The manufacturing labor costs for the December 31 working day: direct manufacturing labor, $3,850, and indirect manufacturing labor, $950.

f. Manufacturing overhead has been allocated at 120% of direct manufacturing labor costs through December 30.

1. Prepare journal entries for the December 31 payroll.
2. Use T-accounts to compute the following:
   a. The total amount of materials requisitioned into work in process during December
   b. The total amount of direct manufacturing labor recorded in work in process during December (Hint: You have to solve requirements **2b** and **2c** simultaneously)
   c. The total amount of manufacturing overhead recorded in work in process during December
   d. Ending balance in work in process, December 31
   e. Cost of goods sold for December before adjustments for under- or overallocated manufacturing overhead
3. Prepare closing journal entries related to manufacturing overhead. Assume that all under- or overallocated manufacturing overhead is closed directly to Cost of Goods Sold.

4-39 Allocation and proration of overhead. Tamden, Inc., prints custom marketing materials. The business was started January 1, 2010. The company uses a normal-costing system. It has two direct cost pools, materials and labor and one indirect cost pool, overhead. Overhead is charged to printing jobs on the basis of direct labor cost. The following information is available for 2010.

Budgeted direct labor costs	$150,000
Budgeted overhead costs	$180,000
Costs of actual material used	$126,500
Actual direct labor costs	$148,750
Actual overhead costs	$176,000

There were two jobs in process on December 31, 2010: Job 11 and Job 12. Costs added to each job as of December 31 are as follows:

	Direct materials	Direct labor
Job 11	$3,620	$4,500
Job 12	$6,830	$7,250

Tamden, Inc., has no finished goods inventories because all printing jobs are transferred to cost of goods sold when completed.

1. Compute the overhead allocation rate.
2. Calculate the balance in ending work in process and cost of goods sold before any adjustments for under- or overallocated overhead.
3. Calculate under- or overallocated overhead.
4. Calculate the ending balances in work in process and cost of goods sold if the under- or overallocated overhead amount is as follows:
   a. Written off to cost of goods sold
   b. Prorated using the ending balance (before proration) in cost of goods sold and work-in-process control accounts
5. Which of the methods in requirement 4 would you choose? Explain.

4-40 Job costing, contracting, ethics. Kingston Company manufactures modular homes. The company has two main products that it sells commercially: a 1,000 square foot, one-bedroom model and a 1,500 square foot, two-bedroom model. The company recently began providing emergency housing (huts) to FEMA. The emergency housing is similar to the 1,000 square foot model.

FEMA has requested Kingston to create a bid for 150 emergency huts to be sent for flood victims in the south. Your boss has asked that you prepare this bid. In preparing the bid, you find a recent invoice to FEMA for 200 huts provided after hurricane Katrina. You also have a standard cost sheet for the 1,000 square foot model sold commercially. Both are provided as follows:

Standard cost sheet: 1,000 sq. ft. one-bedroom model		
Direct materials		$ 8,000
Direct manufacturing labor	30 hours	600
Manufacturing overhead*	$3 per direct labor dollar	1,800
Total cost		$10,400
Retail markup on total cost		20%
Retail price		$12,480

*Overhead cost pool includes inspection labor ($15 per hour), setup labor ($12 per hour), and other indirect costs associated with production.

INVOICE:
DATE: September 15, 2005
BILL TO: FEMA
FOR: 200 Emergency Huts
SHIP TO: New Orleans, Louisiana

Direct materials	$1,840,000
Direct manufacturing labor**	138,400
Manufacturing overhead	415,200
Total cost	2,393,600
Government contract markup on total cost	15%
Total due	$2,752,640

**Direct manufacturing labor includes 28 production hours per unit, 4 inspection hours per unit, and 6 setup hours per unit

1. Calculate the total bid if you base your calculations on the standard cost sheet assuming a cost plus 15% government contract.
2. Calculate the total bid if you base your calculations on the September 15, 2005, invoice assuming a cost plus 15% government contract.
3. What are the main discrepancies between the bids you calculated in #1 and #2?
4. What bid should you present to your boss? What principles from the IMA *Standards of Ethical Conduct for Practitioners of Management Accounting and Financial Management* should guide your decision?

Collaborative Learning Problem

4-41 Job costing—service industry. Cam Cody schedules book signings for science fiction authors and creates e-books and books on CD to sell at each signing. Cody uses a normal-costing system with two direct cost pools, labor and materials, and one indirect cost pool, general overhead. General overhead is allocated to each signing based on 80% of labor cost. Actual overhead equaled allocated overhead in March 2010. Actual overhead in April was $1,980. All costs incurred during the planning stage for a signing and during the signing are gathered in a balance sheet account called "Signings in Progress (SIP)." When a signing is completed, the costs are transferred to an income statement account called "Cost of Completed Signings (CCS)." Following is cost information for April 2010:

Author	From Beginning SIP Materials	From Beginning SIP Labor	Incurred in April Materials	Incurred in April Labor
N. Asher	$425	$750	$ 90	$225
T. Bucknell	710	575	150	75
S. Brown	200	550	320	450
S. King	—	—	650	400
D. Sherman	—	—	150	200

The following information relates to April 2010.

As of April 1, there were three signings in progress, *N. Asher, T. Bucknell,* and *S. Brown.* Signings for *S. King* and *D. Sherman* were started during April. The signings for *T. Bucknell* and *S. King* were completed during April.

1. Calculate SIP at the end of April.
2. Calculate CCS for April.
3. Calculate under/overallocated overhead at the end of April.
4. Calculate the ending balances in SIP and CCS if the under/overallocated overhead amount is as follows:
   a. Written off to CCS
   b. Prorated based on the ending balances (before proration) in SIP and CCS
   c. Prorated based on the overhead allocated in April in the ending balances of SIP and CCS (before proration)
5. Which of the methods in requirement 4 would you choose?

Activity-Based Costing and Activity-Based Management

From Chapter 5 of *Cost Accounting: A Managerial Emphasis*, 14/e. Charles T. Horngren. Srikant M. Datar. Madhav Rajan.

Activity-Based Costing and Activity-Based Management

A good mystery never fails to capture the imagination.

Money is stolen or lost, property disappears, or someone meets with foul play. On the surface, what appears unremarkable to the untrained eye can turn out to be quite a revelation once the facts and details are uncovered. Getting to the bottom of the case, understanding what happened and why, and taking action can make the difference between a solved case and an unsolved one. Business and organizations are much the same. Their costing systems are often mysteries with unresolved questions: Why are we bleeding red ink? Are we pricing our products accurately? Activity-based costing can help unravel the mystery and result in improved operations, as LG Electronics discovers in the following article.

LG Electronics Reduces Costs and Inefficiencies Through Activity-Based Costing[1]

LG Electronics is one of the world's largest manufacturers of flat-screen televisions and mobile phones. In 2009, the Seoul, South Korea-based company sold 16 million liquid crystal display televisions and 117 million mobile phones worldwide.

To make so many electronic devices, LG Electronics spends nearly $40 billion annually on the procurement of semiconductors, metals, connectors, and other materials. Costs for many of these components have soared in recent years. Until 2008, however, LG Electronics did not have a centralized procurement system to leverage its scale and to control supply costs. Instead, the company had a decentralized system riddled with wasteful spending and inefficiencies.

To respond to these challenges, LG Electronics hired its first chief procurement officer who turned to activity-based costing ("ABC") for answers. ABC analysis of the company's procurement system revealed that most company resources were applied to administrative and not strategic tasks. Furthermore, the administrative tasks were done manually and at a very high cost.

The ABC analysis led LG Electronics to change many of its procurement practices and processes, improve efficiency and focus

[1] *Sources:* Carbone, James. 2009. LG Electronics centralizes purchasing to save. *Purchasing*, April. http://www.purchasing.com/article/217108-LG_Electronics_centralizes_purchasing_to_save.php; Linton's goals. 2009. Supply Management, May 12. http://www.supplymanagement.com/analysis/features/2009/lintons-goals/; Yoou-chul, Kim. 2009. CPO expects to save $1 billion in procurement. *The Korea Times*, April 1. http://www.koreatimes.co.kr/www/news/biz/2009/04/123_42360.html

on the highest-value tasks such as managing costs of commodity products and negotiating with suppliers. Furthermore, the company developed a global procurement strategy for its televisions, mobile phones, computers, and home theatre systems by implementing competitive bidding among suppliers, standardizing parts across product lines, and developing additional buying capacity in China.

The results so far have been staggering. In 2008 alone, LG Electronics reduced its materials costs by 16%, and expects to further reduce costs by $5 billion by the end of 2011.

Ethan Miller \Getty Images, Inc.—Liaison

Most companies—such as Dell, Oracle, JP Morgan Chase, and Honda—offer more than one product (or service). Dell Computer, for example, produces desktops, laptops, and servers. The three basic activities for manufacturing computers are (a) designing computers, (b) ordering component parts, and (c) assembly. The different products, however, require different quantities of the three activities. For example, a server has a more complex design, many more parts, and a more complex assembly than a desktop.

To measure the cost of producing each product, Dell separately tracks activity costs for each product. In this chapter, we describe activity-based costing systems and how they help companies make better decisions about pricing and product mix. And, just as in the case of LG Electronics, we show how ABC systems assist in cost management decisions by improving product designs, processes, and efficiency.

Broad Averaging and Its Consequences

Historically, companies (such as television and automobile manufacturers) produced a limited variety of products. Indirect (or overhead) costs were a relatively small percentage of total costs. Using simple costing systems to allocate costs broadly was easy, inexpensive, and reasonably accurate. However, as product diversity and indirect costs have increased, broad averaging has resulted in greater inaccuracy of product costs. For example, the use of a single, plant-wide manufacturing overhead rate to allocate costs to products often produces unreliable cost data. The term *peanut-butter costing* (yes, that's what it's called) describes a particular costing approach that uses broad averages for assigning (or spreading, as in spreading peanut butter) the cost of resources uniformly to cost objects (such as products or services) when the individual products or services, may in fact, use those resources in nonuniform ways.

Undercosting and Overcosting

The following example illustrates how averaging can result in inaccurate and misleading cost data. Consider the cost of a restaurant bill for four colleagues who meet monthly to discuss business developments. Each diner orders separate entrees, desserts, and drinks. The restaurant bill for the most recent meeting is as follows:

	Emma	James	Jessica	Matthew	Total	Average
Entree	$11	$20	$15	$14	$ 60	$15
Dessert	0	8	4	4	16	4
Drinks	4	14	8	6	32	8
Total	$15	$42	$27	$24	$108	$27

If the $108 total restaurant bill is divided evenly, $27 is the average cost per diner. This cost-averaging approach treats each diner the same. Emma would probably object to paying $27 because her actual cost is only $15; she ordered the lowest-cost entree, had no dessert, and had the lowest-cost drink. When costs are averaged across all four diners, both Emma and Matthew are overcosted, James is undercosted, and Jessica is (by coincidence) accurately costed.

Broad averaging can lead to undercosting or overcosting of products or services:

- **Product undercosting**—a product consumes a high level of resources but is reported to have a low cost per unit (James's dinner).
- **Product overcosting**—a product consumes a low level of resources but is reported to have a high cost per unit (Emma's dinner).

What are the strategic consequences of product undercosting and overcosting? Think of a company that uses cost information about its products to guide pricing decisions. Undercosted products will be underpriced and may even lead to sales that actually result in losses—sales bring in less revenue than the cost of resources they use. Overcosted products lead to overpricing, causing these products to lose market share to competitors producing similar products. Worse still, product undercosting and overcosting causes managers to focus on the wrong products, drawing attention to overcosted products whose costs may in fact be perfectly reasonable and ignoring undercosted products that in fact consume large amounts of resources.

Product-Cost Cross-Subsidization

Product-cost cross-subsidization means that if a company undercosts one of its products, it will overcost at least one of its other products. Similarly, if a company overcosts one of its products, it will undercost at least one of its other products. Product-cost cross-subsidization is very common in situations in which a cost is uniformly spread—meaning it is broadly averaged—across multiple products without recognizing the amount of resources consumed by each product.

In the restaurant-bill example, the amount of cost cross-subsidization of each diner can be readily computed *because all cost items can be traced as direct costs to each diner*. If all diners pay $27, Emma is paying $12 more than her actual cost of $15. She is cross-subsidizing James who is paying $15 less than his actual cost of $42. Calculating the amount of cost cross-subsidization takes more work when there are indirect costs to be considered. Why? Because when the resources represented by indirect costs are used by two or more diners, we need to find a way to allocate costs to each diner. Consider, for example, a $40 bottle of wine whose cost is shared equally. Each diner would pay $10 ($40 ÷ 4). Suppose Matthew drinks 2 glasses of wine while Emma, James, and Jessica drink one glass each for a total of 5 glasses. Allocating the cost of the bottle of wine on the basis of the glasses of wine that each diner drinks would result in Matthew paying $16 ($40 × 2/5) and each of the others $8 ($40 × 1/5). In this case, by sharing the cost equally, Emma, James, and Jessica are each paying $2 ($10 – $8) more and are cross-subsidizing Matthew who is paying $6 ($16 – $10) less for the wine he consumes.

To see the effects of broad averaging on direct and indirect costs, we consider Plastim Corporation's costing system.

Decision Point

When does product undercosting or overcosting occur?

Simple Costing System at Plastim Corporation

Plastim Corporation manufactures lenses for the rear taillights of automobiles. A lens, made from black, red, orange, or white plastic, is the part of the lamp visible on the automobile's exterior. Lenses are made by injecting molten plastic into a mold to give the lamp its desired shape. The mold is cooled to allow the molten plastic to solidify, and the lens is removed.

Under its contract with Giovanni Motors, a major automobile manufacturer, Plastim makes two types of lenses: a complex lens, CL5, and a simple lens, S3. The complex lens is a large lens with special features, such as multicolor molding (when more than one color is injected into the mold) and a complex shape that wraps around the corner of the car. Manufacturing CL5 lenses is more complex because various parts in the mold must align and fit precisely. The S3 lens is simpler to make because it has a single color and few special features.

Design, Manufacturing, and Distribution Processes

The sequence of steps to design, produce, and distribute lenses, whether simple or complex, is as follows:

- **Design products and processes.** Each year Giovanni Motors specifies some modifications to the simple and complex lenses. Plastim's design department designs the molds from which the lenses will be made and specifies the processes needed (that is, details of the manufacturing operations).
- **Manufacture lenses.** The lenses are molded, finished, cleaned, and inspected.
- **Distribute lenses.** Finished lenses are packed and sent to Giovanni Motors.

Plastim is operating at capacity and incurs very low marketing costs. Because of its high-quality products, Plastim has minimal customer-service costs. Plastim's business environment is very competitive with respect to simple lenses. At a recent meeting, Giovanni's purchasing manager indicated that a new supplier, Bandix, which makes only simple lenses, is offering to supply the S3 lens to Giovanni at a price of $53, well below the $63 price that Plastim is currently projecting and budgeting for 2011. Unless Plastim can lower its selling price, it will lose the Giovanni business for the simple lens for the upcoming model year. Fortunately, the same competitive pressures do not exist for the complex lens, which Plastim currently sells to Giovanni at $137 per lens.

Plastim's management has two primary options:

- Plastim can give up the Giovanni business in simple lenses if selling simple lenses is unprofitable. Bandix makes only simple lenses and perhaps, therefore, uses simpler technology and processes than Plastim. The simpler operations may give Bandix a cost advantage that Plastim cannot match. If so, it is better for Plastim to not supply the S3 lens to Giovanni.
- Plastim can reduce the price of the simple lens and either accept a lower margin or aggressively seek to reduce costs.

To make these long-run strategic decisions, management needs to first understand the costs to design, make, and distribute the S3 and CL5 lenses.

While Bandix makes only simple lenses and can fairly accurately calculate the cost of a lens by dividing total costs by units produced, Plastim's costing environment is more challenging. The processes to make both simple and complex lenses are more complicated than the processes required to make only simple lenses. Plastim needs to find a way to allocate costs to each type of lens.

In computing costs, Plastim assigns both variable costs and costs that are fixed in the short run to the S3 and CL5 lenses. Managers cost products and services to guide long-run strategic decisions (for example, what mix of products and services to produce and sell and what prices to charge for them). In the long-run, managers want revenues to exceed total costs (variable and fixed) to design, make, and distribute the lenses.

To guide their pricing and cost-management decisions, Plastim's managers assign all costs, both manufacturing and nonmanufacturing, to the S3 and CL5 lenses. If managers had wanted to calculate the cost of inventory, Plastim's management accountants would have assigned only manufacturing costs to the lenses, as required by generally accepted accounting principles. Surveys of company practice across the globe overwhelmingly indicate that the vast majority of companies use costing systems not just for inventory costing but also for strategic purposes such as pricing and product-mix decisions and decisions about cost reduction, process improvement, design, and planning and budgeting. As a result, even merchandising-sector companies (for whom inventory costing is straightforward) and service-sector companies (who have no inventory) expend considerable resources in designing and operating their costing systems. In this chapter, we take this more strategic focus and allocate costs in all functions of the value chain to the S3 and CL5 lenses.

Simple Costing System Using a Single Indirect-Cost Pool

Plastim has historically had a simple costing system that allocates indirect costs using a single indirect-cost rate. We calculate budgeted costs for each type of lens in 2011 using Plastim's simple costing system and later contrast it with activity-based costing. (Note that instead of jobs, we now have products as the cost objects.) Exhibit 1 shows an overview of Plastim's simple costing system. Use this exhibit as a guide as you study the following steps, each of which is marked in Exhibit 1.

Exhibit 1

Overview of Plastim's Simple Costing System

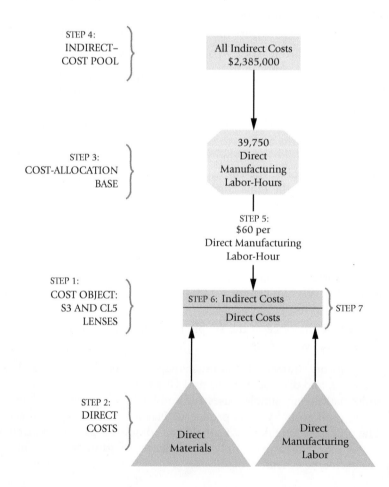

Step 1: Identify the Products That Are the Chosen Cost Objects. The cost objects are the 60,000 simple S3 lenses and the 15,000 complex CL5 lenses that Plastim will produce in 2011. Plastim's goal is to first calculate the total costs and then the unit cost of designing, manufacturing, and distributing these lenses.

Step 2: Identify the Direct Costs of the Products. Plastim identifies the direct costs—direct materials and direct manufacturing labor—of the lenses. Exhibit 2 shows the direct and indirect costs for the S3 and the CL5 lenses using the simple costing system. The direct cost calculations appear on lines 5, 6, and 7 of Exhibit 2. Plastim classifies all other costs as indirect costs.

Step 3: Select the Cost-Allocation Bases to Use for Allocating Indirect (or Overhead) Costs to the Products. A majority of the indirect costs consist of salaries paid to supervisors, engineers, manufacturing support, and maintenance staff, all supporting direct manufacturing labor. Plastim uses direct manufacturing labor-hours as the only allocation base to allocate all manufacturing and nonmanufacturing indirect costs to S3 and CL5. In 2011, Plastim plans to use 39,750 direct manufacturing labor-hours.

Step 4: Identify the Indirect Costs Associated with Each Cost-Allocation Base. Because Plastim uses only a single cost-allocation base, Plastim groups all budgeted indirect costs of $2,385,000 for 2011 into a single overhead cost pool.

Step 5: Compute the Rate per Unit of Each Cost-Allocation Base.

$$\text{Budgeted indirect-cost rate} = \frac{\text{Budgeted total costs in indirect-cost pool}}{\text{Budgeted total quantity of cost-allocation base}}$$

$$= \frac{\$2,385,000}{39,750 \text{ direct manufacturing labor-hours}}$$

$$= \$60 \text{ per direct manufacturing labor-hour}$$

Step 6: Compute the Indirect Costs Allocated to the Products. Plastim expects to use 30,000 total direct manufacturing labor-hours to make the 60,000 S3 lenses and 9,750 total direct manufacturing labor-hours to make the 15,000 CL5 lenses. Exhibit 2 shows indirect costs of $1,800,000 ($60 per direct manufacturing labor-hour × 30,000 direct manufacturing labor-hours) allocated to the simple lens and $585,000 ($60 per direct manufacturing labor-hour × 9,750 direct manufacturing labor-hours) allocated to the complex lens.

Step 7: Compute the Total Cost of the Products by Adding All Direct and Indirect Costs Assigned to the Products. Exhibit 2 presents the product costs for the simple and complex lenses. The direct costs are calculated in Step 2 and the indirect costs in Step 6. Be sure you see the parallel between the simple costing system overview diagram (Exhibit 1)

Exhibit 2   Plastim's Product Costs Using the Simple Costing System

	Home	Insert	Page Layout	Formulas	Data	Review	View		
	A		B	C	D	E	F		G
1			60,000			15,000			
2			Simple Lenses (S3)			Complex Lenses (CL5)			
3			Total	per Unit		Total	per Unit		Total
4			(1)	(2) = (1) ÷ 60,000		(3)	(4) = (3) ÷ 15,000		(5) = (1) + (3)
5	Direct materials		$1,125,000	$18.75		$ 675,000	$45.00		$1,800,000
6	Direct manufacturing labor		600,000	10.00		195,000	13.00		795,000
7	Total direct costs (Step 2)		1,725,000	28.75		870,000	58.00		2,595,000
8	Indirect costs allocated (Step 6)		1,800,000	30.00		585,000	39.00		2,385,000
9	Total costs (Step 7)		$3,525,000	$58.75		$1,455,000	$97.00		$4,980,000
10									

and the costs calculated in Step 7. Exhibit 1 shows two direct-cost categories and one indirect-cost category. Hence, the budgeted cost of each type of lens in Step 7 (Exhibit 2) has three line items: two for direct costs and one for allocated indirect costs. The budgeted cost per S3 lens is $58.75, well above the $53 selling price quoted by Bandix. The budgeted cost per CL5 lens is $97.

Applying the Five-Step Decision-Making Process at Plastim

To decide how it should respond to the threat that Bandix poses to its S3 lens business, Plastim's management works through the five-step decision-making process.

Step 1: Identify the problem and uncertainties. The problem is clear: If Plastim wants to retain the Giovanni business for S3 lenses and make a profit, it must find a way to reduce the price and costs of the S3 lens. The two major uncertainties Plastim faces are (1) whether Plastim's technology and processes for the S3 lens are competitive with Bandix's and (2) whether the S3 lens is overcosted by the simple costing system.

Step 2: Obtain information. Management asks a team of its design and process engineers to analyze and evaluate the design, manufacturing, and distribution operations for the S3 lens. The team is very confident that the technology and processes for the S3 lens are not inferior to those of Bandix and other competitors because Plastim has many years of experience in manufacturing and distributing the S3 with a history and culture of continuous process improvements. If anything, the team is less certain about Plastim's capabilities in manufacturing and distributing complex lenses, because it only recently started making this type of lens. Given these doubts, management is happy that Giovanni Motors considers the price of the CL5 lens to be competitive. It is somewhat of a puzzle, though, how at the currently budgeted prices, Plastim is expected to earn a very large profit margin percentage (operating income ÷ revenues) on the CL5 lenses and a small profit margin on the S3 lenses:

| | 60,000 Simple Lenses (S3) | | 15,000 Complex Lenses (CL5) | | |
	Total (1)	per Unit (2) = (1) ÷ 60,000	Total (3)	per Unit (4) = (3) ÷ 15,000	Total (5) = (1) + (3)
Revenues	$3,780,000	$63.00	$2,055,000	$137.00	$5,835,000
Total costs	3,525,000	58.75	1,455,000	97.00	4,980,000
Operating income	$ 255,000	$ 4.25	$ 600,000	$ 40.00	$ 855,000
Profit margin percentage		6.75%		29.20%	

As it continues to gather information, Plastim's management begins to ponder why the profit margins (and process) are under so much pressure for the S3 lens, where the company has strong capabilities, but high on the newer, less-established CL5 lens. Plastim is not deliberately charging a low price for S3, so management starts to believe that perhaps the problem lies with its costing system. Plastim's simple costing system may be overcosting the simple S3 lens (assigning too much cost to it) and undercosting the complex CL5 lens (assigning too little cost to it).

Step 3: Make predictions about the future. Plastim's key challenge is to get a better estimate of what it will cost to design, make, and distribute the S3 and CL5 lenses. Management is fairly confident about the direct material and direct manufacturing labor costs of each lens because these costs are easily traced to the lenses. But management is quite concerned about how accurately the simple costing system measures the indirect resources used by each type of lens. It believes it can do much better.

At the same time, management wants to ensure that no biases enter its thinking. In particular, it wants to be careful that the desire to be competitive on the S3 lens should not lead to assumptions that bias in favor of lowering costs of the S3 lens.

Step 4:   Make decisions by choosing among alternatives. On the basis of predicted costs, and taking into account how Bandix might respond, Plastim's managers must decide whether they should bid for Giovanni Motors' S3 lens business and if they do bid, what price they should offer.

Step 5:   Implement the decision, evaluate performance, and learn. If Plastim bids and wins Giovanni's S3 lens business, it must compare actual costs, as it makes and ships S3 lenses, to predicted costs and learn why actual costs deviate from predicted costs. Such evaluation and learning form the basis for future improvements.

The next few sections focus on Steps 3, 4, and 5—how Plastim improves the allocation of indirect costs to the S3 and CL5 lenses, how it uses these predictions to bid for the S3 lens business, and how it makes product design and process improvements.

Refining a Costing System

A **refined costing system** reduces the use of broad averages for assigning the cost of resources to cost objects (such as jobs, products, and services) and provides better measurement of the costs of indirect resources used by different cost objects—no matter how differently various cost objects use indirect resources.

Reasons for Refining a Costing System

There are three principal reasons that have accelerated the demand for such refinements.

1. **Increase in product diversity.** The growing demand for customized products has led companies to increase the variety of products and services they offer. Kanthal, the Swedish manufacturer of heating elements, for example, produces more than 10,000 different types of electrical heating wires and thermostats. Banks, such as the Cooperative Bank in the United Kingdom, offer many different types of accounts and services: special passbook accounts, ATMs, credit cards, and electronic banking. These products differ in the demands they place on the resources needed to produce them, because of differences in volume, process, and complexity. The use of broad averages is likely to lead to distorted and inaccurate cost information.

2. **Increase in indirect costs.** The use of product and process technology such as computer-integrated manufacturing (CIM) and flexible manufacturing systems (FMS), has led to an increase in indirect costs and a decrease in direct costs, particularly direct manufacturing labor costs. In CIM and FMS, computers on the manufacturing floor give instructions to set up and run equipment quickly and automatically. The computers accurately measure hundreds of production parameters and directly control the manufacturing processes to achieve high-quality output. Managing more complex technology and producing very diverse products also requires committing an increasing amount of resources for various support functions, such as production scheduling, product and process design, and engineering. Because direct manufacturing labor is not a cost driver of these costs, allocating indirect costs on the basis of direct manufacturing labor (which was the common practice) does not accurately measure how resources are being used by different products.

3. **Competition in product markets.** As markets have become more competitive, managers have felt the need to obtain more accurate cost information to help them make important strategic decisions, such as how to price products and which products to sell. Making correct pricing and product mix decisions is critical in competitive markets because competitors quickly capitalize on a company's mistakes.

   Whereas the preceding factors point to reasons for the increase in *demand* for refined cost systems, *advances in information technology* have enabled companies to implement these refinements. Costing system refinements require more data gathering and more analysis, and improvements in information technology have drastically reduced the costs to gather, validate, store, and analyze vast quantities of data.

Learning Objective 2

Present three guidelines for refining a costing system

. . . classify more costs as direct costs, expand the number of indirect-cost pools, and identify cost drivers

Guidelines for Refining a Costing System

There are three main guidelines for refining a costing system. In the following sections, we delve more deeply into each in the context of the Plastim example.

1. **Direct-cost tracing.** Identify as many direct costs as is economically feasible. This guideline aims to reduce the amount of costs classified as indirect, thereby minimizing the extent to which costs have to be allocated, rather than traced.

2. **Indirect-cost pools.** Expand the number of indirect-cost pools until each pool is more homogeneous. All costs in a *homogeneous cost pool* have the same or a similar cause-and-effect (or benefits-received) relationship with a single cost driver that is used as the cost-allocation base. Consider, for example, a single indirect-cost pool containing both indirect machining costs and indirect distribution costs that are allocated to products using machine-hours. This pool is not homogeneous because machine-hours are a cost driver of machining costs but not of distribution costs, which has a different cost driver, number of shipments. If, instead, machining costs and distribution costs are separated into two indirect-cost pools (with machine-hours as the cost-allocation base for the machining cost pool and number of shipments as the cost-allocation base for the distribution cost pool), each indirect-cost pool would become homogeneous.

3. **Cost-allocation bases.** As we describe later in the chapter, whenever possible, use the cost driver (the cause of indirect costs) as the cost-allocation base for each homogenous indirect-cost pool (the effect).

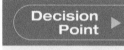

Decision Point ▶

How do managers refine a costing system?

Learning Objective 3

Distinguish between simple and activity-based costing systems

. . . unlike simple systems, ABC systems calculate costs of individual activities to cost products

Activity-Based Costing Systems

One of the best tools for refining a costing system is activity-based costing. **Activity-based costing (ABC)** refines a costing system by identifying individual activities as the fundamental cost objects. An **activity** is an event, task, or unit of work with a specified purpose—for example, designing products, setting up machines, operating machines, and distributing products. More informally, activities are verbs; they are things that a firm does. To help make strategic decisions, ABC systems identify activities in all functions of the value chain, calculate costs of individual activities, and assign costs to cost objects such as products and services on the basis of the mix of activities needed to produce each product or service.[2]

Plastim's ABC System

After reviewing its simple costing system and the potential miscosting of product costs, Plastim decides to implement an ABC system. Direct material costs and direct manufacturing labor costs can be traced to products easily, so the ABC system focuses on refining the assignment of indirect costs to departments, processes, products, or other cost objects. Plastim's ABC system identifies various activities that help explain why Plastim incurs the costs it currently classifies as indirect in its simple costing system. In other words, it breaks up the current indirect cost pool into finer pools of costs related to various activities. To identify these activities, Plastim organizes a team comprised of managers from design, manufacturing, distribution, accounting, and administration.

---

[2] For more details on ABC systems, see R. Cooper and R. S. Kaplan, *The Design of Cost Management Systems* (Upper Saddle River, NJ: Prentice Hall, 1999); G. Cokins, *Activity-Based Cost Management: An Executive's Guide* (Hoboken, NJ: John Wiley & Sons, 2001); and R. S. Kaplan and S. Anderson, *Time-Driven Activity-Based Costing: A Simpler and More Powerful Path to Higher Profits* (Boston: Harvard Business School Press, 2007).

Defining activities is not a simple matter. The team evaluates hundreds of tasks performed at Plastim before choosing the activities that form the basis of its ABC system. For example, it decides if maintenance of molding machines, operations of molding machines, and process control should each be regarded as a separate activity or should be combined into a single activity. An activity-based costing system with many activities becomes overly detailed and unwieldy to operate. An activity-based costing system with too few activities may not be refined enough to measure cause-and-effect relationships between cost drivers and various indirect costs. Plastim's team focuses on activities that account for a sizable fraction of indirect costs and combines activities that have the same cost driver into a single activity. For example, the team decides to combine maintenance of molding machines, operations of molding machines, and process control into a single activity—molding machine operations—because all these activities have the same cost driver: molding machine-hours.

The team identifies the following seven activities by developing a flowchart of all the steps and processes needed to design, manufacture, and distribute S3 and CL5 lenses.

a. Design products and processes
b. Set up molding machines to ensure that the molds are properly held in place and parts are properly aligned before manufacturing starts
c. Operate molding machines to manufacture lenses
d. Clean and maintain the molds after lenses are manufactured
e. Prepare batches of finished lenses for shipment
f. Distribute lenses to customers
g. Administer and manage all processes at Plastim

These activity descriptions form the basis of the activity-based costing system—sometimes called an *activity list* or *activity dictionary*. Compiling the list of tasks, however, is only the first step in implementing activity-based costing systems. Plastim must also identify the cost of each activity and the related cost driver. To do so, Plastim uses the three guidelines for refining a costing system.

1. **Direct-cost tracing.** Plastim's ABC system subdivides the single indirect cost pool into seven smaller cost pools related to the different activities. The costs in the cleaning and maintenance activity cost pool (item d) consist of salaries and wages paid to workers who clean the mold. These costs are direct costs, because they can be economically traced to a specific mold and lens.

2. **Indirect-cost pools.** The remaining six activity cost pools are indirect cost pools. Unlike the single indirect cost pool of Plastim's simple costing system, each of the activity-related cost pools is homogeneous. That is, each activity cost pool includes only those narrow and focused set of costs that have the same cost driver. For example, the distribution cost pool includes only those costs (such as wages of truck drivers) that, over time, increase as the cost driver of distribution costs, cubic feet of packages delivered, increases. In the simple costing system, all indirect costs were lumped together and the cost-allocation base, direct manufacturing labor-hours, was not a cost driver of the indirect costs.

   Determining costs of activity pools requires assigning and reassigning costs accumulated in support departments, such as human resources and information systems, to each of the activity cost pools on the basis of how various activities use support department resources. This is commonly referred to as *first-stage allocation*. We focus here on the *second-stage allocation*, the allocation of costs of activity cost pools to products.

3. **Cost-allocation bases.** For each activity cost pool, the cost driver is used (whenever possible) as the cost-allocation base. To identify cost drivers, Plastim's managers consider various alternatives and use their knowledge of operations to choose among them. For example, Plastim's managers choose setup-hours rather than the number of setups as the cost driver of setup costs, because Plastim's managers believe that more complex setups take more time and are more costly. Over time, Plastim's managers can use data to test their beliefs.

The logic of ABC systems is twofold. First, structuring activity cost pools more finely with cost drivers for each activity cost pool as the cost-allocation base leads to more accurate costing of activities. Second, allocating these costs to products by measuring the cost-allocation bases of different activities used by different products leads to more accurate product costs. We illustrate this logic by focusing on the setup activity at Plastim.

Setting up molding machines frequently entails trial runs, fine-tuning, and adjustments. Improper setups cause quality problems such as scratches on the surface of the lens. The resources needed for each setup depend on the complexity of the manufacturing operation. Complex lenses require more setup resources (setup-hours) per setup than simple lenses. Furthermore, complex lenses can be produced only in small batches because the molds for complex lenses need to be cleaned more often than molds for simple lenses. Thus, relative to simple lenses, complex lenses not only use more setup-hours per setup, but they also require more frequent setups.

Setup data for the simple S3 lens and the complex CL5 lens are as follows:

		Simple S3 Lens	Complex CL5 Lens	Total
1	Quantity of lenses produced	60,000	15,000	
2	Number of lenses produced per batch	240	50	
3 = (1) ÷ (2)	Number of batches	250	300	
4	Setup time per batch	2 hours	5 hours	
5 = (3) × (4)	Total setup-hours	500 hours	1,500 hours	2,000 hours

Of the $2,385,000 in the total indirect-cost pool, Plastim identifies the total costs of setups (consisting mainly of depreciation on setup equipment and allocated costs of process engineers, quality engineers, and supervisors) to be $300,000. Recall that in its simple costing system, Plastim uses direct manufacturing labor-hours to allocate all indirect costs to products. The following table compares how setup costs allocated to simple and complex lenses will be different if Plastim allocates setup costs to lenses based on setup-hours rather than direct manufacturing labor-hours. Of the $60 total rate per direct manufacturing labor-hour, the setup cost per direct manufacturing labor-hour amounts to $7.54717 ($300,000 ÷ 39,750 total direct manufacturing labor-hours). The setup cost per setup-hour equals $150 ($300,000 ÷ 2,000 total setup-hours).

	Simple S3 Lens	Complex CL5 Lens	Total
Setup cost allocated using direct manufacturing labor-hours:			
$7.54717 × 30,000; $7.54717 × 9,750	$226,415	$ 73,585	$300,000
Setup cost allocated using setup-hours:			
$150 × 500; $150 × 1,500	$ 75,000	$225,000	$300,000

As we have already discussed when presenting guidelines 2 and 3, setup-hours, not direct manufacturing labor-hours, are the cost driver of setup costs.. The CL5 lens uses substantially more setup-hours than the S3 lens (1,500 hours ÷ 2,000 hours = 75% of the total setup-hours) because the CL5 requires a greater number of setups (batches) and each setup is more challenging and requires more setup-hours.

The ABC system therefore allocates substantially more setup costs to CL5 than to S3. When direct manufacturing labor-hours rather than setup-hours are used to allocate setup costs in the simple costing system, it is the S3 lens that is allocated a very large share of the setup costs because the S3 lens uses a larger proportion of direct manufacturing labor-hours (30,000 ÷ 39,750 = 75.47%). As a result, the simple costing system overcosts the S3 lens with regard to setup costs.

Note that setup-hours are related to batches (or groups) of lenses made, not the number of individual lenses. Activity-based costing attempts to identify the most relevant cause-and-effect relationship for each activity pool, without restricting the cost driver to only units of output or variables related to units of output (such as direct manufacturing labor-hours). As our discussion of setups illustrates, limiting cost-allocation bases in this manner weakens the cause-and-effect relationship between the cost-allocation base and the costs in a cost pool.

Decision Point ▶

What is the difference between the design of a simple costing system and an activity-based costing (ABC) system?

Cost Hierarchies

A **cost hierarchy** categorizes various activity cost pools on the basis of the different types of cost drivers, or cost-allocation bases, or different degrees of difficulty in determining cause-and-effect (or benefits-received) relationships. ABC systems commonly use a cost hierarchy with four levels—output unit-level costs, batch-level costs, product-sustaining costs, and facility-sustaining costs—to identify cost-allocation bases that are cost drivers of the activity cost pools.

Output unit-level costs are the costs of activities performed on each individual unit of a product or service. Machine operations costs (such as the cost of energy, machine depreciation, and repair) related to the activity of running the automated molding machines are output unit-level costs. They are output unit-level costs because, over time, the cost of this activity increases with additional units of output produced (or machine-hours used). Plastim's ABC system uses molding machine-hours—an output-unit level cost-allocation base—to allocate machine operations costs to products.

Batch-level costs are the costs of activities related to a group of units of a product or service rather than each individual unit of product or service. In the Plastim example, setup costs are batch-level costs because, over time, the cost of this setup activity increases with setup-hours needed to produce batches (groups) of lenses. As described in the table on the previous page, the S3 lens requires 500 setup-hours (2 setup-hours per batch × 250 batches). The CL5 lens requires 1,500 setup-hours (5 setup-hours per batch × 300 batches). The total setup costs allocated to S3 and CL5 depend on the total setup-hours required by each type of lens, not on the number of units of S3 and CL5 produced. (Setup costs being a batch-level cost cannot be avoided by producing one less unit of S3 or CL5.) Plastim's ABC system uses setup-hours—a batch-level cost-allocation base—to allocate setup costs to products. Other examples of batch-level costs are material-handling and quality-inspection costs associated with batches (not the quantities) of products produced, and costs of placing purchase orders, receiving materials, and paying invoices related to the number of purchase orders placed rather than the quantity or value of materials purchased.

Product-sustaining costs (service-sustaining costs) are the costs of activities undertaken to support individual products or services regardless of the number of units or batches in which the units are produced. In the Plastim example, design costs are product-sustaining costs. Over time, design costs depend largely on the time designers spend on designing and modifying the product, the mold, and the process. These design costs are a function of the complexity of the mold, measured by the number of parts in the mold multiplied by the area (in square feet) over which the molten plastic must flow (12 parts × 2.5 square feet, or 30 parts-square feet for the S3 lens, and 14 parts × 5 square feet, or 70 parts-square feet for the CL5 lens). As a result, the total design costs allocated to S3 and CL5 depend on the complexity of the mold, regardless of the number of units or batches of production. Design costs cannot be avoided by producing fewer units or running fewer batches. Plastim's ABC system uses parts-square feet—a product-sustaining cost-allocation base—to allocate design costs to products. Other examples of product-sustaining costs are product research and development costs, costs of making engineering changes, and marketing costs to launch new products.

Facility-sustaining costs are the costs of activities that cannot be traced to individual products or services but that support the organization as a whole. In the Plastim example, the general administration costs (including top management compensation, rent, and building security) are facility-sustaining costs. It is usually difficult to find a good cause-and-effect relationship between these costs and the cost-allocation base. This lack of a cause-and-effect relationship causes some companies not to allocate these costs to products and instead to deduct them as a separate lump-sum amount from operating income. Other companies, such as Plastim, allocate facility-sustaining costs to products on some basis—for example, direct manufacturing labor-hours—because management believes all costs should be allocated to products. Allocating all costs to products or services becomes important when management wants to set selling prices on the basis of an amount of cost that includes all costs.

Learning Objective 4

Describe a four-part cost hierarchy

. . . a four-part cost hierarchy is used to categorize costs based on different types of cost drivers—for example, costs that vary with each unit of a product versus costs that vary with each batch of products

◄ Decision Point

What is a cost hierarchy?

Implementing Activity-Based Costing

Learning
Objective 5

Cost products or
services using activity-
based costing

... use cost rates for
different activities to
compute indirect costs
of a product

Now that you understand the basic concepts of ABC, let's use it to refine Plastim's simple costing system, compare it to alternative costing systems, and examine what managers look for when deciding whether or not to develop ABC systems.

Implementing ABC at Plastim

In order to apply ABC to Plastim's costing system, we follow the seven-step approach to
costing and the three guidelines for refining costing systems (increasing direct-cost tracing, creating homogeneous indirect-cost pools, and identifying cost-allocation bases that
have cause-and-effect relationships with costs in the cost pool). Exhibit 3 shows an
overview of Plastim's ABC system. Use this exhibit as a guide as you study the following
steps, each of which is marked in Exhibit 3.

Step 1: Identify the Products That Are the Chosen Cost Objects. The cost objects are the
60,000 S3 and the 15,000 CL5 lenses that Plastim will produce in 2011. Plastim's goal is
to first calculate the total costs and then the per-unit cost of designing, manufacturing,
and distributing these lenses.

Step 2: Identify the Direct Costs of the Products. Plastim identifies as direct costs of the
lenses: direct material costs, direct manufacturing labor costs, and mold cleaning and maintenance costs because these costs can be economically traced to a specific lens or mold.

Exhibit 5 shows the direct and indirect costs for the S3 and CL5 lenses using the
ABC system. The direct costs calculations appear on lines 6, 7, 8, and 9 of Exhibit 5.
Plastim classifies all other costs as indirect costs, as we will see in Exhibit 4.

**Step 3: Select the Activities and Cost-Allocation Bases to Use for Allocating Indirect
Costs to the Products.** Following guidelines 2 and 3 for refining a costing system, Plastim
identifies six activities—(a) design, (b) molding machine setups, (c) machine operations,
(d) shipment setup, (e) distribution, and (f) administration—for allocating indirect costs
to products. Exhibit 4, column 2, shows the cost hierarchy category, and column 4

Exhibit 3 Overview of Plastim's Activity-Based Costing System

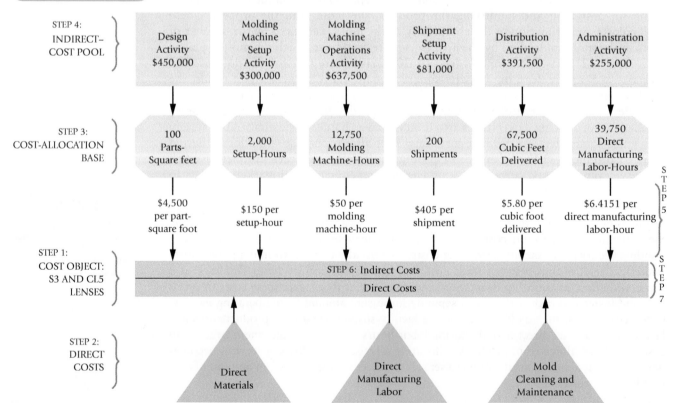

Exhibit 4 Activity-Cost Rates for Indirect-Cost Pools

	A	B	C	D	E	F	G	H
1			(Step 4)	(Step 3)		(Step 5)		
2	Activity	Cost Hierarchy Category	Total Budgeted Indirect Costs	Budgeted Quantity of Cost-Allocation Base		Budgeted Indirect Cost Rate		Cause-and-Effect Relationship Between Allocation Base and Activity Cost
3	(1)	(2)	(3)	(4)		(5) = (3) ÷ (4)		(6)
4	Design	Product-sustaining	$450,000	100	parts-square feet	$ 4,500	per part-square foot	Design Department indirect costs increase with more complex molds (more parts, larger surface area).
5	Setup molding machines	Batch-level	$300,000	2,000	setup-hours	$ 150	per setup-hour	Indirect setup costs increase with setup-hours.
6	Machine operations	Output unit-level	$637,500	12,750	molding machine-hours	$ 50	per molding machine-hour	Indirect costs of operating molding machines increases with molding machine-hours.
7	Shipment setup	Batch-level	$ 81,000	200	shipments	$ 405	per shipment	Shipping costs incurred to prepare batches for shipment increase with the number of shipments.
8	Distribution	Output-unit-level	$391,500	67,500	cubic feet delivered	$ 5.80	per cubic foot delivered	Distribution costs increase with the cubic feet of packages delivered.
9	Administration	Facility sustaining	$255,000	39,750	direct manuf. labor-hours	$6.4151	per direct manuf. labor-hour	The demand for administrative resources increases with direct manufacturing labor-hours.

shows the cost-allocation base and the budgeted quantity of the cost-allocation base for each activity described in column 1.

Identifying the cost-allocation bases defines the number of activity pools into which costs must be grouped in an ABC system. For example, rather than define the design activities of product design, process design, and prototyping as separate activities, Plastim defines these three activities together as a combined "design" activity and forms a homogeneous design cost pool. Why? Because the same cost driver, the complexity of the mold, drives costs of each design activity. A second consideration for choosing a cost-allocation base is the availability of reliable data and measures. For example, in its ABC system, Plastim measures mold complexity in terms of the number of parts in the mold and the surface area of the mold (parts-square feet). If these data are difficult to obtain or measure, Plastim may be forced to use some other measure of complexity, such as the amount of material flowing through the mold that may only be weakly related to the cost of the design activity.

Step 4: Identify the Indirect Costs Associated with Each Cost-Allocation Base. In this step, Plastim assigns budgeted indirect costs for 2011 to activities (see Exhibit 4, column 3), to the extent possible, on the basis of a cause-and-effect relationship between the cost-allocation base for an activity and the cost. For example, all costs that have a cause-and-effect relationship to cubic feet of packages moved are assigned to the distribution cost pool. Of course, the strength of the cause-and-effect relationship between the cost-allocation base and the cost of an activity varies across cost pools. For example, the cause-and-effect relationship between direct manufacturing labor-hours and administration activity costs is not as strong as the relationship between setup-hours and setup activity costs.

Some costs can be directly identified with a particular activity. For example, cost of materials used when designing products, salaries paid to design engineers, and depreciation of equipment used in the design department are directly identified with the design activity. Other costs need to be allocated across activities. For example, on the basis of interviews or time records, manufacturing engineers and supervisors estimate the time they will spend on design, molding machine setup, and machine operations. The time to be spent on these activities serves as a basis for allocating each manufacturing engineer's and supervisor's salary

Exhibit 5 Plastim's Product Costs Using Activity-Based Costing System

	Home	Insert	Page Layout	Formulas	Data	Review	View				

	A	B	C	D	E	F	G
1		60,000			15,000		
2		Simple Lenses (S3)			Complex Lenses (CL5)		
3		Total	per Unit		Total	per Unit	Total
4	**Cost Description**	(1)	(2) = (1) ÷ 60,000		(3)	(4) = (3) ÷ 15,000	(5) = (1) + (3)
5	Direct costs						
6	Direct materials	$1,125,000	$18.75		$ 675,000	$ 45.00	$1,800,000
7	Direct manufacturing labor	600,000	10.00		195,000	13.00	795,000
8	Direct mold cleaning and maintenance costs	120,000	2.00		150,000	10.00	270,000
9	Total direct costs (Step 2)	1,845,000	30.75		1,020,000	68.00	2,865,000
10	Indirect Costs of Activities						
11	Design						
12	S3, 30 parts-sq.ft. × $4,500	135,000	2.25				} 450,000
13	CL5, 70 parts-sq.ft. × $4,500				315,000	21.00	
14	Setup of molding machines						
15	S3, 500 setup-hours × $150	75,000	1.25				} 300,000
16	CL5, 1,500 setup-hours × $150				225,000	15.00	
17	Machine operations						
18	S3, 9,000 molding machine-hours × $50	450,000	7.50				} 637,500
19	CL5, 3,750 molding machine-hours × $50				187,500	12.50	
20	Shipment setup						
21	S3, 100 shipments × $405	40,500	0.67				} 81,000
22	CL5, 100 shipments × $405				40,500	2.70	
23	Distribution						
24	S3, 45,000 cubic feet delivered × $5.80	261,000	4.35				} 391,500
25	CL5, 22,500 cubic feet delivered × $5.80				130,500	8.70	
26	Administration						
27	S3, 30,000 dir. manuf. labor-hours × $6.4151	192,453	3.21				} 255,000
28	CL5, 9,750 dir. manuf. labor-hours × $6.4151				62,547	4.17	
29	Total indirect costs allocated (Step 6)	1,153,953	19.23		961,047	64.07	2,115,000
30	Total Costs (Step 7)	$2,998,953	$49.98		$1,981,047	$132.07	$4,980,000
31							

costs to various activities. Still other costs are allocated to activity-cost pools using allocation bases that measure how these costs support different activities. For example, rent costs are allocated to activity cost pools on the basis of square-feet area used by different activities.

The point here is that all costs do not fit neatly into activity categories. Often, costs may first need to be allocated to activities (Stage 1 of the 2-stage cost-allocation model) before the costs of the activities can be allocated to products (Stage 2).

Step 5: Compute the Rate per Unit of Each Cost-Allocation Base. Exhibit 4, column 5, summarizes the calculation of the budgeted indirect cost rates using the budgeted quantity of the cost-allocation base from Step 3 and the total budgeted indirect costs of each activity from Step 4.

Step 6: Compute the Indirect Costs Allocated to the Products. Exhibit 5 shows total budgeted indirect costs of $1,153,953 allocated to the simple lens and $961,047 allocated to the complex lens. Follow the budgeted indirect cost calculations for each lens in Exhibit 5. For each activity, Plastim's operations personnel indicate the total quantity of the cost-allocation base that will be used by each type of lens (recall that Plastim operates at capacity). For example, lines 15 and 16 of Exhibit 5 show that of the 2,000 total setup-hours, the S3 lens is budgeted to use 500 hours and the CL5 lens 1,500 hours. The budgeted indirect cost rate is $150 per setup-hour (Exhibit 4, column 5, line 5). Therefore, the total budgeted cost of the setup activity allocated to the S3 lens is $75,000 (500 setup-hours × $150 per setup-hour) and to the CL5 lens is $225,000 (1,500 setup-hours × $150 per setup-hour). Budgeted setup cost per unit equals $1.25 ($75,000 ÷ 60,000 units) for the S3 lens and $15 ($225,000 ÷ 15,000 units) for the CL5 lens.

Step 7: Compute the Total Cost of the Products by Adding All Direct and Indirect Costs Assigned to the Products. Exhibit 5 presents the product costs for the simple and complex lenses. The direct costs are calculated in Step 2, and the indirect costs are calculated in Step 6. The ABC system overview in Exhibit 3 shows three direct-cost categories and six indirect-cost categories. The budgeted cost of each lens type in Exhibit 5 has nine line items, three for direct costs and six for indirect costs. The differences between the ABC product costs of S3 and CL5 calculated in Exhibit 5 highlight how each of these products uses different amounts of direct and indirect costs in each activity area.

We emphasize two features of ABC systems. First, these systems identify all costs used by products, whether the costs are variable or fixed in the short run. When making long-run strategic decisions using ABC information, managers want revenues to exceed total costs. Second, recognizing the hierarchy of costs is critical when allocating costs to products. It is easiest to use the cost hierarchy to first calculate the total costs of each product. The per-unit costs can then be derived by dividing total costs by the number of units produced.

Comparing Alternative Costing Systems

Exhibit 6 compares the simple costing system using a single indirect-cost pool (Exhibit 1 and Exhibit 2) Plastim had been using and the ABC system (Exhibit 3 and Exhibit 5). Note three points in Exhibit 6, consistent with the guidelines for refining

> ◀ **Decision Point**
>
> How do managers cost products or services using ABC systems?

Exhibit 6

Comparing Alternative Costing Systems

	Simple Costing System Using a Single Indirect-Cost Pool (1)	ABC System (2)	Difference (3) = (2) − (1)
Direct-cost categories	2	3	1
	Direct materials Direct manufacturing labor	Direct materials Direct manufacturing labor Direct mold cleaning and maintenance labor	
Total direct costs	$2,595,000	$2,865,000	$270,000
Indirect-cost pools	1	6	5
	Single indirect-cost pool allocated using direct manufacturing labor-hours	Design (parts-square feet)[1] Molding machine setup (setup-hours) Machine operations (molding machine-hours) Shipment setup (number of shipments) Distribution (cubic feet delivered) Administration (direct manufacturing labor-hours)	
Total indirect costs	$2,385,000	$2,115,000	($270,000)
Total costs assigned to simple (S3) lens	$3,525,000	$2,998,953	($526,047)
Cost per unit of simple (S3) lens	$58.75	$49.98	($8.77)
Total costs assigned to complex (CL5) lens	$1,455,000	$1,981,047	$526,047
Cost per unit of complex (CL5) lens	$97.00	$132.07	$35.07

[1]Cost drivers for the various indirect-cost pools are shown in parentheses.

a costing system: (1) ABC systems trace more costs as direct costs; (2) ABC systems create homogeneous cost pools linked to different activities; and (3) for each activity-cost pool, ABC systems seek a cost-allocation base that has a cause-and-effect relationship with costs in the cost pool.

The homogeneous cost pools and the choice of cost-allocation bases, tied to the cost hierarchy, give Plastim's managers greater confidence in the activity and product cost numbers from the ABC system. The bottom part of Exhibit 6 shows that allocating costs to lenses using only an output unit-level allocation base—direct manufacturing labor-hours, as in the single indirect-cost pool system used prior to ABC—overcosts the simple S3 lens by $8.77 per unit and undercosts the complex CL5 lens by $35.07 per unit. The CL5 lens uses a disproportionately larger amount of output unit-level, batch-level, and product-sustaining costs than is represented by the direct manufacturing labor-hour cost-allocation base. The S3 lens uses a disproportionately smaller amount of these costs.

The benefit of an ABC system is that it provides information to make better decisions. But this benefit must be weighed against the measurement and implementation costs of an ABC system.

Considerations in Implementing Activity-Based-Costing Systems

Managers choose the level of detail to use in a costing system by evaluating the expected costs of the system against the expected benefits that result from better decisions. There are telltale signs of when an ABC system is likely to provide the most benefits. Here are some of these signs:

- Significant amounts of indirect costs are allocated using only one or two cost pools.
- All or most indirect costs are identified as output unit-level costs (few indirect costs are described as batch-level costs, product-sustaining costs, or facility-sustaining costs).
- Products make diverse demands on resources because of differences in volume, process steps, batch size, or complexity.
- Products that a company is well-suited to make and sell show small profits; whereas products that a company is less suited to produce and sell show large profits.
- Operations staff has substantial disagreement with the reported costs of manufacturing and marketing products and services.

When a company decides to implement ABC, it must make important choices about the level of detail to use. Should it choose many finely specified activities, cost drivers, and cost pools, or would a few suffice? For example, Plastim could identify a different molding machine-hour rate for each different type of molding machine. In making such choices, managers weigh the benefits against the costs and limitations of implementing a more detailed costing system.

The main costs and limitations of an ABC system are the measurements necessary to implement it. ABC systems require management to estimate costs of activity pools and to identify and measure cost drivers for these pools to serve as cost-allocation bases. Even basic ABC systems require many calculations to determine costs of products and services. These measurements are costly. Activity cost rates also need to be updated regularly.

As ABC systems get very detailed and more cost pools are created, more allocations are necessary to calculate activity costs for each cost pool. This increases the chances of misidentifying the costs of different activity cost pools. For example, supervisors are more prone to incorrectly identify the time they spent on different activities if they have to allocate their time over five activities rather than only two activities.

At times, companies are also forced to use allocation bases for which data are readily available rather than allocation bases they would have liked to use. For example, a company might be forced to use the number of loads moved, instead of the degree of difficulty and distance of different loads moved, as the allocation base for

Concepts in Action   Successfully Championing ABC

Successfully implementing ABC systems requires more than an understanding of the technical details. ABC implementation often represents a significant change in the costing system and, as the chapter indicates, it requires a manager to make major choices with respect to the definition of activities and the level of detail. What then are some of the behavioral issues that the management accountant must be sensitive to?

1. **Gaining support of top management and creating a sense of urgency for the ABC effort.** This requires management accountants to lay out the vision for the ABC project and to clearly communicate its strategic benefits (for example, the resulting improvements in product and process design). It also requires selling the idea to end users and working with members of other departments as business partners of the managers in the various areas affected by the ABC project. For example, at USAA Federal Savings Bank, project managers demonstrated how the information gained from ABC would provide insights into the efficiency of bank operations, which was previously unavailable. Now the finance area communicates regularly with operations about new reports and proposed changes to the financial reporting package that managers receive.

2. **Creating a guiding coalition of managers throughout the value chain for the ABC effort.** ABC systems measure how the resources of an organization are used. Managers responsible for these resources have the best knowledge about activities and cost drivers. Getting managers to cooperate and take the initiative for implementing ABC is essential for gaining the required expertise, the proper credibility, and the necessary leadership.

   Gaining wider participation among managers has other benefits. Managers who feel more involved in the process are likely to commit more time to and be less skeptical of the ABC effort. Engaging managers throughout the value chain also creates greater opportunities for coordination and cooperation across the different functions, for example, design and manufacturing.

3. **Educating and training employees in ABC as a basis for employee empowerment.** Disseminating information about ABC throughout an organization allows workers in all areas of a business to use their knowledge of ABC to make improvements. For example, WS Industries, an Indian manufacturer of insulators, not only shared ABC information with its workers but also established an incentive plan that gave employees a percentage of the cost savings. The results were dramatic because employees were empowered and motivated to implement numerous cost-saving projects.

4. **Seeking small short-run successes as proof that the ABC implementation is yielding results.** Too often, managers and management accountants seek big results and major changes far too quickly. In many situations, achieving a significant change overnight is difficult. However, showing how ABC information has helped improve a process and save costs, even if only in small ways, motivates the team to stay on course and build momentum. The credibility gained from small victories leads to additional and bigger improvements involving larger numbers of people and different parts of the organization. Eventually ABC and ABM become rooted in the culture of the organization. Sharing short-term successes may also help motivate employees to be innovative. At USAA Federal Savings Bank, managers created a "process improvement" mailbox in Microsoft Outlook to facilitate the sharing of process improvement ideas.

5. **Recognizing that ABC information is not perfect because it balances the need for better information against the costs of creating a complex system that few managers and employees can understand.** The management accountant must help managers recognize both the value and the limitations of ABC and not oversell it. Open and honest communication about ABC ensures that managers use ABC thoughtfully to make good decisions. Critical judgments can then be made without being adversarial, and tough questions can be asked to help drive better decisions about the system.

material-handling costs, because data on degree of difficulty and distance of moves are difficult to obtain. When erroneous cost-allocation bases are used, activity-cost information can be misleading. For example, if the cost per load moved decreases, a company may conclude that it has become more efficient in its materials-handling operations. In fact, the lower cost per load move may have resulted solely from moving many lighter loads over shorter distances.

Many companies, such as Kanthal, the Swedish manufacturer of heating elements, have found the strategic and operational benefits of a less-detailed ABC system to be good enough to not warrant incurring the costs and challenges of operating a more-detailed system. Other organizations, such as Hewlett-Packard, implement ABC in chosen divisions or functions. As improvements in information technology and accompanying declines in measurement costs continue, more-detailed ABC systems have become a practical alternative in many companies. As such trends persist, more detailed ABC systems will be better able to pass the cost–benefit test.

Global surveys of company practice suggest that ABC implementation varies among companies. Nevertheless, its framework and ideas provide a standard for judging whether any simple costing system is good enough for a particular management's purposes. Any contemplated changes in a simple costing system will inevitably be improved by ABC thinking. The Concepts in Action box describes some of the behavioral issues that management accountants must be sensitive to as they seek to immerse an organization in ABC thinking.

Using ABC Systems for Improving Cost Management and Profitability

The emphasis of this chapter so far has been on the role of ABC systems in obtaining better product costs. However, Plastim's managers must now use this information to make decisions (Step 4 of the 5-step decision process) and to implement the decision, evaluate performance, and learn (Step 5). **Activity-based management (ABM)** is a method of management decision making that uses activity-based costing information to improve customer satisfaction and profitability. We define ABM broadly to include decisions about pricing and product mix, cost reduction, process improvement, and product and process design.

Pricing and Product-Mix Decisions

An ABC system gives managers information about the costs of making and selling diverse products. With this information, managers can make pricing and product-mix decisions. For example, the ABC system indicates that Plastim can match its competitor's price of $53 for the S3 lens and still make a profit because the ABC cost of S3 is $49.98 (see Exhibit 5).

Plastim's managers offer Giovanni Motors a price of $52 for the S3 lens. Plastim's managers are confident that they can use the deeper understanding of costs that the ABC system provides to improve efficiency and further reduce the cost of the S3 lens. Without information from the ABC system, Plastim managers might have erroneously concluded that they would incur an operating loss on the S3 lens at a price of $53. This incorrect conclusion would have probably caused Plastim to reduce its business in simple lenses and focus instead on complex lenses, where its single indirect-cost-pool system indicated it is very profitable.

Focusing on complex lenses would have been a mistake. The ABC system indicates that the cost of making the complex lens is much higher—$132.07 versus $97 indicated by the direct manufacturing labor-hour-based costing system Plastim had been using. As Plastim's operations staff had thought all along, Plastim has no competitive advantage in making CL5 lenses. At a price of $137 per lens for CL5, the profit margin is very small ($137.00 – $132.07 = $4.93). As Plastim reduces its prices on simple lenses, it would need to negotiate a higher price for complex lenses with Giovanni Motors.

Cost Reduction and Process Improvement Decisions

Manufacturing and distribution personnel use ABC systems to focus on how and where to reduce costs. Managers set cost reduction targets in terms of reducing the cost per unit of the cost-allocation base in different activity areas. For example, the supervisor of the distribution activity area at Plastim could have a performance target of decreasing distribution cost per cubic foot of products delivered from $5.80 to $5.40 by reducing distribution labor and warehouse rental costs. The goal is to reduce these costs by improving the way work is done without compromising customer service or the actual or perceived value (usefulness) customers obtain from the product or service. That is, Plastim will attempt to take out only those costs that are *nonvalue added*. Controlling physical cost drivers, such as setup-hours or cubic feet delivered, is another fundamental way that operating personnel manage costs. For example, Plastim can decrease distribution costs by packing the lenses in a way that reduces the bulkiness of the packages delivered.

The following table shows the reduction in distribution costs of the S3 and CL5 lenses as a result of actions that lower cost per cubic foot delivered (from $5.80 to $5.40) and total cubic feet of deliveries (from 45,000 to 40,000 for S3 and 22,500 to 20,000 for CL5).

| | 60,000 (S3) Lenses | | 15,000 (CL5) Lenses | |
	Total (1)	per Unit (2) = (1) ÷ 60,000	Total (3)	per Unit (4) = (3) ÷ 15,000
Distribution costs (from Exhibit 5)				
S3, 45,000 cubic feet × $5.80/cubic foot	$261,000	$4.35		
CL5, 22,500 cubic feet × $5.80/cubic foot			$130,500	$8.70
Distribution costs as a result of process improvements				
S3, 40,000 cubic feet × $5.40/cubic foot	216,000	3.60		
CL5, 20,000 cubic feet × $5.40/cubic foot			108,000	7.20
Savings in distribution costs from process improvements	$ 45,000	$0.75	$ 22,500	$1.50

In the long run, total distribution costs will decrease from $391,500 ($261,000 + $130,500) to $324,000 ($216,000 + $108,000). In the short run, however, distribution costs may be fixed and may not decrease. Suppose all $391,500 of distribution costs are fixed costs in the short run. The efficiency improvements (using less distribution labor and space) mean that the same $391,500 of distribution costs can now be used to distribute $72,500 \left(\dfrac{\$391,500}{\$5.40 \text{ per cubic feet}} \right)$ cubic feet of lenses. In this case, how should costs be allocated to the S3 and CL5 lenses?

ABC systems distinguish *costs incurred* from *resources used* to design, manufacture, and deliver products and services. For the distribution activity, after process improvements,

Costs incurred = $391,500

Resources used = $216,000 (for S3 lens) + $108,000 (for CL5 lens) = $324,000

On the basis of the resources used by each product, Plastim's ABC system allocates $216,000 to S3 and $108,000 to CL5 for a total of $324,000. The difference of $67,500 ($391,500 – $324,000) is shown as costs of unused but available distribution capacity. Plastim's ABC system does not allocate the costs of unused capacity to products so as not to burden the product costs of S3 and CL5 with the cost of resources not used by these products. Instead, the system highlights the amount of unused capacity as a separate line item to signal to managers the need to reduce these costs, such as by redeploying labor to other uses or laying off workers.

Design Decisions

Management can evaluate how its current product and process designs affect activities and costs as a way of identifying new designs to reduce costs. For example, design decisions that decrease complexity of the mold reduce costs of design, materials, labor, machine setups, machine operations, and mold cleaning and maintenance. Plastim's customers may be willing to give up some features of the lens in exchange for a lower price. Note that Plastim's previous costing system, which used direct manufacturing labor-hours as the cost-allocation base for all indirect costs, would have mistakenly signaled that Plastim choose those designs that most reduce direct manufacturing labor-hours when, in fact, there is a weak cause-and-effect relationship between direct manufacturing labor-hours and indirect costs.

Planning and Managing Activities

Many companies implementing ABC systems for the first time analyze actual costs to identify activity-cost pools and activity-cost rates. To be useful for planning, making decisions, and managing activities, companies calculate a budgeted cost rate for each activity and use these budgeted cost rates to cost products as we saw in the Plastim example. At year-end, budgeted costs and actual costs are compared to provide feedback on how well activities were managed and to make adjustments for underallocated or overallocated indirect costs for each activity. As activities and processes are changed, new activity-cost rates are calculated.

Decision Point ▶

How can ABC systems be used to manage better?

Activity-Based Costing and Department Costing Systems

Companies often use costing systems that have features of ABC systems—such as multiple cost pools and multiple cost-allocation bases—but that do not emphasize individual activities. Many companies have evolved their costing systems from using a single indirect cost rate system to using separate indirect cost rates for each department (such as design, manufacturing, distribution, and so on) or each subdepartment (such as machining and assembly departments within manufacturing) that can be thought of as representing broad tasks. ABC systems, with its focus on specific activities, are a further refinement of department costing systems. In this section, we compare ABC systems and department costing systems.

Learning Objective 8

Compare activity-based costing systems and department costing systems

. . . activity-based costing systems are a refinement of department costing systems into more-focused and homogenous cost pools

Plastim uses the design department indirect cost rate to cost its design activity. Plastim calculates the design activity rate by dividing total design department costs by total parts-square feet, a measure of the complexity of the mold and the driver of design department costs. Plastim does not find it worthwhile to calculate separate activity rates within the design department for the different design activities, such as designing products, making temporary molds, and designing processes. Why? Because complexity of a mold is an appropriate cost-allocation base for costs incurred in each design activity. Design department costs are homogeneous with respect to this cost-allocation base.

In contrast, the manufacturing department identifies two activity cost pools—a setup cost pool and a machine operations cost pool—instead of a single manufacturing department overhead cost pool. It identifies these activity cost pools for two reasons. First, each of these activities within manufacturing incurs significant costs and has a different cost driver, setup-hours for the setup cost pool and machine-hours for the machine operations cost pool. Second, the S3 and CL5 lenses do not use resources from these two activity areas in the same proportion. For example, CL5 uses 75% ($1,500 \div 2,000$) of the setup-hours but only 29.4% ($3,750 \div 12,750$) of the machine-hours. Using only machine-hours, say, to allocate all manufacturing department costs at Plastim would result in CL5 being undercosted because it would not be charged for the significant amounts of setup resources it actually uses.

Based on what we just explained, using department indirect cost rates to allocate costs to products results in similar information as activity cost rates if (1) a single activity accounts for a sizable proportion of the department's costs; or (2) significant costs are incurred on different activities within a department, but each activity has the same cost driver and hence cost-allocation base (as was the case in Plastim's design department). From a purely product costing standpoint, department and activity indirect cost rates will also result in the same product costs if (1) significant costs are incurred for different activities with different cost-allocation bases within a department but (2) different products use resources from the different activity areas in the same proportions (for example, if CL5 had used 65%, say, of the setup-hours and 65% of the machine-hours). In this case, though, not identifying activities and cost drivers within departments conceals activity cost information that would be valuable for cost management and design and process improvements.

We close this section with a note of caution. Do not assume that because department costing systems require the creation of multiple indirect cost pools that they properly recognize the drivers of costs within departments as well as how resources are used by products. As we have indicated, in many situations, department costing systems can be refined using ABC. Emphasizing activities leads to more-focused and homogeneous cost pools, aids in identifying cost-allocation bases for activities that have a better cause-and-effect relationship with the costs in activity cost pools, and leads to better design and process decisions. But these benefits of an ABC system would need to be balanced against its costs and limitations.

> **◄ Decision Point**
>
> When can department costing systems be used instead of ABC systems?

ABC in Service and Merchandising Companies

Although many of the early examples of ABC originated in manufacturing, ABC has many applications in service and merchandising companies. In addition to manufacturing activities, the Plastim example includes the application of ABC to a service activity—design—and to a merchandising activity—distribution. Companies such as the Cooperative Bank, Braintree Hospital, BCTel in the telecommunications industry, and Union Pacific in the railroad industry have implemented some form of ABC system to identify profitable product mixes, improve efficiency, and satisfy customers. Similarly, many retail and wholesale companies—for example, Supervalu, a retailer and distributor of grocery store products, and Owens and Minor, a medical supplies distributor—have used ABC systems. Finally, a large number of financial services companies (as well as other companies) employ variations of ABC systems to analyze and improve the profitability of their customer interactions.

The widespread use of ABC systems in service and merchandising companies reinforces the idea that ABC systems are used by managers for strategic decisions rather than for inventory valuation. (Inventory valuation is fairly straightforward in merchandising companies and not needed in service companies.) Service companies, in particular, find great value from ABC because a vast majority of their cost structure comprises indirect costs. After all, there are few direct costs when a bank makes a loan, or when a representative answers a phone call at a call center. As we have seen, a major benefit of ABC is its ability to assign indirect costs to cost objects by identifying activities and cost drivers. As a result, ABC systems provide greater insight than traditional systems into the management of these indirect costs. The general approach to ABC in service and merchandising companies is similar to the ABC approach in manufacturing.

The Cooperative Bank followed the approach described in this chapter when it implemented ABC in its retail banking operations. It calculated the costs of various activities, such as performing ATM transactions, opening and closing accounts, administering mortgages, and processing Visa transactions. It then used the activity cost rates to calculate costs of various products, such as checking accounts, mortgages, and Visa cards and the costs of supporting different customers. ABC information helped the Cooperative Bank to improve its processes and to identify profitable products and customer segments. The Concepts in Action describes how Charles Schwab has similarly benefited from using ABC analysis.

Activity-based costing raises some interesting issues when it is applied to a public service institution such as the U.S. Postal Service. The costs of delivering mail to remote locations are far greater than the costs of delivering mail within urban areas. However, for fairness and community-building reasons, the Postal Service cannot charge higher prices to customers in remote areas. In this case, activity-based costing is valuable for understanding, managing, and reducing costs but not for pricing decisions.

Concepts in Action

Time-Driven Activity-Based Costing at Charles Schwab

James Leynse\CORBIS- NY

Time-driven activity-based costing ("TDABC") helps Charles Schwab, the leading stock brokerage, with strategic-analysis, measurement, and management of its stock trading activity across multiple channels such as branches, call centers, and the Internet. Because the costs for each channel are different, TDABC helps answer questions such as the following: What are the total costs of branch transactions versus online transactions? Which channels help reduce overall costs? How can Charles Schwab price its services to drive changes in customer behavior?

TDABC assigns all of the company's resource costs to cost objects using a framework that requires two sets of estimates. TDABC first calculates the cost of supplying resource capacity, such as broker time. The total cost of resources including personnel, management, occupancy, technology, and supplies is divided by the available capacity—the time available for brokers to do the work—to obtain the capacity cost rate. Next, TDABC uses the capacity cost rate to drive resource costs to cost objects, such as stock trades executed through brokers at a branch, by estimating the demand for resource capacity (time) that the cost object requires.

Realizing that trades executed online cost much less than trades completed through brokers, Charles Schwab developed a fee structure for trading of mutual funds to stimulate the use of cheaper channels. Charles Schwab also used TDABC information to lower process costs by several hundred million dollars annually and to better align product pricing and account management to the company's diverse client segments. The company is working on other opportunities, including priority-call routing and email marketing, to further reduce costs while maintaining or enhancing Charles Schwab's already top-rated customer service.

Sources: Kaplan, R. S. and S. R., Anderson. 2007. The innovation of time-driven activity-based costing. *Cost Management,* March–April: 5–15; Kaplan R. S. and S.R. Anderson. 2007. *Time-driven activity-based costing.* Boston, MA: Harvard Business School Press; Martinez-Jerez, F. Asis. 2007. Understanding customer profitability at Charles Schwab. Harvard Business School Case Study No. 9-106-102, January.

Problem for Self-Study

Family Supermarkets (FS) has decided to increase the size of its Memphis store. It wants information about the profitability of individual product lines: soft drinks, fresh produce, and packaged food. FS provides the following data for 2011 for each product line:

	Soft Drinks	Fresh Produce	Packaged Food
Revenues	$317,400	$840,240	$483,960
Cost of goods sold	$240,000	$600,000	$360,000
Cost of bottles returned	$ 4,800	$ 0	$ 0
Number of purchase orders placed	144	336	144
Number of deliveries received	120	876	264
Hours of shelf-stocking time	216	2,160	1,080
Items sold	50,400	441,600	122,400

FS also provides the following information for 2011:

Activity (1)	Description of Activity (2)	Total Support Costs (3)	Cost-Allocation Base (4)
1. Bottle returns	Returning of empty bottles to store	$ 4,800	Direct tracing to soft-drink line
2. Ordering	Placing of orders for purchases	$ 62,400	624 purchase orders
3. Delivery	Physical delivery and receipt of merchandise	$100,800	1,260 deliveries
4. Shelf-stocking	Stocking of merchandise on store shelves and ongoing restocking	$ 69,120	3,456 hours of shelf-stocking time
5. Customer support	Assistance provided to customers, including checkout and bagging	$122,880	614,400 items sold
Total		$360,000	

Required

1. Family Supermarkets currently allocates store support costs (all costs other than cost of goods sold) to product lines on the basis of cost of goods sold of each product line. Calculate the operating income and operating income as a percentage of revenues for each product line.
2. If Family Supermarkets allocates store support costs (all costs other than cost of goods sold) to product lines using an ABC system, calculate the operating income and operating income as a percentage of revenues for each product line.
3. Comment on your answers in requirements 1 and 2.

Solution

1. The following table shows the operating income and operating income as a percentage of revenues for each product line. All store support costs (all costs other than cost of goods sold) are allocated to product lines using cost of goods sold of each product line as the cost-allocation base. Total store support costs equal $360,000 (cost of bottles returned, $4,800 + cost of purchase orders, $62,400 + cost of deliveries, $100,800 + cost of shelf-stocking, $69,120 + cost of customer support, $122,880). The allocation rate for store support costs = $360,000 ÷ $1,200,000 (soft drinks $240,000 + fresh produce $600,000 + packaged food, $360,000) = 30% of cost of goods sold. To allocate support costs to each product line, FS multiplies the cost of goods sold of each product line by 0.30.

	Soft Drinks	Fresh Produce	Packaged Food	Total
Revenues	$317,400	$840,240	$483,960	$1,641,600
Cost of goods sold	240,000	600,000	360,000	1,200,000
Store support cost ($240,000; $600,000; $360,000) × 0.30	72,000	180,000	108,000	360,000
Total costs	312,000	780,000	468,000	1,560,000
Operating income	$ 5,400	$ 60,240	$ 15,960	$ 81,600
Operating income ÷ Revenues	1.70%	7.17%	3.30%	4.97%

2. Under an ABC system, FS identifies bottle-return costs as a direct cost because these costs can be traced to the soft drink product line. FS then calculates cost-allocation rates for each activity area (as in Step 5 of the seven-step costing system, described in the chapter). The activity rates are as follows:

Activity (1)	Cost Hierarchy (2)	Total Costs (3)	Quantity of Cost-Allocation Base (4)	Overhead Allocation Rate (5) = (3) ÷ (4)
Ordering	Batch-level	$ 62,400	624 purchase orders	$100 per purchase order
Delivery	Batch-level	$100,800	1,260 deliveries	$80 per delivery
Shelf-stocking	Output unit-level	$ 69,120	3,456 shelf-stocking-hours	$20 per stocking-hour
Customer support	Output unit-level	$122,880	614,400 items sold	$0.20 per item sold

Store support costs for each product line by activity are obtained by multiplying the total quantity of the cost-allocation base for each product line by the activity cost rate. Operating income and operating income as a percentage of revenues for each product line are as follows:

	Soft Drinks	Fresh Produce	Packaged Food	Total
Revenues	$317,400	$840,240	$483,960	$1,641,600
Cost of goods sold	240,000	600,000	360,000	1,200,000
Bottle-return costs	4,800	0	0	4,800
Ordering costs				
(144; 336; 144) purchase orders × $100	14,400	33,600	14,400	62,400
Delivery costs				
(120; 876; 264) deliveries × $80	9,600	70,080	21,120	100,800
Shelf-stocking costs				
(216; 2,160; 1,080) stocking-hours × $20	4,320	43,200	21,600	69,120
Customer-support costs				
(50,400; 441,600; 122,400) items sold × $0.20	10,080	88,320	24,480	122,880
Total costs	283,200	835,200	441,600	1,560,000
Operating income	$ 34,200	$ 5,040	$ 42,360	$ 81,600
Operating income ÷ Revenues	10.78%	0.60%	8.75%	4.97%

3. Managers believe the ABC system is more credible than the simple costing system. The ABC system distinguishes the different types of activities at FS more precisely. It also tracks more accurately how individual product lines use resources. Rankings of relative profitability—operating income as a percentage of revenues—of the three product lines under the simple costing system and under the ABC system are as follows:

Simple Costing System		ABC System	
1. Fresh produce	7.17%	1. Soft drinks	10.78%
2. Packaged food	3.30%	2. Packaged food	8.75%
3. Soft drinks	1.70%	3. Fresh produce	0.60%

The percentage of revenues, cost of goods sold, and activity costs for each product line are as follows:

	Soft Drinks	Fresh Produce	Packaged Food
Revenues	19.34%	51.18%	29.48%
Cost of goods sold	20.00	50.00	30.00
Bottle returns	100.00	0	0
Activity areas:			
Ordering	23.08	53.84	23.08
Delivery	9.53	69.52	20.95
Shelf-stocking	6.25	62.50	31.25
Customer-support	8.20	71.88	19.92

Soft drinks have fewer deliveries and require less shelf-stocking time and customer support than either fresh produce or packaged food. Most major soft-drink suppliers deliver merchandise to the store shelves and stock the shelves themselves. In contrast, the fresh produce area has the most deliveries and consumes a large percentage of shelf-stocking time. It also has the highest number of individual sales items and so requires the most customer support. The simple costing system assumed that each product line used the resources in each activity area in the same ratio as their respective individual cost of goods sold to total cost of goods sold. Clearly, this assumption is incorrect. Relative to cost of goods sold, soft drinks and packaged food use fewer resources while fresh produce uses more resources. As a result, the ABC system reduces the costs assigned to soft drinks and packaged food and increases the costs assigned to fresh produce. The simple costing system is an example of averaging that is too broad.

FS managers can use the ABC information to guide decisions such as how to allocate a planned increase in floor space. An increase in the percentage of space allocated to soft drinks is warranted. Note, however, that ABC information should be but one input into decisions about shelf-space allocation. FS may have minimum limits on the shelf space allocated to fresh produce because of shoppers' expectations that supermarkets will carry products from this product line. In many situations, companies cannot make product decisions in isolation but must consider the effect that dropping or deemphasizing a product might have on customer demand for other products.

Pricing decisions can also be made in a more informed way with ABC information. For example, suppose a competitor announces a 5% reduction in soft-drink prices. Given the 10.78% margin FS currently earns on its soft-drink product line, it has flexibility to reduce prices and still make a profit on this product line. In contrast, the simple costing system erroneously implied that soft drinks only had a 1.70% margin, leaving little room to counter a competitor's pricing initiatives.

Decision Points

The following question-and-answer format summarizes the chapter's learning objectives. Each decision presents a key question related to a learning objective. The guidelines are the answer to that question.

Decision	Guidelines
1. When does product under-costing or overcosting occur?	Product undercosting (overcosting) occurs when a product or service consumes a high (low) level of resources but is reported to have a low (high) cost. Broad averaging, or peanut-butter costing, a common cause of undercosting or overcosting, is the result of using broad averages that uniformly assign, or spread, the cost of resources to products when the individual products use those resources in a nonuniform way. Product-cost cross-subsidization exists when one undercosted (overcosted) product results in at least one other product being overcosted (undercosted).
2. How do managers refine a costing system?	Refining a costing system means making changes that result in cost numbers that better measure the way different cost objects, such as products, use different amounts of resources of the company. These changes can require additional direct-cost tracing, the choice of more-homogeneous indirect cost pools, or the use of cost drivers as cost-allocation bases.
3. What is the difference between the design of a simple costing system and an activity-based costing (ABC) system?	The ABC system differs from the simple system by its fundamental focus on activities. The ABC system typically has more-homogeneous indirect-cost pools than the simple system, and more cost drivers are used as cost-allocation bases.

4. What is a cost hierarchy?

A cost hierarchy categorizes costs into different cost pools on the basis of the different types of cost-allocation bases or different degrees of difficulty in determining cause-and-effect (or benefits-received) relationships. A four-part hierarchy to cost products consists of output unit-level costs, batch-level costs, product-sustaining or service-sustaining costs, and facility-sustaining costs.

5. How do managers cost products or services using ABC systems?

In ABC, costs of activities are used to assign costs to other cost objects such as products or services based on the activities the products or services consume.

6. What should managers consider when deciding to implement ABC systems?

ABC systems are likely to yield the most decision-making benefits when indirect costs are a high percentage of total costs or when products and services make diverse demands on indirect resources. The main costs of ABC systems are the difficulties of the measurements necessary to implement and update the systems.

7. How can ABC systems be used to manage better?

Activity-based management (ABM) is a management method of decision making that uses ABC information to satisfy customers and improve profits. ABC systems are used for such management decisions as pricing, product-mix, cost reduction, process improvement, product and process redesign, and planning and managing activities.

8. When can department costing systems be used instead of ABC systems?

Activity-based costing systems are a refinement of department costing systems into more-focused and homogeneous cost pools. Cost information in department costing systems approximates cost information in ABC systems only when each department has a single activity (or a single activity accounts for a significant proportion of department costs), a single cost driver for different activities, or when different products use the different activities of the department in the same proportions.

Terms to Learn

This chapter contains definitions of the following important terms:

activity	cost hierarchy	product overcosting
activity-based costing (ABC)	facility-sustaining costs	product-sustaining costs
activity-based management (ABM)	output unit-level costs	product undercosting
batch-level costs	product-cost cross-subsidization	refined costing system
		service-sustaining costs

Assignment Material

MyAccountingLab

Questions

5-1 What is broad averaging and what consequences can it have on costs?

5-2 Why should managers worry about product overcosting or undercosting?

5-3 What is costing system refinement? Describe three guidelines for refinement.

5-4 What is an activity-based approach to designing a costing system?

5-5 Describe four levels of a cost hierarchy.

5-6 Why is it important to classify costs into a cost hierarchy?

5-7 What are the key reasons for product cost differences between simple costing systems and ABC systems?

5-8 Describe four decisions for which ABC information is useful.

5-9 "Department indirect-cost rates are never activity-cost rates." Do you agree? Explain.

5-10 Describe four signs that help indicate when ABC systems are likely to provide the most benefits.

5-11 What are the main costs and limitations of implementing ABC systems?

5-12 "ABC systems only apply to manufacturing companies." Do you agree? Explain.

5-13 "Activity-based costing is the wave of the present and the future. All companies should adopt it." Do you agree? Explain.

5-14 "Increasing the number of indirect-cost pools is guaranteed to sizably increase the accuracy of product or service costs." Do you agree? Why?

5-15 The controller of a retail company has just had a $50,000 request to implement an ABC system quickly turned down. A senior vice president, in rejecting the request, noted, "Given a choice, I will always prefer a $50,000 investment in improving things a customer sees or experiences, such as our shelves or our store layout. How does a customer benefit by our spending $50,000 on a supposedly better accounting system?" How should the controller respond?

Exercises

5-16 Cost hierarchy. Hamilton, Inc., manufactures boom boxes (music systems with radio, cassette, and compact disc players) for several well-known companies. The boom boxes differ significantly in their complexity and their manufacturing batch sizes. The following costs were incurred in 2011:

- **a.** Indirect manufacturing labor costs such as supervision that supports direct manufacturing labor, $1,450,000
- **b.** Procurement costs of placing purchase orders, receiving materials, and paying suppliers related to the number of purchase orders placed, $850,000
- **c.** Cost of indirect materials, $275,000
- **d.** Costs incurred to set up machines each time a different product needs to be manufactured, $630,000
- **e.** Designing processes, drawing process charts, making engineering process changes for products, $775,000
- **f.** Machine-related overhead costs such as depreciation, maintenance, production engineering, $1,500,000 (These resources relate to the activity of running the machines.)
- **g.** Plant management, plant rent, and plant insurance, $925,000

1. Classify each of the preceding costs as output unit-level, batch-level, product-sustaining, or facility-sustaining. Explain each answer. **Required**
2. Consider two types of boom boxes made by Hamilton, Inc. One boom box is complex to make and is produced in many batches. The other boom box is simple to make and is produced in few batches. Suppose that Hamilton needs the same number of machine-hours to make each type of boom box and that Hamilton allocates all overhead costs using machine-hours as the only allocation base. How, if at all, would the boom boxes be miscosted? Briefly explain why.
3. How is the cost hierarchy helpful to Hamilton in managing its business?

5-17 ABC, cost hierarchy, service. (CMA, adapted) Vineyard Test Laboratories does heat testing (HT) and stress testing (ST) on materials and operates at capacity. Under its current simple costing system, Vineyard aggregates all operating costs of $1,190,000 into a single overhead cost pool. Vineyard calculates a rate per test-hour of $17 ($1,190,000 ÷ 70,000 total test-hours). HT uses 40,000 test-hours, and ST uses 30,000 test-hours. Gary Celeste, Vineyard's controller, believes that there is enough variation in test procedures and cost structures to establish separate costing and billing rates for HT and ST. The market for test services is becoming competitive. Without this information, any miscosting and mispricing of its services could cause Vineyard to lose business. Celeste divides Vineyard's costs into four activity-cost categories.

- **a.** Direct-labor costs, $146,000. These costs can be directly traced to HT, $100,000, and ST, $46,000.
- **b.** Equipment-related costs (rent, maintenance, energy, and so on), $350,000. These costs are allocated to HT and ST on the basis of test-hours.
- **c.** Setup costs, $430,000. These costs are allocated to HT and ST on the basis of the number of setup-hours required. HT requires 13,600 setup-hours, and ST requires 3,600 setup-hours.
- **d.** Costs of designing tests, $264,000. These costs are allocated to HT and ST on the basis of the time required for designing the tests. HT requires 3,000 hours, and ST requires 1,400 hours.

1. Classify each activity cost as output unit-level, batch-level, product- or service-sustaining, or facility-sustaining. Explain each answer. **Required**
2. Calculate the cost per test-hour for HT and ST. Explain briefly the reasons why these numbers differ from the $17 per test-hour that Vineyard calculated using its simple costing system.
3. Explain the accuracy of the product costs calculated using the simple costing system and the ABC system. How might Vineyard's management use the cost hierarchy and ABC information to better manage its business?

5-18 Alternative allocation bases for a professional services firm. The Walliston Group (WG) provides tax advice to multinational firms. WG charges clients for (a) direct professional time (at an hourly rate) and (b) support services (at 30% of the direct professional costs billed). The three professionals in WG and their rates per professional hour are as follows:

Professional	Billing Rate per Hour
Max Walliston	$640
Alexa Boutin	220
Jacob Abbington	100

WG has just prepared the May 2011 bills for two clients. The hours of professional time spent on each client are as follows:

	Hours per Client	
Professional	San Antonio Dominion	Amsterdam Enterprises
Walliston	26	4
Boutin	5	14
Abbington	39	52
Total	70	70

Required

1. What amounts did WG bill to San Antonio Dominion and Amsterdam Enterprises for May 2011?
2. Suppose support services were billed at $75 per professional labor-hour (instead of 30% of professional labor costs). How would this change affect the amounts WG billed to the two clients for May 2011? Comment on the differences between the amounts billed in requirements 1 and 2.
3. How would you determine whether professional labor costs or professional labor-hours is the more appropriate allocation base for WG's support services?

5-19 Plant-wide, department, and ABC indirect cost rates. Automotive Products (AP) designs and produces automotive parts. In 2011, actual variable manufacturing overhead is $308,600. AP's simple costing system allocates variable manufacturing overhead to its three customers based on machine-hours and prices its contracts based on full costs. One of its customers has regularly complained of being charged noncompetitive prices, so AP's controller Devon Smith realizes that it is time to examine the consumption of overhead resources more closely. He knows that there are three main departments that consume overhead resources: design, production, and engineering. Interviews with the department personnel and examination of time records yield the following detailed information:

Department	Cost Driver	Variable Manufacturing Overhead in 2011	Usage of Cost Drivers by Customer Contract		
			United Motors	Holden Motors	Leland Vehicle
Design	CAD-design-hours	$ 39,000	110	200	80
Production	Engineering-hours	29,600	70	60	240
Engineering	Machine-hours	240,000	120	2,800	1,080
Total		$308,600			

Required

1. Compute the variable manufacturing overhead allocated to each customer in 2011 using the simple costing system that uses machine-hours as the allocation base.
2. Compute the variable manufacturing overhead allocated to each customer in 2011 using department-based variable manufacturing overhead rates.
3. Comment on your answers in requirements 1 and 2. Which customer do you think was complaining about being overcharged in the simple system? If the new department-based rates are used to price contracts, which customer(s) will be unhappy? How would you respond to these concerns?

4. How else might AP use the information available from its department-by-department analysis of variable manufacturing overhead costs?
5. AP's managers are wondering if they should further refine the department-by-department costing system into an ABC system by identifying different activities within each department. Under what conditions would it not be worthwhile to further refine the department costing system into an ABC system?

5-20 Plant-wide, department, and activity-cost rates. Tarquin's Trophies makes trophies and plaques and operates at capacity. Tarquin does large custom orders, such as the participant trophies for the Mishawaka Little League. The controller has asked you to compare plant-wide, department, and activity-based cost allocation.

Tarquin's Trophies
Budgeted Information
For the Year Ended November 30, 2011

Forming Department	Trophies	Plaques	Total
Direct materials	$13,000	$11,250	$24,250
Direct labor	15,600	9,000	24,600
Overhead Costs			
Setup			12,000
Supervision			10,386

Assembly Department	Trophies	Plaques	Total
Direct materials	$ 2,600	$ 9,375	$11,975
Direct labor	7,800	10,500	18,300
Overhead costs			
Setup			23,000
Supervision			10,960

Other information follows:

Setup costs vary with the number of batches processed in each department. The budgeted number of batches for each product line in each department is as follows:

	Trophies	Plaques
Forming department	40	116
Assembly department	43	103

Supervision costs vary with direct labor costs in each department.

1. Calculate the budgeted cost of trophies and plaques based on a single plant-wide overhead rate, if total overhead is allocated based on total direct costs.
2. Calculate the budgeted cost of trophies and plaques based on departmental overhead rates, where forming department overhead costs are allocated based on direct labor costs of the forming department, and assembly department overhead costs are allocated based on total direct costs of the assembly department.
3. Calculate the budgeted cost of trophies and plaques if Tarquin allocates overhead costs in each department using activity-based costing.
4. Explain how the disaggregation of information could improve or reduce decision quality.

Required

5-21 ABC, process costing. Parker Company produces mathematical and financial calculators and operates at capacity. Data related to the two products are presented here:

	Mathematical	Financial
Annual production in units	50,000	100,000
Direct material costs	$150,000	$300,000
Direct manufacturing labor costs	$ 50,000	$100,000
Direct manufacturing labor-hours	2,500	5,000
Machine-hours	25,000	50,000
Number of production runs	50	50
Inspection hours	1,000	500

Total manufacturing overhead costs are as follows:

	Total
Machining costs	$375,000
Setup costs	120,000
Inspection costs	105,000

Required

1. Choose a cost driver for each overhead cost pool and calculate the manufacturing overhead cost per unit for each product.
2. Compute the manufacturing cost per unit for each product.

5-22 Activity-based costing, service company. Quikprint Corporation owns a small printing press that prints leaflets, brochures, and advertising materials. Quikprint classifies its various printing jobs as standard jobs or special jobs. Quikprint's simple job-costing system has two direct-cost categories (direct materials and direct labor) and a single indirect-cost pool. Quikprint operates at capacity and allocates all indirect costs using printing machine-hours as the allocation base.

Quikprint is concerned about the accuracy of the costs assigned to standard and special jobs and therefore is planning to implement an activity-based costing system. Quickprint's ABC system would have the same direct-cost categories as its simple costing system. However, instead of a single indirect-cost pool there would now be six categories for assigning indirect costs: design, purchasing, setup, printing machine operations, marketing, and administration. To see how activity-based costing would affect the costs of standard and special jobs, Quikprint collects the following information for the fiscal year 2011 that just ended.

	Home Insert Page Layout Formulas Data Review View							
	A	B	C	D	E	F	G	H
1		Standard Job	Special Job	Total	**Cause-and-Effect Relationship Between Allocation Base and Activity Cost**			
2	Number of printing jobs	400	200					
3	Price per job	$1,200	$ 1,500					
4	Cost of supplies per job	$ 200	$ 250					
5	Direct labor costs per job	$ 180	$ 200					
6	Printing machine-hours per job	10	10					
7	Cost of printing machine operations			$150,000	Indirect costs of operating printing machines			
8					increase with printing machine hours			
9	Setup-hours per job	4	7					
10	Setup costs			$ 90,000	Indirect setup costs increase with setup hours			
11	Total number of purchase orders	400	500					
12	Purchase order costs			$ 36,000	Indirect purchase order costs increase with			
13					number of purchase orders			
14	Design costs	$8,000	$32,000	$ 40,000	Design costs are allocated to standard and special			
15					jobs based on a special study of the design department			
16	Marketing costs as a percentage of revenues	5%	5%	$ 39,000				
17	Administration costs			$ 48,000	Demand for administrative resources increases with direct labor costs			

Required

1. Calculate the cost of a standard job and a special job under the simple costing system.
2. Calculate the cost of a standard job and a special job under the activity-based costing system.
3. Compare the costs of a standard job and a special job in requirements 1 and 2. Why do the simple and activity-based costing systems differ in the cost of a standard job and a special job?
4. How might Quikprint use the new cost information from its activity-based costing system to better manage its business?

5-23 Activity-based costing, manufacturing. Open Doors, Inc., produces two types of doors, interior and exterior. The company's simple costing system has two direct cost categories (materials and labor) and one indirect cost pool. The simple costing system allocates indirect costs on the basis of machine-hours. Recently, the owners of Open Doors have been concerned about a decline in the market share for their interior doors, usually their biggest seller. Information related to Open Doors production for the most recent year follows:

	Interior	Exterior
Units sold	3,200	1,800
Selling price	$ 125	$ 200
Direct material cost per unit	$ 30	$ 45
Direct manufacturing labor cost per hour	$ 16	$ 16
Direct manufacturing labor-hours per unit	1.50	2.25
Production runs	40	85
Material moves	72	168
Machine setups	45	155
Machine-hours	5,500	4,500
Number of inspections	250	150

The owners have heard of other companies in the industry that are now using an activity-based costing system and are curious how an ABC system would affect their product costing decisions. After analyzing the indirect cost pool for Open Doors, six activities were identified as generating indirect costs: production scheduling, material handling, machine setup, assembly, inspection, and marketing. Open Doors collected the following data related to the indirect cost activities:

Activity	Activity Cost	Activity Cost Driver
Production scheduling	$95,000	Production runs
Material handling	$45,000	Material moves
Machine setup	$25,000	Machine setups
Assembly	$60,000	Machine-hours
Inspection	$ 8,000	Number of inspections

Marketing costs were determined to be 3% of the sales revenue for each type of door.

1. Calculate the cost of an interior door and an exterior door under the existing simple costing system.
2. Calculate the cost of an interior door and an exterior door under an activity-based costing system.
3. Compare the costs of the doors in requirements 1 and 2. Why do the simple and activity-based costing systems differ in the cost of an interior and exterior door?
4. How might Open Door, Inc., use the new cost information from its activity-based costing system to address the declining market share for interior doors?

5-24 ABC, retail product-line profitability. Family Supermarkets (FS) operates at capacity and decides to apply ABC analysis to three product lines: baked goods, milk and fruit juice, and frozen foods. It identifies four activities and their activity cost rates as follows:

Ordering $100 per purchase order
Delivery and receipt of merchandise $ 80 per delivery
Shelf-stocking $ 20 per hour
Customer support and assistance $ 0.20 per item sold

The revenues, cost of goods sold, store support costs, the activities that account for the store support costs, and activity-area usage of the three product lines are as follows:

	Baked Goods	Milk and Fruit Juice	Frozen Products
Financial data			
Revenues	$57,000	$63,000	$52,000
Cost of goods sold	$38,000	$47,000	$35,000
Store support	$11,400	$14,100	$10,500
Activity-area usage (cost-allocation base)			
Ordering (purchase orders)	30	25	13
Delivery (deliveries)	98	36	28
Shelf-stocking (hours)	183	166	24
Customer support (items sold)	15,500	20,500	7,900

113

ACTIVITY-BASED COSTING AND ACTIVITY-BASED MANAGEMENT

Under its simple costing system, FS allocated support costs to products at the rate of 30% of cost of goods sold.

Required

1. Use the simple costing system to prepare a product-line profitability report for FS.
2. Use the ABC system to prepare a product-line profitability report for FS.
3. What new insights does the ABC system in requirement 2 provide to FS managers?

5-25 ABC, wholesale, customer profitability. Ramirez Wholesalers operates at capacity and sells furniture items to four department-store chains (customers). Mr. Ramirez commented, "We apply ABC to determine product-line profitability. The same ideas apply to customer profitability, and we should find out our customer profitability as well." Ramirez Wholesalers sends catalogs to corporate purchasing departments on a monthly basis. The customers are entitled to return unsold merchandise within a six-month period from the purchase date and receive a full purchase price refund. The following data were collected from last year's operations:

	Chain			
	1	2	3	4
Gross sales	$55,000	$25,000	$100,000	$75,000
Sales returns:				
Number of items	101	25	65	35
Amount	$11,000	$ 3,500	$ 7,000	$ 6,500
Number of orders:				
Regular	45	175	52	75
Rush	11	48	11	32

Ramirez has calculated the following activity rates:

Activity	Cost-Driver Rate
Regular order processing	$25 per regular order
Rush order processing	$125 per rush order
Returned items processing	$15 per item
Catalogs and customer support	$1,100 per customer

Customers pay the transportation costs. The cost of goods sold averages 70% of sales.

Required Determine the contribution to profit from each chain last year. Comment on your solution.

5-26 ABC, activity area cost-driver rates, product cross-subsidization. Idaho Potatoes (IP) operates at capacity and processes potatoes into potato cuts at its highly automated Pocatello plant. It sells potatoes to the retail consumer market and to the institutional market, which includes hospitals, cafeterias, and university dormitories.

IP's simple costing system, which does not distinguish between potato cuts processed for retail and institutional markets, has a single direct-cost category (direct materials, i.e. raw potatoes) and a single indirect-cost pool (production support). Support costs, which include packaging materials, are allocated on the basis of pounds of potato cuts processed. The company uses 1,200,000 pounds of raw potatoes to process 1,000,000 pounds of potato cuts. At the end of 2011, IP unsuccessfully bid for a large institutional contract. Its bid was reported to be 30% above the winning bid. This feedback came as a shock because IP included only a minimum profit margin on its bid and the Pocatello plant was acknowledged as the most efficient in the industry.

As a result of its review process of the lost contract bid, IP decided to explore ways to refine its costing system. The company determined that 90% of the direct materials (raw potatoes) related to the retail market and 10% to the institutional market. In addition, the company identified that packaging materials could be directly traced to individual jobs ($180,000 for retail and $8,000 for institutional). Also, the company used ABC to identify three main activity areas that generated support costs: cleaning, cutting, and packaging.

- **Cleaning Activity Area**—The cost-allocation base is pounds of raw potatoes cleaned.
- **Cutting Activity Area**—The production line produces (a) 250 pounds of retail potato cuts per cutting-hour and (b) 400 pounds of institutional potato cuts per cutting-hour. The cost-allocation base is cutting-hours on the production line.
- **Packaging Activity Area**—The packaging line packages (a) 25 pounds of retail potato cuts per packaging-hour and (b) 100 pounds of institutional potato cuts per packaging-hour. The cost-allocation base is packaging-hours on the production line.

114

The following table summarizes the actual costs for 2011 before and after the preceding cost analysis:

| | Before the cost analysis | After the cost analysis | | | |
		Production Support	Retail	Institutional	Total
Direct materials used					
Potatoes	$ 150,000		$135,000	$15,000	$ 150,000
Packaging			180,000	8,000	188,000
Production support	983,000				
Cleaning		$120,000			120,000
Cutting		231,000			231,000
Packaging		444,000			444,000
Total	$1,133,000	$795,000	$315,000	$23,000	$1,133,000

Required

1. Using the simple costing system, what is the cost per pound of potato cuts produced by IP?
2. Calculate the cost rate per unit of the cost driver in the (a) cleaning, (b) cutting, and (c) packaging activity areas.
3. Suppose IP uses information from its activity cost rates to calculate costs incurred on retail potato cuts and institutional potato cuts. Using the ABC system, what is the cost per pound of (a) retail potato cuts and (b) institutional potato cuts?
4. Comment on the cost differences between the two costing systems in requirements 1 and 3. How might IP use the information in requirement 3 to make better decisions?

5-27 Activity-based costing. The job costing system at Smith's Custom Framing has five indirect cost pools (purchasing, material handling, machine maintenance, product inspection, and packaging). The company is in the process of bidding on two jobs; Job 215, an order of 15 intricate personalized frames, and Job 325, an order of 6 standard personalized frames. The controller wants you to compare overhead allocated under the current simple job-costing system and a newly-designed activity-based job-costing system. Total budgeted costs in each indirect cost pool and the budgeted quantity of activity driver are as follows:

	Budgeted Overhead	Activity Driver	Budgeted Quantity of Activity Driver
Purchasing	$ 70,000	Purchase orders processed	2,000
Material handling	87,500	Material moves	5,000
Machine maintenance	237,300	Machine-hours	10,500
Product inspection	18,900	Inspections	1,200
Packaging	39,900	Units produced	3,800
	$453,600		

Information related to Job 215 and Job 325 follows. Job 215 incurs more batch-level costs because it uses more types of materials that need to be purchased, moved, and inspected relative to Job 325.

	Job 215	Job 325
Number of purchase orders	25	8
Number of material moves	10	4
Machine-hours	40	60
Number of inspections	9	3
Units produced	15	6

1. Compute the total overhead allocated to each job under a simple costing system, where overhead is allocated based on machine-hours.
2. Compute the total overhead allocated to each job under an activity-based costing system using the appropriate activity drivers.
3. Explain why Smith's Custom Framing might favor the ABC job-costing system over the simple job-costing system, especially in its bidding process.

5-28 ABC, product costing at banks, cross-subsidization. National Savings Bank (NSB) is examining the profitability of its Premier Account, a combined savings and checking account. Depositors receive a 7% annual interest rate on their average deposit. NSB earns an interest rate spread of 3% (the difference between the rate at which it lends money and the rate it pays depositors) by lending money for home loan purposes at 10%. Thus, NSB would gain $60 on the interest spread if a depositor had an average Premier Account balance of $2,000 in 2011 ($2,000 × 3% = $60).

The Premier Account allows depositors unlimited use of services such as deposits, withdrawals, checking accounts, and foreign currency drafts. Depositors with Premier Account balances of $1,000 or more receive unlimited free use of services. Depositors with minimum balances of less than $1,000 pay a $22-a-month service fee for their Premier Account.

NSB recently conducted an activity-based costing study of its services. It assessed the following costs for six individual services. The use of these services in 2011 by three customers is as follows:

	Activity-Based Cost per "Transaction"	Account Usage		
		Holt	Turner	Graham
Deposit/withdrawal with teller	$ 2.30	42	48	5
Deposit/withdrawal with automatic teller machine (ATM)	0.70	7	19	17
Deposit/withdrawal on prearranged monthly basis	0.40	0	13	62
Bank checks written	8.40	11	1	3
Foreign currency drafts	12.40	4	2	6
Inquiries about account balance	1.40	12	20	9
Average Premier Account balance for 2011		$1,100	$700	$24,600

Assume Holt and Graham always maintain a balance above $1,000, whereas Turner always has a balance below $1,000.

Required

1. Compute the 2011 profitability of the Holt, Turner, and Graham Premier Accounts at NSB.
2. Why might NSB worry about the profitability of individual customers if the Premier Account product offering is profitable as a whole?
3. What changes would you recommend for NSB's Premier Account?

MyAccountingLab

Problems

5-29 Job costing with single direct-cost category, single indirect-cost pool, law firm. Wigan Associates is a recently formed law partnership. Ellery Hanley, the managing partner of Wigan Associates, has just finished a tense phone call with Martin Offiah, president of Widnes Coal. Offiah strongly complained about the price Wigan charged for some legal work done for Widnes Coal.

Hanley also received a phone call from its only other client (St. Helen's Glass), which was very pleased with both the quality of the work and the price charged on its most recent job.

Wigan Associates operates at capacity and uses a cost-based approach to pricing (billing) each job. Currently it uses a simple costing system with a single direct-cost category (professional labor-hours) and a single indirect-cost pool (general support). Indirect costs are allocated to cases on the basis of professional labor-hours per case. The job files show the following:

	Widnes Coal	St. Helen's Glass
Professional labor	104 hours	96 hours

Professional labor costs at Wigan Associates are $70 an hour. Indirect costs are allocated to cases at $105 an hour. Total indirect costs in the most recent period were $21,000.

Required

1. Why is it important for Wigan Associates to understand the costs associated with individual jobs?
2. Compute the costs of the Widnes Coal and St. Helen's Glass jobs using Wigan's simple costing system.

5-30 Job costing with multiple direct-cost categories, single indirect-cost pool, law firm (continuation of 5-29). Hanley asks his assistant to collect details on those costs included in the $21,000 indirect-cost pool that can be traced to each individual job. After analysis, Wigan is able to reclassify $14,000 of the $21,000 as direct costs:

Other Direct Costs	Widnes Coal	St. Helen's Glass
Research support labor	$1,600	$ 3,400
Computer time	500	1,300
Travel and allowances	600	4,400
Telephones/faxes	200	1,000
Photocopying	250	750
Total	$3,150	$10,850

Hanley decides to calculate the costs of each job as if Wigan had used six direct cost-pools and a single indirect-cost pool. The single indirect-cost pool would have $7,000 of costs and would be allocated to each case using the professional labor-hours base.

Required

1. What is the revised indirect-cost allocation rate per professional labor-hour for Wigan Associates when total indirect costs are $7,000?
2. Compute the costs of the Widnes and St. Helen's jobs if Wigan Associates had used its refined costing system with multiple direct-cost categories and one indirect-cost pool.
3. Compare the costs of Widnes and St. Helen's jobs in requirement 2 with those in requirement 2 of Problem 5-29. Comment on the results.

5-31 Job costing with multiple direct-cost categories, multiple indirect-cost pools, law firm (continuation of 5-29 and 5-30). Wigan has two classifications of professional staff: partners and associates. Hanley asks his assistant to examine the relative use of partners and associates on the recent Widnes Coal and St. Helen's jobs. The Widnes job used 24 partner-hours and 80 associate-hours. The St. Helen's job used 56 partner-hours and 40 associate-hours. Therefore, totals of the two jobs together were 80 partner-hours and 120 associate-hours. Hanley decides to examine how using separate direct-cost rates for partners and associates and using separate indirect-cost pools for partners and associates would have affected the costs of the Widnes and St. Helen's jobs. Indirect costs in each indirect-cost pool would be allocated on the basis of total hours of that category of professional labor. From the total indirect cost-pool of $7,000, $4,600 is attributable to the activities of partners, and $2,400 is attributable to the activities of associates.

The rates per category of professional labor are as follows:

Category of Professional Labor	Direct Cost per Hour	Indirect Cost per Hour
Partner	$100.00	$4,600 ÷ 80 hours = $57.50
Associate	50.00	$2,400 ÷ 120 hours = $20.00

Required

1. Compute the costs of the Widnes and St. Helen's cases using Wigan's further refined system, with multiple direct-cost categories and multiple indirect-cost pools.
2. For what decisions might Wigan Associates find it more useful to use this job-costing approach rather than the approaches in Problem 5-29 or 5-30?

5-32 Plant-wide, department, and activity-cost rates. Allen's Aero Toys makes two models of toy airplanes, fighter jets, and cargo planes. The fighter jets are more detailed and require smaller batch sizes. The controller has asked you to compare plant-wide, department, and activity-based cost allocations.

Allen's Aero Toys
Budgeted Information per unit
For the Year Ended 30 November 2010

Assembly Department	Fighters	Cargo	Total
Direct materials	$2.50	$3.75	$ 6.25
Direct manufacturing labor	3.50	2.00	5.50
Total direct cost per unit	$6.00	$5.75	$11.75

Painting Department	Fighters	Cargo	
Direct materials	$0.50	$1.00	$ 1.50
Direct manufacturing labor	2.25	1.50	3.75
Total direct cost per unit	$2.75	$2.50	$ 5.25

Number of units produced	800	740	

The budgeted overhead cost for each department is as follows:

	Assembly Department	Painting Department	Total
Materials handling	$1,700	$ 900	$ 2,600
Quality inspection	2,750	1,150	3,900
Utilities	2,580	2,100	4,680
	$7,030	$4,150	$11,180

Other information follows:

Materials handling and quality inspection costs vary with the number of batches processed in each department. The budgeted number of batches for each product line in each department is as follows:

	Fighters	Cargo	Total
Assembly department	150	48	198
Painting department	100	32	132
Total	250	80	330

Utilities costs vary with direct manufacturing labor cost in each department.

Required

1. Calculate the budgeted cost per unit for fighter jets and cargo planes based on a single plant-wide overhead rate, if total overhead is allocated based on total direct costs.
2. Calculate the budgeted cost per unit for fighter jets and cargo planes based on departmental overhead rates, where assembly department overhead costs are allocated based on direct manufacturing labor costs of the assembly department and painting department overhead costs are allocated based on total direct costs of the painting department.
3. Calculate the budgeted cost per unit for fighter jets and cargo planes if Allen's Aero Toys allocates overhead costs using activity-based costing.
4. Explain how activity-based costing could improve or reduce decision quality.

5-33 Department and activity-cost rates, service sector. Roxbury's Radiology Center (RRC) performs X-rays, ultrasounds, CT scans, and MRIs. RRC has developed a reputation as a top Radiology Center in the state. RRC has achieved this status because it constantly reexamines its processes and procedures. RRC has been using a single, facility-wide overhead allocation rate. The VP of Finance believes that RRC can make better process improvements if it uses more disaggregated cost information. She says, "We have state of the art medical imaging technology. Can't we have state of the art accounting technology?"

Roxbury's Radiology Center
Budgeted Information
For the Year Ended May 30, 2011

	X-rays	Ultrasound	CT scan	MRI	Total
Technician labor	$ 64,000	$104,000	$119,000	$106,000	$ 393,000
Depreciation	136,800	231,000	400,200	792,000	1560,000
Materials	22,400	16,500	23,900	30,800	93,600
Administration					19,000
Maintenance					260,000
Sanitation					267,900
Utilities					121,200
	$223,200	$351,500	$543,100	$928,800	$2,714,700
Number of procedures	2,555	4,760	3,290	2,695	
Minutes to clean after each procedure	10	10	20	40	
Minutes for each procedure	5	20	15	40	

RRC operates at capacity. The proposed allocation bases for overhead are as follows:

Administration	Number of procedures
Maintenance (including parts)	Capital cost of the equipment (use Depreciation)
Sanitation	Total cleaning minutes
Utilities	Total procedure minutes

Required

1. Calculate the budgeted cost per service for X-rays, Ultrasounds, CT scans, and MRIs using direct technician labor costs as the allocation basis.
2. Calculate the budgeted cost per service of X-rays, Ultrasounds, CT scans, and MRIs if RRC allocated overhead costs using activity-based costing.
3. Explain how the disaggregation of information could be helpful to RRC's intention to continuously improve its services.

5-34 Choosing cost drivers, activity-based costing, activity-based management. Annie Warbucks runs a dance studio with childcare and adult fitness classes. Annie's budget for the upcoming year is as follows:

Annie Warbuck's Dance Studio
Budgeted Costs and Activities
For the Year Ended June 30, 2010

Dance teacher salaries	$62,100	
Child care teacher salaries	24,300	
Fitness instructor salaries	39,060	
Total salaries		$125,460
Supplies (art, dance accessories, fitness)		21,984
Rent, maintenance, and utilities		97,511
Administration salaries		50,075
Marketing expenses		21,000
Total		$316,030

Other budget information follows:

	Dance	Childcare	Fitness	Total
Square footage	6,000	3,150	2,500	11,650
Number of participants	1,485	450	270	2,205
Teachers per hour	3	3	1	7
Number of advertisements	26	24	20	70

Required

1. Determine which costs are direct costs and which costs are indirect costs of different programs.
2. Choose a cost driver for the indirect costs and calculate the budgeted cost per unit of the cost driver. Explain briefly your choice of cost driver.
3. Calculate the budgeted costs of each program.
4. How can Annie use this information for pricing? What other factors should she consider?

5-35 Activity-based costing, merchandising. Pharmacare, Inc., a distributor of special pharmaceutical products, operates at capacity and has three main market segments:

a. General supermarket chains
b. Drugstore chains
c. Mom-and-Pop single-store pharmacies

Rick Flair, the new controller of Pharmacare, reported the following data for 2011:

	A	B	C	D	E
1					
2	**Pharmacare, 2011**	**General**			
3		**Supermarket**	**Drugstore**	**Mom-and-Pop**	
4		**Chains**	**Chains**	**Single Stores**	**Pharmacare**
5	Revenues	$3,708,000	$3,150,000	$1,980,000	$8,838,000
6	Cost of goods sold	3,600,000	3,000,000	1,800,000	8,400,000
7	Gross margin	$ 108,000	$ 150,000	$ 180,000	438,000
8	Other operating costs				301,080
9	Operating income				$ 136,920

For many years, Pharmacare has used gross margin percentage [(Revenue − Cost of goods sold) ÷ Revenue] to evaluate the relative profitability of its market segments. But, Flair recently attended a seminar on activity-based costing and is considering using it at Pharmacare to analyze and allocate "other operating costs." He meets with all the key managers and several of his operations and sales staff and they agree that there are five key activities that drive other operating costs at Pharmacare:

Activity Area	Cost Driver
Order processing	Number of customer purchase orders
Line-item processing	Number of line items ordered by customers
Delivering to stores	Number of store deliveries
Cartons shipped to store	Number of cartons shipped
Stocking of customer store shelves	Hours of shelf-stocking

Each customer order consists of one or more line items. A line item represents a single product (such as Extra-Strength Tylenol Tablets). Each product line item is delivered in one or more separate cartons. Each store delivery entails the delivery of one or more cartons of products to a customer. Pharmacare's staff stacks cartons directly onto display shelves in customers' stores. Currently, there is no additional charge to the customer for shelf-stocking and not all customers use Pharmacare for this activity. The level of each activity in the three market segments and the total cost incurred for each activity in 2011 is as follows:

	Home	Insert	Page Layout	Formulas	Data	Review	View	
	A		B	C	D	E		
13								
14	Activity-based Cost Data			Activity Level				
15	Pharmacare 2011		General			Total Cost		
16			Supermarket	Drugstore	Mom-and-Pop	of Activity		
17	Activity		Chains	Chains	Single Stores	in 2011		
18	Orders processed (number)		140	360	1,500	$ 80,000		
19	Line-items ordered (number)		1,960	4,320	15,000	63,840		
20	Store deliveries made (number)		120	360	1,000	71,000		
21	Cartons shipped to stores (number)		36,000	24,000	16,000	76,000		
22	Shelf stocking (hours)		360	180	100	10,240		
23						$301,080		

Required

1. Compute the 2011 gross-margin percentage for each of Pharmacare's three market segments.
2. Compute the cost driver rates for each of the five activity areas.
3. Use the activity-based costing information to allocate the $301,080 of "other operating costs" to each of the market segments. Compute the operating income for each market segment.
4. Comment on the results. What new insights are available with the activity-based costing information?

5-36 Choosing cost drivers, activity-based costing, activity-based management. Pumpkin Bags (PB) is a designer of high quality backpacks and purses. Each design is made in small batches. Each spring, PB comes out with new designs for the backpack and for the purse. The company uses these designs for a year, and then moves on to the next trend. The bags are all made on the same fabrication equipment that is expected to operate at capacity. The equipment must be switched over to a new design and set up to prepare for the production of each new batch of products. When completed, each batch of products is immediately shipped to a wholesaler. Shipping costs vary with the number of shipments. Budgeted information for the year is as follows:

Pumpkin Bags
Budget for costs and Activities
For the Year Ended February 28, 2011

Direct materials—purses	$ 379,290
Direct materials—backpacks	412,920
Direct manufacturing labor—purses	98,000
Direct manufacturing labor—backpacks	120,000
Setup	65,930
Shipping	73,910
Design	166,000
Plant utilities and administration	243,000
Total	$1,559,050

Other budget information follows:

	Backpacks	Purses	Total
Number of bags	6,050	3,350	9,400
Hours of production	1,450	2,600	4,050
Number of batches	130	60	190
Number of designs	2	2	4

Required

1. Identify the cost hierarcy level for each cost category.
2. Identify the most appropriate cost driver for each cost category. Explain briefly your choice of cost driver.
3. Calculate the budgeted cost per unit of cost driver for each cost category.
4. Calculate the budgeted total costs and cost per unit for each product line.
5. Explain how you could use the information in requirement 4 to reduce costs.

5-37 ABC, health care. Uppervale Health Center runs two programs: drug addict rehabilitation and aftercare (counseling and support of patients after release from a mental hospital). The center's budget for 2010 follows:

Professional salaries:		
4 physicians × $150,000	$600,000	
12 psychologists × $75,000	900,000	
16 nurses × $30,000	480,000	$1,980,000
Medical supplies		220,000
Rent and clinic maintenance		126,000
Administrative costs to manage patient charts, food, laundry		440,000
Laboratory services		84,000
Total		$2,850,000

Muriel Clayton, the director of the center, is keen on determining the cost of each program. Clayton compiled the following data describing employee allocations to individual programs:

	Drug	Aftercare	Total Employees
Physicians	4		4
Psychologists	4	8	12
Nurses	6	10	16

Clayton has recently become aware of activity-based costing as a method to refine costing systems. She asks her accountant, Huey Deluth, how she should apply this technique. Deluth obtains the following budgeted information for 2010:

	Drug	Aftercare	Total
Square feet of space occupied by each program	9,000	12,000	21,000
Patient-years of service	50	60	110
Number of laboratory tests	1,400	700	2,100

Required

1. **a.** Selecting cost-allocation bases that you believe are the most appropriate for allocating indirect costs to programs, calculate the budgeted indirect cost rates for medical supplies; rent and clinic maintenance; administrative costs for patient charts, food, and laundry; and laboratory services.
   b. Using an activity-based costing approach to cost analysis, calculate the budgeted cost of each program and the budgeted cost per patient-year of the drug program.
   c. What benefits can Uppervale Health Center obtain by implementing the ABC system?
2. What factors, other than cost, do you think Uppervale Health Center should consider in allocating resources to its programs?

5-38 Unused capacity, activity-based costing, activity-based management. Nivag's Netballs is a manufacturer of high quality basketballs and volleyballs. Setup costs are driven by the number of batches. Equipment and maintenance costs increase with the number of machine-hours, and lease rent is paid per square foot. Capacity of the facility is 12,000 square feet and Nivag is using only 70% of this capacity. Nivag records the cost of unused capacity as a separate line item, and not as a product cost. The following is the budgeted information for Nivag:

Nivag's Netballs
Budgeted Costs and Activities
For the Year Ended August 31, 2012

Direct materials—basketballs	$ 209,750
Direct materials—volleyballs	358,290
Direct manufacturing labor—basketballs	107,333
Direct manufacturing labor—volleyballs	102,969
Setup	143,500
Equipment and maintenance costs	109,900
Lease rent	216,000
Total	$1,247,742

Other budget information follows:

	Basketballs	Volleyballs
Number of balls	66,000	100,000
Machine-hours	11,000	12,500
Number of batches	300	400
Square footage of production space used	3,360	5,040

Required

1. Calculate the budgeted cost per unit of cost driver for each indirect cost pool.
2. What is the budgeted cost of unused capacity?
3. What is the budgeted total cost and the cost per unit of resources used to produce (a) basketballs and (b) volleyballs?
4. What factors should Nivag consider if it has the opportunity to manufacture a new line of footballs?

5-39 Activity-based job costing, unit-cost comparisons. The Tracy Corporation has a machining facility specializing in jobs for the aircraft-components market. Tracy's previous simple job-costing system had two direct-cost categories (direct materials and direct manufacturing labor) and a single indirect-cost pool (manufacturing overhead, allocated using direct manufacturing labor-hours). The indirect cost-allocation rate of the simple system for 2010 would have been $115 per direct manufacturing labor-hour.

Recently a team with members from product design, manufacturing, and accounting used an ABC approach to refine its job-costing system. The two direct-cost categories were retained. The team decided to replace the single indirect-cost pool with five indirect-cost pools. The cost pools represent five activity areas at the plant, each with its own supervisor and budget responsibility. Pertinent data are as follows:

Activity Area	Cost-Allocation Base	Cost-Allocation Rate
Materials handling	Parts	$ 0.40
Lathe work	Lathe turns	0.20
Milling	Machine-hours	20.00
Grinding	Parts	0.80
Testing	Units tested	15.00

Information-gathering technology has advanced to the point at which the data necessary for budgeting in these five activity areas are collected automatically.

Two representative jobs processed under the ABC system at the plant in the most recent period had the following characteristics:

	Job 410	Job 411
Direct material cost per job	$ 9,700	$59,900
Direct manufacturing labor cost per job	$750	$11,250
Number of direct manufacturing labor-hours per job	25	375
Parts per job	500	2,000
Lathe turns per job	20,000	59,250
Machine-hours per job	150	1,050
Units per job (all units are tested)	10	200

Required

1. Compute the manufacturing cost per unit for each job under the previous simple job-costing system.
2. Compute the manufacturing cost per unit for each job under the activity-based costing system.
3. Compare the per-unit cost figures for Jobs 410 and 411 computed in requirements 1 and 2. Why do the simple and the activity-based costing systems differ in the manufacturing cost per unit for each job? Why might these differences be important to Tracy Corporation?
4. How might Tracy Corporation use information from its ABC system to better manage its business?

5-40 ABC, implementation, ethics. (CMA, adapted) Applewood Electronics, a division of Elgin Corporation, manufactures two large-screen television models: the Monarch, which has been produced since 2006 and sells for $900, and the Regal, a newer model introduced in early 2009 that sells for $1,140. Based on the following income statement for the year ended November 30, 2010, senior management at Elgin have decided to concentrate Applewood's marketing resources on the Regal model and to begin to phase out the Monarch model because Regal generates a much bigger operating income per unit.

Applewood Electronics
Income Statement
For the Fiscal Year Ended November 30, 2010

	Monarch	Regal	Total
Revenues	$19,800,000	$4,560,000	$24,360,000
Cost of goods sold	12,540,000	3,192,000	15,732,000
Gross margin	7,260,000	1,368,000	8,628,000
Selling and administrative expense	5,830,000	978,000	6,808,000
Operating income	$ 1,430,000	$ 390,000	$ 1,820,000
Units produced and sold	22,000	4,000	
Operating income per unit sold	$65.00	$97.50	

Details for cost of goods sold for Monarch and Regal are as follows:

	Monarch		Regal	
	Total	Per unit	Total	Per unit
Direct materials	$ 4,576,000	$208	$2,336,000	$584
Direct manufacturing labor[a]	396,000	18	168,000	42
Machine costs[b]	3,168,000	144	288,000	72
Total direct costs	$ 8,140,000	$370	$2,792,000	$698
Manufacturing overhead costs[c]	$ 4,400,000	$200	$ 400,000	$100
Total cost of goods sold	$12,540,000	$570	$3,192,000	$798

---

[a] Monarch requires 1.5 hours per unit and Regal requires 3.5 hours per unit. The direct manufacturing labor cost is $12 per hour.
[b] Machine costs include lease costs of the machine, repairs, and maintenance. Monarch requires 8 machine-hours per unit and Regal requires 4 machine-hours per unit. The machine hour rate is $18 per hour.
[c] Manufacturing overhead costs are allocated to products based on machine-hours at the rate of $25 per hour.

Applewood's controller, Susan Benzo, is advocating the use of activity-based costing and activity-based management and has gathered the following information about the company's manufacturing overhead costs for the year ended November 30, 2010.

Activity Center (Cost-Allocation Base)	Total Activity Costs	Units of the Cost-Allocation Base		
		Monarch	Regal	Total
Soldering (number of solder points)	$ 942,000	1,185,000	385,000	1,570,000
Shipments (number of shipments)	860,000	16,200	3,800	20,000
Quality control (number of inspections)	1,240,000	56,200	21,300	77,500
Purchase orders (number of orders)	950,400	80,100	109,980	190,080
Machine power (machine-hours)	57,600	176,000	16,000	192,000
Machine setups (number of setups)	750,000	16,000	14,000	30,000
Total manufacturing overhead	$4,800,000			

After completing her analysis, Benzo shows the results to Fred Duval, the Applewood division president. Duval does not like what he sees. "If you show headquarters this analysis, they are going to ask us to phase out the Regal line, which we have just introduced. This whole costing stuff has been a major problem for us. First Monarch was not profitable and now Regal."

"Looking at the ABC analysis, I see two problems. First, we do many more activities than the ones you have listed. If you had included all activities, maybe your conclusions would be different. Second, you used number of setups and number of inspections as allocation bases. The numbers would be different had you used setup-hours and inspection-hours instead. I know that measurement problems precluded you from using these other cost-allocation bases, but I believe you ought to make some adjustments to our current numbers to compensate for these issues. I know you can do better. We can't afford to phase out either product."

Benzo knows that her numbers are fairly accurate. As a quick check, she calculates the profitability of Regal and Monarch using more and different allocation bases. The set of activities and activity rates she had used results in numbers that closely approximate those based on more detailed analyses. She is confident that headquarters, knowing that Regal was introduced only recently, will not ask Applewood to phase it out. She is also aware that a sizable portion of Duval's bonus is based on division revenues. Phasing out either product would adversely affect his bonus. Still, she feels some pressure from Duval to do something.

Required

1. Using activity-based costing, calculate the gross margin per unit of the Regal and Monarch models.
2. Explain briefly why these numbers differ from the gross margin per unit of the Regal and Monarch models calculated using Applewood's existing simple costing system.
3. Comment on Duval's concerns about the accuracy and limitations of ABC.
4. How might Applewood find the ABC information helpful in managing its business?
5. What should Susan Benzo do in response to Duval's comments?

Collaborative Learning Problem

5-41 Activity-based costing, activity-based management, merchandising. Super Bookstore (SB) is a large city bookstore that sells books and music CDs, and has a café. SB operates at capacity and allocates selling, general, and administration (S, G & A) costs to each product line using the cost of merchandise of each product line. SB wants to optimize the pricing and cost management of each product line. SB is wondering if its accounting system is providing it with the best information for making such decisions.

Super Bookstore
Product Line Information
For the Year Ended December 31, 2010

	Books	CDs	Café
Revenues	$3,720,480	$2,315,360	$736,216
Cost of merchandise	$2,656,727	$1,722,311	$556,685
Cost of café cleaning	—	—	$ 18,250
Number of purchase orders placed	2,800	2,500	2,000
Number of deliveries received	1,400	1,700	1,600
Hours of shelf stocking time	15,000	14,000	10,000
Items sold	124,016	115,768	368,108

Super Bookstore incurs the following selling, general, and administration costs:

Super Bookstore
Selling, General, & Administration (S, G & A) Costs
For the Year Ended December 31, 2010

Purchasing department expenses	$ 474,500
Receiving department expenses	432,400
Shelf stocking labor expense	487,500
Customer support expense (cashiers and floor employees)	91,184
	$1,485,584

Required

1. Suppose Super Bookstore uses cost of merchandise to allocate all S, G & A costs. Prepare product line and total company income statements.
2. Identify an improved method for allocating costs to the three product lines. Explain. Use the method for allocating S, G & A costs that you propose to prepare new product line and total company income statements. Compare your results to the results in requirement 1.
3. Write a memo to Super Bookstore's management describing how the improved system might be useful for managing Super Bookstore.

Master Budget and Responsibility Accounting

From Chapter 6 of *Cost Accounting: A Managerial Emphasis*, 14/e. Charles T. Horngren. Srikant M. Datar. Madhav Rajan.

Master Budget and Responsibility Accounting

Amid the recent recession, one of the hottest innovations was the growth of Web sites that enable users to get an aggregate picture of their financial data and to set up budgets to manage their spending and other financial decisions online. (Mint.com, a pioneer in this market, was acquired by Intuit for $170 million in September 2009.)

Budgets play a similar crucial role in businesses. Without budgets, it's difficult for managers and their employees to know whether they're on target for their growth and spending goals. You might think a budget is only for companies that are in financial difficulty (such as Citigroup) or whose profit margins are slim—Wal-Mart, for example. As the following article shows, even companies that sell high-dollar value goods and services adhere to budgets.

"Scrimping" at the Ritz: Master Budgets

"Ladies and gentlemen serving ladies and gentlemen." That's the motto of the Ritz-Carlton. With locations ranging from South Beach (Miami) to South Korea, the grand hotel chain is known for its indulgent luxury and sumptuous surroundings. However, the aura of the chain's old-world elegance stands in contrast to its rather heavy emphasis—behind the scenes, of course—on cost control and budgets. It is this very approach, however, that makes it possible for the Ritz to offer the legendary grandeur its guests expect during their stay.

A Ritz hotel's performance is the responsibility of its general manager and controller at each location worldwide. Local forecasts and budgets are prepared annually and are the basis of subsequent performance evaluations for the hotel and people who work there.

The preparation of a hotel's budget begins with the hotel's sales director, who is responsible for all hotel revenues. Sources of revenue include hotel rooms, conventions, weddings, meeting facilities, merchandise, and food and beverage. The controller then seeks input about costs. Standard costs, based on cost per occupied room, are used to build the budget for guest room stays. Other standard costs are used to calculate costs for meeting rooms and food and beverages. The completed sales budget and annual operating budget are sent to corporate headquarters. From there, the hotel's actual monthly performance is monitored against the approved budget.

The managers of each hotel meet daily to review the hotel's performance to date relative to plan. They have the ability to adjust prices in the reservation system if they so choose. Adjusting prices can be particularly important if a hotel experiences unanticipated changes in occupancy rates.

Each month, the hotel's actual performance is monitored against the approved budget. The controller of each hotel receives a report from corporate headquarters that shows how the hotel performed against budget, as well as against the actual

Michael Blann\Getty Images, Inc.—Liaison

performance of other Ritz hotels. Any ideas for boosting revenues and reducing costs are regularly shared among hotel controllers.

Why does a successful company feel the need to watch its spending so closely? In many profitable companies, a strict budget is actually a key to their success. As the Ritz-Carlton example illustrates, budgeting is a critical function in organizations. Southwest Airlines, for example, uses budgets to monitor and manage fuel costs. Wal-Mart depends on its budget to maintain razor-thin margins as it competes with Target. Gillette uses budgets to plan marketing campaigns for its razors and blades.

Budgeting is a common accounting tool that companies use for implementing strategy. Management uses budgets to communicate directions and goals throughout a company. Budgets turn managers' perspectives forward and aid in planning and controlling the actions managers must undertake to satisfy their customers and succeed in the marketplace. Budgets provide measures of the financial results a company expects from its planned activities and help define objectives and timelines against which progress can be measured. Through budgeting, managers learn to anticipate and avoid potential problems. Interestingly, even when it comes to entrepreneurial activities, business planning has been shown to increase a new venture's probability of survival, as well as its product development and venture organizing activities.[1] As the old adage goes: "If you fail to plan, you plan to fail."

---

[1] For more details, take a look at F. Delmar and S. Shane, "Does Business Planning Facilitate the Development of New Ventures?" *Strategic Management Journal*, December 2003.

Budgets and the Budgeting Cycle

A *budget* is (a) the quantitative expression of a proposed plan of action by management for a specified period and (b) an aid to coordinate what needs to be done to implement that plan. A budget generally includes both financial and nonfinancial aspects of the plan, and it serves as a blueprint for the company to follow in an upcoming period. A financial budget quantifies management's expectations regarding income, cash flows, and financial position. Just as financial statements are prepared for past periods, financial statements can be prepared for future periods—for example, a budgeted income statement, a budgeted statement of cash flows, and a budgeted balance sheet. Underlying these financial budgets are nonfinancial budgets for, say, units manufactured or sold, number of employees, and number of new products being introduced to the marketplace.

Strategic Plans and Operating Plans

Budgeting is most useful when it is integrated with a company's strategy. *Strategy* specifies how an organization matches its own capabilities with the opportunities in the marketplace to accomplish its objectives. In developing successful strategies, managers consider questions such as the following:

- What are our objectives?
- How do we create value for our customers while distinguishing ourselves from our competitors?
- Are the markets for our products local, regional, national, or global? What trends affect our markets? How are we affected by the economy, our industry, and our competitors?
- What organizational and financial structures serve us best?
- What are the risks and opportunities of alternative strategies, and what are our contingency plans if our preferred plan fails?

A company, such as Home Depot, can have a strategy of providing quality products or services at a low price. Another company, such as Pfizer or Porsche, can have a strategy of providing a unique product or service that is priced higher than the products or services of competitors. Exhibit 1 shows that strategic plans are expressed through long-run budgets and operating plans are expressed via short-run budgets. But there is more to the story! The exhibit shows arrows pointing backward as well as forward. The backward arrows are a way of graphically indicating that budgets can lead to changes in plans and strategies. Budgets help managers assess strategic risks and opportunities by providing them with feedback about the likely effects of their strategies and plans. Sometimes the feedback signals to managers that they need to revise their plans and possibly their strategies.

Boeing's experience with the 747-8 program illustrates how budgets can help managers rework their operating plans. Boeing viewed updating its 747 jumbo jet by sharing design synergies with the ongoing 787 Dreamliner program as a relatively inexpensive way to take sales from Airbus' A380 superjumbo jet. However, continued cost overruns and delays have undermined that strategy: The 747-8 program is already $2 billion over budget and a year behind schedule. The company recently revealed that it expects to earn no profit on virtually any of the 105 747-8 planes on its order books. With the budget for 2010 revealing higher-than-expected costs in design, rework, and production, Boeing has postponed plans to accelerate the jumbo's production to 2013. Some aerospace experts are urging Boeing to consider more dramatic steps, including discontinuing the passenger aircraft version of the 747-8 program.

Exhibit 1

Strategy, Planning, and Budgets

Budgeting Cycle and Master Budget

Well-managed companies usually cycle through the following budgeting steps during the course of the fiscal year:

1. Working together, managers and management accountants plan the performance of the company as a whole and the performance of its subunits (such as departments or divisions). Taking into account past performance and anticipated changes in the future, managers at all levels reach a common understanding on what is expected.

2. Senior managers give subordinate managers a frame of reference, a set of specific financial or nonfinancial expectations against which actual results will be compared.

3. Management accountants help managers investigate variations from plans, such as an unexpected decline in sales. If necessary, corrective action follows, such as a reduction in price to boost sales or cutting of costs to maintain profitability.

4. Managers and management accountants take into account market feedback, changed conditions, and their own experiences as they begin to make plans for the next period. For example, a decline in sales may cause managers to make changes in product features for the next period.

The preceding four steps describe the ongoing budget process. The working document at the core of this process is called the *master budget*. The **master budget** expresses management's operating and financial plans for a specified period (usually a fiscal year), and it includes a set of budgeted financial statements. The master budget is the initial plan of what the company intends to accomplish in the budget period. The master budget evolves from both operating and financing decisions made by managers.

■ Operating decisions deal with how to best use the limited resources of an organization.

■ Financing decisions deal with how to obtain the funds to acquire those resources.

The terminology used to describe budgets varies among companies. For example, budgeted financial statements are sometimes called **pro forma statements**. Some companies, such as Hewlett-Packard, refer to budgeting as *targeting*. And many companies, such as Nissan Motor Company and Owens Corning, refer to the budget as a *profit plan*. Microsoft refers to goals as *commitments* and distributes firm-level goals across the company, connecting them to organizational, team, and ultimately individual commitments.

This book's focus centers on how management accounting helps managers make operating decisions, which is why this chapter emphasizes operating budgets. Managers spend a significant part of their time preparing and analyzing budgets. The many advantages of budgeting make spending time on the budgeting process a worthwhile investment of managers' energies.

Decision Point

What is the master budget and why is it useful?

Advantages of Budgets

Budgets are an integral part of management control systems. When administered thoughtfully by managers, budgets do the following:

■ Promote coordination and communication among subunits within the company

■ Provide a framework for judging performance and facilitating learning

■ Motivate managers and other employees

Coordination and Communication

Coordination is meshing and balancing all aspects of production or service and all departments in a company in the best way for the company to meet its goals. *Communication* is making sure those goals are understood by all employees.

Coordination forces executives to think of relationships among individual departments within the company, as well as between the company and its supply chain partners. Consider budgeting at Pace, a United Kingdom-based manufacturer of electronic products. A key product is Pace's digital set-top box for decoding satellite broadcasts. The production manager can achieve more timely production by coordinating and

Learning Objective 2

Describe the advantages of budgets

. . . advantages include coordination, communication, performance evaluation, and managerial motivation

communicating with the company's marketing team to understand when set-top boxes will be needed. In turn, the marketing team can make better predictions of future demand for set-top boxes by coordinating and communicating with Pace's customers.

Suppose BSkyB, one of Pace's largest customers, is planning to launch a new high-definition personal video recorder service. If Pace's marketing group is able to obtain information about the launch date for the service, it can share this information with Pace's manufacturing group. The manufacturing group must then coordinate and communicate with Pace's materials-procurement group, and so on. The point to understand is that Pace is more likely to have satisfied customers (by having personal video recorders in the demanded quantities at the times demanded) if Pace coordinates and communicates both within its business functions and with its suppliers and customers during the budgeting process as well as during the production process.

Framework for Judging Performance and Facilitating Learning

Budgets enable a company's managers to measure actual performance against predicted performance. Budgets can overcome two limitations of using past performance as a basis for judging actual results. One limitation is that past results often incorporate past miscues and substandard performance. Consider a cellular telephone company (Mobile Communications) examining the current-year (2012) performance of its sales force. Suppose the performance for 2011 incorporated the efforts of many salespeople who have since left Mobile because they did not have a good understanding of the marketplace. (The president of Mobile said, "They could not sell ice cream in a heat wave.") Using the sales record of those departed employees would set the performance bar for 2012 much too low.

The other limitation of using past performance is that future conditions can be expected to differ from the past. Consider again Mobile Communications. Suppose, in 2012, Mobile had a 20% revenue increase, compared with a 10% revenue increase in 2011. Does this increase indicate outstanding sales performance? Before you say yes, consider the following facts. In November 2011, an industry trade association forecasts that the 2012 growth rate in industry revenues will be 40%, which also turned out to be the actual growth rate. As a result, Mobile's 20% actual revenue gain in 2012 takes on a negative connotation, even though it exceeded the 2011 actual growth rate of 10%. Using the 40% budgeted sales growth rate provides a better measure of the 2012 sales performance than using the 2011 actual growth rate of 10%.

It is important to remember that a company's budget should not be the only benchmark used to evaluate performance. Many companies also consider performance relative to peers as well as improvement over prior years. The problem with evaluating performance relative only to a budget is it creates an incentive for subordinates to set a target that is relatively easy to achieve.[2] Of course, managers at all levels recognize this incentive, and therefore work to make the budget more challenging to achieve for the individuals who report to them. Negotiations occur among managers at each of these levels to understand what is possible and what is not. The budget is the end product of these negotiations.

One of the most valuable benefits of budgeting is that it helps managers gather relevant information for improving future performance. When actual outcomes fall short of budgeted or planned results, it prompts thoughtful senior managers to ask questions about what happened and why, and how this knowledge can be used to ensure that such shortfalls do not occur again. This probing and learning is one of the most important reasons why budgeting helps improve performance.

Motivating Managers and Other Employees

Research shows that challenging budgets improve employee performance because employees view falling short of budgeted numbers as a failure. Most employees are motivated to work more intensely to avoid failure than to achieve success. As employees get

---

[2] For several examples, see J. Hope and R. Fraser, *Beyond Budgeting* (Boston, MA: Harvard Business School Press, 2003). The authors also criticize the tendency for managers to administer budgets rigidly even when changing market conditions have rendered the budget obsolete.

closer to a goal, they work harder to achieve it. Therefore, many executives like to set demanding but achievable goals for their subordinate managers and employees.[3] Creating a little anxiety improves performance, but overly ambitious and unachievable budgets increase anxiety without motivation because employees see little chance of avoiding failure. General Electric's former CEO, Jack Welch, describes challenging, yet achievable, budgets as energizing, motivating, and satisfying for managers and other employees, and capable of unleashing out-of-the-box and creative thinking.

Challenges in Administering Budgets

The budgeting process involves all levels of management. Top managers want lower-level managers to participate in the budgeting process because lower-level managers have more specialized knowledge and first-hand experience with day-to-day aspects of running the business. Participation creates greater commitment and accountability toward the budget among lower-level managers. This is the bottom-up aspect of the budgeting process.

The budgeting process, however, is a time-consuming one. It has been estimated that senior managers spend about 10% to 20% of their time on budgeting, and finance planning departments spend as much as 50% of their time on it.[4] For most organizations, the annual budget process is a months-long exercise that consumes a tremendous amount of resources. Despite his admiration for setting challenging targets, Jack Welch has also referred to the budgeting process as "the most ineffective process in management," and as "the bane of corporate America."

The widespread prevalence of budgets in companies ranging from major multinational corporations to small local businesses indicates that the advantages of budgeting systems outweigh the costs. To gain the benefits of budgeting, management at all levels of a company should understand and support the budget and all aspects of the management control system. This is critical for obtaining lower-level management's participation in the formulation of budgets and for successful administration of budgets. Lower-level managers who feel that top management does not "believe" in a budget are unlikely to be active participants in a budget process.

Budgets should not be administered rigidly. Attaining the budget is not an end in itself, especially when conditions change dramatically. A manager may commit to a budget, but if a situation arises in which some unplanned repairs or an unplanned advertising program would serve the long-run interests of the company, the manager should undertake the additional spending. On the flip side, the dramatic decline in consumer demand during the recent recession led designers such as Gucci to slash their ad budgets and put on hold planned new boutiques. Macy's and other retailers, stuck with shelves of merchandise ordered before the financial crisis, had no recourse but to slash prices and cut their workforce. JCPenney eventually missed its sales projections for 2008–09 by $2 billion. However, its aggressive actions during the year enabled it to survive the recession and emerge with sophisticated new inventory management plans to profit from the next holiday season.

Developing an Operating Budget

Budgets are typically developed for a set period, such as a month, quarter, year, and so on. The set period can itself be broken into subperiods. For example, a 12-month cash budget may be broken into 12 monthly periods so that cash inflows and outflows can be better coordinated.

Time Coverage of Budgets

The motive for creating a budget should guide a manager in choosing the period for the budget. For example, consider budgeting for a new Harley-Davidson 500-cc motorcycle. If the purpose is to budget for the total profitability of this new model, a five-year period (or more) may be suitable and long enough to cover the product from design through to manufacture, sales, and after-sales support. In contrast, consider budgeting for a school

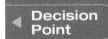

Decision Point

When should a company prepare budgets? What are the advantages of preparing budgets?

Learning Objective 3

Prepare the operating budget

. . . the budgeted income statement

and its supporting schedules

. . . such as cost of goods sold and nonmanufacturing costs

---

[3] For a detailed discussion and several examples of the merits of setting specific hard goals, see G. Latham, "The Motivational Benefits of Goal-Setting," *Academy of Management Executive* 18, no. 4, (2004).
[4] See P. Horvath and R. Sauter, "Why Budgeting Fails: One Management System is Not Enough," Balanced Scorecard Report, (September 2004).

play. If the purpose is to estimate all cash outlays, a six-month period from the planning stage to the final performance may suffice.

The most frequently used budget period is one year, which is often subdivided into months and quarters. The budgeted data for a year are frequently revised as the year goes on. At the end of the second quarter, management may change the budget for the next two quarters in light of new information obtained during the first six months. For example, Amerigroup, a health insurance firm, had to make substantial revisions to its third-quarter and annual cost projections for 2009 because of higher-than-expected costs related to the H1N1 virus.

Businesses are increasingly using rolling budgets. A **rolling budget**, also called a **continuous budget**, is a budget that is always available for a specified future period. It is created by continually adding a month, quarter, or year to the period that just ended. Consider Electrolux, the global appliance company, which has a three- to five-year strategic plan and a four-quarter rolling budget. A four-quarter rolling budget for the April 2011 to March 2012 period is superseded in the next quarter—that is in June 2011—by a four-quarter rolling budget for July 2011 to June 2012, and so on. There is always a 12-month budget (for the next year) in place. Rolling budgets constantly force Electrolux's management to think about the forthcoming 12 months, regardless of the quarter at hand. Some companies prepare rolling financial forecasts that look ahead five quarters. Examples are Borealis, Europe's leading polyolefin plastics manufacturer; Millipore, a life sciences research and manufacturing firm headquartered in Massachusetts; and Nordea, the largest financial services group in the Nordic and Baltic Sea region. Others, such as EMC Corporation, the information infrastructure giant, employ a six-quarter rolling-forecast process so that budget allocations can be constantly adjusted to meet changing market conditions.

Steps in Preparing an Operating Budget

The best way to explain how to prepare an operating budget is by walking through the steps a company would take to do so. Consider Stylistic Furniture, a company that makes two types of granite-top coffee tables: Casual and Deluxe. It is late 2011 and Stylistic's CEO, Rex Jordan, is very concerned about how he is going to respond to the board of directors' mandate to increase profits by 10% in the coming year. Jordan goes through the five-step decision-making process.

1. **Identify the problem and uncertainties.** The problem is to identify a strategy and to build a budget to achieve a 10% profit growth. There are several uncertainties. Can Stylistic dramatically increase sales for its more profitable Deluxe tables? What price pressures is Stylistic likely to face? Will the cost of materials increase? Can costs be reduced through efficiency improvements?

2. **Obtain information.** Stylistic's managers gather information about sales of Deluxe tables in the current year. They are delighted to learn that sales have been stronger than expected. Moreover, one of the key competitors in Stylistic's Casual tables line has had quality problems that are unlikely to be resolved until early 2012. Unfortunately, they also discover that the prices of direct materials have increased slightly during 2011.

3. **Make predictions about the future.** Stylistic's managers feel confident that with a little more marketing, they will be able to grow the Deluxe tables business and even increase prices slightly relative to 2011. They also do not expect significant price pressures on Casual tables in the early part of the year, because of the quality problems faced by a key competitor. They are concerned, however, that when the competitor does start selling again, pressure on prices could increase.

   The purchasing manager anticipates that prices of direct materials will be about the same as in 2011. The manufacturing manager believes that efficiency improvements would allow costs of manufacturing tables to be maintained at 2011 costs despite an increase in the prices of other inputs. Achieving these efficiency improvements is important if Stylistic is to maintain its 12% operating margin (that is, operating income ÷ sales = 12%) and to grow sales and operating income.

4. **Make decisions by choosing among alternatives.** Jordan and his managers feel confident in their strategy of pushing sales of Deluxe tables. This decision has some risks but is easily the best option available for Stylistic to increase profits by 10%.

5. **Implement the decision, evaluate performance, and learn.** Managers compare actual to predicted performance to learn about why things turned out the way they did and how to do things better. Stylistic's managers would want to know whether their predictions about prices of Casual and Deluxe tables were correct. Did prices of direct materials increase more or less than anticipated? Did efficiency improvements occur? Such learning would be very helpful as Stylistic plans its budgets in subsequent years.

Stylistic's managers begin their work toward the 2012 budget. Exhibit 2 shows a diagram of the various parts of the *master budget*. The master budget comprises the financial projections of all the individual budgets for a company for a specified period, usually a fiscal year. The light, medium, and dark purple boxes in Exhibit 2 represent the budgeted income statement and its supporting budget schedules—together called the **operating budget**.

We show the revenues budget box in a light purple color to indicate that it is often the starting point of the operating budget. The supporting schedules—shown in medium purple—quantify the budgets for various business functions of the value chain, from research and development to distribution costs. These schedules build up to the budgeted income statement—the key summary statement in the operating budget—shown in dark purple.

The light and dark blue boxes in the exhibit are the **financial budget**, which is that part of the master budget made up of the capital expenditures budget, the cash budget, the budgeted balance sheet, and the budgeted statement of cash flows. A financial budget focuses on how operations and planned capital outlays affect cash—shown in light blue.

The cash budget and the budgeted income statement can then be used to prepare two other summary financial statements—the budgeted balance sheet and the budgeted statement of cash flows—shown in dark blue. The master budget is finalized only after several rounds of discussions between top management and managers responsible for various business functions in the value chain.

We next present the steps in preparing an operating budget for Stylistic Furniture for 2012. Use Exhibit 2 as a guide for the steps that follow. The appendix to this chapter presents Stylistic's cash budget, which is another key component of the master budget. Details needed to prepare the budget follow:

- Stylistic sells two models of granite-top coffee tables: Casual and Deluxe. Revenue unrelated to sales, such as interest income, is zero.
- Work-in-process inventory is negligible and is ignored.
- Direct materials inventory and finished goods inventory are costed using the first-in, first-out (FIFO) method. Unit costs of direct materials purchased and unit costs of finished goods sold remain unchanged throughout each budget year but can change from year to year.
- There are two types of direct materials: red oak (RO) and granite slabs (GS). Direct material costs are variable with respect to units of output—coffee tables.
- Direct manufacturing labor workers are hired on an hourly basis; no overtime is worked.
- There are two cost drivers for manufacturing overhead costs—direct manufacturing labor-hours and setup labor-hours.
- Direct manufacturing labor-hours is the cost driver for the variable portion of manufacturing operations overhead. The fixed component of manufacturing operations overhead is tied to the manufacturing capacity of 300,000 direct manufacturing labor-hours that Stylistic has planned for 2012.
- Setup labor-hours is the cost driver for the variable portion of machine setup overhead. The fixed component of machine setup overhead is tied to the setup capacity of 15,000 setup labor-hours that Stylistic has planned for 2012.
- For computing inventoriable costs, Stylistic allocates all (variable and fixed) manufacturing operations overhead costs using direct manufacturing labor-hours and machine setup overhead costs using setup labor-hours.

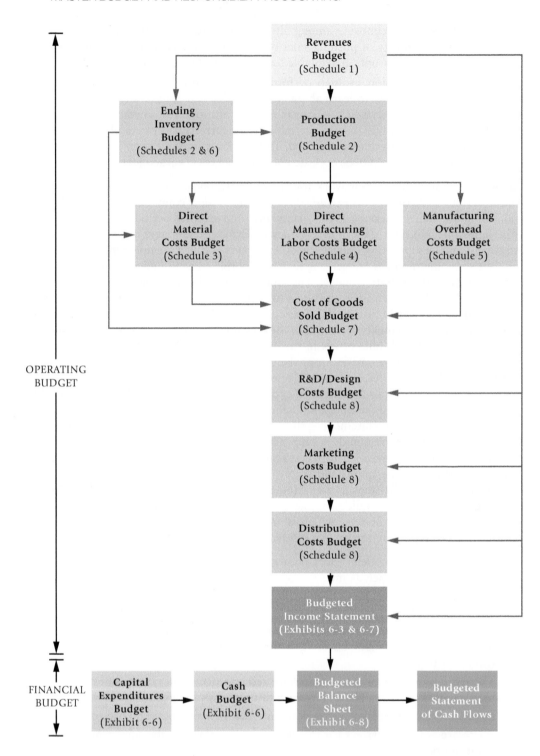

Overview of the Master Budget for Stylistic Furniture

OPERATING BUDGET

FINANCIAL BUDGET

- Nonmanufacturing costs consist of product design, marketing, and distribution costs. All product design costs are fixed costs for 2012. The variable component of marketing costs equals the 6.5% sales commission on revenues paid to salespeople. The variable portion of distribution costs varies with cubic feet of tables moved.

The following data are available for the 2012 budget:

Direct materials	
Red Oak	$ 7 per board foot (b.f.) (same as in 2011)
Granite	$10 per square foot (sq. ft.) (same as in 2011)
Direct manufacturing labor	$20 per hour

Content of Each Product Unit

	Product	
	Casual Granite Table	Deluxe Granite Table
Red Oak	12 board feet	12 board feet
Granite	6 square feet	8 square feet
Direct manufacturing labor	4 hours	6 hours

	Product	
	Casual Granite Table	Deluxe Granite Table
Expected sales in units	50,000	10,000
Selling price	$ 600	$ 800
Target ending inventory in units	11,000	500
Beginning inventory in units	1,000	500
Beginning inventory in dollars	$384,000	$262,000

	Direct Materials	
	Red Oak	Granite
Beginning inventory	70,000 b.f.	60,000 sq. ft.
Target ending inventory	80,000 b.f.	20,000 sq. ft.

Stylistic bases its budgeted cost information on the costs it predicts it will incur to support its revenue budget, taking into account the efficiency improvements it expects to make in 2012. Recall from Step 3 in the decision-making process that efficiency improvements are critical to offset anticipated increases in the cost of inputs and to maintain Stylistic's 12% operating margin. Some companies rely heavily on past results when developing budgeted amounts; others rely on detailed engineering studies. Companies differ in how they compute their budgeted amounts.

Most companies have a budget manual that contains a company's particular instructions and relevant information for preparing its budgets. Although the details differ among companies, the following basic steps are common for developing the operating budget for a manufacturing company. Beginning with the revenues budget, each of the other budgets follows step-by-step in logical fashion.

Step 1: Prepare the Revenues Budget. A revenues budget, calculated in Schedule 1, is the usual starting point for the operating budget. That's because the production level and the inventory level—and therefore manufacturing costs—as well as nonmanufacturing costs, generally depend on the forecasted level of unit sales or revenues. Many factors influence the sales forecast, including the sales volume in recent periods, general economic and industry conditions, market research studies, pricing policies, advertising and sales promotions, competition, and regulatory policies. In Stylistic's case, the revenues budget for 2012 reflects Stylistic's strategy to grow revenues by increasing sales of Deluxe tables from 8,000 tables in 2011 to 10,000 tables in 2012.

Schedule 1: Revenues Budget
For the Year Ending December 31, 2012

	Units	Selling Price	Total Revenues
Casual	50,000	$600	$30,000,000
Deluxe	10,000	800	8,000,000
Total			$38,000,000

The $38,000,000 is the amount of revenues in the budgeted income statement. The revenues budget is often the result of elaborate information gathering and discussions among sales managers and sales representatives who have a detailed understanding of customer needs, market potential, and competitors' products. This information is often gathered through a customer response management (CRM) or sales management system. Statistical approaches such as regression and trend analysis can also help in sales forecasting. These techniques use indicators of economic activity and past sales data to forecast future sales. Managers should use statistical analysis only as one input to forecast sales. In the final analysis, the sales forecast should represent the collective experience and judgment of managers.

The usual starting point for Step 1 is to base revenues on expected demand. Occasionally, a factor other than demand limits budgeted revenues. For example, when demand is greater than available production capacity or a manufacturing input is in short supply, the revenues budget would be based on the maximum units that could be produced. Why? Because sales would be limited by the amount produced.

Step 2: Prepare the Production Budget (in Units). After revenues are budgeted, the manufacturing manager prepares the production budget, which is calculated in Schedule 2. The total finished goods units to be produced depend on budgeted unit sales and expected changes in units of inventory levels:

$$\begin{array}{c} \text{Budget} \\ \text{production} \\ \text{(units)} \end{array} = \begin{array}{c} \text{Budget} \\ \text{sales} \\ \text{(units)} \end{array} + \begin{array}{c} \text{Target ending} \\ \text{finished goods} \\ \text{inventory} \\ \text{(units)} \end{array} - \begin{array}{c} \text{Beginning} \\ \text{finished goods} \\ \text{inventory} \\ \text{(units)} \end{array}$$

Schedule 2: Production Budget (in Units)
For the Year Ending December 31, 2012

	Product	
	Casual	Deluxe
Budgeted unit sales (Schedule 1)	50,000	10,000
Add target ending finished goods inventory	11,000	500
Total required units	61,000	10,500
Deduct beginning finished goods inventory	1,000	500
Units of finished goods to be produced	60,000	10,000

Step 3: Prepare the Direct Material Usage Budget and Direct Material Purchases Budget. The number of units to be produced, calculated in Schedule 2, is the key to computing the usage of direct materials in quantities and in dollars. The direct material quantities used depend on the efficiency with which materials are consumed to produce a table. In determining budgets, managers are constantly anticipating ways to make process improvements that increase quality and reduce waste, thereby reducing direct material usage and costs.

Like many companies, Stylistic has a *bill of materials*, stored and updated in its computer systems. This document identifies how each product is manufactured, specifying all materials (and components), the sequence in which the materials are used, the quantity of materials in each finished unit, and the work centers where the operations are performed. For example, the bill of materials would indicate that 12 board feet of red oak and 6 square feet of granite are needed to produce each Casual coffee table, and 12 board feet of red oak and 8 square feet of granite to produce each Deluxe coffee table. This information is then used to calculate the amounts in Schedule 3A.

Schedule 3A: Direct Material Usage Budget in Quantity and Dollars
For the Year Ending December 31, 2012

	Material		
	Red Oak	Granite	Total
Physical Units Budget			
Direct materials required for Casual tables (60,000 units × 12 b.f. and 6 sq. ft.)	720,000 b.f.	360,000 sq. ft.	
Direct materials required for Deluxe tables (10,000 units × 12 b.f. and 8 sq. ft.)	120,000 b.f.	80,000 sq. ft.	
Total quantity of direct materials to be used	840,000 b.f.	440,000 sq. ft.	
Cost Budget			
Available from beginning direct materials inventory (under a FIFO cost-flow assumption)			
Red Oak: 70,000 b.f. × $7 per b.f.	$ 490,000		
Granite: 60,000 sq. ft. × $10 per sq. ft.		$ 600,000	
To be purchased this period			
Red Oak: (840,000 − 70,000) b.f. × $7 per b.f.	5,390,000		
Granite: (440,000 − 60,000) sq. ft. × $10 per sq. ft.		3,800,000	
Direct materials to be used this period	$5,880,000	$4,400,000	$10,280,000

The purchasing manager prepares the budget for direct material purchases, calculated in Schedule 3B, based on the budgeted direct materials to be used, the beginning inventory of direct materials, and the target ending inventory of direct materials:

$$\begin{matrix} \text{Purchases} \\ \text{of direct} \\ \text{materials} \end{matrix} = \begin{matrix} \text{Direct} \\ \text{materials} \\ \text{used in} \\ \text{production} \end{matrix} + \begin{matrix} \text{Target ending} \\ \text{inventory} \\ \text{of direct} \\ \text{materials} \end{matrix} - \begin{matrix} \text{Beginning} \\ \text{inventory} \\ \text{of direct} \\ \text{materials} \end{matrix}$$

Schedule 3B: Direct Material Purchases Budget
For the Year Ending December 31, 2012

	Material Red Oak	Material Granite	Total
Physical Units Budget			
To be used in production (from Schedule 3A)	840,000 b.f.	440,000 sq. ft.	
Add target ending inventory	80,000 b.f.	20,000 sq. ft.	
Total requirements	920,000 b.f.	460,000 sq. ft.	
Deduct beginning inventory	70,000 b.f.	60,000 sq. ft.	
Purchases to be made	850,000 b.f.	400,000 sq. ft.	
Cost Budget			
Red Oak: 850,000 b.f. × $7 per b.f.	$5,950,000		
Granite: 400,000 sq. ft. × $10 per sq. ft.		$4,000,000	
Purchases	$5,950,000	$4,000,000	$9,950,000

Step 4: Prepare the Direct Manufacturing Labor Costs Budget. In this step, manufacturing managers use *labor standards*, the time allowed per unit of output, to calculate the direct manufacturing labor costs budget in Schedule 4. These costs depend on wage rates, production methods, process and efficiency improvements, and hiring plans.

Schedule 4: Direct Manufacturing Labor Costs Budget
For the Year Ending December 31, 2012

	Output Units Produced (Schedule 2)	Direct Manufacturing Labor-Hours per Unit	Total Hours	Hourly Wage Rate	Total
Casual	60,000	4	240,000	$20	$4,800,000
Deluxe	10,000	6	60,000	20	1,200,000
Total			300,000		$6,000,000

Step 5: Prepare the Manufacturing Overhead Costs Budget. As we described earlier, direct manufacturing labor-hours is the cost driver for the variable portion of manufacturing operations overhead and setup labor-hours is the cost driver for the variable portion of machine setup overhead costs. The use of activity-based cost drivers such as these gives rise to *activity-based budgeting*. **Activity-based budgeting (ABB)** focuses on the budgeted cost of the activities necessary to produce and sell products and services.

For the 300,000 direct manufacturing labor-hours, Stylistic's manufacturing managers estimate various line items of overhead costs that constitute manufacturing operations overhead (that is, all costs for which direct manufacturing labor-hours is the cost driver). Managers identify opportunities for process improvements and determine budgeted manufacturing operations overhead costs in the operating department. They also determine the resources that they will need from the two support departments—kilowatt hours of energy from the power department and hours of maintenance service from the maintenance department. The support department managers, in turn, plan the costs of personnel and supplies that they will need in order to provide the operating department with the support services it requires. The costs of the support departments are then allocated (first-stage cost allocation) as part of manufacturing operations overhead. The allocation of support department costs to operating departments is done when support departments provide services to each other and to operating departments. The upper half of Schedule 5 shows the various line items of costs that constitute manufacturing operations overhead costs—that is, all overhead costs that are caused by the 300,000 direct manufacturing labor-hours (the cost driver).

Stylistic's managers determine how setups should be done for the Casual and Deluxe line of tables, taking into account past experiences and potential improvements in setup efficiency.

For example, managers consider the following:

- Increasing the length of the production run per batch so that fewer batches (and therefore fewer setups) are needed for the budgeted production of tables
- Decreasing the setup time per batch
- Reducing the supervisory time needed, for instance by increasing the skill base of workers

Stylistic's managers forecast the following setup information for the Casual and Deluxe tables:

	Casual Tables	Deluxe Tables	Total
1. Quantity of tables to be produced	60,000 tables	10,000 tables	
2. Number of tables to be produced per batch	50 tables/batch	40 tables/batch	
3. Number of batches (1) ÷ (2)	1,200 batches	250 batches	
4. Setup time per batch	10 hours/batch	12 hours/batch	
5. Total setup-hours (3) × (4)	12,000 hours	3,000 hours	15,000 hours
6. Setup-hours per table (5) ÷ (1)	0.2 hour	0.3 hour	

Using an approach similar to the one described for manufacturing operations overhead costs, Stylistic's managers estimate various line items of costs that comprise machine setup overhead costs—that is, all costs that are caused by the 15,000 setup labor-hours (the cost driver). Note how using activity-based cost drivers provide additional and detailed information that improves decision making compared with budgeting based solely on output-based cost drivers. Of course, managers must always evaluate whether the expected benefit of adding more cost drivers exceeds the expected cost.[5] The bottom half of Schedule 5 summarizes these costs.

Schedule 5: Manufacturing Overhead Costs Budget
For the Year Ending December 31, 2012
Manufacturing Operations Overhead Costs

Variable costs		
Supplies	$1,500,000	
Indirect manufacturing labor	1,680,000	
Power (support department costs)	2,100,000	
Maintenance (support department costs)	1,200,000	$6,480,000
Fixed costs (to support capacity of 300,000 direct manufacturing labor-hours)		
Depreciation	1,020,000	
Supervision	390,000	
Power (support department costs)	630,000	
Maintenance (support department costs)	480,000	2,520,000
Total manufacturing operations overhead costs		$9,000,000

Machine Setup Overhead Costs

Variable costs		
Supplies	$ 390,000	
Indirect manufacturing labor	840,000	
Power (support department costs)	90,000	$ 1,320,000
Fixed costs (to support capacity of 15,000 setup labor-hours)		
Depreciation	603,000	
Supervision	1,050,000	
Power (support department costs)	27,000	1,680,000
Total machine setup overhead costs		$ 3,000,000
Total manufacturing operations overhead costs		$12,000,000

[5] The Stylistic example illustrates ABB using setup costs included in Stylistic's manufacturing overhead costs budget. ABB implementations in practice include costs in many parts of the value chain. For an example, see S. Borjesson, "A Case Study on Activity-Based Budgeting," *Journal of Cost Management* 10, no. 4: 7–18.

Step 6:   Prepare the Ending Inventories Budget. The management accountant prepares the ending inventories budget, calculated in Schedules 6A and 6B. In accordance with generally accepted accounting principles, Stylistic treats both variable and fixed manufacturing overhead as inventoriable (product) costs. Stylistic is budgeted to operate at capacity. Manufacturing operations overhead costs are allocated to finished goods inventory at the budgeted rate of $30 per direct manufacturing labor-hour (total budgeted manufacturing operations overhead, $9,000,000 ÷ 300,000 budgeted direct manufacturing labor-hours). Machine setup overhead costs are allocated to finished goods inventory at the budgeted rate of $200 per setup-hour (total budgeted machine setup overhead, $3,000,000 ÷ 15,000 budgeted setup labor-hours). Schedule 6A shows the computation of the unit cost of coffee tables started and completed in 2012.

Schedule 6A: Unit Costs of Ending Finished Goods Inventory
December 31, 2012

		Product			
		Casual Tables		Deluxe Tables	
	Cost per Unit of Input	Input per Unit of Output	Total	Input per Unit of Output	Total
Red Oak	$ 7	12 b.f.	$ 84	12 b.f.	$ 84
Granite	10	6 sq. ft.	60	8 sq. ft.	80
Direct manufacturing labor	20	4 hrs.	80	6 hrs.	120
Manufacturing overhead	30	4 hrs.	120	6 hrs.	180
Machine setup overhead	200	0.2 hrs.	40	0.3 hrs.	60
Total			$384		$524

Under the FIFO method, this unit cost is used to calculate the cost of target ending inventories of finished goods in Schedule 6B.

Schedule 6B: Ending Inventories Budget
December 31, 2012

	Quantity	Cost per Unit		Total
Direct materials				
Red Oak	80,000*	$ 7	$ 560,000	
Granite	20,000*	10	200,000	$ 760,000
Finished goods				
Casual	11,000**	$384***	$4,224,000	
Deluxe	500**	524***	262,000	4,486,000
Total ending inventory				$5,246,000

*Data are from page 191. **Data are from page 191 ***From Schedule 6A, this is based on 2012 costs of manufacturing finished goods because under the FIFO costing method, the units in finished goods ending inventory consists of units that are produced during 2012.

Step 7:   Prepare the Cost of Goods Sold Budget. The manufacturing and purchase managers, together with the management accountant, use information from Schedules 3 through 6 to prepare Schedule 7.

Schedule 7: Cost of Goods Sold Budget
For the Year Ending December 31, 2012

	From Schedule		Total
Beginning finished goods inventory, January 1, 2012	Given*		$ 646,000
Direct materials used	3A	$10,280,000	
Direct manufacturing labor	4	6,000,000	
Manufacturing overhead	5	12,000,000	
Cost of goods manufactured			28,280,000
Cost of goods available for sale			28,926,000
Deduct ending finished goods inventory, December 31, 2012	6B		4,486,000
Cost of goods sold			$24,440,000

*Given in the description of basic data and requirements (Casual, $384,000, Deluxe $262,000).

Step 8: Prepare the Nonmanufacturing Costs Budget. Schedules 2 through 7 cover budgeting for Stylistic's production function of the value chain. For brevity, other parts of the value chain—product design, marketing, and distribution—are combined into a single schedule. Just as in the case of manufacturing costs, managers in other functions of the value chain build in process and efficiency improvements and prepare nonmanufacturing cost budgets on the basis of the quantities of cost drivers planned for 2012.

Product design costs are fixed costs, determined on the basis of the product design work anticipated for 2012. The variable component of budgeted marketing costs is the commissions paid to sales people equal to 6.5% of revenues. The fixed component of budgeted marketing costs equal to $1,330,000 is tied to the marketing capacity for 2012. The cost driver of the variable component of budgeted distribution costs is cubic feet of tables moved (Casual: 18 cubic feet × 50,000 tables + Deluxe: 24 cubic feet × 10,000 tables = 1,140,000 cubic feet). Variable distribution costs equal $2 per cubic foot. The fixed component of budgeted distribution costs equals $1,596,000 and is tied to the distribution capacity for 2012. Schedule 8 shows the product design, marketing, and distribution costs budget for 2012.

Schedule 8: Nonmanufacturing Costs Budget
For the Year Ending December 31, 2012

Business Function	Variable Costs	Fixed Costs	Total Costs
Product design	—	$1,024,000	$1,024,000
Marketing (Variable cost: $38,000,000 × 0.065)	$2,470,000	1,330,000	3,800,000
Distribution (Variable cost: $2 × 1,140,000 cu. ft.)	2,280,000	1,596,000	3,876,000
	$4,750,000	$3,950,000	$8,700,000

Step 9: Prepare the Budgeted Income Statement. The CEO and managers of various business functions, with help from the management accountant, use information in Schedules 1, 7, and 8 to finalize the budgeted income statement, shown in Exhibit 3. The style used in Exhibit 3 is typical, but more details could be included in the income statement; the more details that are put in the income statement, the fewer supporting schedules that are needed for the income statement.

Budgeting is a cross-functional activity. Top management's strategies for achieving revenue and operating income goals influence the costs planned for the different business functions of the value chain. For example, a budgeted increase in sales based on spending more for marketing must be matched with higher production costs to ensure that there is an adequate supply of tables and with higher distribution costs to ensure timely delivery of tables to customers.

Rex Jordan, the CEO of Stylistic Furniture, is very pleased with the 2012 budget. It calls for a 10% increase in operating income compared with 2011. The keys to achieving a higher operating income are a significant increase in sales of Deluxe tables, and process improvements and efficiency gains throughout the value chain. As Rex studies the budget

Exhibit 3

Budgeted Income Statement for Stylistic Furniture

	A	B	C	D
1	Budgeted Income Statement for Stylistic Furniture			
2	For the Year Ending December 31, 2012			
3	Revenues	Schedule 1		$38,000,000
4	Cost of goods sold	Schedule 7		24,440,000
5	Gross margin			13,560,000
6	Operating costs			
7	Product design costs	Schedule 8	$1,024,000	
8	Marketing costs	Schedule 8	3,800,000	
9	Distribution costs	Schedule 8	3,876,000	8,700,000
10	Operating income			$ 4,860,000

more carefully, however, he is struck by two comments appended to the budget: First, to achieve the budgeted number of tables sold, Stylistic may need to reduce its selling prices by 3% to $582 for Casual tables and to $776 for Deluxe tables. Second, a supply shortage in direct materials may result in a 5% increase in the prices of direct materials (red oak and granite) above the material prices anticipated in the 2012 budget. If direct materials prices increase, however, no reduction in selling prices is anticipated. He asks Tina Larsen, the management accountant, to use Stylistic's financial planning model to evaluate how these outcomes will affect budgeted operating income.

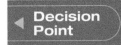

Decision Point

What is the operating budget and what are its components?

Financial Planning Models and Sensitivity Analysis

Financial planning models are mathematical representations of the relationships among operating activities, financing activities, and other factors that affect the master budget. Companies can use computer-based systems, such as Enterprise Resource Planning (ERP) systems, to perform calculations for these planning models. Companies that use ERP systems, and other such budgeting tools, find that these systems simplify budgeting and reduce the computational burden and time required to prepare budgets. The Concepts in Action box on the next page provides an example of one such company. ERP systems store vast quantities of information about the materials, machines and equipment, labor, power, maintenance, and setups needed to manufacture different products. Once sales quantities for different products have been identified, the software can quickly compute the budgeted costs for manufacturing these products.

Learning Objective 4

Use computer-based financial planning models in sensitivity analysis

. . . for example, understand the effects of changes in selling prices and direct material prices on budgeted income

Software packages typically have a module on sensitivity analysis to assist managers in their planning and budgeting activities. *Sensitivity analysis* is a "what-if" technique that examines how a result will change if the original predicted data are not achieved or if an underlying assumption changes.

To see how sensitivity analysis works, we consider two scenarios identified as possibly affecting Stylistic Furniture's budget model for 2012.

Scenario 1: A 3% decrease in the selling price of the Casual table and a 3% decrease in the selling price of the Deluxe table.

Scenario 2: A 5% increase in the price per board foot of red oak and a 5% increase in the price per square foot of granite.

Exhibit 4 presents the budgeted operating income for the two scenarios.

Note that under Scenario 1, a change in selling prices per table affects revenues (Schedule 1) as well as variable marketing costs (sales commissions, Schedule 8). The Problem for Self-Study at the end of the chapter shows the revised schedules for Scenario 1. Similarly, a change in the price of direct materials affects the direct material usage budget (Schedule 3A), the unit cost of ending finished goods inventory (Schedule 6A), the ending

Exhibit 4   Effect of Changes in Budget Assumptions on Budgeted Operating Income for Stylistic Furniture

	Home	Insert	Page Layout	Formulas	Data	Review	View		
	A	B	C	D	E	F	G	H	I
1	Key Assumptions								
2		Units Sold		Selling Price		Direct Material Cost		Budgeted Operating Income	
3	What-If Scenario	Casual	Deluxe	Casual	Deluxe	Red Oak	Granite	Dollars	Change from Master Budget
4	Master budget	50,000	10,000	$600	$800	$7.00	$10.00	$4,860,000	
5	Scenario 1	50,000	10,000	582	776	$7.00	$10.00	3,794,100	22% decrease
6	Scenario 2	50,000	10,000	600	800	$7.35	$10.50	4,483,800	8% decrease

Concepts in Action   Web-Enabled Budgeting and Hendrick Motorsports

Getty Images, Inc.

In recent years, an increasing number of companies have implemented comprehensive software packages that manage budgeting and forecasting functions across the organization. One such option is Microsoft Forecaster, which was originally designed by FRx Software for businesses looking to gain control over their budgeting and forecasting process within a fully integrated Web-based environment.

Among the more unique companies implementing Web-enabled budgeting is Hendrick Motorsports. Featuring champion drivers Jeff Gordon and Jimmie Johnson, Hendrick is the premier NASCAR Sprint Cup stock car racing organization. According to Forbes magazine, Hendrick is NASCAR's most valuable team, with an estimated value of $350 million. Headquartered on a 12 building, 600,000-square-foot campus near Charlotte, North Carolina, Hendrick operates four full-time teams in the Sprint Cup series, which runs annually from February through November and features 36 races at 22 speedways across the United States. The Hendrick organization has annual revenues of close to $195 million and more than 500 employees, with tasks ranging from accounting and marketing to engine building and racecar driving. Such an environment features multiple functional areas and units, varied worksites, and ever-changing circumstances. Patrick Perkins, director of marketing, noted, "Racing is a fast business. It's just as fast off the track as it is on it. With the work that we put into development of our teams and technologies, and having to respond to change as well as anticipate change, I like to think of us in this business as change experts."

Microsoft Forecaster, Hendrick's Web-enabled budgeting package, has allowed Hendrick's financial managers to seamlessly manage the planning and budgeting process. Authorized users from each functional area or team sign on to the application through the corporate intranet. Security on the system is tight: Access is limited to only the accounts that a manager is authorized to budget. (For example, Jeff Gordon's crew chief is not able to see what Jimmie Johnson's team members are doing.) Forecaster also allows users at the racetrack to access the application remotely, which allows mangers to receive or update real-time "actuals" from the system. This way, team managers know their allotted expenses for each race. Forecaster also provides users with additional features, including seamless links with general ledger accounts and the option to perform what-if (sensitivity) analyses. Scott Lampe, chief financial officer, said, "Forecaster allows us to change our forecasts to respond to changes, either rule changes [such as changes in the series' points system] or technology changes [such as pilot testing NASCAR's new, safer "Car of Tomorrow"] throughout the racing season."

Hendrick's Web-enabled budgeting system frees the finance department so it can work on strategy, analysis, and decision making. It also allows Hendrick to complete its annual budgeting process in only six weeks, a 50% reduction in the time spent budgeting and planning, which is critical given NASCAR's extremely short off-season. Patrick Pearson from Hendrick Motorsports believes the system gives the organization a competitive advantage: "In racing, the team that wins is not only the team with the fastest car, but the team that is the most disciplined and prepared week in and week out. Forecaster allows us to respond to that changing landscape."

Sources: Gage, Jack. 2009. Nascar's most valuable teams. Forbes.com, June 3. http://www.forbes.com/2009/06/03/nascar-most-valuable-teams-business-sports-nascar.html; Goff, John. 2004. In the fast lane. *CFO Magazine*, December 1; Hendrick Motorsports. 2010. About Hendrick Motorsports. Hendrick Motorsports Web site, May 28. www.hendrickmotorsports.com; Lampe, Scott. 2003. NASCAR racing team stays on track with FRx Software's comprehensive budget planning solution. *DM Review*, July 1; Microsoft Corporation. 2009. Microsoft Forecaster: Hendrick Motorsports customer video. October 8. http://www.microsoft.com/BusinessSolutions/frx_hendrick_video.mspx; Ryan, Nate. 2006. Hendrick empire strikes back with three contenders in chase for the Nextel Cup. *USA Today*, September 17.

finished goods inventories budget (in Schedule 6B) and the cost of goods sold budget (Schedule 7). Sensitivity analysis is especially useful in incorporating such interrelationships into budgeting decisions by managers.

Exhibit 4 shows a substantial decrease in operating income as a result of decreases in selling prices but a smaller decline in operating income if direct material prices increase by 5%. The sensitivity analysis prompts Stylistic's managers to put in place contingency plans. For example, should selling prices decline in 2012, Stylistic may choose to postpone some product development programs that it had included in its 2012 budget but that could be deferred to a later year. More generally, when the success or viability of a venture is highly dependent on attaining one or more targets, managers should frequently update their budgets as uncertainty is resolved. These updated budgets can help managers to adjust expenditure levels as circumstances change.

Instructors and students who, at this point, want to explore the cash budget and the budgeted balance sheet for the Stylistic Furniture example can skip ahead to the appendix at the end of this chapter.

Budgeting and Responsibility Accounting

To attain the goals described in the master budget, a company must coordinate the efforts of all its employees—from the top executive through all levels of management to every supervised worker. Coordinating the company's efforts means assigning responsibility to managers who are accountable for their actions in planning and controlling human and other resources. How each company structures its own organization significantly shapes how the company's efforts will be coordinated.

Organization Structure and Responsibility

Organization structure is an arrangement of lines of responsibility within the organization. A company such as ExxonMobil is organized by business function—exploration, refining, marketing, and so on—with the president of each business-line company having decision-making authority over his or her function. Another company, such as Procter & Gamble, the household-products giant, is organized primarily by product line or brand. The managers of the individual divisions (toothpaste, soap, and so on) would each have decision-making authority concerning all the business functions (manufacturing, marketing, and so on) within that division.

Each manager, regardless of level, is in charge of a responsibility center. A **responsibility center** is a part, segment, or subunit of an organization whose manager is accountable for a specified set of activities. The higher the manager's level, the broader the responsibility center and the larger the number of his or her subordinates. **Responsibility accounting** is a system that measures the plans, budgets, actions, and actual results of each responsibility center. Four types of responsibility centers are as follows:

1. **Cost center**—the manager is accountable for costs only.
2. **Revenue center**—the manager is accountable for revenues only.
3. **Profit center**—the manager is accountable for revenues and costs.
4. **Investment center**—the manager is accountable for investments, revenues, and costs.

The maintenance department of a Marriott hotel is a cost center because the maintenance manager is responsible only for costs, so this budget is based on costs. The sales department is a revenue center because the sales manager is responsible primarily for revenues, so this budget is based on revenues. The hotel manager is in charge of a profit center because the manager is accountable for both revenues and costs, so this budget is based on revenues and costs. The regional manager responsible for determining the amount to be invested in new hotel projects and for revenues and costs generated from these investments is in charge of an investment center, so this budget is based on revenues, costs, and the investment base.

A responsibility center can be structured to promote better alignment of individual and company goals. For example, until recently, OPD, an office products distributor, operated its sales department as a revenue center. Each salesperson received a commission of 3% of the revenues per order, regardless of its size, the cost of processing it, or the cost of delivering the office products. An analysis of customer profitability at OPD found that many customers were unprofitable. The main reason was the high ordering and delivery costs of small orders. OPD's managers decided to make the sales department a profit center, accountable for revenues and costs, and to change the incentive system for salespeople

Decision Point

How can managers plan for changes in the assumptions underlying the budget?

Learning Objective 5

Describe responsibility centers

. . . a part of an organization that a manager is accountable for

and responsibility accounting

. . . measurement of plans and actual results that a manager is accountable for

to 15% of the monthly profits per customer. The costs for each customer included the ordering and delivery costs. The effect of this change was immediate. The sales department began charging customers for ordering and delivery, and salespeople at OPD actively encouraged customers to consolidate their purchases into fewer orders. As a result, each order began producing larger revenues. Customer profitability increased because of a 40% reduction in ordering and delivery costs in one year.

Feedback

Budgets coupled with responsibility accounting provide feedback to top management about the performance relative to the budget of different responsibility center managers.

Differences between actual results and budgeted amounts—called *variances*—if properly used, can help managers implement and evaluate strategies in three ways:

1. *Early warning.* Variances alert managers early to events not easily or immediately evident. Managers can then take corrective actions or exploit the available opportunities. For example, after observing a small decline in sales this period, managers may want to investigate if this is an indication of an even steeper decline to follow later in the year.

2. *Performance evaluation.* Variances prompt managers to probe how well the company has performed in implementing its strategies. Were materials and labor used efficiently? Was R&D spending increased as planned? Did product warranty costs decrease as planned?

3. *Evaluating strategy.* Variances sometimes signal to managers that their strategies are ineffective. For example, a company seeking to compete by reducing costs and improving quality may find that it is achieving these goals but that it is having little effect on sales and profits. Top management may then want to reevaluate the strategy.

Responsibility and Controllability

Controllability is the degree of influence that a specific manager has over costs, revenues, or related items for which he or she is responsible. A **controllable cost** is any cost that is primarily subject to the influence of a given *responsibility center manager* for a given *period.* A responsibility accounting system could either exclude all uncontrollable costs from a manager's performance report or segregate such costs from the controllable costs. For example, a machining supervisor's performance report might be confined to direct materials, direct manufacturing labor, power, and machine maintenance costs and might exclude costs such as rent and taxes paid on the plant.

In practice, controllability is difficult to pinpoint for at least two reasons:

1. Few costs are clearly under the sole influence of one manager. For example, prices of direct materials may be influenced by a purchasing manager, but these prices also depend on market conditions beyond the manager's control. Quantities used may be influenced by a production manager, but quantities used also depend on the quality of materials purchased. Moreover, managers often work in teams. Think about how difficult it is to evaluate individual responsibility in a team situation.

2. With a long enough time span, all costs will come under somebody's control. However, most performance reports focus on periods of a year or less. A current manager may benefit from a predecessor's accomplishments or may inherit a predecessor's problems and inefficiencies. For example, present managers may have to work under undesirable contracts with suppliers or labor unions that were negotiated by their predecessors. How can we separate what the current manager actually controls from the results of decisions made by others? Exactly what is the current manager accountable for? Answers may not be clear-cut.

Executives differ in how they embrace the controllability notion when evaluating those reporting to them. Some CEOs regard the budget as a firm commitment that subordinates must meet. Failure to meet the budget is viewed unfavorably. Other CEOs believe a more risk-sharing approach with managers is preferable, in which noncontrollable factors and performance relative to competitors are taken into account when judging the performance of managers who fail to meet their budgets.

Managers should avoid overemphasizing controllability. Responsibility accounting is more far-reaching. It focuses on gaining *information and knowledge*, not only on control. *Responsibility accounting helps managers to first focus on whom they should ask to obtain information and not on whom they should blame.* For example, if actual revenues at a Marriott hotel are less than budgeted revenues, the managers of the hotel may be tempted to blame the sales manager for the poor performance. The fundamental purpose of responsibility accounting, however, is not to fix blame but to gather information to enable future improvement.

Managers want to know who can tell them the most about the specific item in question, regardless of that person's ability to exert personal control over that item. For instance, purchasing managers may be held accountable for total purchase costs, not because of their ability to control market prices, but because of their ability to predict uncontrollable prices and to explain uncontrollable price changes. Similarly, managers at a Pizza Hut unit may be held responsible for operating income of their units, even though they (a) do not fully control selling prices or the costs of many food items and (b) have minimal flexibility about what items to sell or the ingredients in the items they sell. They are, however, in the best position to explain differences between their actual operating incomes and their budgeted operating incomes.

Performance reports for responsibility centers are sometimes designed to change managers' behavior in the direction top management desires. A cost-center manager may emphasize efficiency and deemphasize the pleas of sales personnel for faster service and rush orders. When evaluated as a profit center, the manager will more likely consider ways to influence activities that affect sales and weigh the impact of decisions on costs and revenues rather than on costs alone. To induce that change, some companies have changed the accountability of a cost center to a profit center. Call centers are an interesting example of this trend. As firms continue to differentiate on customer service while attempting to control operating expenses, driving efficiency wherever possible in the call centers has become a critical issue—as has driving revenue through this unique channel. There is increasing pressure for customer service representatives to promote new offers through upsell and cross-sell tactics. Microsoft, Oracle, and others offer software platforms that seek to evolve the call center from cost center to profit center. The new adage is, "Every service call is a sales call."

Decision Point

How do companies use responsibility centers? Should performance reports of responsibility center managers include only costs the manager can control?

Human Aspects of Budgeting

Why did we discuss the two major topics, the master budget and responsibility accounting, in the same chapter? Primarily to emphasize that human factors are crucial in budgeting. Too often, budgeting is thought of as a mechanical tool as the budgeting techniques themselves are free of emotion. However, the administration of budgeting requires education, persuasion, and intelligent interpretation.

Learning Objective 6

Recognize the human aspects of budgeting

. . . to engage subordinate managers in the budgeting process

Budgetary Slack

As we discussed earlier in this chapter, budgeting is most effective when lower-level managers actively participate and meaningfully engage in the budgeting process. Participation adds credibility to the budgeting process and creates greater commitment and accountability toward the budget. But participation requires "honest" communication about the business from subordinates and lower-level managers to their bosses.

At times, subordinates may try to "play games" and build in *budgetary slack*. **Budgetary slack** describes the practice of underestimating budgeted revenues, or overestimating budgeted costs, to make budgeted targets more easily achievable. It frequently occurs when budget variances (the differences between actual results and budgeted amounts) are used to evaluate performance. Line managers are also unlikely to be fully honest in their budget communications if top management mechanically institutes across-the-board cost reductions (say, a 10% reduction in all areas) in the face of projected revenue reductions.

Budgetary slack provides managers with a hedge against unexpected adverse circumstances. But budgetary slack also misleads top management about the true profit potential of the company, which leads to inefficient resource planning and allocation and poor coordination of activities across different parts of the company.

To avoid problems of budgetary slack, some companies use budgets primarily for planning purposes. They evaluate managerial performance using multiple indicators that take into account various factors such as the prevailing business environment and performance relative to competitors. Evaluating performance in this way takes time and requires careful exercise of judgment. Other companies use budgets for both planning and performance evaluation and use different approaches to obtain accurate information.

To explain one approach, let's consider the plant manager of a beverage bottler who is suspected by top management of understating the productivity potential of the bottling lines in his forecasts for the coming year. His presumed motivation is to increase the likelihood of meeting next year's production bonus targets. Suppose top management could purchase a consulting firm's study that reports productivity levels—such as the number of bottles filled per hour—at a number of comparable plants owned by other bottling companies. This report shows that its own plant manager's productivity forecasts are well below the actual productivity levels being achieved at other comparable plants.

Top management could share this independent information source with the plant manager and ask him to explain why his productivity differs from that at other similar plants. Management could also base part of the plant manager's compensation on his plant's productivity in comparison with other "benchmark" plants rather than on the forecasts he provided. Using external benchmark performance measures reduces a manager's ability to set budget levels that are easy to achieve.[6]

Another approach to reducing budgetary slack is for managers to involve themselves regularly in understanding what their subordinates are doing. Such involvement should not result in managers dictating the decisions and actions of subordinates. Rather, a manager's involvement should take the form of providing support, challenging in a motivational way the assumptions subordinates make, and enhancing mutual learning about the operations. Regular interaction with subordinates allows managers to become knowledgeable about the operations and diminishes the ability of subordinates to create slack in their budgets.

Part of top management's responsibility is to promote commitment among the employees to a set of core values and norms. These values and norms describe what constitutes acceptable and unacceptable behavior. For example, Johnson & Johnson (J&J) has a credo that describes its responsibilities to doctors, patients, employees, communities, and shareholders. Employees are trained in the credo to help them understand the behavior that is expected of them. Managers are often promoted from within and are therefore very familiar with the work of the employees reporting to them. Managers also have the responsibility to interact with and mentor their subordinates. These values and practices create a culture at J&J that discourages budgetary slack.

Some companies, such as IBM and Kodak, have designed innovative performance evaluation measures that reward managers based on the subsequent accuracy of the forecasts used in preparing budgets. For example, the *higher and more accurate* the budgeted profit forecasts of division managers, the higher their incentive bonuses.

Many of the best performing companies, such as General Electric, Microsoft, and Novartis, set "stretch" targets. Stretch targets are challenging but achievable levels of expected performance, intended to create a little discomfort and to motivate employees to exert extra effort and attain better performance. Organizations such as Goldman Sachs also use "horizontal" stretch goal initiatives. The aim is to enhance professional development of employees by asking them to take on significantly different responsibilities or roles outside their comfort zone.

Many managers regard budgets negatively. To them, the word budget is about as popular as, say, *downsizing, layoff,* or *strike.* Top managers must convince their subordinates that the budget is a tool designed to help them set and reach goals. Whatever the manager's perspective on budgets—pro or con—budgets are not remedies for weak management talent, faulty organization, or a poor accounting system.

---

[6] For an excellent discussion of these issues, see Chapter 14 ("Formal Models in Budgeting and Incentive Contracts") of R. S. Kaplan and A. A. Atkinson, *Advanced Management Accounting,* 3rd ed. (Upper Saddle River, NJ: Prentice Hall, 1998).

The management style of executives is a factor in how budgets are perceived in companies. Some CEOs argue that "numbers always tell the story." An executive once noted, "You can miss your plan once, but you wouldn't want to miss it twice." Other CEOs believe "too much focus on making the numbers in a budget" can lead to poor decision making and unethical practices.

Kaizen Budgeting

We have noted the importance of continuous improvement, or *kaizen* in Japanese. **Kaizen budgeting** explicitly incorporates continuous improvement anticipated during the budget period into the budget numbers. Many companies that have cost reduction as a strategic focus, including General Electric in the United States and Citizens Watch and Toyota in Japan, use kaizen budgeting to continuously reduce costs. Much of the cost reduction associated with kaizen budgeting arises from many small improvements rather than "quantum leaps."

A significant aspect of kaizen budgeting is employee suggestions. Companies implementing kaizen budgeting believe that employees who actually do the job, whether in manufacturing, sales, or distribution, have the best information and knowledge of how the job can be done better. These companies create a culture in which employee suggestions are valued, recognized, and rewarded.

As an example, throughout our nine budgeting steps for Stylistic Furniture, we assumed four hours of direct labor time to manufacture each Casual coffee table. A kaizen budgeting approach would incorporate continuous improvement resulting from, for example, employee suggestions for doing the work faster or reducing idle time. The kaizen budget might then prescribe 4.00 direct manufacturing labor-hours per table for the first quarter of 2012, 3.95 hours for the second quarter, 3.90 hours for the third quarter, and so on. The implications of these reductions would be lower direct manufacturing labor costs, as well as lower variable manufacturing overhead costs, because direct manufacturing labor is the driver of these costs. If these continuous improvement goals are not met, Stylistic's managers will explore the reasons behind it and either adjust the targets or implement process changes that will accelerate continuous improvement.

Kaizen budgeting can also be applied to activities such as setups with the goal of reducing setup time and setup costs, or distribution with the goal of reducing the cost of moving each cubic foot of table. Kaizen budgeting and budgeting for specific activities are key building blocks of the master budget. Interestingly, companies are not the only ones interested in kaizen techniques. A growing number of cash-strapped states in the United States are bringing together government workers, regulators, and end users of government processes to identify ways to attack inefficiencies arising from bureaucratic procedures. Environmental regulators, whose cumbersome processes have long been the targets of business developers, have taken particular interest in kaizen. By the end of 2008, 29 state environmental agencies had conducted a kaizen session or were planning one.[7] How successful these efforts will be depends heavily on human factors such as the commitment and engagement of the individuals involved.

◄ Decision Point

Why are human factors crucial in budgeting?

Budgeting in Multinational Companies

Multinational companies, such as Federal Express, Kraft, and Pfizer, have operations in many countries. An international presence carries with it positives—access to new markets and resources—and negatives—operating in less-familiar business environments and exposure to currency fluctuations. For example, multinational companies earn revenues and incur expenses in many different currencies, and they must translate their operating performance into a single currency (say, U.S. dollars) for reporting results to their shareholders each quarter. This translation is based on the average exchange rates that prevail during the quarter. That is, in addition to budgeting in different currencies, management accountants in multinational companies also need to budget for foreign exchange rates. This is difficult because management accountants need to anticipate potential changes

Learning Objective 7

Appreciate the special challenges of budgeting in multinational companies

. . . exposure to currency fluctuations and to different legal, political, and economic environments

---

[7] For details, see "State governments, including Ohio's, embrace Kaizen to seek efficiency via Japanese methods," www.cleveland.com, (December 12, 2008).

that might take place during the year. Exchange rates are constantly fluctuating, so to reduce the possible negative impact on performance caused by unfavorable exchange rate movements, finance managers will frequently use sophisticated techniques such as forward, future, and option contracts to minimize exposure to foreign currency fluctuations. Besides currency issues, multinational companies need to understand the political, legal, and, in particular, economic environments of the different countries in which they operate. For example, in countries such as Zimbabwe, Iraq, and Guinea, annual inflation rates are very high, resulting in sharp declines in the value of the local currency. Issues related to differences in tax regimes are also critical, especially when the company transfers goods or services across the many countries in which it operates.

Multinational companies find budgeting to be a valuable tool when operating in very uncertain environments. As circumstances and conditions change, companies revise their budgets. The purpose of budgeting in such environments is not to evaluate performance relative to budgets, which is a meaningless comparison when conditions are so volatile, but to help managers throughout the organization to learn and to adapt their plans to the changing conditions and to communicate and coordinate the actions that need to be taken throughout the company. Senior managers evaluate performance more subjectively, based on how well subordinate managers have managed in these uncertain environments.

Decision Point

What are the special challenges involved in budgeting at multinational companies?

Problem for Self-Study

Consider the Stylistic Furniture example described earlier. Suppose that to maintain its sales quantities, Stylistic needs to decrease selling prices to $582 per Casual table and $776 per Deluxe table, a 3% decrease in the selling prices used in the chapter illustration. All other data are unchanged.

Required Prepare a budgeted income statement, including all necessary detailed supporting budget schedules that are different from the schedules presented in the chapter. Indicate those schedules that will remain unchanged.

Solution

Schedules 1 and 8 will change. Schedule 1 changes because a change in selling price affects revenues. Schedule 8 changes because revenues are a cost driver of marketing costs (sales commissions). The remaining schedules will not change because a change in selling price has no effect on manufacturing costs. The revised schedules and the new budgeted income statement follow:

Schedule 1: Revenue Budget
For the Year Ending December 31, 2012

	Selling Price	Units	Total Revenues
Casual tables	$582	50,000	$29,100,000
Deluxe tables	776	10,000	7,760,000
Total			$36,860,000

Schedule 8: Nonmanufacturing Costs Budget
For the Year Ending December 31, 2012

Business Function	Variable Costs	Fixed Costs (as in Schedule 8, p. 196)	Total Costs
Product design		$1,024,000	$1,024,000
Marketing (Variable cost: $36,860,000 × 0.065)	$2,395,900	1,330,000	3,725,900
Distribution (Variable cost: $2 × 1,140,000 cu. ft.)	2,280,000	1,596,000	3,876,000
	$4,675,900	$3,950,000	$8,625,900

Stylistic Furniture
Budgeted Income Statement
For the Year Ending December 31, 2012

Revenues	Schedule 1		$36,860,000
Cost of goods sold	Schedule 7		24,440,000
Gross margin			12,420,000
Operating costs			
Product design	Schedule 8	$1,024,000	
Marketing costs	Schedule 8	3,725,900	
Distribution costs	Schedule 8	3,876,000	8,625,900
Operating income			$ 3,794,100

Decision Points

The following question-and-answer format summarizes the chapter's learning objectives. Each decision presents a key question related to a learning objective. The guidelines are the answer to that question.

Decision	Guidelines
1. What is the master budget and why is it useful?	The master budget summarizes the financial projections of all the company's budgets. It expresses management's operating and financing plans—the formalized outline of the company's financial objectives and how they will be attained. Budgets are tools that, by themselves, are neither good nor bad. Budgets are useful when administered skillfully.
2. When should a company prepare budgets? What are the advantages of preparing budgets?	Budgets should be prepared when their expected benefits exceed their expected costs. The advantages of budgets include the following: (a) they compel strategic analysis and planning, (b) they promote coordination and communication among subunits of the company, (c) they provide a framework for judging performance and facilitating learning, and (d) they motivate managers and other employees.
3. What is the operating budget and what are its components?	The operating budget is the budgeted income statement and its supporting budget schedules. The starting point for the operating budget is generally the revenues budget. The following supporting schedules are derived from the revenues budget and the activities needed to support the revenues budget: production budget, direct material usage budget, direct material purchases budget, direct manufacturing labor cost budget, manufacturing overhead costs budget, ending inventories budget, cost of goods sold budget, R&D/product design cost budget, marketing cost budget, distribution cost budget, and customer-service cost budget.
4. How can managers plan for changes in the assumptions underlying the budget?	Managers can use financial planning models—mathematical statements of the relationships among operating activities, financing activities, and other factors that affect the budget. These models make it possible for management to conduct what-if (sensitivity) analysis of the effects that changes in the original predicted data or changes in underlying assumptions would have on the master budget and to develop plans to respond to changed conditions.

5. How do companies use responsibility centers? Should performance reports of responsibility center managers include only costs the manager can control?	A responsibility center is a part, segment, or subunit of an organization whose manager is accountable for a specified set of activities. Four types of responsibility centers are cost centers, revenue centers, profit centers, and investment centers. Responsibility accounting systems are useful because they measure the plans, budgets, actions, and actual results of each responsibility center. Controllable costs are costs primarily subject to the influence of a given responsibility center manager for a given time period. Performance reports of responsibility center managers often include costs, revenues, and investments that the managers cannot control. Responsibility accounting associates financial items with managers on the basis of which manager has the most knowledge and information about the specific items, regardless of the manager's ability to exercise full control.
6. Why are human factors crucial in budgeting?	The administration of budgets requires education, participation, persuasion, and intelligent interpretation. When wisely administered, budgets create commitment, accountability, and honest communication, and can be used as the basis for continuous improvement efforts. When badly managed, budgeting can lead to game-playing and budgetary slack—the practice of making budget targets more easily achievable.
7. What are the special challenges involved in budgeting at multinational companies?	Budgeting is a valuable tool for multinational companies but is made difficult by the enormous uncertainties inherent in operating in multiple countries. In addition to budgeting in different currencies, management accountants in multinational companies also need to budget for foreign exchange rates. Besides currency issues, multinational companies need to understand the political, legal, and economic environments of the different countries in which they operate.

Appendix

The Cash Budget

The chapter illustrated the operating budget, which is one part of the master budget. The other part is the financial budget, which comprises the capital expenditures budget, the cash budget, the budgeted balance sheet, and the budgeted statement of cash flows. This appendix focuses on the cash budget and the budgeted balance sheet. The budgeted statement of cash flows is beyond the scope of this book, and generally is covered in financial accounting and corporate finance courses.

Suppose Stylistic Furniture had the balance sheet for the year ended December 31, 2011, shown in Exhibit 5. The budgeted cash flows for 2012 are as follows:

	Quarters			
	1	2	3	4
Collections from customers	$9,136,600	$10,122,000	$10,263,200	$8,561,200
Disbursements				
Direct materials	2,947,605	2,714,612	2,157,963	2,155,356
Payroll	3,604,512	2,671,742	2,320,946	2,562,800
Manufacturing overhead costs	2,109,018	1,530,964	1,313,568	1,463,450
Nonmanufacturing costs	1,847,750	1,979,000	1,968,250	1,705,000
Machinery purchase	—	—	758,000	—
Income taxes	725,000	400,000	400,000	400,000

The quarterly data are based on the budgeted cash effects of the operations formulated in Schedules 1 through 8 in the chapter, but the details of that formulation are not shown here to keep this illustration as brief and as focused as possible.

The company wants to maintain a $350,000 minimum cash balance at the end of each quarter. The company can borrow or repay money at an interest rate of 12% per year. Management does not want to borrow any more short-term cash than is necessary. By special arrangement, interest is computed and paid when the principal is repaid.

Exhibit 5

Balance Sheet for
Stylistic Furniture,
December 31, 2011

	A	B	C	D
1	Stylistic Furniture			
1	Balance Sheet			
2	December 31, 2011			
3	Assets			
4	Current assets			
5	Cash		$ 300,000	
6	Accounts receivable		1,711,000	
7	Direct materials inventory		1,090,000	
8	Finished goods inventory		646,000	$ 3,747,000
9	Property, plant, and equipment:			
10	Land		2,000,000	
11	Building and equipment	$22,000,000		
12	Accumulated depreciation	(6,900,000)	15,100,000	17,100,000
13	Total			$20,847,000
14	Liabilities and Stockholders' Equity			
15	Current liabilities			
16	Accounts payable		$ 904,000	
17	Income taxes payable		325,000	$ 1,229,000
18	Stockholders' equity			
19	Common stock, no-par,			
20	25,000 shares outstanding		3,500,000	
21	Retained earnings		16,118,000	19,618,000
22	Total			$20,847,000

Assume, for simplicity, that borrowing takes place at the beginning and repayment at the end of the quarter under consideration (in multiples of $1,000). Interest is computed to the nearest dollar.

Suppose the management accountant at Stylistic is given the preceding data and the other data contained in the budgets in the chapter. She is instructed as follows:

1. Prepare a cash budget for 2012 by quarter. That is, prepare a statement of cash receipts and disbursements by quarter, including details of borrowing, repayment, and interest.

2. Prepare a budgeted income statement for the year ending December 31, 2012. This statement should include interest expense and income taxes (at a rate of 40% of operating income).

3. Prepare a budgeted balance sheet on December 31, 2012.

Preparation of Budgets

1. The **cash budget** (Exhibit 6) is a schedule of expected cash receipts and disbursements. It predicts the effects on the cash position at the given level of operations. Exhibit 6 presents the cash budget by quarters to show the impact of cash flow timing on bank loans and their repayment. In practice, monthly—and sometimes weekly or even daily—cash budgets are critical for cash planning and control. Cash budgets help avoid unnecessary idle cash and unexpected cash deficiencies. They thus keep cash balances in line with needs. Ordinarily, the cash budget has these main sections:

    a. **Cash available for needs (before any financing).** The beginning cash balance plus cash receipts equals the total cash available for needs before any financing. Cash receipts depend on collections of accounts receivable, cash sales, and miscellaneous recurring sources, such as rental or royalty receipts. Information on the expected collectibility of accounts receivable is needed for accurate predictions. Key factors include bad-debt (uncollectible accounts) experience (not an issue in the Stylistic case because Stylistic sells to only a few large wholesalers) and average time lag between sales and collections.

    b. **Cash disbursements.** Cash disbursements by Stylistic Furniture include the following:
        i. *Direct material purchases.* Suppliers are paid in full three weeks after the goods are delivered.

Exhibit 6   Cash Budget for Stylistic Furniture for the Year Ending December 31, 2012

		Home	Insert	Page Layout	Formulas	Data	Review	View	

	A	B	C	D	E	F
1				Stylistic Furniture		
2				Cash Budget		
3				For Year Ending December 31, 2012		
4				Quarters		Year as a
5		1	2	3	4	Whole
6	Cash balance, beginning	$ 300,000	$ 350,715	$ 350,657	$ 350,070	$ 300,000
7	Add receipts					
8	Collections from customers	9,136,600	10,122,000	10,263,200	8,561,200	38,083,000
9	Total cash available for needs (x)	9,436,600	10,472,715	10,613,857	8,911,270	38,383,000
10	Deduct disbursements					
11	Direct materials	2,947,605	2,714,612	2,157,963	2,155,356	9,975,536
12	Payroll	3,604,512	2,671,742	2,320,946	2,562,800	11,160,000
13	Manufacturing overhead costs	2,109,018	1,530,964	1,313,568	1,463,450	6,417,000
14	Nonmanufacturing costs	1,847,750	1,979,000	1,968,250	1,705,000	7,500,000
15	Machinery purchase			758,000		758,000
16	Income taxes	725,000	400,000	400,000	400,000	1,925,000
17	Total disbursements (y)	11,233,885	9,296,318	8,918,727	8,286,606	37,735,536
18	Minimum cash balance desired	350,000	350,000	350,000	350,000	350,000
19	Total cash needed	11,583,885	9,646,318	9,268,727	8,636,606	38,085,536
20	Cash excess (deficiency)*	$ (2,147,285)	$ 826,397	$ 1,345,130	$ 274,664	$ 297,464
21	Financing					
22	Borrowing (at beginning)	$ 2,148,000	$ 0	$ 0	$ 0	$ 2,148,000
23	Repayment (at end)	0	(779,000)	(1,234,000)	(135,000)	(2,148,000)
24	Interest (at 12% per year)**	0	(46,740)	(111,060)	(16,200)	(174,000)
25	Total effects of financing (z)	$ 2,148,000	$ (825,740)	$ (1,345,060)	$ (151,200)	$ (174,000)
26	Cash balance, ending***	$ 350,715	$ 350,657	$ 350,070	$ 473,464	$ 473,464
27	*Excess of total cash available for needs − Total cash needed before financing.					
28	**Note that the short-term interest payments pertain only to the amount of principal being repaid at the end of a quarter. The specific computations regarding interest are $779,000 × 0.12 × 0.5 = $46,740; $1,234,000 × 0.12 × 0.75 = $111,060; $135,000 × 0.12 = $16,200. Also note that *depreciation does not require a cash outlay.*					
29	***Ending cash balance = Total cash available for needs (x) − Total disbursements (y) + Total effects of financing (z)					

ii. *Direct labor and other wage and salary outlays.* All payroll-related costs are paid in the month in which the labor effort occurs.

iii. *Other costs.* These depend on timing and credit terms. (In the Stylistic case, all other costs are paid in the month in which the cost is incurred.) *Note, depreciation does not require a cash outlay.*

iv. *Other disbursements.* These include outlays for property, plant, equipment, and other long-term investments.

v. Income tax payments.

c. **Financing effects.** Short-term financing requirements depend on how the total cash available for needs [keyed as (x) in Exhibit 6] compares with the total cash disbursements [keyed as (y)], plus the minimum ending cash balance desired. The financing plans will depend on the relationship between total cash available for needs and total cash needed. If there is a deficiency of cash, loans will be obtained. If there is excess cash, any outstanding loans will be repaid.

d. **Ending cash balance.** The cash budget in Exhibit 6 shows the pattern of short-term "self-liquidating" cash loans. In quarter 1, Stylistic budgets a $2,147,285 cash deficiency. Hence, it undertakes short-term borrowing of $2,148,000 that it pays off over the course of the year. Seasonal peaks of production or sales often result in heavy cash disbursements for purchases, payroll, and other operating outlays as the products are produced and sold. Cash receipts from customers typically lag behind sales. The loan is *self-liquidating* in the sense that the borrowed money is used to acquire resources that are used to produce and sell finished goods, and the proceeds from sales are used to repay the loan. This self-liquidating cycle is the movement from cash to inventories to receivables and back to cash.

2. The budgeted income statement is presented in Exhibit 7. It is merely the budgeted operating income statement in Exhibit 3 expanded to include interest expense and income taxes.

3. The budgeted balance sheet is presented in Exhibit 8. Each item is projected in light of the details of the business plan as expressed in all the previous budget schedules. For example, the ending balance of accounts receivable of $1,628,000 is computed by adding the budgeted revenues of $38,000,000 (from Schedule 1) to the beginning balance of accounts receivable of $1,711,000 (from Exhibit 5) and subtracting cash receipts of $38,083,000 (from Exhibit 6).

For simplicity, the cash receipts and disbursements were given explicitly in this illustration. Usually, the receipts and disbursements are calculated based on the lags between the items reported on the accrual basis of accounting in an income statement and balance sheet and their related cash receipts and disbursements. Consider accounts receivable. In the first three quarters, Stylistic estimates that 80% of all sales made in a quarter are collected in the same quarter and 20% are collected in the following quarter. Estimated collections from customers each quarter are calculated in the following table (assuming sales by quarter of $9,282,000; $10,332,000; $10,246,000; and $8,140,000 that equal 2012 budgeted sales of $38,000,000).

Schedule of Cash Collections

	Quarters			
	1	2	3	4
Accounts receivable balance on 1-1-2012 (p. 207)				
(Fourth quarter sales from prior year collected in first quarter of 2012)	$1,711,000			
From first-quarter 2012 sales (9,282,000 × 0.80; 9,282,000 × 0.20)	7,425,600	$ 1,856,400		
From second-quarter 2012 sales (10,332,000 × 0.80; 10,332,000 × 0.20)		8,265,600	$ 2,066,400	
From third-quarter 2012 sales (10,246,000 × 0.80; 10,246,000 × 0.20)			8,196,800	$2,049,200
From fourth-quarter 2012 sales (8,140,000 × 0.80)				6,512,000
Total collections	$9,136,600	$10,122,000	$10,263,200	$8,561,200

Note that the quarterly cash collections from customers calculated in this schedule equal the cash collections by quarter shown on page 206. Furthermore, the difference between fourth-quarter sales and the cash collected from fourth-quarter sales, $8,140,000 – $6,512,000 = $1,628,000 appears as accounts receivable in the budgeted balance sheet as of December 31, 2012 (see Exhibit 8).

Exhibit 7
Budgeted Income Statement for Stylistic Furniture for the Year Ending December 31, 2012

	A	B	C	D
1	Stylistic Furniture			
2	Budgeted Income Statement			
3	For the Year Ending December 31, 2012			
4	Revenues	Schedule 1		$38,000,000
5	Cost of goods sold	Schedule 7		24,440,000
6	Gross margin			13,560,000
7	Operating costs			
8	Product design costs	Schedule 8	$1,024,000	
9	Marketing costs	Schedule 8	3,800,000	
10	Distribution costs	Schedule 8	3,876,000	8,700,000
11	Operating income			4,860,000
12	Interest expense	Exhibit 6-6		174,000
13	Income before income taxes			4,686,000
14	Income taxes (at 40%)			1,874,400
15	Net income			$ 2,811,600

Exhibit 8   Budgeted Balance Sheet for Stylistic Furniture, December 31, 2012

	Home	Insert	Page Layout	Formulas	Data	Review	View		
	A					B	C	D	
1	Stylistic Furniture								
2	Budgeted Balance Sheet								
3	December 31, 2012								
4	Assets								
5	Current assets								
6	Cash (from Exhibit 6-6)						$ 473,464		
7	Accounts receivable (1)						1,628,000		
8	Direct materials inventory (2)						760,000		
9	Finished goods inventory (2)						4,486,000	$ 7,347,464	
10	Property, plant, and equipment								
11	Land (3)						2,000,000		
12	Building and equipment (4)					$22,758,000			
13	Accumulated depreciation (5)					(8,523,000)	14,235,000	16,235,000	
14	Total							$23,582,464	
15	Liabilities and Stockholders' Equity								
16	Current liabilities								
17	Accounts payable (6)						$ 878,464		
18	Income taxes payable (7)						274,400	$ 1,152,864	
19	Stockholders' equity								
20	Common stock, no-par, 25,000 shares outstanding (8)						3,500,000		
21	Retained earnings (9)						18,929,600	22,429,600	
22	Total							$23,582,464	
23									
24	Notes:								
25	Beginning balances are used as the starting point for most of the following computations:								
26	(1) $1,711,000 + $38,000,000 revenues − $38,083,000 receipts (Exhibit 6-6) = $1,628,000								
27	(2) From Schedule 6B, p. 195								
28	(3) From beginning balance sheet, p. 207								
29	(4) $22,000,000 + $758,000 purchases = $22,758,0000								
30	(5) $6,900,000 + $1,020,000 + $603,000 depreciation from Schedule 5, p. 194								
31	(6) $904,000 + $9,950,000 (Schedule 3B) − $9,975,536 (Exhibit 6-6) = $878,464								
32	There are no other current liabilities. Cash flows for payroll, manufacturing overhead and nonmanufacturing costs totaling $25,077,000 on the cash budget (Exhibit 6-6) consists of direct manufacturing labor costs of $6,000,000 from Schedule 4 + cash manufacturing overhead costs of $10,377,000 ($12,000,000 − depreciation of $1,623,000) from Schedule 5 + cash nonmanufacturing costs of $8,700,000 from Schedule 8.								
33	(7) $325,000 + $1,874,400 current year − $1,925,0000 payment = $274,400.								
34	(8) From beginning balance sheet.								
35	(9) $16,118,000 + $2,811,600 net income per Exhibit 7 = $18,929,600								

Sensitivity Analysis and Cash Flows

Exhibit 4 shows how differing assumptions about selling prices of coffee tables and direct material prices led to differing amounts for budgeted operating income for Stylistic Furniture. A key use of sensitivity analysis is to budget cash flow. Exhibit 9 outlines the short-term borrowing implications of the two combinations examined in Exhibit 4. Scenario 1, with the lower selling prices per table ($582 for the Casual table and $776 for the Deluxe table), requires $2,352,000 of short-term borrowing in quarter 1 that cannot be fully repaid as of December 31, 2012. Scenario 2, with the 5% higher direct material costs, requires $2,250,000 borrowing by Stylistic Furniture that also cannot be repaid by December 31, 2012. Sensitivity analysis helps managers anticipate such outcomes and take steps to minimize the effects of expected reductions in cash flows from operations.

Exhibit 9 Sensitivity Analysis: Effects of Key Budget Assumptions in Exhibit 4 on 2012 Short-Term Borrowing for Stylistic Furniture

	Home	Insert	Page Layout	Formulas	Data	Review	View			
	A	B	C	D	E	F	G	H	I	J
1				Direct Material			Short-Term Borrowing and Repayment by Quarter			
2		Selling Price		Purchase Costs		Budgeted	Quarters			
3	Scenario	Casual	Deluxe	Red Oak	Granite	Operating Income	1	2	3	4
4	1	$582	$776	$7.00	$10.00	$3,794,100	$2,352,000	($511,000)	($ 969,000)	($ 30,000)
5	2	$600	$800	7.35	10.50	4,483,800	2,250,000	(651,000)	(1,134,000)	(149,000)

Terms to Learn

The chapter contains definitions of the following important terms:

activity-based budgeting (ABB)
budgetary slack
cash budget
continuous budget
controllability
controllable cost
cost center

financial budget
financial planning models
investment center
kaizen budgeting
master budget
operating budget
organization structure

pro forma statements
profit center
responsibility accounting
responsibility center
revenue center
rolling budget

Assignment Material

Questions

6-1 What are the four elements of the budgeting cycle?
6-2 Define master budget.
6-3 "Strategy, plans, and budgets are unrelated to one another." Do you agree? Explain.
6-4 "Budgeted performance is a better criterion than past performance for judging managers." Do you agree? Explain.
6-5 "Production managers and marketing managers are like oil and water. They just don't mix." How can a budget assist in reducing battles between these two areas?
6-6 "Budgets meet the cost-benefit test. They force managers to act differently." Do you agree? Explain.
6-7 Define rolling budget. Give an example.
6-8 Outline the steps in preparing an operating budget.
6-9 "The sales forecast is the cornerstone for budgeting." Why?
6-10 How can sensitivity analysis be used to increase the benefits of budgeting?
6-11 Define kaizen budgeting.
6-12 Describe how nonoutput-based cost drivers can be incorporated into budgeting.
6-13 Explain how the choice of the type of responsibility center (cost, revenue, profit, or investment) affects behavior.
6-14 What are some additional considerations that arise when budgeting in multinational companies?
6-15 "Cash budgets must be prepared before the operating income budget." Do you agree? Explain.

Exercises

6-16 **Sales budget, service setting.** In 2011, Rouse & Sons, a small environmental-testing firm, performed 12,200 radon tests for $290 each and 16,400 lead tests for $240 each. Because newer homes are being built with lead-free pipes, lead-testing volume is expected to decrease by 10% next year. However, awareness of radon-related health hazards is expected to result in a 6% increase in radon-test volume each year in the near future. Jim Rouse feels that if he lowers his price for lead testing to $230 per test, he will have to face only a 7% decline in lead-test sales in 2012.

1. Prepare a 2012 sales budget for Rouse & Sons assuming that Rouse holds prices at 2011 levels.
2. Prepare a 2012 sales budget for Rouse & Sons assuming that Rouse lowers the price of a lead test to $230. Should Rouse lower the price of a lead test in 2012 if its goal is to maximize sales revenue?

Required

157

6-17 Sales and production budget. The Mendez Company expects sales in 2012 of 200,000 units of serving trays. Mendez's beginning inventory for 2012 is 15,000 trays and its target ending inventory is 25,000 trays. Compute the number of trays budgeted for production in 2012.

6-18 Direct material budget. Inglenook Co. produces wine. The company expects to produce 2,500,000 two-liter bottles of Chablis in 2012. Inglenook purchases empty glass bottles from an outside vendor. Its target ending inventory of such bottles is 80,000; its beginning inventory is 50,000. For simplicity, ignore breakage. Compute the number of bottles to be purchased in 2012.

6-19 Budgeting material purchases. The Mahoney Company has prepared a sales budget of 45,000 finished units for a three-month period. The company has an inventory of 16,000 units of finished goods on hand at December 31 and has a target finished goods inventory of 18,000 units at the end of the succeeding quarter.

It takes three gallons of direct materials to make one unit of finished product. The company has an inventory of 60,000 gallons of direct materials at December 31 and has a target ending inventory of 50,000 gallons at the end of the succeeding quarter. How many gallons of direct materials should be purchased during the three months ending March 31?

6-20 Revenues and production budget. Purity, Inc., bottles and distributes mineral water from the company's natural springs in northern Oregon. Purity markets two products: twelve-ounce disposable plastic bottles and four-gallon reusable plastic containers.

Required

1. For 2012, Purity marketing managers project monthly sales of 400,000 twelve-ounce bottles and 100,000 four-gallon containers. Average selling prices are estimated at $0.25 per twelve-ounce bottle and $1.50 per four-gallon container. Prepare a revenues budget for Purity, Inc., for the year ending December 31, 2012.
2. Purity begins 2012 with 900,000 twelve-ounce bottles in inventory. The vice president of operations requests that twelve-ounce bottles ending inventory on December 31, 2012, be no less than 600,000 bottles. Based on sales projections as budgeted previously, what is the minimum number of twelve-ounce bottles Purity must produce during 2012?
3. The VP of operations requests that ending inventory of four-gallon containers on December 31, 2012, be 200,000 units. If the production budget calls for Purity to produce 1,300,000 four-gallon containers during 2012, what is the beginning inventory of four-gallon containers on January 1, 2012?

6-21 Budgeting; direct material usage, manufacturing cost and gross margin. Xerxes Manufacturing Company manufactures blue rugs, using wool and dye as direct materials. One rug is budgeted to use 36 skeins of wool at a cost of $2 per skein and 0.8 gallons of dye at a cost of $6 per gallon. All other materials are indirect. At the beginning of the year Xerxes has an inventory of 458,000 skeins of wool at a cost of $961,800 and 4,000 gallons of dye at a cost of $23,680. Target ending inventory of wool and dye is zero. Xerxes uses the FIFO inventory cost flow method.

Xerxes blue rugs are very popular and demand is high, but because of capacity constraints the firm will produce only 200,000 blue rugs per year. The budgeted selling price is $2,000 each. There are no rugs in beginning inventory. Target ending inventory of rugs is also zero.

Xerxes makes rugs by hand, but uses a machine to dye the wool. Thus, overhead costs are accumulated in two cost pools—one for weaving and the other for dyeing. Weaving overhead is allocated to products based on direct manufacturing labor-hours (DMLH). Dyeing overhead is allocated to products based on machine-hours (MH).

There is no direct manufacturing labor cost for dyeing. Xerxes budgets 62 direct manufacturing labor-hours to weave a rug at a budgeted rate of $13 per hour. It budgets 0.2 machine-hours to dye each skein in the dyeing process.

The following table presents the budgeted overhead costs for the dyeing and weaving cost pools:

	Dyeing (based on 1,440,000 MH)	Weaving (based on 12,400,000 DMLH)
Variable costs		
Indirect materials	$ 0	$15,400,000
Maintenance	6,560,000	5,540,000
Utilities	7,550,000	2,890,000
Fixed costs		
Indirect labor	347,000	1,700,000
Depreciation	2,100,000	274,000
Other	723,000	5,816,000
Total budgeted costs	$17,280,000	$31,620,000

Required

1. Prepare a direct material usage budget in both units and dollars.

2. Calculate the budgeted overhead allocation rates for weaving and dyeing.
3. Calculate the budgeted unit cost of a blue rug for the year.
4. Prepare a revenue budget for blue rugs for the year, assuming Xerxes sells (a) 200,000 or (b) 185,000 blue rugs (that is, at two different sales levels).
5. Calculate the budgeted cost of goods sold for blue rugs under each sales assumption.
6. Find the budgeted gross margin for blue rugs under each sales assumption.

6-22 Revenues, production, and purchases budgets. The Suzuki Co. in Japan has a division that manufactures two-wheel motorcycles. Its budgeted sales for Model G in 2013 is 900,000 units. Suzuki's target ending inventory is 80,000 units, and its beginning inventory is 100,000 units. The company's budgeted selling price to its distributors and dealers is 400,000 yen (¥) per motorcycle.

Suzuki buys all its wheels from an outside supplier. No defective wheels are accepted. (Suzuki's needs for extra wheels for replacement parts are ordered by a separate division of the company.) The company's target ending inventory is 60,000 wheels, and its beginning inventory is 50,000 wheels. The budgeted purchase price is 16,000 yen (¥) per wheel.

Required

1. Compute the budgeted revenues in yen.
2. Compute the number of motorcycles to be produced.
3. Compute the budgeted purchases of wheels in units and in yen.

6-23 Budgets for production and direct manufacturing labor. (CMA, adapted) Roletter Company makes and sells artistic frames for pictures of weddings, graduations, and other special events. Bob Anderson, the controller, is responsible for preparing Roletter's master budget and has accumulated the following information for 2013:

	2013				
	January	February	March	April	May
Estimated sales in units	10,000	12,000	8,000	9,000	9,000
Selling price	$54.00	$51.50	$51.50	$51.50	$51.50
Direct manufacturing labor-hours per unit	2.0	2.0	1.5	1.5	1.5
Wage per direct manufacturing labor-hour	$10.00	$10.00	$10.00	$11.00	$11.00

In addition to wages, direct manufacturing labor-related costs include pension contributions of $0.50 per hour, worker's compensation insurance of $0.15 per hour, employee medical insurance of $0.40 per hour, and Social Security taxes. Assume that as of January 1, 2013, the Social Security tax rates are 7.5% for employers and 7.5% for employees. The cost of employee benefits paid by Roletter on its employees is treated as a direct manufacturing labor cost.

Roletter has a labor contract that calls for a wage increase to $11 per hour on April 1, 2013. New labor-saving machinery has been installed and will be fully operational by March 1, 2013. Roletter expects to have 16,000 frames on hand at December 31, 2012, and it has a policy of carrying an end-of-month inventory of 100% of the following month's sales plus 50% of the second following month's sales.

Required

Prepare a production budget and a direct manufacturing labor budget for Roletter Company by month and for the first quarter of 2013. Both budgets may be combined in one schedule. The direct manufacturing labor budget should include labor-hours, and show the details for each labor cost category.

6-24 Activity-based budgeting. The Chelsea store of Family Supermarket (FS), a chain of small neighborhood grocery stores, is preparing its activity-based budget for January 2011. FS has three product categories: soft drinks, fresh produce, and packaged food. The following table shows the four activities that consume indirect resources at the Chelsea store, the cost drivers and their rates, and the cost-driver amount budgeted to be consumed by each activity in January 2011.

	Home	Insert	Page Layout	Formulas	Data	Review	View

	A	B	C	D	E	F
1			January 2011	January 2011 Budgeted		
2			Budgeted	Amount of Cost Driver Used		
3	Activity	Cost Driver	Cost-Driver Rate	Soft Drinks	Fresh Produce	Packaged Food
4	Ordering	Number of purchase orders	$90	14	24	14
5	Delivery	Number of deliveries	$82	12	62	19
6	Shelf stocking	Hours of stocking time	$21	16	172	94
7	Customer support	Number of items sold	$ 0.18	4,600	34,200	10,750

Required

1. What is the total budgeted indirect cost at the Chelsea store in January 2011? What is the total budgeted cost of each activity at the Chelsea store for January 2011? What is the budgeted indirect cost of each product category for January 2011?
2. Which product category has the largest fraction of total budgeted indirect costs?
3. Given your answer in requirement 2, what advantage does FS gain by using an activity-based approach to budgeting over, say, allocating indirect costs to products based on cost of goods sold?

6-25 Kaizen approach to activity-based budgeting (continuation of 6-24). Family Supermarkets (FS) has a kaizen (continuous improvement) approach to budgeting monthly activity costs for each month of 2011. Each successive month, the budgeted cost-driver rate decreases by 0.4% relative to the preceding month. So, for example, February's budgeted cost-driver rate is 0.996 times January's budgeted cost-driver rate, and March's budgeted cost-driver rate is 0.996 times the budgeted February 2011 rate. FS assumes that the budgeted amount of cost-driver usage remains the same each month.

Required

1. What is the total budgeted cost for each activity and the total budgeted indirect cost for March 2011?
2. What are the benefits of using a kaizen approach to budgeting? What are the limitations of this approach, and how might FS management overcome them?

6-26 Responsibility and controllability. Consider each of the following independent situations for Anderson Forklifts. Anderson manufactures and sells forklifts. The company also contracts to service both its own and other brands of forklifts. Anderson has a manufacturing plant, a supply warehouse that supplies both the manufacturing plant and the service technicians (who often need parts to repair forklifts) and 10 service vans. The service technicians drive to customer sites to service the forklifts. Anderson owns the vans, pays for the gas, and supplies forklift parts, but the technicians own their own tools.

1. In the manufacturing plant the production manager is not happy with the engines that the purchasing manager has been purchasing. In May the production manager stops requesting engines from the supply warehouse, and starts purchasing them directly from a different engine manufacturer. Actual materials costs in May are higher than budgeted.
2. Overhead costs in the manufacturing plant for June are much higher than budgeted. Investigation reveals a utility rate hike in effect that was not figured into the budget.
3. Gasoline costs for each van are budgeted based on the service area of the van and the amount of driving expected for the month. The driver of van 3 routinely has monthly gasoline costs exceeding the budget for van 3. After investigating, the service manager finds that the driver has been driving the van for personal use.
4. At Bigstore Warehouse, one of Anderson's forklift service customers, the service people are only called in for emergencies and not for routine maintenance. Thus, the materials and labor costs for these service calls exceeds the monthly budgeted costs for a contract customer.
5. Anderson's service technicians are paid an hourly wage, with overtime pay if they exceed 40 hours per week, excluding driving time. Fred Snert, one of the technicians, frequently exceeds 40 hours per week. Service customers are happy with Fred's work, but the service manager talks to him constantly about working more quickly. Fred's overtime causes the actual costs of service to exceed the budget almost every month.
6. The cost of gasoline has increased by 50% this year, which caused the actual gasoline costs to greatly exceed the budgeted costs for the service vans.

Required

For each situation described, determine where (that is, with whom) (a) responsibility and (b) controllability lie. Suggest what might be done to solve the problem or to improve the situation.

6-27 Cash flow analysis, sensitivity analysis. Game Guys is a retail store selling video games. Sales are uniform for most of the year, but pick up in June and December, both because new releases come out and because games are purchased in anticipation of summer or winter holidays. Game Guys also sells and repairs game systems. The forecast of sales and service revenue for the second quarter of 2012 is as follows:

Sales and Service Revenue Budget
Second Quarter, 2012

Month	Expected Sales Revenue	Expected Service Revenue	Total Revenue
April	$ 5,500	$1,000	$ 6,500
May	6,200	1,400	7,600
June	9,700	2,600	12,300
Total	$21,400	$5,000	$26,400

Almost all the service revenue is paid for by bank credit card, so Game Guys budgets this as 100% bank card revenue. The bank cards charge an average fee of 3% of the total. Half of the sales revenue is also paid for by bank credit card, for which the fee is also 3% on average. About 10% of the sales are paid in cash, and the rest (the remaining 40%) are carried on a store account. Although the store tries to give store credit only to the best customers, it still averages about 2% for uncollectible accounts; 90% of store accounts are paid in the month following the purchase, and 8% are paid two months after purchase.

1. Calculate the cash that Game Guys expects to collect in May and in June of 2012. Show calculations for each month. **Required**

2. Game Guys has budgeted expenditures for May of $4,350 for the purchase of games and game systems, $1,400 for rent and utilities and other costs, and $1,000 in wages for the two part time employees.

   a. Given your answer to requirement 1, will Game Guys be able to cover its payments for May?

   b. The projections for May are a budget. Assume (independently for each situation) that May revenues might also be 5% less and 10% less, and that costs might be 8% higher. Under each of those three scenarios show the total net cash for May and the amount Game Guys would have to borrow if cash receipts are less than cash payments. Assume the beginning cash balance for May is $100.

3. Suppose the costs for May are as described in requirement 2, but the expected cash receipts for May are $6,200 and beginning cash balance is $100. Game Guys has the opportunity to purchase the games and game systems on account in May, but the supplier offers the company credit terms of 2/10 net 30, which means if Game Guys pays within 10 days (in May) it will get a 2% discount on the price of the merchandise. Game Guys can borrow money at a rate of 24%. Should Game Guys take the purchase discount?

Problems

6-28 **Budget schedules for a manufacturer.** Logo Specialties manufactures, among other things, woolen blankets for the athletic teams of the two local high schools. The company sews the blankets from fabric and sews on a logo patch purchased from the licensed logo store site. The teams are as follows:

- ▪ Knights, with red blankets and the Knights logo
- ▪ Raiders, with black blankets and the Raider logo

Also, the black blankets are slightly larger than the red blankets.

The budgeted direct-cost inputs for each product in 2012 are as follows:

	Knights Blanket	Raiders Blanket
Red wool fabric	3 yards	0
Black wool fabric	0	3.3 yards
Knight logo patches	1	0
Raider logo patches	0	1
Direct manufacturing labor	1.5 hours	2 hours

Unit data pertaining to the direct materials for March 2012 are as follows:

Actual Beginning Direct Materials Inventory (3/1/2012)

	Knights Blanket	Raiders Blanket
Red wool fabric	30 yards	0
Black wool fabric	0	10 yards
Knight logo patches	40	0
Raider logo patches	0	55

Target Ending Direct Materials Inventory (3/31/2012)

	Knights Blanket	Raiders Blanket
Red wool fabric	20 yards	0
Black wool fabric	0	20 yards
Knight logo patches	20	0
Raider logo patches	0	20

Unit cost data for direct-cost inputs pertaining to February 2012 and March 2012 are as follows:

	February 2012 (actual)	March 2012 (budgeted)
Red wool fabric (per yard)	$8	$9
Black wool fabric (per yard)	10	9
Knight logo patches (per patch)	6	6
Raider logo patches (per patch)	5	7
Manufacturing labor cost per hour	25	26

Manufacturing overhead (both variable and fixed) is allocated to each blanket on the basis of budgeted direct manufacturing labor-hours per blanket. The budgeted variable manufacturing overhead rate for March 2012 is $15 per direct manufacturing labor-hour. The budgeted fixed manufacturing overhead for March 2012 is $9,200. Both variable and fixed manufacturing overhead costs are allocated to each unit of finished goods.

Data relating to finished goods inventory for March 2012 are as follows:

	Knights Blankets	Raiders Blankets
Beginning inventory in units	10	15
Beginning inventory in dollars (cost)	$1,210	$2,235
Target ending inventory in units	20	25

Budgeted sales for March 2012 are 120 units of the Knights blankets and 180 units of the Raiders blankets. The budgeted selling prices per unit in March 2012 are $150 for the Knights blankets and $175 for the Raiders blankets. Assume the following in your answer:

■ Work-in-process inventories are negligible and ignored.

■ Direct materials inventory and finished goods inventory are costed using the FIFO method.

■ Unit costs of direct materials purchased and finished goods are constant in March 2012.

Required

1. Prepare the following budgets for March 2012:
   a. Revenues budget
   b. Production budget in units
   c. Direct material usage budget and direct material purchases budget
   d. Direct manufacturing labor budget
   e. Manufacturing overhead budget
   f. Ending inventories budget (direct materials and finished goods)
   g. Cost of goods sold budget

2. Suppose Logo Specialties decides to incorporate continuous improvement into its budgeting process. Describe two areas where it could incorporate continuous improvement into the budget schedules in requirement 1.

6-29 Budgeted costs; kaizen improvements. DryPool T-Shirt Factory manufactures plain white and solid colored T-shirts. Inputs include the following:

	Price	Quantity	Cost per unit of output
Fabric	$ 6 per yard	1 yard per unit	$6 per unit
Labor	$12 per DMLH	0.25 DMLH per unit	$3 per unit

Additionally, the colored T-shirts require 3 ounces of dye per shirt at a cost of $0.20 per ounce. The shirts sell for $15 each for white and $20 each for colors. The company expects to sell 12,000 white T-shirts and 60,000 colored T-shirts uniformly over the year.

DryPool has the opportunity to switch from using the dye it currently uses to using an environmentally friendly dye that costs $1.00 per ounce. The company would still need three ounces of dye per shirt. DryPool is reluctant to change because of the increase in costs (and decrease in profit) but the Environmental Protection Agency has threatened to fine them $102,000 if they continue to use the harmful but less expensive dye.

Required

1. Given the preceding information, would DryPool be better off financially by switching to the environmentally friendly dye? (Assume all other costs would remain the same.)

2. Assume DryPool chooses to be environmentally responsible regardless of cost, and it switchs to the new dye. The production manager suggests trying Kaizen costing. If DryPool can reduce fabric and labor costs each by 1% per month, how close will it be at the end of 12 months to the gross profit it would have earned before switching to the more expensive dye? (Round to the nearest dollar for calculating cost reductions)

3. Refer to requirement 2. How could the reduction in material and labor costs be accomplished? Are there any problems with this plan?

6-30 Revenue and production budgets. (CPA, adapted) The Scarborough Corporation manufactures and sells two products: Thingone and Thingtwo. In July 2011, Scarborough's budget department gathered the following data to prepare budgets for 2012:

2012 Projected Sales

Product	Units	Price
Thingone	60,000	$165
Thingtwo	40,000	$250

2012 Inventories in Units

	Expected Target	
Product	January 1, 2012	December 31, 2012
Thingone	20,000	25,000
Thingtwo	8,000	9,000

The following direct materials are used in the two products:

		Amount Used per Unit	
Direct Material	Unit	Thingone	Thingtwo
A	pound	4	5
B	pound	2	3
C	each	0	1

Projected data for 2012 with respect to direct materials are as follows:

Direct Material	Anticipated Purchase Price	Expected Inventories January 1, 2012	Target Inventories December 31, 2012
A	$12	32,000 lb.	36,000 lb.
B	5	29,000 lb.	32,000 lb.
C	3	6,000 units	7,000 units

Projected direct manufacturing labor requirements and rates for 2012 are as follows:

Product	Hours per Unit	Rate per Hour
Thingone	2	$12
Thingtwo	3	16

Manufacturing overhead is allocated at the rate of $20 per direct manufacturing labor-hour.

Based on the preceding projections and budget requirements for Thingone and Thingtwo, prepare the following budgets for 2012:   **Required**

1. Revenues budget (in dollars)
2. Production budget (in units)
3. Direct material purchases budget (in quantities)
4. Direct material purchases budget (in dollars)
5. Direct manufacturing labor budget (in dollars)
6. Budgeted finished goods inventory at December 31, 2012 (in dollars)

6-31 Budgeted income statement. (CMA, adapted) Easecom Company is a manufacturer of videoconferencing products. Regular units are manufactured to meet marketing projections, and specialized units are made after an order is received. Maintaining the videoconferencing equipment is an important area of customer satisfaction. With the recent downturn in the computer industry, the videoconferencing equipment segment has suffered, leading to a decline in Easecom's financial performance. The following income statement shows results for 2011:

Easecom Company
Income Statement
For the Year Ended December 31, 2011 (in thousands)

Revenues:		
Equipment	$6,000	
Maintenance contracts	1,800	
Total revenues		$7,800
Cost of goods sold		4,600
Gross margin		3,200
Operating costs		
Marketing	600	
Distribution	150	
Customer maintenance	1,000	
Administration	900	
Total operating costs		2,650
Operating income		$ 550

Easecom's management team is in the process of preparing the 2012 budget and is studying the following information:

1. Selling prices of equipment are expected to increase by 10% as the economic recovery begins. The selling price of each maintenance contract is expected to remain unchanged from 2011.
2. Equipment sales in units are expected to increase by 6%, with a corresponding 6% growth in units of maintenance contracts.
3. Cost of each unit sold is expected to increase by 3% to pay for the necessary technology and quality improvements.
4. Marketing costs are expected to increase by $250,000, but administration costs are expected to remain at 2011 levels.
5. Distribution costs vary in proportion to the number of units of equipment sold.
6. Two maintenance technicians are to be hired at a total cost of $130,000, which covers wages and related travel costs. The objective is to improve customer service and shorten response time.
7. There is no beginning or ending inventory of equipment.

Required Prepare a budgeted income statement for the year ending December 31, 2012.

6-32 Responsibility in a restaurant. Barney Briggs owns a restaurant franchise that is part of a chain of "southern homestyle" restaurants. One of the chain's popular breakfast items is biscuits and gravy. Central Warehouse makes and freezes the biscuit dough, which is then sold to the franchise stores; there, it is thawed and baked in the individual stores by the cook. Each franchise also has a purchasing agent who orders the biscuits (and other items) based on expected demand. In March, 2012, one of the freezers in Central Warehouse breaks down and biscuit production is reduced by 25% for three days. During those three days, Barney's franchise runs out of biscuits but demand does not slow down. Barney's franchise cook, Janet Trible, sends one of the kitchen helpers to the local grocery store to buy refrigerated ready-to-bake biscuits. Although the customers are kept happy, the refrigerated biscuits cost Barney's franchise three times the cost of the Central Warehouse frozen biscuits, and the franchise loses money on this item for those three days. Barney is angry with the purchasing agent for not ordering enough biscuits to avoid running out of stock, and with Janet for spending too much money on the replacement biscuits.

Required Who is responsible for the cost of the biscuits? At what level is the cost controllable? Do you agree that Barney should be angry with the purchasing agent? With Janet? Why or why not?

6-33 Comprehensive problem with ABC costing. Pet Luggage Company makes two pet carriers, the Cat-allac and the Dog-eriffic. They are both made of plastic with metal doors, but the Cat-allac is smaller. Information for the two products for the month of April is given in the following tables:

Input Prices

Direct materials	
Plastic	$ 4 per pound
Metal	$ 3 per pound
Direct manufacturing labor	$14 per direct manufacturing labor-hour

Input Quantities per Unit of Output

	Cat-allac	Dog-eriffic
Direct materials		
Plastic	3 pounds	5 pounds
Metal	0.5 pounds	1 pound
Direct manufacturing labor-hours (DMLH)	3 hours	5 hours
Machine-hours (MH)	13 MH	20 MH

Inventory Information, Direct Materials

	Plastic	Metal
Beginning inventory	230 pounds	70 pounds
Target ending inventory	400 pounds	65 pounds
Cost of beginning inventory	$874	$224

Pet Luggage accounts for direct materials using a FIFO cost flow assumption.

Sales and Inventory Information, Finished Goods

	Cat-allac	Dog-eriffic
Expected sales in units	580	240
Selling price	$ 190	$ 275
Target ending inventory in units	45	25
Beginning inventory in units	25	40
Beginning inventory in dollars	$2,500	$7,440

Pet Luggage uses a FIFO cost flow assumption for finished goods inventory.

Pet Luggage uses an activity-based costing system and classifies overhead into three activity pools: Setup, Processing, and Inspection. Activity rates for these activities are $130 per setup-hour, $5 per machine-hour, and $20 per inspection-hour, respectively. Other information follows:

Cost Driver Information

	Cat-allac	Dog-eriffic
Number of units per batch	25	13
Setup time per batch	1.25 hours	2.00 hours
Inspection time per batch	0.5 hour	0.6 hour

Nonmanufacturing fixed costs for March equal $32,000, of which half are salaries. Salaries are expected to increase 5% in April. The only variable nonmanufacturing cost is sales commission, equal to 1% of sales revenue.

Prepare the following for April:

Required

1. Revenues budget
2. Production budget in units
3. Direct material usage budget and direct material purchases budget
4. Direct manufacturing labor cost budget
5. Manufacturing overhead cost budgets for each of the three activities
6. Budgeted unit cost of ending finished goods inventory and ending inventories budget
7. Cost of goods sold budget
8. Nonmanufacturing costs budget
9. Budgeted income statement (ignore income taxes)

6-34 Cash budget (continuation of 6-33). Refer to the information in Problem 6-33.

Assume the following: Pet Luggage (PL) does not make any sales on credit. PL sells only to the public, and accepts cash and credit cards; 90% of its sales are to customers using credit cards, for which PL gets the cash right away less a 2% transaction fee.

Purchases of materials are on account. PL pays for half the purchases in the period of the purchase, and the other half in the following period. At the end of March, PL owes suppliers $8,400.

PL plans to replace a machine in April at a net cash cost of $13,800.

Labor, other manufacturing costs, and nonmanufacturing costs are paid in cash in the month incurred except of course, depreciation, which is not a cash flow. $22,500 of the manufacturing cost and $12,500 of the nonmanufacturing cost for April is depreciation.

PL currently has a $2,600 loan at an annual interest rate of 24%. The interest is paid at the end of each month. If PL has more than $10,000 cash at the end of April it will pay back the loan. PL owes $5,400 in income taxes that need to be remitted in April. PL has cash of $5,200 on hand at the end of March.

Prepare a cash budget for April for Pet Luggage.

Required

6-35 Comprehensive operating budget, budgeted balance sheet. Slopes, Inc., manufactures and sells snowboards. Slopes manufactures a single model, the Pipex. In the summer of 2011, Slopes' management accountant gathered the following data to prepare budgets for 2012:

Materials and Labor Requirements

Direct materials	
Wood	5 board feet (b.f.) per snowboard
Fiberglass	6 yards per snowboard
Direct manufacturing labor	5 hours per snowboard

Slopes' CEO expects to sell 1,000 snowboards during 2012 at an estimated retail price of $450 per board. Further, the CEO expects 2012 beginning inventory of 100 snowboards and would like to end 2012 with 200 snowboards in stock.

Direct Materials Inventories

	Beginning Inventory 1/1/2012	Ending Inventory 12/31/2012
Wood	2,000 b.f.	1,500 b.f.
Fiberglass	1,000 yards	2,000 yards

Variable manufacturing overhead is $7 per direct manufacturing labor-hour. There are also $66,000 in fixed manufacturing overhead costs budgeted for 2012. Slopes combines both variable and fixed manufacturing overhead into a single rate based on direct manufacturing labor-hours. Variable marketing costs are allocated at the rate of $250 per sales visit. The marketing plan calls for 30 sales visits during 2012. Finally, there are $30,000 in fixed nonmanufacturing costs budgeted for 2012.

Other data include the following:

	2011 Unit Price	2012 Unit Price
Wood	$28.00 per b.f.	$30.00 per b.f.
Fiberglass	$ 4.80 per yard	$ 5.00 per yard
Direct manufacturing labor	$24.00 per hour	$25.00 per hour

The inventoriable unit cost for ending finished goods inventory on December 31, 2011, is $374.80. Assume Slopes uses a FIFO inventory method for both direct materials and finished goods. Ignore work in process in your calculations.

Budgeted balances at December 31, 2012, in the selected accounts are as follows:

Cash	$ 10,000
Property, plant, and equipment (net)	850,000
Current liabilities	17,000
Long-term liabilities	178,000
Stockholders' equity	800,000

Required

1. Prepare the 2012 revenues budget (in dollars).
2. Prepare the 2012 production budget (in units).
3. Prepare the direct material usage and purchases budgets for 2012.
4. Prepare a direct manufacturing labor budget for 2012.
5. Prepare a manufacturing overhead budget for 2012.
6. What is the budgeted manufacturing overhead rate for 2012?
7. What is the budgeted manufacturing overhead cost per output unit in 2012?
8. Calculate the cost of a snowboard manufactured in 2012.
9. Prepare an ending inventory budget for both direct materials and finished goods for 2012.
10. Prepare a cost of goods sold budget for 2012.
11. Prepare the budgeted income statement for Slopes, Inc., for the year ending December 31, 2012.
12. Prepare the budgeted balance sheet for Slopes, Inc., as of December 31, 2012.

6-36 Cash budgeting. Retail outlets purchase snowboards from Slopes, Inc., throughout the year. However, in anticipation of late summer and early fall purchases, outlets ramp up inventories from May through August. Outlets are billed when boards are ordered. Invoices are payable within 60 days. From past experience, Slopes' accountant projects 20% of invoices will be paid in the month invoiced, 50% will be paid in the following month, and 30% of invoices will be paid two months after the month of invoice. The average selling price per snowboard is $450.

To meet demand, Slopes increases production from April through July, because the snowboards are produced a month prior to their projected sale. Direct materials are purchased in the month of production and are paid for during the following month (terms are payment in full within 30 days of the invoice date). During this period there is no production for inventory, and no materials are purchased for inventory.

Direct manufacturing labor and manufacturing overhead are paid monthly. Variable manufacturing overhead is incurred at the rate of $7 per direct manufacturing labor-hour. Variable marketing costs are driven by the number of sales visits. However, there are no sales visits during the months studied. Slopes, Inc., also incurs fixed manufacturing overhead costs of $5,500 per month and fixed nonmanufacturing overhead costs of $2,500 per month.

Projected Sales

May 80 units	August 100 units
June 120 units	September 60 units
July 200 units	October 40 units

Direct Materials and Direct Manufacturing Labor Utilization and Cost

	Units per Board	Price per Unit	Unit
Wood	5	$30	board feet
Fiberglass	6	5	yard
Direct manufacturing labor	5	25	hour

The beginning cash balance for July 1, 2012, is $10,000. On October 1, 2011, Slopes had a cash crunch and borrowed $30,000 on a 6% one-year note with interest payable monthly. The note is due October 1, 2012. Using the information provided, you will need to determine whether Slopes will be in a position to pay off this short-term debt on October 1, 2012.

Required

1. Prepare a cash budget for the months of July through September 2012. Show supporting schedules for the calculation of receivables and payables.
2. Will Slopes be in a position to pay off the $30,000 one-year note that is due on October 1, 2012? If not, what actions would you recommend to Slopes' management?
3. Suppose Slopes is interested in maintaining a minimum cash balance of $10,000. Will the company be able to maintain such a balance during all three months analyzed? If not, suggest a suitable cash management strategy.

6-37 Cash budgeting. On December 1, 2011, the Itami Wholesale Co. is attempting to project cash receipts and disbursements through January 31, 2012. On this latter date, a note will be payable in the amount of $100,000. This amount was borrowed in September to carry the company through the seasonal peak in November and December.

Selected general ledger balances on December 1 are as follows:

Cash	$ 88,000
Inventory	65,200
Accounts payable	136,000

Sales terms call for a 3% discount if payment is made within the first 10 days of the month after sale, with the balance due by the end of the month after sale. Experience has shown that 50% of the billings will be collected within the discount period, 30% by the end of the month after purchase, and 14% in the following month. The remaining 6% will be uncollectible. There are no cash sales.

The average selling price of the company's products is $100 per unit. Actual and projected sales are as follows:

October actual	$ 280,000
November actual	320,000
December estimated	330,000
January estimated	250,000
February estimated	240,000
Total estimated for year ending June 30, 2012	$2,400,000

All purchases are payable within 15 days. Approximately 60% of the purchases in a month are paid that month, and the rest the following month. The average unit purchase cost is $80. Target ending inventories are 500 units plus 10% of the next month's unit sales.

Total budgeted marketing, distribution, and customer-service costs for the year are $600,000. Of this amount, $120,000 are considered fixed (and include depreciation of $30,000). The remainder varies with sales. Both fixed and variable marketing, distribution, and customer-service costs are paid as incurred.

Required

Prepare a cash budget for December 2011 and January 2012. Supply supporting schedules for collections of receivables; payments for merchandise; and marketing, distribution, and customer-service costs.

6-38 Comprehensive problem; ABC manufacturing, two products. Follete Inc. operates at capacity and makes plastic combs and hairbrushes. Although the combs and brushes are a matching set, they are sold individually and so the sales mix is not 1:1. Follette Inc. is planning its annual budget for fiscal year 2011. Information for 2011 follows:

Input Prices
Direct materials
    Plastic $ 0.20 per ounce
    Bristles $ 0.50 per bunch
Direct manufacturing labor $12 per direct manufacturing labor-hour

Input Quantities per Unit of Output

	Combs	Brushes
Direct materials		
Plastic	5 ounces	8 ounces
Bristles	—	16 bunches
Direct manufacturing labor	0.05 hours	0.2 hours
Machine-hours (MH)	0.025 MH	0.1 MH

Inventory Information, Direct Materials

	Plastic	Bristles
Beginning inventory	1,600 ounces	1,820 bunches
Target ending inventory	1,766 ounces	2,272 bunches
Cost of beginning inventory	$304	$946

Folette Inc. accounts for direct materials using a FIFO cost flow.

Sales and Inventory Information, Finished Goods

	Combs	Brushes
Expected sales in units	12,000	14,000
Selling price	$ 6	$ 20
Target ending inventory in units	1,200	1,400
Beginning inventory in units	600	1,200
Beginning inventory in dollars	$ 1,800	$18,120

Folette Inc. uses a FIFO cost flow assumption for finished goods inventory.

Combs are manufactured in batches of 200, and brushes are manufactured in batches of 100. It takes 20 minutes to set up for a batch of combs, and one hour to set up for a batch of brushes.

Folette Inc. uses activity-based costing and has classified all overhead costs as shown in the following table:

Cost Type	Budgeted Variable	Budgeted Fixed	Cost Driver/Allocation Base
Manufacturing:			
Materials handling	$11,490	$15,000	Number of ounces of plastic used
Setup	6,830	11,100	Setup-hours
Processing	7,760	20,000	Machine-hours
Inspection	7,000	1,040	Number of units produced
Nonmanufacturing:			
Marketing	14,100	60,000	Sales revenue
Distribution	0	780	Number of deliveries

Delivery trucks transport units sold in delivery sizes of 1,000 combs or 1,000 brushes.

Required Do the following for the year 2011:

1. Prepare the revenues budget.
2. Use the revenue budget to
   a. find the budgeted allocation rate for marketing costs.
   b. find the budgeted number of deliveries and allocation rate for distribution costs.
3. Prepare the production budget in units.
4. Use the production budget to
   a. find the budgeted number of setups, setup-hours, and the allocation rate for setup costs.
   b. find the budgeted total machine-hours and the allocation rate for processing costs.
   c. find the budgeted total units produced and the allocation rate for inspection costs.
5. Prepare the direct material usage budget and the direct material purchases budgets in both units and dollars; round to whole dollars.
6. Use the direct material usage budget to find the budgeted allocation rate for materials handling costs.
7. Prepare the direct manufacturing labor cost budget.
8. Prepare the manufacturing overhead cost budget for materials handling, setup, and processing.
9. Prepare the budgeted unit cost of ending finished goods inventory and ending inventories budget.

10. Prepare the cost of goods sold budget.
11. Prepare the nonmanufacturing overhead costs budget for marketing and distribution.
12. Prepare a budgeted income statement (ignore income taxes).

6-39 Budgeting and ethics. Delma Company manufactures a variety of products in a variety of departments, and evaluates departments and departmental managers by comparing actual cost and output relative to the budget. Departmental managers help create the budgets, and usually provide information about input quantities for materials, labor, and overhead costs.

Wert Mimble is the manager of the department that produces product Z. Wert has estimated these inputs for product Z:

Input	Budget Quantity per Unit of Output
Direct material	4 pounds
Direct manufacturing labor	15 minutes
Machine time	12 minutes

The department produces about 100 units of product Z each day. Wert's department always gets excellent evaluations, sometimes exceeding budgeted production quantities. Each 100 units of product Z uses, on average, about 24 hours of direct manufacturing labor (four people working six hours each), 395 pounds of material, and 19.75 machine-hours.

Top management of Delma Company has decided to implement budget standards that will challenge the workers in each department, and it has asked Wert to design more challenging input standards for product Z. Wert provides top management with the following input quantities:

Input	Budget Quantity per Unit of Output
Direct material	3.95 pounds
Direct manufacturing labor	14.5 minutes
Machine time	11.8 minutes

Discuss the following:

Required

1. Are these standards challenging standards for the department that produces product Z?
2. Why do you suppose Wert picked these particular standards?
3. What steps can Delma Company's top management take to make sure Wert's standards really meet the goals of the firm?

6-40 Human Aspects of Budgeting in a Service Firm. Jag Meerkat owns three upscale hair salons: Hair Suite I, II, and III. Each of the salons has a manager and 10 stylists who rent space in the salons as independent contractors and who pay a fee of 10% of each week's revenue to the salon as rent. In exchange they get to use the facility and utilities, but must bring their own equipment.

The manager of each salon schedules each customer appointment to last an hour, and then allows the stylist 10 minutes between appointments to clean up, rest, and prepare for the next appointment. The salons are open from 10 A.M. to 6 P.M., so each stylist can serve seven customers per day. Stylists each work five days a week on a staggered schedule, so the salon is open seven days a week. Everyone works on Saturdays, but some stylists have Sunday and Monday off, some have Tuesday and Wednesday off, and some have Thursday and Friday off.

Jag Meerkat knows that utility costs are rising. Jag wants to increase revenues to cover at least some part of rising utility costs, so Jag tells each of the managers to find a way to increase productivity in the salons so that the stylists will pay more to the salons. Jag does not want to increase the rental fee above 10% of revenue for fear the stylists will leave, and each salon has only 10 stations, so he feels each salon cannot hire more than 10 full-time stylists.

The manager of Hair Suite I attacks the problem by simply telling the stylists that, from now on, customers will be scheduled for 40 minute appointments and breaks will be five minutes. This will allow each stylist to add one more customer per day.

The manager of Hair Suite II asks the stylists on a voluntary basis to work one extra hour per day, from 10 A.M. to 7 P.M., to add an additional customer per stylist per day.

The manager of Hair Suite III sits down with the stylists and discusses the issue. After considering shortening the appointment and break times, or lengthening the hours of operation, one of the stylists says, "I know we rent stations in your store, but I am willing to share my station. You could hire an eleventh stylist, who will simply work at whatever station is vacant during our days off. Since we use our own equipment, this will not be a problem for me as long as there is a secure place I can leave my equipment on my days off." Most of the other stylists agree that this is a good solution.

Required

1. Which manager's style do you think is most effective? Why?
2. How do you think the stylists will react to the managers of salons I and II? What can they do to indicate their displeasure, assuming they are displeased?
3. In Hair Suite III, if the stylists did not want to share their stations with another party, how else could they find a way to increase revenues?
4. Refer again to the action that the manager of Hair Suite I has chosen. How does this relate to the concept of stretch targets?

Collaborative Learning Problem

6-41 Comprehensive budgeting problem; activity based costing, operating and financial budgets. Borkenstick makes a very popular undyed cloth sandal in one style, but in Regular and Deluxe. The Regular sandals have cloth soles and the Deluxe sandals have cloth covered wooden soles. Borkenstick is preparing its budget for June 2012, and has estimated sales based on past experience.

Other information for the month of June follows:

Input Prices

Direct materials

Cloth	$3.50 per yard
Wood	$5.00 per board foot
Direct manufacturing labor	$10 per direct manufacturing labor-hour

Input Quantities per Unit of Output (per pair of sandals)

	Regular	Deluxe
Direct materials		
Cloth	1.3 yards	1.5 yards
Wood	0	2 b.f.
Direct manufacturing labor-hours (DMLH)	5 hours	7 hours
Setup-hours per batch	2 hours	3 hours

Inventory Information, Direct Materials

	Cloth	Wood
Beginning inventory	610 yards	800 b.f.
Target ending inventory	386 yards	295 b.f.
Cost of beginning inventory	$2,146	$4,040

Borkenstick accounts for direct materials using a FIFO cost flow assumption.

Sales and Inventory Information, Finished Goods

	Regular	Deluxe
Expected sales in units (pairs of sandals)	2,000	3,000
Selling price	$ 80	$ 130
Target ending inventory in units	400	600
Beginning inventory in units	250	650
Beginning inventory in dollars	$15,500	$61,750

Borkenstick uses a FIFO cost flow assumption for finished goods inventory.

All the sandals are made in batches of 50 pairs of sandals. Borkenstick incurs manufacturing overhead costs, marketing and general administration, and shipping costs. Besides materials and labor, manufacturing costs include setup, processing, and inspection costs. Borkenstick ships 40 pairs of sandals per shipment. Borkenstick uses activity-based costing and has classified all overhead costs for the month of June as shown in the following chart:

Cost type	Denominator Activity	Rate
Manufacturing:		
Setup	Setup-hours	$12 per setup-hour
Processing	Direct manufacturing labor-hours	$1.20 per DMLH
Inspection	Number of pairs of sandals	$0.90 per pair
Nonmanufacturing:		
Marketing and general administration	Sales revenue	8%
Shipping	Number of shipments	$10 per shipment

1. Prepare each of the following for June:
   a. Revenues budget
   b. Production budget in units
   c. Direct material usage budget and direct material purchases budget in both units and dollars; round to dollars
   d. Direct manufacturing labor cost budget
   e. Manufacturing overhead cost budgets for processing and setup activities
   f. Budgeted unit cost of ending finished goods inventory and ending inventories budget
   g. Cost of goods sold budget
   h. Marketing and general administration costs budget

Required

2. Borkenstick's balance sheet for May 31 follows. Use it and the following information to prepare a cash budget for Borkenstick for June. Round to dollars.
   - All sales are on account; 60% are collected in the month of the sale, 38% are collected the following month, and 2% are never collected and written off as bad debts.
   - All purchases of materials are on account. Borkenstick pays for 80% of purchases in the month of purchase and 20% in the following month.
   - All other costs are paid in the month incurred, including the declaration and payment of a $10,000 cash dividend in June.
   - Borkenstick is making monthly interest payments of 0.5% (6% per year) on a $100,000 long term loan.
   - Borkenstick plans to pay the $7,200 of taxes owed as of May 31 in the month of June. Income tax expense for June is zero.
   - 30% of processing and setup costs, and 10% of marketing and general administration costs are depreciation.

Borkenstick
Balance Sheet
as of May 31

Assets

Cash		$ 6,290
Accounts receivable	$216,000	
Less: Allowance for bad debts	10,800	205,200
Inventories		
Direct materials		6,186
Finished goods		77,250
Fixed assets	$580,000	
Less: Accumulated depreciation	90,890	489,110
Total assets		$784,036

Liabilities and Equity

Accounts payable	$ 10,400
Taxes payable	7,200
Interest payable	500
Long-term debt	100,000
Common stock	200,000
Retained earnings	465,936
Total liabilities and equity	$784,036

3. Prepare a budgeted income statement for June and a budgeted balance sheet for Borkenstick as of June 30.

Flexible Budgets, Direct-Cost Variances, and Management Control

From Chapter 7 of *Cost Accounting: A Managerial Emphasis*, 14/e. Charles T. Horngren. Srikant M. Datar. Madhav Rajan.

Flexible Budgets, Direct-Cost Variances, and Management Control

Professional sports leagues thrive on providing excitement for their fans.

It seems that no expense is spared to entertain spectators and keep them occupied before, during, and after games. Professional basketball has been at the forefront of this trend, popularizing such crowd-pleasing distractions as pregame pyrotechnics, pumped-in noise, fire-shooting scoreboards, and T-shirt-shooting cheerleaders carrying air guns. What is the goal of investing millions in such "game presentation" activities? Such showcasing attracts and maintains the loyalty of younger fans. But eventually, every organization, regardless of its growth, has to step back and take a hard look at the wisdom of its spending choices. And when customers are affected by a recession, the need for an organization to employ budgeting and variance analysis tools for cost control becomes especially critical, as the following article shows.

The NBA: Where Frugal Happens[1]

For more than 20 years, the National Basketball Association (NBA) flew nearly as high as one of LeBron James's slam dunks. The league expanded from 24 to 30 teams, negotiated lucrative TV contracts, and made star players like Kobe Bryant and Dwayne Wade household names and multimillionaires. The NBA was even advertised as "where amazing happens." While costs for brand new arenas and player contracts increased, fans continued to pay escalating ticket prices to see their favorite team. But when the economy nosedived in 2008, the situation changed dramatically.

In the season that followed (2008–2009), more than half of the NBA's franchises lost money. Fans stopped buying tickets and many companies could no longer afford pricy luxury suites. NBA commissioner David Stern announced that overall league revenue for the 2009–2010 season was expected to fall by an additional 5% over the previous disappointing campaign. With revenues dwindling and operating profits tougher to achieve, NBA teams began to heavily emphasize cost control and operating-variance reduction for the first time since the 1980s.

Some of the changes were merely cosmetic. The Charlotte Bobcats stopped paying for halftime entertainment, which cost up to

---

[1] *Sources:* Arnold, Gregory. 2009. NBA teams cut rosters, assistants, scouts to reduce costs. *The Oregonian*, October 26; Biderman, David. 2009. The NBA: Where frugal happens. *Wall Street Journal*, October 27.

$15,000 per game, while the Cleveland Cavaliers saved $40,000 by switching from paper holiday cards to electronic ones. Many other teams—including the Dallas Mavericks, Indiana Pacers, and Miami Heat—reduced labor costs by laying off front-office staff.

Other changes, however, affected play on the court. While NBA teams were allowed to have 15 players on their respective rosters, 10 teams chose to save money by employing fewer players. For example, the Memphis Grizzlies eliminated its entire scouting department, which provided important information on upcoming opponents and potential future players, while the New Jersey Nets traded away most of its high-priced superstars and chose to play with lower-salaried younger players. Each team cutting costs experienced different results. The Grizzlies were a playoff contender, but the Nets were on pace for one of the worst seasons in NBA history.

Just as companies like General Electric and Bank of America have to manage costs and analyze variances for long-term sustainability, so, too, do sports teams. "The NBA is a business just like any other business," Sacramento Kings co-owner Joe Maloof said. "We have to watch our costs and expenses, especially during this trying economic period. It's better to be safe and watch your expenses and make sure you keep your franchise financially strong."

You saw how budgets help managers with their planning function. We now explain how budgets, specifically flexible budgets, are used to compute variances, which assist managers in their control function. Flexible budgets and variances enable managers to make meaningful comparisons of actual results with planned performance, and to obtain insights into why actual results differ from planned performance. They form the critical final function in the five-step decision-making process, by making it possible for managers to *evaluate performance and learn* after decisions are implemented. In this chapter, we explain how.

Eric Gay/AP Wide World Photos

Static Budgets and Variances

A **variance** is the difference between actual results and expected performance. The expected performance is also called **budgeted performance**, which is a point of reference for making comparisons.

The Use of Variances

Variances lie at the point where the planning and control functions of management come together. They assist managers in implementing their strategies by enabling **management by exception**. This is the practice of focusing management attention on areas that are not operating as expected (such as a large shortfall in sales of a product) and devoting less time to areas operating as expected. In other words, by highlighting the areas that have deviated most from expectations, variances enable managers to focus their efforts on the most critical areas. Consider scrap and rework costs at a Maytag appliances plant. If actual costs are much higher than budgeted, the variances will guide managers to seek explanations and to take early corrective action, ensuring that future operations result in less scrap and rework. Sometimes a large positive variance may occur, such as a significant decrease in manufacturing costs of a product. Managers will try to understand the reasons for this decrease (better operator training or changes in manufacturing methods for example), so these practices can be appropriately continued and transferred to other divisions within the organization.

Variances are also used in performance evaluation and to motivate managers. Production-line managers at Maytag may have quarterly efficiency incentives linked to achieving a budgeted amount of operating costs.

Sometimes variances suggest that the company should consider a change in strategy. For example, large negative variances caused by excessive defect rates for a new product may suggest a flawed product design. Managers may then want to investigate the product design and potentially change the mix of products being offered.

Variance analysis contributes in many ways to making the five-step decision-making process more effective. It allows managers to evaluate performance and learn by providing a framework for correctly assessing current performance. In turn, managers take corrective actions to ensure that decisions are implemented correctly and that previously budgeted results are attained. Variances also enable managers to generate more informed predictions about the future, and thereby improve the quality of the five-step decision-making process.

The benefits of variance analysis are not restricted to companies. In today's difficult economic environment, public officials have realized that the ability to make timely tactical alterations based on variance information guards against having to make more draconian adjustments later. For example, the city of Scottsdale, Arizona, monitors its tax and fee performance against expenditures monthly. Why? One of the city's goals is to keep its water usage rates stable. By monitoring the extent to which water revenues are meeting current expenses and obligations, while simultaneously building up funds for future infrastructure projects, the city can avoid rate spikes and achieve long-run rate stability.[2]

How important is variance analysis? A survey by the United Kingdom's Chartered Institute of Management Accountants in July 2009 found that variance analysis was easily the most popular costing tool in practice, and retained that distinction across organizations of all sizes.

Static Budgets and Static-Budget Variances

We will take a closer look at variances by examining one company's accounting system. Note as you study the exhibits in this chapter that "level" followed by a number denotes the amount of detail shown by a variance analysis. Level 1 reports the least detail; level 2 offers more information; and so on.

Consider Webb Company, a firm that manufactures and sells jackets. The jackets require tailoring and many other hand operations. Webb sells exclusively to distributors, who in turn sell to independent clothing stores and retail chains. For simplicity, we assume that Webb's only costs are in the manufacturing function; Webb incurs no costs in other value-chain functions, such as marketing and distribution. We also assume that all units manufactured in April 2011 are sold in April 2011. Therefore, all direct materials are purchased and used in the same budget period, and there is no direct materials inventory at either the beginning or the end of the period. No work-in-process or finished goods inventories exist at either the beginning or the end of the period.

---

[2] For an excellent discussion and other related examples from governmental settings, see S. Kavanagh and C. Swanson, "Tactical Financial Management: Cash Flow and Budgetary Variance Analysis," *Government Finance Review* (October 1, 2009).

Webb has three variable-cost categories. The budgeted variable cost per jacket for each category is as follows:

Cost Category	Variable Cost per Jacket
Direct material costs	$60
Direct manufacturing labor costs	16
Variable manufacturing overhead costs	12
Total variable costs	$88

The *number of units manufactured* is the cost driver for direct materials, direct manufacturing labor, and variable manufacturing overhead. The relevant range for the cost driver is from 0 to 12,000 jackets. Budgeted and actual data for April 2011 follow:

Budgeted fixed costs for production between 0 and 12,000 jackets	$276,000
Budgeted selling price	$ 120 per jacket
Budgeted production and sales	12,000 jackets
Actual production and sales	10,000 jackets

The **static budget,** or master budget, is based on the level of output planned at the start of the budget period. The master budget is called a static budget because the budget for the period is developed around a single (static) planned output level. Exhibit 1, column 3, presents the static budget for Webb Company for April 2011 that was prepared at the end of 2010. For each line item in the income statement, Exhibit 1, column 1, displays data for the actual April results. For example, actual revenues are $1,250,000, and the actual selling price is $1,250,000 ÷ 10,000 jackets = $125 per jacket—compared with the budgeted selling price of $120 per jacket. Similarly, actual direct material costs are $621,600, and the direct material cost per jacket is $621,600 ÷ 10,000 = $62.16 per jacket—compared with the budgeted direct material cost per jacket of $60. We describe potential reasons and explanations for these differences as we discuss different variances throughout the chapter.

The **static-budget variance** (see Exhibit 1, column 2) is the difference between the actual result and the corresponding budgeted amount in the static budget.

A **favorable variance**—denoted F in this book—has the effect, when considered in isolation, of increasing operating income relative to the budgeted amount. For revenue

Level 1 Analysis

	Actual Results (1)	Static-Budget Variances (2) = (1) – (3)	Static Budget (3)
Units sold	10,000	2,000 U	12,000
Revenues	$ 1,250,000	$190,000 U	$1,440,000
Variable costs			
Direct materials	621,600	98,400 F	720,000
Direct manufacturing labor	198,000	6,000 U	192,000
Variable manufacturing overhead	130,500	13,500 F	144,000
Total variable costs	950,100	105,900 F	1,056,000
Contribution margin	299,900	84,100 U	384,000
Fixed costs	285,000	9,000 U	276,000
Operating income	$ 14,900	$ 93,100 U	$ 108,000

$ 93,100 U

Static-budget variance

Exhibit 1

Static-Budget-Based Variance Analysis for Webb Company for April 2011

items, F means actual revenues exceed budgeted revenues. For cost items, F means actual costs are less than budgeted costs. An **unfavorable variance**—denoted U in this book—has the effect, when viewed in isolation, of decreasing operating income relative to the budgeted amount. Unfavorable variances are also called *adverse variances* in some countries, such as the United Kingdom.

The unfavorable static-budget variance for operating income of $93,100 in Exhibit 1 is calculated by subtracting static-budget operating income of $108,000 from actual operating income of $14,900:

$$\begin{array}{c} \text{Static-budget} \\ \text{variance for} \\ \text{operating income} \end{array} = \begin{array}{c} \text{Actual} \\ \text{result} \end{array} - \begin{array}{c} \text{Static-budget} \\ \text{amount} \end{array}$$

$$= \$14,900 - \$108,000$$

$$= \$93,100 \text{ U.}$$

The analysis in Exhibit 1 provides managers with additional information on the static-budget variance for operating income of $93,100 U. The more detailed breakdown indicates how the line items that comprise operating income—revenues, individual variable costs, and fixed costs—add up to the static-budget variance of $93,100.

Remember, Webb produced and sold only 10,000 jackets, although managers anticipated an output of 12,000 jackets in the static budget. *Managers want to know how much of the static-budget variance is because of inaccurate forecasting of output units sold and how much is due to Webb's performance in manufacturing and selling 10,000 jackets.* Managers, therefore, create a flexible budget, which enables a more in-depth understanding of deviations from the static budget.

Flexible Budgets

A **flexible budget** calculates budgeted revenues and budgeted costs based on *the actual output in the budget period*. The flexible budget is prepared at the end of the period (April 2011), after the actual output of 10,000 jackets is known. The flexible budget is the *hypothetical* budget that Webb would have prepared at the start of the budget period if it had correctly forecast the actual output of 10,000 jackets. In other words, the flexible budget is not the plan Webb initially had in mind for April 2011 (remember Webb planned for an output of 12,000 jackets instead). Rather, it is the budget Webb *would have* put together for April if it knew in advance that the output for the month would be 10,000 jackets. In preparing the flexible budget, note that:

- The budgeted selling price is the same $120 per jacket used in preparing the static budget.
- The budgeted unit variable cost is the same $88 per jacket used in preparing the static budget.
- The budgeted *total* fixed costs are the same static-budget amount of $276,000. Why? Because the 10,000 jackets produced falls within the relevant range of 0 to 12,000 jackets. Therefore, Webb would have budgeted the same amount of fixed costs, $276,000, whether it anticipated making 10,000 or 12,000 jackets.

The *only* difference between the static budget and the flexible budget is that the static budget is prepared for the planned output of 12,000 jackets, whereas the flexible budget is based on the actual output of 10,000 jackets. The static budget is being "flexed," or adjusted, from 12,000 jackets to 10,000 jackets.[3] The flexible budget for 10,000 jackets assumes that all costs are either completely variable or completely fixed with respect to the number of jackets produced.

Webb develops its flexible budget in three steps.

Step 1: Identify the Actual Quantity of Output. In April 2011, Webb produced and sold 10,000 jackets.

---

[3] Suppose Webb, when preparing its next year's budget at the end of 2010, had perfectly anticipated that its output in April 2011 would equal 10,000 jackets. Then, the flexible budget for April 2011 would be identical to the static budget.

Decision Point ▶

What are static budgets and static-budget variances?

Learning Objective 2

Examine the concept of a flexible budget

. . . the budget that is adjusted (flexed) to recognize the actual output level

and learn how to develop it

. . . proportionately increase variable costs; keep fixed costs the same

Step 2: Calculate the Flexible Budget for Revenues Based on Budgeted Selling Price and Actual Quantity of Output.

$$\text{Flexible-budget revenues} = \$120 \text{ per jacket} \times 10,000 \text{ jackets}$$

$$= \$1,200,000$$

Step 3: Calculate the Flexible Budget for Costs Based on Budgeted Variable Cost per Output Unit, Actual Quantity of Output, and Budgeted Fixed Costs.

Flexible-budget variable costs	
Direct materials, $60 per jacket × 10,000 jackets	$ 600,000
Direct manufacturing labor, $16 per jacket × 10,000 jackets	160,000
Variable manufacturing overhead, $12 per jacket × 10,000 jackets	120,000
Total flexible-budget variable costs	880,000
Flexible-budget fixed costs	276,000
Flexible-budget total costs	$1,156,000

These three steps enable Webb to prepare a flexible budget, as shown in Exhibit 2, column 3. The flexible budget allows for a more detailed analysis of the $93,100 unfavorable static-budget variance for operating income.

> **Decision Point**
>
> How can managers develop a flexible budget and why is it useful to do so?

Flexible-Budget Variances and Sales-Volume Variances

Exhibit 2 shows the flexible-budget-based variance analysis for Webb, which subdivides the $93,100 unfavorable static-budget variance for operating income into two parts: a flexible-budget variance of $29,100 U and a sales-volume variance of $64,000 U. The **sales-volume variance** is the difference between a flexible-budget amount and the corresponding static-budget amount. The **flexible-budget variance** is the difference between an actual result and the corresponding flexible-budget amount.

Exhibit 2	Level 2 Flexible-Budget-Based Variance Analysis for Webb Company for April 2011[a]

Level 2 Analysis

	Actual Results (1)	Flexible-Budget Variances (2) = (1) – (3)	Flexible Budget (3)	Sales-Volume Variances (4) = (3) – (5)	Static Budget (5)
Units sold	10,000	0	10,000	2,000 U	12,000
Revenues	$1,250,000	$50,000 F	$1,200,000	$240,000 U	$1,440,000
Variable costs					
Direct materials	621,600	21,600 U	600,000	120,000 F	720,000
Direct manufacturing labor	198,000	38,000 U	160,000	32,000 F	192,000
Variable manufacturing overhead	130,500	10,500 U	120,000	24,000 F	144,000
Total variable costs	950,100	70,100 U	880,000	176,000 F	1,056,000
Contribution margin	299,900	20,100 U	320,000	64,000 U	384,000
Fixed manufacturing costs	285,000	9,000 U	276,000	0	276,000
Operating income	$ 14,900	$29,100 U	$ 44,000	$ 64,000 U	$ 108,000
Level 2		$29,100 U		$ 64,000 U	
		Flexible-budget variance		Sales-volume variance	
Level 1			$93,100 U		
			Static-budget variance		

[a]F = favorable effect on operating income; U = unfavorable effect on operating income.

Sales-Volume Variances

Keep in mind that the flexible-budget amounts in column 3 of Exhibit 2 and the static-budget amounts in column 5 are both computed using budgeted selling prices, budgeted variable cost per jacket, and budgeted fixed costs. The difference between the static-budget and the flexible-budget amounts is called the sales-volume variance because it arises *solely* from the difference between the 10,000 actual quantity (or volume) of jackets sold and the 12,000 quantity of jackets expected to be sold in the static budget.

$$\text{Sales-volume variance for operating income} = \text{Flexible-budget amount} - \text{Static-budget amount}$$

$$= \$44{,}000 - \$108{,}000$$

$$= \$64{,}000 \text{ U}$$

The sales-volume variance in operating income for Webb measures the change in budgeted contribution margin because Webb sold only 10,000 jackets rather than the budgeted 12,000.

$$\text{Sales-volume variance for operating income} = \left(\begin{array}{c}\text{Budgeted contribution}\\ \text{margin per unit}\end{array}\right) \times \left(\begin{array}{c}\text{Actual units}\\ \text{sold}\end{array} - \begin{array}{c}\text{Static-budget}\\ \text{units sold}\end{array}\right)$$

$$= \left(\begin{array}{c}\text{Budgeted selling}\\ \text{price}\end{array} - \begin{array}{c}\text{Budgeted variable}\\ \text{cost per unit}\end{array}\right) \times \left(\begin{array}{c}\text{Actual units}\\ \text{sold}\end{array} - \begin{array}{c}\text{Static-budget}\\ \text{units sold}\end{array}\right)$$

$$= (\$120 \text{ per jacket} - \$88 \text{ per jacket}) \times (10{,}000 \text{ jackets} - 12{,}000 \text{ jackets})$$

$$= \$32 \text{ per jacket} \times (-2{,}000 \text{ jackets})$$

$$= \$64{,}000 \text{ U}$$

Exhibit 2, column 4, shows the components of this overall variance by identifying the sales-volume variance for each of the line items in the income statement. Webb's managers determine that the unfavorable sales-volume variance in operating income could be because of one or more of the following reasons:

1. The overall demand for jackets is not growing at the rate that was anticipated.
2. Competitors are taking away market share from Webb.
3. Webb did not adapt quickly to changes in customer preferences and tastes.
4. Budgeted sales targets were set without careful analysis of market conditions.
5. Quality problems developed that led to customer dissatisfaction with Webb's jackets.

How Webb responds to the unfavorable sales-volume variance will be influenced by what management believes to be the cause of the variance. For example, if Webb's managers believe the unfavorable sales-volume variance was caused by market-related reasons (reasons 1, 2, 3, or 4), the sales manager would be in the best position to explain what happened and to suggest corrective actions that may be needed, such as sales promotions or market studies. If, however, managers believe the unfavorable sales-volume variance was caused by quality problems (reason 5), the production manager would be in the best position to analyze the causes and to suggest strategies for improvement, such as changes in the manufacturing process or investments in new machines. The appendix shows how to further analyze the sales volume variance to identify the reasons behind the unfavorable outcome.

The static-budget variances compared actual revenues and costs for 10,000 jackets against budgeted revenues and costs for 12,000 jackets. A portion of this difference, the sales-volume variance, reflects the effects of inaccurate forecasting of output units sold.

By removing this component from the static-budget variance, managers can compare actual revenues earned and costs incurred for April 2011 against the flexible budget—the revenues and costs Webb would have budgeted for the 10,000 jackets actually produced and sold. *These flexible-budget variances are a better measure of operating performance than static-budget variances because they compare actual revenues to budgeted revenues and actual costs to budgeted costs for the same 10,000 jackets of output.*

Flexible-Budget Variances

The first three columns of Exhibit 2 compare actual results with flexible-budget amounts. Flexible-budget variances are in column 2 for each line item in the income statement:

$$\text{Flexible-budget variance} = \text{Actual result} - \text{Flexible-budget amount}$$

The operating income line in Exhibit 2 shows the flexible-budget variance is $29,100 U ($14,900 − $44,000). The $29,100 U arises because actual selling price, actual variable cost per unit, and actual fixed costs differ from their budgeted amounts. The actual results and budgeted amounts for the selling price and variable cost per unit are as follows:

	Actual Result	Budgeted Amount
Selling price	$125.00 ($1,250,000 ÷ 10,000 jackets)	$120.00 ($1,200,000 ÷ 10,000 jackets)
Variable cost per jacket	$ 95.01 ($ 950,100 ÷ 10,000 jackets)	$ 88.00 ($ 880,000 ÷ 10,000 jackets)

The flexible-budget variance for revenues is called the **selling-price variance** because it arises solely from the difference between the actual selling price and the budgeted selling price:

$$\text{Selling-price variance} = \left(\text{Actual selling price} - \text{Budgeted selling price} \right) \times \text{Actual units sold}$$

$$= (\$125 \text{ per jacket} - \$120 \text{ per jacket}) \times 10,000 \text{ jackets}$$

$$= \$50,000 \text{ F}$$

Webb has a favorable selling-price variance because the $125 actual selling price exceeds the $120 budgeted amount, which increases operating income. Marketing managers are generally in the best position to understand and explain the reason for this selling price difference. For example, was the difference due to better quality? Or was it due to an overall increase in market prices? Webb's managers concluded it was due to a general increase in prices.

The flexible-budget variance for total variable costs is unfavorable ($70,100 U) for the actual output of 10,000 jackets. It's unfavorable because of one or both of the following:

- Webb used greater quantities of inputs (such as direct manufacturing labor-hours) compared to the budgeted quantities of inputs.
- Webb incurred higher prices per unit for the inputs (such as the wage rate per direct manufacturing labor-hour) compared to the budgeted prices per unit of the inputs.

Higher input quantities and/or higher input prices relative to the budgeted amounts could be the result of Webb deciding to produce a better product than what was planned or the result of inefficiencies in Webb's manufacturing and purchasing, or both. *You should always think of variance analysis as providing suggestions for further investigation rather than as establishing conclusive evidence of good or bad performance.*

The actual fixed costs of $285,000 are $9,000 more than the budgeted amount of $276,000. This unfavorable flexible-budget variance reflects unexpected increases in the cost of fixed indirect resources, such as factory rent or supervisory salaries.

In the rest of this chapter, we will focus on variable direct-cost input variances.

Decision Point

How are flexible-budget and sales-volume variances calculated?

Price Variances and Efficiency Variances for Direct-Cost Inputs

To gain further insight, almost all companies subdivide the flexible-budget variance for direct-cost inputs into two more-detailed variances:

1. A price variance that reflects the difference between an actual input price and a budgeted input price

2. An efficiency variance that reflects the difference between an actual input quantity and a budgeted input quantity

The information available from these variances (which we call level 3 variances) helps managers to better understand past performance and take corrective actions to implement superior strategies in the future. Managers generally have more control over efficiency variances than price variances because the quantity of inputs used is primarily affected by factors inside the company (such as the efficiency with which operations are performed), while changes in the price of materials or in wage rates may be largely dictated by market forces outside the company (see the Concepts in Action feature).

Obtaining Budgeted Input Prices and Budgeted Input Quantities

Learning Objective 4

Explain why standard costs are often used in variance analysis

. . . standard costs exclude past inefficiencies and take into account expected future changes

To calculate price and efficiency variances, Webb needs to obtain budgeted input prices and budgeted input quantities. Webb's three main sources for this information are past data, data from similar companies, and standards.

1. **Actual input data from past periods.** Most companies have past data on actual input prices and actual input quantities. These historical data could be analyzed for trends or patterns to obtain estimates of budgeted prices and quantities. The advantage of past data is that they represent quantities and prices that are real rather than hypothetical and can serve as benchmarks for continuous improvement. Another advantage is that past data are typically available at low cost. However, there are limitations to using past data. Past data can include inefficiencies such as wastage of direct materials. They also do not incorporate any changes expected for the budget period.

2. **Data from other companies that have similar processes.** The benefit of using data from peer firms is that the budget numbers represent competitive benchmarks from other companies. For example, Baptist Healthcare System in Louisville, Kentucky, maintains detailed flexible budgets and benchmarks its labor performance against hospitals that provide similar types of services and volumes and are in the upper quartile of a national benchmark. The main difficulty of using this source is that input-price and input quantity data from other companies are often not available or may not be comparable to a particular company's situation. Consider American Apparel, which makes over 1 million articles of clothing a week. At its sole factory, in Los Angeles, workers receive hourly wages, piece rates, and medical benefits well in excess of those paid by its competitors, virtually all of whom are offshore. Moreover, because sourcing organic cotton from overseas results in too high of a carbon footprint, American Apparel purchases more expensive domestic cotton in keeping with its sustainability programs.

3. **Standards developed by Webb.** A **standard** is a carefully determined price, cost, or quantity that is used as a benchmark for judging performance. Standards are usually expressed on a per-unit basis. Consider how Webb determines its direct manufacturing labor standards. Webb conducts engineering studies to obtain a detailed breakdown of the steps required to make a jacket. Each step is assigned a standard time based on work performed by a *skilled* worker using equipment operating in an *efficient* manner. There are two advantages of using standard times: (i) They aim to exclude past inefficiencies and (ii) they aim to take into account changes expected to occur in the budget period. An example of (ii) is the decision by Webb, for strategic reasons, to lease new

sewing machines that operate at a faster speed and enable output to be produced with lower defect rates. Similarly, Webb determines the standard quantity of square yards of cloth required by a skilled operator to make each jacket.

The term "standard" refers to many different things. Always clarify its meaning and how it is being used. A **standard input** is a carefully determined quantity of input—such as square yards of cloth or direct manufacturing labor-hours—required for one unit of output, such as a jacket. A **standard price** is a carefully determined price that a company expects to pay for a unit of input. In the Webb example, the standard wage rate that Webb expects to pay its operators is an example of a standard price of a direct manufacturing labor-hour. A **standard cost** is a carefully determined cost of a unit of output—for example, the standard direct manufacturing labor cost of a jacket at Webb.

$$\begin{array}{c} \text{Standard cost per output unit for} \\ \text{each variable direct-cost input} \end{array} = \begin{array}{c} \text{Standard input allowed} \\ \text{for one output unit} \end{array} \times \begin{array}{c} \text{Standard price} \\ \text{per input unit} \end{array}$$

Standard direct material cost per jacket: 2 square yards of cloth input allowed per output unit (jacket) manufactured, at $30 standard price per square yard

Standard direct material cost per jacket = 2 square yards × $30 per square yard = $60

Standard direct manufacturing labor cost per jacket: 0.8 manufacturing labor-hour of input allowed per output unit manufactured, at $20 standard price per hour

Standard direct manufacturing labor cost per jacket = 0.8 labor-hour × $20 per labor-hour = $16

How are the words "budget" and "standard" related? Budget is the broader term. To clarify, budgeted input prices, input quantities, and costs need *not* be based on standards. As we saw previously, they could be based on past data or competitive benchmarks, for example. However, when standards *are* used to obtain budgeted input quantities and prices, the terms "standard" and "budget" are used interchangeably. The standard cost of each input required for one unit of output is determined by the standard quantity of the input required for one unit of output and the standard price per input unit. See how the standard-cost computations shown previously for direct materials and direct manufacturing labor result in the budgeted direct material cost per jacket of $60 and the budgeted direct manufacturing labor cost of $16 referred to earlier.

In its standard costing system, Webb uses standards that are attainable through efficient operations but that allow for normal disruptions. An alternative is to set more-challenging standards that are more difficult to attain. Setting challenging standards can increase motivation and performance. If, however, standards are regarded by workers as essentially unachievable, it can increase frustration and hurt performance.

Data for Calculating Webb's Price Variances and Efficiency Variances

Consider Webb's two direct-cost categories. The actual cost for each of these categories for the 10,000 jackets manufactured and sold in April 2011 is as follows:

Direct Materials Purchased and Used[4]

1. Square yards of cloth input purchased and used	22,200
2. Actual price incurred per square yard	$ 28
3. Direct material costs (22,200 × $28) [shown in Exhibit 2, column 1]	$621,600

Direct Manufacturing Labor

1. Direct manufacturing labor-hours	9,000
2. Actual price incurred per direct manufacturing labor-hour	$ 22
3. Direct manufacturing labor costs (9,000 × $22) [shown in Exhibit 2, column 1]	$198,000

---

[4] The Problem for Self-Study relaxes the assumption that the quantity of direct materials used equals the quantity of direct materials purchased.

◀ **Decision Point**

What is a standard cost and what are its purposes?

Learning Objective 5

Compute price variances

. . . each price variance is the difference between an actual input price and a budgeted input price

and efficiency variances

. . . each efficiency variance is the difference between an actual input quantity and a budgeted input quantity for actual output

for direct-cost categories

Let's use the Webb Company data to illustrate the price variance and the efficiency variance for direct-cost inputs.

A **price variance** is the difference between actual price and budgeted price, multiplied by actual input quantity, such as direct materials purchased or used. A price variance is sometimes called an **input-price variance** or **rate variance**, especially when referring to a price variance for direct manufacturing labor. An **efficiency variance** is the difference between actual input quantity used—such as square yards of cloth of direct materials—and budgeted input quantity allowed for actual output, multiplied by budgeted price. An efficiency variance is sometimes called a **usage variance**. Let's explore price and efficiency variances in greater detail so we can see how managers use these variances to improve their future performance.

Price Variances

The formula for computing the price variance is as follows:

$$\text{Price variance} = \left(\begin{array}{c} \text{Actual price} \\ \text{of input} \end{array} - \begin{array}{c} \text{Budgeted price} \\ \text{of input} \end{array} \right) \times \begin{array}{c} \text{Actual quantity} \\ \text{of input} \end{array}$$

Price variances for Webb's two direct-cost categories are as follows:

Direct-Cost Category	$\left(\begin{array}{c}\text{Actual price} \\ \text{of input} \end{array} - \begin{array}{c}\text{Budgeted price} \\ \text{of input} \end{array} \right)$	×	Actual quantity of input	Price = Variance
Direct materials	($28 per sq. yard − $30 per sq. yard)	×	22,200 square yards	= $44,400 F
Direct manufacturing labor	($22 per hour − $20 per hour)	×	9,000 hours	= $18,000 U

The direct materials price variance is favorable because actual price of cloth is less than budgeted price, resulting in an increase in operating income. The direct manufacturing labor price variance is unfavorable because actual wage rate paid to labor is more than the budgeted rate, resulting in a decrease in operating income.

Always consider a broad range of possible causes for a price variance. For example, Webb's favorable direct materials price variance could be due to one or more of the following:

- Webb's purchasing manager negotiated the direct materials prices more skillfully than was planned for in the budget.
- The purchasing manager changed to a lower-price supplier.
- Webb's purchasing manager ordered larger quantities than the quantities budgeted, thereby obtaining quantity discounts.
- Direct material prices decreased unexpectedly because of, say, industry oversupply.
- Budgeted purchase prices of direct materials were set too high without careful analysis of market conditions.
- The purchasing manager received favorable prices because he was willing to accept unfavorable terms on factors other than prices (such as lower-quality material).

Webb's response to a direct materials price variance depends on what is believed to be the cause of the variance. Assume Webb's managers attribute the favorable price variance to the purchasing manager ordering in larger quantities than budgeted, thereby receiving quantity discounts. Webb could examine if purchasing in these larger quantities resulted in higher storage costs. If the increase in storage and inventory holding costs exceeds the quantity discounts, purchasing in larger quantities is not beneficial. Some companies have reduced their materials storage areas to prevent their purchasing managers from ordering in larger quantities.

Efficiency Variance

For any actual level of output, the efficiency variance is the difference between actual quantity of input used and the budgeted quantity of input allowed for that output level, multiplied by the budgeted input price:

$$\text{Efficiency Variance} = \left(\begin{array}{c} \text{Actual} \\ \text{quantity of} \\ \text{input used} \end{array} - \begin{array}{c} \text{Budgeted quantity} \\ \text{of input allowed} \\ \text{for actual output} \end{array} \right) \times \begin{array}{c} \text{Budgeted price} \\ \text{of input} \end{array}$$

Concepts in Action | Starbucks Reduces Direct-Cost Variances to Brew a Turnaround

Stephen Chernin/Newscom

Along with coffee, Starbucks brewed profitable growth for many years. From Seattle to Singapore, customers lined up to buy $4 lattes and Frappuccinos. Walking around with a coffee drink from Starbucks became an affordable-luxury status symbol. But when consumers tightened their purse strings amid the recession, the company was in serious trouble. With customers cutting back and lower-priced competition—from Dunkin' Donuts and McDonald's among others—increasing, Starbucks' profit margins were under attack.

For Starbucks, profitability depends on making each high-quality beverage at the lowest possible costs. As a result, an intricate understanding of direct costs is critical. Variance analysis helps managers assess and maintain profitability at desired levels. In each Starbucks store, the two key direct costs are materials and labor.

Materials costs at Starbucks include coffee beans, milk, flavoring syrups, pastries, paper cups, and lids. To reduce budgeted costs for materials, Starbucks focused on two key inputs: coffee and milk. For coffee, Starbucks sought to avoid waste and spoilage by no longer brewing decaffeinated and darker coffee blends in the afternoon and evening, when store traffic is slower. Instead, baristas were instructed to brew a pot only when a customer ordered it. With milk prices rising (and making up around 10% of Starbucks' cost of sales), the company switched to 2% milk, which is healthier and costs less, and redoubled efforts to reduce milk-related spoilage.

Labor costs at Starbucks, which cost 24% of company revenue annually, were another area of variance focus. Many stores employed fewer baristas. In other stores, Starbucks adopted many "lean" production techniques. With 30% of baristas' time involved in walking around behind the counter, reaching for items, and blending drinks, Starbucks sought to make its drink-making processes more efficient. While the changes seem small—keeping bins of coffee beans on top of the counter so baristas don't have to bend over, moving bottles of flavored syrups closer to where drinks are made, and using colored tape to quickly differentiate between pitchers of soy, nonfat, and low-fat milk—some stores experienced a 10% increase in transactions using the same number of workers or fewer.

The company took additional steps to align labor costs with its pricing. Starbucks cut prices on easier-to-make drinks like drip coffee, while lifting prices by as much as 30 cents for larger and more complex drinks, such as a venti caramel macchiato.

Starbucks' focus on reducing year-over-year variances paid off. In fiscal year 2009, the company reduced its store operating expenses by $320 million, or 8.5%. Continued focus on direct-cost variances will be critical to the company's future success in any economic climate.

Sources: Adamy, Janet. 2009. Starbucks brews up new cost cuts by putting lid on afternoon decaf. *Wall Street Journal*, January 28; Adamy, Janet. 2008. New Starbucks brew attracts customers, flak. *Wall Street Journal*, July 1; Harris, Craig. 2007. Starbucks slips; lattes rise. *Seattle Post Intelligencer*, July 23; Jargon, Julie. 2010. Starbucks growth revives, perked by Via. *Wall Street Journal*, January 21; Jargon, Julie. 2009. Latest Starbucks buzzword: 'Lean' Japanese techniques. *Wall Street Journal*, August 4; Kesmodel, David. 2009. Starbucks sees demand stirring again. *Wall Street Journal*, November 6.

The idea here is that a company is inefficient if it uses a larger quantity of input than the budgeted quantity for its actual level of output; the company is efficient if it uses a smaller quantity of input than was budgeted for that output level.

The efficiency variances for each of Webb's direct-cost categories are as follows:

Direct-Cost Category	$\left(\begin{array}{c}\text{Actual} \\ \text{quantity of} \\ \text{input used}\end{array} - \begin{array}{c}\text{Budgeted quantity} \\ \text{of input allowed} \\ \text{for actual output}\end{array}\right)$	$\times$	Budgeted price of input	=	Efficiency Variance
Direct materials	[22,200 sq. yds. − (10,000 units × 2 sq. yds./unit)]	× $30 per sq. yard			
	= (22,200 sq. yds. − 20,000 sq. yds.)	× $30 per sq. yard	=	$66,000 U	
Direct manufacturing labor	[9,000 hours − (10,000 units × 0.8 hour/unit)]	× $20 per hour			
	= (9,000 hours − 8,000 hours)	× $20 per hour	=	20,000 U	

The two manufacturing efficiency variances—direct materials efficiency variance and direct manufacturing labor efficiency variance—are each unfavorable because more input was used than was budgeted for the actual output, resulting in a decrease in operating income.

As with price variances, there is a broad range of possible causes for these efficiency variances. For example, Webb's unfavorable efficiency variance for direct manufacturing labor could be because of one or more of the following:

- Webb's personnel manager hired underskilled workers.

- Webb's production scheduler inefficiently scheduled work, resulting in more manufacturing labor time than budgeted being used per jacket.

- Webb's maintenance department did not properly maintain machines, resulting in more manufacturing labor time than budgeted being used per jacket.

- Budgeted time standards were set too tight without careful analysis of the operating conditions and the employees' skills.

Decision Point ▶

Why should a company calculate price and efficiency variances?

Suppose Webb's managers determine that the unfavorable variance is due to poor machine maintenance. Webb may then establish a team consisting of plant engineers and machine operators to develop a maintenance schedule that will reduce future breakdowns and thereby prevent adverse effects on labor time and product quality.

Exhibit 3 provides an alternative way to calculate price and efficiency variances. It also illustrates how the price variance and the efficiency variance subdivide the flexible-budget variance. Consider direct materials. The direct materials flexible-budget variance of $21,600 U is the difference between actual costs incurred (actual input quantity × actual price) of $621,600 shown in column 1 and the flexible budget (budgeted input quantity allowed for actual output × budgeted price) of $600,000 shown in column 3. Column 2 (actual input quantity × budgeted price) is inserted between column 1 and column 3. The difference between columns 1 and 2 is the price variance of $44,400 F. This price variance occurs because the same actual input quantity (22,200 sq. yds.) is multiplied by *actual price* ($28) in column 1 and *budgeted price* ($30) in column 2. The difference between columns 2 and 3 is the efficiency variance of $66,000 U because the same budgeted price ($30) is multiplied by *actual input quantity* (22,200 sq. yds) in column 2

Exhibit 3   Columnar Presentation of Variance Analysis: Direct Costs for Webb Company for April 2011[a]

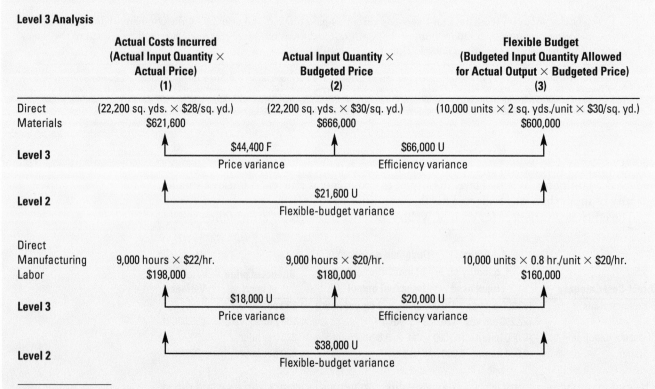

Level 3 Analysis

	Actual Costs Incurred (Actual Input Quantity × Actual Price) (1)	Actual Input Quantity × Budgeted Price (2)	Flexible Budget (Budgeted Input Quantity Allowed for Actual Output × Budgeted Price) (3)
Direct Materials	(22,200 sq. yds. × $28/sq. yd.) $621,600	(22,200 sq. yds. × $30/sq. yd.) $666,000	(10,000 units × 2 sq. yds./unit × $30/sq. yd.) $600,000
Level 3		↑ $44,400 F ↑ Price variance	$66,000 U ↑ Efficiency variance
Level 2		↑ $21,600 U Flexible-budget variance	↑
Direct Manufacturing Labor	9,000 hours × $22/hr. $198,000	9,000 hours × $20/hr. $180,000	10,000 units × 0.8 hr./unit × $20/hr. $160,000
Level 3		↑ $18,000 U ↑ Price variance	$20,000 U ↑ Efficiency variance
Level 2		↑ $38,000 U Flexible-budget variance	↑

[a]F = favorable effect on operating income; U = unfavorable effect on operating income.

and *budgeted input quantity allowed for actual output* (20,000 sq. yds.) in column 3. The sum of the direct materials price variance, $44,400 F, and the direct materials efficiency variance, $66,000 U, equals the direct materials flexible budget variance, $21,600 U.

Summary of Variances

Exhibit 4 provides a summary of the different variances. Note how the variances at each higher level provide disaggregated and more detailed information for evaluating performance.

The following computations show why actual operating income is $14,900 when the static-budget operating income is $108,000. The numbers in the computations can be found in Exhibits 2 and 3.

Static-budget operating income			$108,000
Unfavorable sales-volume variance for operating income			(64,000)
Flexible-budget operating income			44,000
Flexible-budget variances for operating income:			
Favorable selling-price variance		$50,000	
Direct materials variances:			
Favorable direct materials price variance	$ 44,400		
Unfavorable direct materials efficiency variance	(66,000)		
Unfavorable direct materials variance		(21,600)	
Direct manufacturing labor variances:			
Unfavorable direct manufacturing labor price variance	(18,000)		
Unfavorable direct manufacturing labor efficiency variance	(20,000)		
Unfavorable direct manufacturing labor variance		(38,000)	
Unfavorable variable manufacturing overhead variance		(10,500)	
Unfavorable fixed manufacturing overhead variance		(9,000)	
Unfavorable flexible-budget variance for operating income			(29,100)
Actual operating income			$ 14,900

The summary of variances highlights three main effects:

1. Webb sold 2,000 fewer units than budgeted, resulting in an unfavorable sales volume variance of $64,000. Sales declined because of quality problems and new styles of jackets introduced by Webb's competitors.

2. Webb sold units at a higher price than budgeted, resulting in a favorable selling-price variance of $50,000. Webb's prices, however, were lower than the prices charged by Webb's competitors.

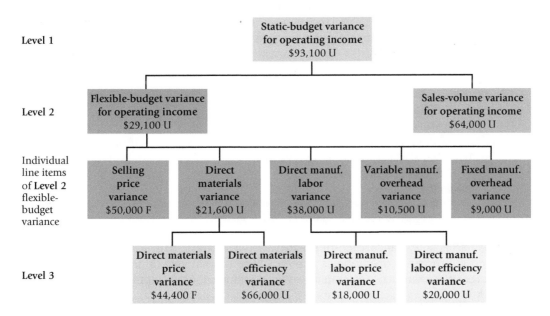

Level 1 — Static-budget variance for operating income $93,100 U

Level 2 — Flexible-budget variance for operating income $29,100 U / Sales-volume variance for operating income $64,000 U

Individual line items of **Level 2** flexible-budget variance — Selling price variance $50,000 F / Direct materials variance $21,600 U / Direct manuf. labor variance $38,000 U / Variable manuf. overhead variance $10,500 U / Fixed manuf. overhead variance $9,000 U

Level 3 — Direct materials price variance $44,400 F / Direct materials efficiency variance $66,000 U / Direct manuf. labor price variance $18,000 U / Direct manuf. labor efficiency variance $20,000 U

Exhibit 4

Summary of Level 1, 2, and 3 Variance Analyses

3. Manufacturing costs for the actual output produced were higher than budgeted—direct materials by $21,600, direct manufacturing labor by $38,000, variable manufacturing overhead by $10,500, and fixed overhead by $9,000 because of poor quality of cloth, poor maintenance of machines, and underskilled workers.

We now present Webb's journal entries under its standard costing system.

Journal Entries Using Standard Costs

We will now illustrate journal entries for Webb Company using standard costs. Our focus is on direct materials and direct manufacturing labor. All the numbers included in the following journal entries are found in Exhibit 3.

Note: In each of the following entries, unfavorable variances are always debits (they decrease operating income), and favorable variances are always credits (they increase operating income).

JOURNAL ENTRY 1A: Isolate the direct materials price variance at the time of purchase by increasing (debiting) Direct Materials Control at standard prices. This is the earliest time possible to isolate this variance.

1a.	Direct Materials Control		
	(22,200 square yards × $30 per square yard)	666,000	
	Direct Materials Price Variance		
	(22,200 square yards × $2 per square yard)		44,400
	Accounts Payable Control		
	(22,200 square yards × $28 per square yard)		621,600
	To record direct materials purchased.		

JOURNAL ENTRY 1B: Isolate the direct materials efficiency variance at the time the direct materials are used by increasing (debiting) Work-in-Process Control at standard quantities allowed for actual output units manufactured times standard prices.

1b.	Work-in-Process Control		
	(10,000 jackets × 2 yards per jacket × $30 per square yard)	600,000	
	Direct Materials Efficiency Variance		
	(2,200 square yards × $30 per square yard)	66,000	
	Direct Materials Control		
	(22,200 square yards × $30 per square yard)		666,000
	To record direct materials used.		

JOURNAL ENTRY 2: Isolate the direct manufacturing labor price variance and efficiency variance at the time this labor is used by increasing (debiting) Work-in-Process Control at standard quantities allowed for actual output units manufactured at standard prices. Note that Wages Payable Control measures the actual amounts payable to workers based on actual hours worked and actual wage rates.

2.	Work-in-Process Control		
	(10,000 jackets × 0.80 hour per jacket × $20 per hour)	160,000	
	Direct Manufacturing Labor Price Variance		
	(9,000 hours × $2 per hour)	18,000	
	Direct Manufacturing Labor Efficiency Variance		
	(1,000 hours × $20 per hour)	20,000	
	Wages Payable Control		
	(9,000 hours × $22 per hour)		198,000
	To record liability for direct manufacturing labor costs.		

We have seen how standard costing and variance analysis help to focus management attention on areas not operating as expected. The journal entries here point to another advantage of standard costing systems—that is, standard costs simplify product costing. As each unit is manufactured, costs are assigned to it using the standard cost of direct materials, the standard cost of direct manufacturing labor and standard manufacturing overhead cost.

From the perspective of control, all variances are isolated at the earliest possible time. For example, by isolating the direct materials price variance at the time of purchase, corrective actions—such as seeking cost reductions from the current supplier or obtaining price quotes from other potential suppliers—can be taken immediately when a large unfavorable variance is first known rather than waiting until after the materials are used in production.

At the end of the fiscal year, the variance accounts are written off to cost of goods sold if they are immaterial in amount. For simplicity, we assume that the balances in the different direct cost variance accounts as of April 2011 are also the balances at the end of 2011 and therefore immaterial in total. Webb would record the following journal entry to write off the direct cost variance accounts to Cost of Goods Sold.

Cost of Goods Sold	59,600	
Direct Materials Price Variance	44,400	
Direct Materials Efficiency Variance		66,000
Direct Manufacturing Labor Price Variance		18,000
Direct Manufacturing Labor Efficiency Variance		20,000

Alternatively, assuming Webb has inventories at the end of the fiscal year, and the variances are material in their amounts, the variance accounts are prorated between cost of goods sold and various inventory accounts. For example, Direct Materials Price Variance is prorated among Materials Control, Work-in-Process Control, Finished Goods Control and Cost of Goods Sold on the basis of the standard costs of direct materials in each account's ending balance. Direct Materials Efficiency Variance is prorated among Work-in-Process Control, Finished Goods Control, and Cost of Goods Sold on the basis of the direct material costs in each account's ending balance (after proration of the direct materials price variance).

Many accountants, industrial engineers, and managers maintain that to the extent that variances measure inefficiency or abnormal efficiency during the year, they should be written off instead of being prorated among inventories and cost of goods sold. This reasoning argues for applying a combination of the write-off and proration methods for each individual variance. Consider the efficiency variance. The portion of the efficiency variance that is due to inefficiency and could have been avoided should be written off to cost of goods sold while the portion that is unavoidable should be prorated. If another variance, such as the direct materials price variance, is considered unavoidable because it is entirely caused by general market conditions, it should be prorated. Unlike full proration, this approach avoids carrying the costs of inefficiency as part of inventoriable costs.

Implementing Standard Costing

Standard costing provides valuable information for the management and control of materials, labor, and other activities related to production.

Standard Costing and Information Technology

Modern information technology promotes the increased use of standard costing systems for product costing and control. Companies such as Dell and Sandoz store standard prices and standard quantities in their computer systems. A bar code scanner records the receipt of materials, immediately costing each material using its stored standard price. The receipt of materials is then matched with the purchase order to record accounts payable and to isolate the direct materials price variance.

The direct materials efficiency variance is calculated as output is completed by comparing the standard quantity of direct materials that should have been used with the computerized request for direct materials submitted by an operator on the production floor. Labor variances are calculated as employees log into production-floor terminals and punch in their employee numbers, start and end times, and the quantity of product they helped produce. Managers use this instantaneous feedback from variances to initiate immediate corrective action, as needed.

Wide Applicability of Standard Costing

Companies that have implemented total quality management and computer-integrated manufacturing (CIM) systems, as well as companies in the service sector, find standard costing to be a useful tool. Companies implementing total quality management programs use standard costing to control materials costs. Service-sector companies such as McDonald's are labor intensive and use standard costs to control labor costs. Companies that have implemented CIM, such as Toyota, use flexible budgeting and standard costing to manage activities such as materials handling and setups. The growing use of Enterprise Resource Planning (ERP) systems has made it easy for firms to keep track of standard, average, and actual costs for inventory items and to make real-time assessments of variances. Managers use variance information to identify areas of the firm's manufacturing or purchasing process that most need attention.

Management Uses of Variances

Learning Objective 6

Understand how managers use variances

. . . managers use variances to improve future performance

Managers and management accountants use variances to evaluate performance after decisions are implemented, to trigger organization learning, and to make continuous improvements. Variances serve as an early warning system to alert managers to existing problems or to prospective opportunities. Variance analysis enables managers to evaluate the effectiveness of the actions and performance of personnel in the current period, as well as to fine-tune strategies for achieving improved performance in the future. To make sure that managers interpret variances correctly and make appropriate decisions based on them, managers need to recognize that variances can have multiple causes.

Multiple Causes of Variances

Managers must not interpret variances in isolation of each other. The causes of variances in one part of the value chain can be the result of decisions made in another part of the value chain. Consider an unfavorable direct materials efficiency variance on Webb's production line. Possible operational causes of this variance across the value chain of the company are as follows:

1. Poor design of products or processes
2. Poor work on the production line because of underskilled workers or faulty machines
3. Inappropriate assignment of labor or machines to specific jobs
4. Congestion due to scheduling a large number of rush orders from Webb's sales representatives
5. Webb's suppliers not manufacturing cloth materials of uniformly high quality

Item 5 offers an even broader reason for the cause of the unfavorable direct materials efficiency variance by considering inefficiencies in the supply chain of companies—in this case, by the cloth suppliers for Webb's jackets. Whenever possible, managers must attempt to understand the root causes of the variances.

When to Investigate Variances

Managers realize that a standard is not a single measure but rather a range of possible acceptable input quantities, costs, output quantities, or prices. Consequently, they expect small variances to arise. A variance within an acceptable range is considered to be an "in control occurrence" and calls for no investigation or action by managers. So when would managers need to investigate variances?

Frequently, managers investigate variances based on subjective judgments or rules of thumb. For critical items, such as product defects, even a small variance may prompt investigations and actions. For other items, such as direct material costs, labor costs, and repair costs, companies generally have rules such as "investigate all variances exceeding $5,000 or 25% of the budgeted cost, whichever is lower." The idea is that a 4% variance in direct material costs of $1 million—a $40,000 variance—deserves more attention than a 20% variance in repair costs of $10,000—a $2,000 variance. Variance analysis is subject to the same cost-benefit test as all other phases of a management control system.

Performance Measurement Using Variances

Managers often use variance analysis when evaluating the performance of their subordinates. Two attributes of performance are commonly evaluated:

1. **Effectiveness:** the degree to which a predetermined objective or target is met—for example, sales, market share and customer satisfaction ratings of Starbucks' new VIA® Ready Brew line of instant coffees.

2. **Efficiency:** the relative amount of inputs used to achieve a given output level—the smaller the quantity of Arabica beans used to make a given number of VIA packets or the greater the number of VIA packets made from a given quantity of beans, the greater the efficiency.

As we discussed earlier, managers must be sure they understand the causes of a variance before using it for performance evaluation. Suppose a Webb purchasing manager has just negotiated a deal that results in a favorable price variance for direct materials. The deal could have achieved a favorable variance for any or all of the following reasons:

1. The purchasing manager bargained effectively with suppliers.

2. The purchasing manager secured a discount for buying in bulk with fewer purchase orders. However, buying larger quantities than necessary for the short run resulted in excessive inventory.

3. The purchasing manager accepted a bid from the lowest-priced supplier after only minimal effort to check quality amid concerns about the supplier's materials.

If the purchasing manager's performance is evaluated solely on price variances, then the evaluation will be positive. Reason 1 would support this favorable conclusion: The purchasing manager bargained effectively. Reasons 2 and 3 have short-run gains, buying in bulk or making only minimal effort to check the supplier's quality-monitoring procedures. However, these short-run gains could be offset by higher inventory storage costs or higher inspection costs and defect rates on Webb's production line, leading to unfavorable direct manufacturing labor and direct materials efficiency variances. Webb may ultimately lose more money because of reasons 2 and 3 than it gains from the favorable price variance.

Bottom line: Managers should not automatically interpret a favorable variance as "good news."

Managers benefit from variance analysis because it highlights individual aspects of performance. However, if any single performance measure (for example, a labor efficiency variance or a consumer rating report) receives excessive emphasis, managers will tend to make decisions that will cause the particular performance measure to look good. These actions may conflict with the company's overall goals, inhibiting the goals from being achieved. This faulty perspective on performance usually arises when top management designs a performance evaluation and reward system that does not emphasize total company objectives.

Organization Learning

The goal of variance analysis is for managers to understand why variances arise, to learn, and to improve future performance. For instance, to reduce the unfavorable direct materials efficiency variance, Webb's managers may seek improvements in product design, in the commitment of workers to do the job right the first time, and in the quality of supplied materials, among other improvements. Sometimes an unfavorable direct materials efficiency variance may signal a need to change product strategy, perhaps because the product cannot be made at a low enough cost. Variance analysis should not be a tool to "play the blame game" (that is, seeking a person to blame for every unfavorable variance). Rather, it should help the company learn about what happened and how to perform better in the future.

Managers need to strike a delicate balance between the two uses of variances we have discussed: performance evaluation and organization learning. Variance analysis is helpful for performance evaluation, but an overemphasis on performance evaluation and meeting individual variance targets can undermine learning and continuous improvement. Why? Because achieving the standard becomes an end in and of itself. As a result, managers will seek targets that are easy to attain rather than targets that are challenging and that require creativity and resourcefulness. For example, if performance evaluation is overemphasized, Webb's manufacturing manager will prefer an easy standard that allows workers ample time to manufacture a jacket; he will then have little incentive to improve processes and methods to reduce manufacturing time and cost.

An overemphasis on performance evaluation may also cause managers to take actions to achieve the budget and avoid an unfavorable variance, even if such actions could hurt the company in the long run. For example, the manufacturing manager may push workers to produce jackets within the time allowed, even if this action could lead to poorer quality jackets being produced, which could later hurt revenues. Such negative impacts are less likely to occur if variance analysis is seen as a way of promoting organization learning.

Continuous Improvement

Managers can also use variance analysis to create a virtuous cycle of continuous improvement. How? By repeatedly identifying causes of variances, initiating corrective actions, and evaluating results of actions. Improvement opportunities are often easier to identify when products are first produced. Once the easy opportunities have been identified ("the low-hanging fruit picked"), much more ingenuity may be required to identify successive improvement opportunities. Some companies use kaizen budgeting to specifically target reductions in budgeted costs over successive periods. The advantage of kaizen budgeting is that it makes continuous improvement goals explicit.

Financial and Nonfinancial Performance Measures

Almost all companies use a combination of financial and nonfinancial performance measures for planning and control rather than relying exclusively on either type of measure. To control a production process, supervisors cannot wait for an accounting report with variances reported in dollars. Instead, timely nonfinancial performance measures are frequently used for control purposes in such situations. For example, a Nissan plant compiles data such as defect rates and production-schedule attainment and broadcasts them in ticker-tape fashion on screens throughout the plant.

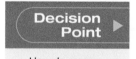

Decision Point

How do managers use variances?

In Webb's cutting room, cloth is laid out and cut into pieces, which are then matched and assembled. Managers exercise control in the cutting room by observing workers and by focusing on *nonfinancial measures*, such as number of square yards of cloth used to produce 1,000 jackets or percentage of jackets started and completed without requiring any rework. Webb production workers find these nonfinancial measures easy to understand. At the same time, Webb production managers will also use *financial measures* to evaluate the overall cost efficiency with which operations are being run and to help guide decisions about, say, changing the mix of inputs used in manufacturing jackets. Financial measures are often critical in a company because they indicate the economic impact of diverse physical activities. This knowledge allows managers to make trade-offs—increase the costs of one physical activity (say, cutting) to reduce the costs of another physical measure (say, defects).

Benchmarking and Variance Analysis

Learning Objective 7

Describe benchmarking and explain its role in cost management

. . . benchmarking compares actual performance against the best levels of performance

The budgeted amounts in the Webb Company illustration are based on analysis of operations within their own respective companies. We now turn to the situation in which companies develop standards based on an analysis of operations at other companies. **Benchmarking** is the continuous process of comparing the levels of performance in producing products and services and executing activities against the best levels of performance in competing companies or in companies having similar processes. When benchmarks are used as standards, managers and management accountants know that the company will be competitive in the marketplace if it can attain the standards.

Companies develop benchmarks and calculate variances on items that are the most important to their businesses. Consider the cost per available seat mile (ASM) for United Airlines; ASMs equal the total seats in a plane multiplied by the distance traveled, and are a measure of airline size. Assume United uses data from each of seven competing U.S. airlines in its benchmark cost comparisons. Summary data are in Exhibit 5. The benchmark

Exhibit 5   Available Seat Mile (ASM) Benchmark Comparison of United Airlines with Seven Other Airlines

	Home	Insert	Page Layout	Formulas	Data	Review	View		
	A	B	C	D	E	F	G		
1		Operating Cost	Operating Revenue	Operating Income	Fuel Cost	Labor Cost	Total ASMs		
2		per ASM	per ASM	per ASM	per ASM	per ASM	(Millions)		
3	Airline	(1)	(2)	(3) = (2) – (1)	(4)	(5)	(6)		
4									
5	United Airlines	$0.1574	$0.1258	–$0.0315	$0.0568	$0.0317	135,861		
6	Airlines used as benchmarks:								
7	JetBlue Airways	$0.1011	$0.1045	$0.0034	$0.0417	$0.0214	32,422		
8	Southwest Airlines	$0.1024	$0.1067	$0.0043	$0.0360	$0.0323	103,271		
9	Continental Airlines	$0.1347	$0.1319	–$0.0027	$0.0425	$0.0258	115,511		
10	Alaska Airlines	$0.1383	$0.1330	–$0.0053	$0.0480	$0.0319	24,218		
11	American Airlines	$0.1387	$0.1301	–$0.0086	$0.0551	$0.0407	163,532		
12	U.S. Airways	$0.1466	$0.1263	–$0.0203	$0.0488	$0.0301	74,151		
13	Delta/Northwest Airlines	$0.1872	$0.1370	–$0.0502	$0.0443	$0.0290	165,639		
14	Average of airlines								
15	used as benchmarks	$0.1356	$0.1242	–$0.0113	$0.0452	$0.0302	96,963		
16									
17									
18	*Source:* Individual companies' 10-K reports for the year ending December 31, 2008								

companies are ranked from lowest to highest operating cost per ASM in column 1. Also reported in Exhibit 5 are operating revenue per ASM, operating income per ASM, labor cost per ASM, fuel cost per ASM, and total available seat miles. The impact of the recession on the travel industry is evident in the fact that only two airlines—JetBlue and Southwest—have positive levels of operating income.

How well did United manage its costs? The answer depends on which specific benchmark is being used for comparison. United's actual operating cost of $0.1574 per ASM is above the average operating cost of $0.1356 per ASM of the seven other airlines. Moreover, United's operating cost per ASM is 55.7% higher than JetBlue Airways, the lowest-cost competitor at $0.1011 per ASM [($0.1574 – $0.1011) ÷ $0.1011 = 55.7%]. So why is United's operating cost per ASM so high? Columns E and F suggest that both fuel cost and labor cost are possible reasons. These benchmarking data alert management at United that it needs to become more efficient in its use of both material and labor inputs to become more cost competitive.

Using benchmarks such as those in Exhibit 5 is not without problems. Finding appropriate benchmarks is a major issue in implementing benchmarking. Many companies purchase benchmark data from consulting firms. Another problem is ensuring the benchmark numbers are comparable. In other words, there needs to be an "apples to apples" comparison. Differences can exist across companies in their strategies, inventory costing methods, depreciation methods, and so on. For example, JetBlue serves fewer cities and has mostly long-haul flights compared with United, which serves almost all major U.S. cities and several international cities and has both long-haul and short-haul flights. Southwest Airlines differs from United because it specializes in short-haul direct flights and offers fewer services on board its planes. Because United's strategy is different from the strategies of JetBlue and Southwest, one might expect its cost per ASM to be different too. United's strategy is more comparable to the strategies of American, Continental, Delta, and U.S. Airways. Note that its costs per ASM are relatively more competitive with these airlines. But United competes head-to-head with JetBlue and Southwest in several cities and markets, so it still needs to benchmark against these carriers as well.

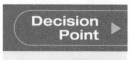

Decision Point

What is benchmarking and why is it useful?

United's management accountants can use benchmarking data to address several questions. How do factors such as plane size and type, or the duration of flights, affect the cost per ASM? Do airlines differ in their fixed cost/variable cost structures? Can performance be improved by rerouting flights, using different types of aircraft on different routes, or changing the frequency or timing of specific flights? What explains revenue differences per ASM across airlines? Is it differences in perceived quality of service or differences in competitive power at specific airports? Management accountants are more valuable to managers when they use benchmarking data to provide insight into *why* costs or revenues differ across companies, or within plants of the same company, as distinguished from simply reporting the magnitude of such differences.

Problem for Self-Study

O'Shea Company manufactures ceramic vases. It uses its standard costing system when developing its flexible-budget amounts. In April 2012, 2,000 finished units were produced. The following information relates to its two direct manufacturing cost categories: direct materials and direct manufacturing labor.

Direct materials used were 4,400 kilograms (kg). The standard direct materials input allowed for one output unit is 2 kilograms at $15 per kilogram. O'Shea purchased 5,000 kilograms of materials at $16.50 per kilogram, a total of $82,500. (This Problem for Self-Study illustrates how to calculate direct materials variances when the quantity of materials *purchased* in a period differs from the quantity of materials *used* in that period.)

Actual direct manufacturing labor-hours were 3,250, at a total cost of $66,300. Standard manufacturing labor time allowed is 1.5 hours per output unit, and the standard direct manufacturing labor cost is $20 per hour.

Required

1. Calculate the direct materials price variance and efficiency variance, and the direct manufacturing labor price variance and efficiency variance. Base the direct materials price variance on a flexible budget for *actual quantity purchased*, but base the direct materials efficiency variance on a flexible budget for *actual quantity used*.
2. Prepare journal entries for a standard costing system that isolates variances at the earliest possible time.

Solution

1. Exhibit 6 shows how the columnar presentation of variances introduced in Exhibit 3 can be adjusted for the difference in timing between purchase and use of materials. Note, in particular, the two sets of computations in column 2 for direct materials—the $75,000 for direct materials purchased and the $66,000 for direct materials used. The direct materials price variance is calculated on purchases so that managers responsible for the purchase can immediately identify and isolate reasons for the variance and initiate any desired corrective action. The efficiency variance is the responsibility of the production manager, so this variance is identified only at the time materials are used.

2.
Materials Control (5,000 kg × $15 per kg)	75,000	
Direct Materials Price Variance (5,000 kg × $1.50 per kg)	7,500	
Accounts Payable Control (5,000 kg × $16.50 per kg)		82,500
Work-in-Process Control (2,000 units × 2 kg per unit × $15 per kg)	60,000	
Direct Materials Efficiency Variance (400 kg × $15 per kg)	6,000	
Materials Control (4,400 kg × $15 per kg)		66,000
Work-in-Process Control (2,000 units × 1.5 hours per unit × $20 per hour)	60,000	
Direct Manufacturing Labor Price Variance (3,250 hours × $0.40 per hour)	1,300	
Direct Manufacturing Labor Efficiency Variance (250 hours × $20 per hour)	5,000	
Wages Payable Control (3,250 hours × $20.40 per hour)		66,300

Note: All the variances are debits because they are unfavorable and therefore reduce operating income.

Exhibit 6 Columnar Presentation of Variance Analysis for O'Shea Company: Direct Materials and Direct Manufacturing Labor for April 2012[a]

Level 3 Analysis

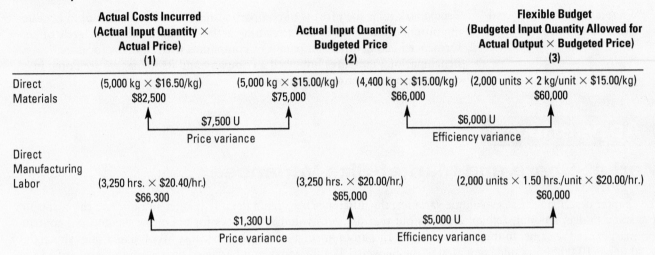

	Actual Costs Incurred (Actual Input Quantity × Actual Price) (1)	Actual Input Quantity × Budgeted Price (2)	Flexible Budget (Budgeted Input Quantity Allowed for Actual Output × Budgeted Price) (3)
Direct Materials	(5,000 kg × $16.50/kg) $82,500	(5,000 kg × $15.00/kg) $75,000 (4,400 kg × $15.00/kg) $66,000	(2,000 units × 2 kg/unit × $15.00/kg) $60,000
	↑____ $7,500 U ____↑ Price variance		↑____ $6,000 U ____↑ Efficiency variance
Direct Manufacturing Labor	(3,250 hrs. × $20.40/hr.) $66,300	(3,250 hrs. × $20.00/hr.) $65,000	(2,000 units × 1.50 hrs./unit × $20.00/hr.) $60,000
	↑____ $1,300 U ____↑ Price variance	↑____ $5,000 U ____↑ Efficiency variance	

[a]F = favorable effect on operating income; U = unfavorable effect on operating income.

Decision Points

The following question-and-answer format summarizes the chapter's learning objectives. Each decision presents a key question related to a learning objective. The guidelines are the answer to that question.

Decision	Guidelines
1. What are static budgets and static-budget variances?	A static budget is based on the level of output planned at the start of the budget period. The static-budget variance is the difference between the actual result and the corresponding budgeted amount in the static budget.
2. How can managers develop a flexible budget and why is it useful to do so?	A flexible budget is adjusted (flexed) to recognize the actual output level of the budget period. Managers use a three-step procedure to develop a flexible budget. When all costs are either variable with respect to output units or fixed, these three steps require only information about budgeted selling price, budgeted variable cost per output unit, budgeted fixed costs, and actual quantity of output units. Flexible budgets help managers gain more insight into the causes of variances than is available from static budgets.
3. How are flexible-budget and sales-volume variances calculated?	The static-budget variance can be subdivided into a flexible-budget variance (the difference between an actual result and the corresponding flexible-budget amount) and a sales-volume variance (the difference between the flexible-budget amount and the corresponding static-budget amount).
4. What is a standard cost and what are its purposes?	A standard cost is a carefully determined cost used as a benchmark for judging performance. The purposes of a standard cost are to exclude past inefficiencies and to take into account changes expected to occur in the budget period.
5. Why should a company calculate price and efficiency variables?	The computation of price and efficiency variances helps managers gain insight into two different—but not independent—aspects of performance. The price variance focuses on the difference between actual input price and budgeted input price. The efficiency variance focuses on the difference between actual quantity of input and budgeted quantity of input allowed for actual output.

6. How do managers use variances?	Managers use variances for control, decision implementation, performance evaluation, organization learning, and continuous improvement. When using variances for these purposes, managers consider several variances together rather than focusing only on an individual variance.
7. What is benchmarking and why is it useful?	Benchmarking is the process of comparing the level of performance in producing products and services and executing activities against the best levels of performance in competing companies or companies with similar processes. Benchmarking measures how well a company and its managers are doing in comparison to other organizations.

Appendix

Market-Share and Market-Size Variances

The chapter described the sales-volume variance, the difference between a flexible-budget amount and the corresponding static-budget amount. Exhibit 2 points out that the sales-volume variances for operating income and contribution margin are the same. In the Webb example, this amount equals 64,000 U, because Webb had a sales shortfall of 2,000 units (10,000 units sold compared to the budgeted 12,000 units), at a budgeted contribution margin of $32 per jacket. Webb's managers can gain more insight into the sales-volume variance by subdividing it. We explore one such analysis here.

Recall that Webb sells a single product, jackets, using a single distribution channel. In this case, the sales-volume variance is also called the *sales-quantity variance*. Sales depend on overall demand for jackets, as well as Webb's share of the market. Assume that Webb derived its total unit sales budget for April 2011 from a management estimate of a 20% market share and a budgeted industry market size of 60,000 units (0.20 × 60,000 units = 12,000 units). For April 2011, actual market size was 62,500 units and actual market share was 16% (10,000 units ÷ 62,500 units = 0.16 or 16%). Exhibit 7 shows the columnar presentation of how Webb's sales-quantity variance can be decomposed into market-share and market-size variances.

Exhibit 7   Market-Share and Market-Size Variance Analysis of Webb Company for April 2011[a]

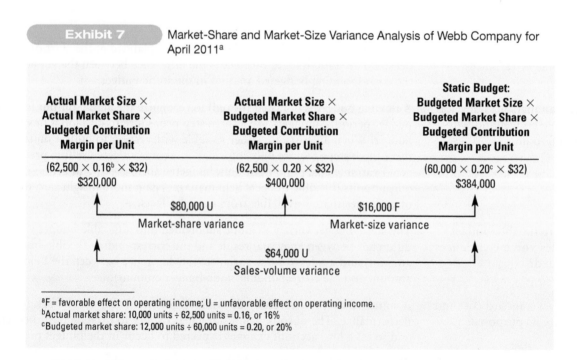

[a]F = favorable effect on operating income; U = unfavorable effect on operating income.
[b]Actual market share: 10,000 units ÷ 62,500 units = 0.16, or 16%
[c]Budgeted market share: 12,000 units ÷ 60,000 units = 0.20, or 20%

Market-Share Variance

The **market-share variance** is the difference in budgeted contribution margin for actual market size in units caused solely by *actual market share* being different from *budgeted market share*. The formula for computing the market-share variance is as follows:

$$\begin{array}{c}\text{Market-share} \\ \text{variance}\end{array} = \begin{array}{c}\text{Actual} \\ \text{market size} \\ \text{in units}\end{array} \times \left(\begin{array}{c}\text{Actual} \\ \text{market} \\ \text{share}\end{array} - \begin{array}{c}\text{Budgeted} \\ \text{market} \\ \text{share}\end{array}\right) \times \begin{array}{c}\text{Budgeted} \\ \text{contribution margin} \\ \text{per unit}\end{array}$$

$$= 62{,}500 \text{ units} \times (0.16 - 0.20) \times \$32 \text{ per unit}$$

$$= \$80{,}000 \text{ U}$$

Webb lost 4.0 market-share percentage points—from the 20% budgeted share to the actual share of 16%. The $80,000 U market-share variance is the decline in contribution margin as a result of those lost sales.

Market-Size Variance

The **market-size variance** is the difference in budgeted contribution margin at budgeted market share caused solely by *actual market size in units* being different from *budgeted market size in units*. The formula for computing the market-size variance is as follows:

$$\begin{array}{c}\text{Market-size} \\ \text{variance}\end{array} = \left(\begin{array}{c}\text{Actual} \\ \text{market} \\ \text{size}\end{array} - \begin{array}{c}\text{Budgeted} \\ \text{market} \\ \text{size}\end{array}\right) \times \begin{array}{c}\text{Budgeted} \\ \text{market} \\ \text{share}\end{array} \times \begin{array}{c}\text{Budgeted} \\ \text{contribution margin} \\ \text{per unit}\end{array}$$

$$= (62{,}500 \text{ units} - 60{,}000 \text{ units}) \times 0.20 \times \$32 \text{ per unit}$$

$$= \$16{,}000 \text{ F}$$

The market-size variance is favorable because actual market size increased 4.17% [(62,500 − 60,000) ÷ 60,000 = 0.417, or 4.17%] compared to budgeted market size.

Managers should probe the reasons for the market-size and market-share variances for April 2011. Is the $16,000 F market-size variance because of an increase in market size that can be expected to continue in the future? If yes, Webb has much to gain by attaining or exceeding its budgeted 20% market share. Was the $80,000 unfavorable market-share variance because of competitors providing better offerings or greater value to customers? We saw earlier that Webb was able to charge a higher selling price than expected, resulting in a favorable selling-price variance. However, competitors introduced new styles of jackets that stimulated market demand and enabled them to charge higher prices than Webb. Webb's products also experienced quality-control problems that were the subject of negative media coverage, leading to a significant drop in market share, even as overall industry sales were growing.

Some companies place more emphasis on the market-share variance than the market-size variance when evaluating their managers. That's because they believe the market-size variance is influenced by economy-wide factors and shifts in consumer preferences that are outside the managers' control, whereas the market-share variance measures how well managers performed relative to their peers.

Be cautious when computing the market-size variance and the market-share variance. Reliable information on market size and market share is available for some, but not all, industries. The automobile, computer, and television industries are cases in which market-size and market-share statistics are widely available. In other industries, such as management consulting and personal financial planning, information about market size and market share is far less reliable.

Terms to Learn

This chapter contains definitions of the following important terms:

benchmarking	flexible budget	price variance
budgeted performance	flexible-budget variance	rate variance
effectiveness	input-price variance	sales-volume variance
efficiency	management by exception	selling-price variance
efficiency variance	market-share variance	standard
favorable variance	market-size variance	standard cost

standard input

standard price

static budget

static-budget variance

unfavorable variance

usage variance

variance

Assignment Material

MyAccountingLab

Questions

7-1 What is the relationship between management by exception and variance analysis?

7-2 What are two possible sources of information a company might use to compute the budgeted amount in variance analysis?

7-3 Distinguish between a favorable variance and an unfavorable variance.

7-4 What is the key difference between a static budget and a flexible budget?

7-5 Why might managers find a flexible-budget analysis more informative than a static-budget analysis?

7-6 Describe the steps in developing a flexible budget.

7-7 List four reasons for using standard costs.

7-8 How might a manager gain insight into the causes of a flexible-budget variance for direct materials?

7-9 List three causes of a favorable direct materials price variance.

7-10 Describe three reasons for an unfavorable direct manufacturing labor efficiency variance.

7-11 How does variance analysis help in continuous improvement?

7-12 Why might an analyst examining variances in the production area look beyond that business function for explanations of those variances?

7-13 Comment on the following statement made by a plant manager: "Meetings with my plant accountant are frustrating. All he wants to do is pin the blame on someone for the many variances he reports."

7-14 How can the sales-volume variance be decomposed further to obtain useful information?

7-15 "Benchmarking against other companies enables a company to identify the lowest-cost producer. This amount should become the performance measure for next year." Do you agree?

MyAccountingLab

Exercises

7-16 Flexible budget. Brabham Enterprises manufactures tires for the Formula I motor racing circuit. For August 2012, it budgeted to manufacture and sell 3,000 tires at a variable cost of $74 per tire and total fixed costs of $54,000. The budgeted selling price was $110 per tire. Actual results in August 2012 were 2,800 tires manufactured and sold at a selling price of $112 per tire. The actual total variable costs were $229,600, and the actual total fixed costs were $50,000.

Required

1. Prepare a performance report (akin to Exhibit 2) that uses a flexible budget and a static budget.
2. Comment on the results in requirement 1.

7-17 Flexible budget. Connor Company's budgeted prices for direct materials, direct manufacturing labor, and direct marketing (distribution) labor per attaché case are $40, $8, and $12, respectively. The president is pleased with the following performance report:

	Actual Costs	Static Budget	Variance
Direct materials	$364,000	$400,000	$36,000 F
Direct manufacturing labor	78,000	80,000	2,000 F
Direct marketing (distribution) labor	110,000	120,000	10,000 F

Actual output was 8,800 attaché cases. Assume all three direct-cost items shown are variable costs.

Required Is the president's pleasure justified? Prepare a revised performance report that uses a flexible budget and a static budget.

7-18 Flexible-budget preparation and analysis. Bank Management Printers, Inc., produces luxury checkbooks with three checks and stubs per page. Each checkbook is designed for an individual customer and is ordered through the customer's bank. The company's operating budget for September 2012 included these data:

Number of checkbooks	15,000
Selling price per book	$ 20
Variable cost per book	$ 8
Fixed costs for the month	$145,000

The actual results for September 2012 were as follows:

Number of checkbooks produced and sold	12,000
Average selling price per book	$ 21
Variable cost per book	$ 7
Fixed costs for the month	$150,000

The executive vice president of the company observed that the operating income for September was much lower than anticipated, despite a higher-than-budgeted selling price and a lower-than-budgeted variable cost per unit. As the company's management accountant, you have been asked to provide explanations for the disappointing September results.

Bank Management develops its flexible budget on the basis of budgeted per-output-unit revenue and per-output-unit variable costs without detailed analysis of budgeted inputs.

Required

1. Prepare a static-budget-based variance analysis of the September performance.
2. Prepare a flexible-budget-based variance analysis of the September performance.
3. Why might Bank Management find the flexible-budget-based variance analysis more informative than the static-budget-based variance analysis? Explain your answer.

7-19 Flexible budget, working backward. The Clarkson Company produces engine parts for car manufacturers. A new accountant intern at Clarkson has accidentally deleted the calculations on the company's variance analysis calculations for the year ended December 31, 2012. The following table is what remains of the data.

	Home	Insert	Page Layout	Formulas	Data	Review	View

	A	B	C	D	E	F
1	Performance Report, Year Ended December 31, 2012					
2						
3		Actual Results	Flexible-Budget Variances	Flexible Budget	Sales-Volume Variances	Static Budget
4	Units sold	130,000				120,000
5	Revenues (sales)	$715,000				$420,000
6	Variable costs	515,000				240,000
7	Contribution margin	200,000				180,000
8	Fixed costs	140,000				120,000
9	Operating income	$ 60,000				$ 60,000

Required

1. Calculate all the required variances. (If your work is accurate, you will find that the total static-budget variance is $0.)
2. What are the actual and budgeted selling prices? What are the actual and budgeted variable costs per unit?
3. Review the variances you have calculated and discuss possible causes and potential problems. What is the important lesson learned here?

7-20 Flexible-budget and sales volume variances, market-share and market-size variances. Marron, Inc., produces the basic fillings used in many popular frozen desserts and treats—vanilla and chocolate ice creams, puddings, meringues, and fudge. Marron uses standard costing and carries over no inventory from one month to the next. The ice-cream product group's results for June 2012 were as follows:

	Home	Insert	Page Layout	Formulas	Data

	A	B	C
1	Performance Report, June 2012		
2		Actual Results	Static Budget
3	Units (pounds)	355,000	345,000
4	Revenues	$1,917,000	$1,880,250
5	Variable manufacturing costs	1,260,250	1,207,500
6	Contribution margin	$ 656,750	$ 672,750

Ted Levine, the business manager for ice-cream products, is pleased that more pounds of ice cream were sold than budgeted and that revenues were up. Unfortunately, variable manufacturing costs went up too. The bottom line is that contribution margin declined by $16,000, which is less than 1% of the budgeted revenues of $1,880,250. Overall, Levine feels that the business is running fine.

Levine would also like to analyze how the company is performing compared to the overall market for ice-cream products. He knows that the expected total market for ice-cream products was 1,150,000 pounds and that the actual total market was 1,109,375 pounds.

Required

1. Calculate the static-budget variance in units, revenues, variable manufacturing costs, and contribution margin. What percentage is each static-budget variance relative to its static-budget amount?
2. Break down each static-budget variance into a flexible-budget variance and a sales-volume variance.
3. Calculate the selling-price variance.
4. Calculate the market-share and market-size variances.
5. Assume the role of management accountant at Marron. How would you present the results to Ted Levine? Should he be more concerned? If so, why?

7-21 Price and efficiency variances. Peterson Foods manufactures pumpkin scones. For January 2012, it budgeted to purchase and use 15,000 pounds of pumpkin at $0.89 a pound. Actual purchases and usage for January 2012 were 16,000 pounds at $0.82 a pound. Peterson budgeted for 60,000 pumpkin scones. Actual output was 60,800 pumpkin scones.

Required

1. Compute the flexible-budget variance.
2. Compute the price and efficiency variances.
3. Comment on the results for requirements 1 and 2 and provide a possible explanation for them.

7-22 Materials and manufacturing labor variances. Consider the following data collected for Great Homes, Inc.:

	Direct Materials	Direct Manufacturing Labor
Cost incurred: Actual inputs × actual prices	$200,000	$90,000
Actual inputs × standard prices	214,000	86,000
Standard inputs allowed for actual output × standard prices	225,000	80,000

Required

Compute the price, efficiency, and flexible-budget variances for direct materials and direct manufacturing labor.

7-23 Direct materials and direct manufacturing labor variances. GloriaDee, Inc., designs and manufactures T-shirts. It sells its T-shirts to brand-name clothes retailers in lots of one dozen. GloriaDee's May 2011 static budget and actual results for direct inputs are as follows:

Static Budget

Number of T-shirt lots (1 lot = 1 dozen)	500

Per Lot of T-shirts:

Direct materials	12 meters at $1.50 per meter = $18.00
Direct manufacturing labor	2 hours at $8.00 per hour = $16.00

Actual Results

Number of T-shirt lots sold	550

Total Direct Inputs:

Direct materials	7,260 meters at $1.75 per meter = $12,705.00
Direct manufacturing labor	1,045 hours at $8.10 per hour = $8,464.50

GloriaDee has a policy of analyzing all input variances when they add up to more than 10% of the total cost of materials and labor in the flexible budget, and this is true in May 2011. The production manager discusses the sources of the variances: "A new type of material was purchased in May. This led to faster cutting and sewing, but the workers used more material than usual as they learned to work with it. For now, the standards are fine."

Required

1. Calculate the direct materials and direct manufacturing labor price and efficiency variances in May 2011. What is the total flexible-budget variance for both inputs (direct materials and direct manufacturing labor) combined? What percentage is this variance of the total cost of direct materials and direct manufacturing labor in the flexible budget?

2. Gloria Denham, the CEO, is concerned about the input variances. But, she likes the quality and feel of the new material and agrees to use it for one more year. In May 2012, GloriaDee again produces 550 lots of T-shirts. Relative to May 2011, 2% less direct material is used, direct material price is down 5%, and 2% less direct manufacturing labor is used. Labor price has remained the same as in May 2011. Calculate the direct materials and direct manufacturing labor price and efficiency variances in May 2012. What is the total flexible-budget variance for both inputs (direct materials and direct manufacturing labor) combined? What percentage is this variance of the total cost of direct materials and direct manufacturing labor in the flexible budget?

3. Comment on the May 2012 results. Would you continue the "experiment" of using the new material?

7-24 Price and efficiency variances, journal entries. The Monroe Corporation manufactures lamps. It has set up the following standards per finished unit for direct materials and direct manufacturing labor:

Direct materials: 10 lb. at $4.50 per lb.	$45.00
Direct manufacturing labor: 0.5 hour at $30 per hour	15.00

The number of finished units budgeted for January 2012 was 10,000; 9,850 units were actually produced. Actual results in January 2012 were as follows:

Direct materials: 98,055 lb. used	
Direct manufacturing labor: 4,900 hours	$154,350

Assume that there was no beginning inventory of either direct materials or finished units.

During the month, materials purchased amounted to 100,000 lb., at a total cost of $465,000. Input price variances are isolated upon purchase. Input-efficiency variances are isolated at the time of usage.

Required

1. Compute the January 2012 price and efficiency variances of direct materials and direct manufacturing labor.
2. Prepare journal entries to record the variances in requirement 1.
3. Comment on the January 2012 price and efficiency variances of Monroe Corporation.
4. Why might Monroe calculate direct materials price variances and direct materials efficiency variances with reference to different points in time?

7-25 Continuous improvement (continuation of 7-24). The Monroe Corporation sets monthly standard costs using a continuous-improvement approach. In January 2012, the standard direct material cost is $45 per unit and the standard direct manufacturing labor cost is $15 per unit. Due to more efficient operations, the standard quantities for February 2012 are set at 0.980 of the standard quantities for January. In March 2012, the standard quantities are set at 0.990 of the standard quantities for February 2012. Assume the same information for March 2012 as in Exercise 7-24, except for these revised standard quantities.

Required

1. Compute the March 2012 standard quantities for direct materials and direct manufacturing labor (to three decimal places).
2. Compute the March 2012 price and efficiency variances for direct materials and direct manufacturing labor (round to the nearest dollar).

7-26 Materials and manufacturing labor variances, standard costs. Dunn, Inc., is a privately held furniture manufacturer. For August 2012, Dunn had the following standards for one of its products, a wicker chair:

Standards per Chair	
Direct materials	2 square yards of input at $5 per square yard
Direct manufacturing labor	0.5 hour of input at $10 per hour

The following data were compiled regarding *actual performance*: actual output units (chairs) produced, 2,000; square yards of input purchased and used, 3,700; price per square yard, $5.10; direct manufacturing labor costs, $8,820; actual hours of input, 900; labor price per hour, $9.80.

1. Show computations of price and efficiency variances for direct materials and direct manufacturing labor. Give a plausible explanation of why each variance occurred.
2. Suppose 6,000 square yards of materials were purchased (at $5.10 per square yard), even though only 3,700 square yards were used. Suppose further that variances are identified at their most timely control point; accordingly, direct materials price variances are isolated and traced at the time of purchase to the purchasing department rather than to the production department. Compute the price and efficiency variances under this approach.

7-27 Journal entries and T-accounts (continuation of 7-26). Prepare journal entries and post them to T-accounts for all transactions in Exercise 7-26, including requirement 2. Summarize how these journal entries differ from normal-costing entries.

7-28 Flexible budget. (Refer to data in Exercise 7-26). Suppose the static budget was for 2,500 units of output. Actual output was 2,000 units. The variances are shown in the following report:

	Actual Results	Static Budget	Variance
Direct materials	$18,870	$25,000	$6,130F
Direct manufacturing labor	$ 8,820	$12,500	$3,680F

Required What are the price, efficiency, and sales-volume variances for direct materials and direct manufacturing labor? Based on your results, explain why the static budget was not achieved.

7-29 Market-Share and Market-Size Variances. Rhaden Company produces sweat-resistant headbands for joggers. Information pertaining to Rhaden's operations for May 2011 follows:

	Actual	Budget
Units sold	230,550	220,000
Sales revenue	$3,412,140	$3,300,000
Variable cost ratio	68%	64%
Market size in units	4,350,000	4,400,000

Required
1. Compute the sales volume variance for May 2011.
2. Compute the market-share and market-size variances for May 2011.
3. Comment on possible reasons for the variances you computed in requirement 2.

MyAccountingLab

Problems

7-30 Flexible budget, direct materials, and direct manufacturing labor variances. Tuscany Statuary manufactures bust statues of famous historical figures. All statues are the same size. Each unit requires the same amount of resources. The following information is from the static budget for 2011:

Expected production and sales	6,000 units
Direct materials	72,000 pounds
Direct manufacturing labor	21,000 hours
Total fixed costs	$1,200,000

Standard quantities, standard prices, and standard unit costs follow for direct materials and direct manufacturing labor:

	Standard Quantity	Standard Price	Standard Unit Cost
Direct materials	12 pounds	$10 per pound	$120
Direct manufacturing labor	3.5 hours	$50 per hour	$175

During 2011, actual number of units produced and sold was 5,500. Actual cost of direct materials used was $668,800, based on 70,400 pounds purchased at $9.50 per pound. Direct manufacturing labor-hours actually used were 18,500, at the rate of $51.50 per hour. As a result, actual direct manufacturing labor costs were $952,750. Actual fixed costs were $1,180,000. There were no beginning or ending inventories.

Required
1. Calculate the sales-volume variance and flexible-budget variance for operating income.
2. Compute price and efficiency variances for direct materials and direct manufacturing labor.

7-31 Variance analysis, nonmanufacturing setting. Stevie McQueen has run Lightning Car Detailing for the past 10 years. His static budget and actual results for June 2011 are provided next. Stevie has one employee who has been with him for all 10 years that he has been in business. In addition, at any given time he also employs two other less experienced workers. It usually takes each employee 2 hours to detail a vehicle, regardless of his or her experience. Stevie pays his experienced employee $40 per vehicle and the other two employees $20 per vehicle. There were no wage increases in June.

Lightning Car Detailing
Actual and Budgeted Income Statements
For the Month Ended June 30, 2011

	Budget	Actual
Cars detailed	200	225
Revenue	$30,000	$39,375
Variable costs		
Costs of supplies	1,500	2,250
Labor	5,600	6,000
Total variable costs	7,100	8,250
Contribution margin	22,900	31,125
Fixed costs	9,500	9,500
Operating income	$13,400	$21,625

1. How many cars, on average, did Stevie budget for each employee? How many cars did each employee **Required** actually detail?
2. Prepare a flexible budget for June 2011.
3. Compute the sales price variance and the labor efficiency variance for each labor type.
4. What information, in addition to that provided in the income statements, would you want Stevie to gather, if you wanted to improve operational efficiency?

7-32 Comprehensive variance analysis, responsibility issues. (CMA, adapted) Styles, Inc., manufactures a full line of well-known sunglasses frames and lenses. Styles uses a standard costing system to set attainable standards for direct materials, labor, and overhead costs. Styles reviews and revises standards annually, as necessary. Department managers, whose evaluations and bonuses are affected by their department's performance, are held responsible to explain variances in their department performance reports.

Recently, the manufacturing variances in the Image prestige line of sunglasses have caused some concern. For no apparent reason, unfavorable materials and labor variances have occurred. At the monthly staff meeting, Jack Barton, manager of the Image line, will be expected to explain his variances and suggest ways of improving performance. Barton will be asked to explain the following performance report for 2011:

	Actual Results	Static-Budget Amounts
Units sold	7,275	7,500
Revenues	$596,550	$600,000
Variable manufacturing costs	351,965	324,000
Fixed manufacturing costs	108,398	112,500
Gross margin	136,187	163,500

Barton collected the following information:
Three items comprised the standard variable manufacturing costs in 2011:

■ Direct materials: Frames. Static budget cost of $49,500. The standard input for 2008 is 3.00 ounces per unit.

■ Direct materials: Lenses. Static budget costs of $139,500. The standard input for 2008 is 6.00 ounces per unit.

■ Direct manufacturing labor: Static budget costs of $135,000. The standard input for 2008 is 1.20 hours per unit.

Assume there are no variable manufacturing overhead costs.
The actual variable manufacturing costs in 2011 were as follows:

■ Direct materials: Frames. Actual costs of $55,872. Actual ounces used were 3.20 ounces per unit.

■ Direct materials: Lenses. Actual costs of $150,738. Actual ounces used were 7.00 ounces per unit.

■ Direct manufacturing labor: Actual costs of $145,355. The actual labor rate was $14.80 per hour.

1. Prepare a report that includes the following: **Required**
   a. Selling-price variance
   b. Sales-volume variance and flexible-budget variance for operating income in the format of the analysis in Exhibit 2

c. Price and efficiency variances for the following:
  - Direct materials: frames
  - Direct materials: lenses
  - Direct manufacturing labor

2. Give three possible explanations for each of the three price and efficiency variances at Styles in requirement 1c.

7-33 Possible causes for price and efficiency variances. You are a student preparing for a job interview with a *Fortune* 100 consumer products manufacturer. You are applying for a job in the finance department. This company is known for its rigorous case-based interview process. One of the students who successfully obtained a job with them upon graduation last year advised you to "know your variances cold!" When you inquired further, she told you that she had been asked to pretend that she was investigating wage and materials variances. Per her advice, you have been studying the causes and consequences of variances. You are excited when you walk in and find that the first case deals with variance analysis. You are given the following data for May for a detergent bottling plant located in Mexico:

Actual

Bottles filled	340,000
Direct materials used in production	6,150,000 oz.
Actual direct material cost	2,275,500 pesos
Actual direct manufacturing labor-hours	26,000 hours
Actual direct labor cost	784,420 pesos

Standards

Purchase price of direct materials	0.36 pesos/oz
Bottle size	15 oz.
Wage rate	29.25 pesos/hour
Bottles per minute	0.50

Required

Please respond to the following questions as if you were in an interview situation:

1. Calculate the materials efficiency and price variance, and the wage and labor efficiency variances for the month of May.
2. You are given the following context: "Union organizers are targeting our detergent bottling plant in Puebla, Mexico, for a union." Can you provide a better explanation for the variances that you have calculated on the basis of this information?

7-34 Material cost variances, use of variances for performance evaluation. Katharine Stanley is the owner of Better Bikes, a company that produces high quality cross-country bicycles. Better Bikes participates in a supply chain that consists of suppliers, manufacturers, distributors, and elite bicycle shops. For several years Better Bikes has purchased titanium from suppliers in the supply chain. Better Bikes uses titanium for the bicycle frames because it is stronger and lighter than other metals and therefore increases the quality of the bicycle. Earlier this year, Better Bikes hired Michael Scott, a recent graduate from State University, as purchasing manager. Michael believed that he could reduce costs if he purchased titanium from an online marketplace at a lower price.

Better Bikes established the following standards based upon the company's experience with previous suppliers. The standards are as follows:

Cost of titanium	$22 per pound
Titanium used per bicycle	8 lb.

Actual results for the first month using the online supplier of titanium are as follows:

Bicycles produced	800
Titanium purchased	8,400 lb. for $159,600
Titanium used in production	7,900 lb.

Required

1. Compute the direct materials price and efficiency variances.
2. What factors can explain the variances identified in requirement 1? Could any other variances be affected?
3. Was switching suppliers a good idea for Better Bikes? Explain why or why not.
4. Should Michael Scott's performance evaluation be based solely on price variances? Should the production manager's evaluation be based solely on efficiency variances? Why it is important for Katharine Stanley to understand the causes of a variance before she evaluates performance?
5. Other than performance evaluation, what reasons are there for calculating variances?
6. What future problems could result from Better Bikes' decision to buy a lower quality of titanium from the online marketplace?

7-35 Direct manufacturing labor and direct materials variances, missing data. (CMA, heavily adapted) Morro Bay Surfboards manufactures fiberglass surfboards. The standard cost of direct materials and direct manufacturing labor is $225 per board. This includes 30 pounds of direct materials, at the budgeted price of $3 per pound, and 9 hours of direct manufacturing labor, at the budgeted rate of $15 per hour. Following are additional data for the month of July:

Units completed	5,500 units
Direct material purchases	190,000 pounds
Cost of direct material purchases	$579,500
Actual direct manufacturing labor-hours	49,000 hours
Actual direct labor cost	$739,900
Direct materials efficiency variance	$ 1,500 F

There were no beginning inventories.

1. Compute direct manufacturing labor variances for July.
2. Compute the actual pounds of direct materials used in production in July.
3. Calculate the actual price per pound of direct materials purchased.
4. Calculate the direct materials price variance.

Required

7-36 Direct materials and manufacturing labor variances, solving unknowns. (CPA, adapted) On May 1, 2012, Bovar Company began the manufacture of a new paging machine known as Dandy. The company installed a standard costing system to account for manufacturing costs. The standard costs for a unit of Dandy follow:

Direct materials (3 lb. at $5 per lb.)	$15.00
Direct manufacturing labor (1/2 hour at $20 per hour)	10.00
Manufacturing overhead (75% of direct manufacturing labor costs)	7.50
	$32.50

The following data were obtained from Bovar's records for the month of May:

	Debit	Credit
Revenues		$125,000
Accounts payable control (for May's purchases of direct materials)		68,250
Direct materials price variance	$3,250	
Direct materials efficiency variance	2,500	
Direct manufacturing labor price variance	1,900	
Direct manufacturing labor efficiency variance		2,000

Actual production in May was 4,000 units of Dandy, and actual sales in May were 2,500 units.

The amount shown for direct materials price variance applies to materials purchased during May. There was no beginning inventory of materials on May 1, 2012.

Compute each of the following items for Bovar for the month of May. Show your computations.

Required

1. Standard direct manufacturing labor-hours allowed for actual output produced
2. Actual direct manufacturing labor-hours worked
3. Actual direct manufacturing labor wage rate
4. Standard quantity of direct materials allowed (in pounds)
5. Actual quantity of direct materials used (in pounds)
6. Actual quantity of direct materials purchased (in pounds)
7. Actual direct materials price per pound

7-37 Direct materials and manufacturing labor variances, journal entries. Shayna's Smart Shawls, Inc., is a small business that Shayna developed while in college. She began hand-knitting shawls for her dorm friends to wear while studying. As demand grew, she hired some workers and began to manage the operation. Shayna's shawls require wool and labor. She experiments with the type of wool that she uses, and she has great variety in the shawls she produces. Shayna has bimodal turnover in her labor. She has some employees who have been with her for a very long time and others who are new and inexperienced.

Shayna uses standard costing for her shawls. She expects that a typical shawl should take 4 hours to produce, and the standard wage rate is $10.00 per hour. An average shawl uses 12 skeins of wool. Shayna shops around for good deals, and expects to pay $3.50 per skein.

Shayna uses a just-in-time inventory system, as she has clients tell her what type and color of wool they would like her to use.

For the month of April, Shayna's workers produced 235 shawls using 925 hours and 3,040 skeins of wool. Shayna bought wool for $10,336 (and used the entire quantity), and incurred labor costs of $9,620.

1. Calculate the price and efficiency variances for the wool, and the price and efficiency variances for direct manufacturing labor.
2. Record the journal entries for the variances incurred.
3. Discuss logical explanations for the combination of variances that Shayna experienced.

7-38 Use of materials and manufacturing labor variances for benchmarking. You are a new junior accountant at Clearview Corporation, maker of lenses for eyeglasses. Your company sells generic-quality lenses for a moderate price. Your boss, the Controller, has given you the latest month's report for the lens trade association. This report includes information related to operations for your firm and three of your competitors within the trade association. The report also includes information related to the industry benchmark for each line item in the report. You do not know which firm is which, except that you know you are Firm A.

Unit Variable Costs
Member Firms
For the Month Ended September 30, 2012

	Firm A	Firm B	Firm C	Firm D	Industry Benchmark
Materials input	2.00	1.95	2.15	2.50	2.0 oz. of glass
Materials price	$ 4.90	$ 5.60	$ 5.00	$ 4.50	$ 5.00 per oz.
Labor-hours used	1.10	1.15	0.95	1.00	1.00 hours
Wage rate	$15.00	$15.50	$16.50	$15.90	$13.00 per DLH
Variable overhead rate	$ 9.00	$13.50	$ 7.50	$11.25	$12.00 per DLH

1. Calculate the total variable cost per unit for each firm in the trade association. Compute the percent of total for the material, labor, and variable overhead components.
2. Using the trade association's industry benchmark, calculate direct materials and direct manufacturing labor price and efficiency variances for the four firms. Calculate the percent over standard for each firm and each variance.
3. Write a brief memo to your boss outlining the advantages and disadvantages of belonging to this trade association for benchmarking purposes. Include a few ideas to improve productivity that you want your boss to take to the department heads' meeting.

7-39 Comprehensive variance analysis review. Sonnet, Inc., has the following budgeted standards for the month of March 2011:

Average selling price per diskette	$ 6.00
Total direct material cost per diskette	$ 1.50
Direct manufacturing labor	
Direct manufacturing labor cost per hour	$ 12.00
Average labor productivity rate (diskettes per hour)	300
Direct marketing cost per unit	$ 0.30
Fixed overhead	$ 800,000

Sales of 1,500,000 units are budgeted for March. The expected total market for this product was 7,500,000 diskettes. Actual March results are as follows:

- Unit sales and production totaled 95% of plan.
- Actual average selling price increased to $6.10.
- Productivity dropped to 250 diskettes per hour.
- Actual direct manufacturing labor cost is $12.20 per hour.
- Actual total direct material cost per unit increased to $1.60.
- Actual direct marketing costs were $0.25 per unit.
- Fixed overhead costs were $10,000 above plan.
- Actual market size was 8,906,250 diskettes.

Calculate the following:

1. Static-budget and actual operating income
2. Static-budget variance for operating income
3. Flexible-budget operating income
4. Flexible-budget variance for operating income
5. Sales-volume variance for operating income
6. Market share and market size variances
7. Price and efficiency variances for direct manufacturing labor
8. Flexible-budget variance for direct manufacturing labor

7-40 Comprehensive variance analysis. (CMA) Iceland, Inc., is a fast-growing ice-cream maker. The company's new ice-cream flavor, Cherry Star, sells for $9 per pound. The standard monthly production level is 300,000 pounds, and the standard inputs and costs are as follows:

	Quantity per Pound of Ice Cream		Standard Unit Costs	
Cost Item				
Direct materials				
Cream	12	oz.	$ 0.03	/oz.
Vanilla extract	4	oz.	0.12	/oz.
Cherry	1	oz.	0.45	/oz.
Direct manufacturing labor[a]				
Preparing	1.2	min.	14.40	/hr.
Stirring	1.8	min.	18.00	/hr.
Variable overhead[b]	3	min.	32.40	/hr.
[a] Direct manufacturing labor rates include employee benefits.				
[b] Allocated on the basis of direct manufacturing labor-hours.				

Molly Cates, the CFO, is disappointed with the results for May 2011, prepared based on these standard costs.

Performance Report, May 2011

	Actual	Budget	Variance	
Units (pounds)	275,000	300,000	25,000	U
Revenues	$2,502,500	$2,700,000	$197,500	U
Direct materials	432,500	387,000	45,500	U
Direct manufacturing labor	174,000	248,400	74,400	F

Cates notes that despite a sizable increase in the pounds of ice cream sold in May, Cherry Star's contribution to the company's overall profitability has been lower than expected. Cates gathers the following information to help analyze the situation:

Usage Report, May 2011

Cost Item	Quantity		Actual Cost
Direct materials			
Cream	3,120,000	oz.	$124,800
Vanilla extract	1,230,000	oz.	184,500
Cherry	325,000	oz.	133,250
Direct manufacturing labor			
Preparing	310,000	min.	77,500
Stirring	515,000	min.	154,500

Required

Compute the following variances. Comment on the variances, with particular attention to the variances that may be related to each other and the controllability of each variance:

1. Selling-price variance
2. Direct materials price variance
3. Direct materials efficiency variance
4. Direct manufacturing labor efficiency variance

7-41 Price and efficiency variances, problems in standard-setting, and benchmarking. Stuckey, Inc., manufactures industrial 55 gallon drums for storing chemicals used in the mining industry. The body of the drums is made from aluminum and the lid is made of chemical resistant plastic. Andy Jorgenson, the controller, is becoming increasingly disenchanted with Stuckey's standard costing system. The budgeted information for direct materials and direct manufacturing labor for June 2011 were as follows:

	Budget
Drums and lids produced	5,200
Direct materials price per sq. ft.	
Aluminum	$ 3.00
Plastic	$ 1.50
Direct materials per unit	
Aluminum (sq. ft.)	20
Plastic (sq. ft.)	7
Direct labor-hours per unit	2.3
Direct labor cost per hour	$12.00

The actual number of drums and lids produced was 4,920. The actual cost of aluminum and plastic was $283,023 (95,940 sq. ft.) and $50,184 (33,456 sq. ft.), respectively. The actual direct labor cost incurred was $118,572 (9,840 hours). There were no beginning or ending inventories of materials.

Standard costs are based on a study of the operations conducted by an independent consultant six months earlier. Jorgenson observes that since that study he has rarely seen an unfavorable variance of any magnitude. He notes that even at their current output levels, the workers seem to have a lot of time for sitting around and gossiping. Jorgenson is concerned that the production manager, Charlie Fenton, is aware of this but does not want to tighten up the standards because the lax standards make his performance look good.

Required

1. Compute the price and efficiency variances of Stuckey, Inc., for each direct material and direct manufacturing labor in June 2011.
2. Describe the types of actions the employees at Stuckey, Inc., may have taken to reduce the accuracy of the standards set by the independent consultant. Why would employees take those actions? Is this behavior ethical?
3. If Jorgenson does nothing about the standard costs, will his behavior violate any of the Standards of Ethical Conduct for Management Accountants?
4. What actions should Jorgenson take?
5. Jorgenson can obtain benchmarking information about the estimated costs of Stuckey's major competitors from Benchmarking Clearing House (BCH). Discuss the pros and cons of using the BCH information to compute the variances in requirement 1.

Collaborative Learning Problem

7-42 Comprehensive variance analysis. Sol Electronics, a fast-growing electronic device producer, uses a standard costing system, with standards set at the beginning of each year.

In the second quarter of 2011, Sol faced two challenges: It had to negotiate and sign a new short-term labor agreement with its workers' union, and it also had to pay a higher rate to its suppliers for direct materials. The new labor contract raised the cost of direct manufacturing labor relative to the company's 2011 standards. Similarly, the new rate for direct materials exceeded the company's 2011 standards. However, the materials were of better quality than expected, so Sol's management was confident that there would be less waste and less rework in the manufacturing process. Management also speculated that the per-unit direct manufacturing labor cost might decline as a result of the materials' improved quality.

At the end of the second quarter, Sol's CFO, Terence Shaw, reviewed the following results:

	A	B	C	D	E	F	G	H	I	J	K	L	M	N	O	P	Q	R	S
1		Variable Costs Per Unit																	
2	Per Unit Variable Costs	Standard						First Quarter 2011 Actual Results						Second Quarter 2011 Actual Results					
3	Direct materials	2.2	lb.	at	$5.70	per lb.	$12.54	2.3	lb.	at	$5.80	per lb.	$13.34	2.0	lb.	at	$6.00	per lb.	$12.00
4	Direct manufacturing labor	0.5	hrs.	at	$12	per hr.	$6.00	0.52	hrs.	at	$12	per hr.	$6.24	0.45	hrs.	at	$14	per hr.	$6.30
5	Other variable costs						$10.00						$10.00						$9.85
6							$28.54						$29.58						$28.15

	U	V	W	X
1				
2		Static Budget for Each Quarter Based on 2011	First Quarter 2011 Results	Second Quarter 2011 Results
3	Units	4,000	4,400	4,800
4	Selling price	$ 70	$ 72	$ 71.50
5	Sales	$280,000	$316,800	$343,200
6	Variable costs			
7	Direct materials	50,160	58,696	57,600
8	Direct manufacturing labor	24,000	27,456	30,240
9	Other variable costs	40,000	44,000	47,280
10	Total variable costs	114,160	130,152	135,120
11	Contribution margin	165,840	186,648	208,080
12	Fixed costs	68,000	66,000	68,400
13	Operating income	$ 97,840	$120,648	$139,680

Shaw was relieved to see that the anticipated savings in material waste and rework seemed to have materialized. But, he was concerned that the union would press hard for higher wages given that actual unit costs came in below standard unit costs and operating income continued to climb.

Required

1. Prepare a detailed variance analysis of the second quarter results relative to the static budget. Show how much of the improvement in operating income arose due to changes in sales volume and how much arose for other reasons. Calculate variances that isolate the effects of price and usage changes in direct materials and direct manufacturing labor.
2. Use the results of requirement 1 to prepare a rebuttal to the union's anticipated demands in light of the second quarter results.
3. Terence Shaw thinks that the company can negotiate better if it changes the standards. Without performing any calculations, discuss the pros and cons of immediately changing the standards.

Flexible Budgets, Overhead Cost Variances, and Management Control

From Chapter 8 of *Cost Accounting: A Managerial Emphasis*, 14/e. Charles T. Horngren. Srikant M. Datar. Madhav Rajan.
Copyright © 2012 by Pearson Education. Published by Prentice Hall. All rights reserved.

Flexible Budgets, Overhead Cost Variances, and Management Control

What do this week's weather forecast and organization performance have in common?

Most of the time, reality doesn't match expectations. Cloudy skies that cancel a little league game may suddenly let the sun shine through just as the vans are packed. Jubilant business owners may change their tune when they tally their monthly bills and discover that skyrocketing operation costs have significantly reduced their profits. Differences, or variances, are all around us.

For organizations, variances are of great value because they highlight the areas where performance most lags expectations. By using this information to make corrective adjustments, companies can achieve significant savings, as the following article shows.

Overhead Cost Variances Force Macy's to Shop for Changes in Strategy[1]

Managers frequently review the differences, or variances, in overhead costs and make changes in the operations of a business. Sometimes staffing levels are increased or decreased, while at other times managers identify ways to use fewer resources like, say, office supplies and travel for business meetings that don't add value to the products and services that customers buy.

At the department-store chain Macy's, however, managers analyzed overhead cost variances and changed the way the company purchased the products it sells. In 2005, when Federated Department Stores and the May Department Store Company merged, Macy's operated seven buying offices across the United States. Each of these offices was responsible for purchasing some of the clothes, cosmetics, jewelry, and many other items Macy's sells. But overlapping responsibilities, seasonal buying patterns (clothes are generally purchased in the spring and fall) and regional differences in costs and salaries (for example, it costs more for employees and rent in San Francisco than Cincinnati) led to frequent and significant variances in overhead costs.

These overhead costs weighed on the company as the retailer struggled with disappointing sales after the merger. As a result, Macy's leaders felt pressured to reduce its costs that were not directly related to selling merchandise in stores and online.

[1] *Sources*: Boyle, Matthew. 2009. A leaner Macy's tries to cater to local tastes. *BusinessWeek.com*, September 3; Kapner, Suzanne. 2009. Macy's looking to cut costs. *Fortune*, January 14. http://money.cnn.com/2009/01/14/news/companies/macys_consolidation.fortune/; *Macy's 2009 Corporate Fact Book*. 2009. Cincinnati: Macy's, Inc., 7.

In early 2009, the company announced plans to consolidate its network of seven buying offices into one location in New York. With all centralized buying and merchandise planning in one location, Macy's buying structure and overhead costs were in line with how many other large chains operate, including JCPenney and Kohl's. All told, the move to centralized buying would generate $100 million in annualized cost savings for the company.

While centralized buying was applauded by industry experts and shareholders, Macy's CEO Terry Lundgren was concerned about keeping a "localized flavor" in his stores. To ensure that nationwide buying accommodated local tastes, a new team of merchants was formed in each Macy's market to gauge local buying habits. That way, the company could reduce its overhead costs while ensuring that Macy's stores near water parks had extra swimsuits.

Companies such as DuPont, International Paper, and U.S. Steel, which invest heavily in capital equipment, or Amazon.com and Yahoo!, which invest large amounts in software, have high overhead costs. As the Macy's example suggests, understanding the behavior of overhead costs, planning for them, performing variance analysis, and acting appropriately on the results are critical for a company.

Jason Kempin/Redux Pictures

In this chapter, we will examine how flexible budgets and variance analysis can help managers plan and control overhead costs. In this chapter, we focus on the indirect-cost categories of variable manufacturing overhead and fixed manufacturing overhead. Finally, we explain why managers should be careful when interpreting variances based on overhead-cost concepts developed primarily for financial reporting purposes.

Learning Objective 1

Explain the similarities and differences in planning variable overhead costs and fixed overhead costs

. . . for both, plan only essential activities and be efficient; fixed overhead costs are usually determined well before the budget period begins

Planning of Variable and Fixed Overhead Costs

We'll use the Webb Company example again to illustrate the planning and control of variable and fixed overhead costs. Recall that Webb manufactures jackets that are sold to distributors who in turn sell to independent clothing stores and retail chains. For simplicity, we assume Webb's only costs are *manufacturing* costs. For ease of exposition, we use the term overhead costs instead of manufacturing overhead costs. Variable (manufacturing) overhead costs for Webb include energy, machine maintenance, engineering support, and indirect materials. Fixed (manufacturing) overhead costs include plant leasing costs, depreciation on plant equipment, and the salaries of the plant managers.

Planning Variable Overhead Costs

To effectively plan variable overhead costs for a product or service, managers must focus attention on the activities that create a superior product or service for their customers and eliminate activities that do not add value. Webb's managers examine how each of their variable overhead costs relates to delivering a superior product or service to customers. For example, customers expect Webb's jackets to last, so managers at Webb consider sewing to be an essential activity. Therefore, maintenance activities for sewing machines—included in Webb's variable overhead costs—are also essential activities for which management must plan. In addition, such maintenance should be done in a cost-effective way, such as by scheduling periodic equipment maintenance rather than waiting for sewing machines to break down. For many companies today, it is critical to plan for ways to become more efficient in the use of energy, a rapidly growing component of variable overhead costs. Webb installs smart meters in order to monitor energy use in real time and steer production operations away from peak consumption periods.

Planning Fixed Overhead Costs

Effective planning of fixed overhead costs is similar to effective planning for variable overhead costs—planning to undertake only essential activities and then planning to be efficient in that undertaking. But in planning fixed overhead costs, there is one more strategic issue that managers must take into consideration: choosing the appropriate level of capacity or investment that will benefit the company in the long run. Consider Webb's leasing of sewing machines, each having a fixed cost per year. Leasing more machines than necessary—if Webb overestimates demand—will result in additional fixed leasing costs on machines not fully used during the year. Leasing insufficient machine capacity—say, because Webb underestimates demand or because of limited space in the plant—will result in an inability to meet demand, lost sales of jackets, and unhappy customers. Consider the example of AT&T, which did not foresee the iPhone's appeal or the proliferation of "apps" and did not upgrade its network sufficiently to handle the resulting data traffic. AT&T has since had to impose limits on how customers can use the iPhone (such as by curtailing tethering and the streaming of Webcasts). In December 2009, AT&T had the lowest customer satisfaction ratings among all major carriers.

The planning of fixed overhead costs differs from the planning of variable overhead costs in one important respect: timing. At the start of a budget period, management will have made most of the decisions that determine the level of fixed overhead costs to be incurred. But, it's the day-to-day, ongoing operating decisions that mainly determine the level of variable overhead costs incurred in that period. In health care settings, for example, variable overhead, which includes disposable supplies, unit doses of medication, suture packets, and medical waste disposal costs, is a function of the number and nature of procedures carried out, as well as the practice patterns of the physicians. However, the majority of the cost of providing hospital service is related to buildings, equipment, and salaried labor, which are fixed overhead items, unrelated to the volume of activity.[2]

Standard Costing at Webb Company

Webb uses standard costing. This chapter discusses the development of standards for Webb's manufacturing overhead costs. **Standard costing** is a costing system that (a) traces direct costs to output produced by multiplying the standard prices or rates by the standard quantities of inputs allowed for actual outputs produced and (b) allocates overhead costs on the basis of the standard overhead-cost rates times the standard quantities of the allocation bases allowed for the actual outputs produced.

Decision Point ▶

How do managers plan variable overhead costs and fixed overhead costs?

Learning Objective 2

Develop budgeted variable overhead cost rates

... budgeted variable costs divided by quantity of cost-allocation base

and budgeted fixed overhead cost rates

... budgeted fixed costs divided by quantity of cost-allocation base

---

[2] Related to this, free-standing surgery centers have thrived because they have an economic advantage of lower fixed overhead when compared to a traditional hospital. For an enlightening summary of costing issues in health care, see A. Macario, "What Does One Minute of Operating Room Time Cost?" Stanford University School of Medicine (2009).

The standard cost of Webb's jackets can be computed at the start of the budget period. This feature of standard costing simplifies record keeping because no record is needed of the actual overhead costs or of the actual quantities of the cost-allocation bases used for making the jackets. What is needed are the standard overhead cost rates for variable and fixed overhead. Webb's management accountants calculate these cost rates based on the planned amounts of variable and fixed overhead and the standard quantities of the allocation bases. We describe these computations next. Note that once standards have been set, the costs of using standard costing are low relative to the costs of using actual costing or normal costing.

Developing Budgeted Variable Overhead Rates

Budgeted variable overhead cost-allocation rates can be developed in four steps. We use the Webb example to illustrate these steps. Throughout the chapter, we use the broader term "budgeted rate" rather than "standard rate" to be consistent with the term used in describing normal costing. In standard costing, the budgeted rates are standard rates.

Step 1: Choose the Period to Be Used for the Budget. Webb uses a 12-month budget period. There are two reasons for using annual overhead rates rather than, say, monthly rates. The first relates to the numerator (such as reducing the influence of seasonality on the cost structure) and the second to the denominator (such as reducing the effect of varying output and number of days in a month). In addition, setting overhead rates once a year saves management the time it would need 12 times during the year if budget rates had to be set monthly.

Step 2: Select the Cost-Allocation Bases to Use in Allocating Variable Overhead Costs to Output Produced. Webb's operating managers select machine-hours as the cost-allocation base because they believe that machine-hours is the only cost driver of variable overhead. Based on an engineering study, Webb estimates it will take 0.40 of a machine-hour per actual output unit. For its budgeted output of 144,000 jackets in 2011, Webb budgets 57,600 (0.40 × 144,000) machine-hours.

Step 3: Identify the Variable Overhead Costs Associated with Each Cost-Allocation Base. Webb groups all of its variable overhead costs, including costs of energy, machine maintenance, engineering support, indirect materials, and indirect manufacturing labor in a single cost pool. Webb's total budgeted variable overhead costs for 2011 are $1,728,000.

Step 4: Compute the Rate per Unit of Each Cost-Allocation Base Used to Allocate Variable Overhead Costs to Output Produced. Dividing the amount in Step 3 ($1,728,000) by the amount in Step 2 (57,600 machine-hours), Webb estimates a rate of $30 per standard machine-hour for allocating its variable overhead costs.

In standard costing, the variable overhead rate per unit of the cost-allocation base ($30 per machine-hour for Webb) is generally expressed as a standard rate per output unit. Webb calculates the budgeted variable overhead cost rate per output unit as follows:

$$\begin{array}{c} \text{Budgeted variable} \\ \text{overhead cost rate} \\ \text{per output unit} \end{array} = \begin{array}{c} \text{Budgeted input} \\ \text{allowed per} \\ \text{output unit} \end{array} \times \begin{array}{c} \text{Budgeted variable} \\ \text{overhead cost rate} \\ \text{per input unit} \end{array}$$

$$= 0.40 \text{ hour per jacket} \times \$30 \text{ per hour}$$

$$= \$12 \text{ per jacket}$$

Webb uses $12 per jacket as the budgeted variable overhead cost rate in both its static budget for 2011 and in the monthly performance reports it prepares during 2011.

The $12 per jacket represents the amount by which Webb's variable overhead costs are expected to change with respect to output units for planning and control purposes. Accordingly, as the number of jackets manufactured increases, variable overhead costs are allocated to output units (for the inventory costing purpose) at the same rate of $12 per jacket. Of course, this presents an overall picture of total variable overhead costs, which in reality consist of many items, including energy, repairs, indirect labor, and so on. Managers help control variable overhead costs by budgeting each line item and then investigating possible causes for any significant variances.

Developing Budgeted Fixed Overhead Rates

Fixed overhead costs are, by definition, a lump sum of costs that remains unchanged in total for a given period, despite wide changes in the level of total activity or volume related to those overhead costs. Fixed costs are included in flexible budgets, but they remain the same total amount within the relevant range of activity regardless of the output level chosen to "flex" the variable costs and revenues. The fixed-cost amount is the same $276,000 in the static budget and in the flexible budget. Do not assume, however, that fixed overhead costs can never be changed. Managers can reduce fixed overhead costs by selling equipment or by laying off employees. But they are fixed in the sense that, unlike variable costs such as direct material costs, fixed costs do not *automatically* increase or decrease with the level of activity within the relevant range.

The process of developing the budgeted fixed overhead rate is the same as that detailed earlier for calculating the budgeted variable overhead rate. The four steps are as follows:

Step 1: Choose the Period to Use for the Budget. As with variable overhead costs, the budget period for fixed overhead costs is typically 12 months to help smooth out seasonal effects.

Step 2: Select the Cost-Allocation Bases to Use in Allocating Fixed Overhead Costs Output Produced. Webb uses machine-hours as the only cost-allocation base for fixed overhead costs. Why? Because Webb's managers believe that, in the long run, fixed overhead costs will increase or decrease to the levels needed to support the amount of machine-hours. Therefore, in the long run, the amount of machine-hours used is the only cost driver of fixed overhead costs. The number of machine-hours is the denominator in the budgeted fixed overhead rate computation and is called the **denominator level** or, in manufacturing settings, the **production-denominator level.** For simplicity, we assume Webb expects to operate at capacity in fiscal year 2011—with a budgeted usage of 57,600 machine-hours for a budgeted output of 144,000 jackets.[3]

Step 3: Identify the Fixed Overhead Costs Associated with Each Cost-Allocation Base. Because Webb identifies only a single cost-allocation base—machine-hours—to allocate fixed overhead costs, it groups all such costs into a single cost pool. Costs in this pool include depreciation on plant and equipment, plant and equipment leasing costs, and the plant manager's salary. Webb's fixed overhead budget for 2011 is $3,312,000.

Step 4: Compute the Rate per Unit of Each Cost-Allocation Base Used to Allocate Fixed Overhead Costs to Output Produced. Dividing the $3,312,000 from Step 3 by the 57,600 machine-hours from Step 2, Webb estimates a fixed overhead cost rate of $57.50 per machine-hour:

$$\frac{\text{Budgeted fixed overhead cost per unit of cost-allocation base}}{} = \frac{\text{Budgeted total costs in fixed overhead cost pool}}{\text{Budgeted total quantity of cost-allocation base}} = \frac{\$3,312,000}{57,600} = \$57.50 \text{ per machine-hour}$$

In standard costing, the $57.50 fixed overhead cost per machine-hour is usually expressed as a standard cost per output unit. Recall that Webb's engineering study estimates that it will take 0.40 machine-hour per output unit. Webb can now calculate the budgeted fixed overhead cost per output unit as follows:

$$\text{Budgeted fixed overhead cost per output unit} = \frac{\text{Budgeted quantity of cost-allocation base allowed per output unit}}{} \times \frac{\text{Budgeted fixed overhead cost per unit of cost-allocation base}}{}$$

$$= 0.40 \text{ of a machine-hour per jacket} \times \$57.50 \text{ per machine-hour}$$

$$= \$23.00 \text{ per jacket}$$

---

[3] Because Webb plans its capacity over multiple periods, anticipated demand in 2011 could be such that budgeted output for 2011 is less than capacity. Companies vary in the denominator levels they choose; some may choose budgeted output and others may choose capacity. In either case, the basic approach and analysis presented in this chapter is unchanged.

When preparing monthly budgets for 2011, Webb divides the $3,312,000 annual total fixed costs into 12 equal monthly amounts of $276,000.

Variable Overhead Cost Variances

We now illustrate how the budgeted variable overhead rate is used in computing Webb's variable overhead cost variances. The following data are for April 2011, when Webb produced and sold 10,000 jackets:

	Actual Result	Flexible-Budget Amount
1. Output units (jackets)	10,000	10,000
2. Machine-hours per output unit	0.45	0.40
3. Machine-hours (1 × 2)	4,500	4,000
4. Variable overhead costs	$130,500	$120,000
5. Variable overhead costs per machine-hour (4 ÷ 3)	$ 29.00	$ 30.00
6. Variable overhead costs per output unit (4 ÷ 1)	$ 13.05	$ 12.00

The flexible budget enables Webb to highlight the differences between actual costs and actual quantities versus budgeted costs and budgeted quantities for the actual output level of 10,000 jackets.

Flexible-Budget Analysis

The **variable overhead flexible-budget variance** measures the difference between actual variable overhead costs incurred and flexible-budget variable overhead amounts.

$$\begin{array}{c} \text{Variable overhead} \\ \text{flexible-budget variance} \end{array} = \begin{array}{c} \text{Actual costs} \\ \text{incurred} \end{array} - \begin{array}{c} \text{Flexible-budget} \\ \text{amount} \end{array}$$

$$= \$130,500 - \$120,000$$

$$= \$10,500 \text{ U}$$

This $10,500 unfavorable flexible-budget variance means Webb's actual variable overhead exceeded the flexible-budget amount by $10,500 for the 10,000 jackets actually produced and sold. Webb's managers would want to know why actual costs exceeded the flexible-budget amount. Did Webb use more machine-hours than planned to produce the 10,000 jackets? If so, was it because workers were less skilled than expected in using machines? Or did Webb spend more on variable overhead costs, such as maintenance?

Just as we illustrated with the flexible-budget variance for direct-cost items, Webb's managers can get further insight into the reason for the $10,500 unfavorable variance by subdividing it into the efficiency variance and spending variance.

Variable Overhead Efficiency Variance

The **variable overhead efficiency variance** is the difference between actual quantity of the cost-allocation base used and budgeted quantity of the cost-allocation base that should have been used to produce actual output, multiplied by budgeted variable overhead cost per unit of the cost-allocation base.

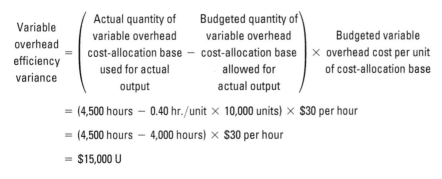

$$= (4,500 \text{ hours} - 0.40 \text{ hr./unit} \times 10,000 \text{ units}) \times \$30 \text{ per hour}$$

$$= (4,500 \text{ hours} - 4,000 \text{ hours}) \times \$30 \text{ per hour}$$

$$= \$15,000 \text{ U}$$

Decision Point

How are budgeted variable overhead and fixed overhead cost rates calculated?

Learning Objective 3

Compute the variable overhead flexible-budget variance,

... difference between actual variable overhead costs and flexible-budget variable overhead amounts

the variable overhead efficiency variance,

... difference between actual quantity of cost-allocation base and budgeted quantity of cost-allocation base

and the variable overhead spending variance

... difference between actual variable overhead cost rate and budgeted variable overhead cost rate

Columns 2 and 3 of Exhibit 1 depict the variable overhead efficiency variance. Note the variance arises solely because of the difference between actual quantity (4,500 hours) and budgeted quantity (4,000 hours) of the cost-allocation base. The variable overhead efficiency variance is computed the same way the efficiency variance for direct-cost items is. However, the interpretation of the variance is quite different. Efficiency variances for direct-cost items are based on differences between actual inputs used and budgeted inputs allowed for actual output produced. For example, a forensic laboratory (the kind popularized by television shows such as *CSI* and *Dexter*) would calculate a direct labor efficiency variance based on whether the lab used more or fewer hours than the standard hours allowed for the actual number of DNA tests. In contrast, the efficiency variance for variable overhead cost is based on the efficiency with which *the cost-allocation base* is used. Webb's unfavorable variable overhead efficiency variance of $15,000 means that the actual machine-hours (the cost-allocation base) of 4,500 hours turned out to be higher than the budgeted machine-hours of 4,000 hours allowed to manufacture 10,000 jackets.

The following table shows possible causes for Webb's actual machine-hours exceeding budgeted machine-hours and management's potential responses to each of these causes.

Possible Causes for Exceeding Budget	Potential Management Responses
1. Workers were less skilled than expected in using machines.	1. Encourage the human resources department to implement better employee-hiring practices and training procedures.
2. Production scheduler inefficiently scheduled jobs, resulting in more machine-hours used than budgeted.	2. Improve plant operations by installing production scheduling software.
3. Machines were not maintained in good operating condition.	3. Ensure preventive maintenance is done on all machines.
4. Webb's sales staff promised a distributor a rush delivery, which resulted in more machine-hours used than budgeted.	4. Coordinate production schedules with sales staff and distributors and share information with them.
5. Budgeted machine time standards were set too tight.	5. Commit more resources to develop appropriate standards.

Management would assess the cause(s) of the $15,000 U variance in April 2011 and respond accordingly. Note how, depending on the cause(s) of the variance, corrective actions may need to be taken not just in manufacturing but also in other business functions of the value chain, such as sales and distribution.

Exhibit 1   Columnar Presentation of Variable Overhead Variance Analysis: Webb Company for April 2011[a]

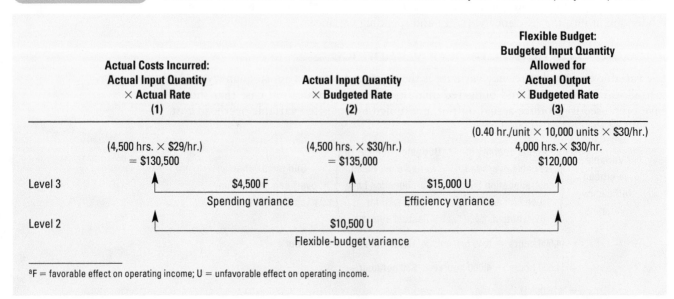

	Actual Costs Incurred: Actual Input Quantity × Actual Rate (1)	Actual Input Quantity × Budgeted Rate (2)	Flexible Budget: Budgeted Input Quantity Allowed for Actual Output × Budgeted Rate (3)
	(4,500 hrs. × $29/hr.) = $130,500	(4,500 hrs. × $30/hr.) = $135,000	(0.40 hr./unit × 10,000 units × $30/hr.) 4,000 hrs.× $30/hr. $120,000
Level 3		$4,500 F	$15,000 U
		Spending variance	Efficiency variance
Level 2		$10,500 U	
		Flexible-budget variance	

[a]F = favorable effect on operating income; U = unfavorable effect on operating income.

Webb's managers discovered that one reason the machines operated below budgeted efficiency levels in April 2011 was insufficient maintenance performed in the prior two months. A former plant manager delayed maintenance in a presumed attempt to meet monthly budget cost targets. Managers should not be focused on meeting short-run budget targets if they are likely to result in harmful long-run consequences. Webb is now strengthening its internal maintenance procedures so that failure to do monthly maintenance as needed will raise a "red flag" that must be immediately explained to management. Another reason for actual machine-hours exceeding budgeted machine-hours was the use of underskilled workers. As a result, Webb is initiating steps to improve hiring and training practices.

Variable Overhead Spending Variance

The **variable overhead spending variance** is the difference between actual variable overhead cost per unit of the cost-allocation base and budgeted variable overhead cost per unit of the cost-allocation base, multiplied by the actual quantity of variable overhead cost-allocation base used for actual output.

$$\begin{pmatrix} \text{Variable} \\ \text{overhead} \\ \text{spending} \\ \text{variance} \end{pmatrix} = \begin{pmatrix} \text{Actual variable} & \text{Budgeted variable} \\ \text{overhead cost per unit} - \text{overhead cost per unit} \\ \text{of cost-allocation base} & \text{of cost-allocation base} \end{pmatrix} \times \begin{pmatrix} \text{Actual quantity of} \\ \text{variable overhead} \\ \text{cost-allocation base} \\ \text{used for actual output} \end{pmatrix}$$

$$= (\$29 \text{ per machine-hour} - \$30 \text{ per machine-hour}) \times 4{,}500 \text{ machine-hours}$$

$$= (-\$1 \text{ per machine-hour}) \times 4{,}500 \text{ machine-hours}$$

$$= \$4{,}500 \text{ F}$$

Since Webb operated in April 2011 with a lower-than-budgeted variable overhead cost per machine-hour, there is a favorable variable overhead spending variance. Columns 1 and 2 in Exhibit 1 depict this variance.

To understand the favorable variable overhead spending variance and its implications, Webb's managers need to recognize why *actual* variable overhead cost per unit of the cost-allocation base ($29 per machine-hour) is *lower* than the *budgeted* variable overhead cost per unit of the cost-allocation base ($30 per machine-hour). Overall, Webb used 4,500 machine-hours, which is 12.5% greater than the flexible-budget amount of 4,000 machine hours. However, actual variable overhead costs of $130,500 are only 8.75% greater than the flexible-budget amount of $120,000. Thus, relative to the flexible budget, the percentage increase in actual variable overhead costs is *less* than the percentage increase in machine-hours. Consequently, actual variable overhead cost per machine-hour is lower than the budgeted amount, resulting in a favorable variable overhead spending variance.

Recall that variable overhead costs include costs of energy, machine maintenance, indirect materials, and indirect labor. Two possible reasons why the percentage increase in actual variable overhead costs is less than the percentage increase in machine-hours are as follows:

1. Actual prices of individual inputs included in variable overhead costs, such as the price of energy, indirect materials, or indirect labor, are lower than budgeted prices of these inputs. For example, the actual price of electricity may only be $0.09 per kilowatt-hour, compared with a price of $0.10 per kilowatt-hour in the flexible budget.

2. Relative to the flexible budget, the percentage increase in the actual usage of individual items in the variable overhead-cost pool is less than the percentage increase in machine-hours. Compared with the flexible-budget amount of 30,000 kilowatt-hours, suppose actual energy used is 32,400 kilowatt-hours, or 8% higher. The fact that this is a smaller percentage increase than the 12.5% increase in machine-hours (4,500 actual machine-hours versus a flexible budget of 4,000 machine hours) will lead to a favorable variable overhead spending variance. The favorable spending variance can be partially or completely traced to the efficient use of energy and other variable overhead items.

As part of the last stage of the five-step decision-making process, Webb's managers will need to examine the signals provided by the variable overhead variances to *evaluate performance and learn*. By understanding the reasons for these variances, Webb can take appropriate actions and make more precise predictions in order to achieve improved results in future periods.

For example, Webb's managers must examine why actual prices of variable overhead cost items are different from budgeted prices. The price effects could be the result of skillful negotiation on the part of the purchasing manager, oversupply in the market, or lower quality of inputs such as indirect materials. Webb's response depends on what is believed to be the cause of the variance. If the concerns are about quality, for instance, Webb may want to put in place new quality management systems.

Similarly, Webb's managers should understand the possible causes for the efficiency with which variable overhead resources are used. These causes include skill levels of workers, maintenance of machines, and the efficiency of the manufacturing process. Webb's managers discovered that Webb used fewer supervision resources per machine-hour because of manufacturing process improvements. As a result, they began organizing crossfunctional teams to see if more process improvements could be achieved.

We emphasize that a favorable variable overhead spending variance is not always desirable. For example, the variable overhead spending variance would be favorable if Webb's managers purchased lower-priced, poor-quality indirect materials, hired less-talented supervisors, or performed less machine maintenance. These decisions, however, are likely to hurt product quality and harm the long-run prospects of the business.

To clarify the concepts of variable overhead efficiency variance and variable overhead spending variance, consider the following example. Suppose that (a) energy is the only item of variable overhead cost and machine-hours is the cost-allocation base; (b) actual machine-hours used equals the number of machine hours under the flexible budget; and (c) the actual price of energy equals the budgeted price. From (a) and (b), it follows that there is no efficiency variance — the company has been efficient with respect to the number of machine-hours (the cost-allocation base) used to produce the actual output. However, and despite (c), there could still be a spending variance. Why? Because even though the company used the correct number of machine hours, the energy consumed *per machine hour* could be higher than budgeted (for example, because the machines have not been maintained correctly). The cost of this higher energy usage would be reflected in an unfavorable spending variance.

Journal Entries for Variable Overhead Costs and Variances

We now prepare journal entries for Variable Overhead Control and the contra account Variable Overhead Allocated.

Entries for variable overhead for April 2011 (data from Exhibit 1) are as follows:

1. Variable Overhead Control	130,500	
Accounts Payable and various other accounts		130,500
To record actual variable overhead costs incurred.		
2. Work-in-Process Control	120,000	
Variable Overhead Allocated		120,000
To record variable overhead cost allocated		
(0.40 machine-hour/unit × 10,000 units × $30/machine-hour). (The costs accumulated in Work-in-Process Control are transferred to Finished Goods Control when production is completed and to Cost of Goods Sold when the products are sold.)		
3. Variable Overhead Allocated	120,000	
Variable Overhead Efficiency Variance	15,000	
Variable Overhead Control		130,500
Variable Overhead Spending Variance		4,500
To record variances for the accounting period.		

These variances are the underallocated or overallocated variable overhead costs. At the end of the fiscal year, the variance accounts are written off to cost of goods sold if immaterial in amount. If the variances are material in amount, they are prorated among Work-in-Process Control, Finished Goods Control, and Cost of Goods Sold on the basis of the variable overhead allocated to these accounts. Only unavoidable costs are prorated. Any part of the variances attributable to avoidable inefficiency are written off in the period. Assume that the balances in the variable overhead variance accounts as of April 2011 are also the balances at the end of the 2011 fiscal year and are immaterial in amount. The following journal entry records the write-off of the variance accounts to cost of goods sold:

Cost of Goods Sold	10,500	
Variable Overhead Spending Variance	4,500	
Variable Overhead Efficiency Variance		15,000

We next consider fixed overhead cost variances.

Fixed Overhead Cost Variances

The flexible-budget amount for a fixed-cost item is also the amount included in the static budget prepared at the start of the period. No adjustment is required for differences between actual output and budgeted output for fixed costs, because fixed costs are unaffected by changes in the output level within the relevant range. At the start of 2011, Webb budgeted fixed overhead costs to be $276,000 per month. The actual amount for April 2011 turned out to be $285,000. The **fixed overhead flexible-budget variance** is the difference between actual fixed overhead costs and fixed overhead costs in the flexible budget:

$$\frac{\text{Fixed overhead}}{\text{flexible-budget variance}} = \frac{\text{Actual costs}}{\text{incurred}} - \frac{\text{Flexible-budget}}{\text{amount}}$$

$$= \$285,000 - \$276,000$$

$$= \$9,000 \text{ U}$$

The variance is unfavorable because $285,000 actual fixed overhead costs exceed the $276,000 budgeted for April 2011, which decreases that month's operating income by $9,000.

The variable overhead flexible-budget variance described earlier in this chapter was subdivided into a spending variance and an efficiency variance. There is not an efficiency variance for fixed overhead costs. That's because a given lump sum of fixed overhead costs will be unaffected by how efficiently machine-hours are used to produce output in a given budget period. As we will see later on, this does not mean that a company cannot be efficient or inefficient in its use of fixed-overhead-cost resources. As Exhibit 2 shows, because there is no efficiency variance, the **fixed overhead spending variance** is the same amount as the fixed overhead flexible-budget variance:

$$\frac{\text{Fixed overhead}}{\text{spending variance}} = \frac{\text{Actual costs}}{\text{incurred}} - \frac{\text{Flexible-budget}}{\text{amount}}$$

$$= \$285,000 - \$276,000$$

$$= \$9,000 \text{ U}$$

Reasons for the unfavorable spending variance could be higher plant-leasing costs, higher depreciation on plant and equipment, or higher administrative costs, such as a higher-than-budgeted salary paid to the plant manager. Webb investigated this variance and found that there was a $9,000 per month unexpected increase in its equipment-leasing costs. However, management concluded that the new lease rates were competitive with lease rates available elsewhere. If this were not the case, management would look to lease equipment from other suppliers.

◀ **Decision Point**

What variances can be calculated for variable overhead costs?

Learning Objective 4

Compute the fixed overhead flexible-budget variance,

. . . difference between actual fixed overhead costs and flexible-budget fixed overhead amounts

the fixed overhead spending variance,

. . . same as the preceding explanation

and the fixed overhead production-volume variance

. . . difference between budgeted fixed overhead and fixed overhead allocated on the basis of actual output produced

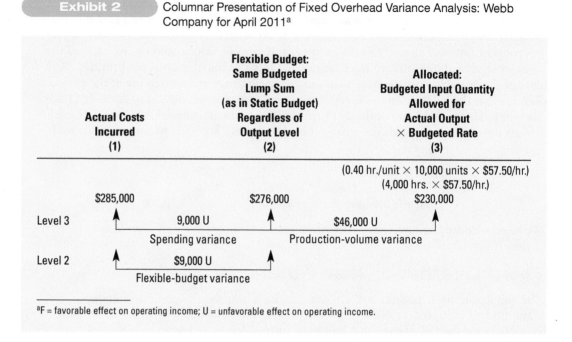

Exhibit 2 Columnar Presentation of Fixed Overhead Variance Analysis: Webb Company for April 2011[a]

[a]F = favorable effect on operating income; U = unfavorable effect on operating income.

Production-Volume Variance

We now examine a variance—the production-volume variance—that arises only for fixed costs. Recall that at the start of the year, Webb calculated a budgeted fixed overhead rate of $57.50 per machine hour. Under standard costing, Webb's budgeted fixed overhead costs are allocated to actual output produced during the period at the rate of $57.50 per standard machine-hour, equivalent to a rate of $23 per jacket (0.40 machine-hour per jacket × $57.50 per machine-hour). If Webb produces 1,000 jackets, $23,000 ($23 per jacket × 1,000 jackets) out of April's budgeted fixed overhead costs of $276,000 will be allocated to the jackets. If Webb produces 10,000 jackets, $230,000 ($23 per jacket × 10,000 jackets) will be allocated. Only if Webb produces 12,000 jackets (that is, operates at capacity), will all $276,000 ($23 per jacket × 12,000 jackets) of the budgeted fixed overhead cost be allocated to the jacket output. The key point here is that even though Webb budgets fixed overhead costs to be $276,000, it does not necessarily allocate all these costs to output. The reason is that Webb budgets $276,000 of fixed costs to support its planned production of 12,000 jackets. If Webb produces fewer than 12,000 jackets, it only allocates the budgeted cost of capacity actually needed and used to produce the jackets.

The **production-volume variance**, also referred to as the **denominator-level variance**, is the difference between budgeted fixed overhead and fixed overhead allocated on the basis of actual output produced. The allocated fixed overhead can be expressed in terms of allocation-base units (machine-hours for Webb) or in terms of the budgeted fixed cost per unit:

$$\frac{\text{Production}}{\text{volume variance}} = \frac{\text{Budgeted}}{\text{fixed overhead}} - \frac{\text{Fixed overhead allocated}}{\text{for actual output units produced}}$$

$$= \$276,000 - (0.40 \text{ hour per jacket} \times \$57.50 \text{ per hour} \times 10,000 \text{ jackets})$$

$$= \$276,000 - (\$23 \text{ per jacket} \times 10,000 \text{ jackets})$$

$$= \$276,000 - \$230,000$$

$$= \$46,000 \text{ U}$$

As shown in Exhibit 2, the budgeted fixed overhead ($276,000) will be the lump sum shown in the static budget and also in any flexible budget within the relevant range. Fixed overhead allocated ($230,000) is the amount of fixed overhead costs allocated; it is calculated by multiplying the number of output units produced during the budget period (10,000 units) by the budgeted cost per output unit ($23). The $46,000 U production-volume variance can also be thought of as $23 per jacket × 2,000 jackets that were *not* produced (12,000 jackets planned – 10,000 jackets produced). We will explore possible causes for the unfavorable production-volume variance and its management implications in the following section.

Exhibit 3 is a graphic presentation of the production-volume variance. Exhibit 3 shows that for planning and control purposes, fixed (manufacturing) overhead costs do not change in the 0- to 12,000-unit relevant range. Contrast this behavior of fixed costs with how these costs are depicted for the inventory costing purpose in Exhibit 3. Under generally accepted accounting principles, fixed (manufacturing) overhead costs are allocated as an inventoriable cost to the output units produced. Every output unit that Webb manufactures will increase the fixed overhead allocated to products by $23. That is, for purposes of allocating fixed overhead costs to jackets, these costs are viewed *as if* they had a variable-cost behavior pattern. As the graph in Exhibit 3 shows, the difference between the fixed overhead costs budgeted of $276,000 and the $230,000 of costs allocated is the $46,000 unfavorable production-volume variance.

Managers should always be careful to distinguish the true behavior of fixed costs from the manner in which fixed costs are assigned to products. In particular, while fixed costs are unitized and allocated for inventory costing purposes in a certain way, as described previously, managers should be wary of using the same unitized fixed overhead costs for planning and control purposes. When forecasting fixed costs, managers should concentrate on total lump-sum costs. Similarly, when managers are looking to assign costs for control purposes or identify the best way to use capacity resources that are fixed in the short run, we will see that the use of unitized fixed costs often leads to incorrect decisions.

Interpreting the Production-Volume Variance

Lump-sum fixed costs represent costs of acquiring capacity that do not decrease automatically if the resources needed turn out to be less than the resources acquired. Sometimes costs are fixed for a specific time period for contractual reasons, such as an annual lease contract for a plant. At other times, costs are fixed because capacity has to be acquired or disposed of in fixed increments, or lumps. For example, suppose that acquiring a sewing machine gives Webb the ability to produce 1,000 jackets. Then, if it is not possible to buy or lease a fraction of a machine, Webb can add capacity only in increments of 1,000 jackets. That is, Webb may choose capacity levels of 10,000; 11,000; or 12,000 jackets, but nothing in between.

Webb's management would want to analyze why this overcapacity occurred. Is demand weak? Should Webb reevaluate its product and marketing strategies? Is there a quality problem? Or did Webb make a strategic mistake by acquiring too much capacity? The causes of the $46,000 unfavorable production-volume variance will drive the actions Webb's managers will take in response to this variance.

In contrast, a favorable production-volume variance indicates an overallocation of fixed overhead costs. That is, the overhead costs allocated to the actual output produced exceed the budgeted fixed overhead costs of $276,000. The favorable production-volume variance comprises the fixed costs recorded in excess of $276,000.

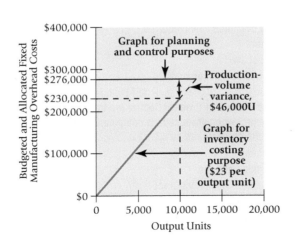

Exhibit 3

Behavior of Fixed Manufacturing Overhead Costs: Budgeted for Planning and Control Purposes and Allocated for Inventory Costing Purposes for Webb Company for April 2011

Be careful when drawing conclusions regarding a company's decisions about capacity planning and usage from the type (that is, favorable, F, or unfavorable, U) or the magnitude associated with a production-volume variance. To interpret the $46,000 unfavorable variance, Webb should consider why it sold only 10,000 jackets in April. Suppose a new competitor had gained market share by pricing below Webb's selling price. To sell the budgeted 12,000 jackets, Webb might have had to reduce its own selling price on all 12,000 jackets. Suppose it decided that selling 10,000 jackets at a higher price yielded higher operating income than selling 12,000 jackets at a lower price. The production-volume variance does not take into account such information. The failure of the production-volume variance to consider such information is why Webb should not interpret the $46,000 U amount as the total economic cost of selling 2,000 jackets fewer than the 12,000 jackets budgeted. If, however, Webb's managers anticipate they will not need capacity beyond 10,000 jackets, they may reduce the excess capacity, say, by canceling the lease on some of the machines.

Companies plan their plant capacity strategically on the basis of market information about how much capacity will be needed over some future time horizon. For 2011, Webb's budgeted quantity of output is equal to the maximum capacity of the plant for that budget period. Actual demand (and quantity produced) turned out to be below the budgeted quantity of output, so Webb reports an unfavorable production-volume variance for April 2011. However, it would be incorrect to conclude that Webb's management made a poor planning decision regarding plant capacity. Demand for Webb's jackets might be highly uncertain. Given this uncertainty and the cost of not having sufficient capacity to meet sudden demand surges (including lost contribution margins as well as reduced repeat business), Webb's management may have made a wise choice in planning 2011 plant capacity. Of course, if demand is unlikely to pick up again, Webb's managers may look to cancel the lease on some of the machines or to sublease the machines to other parties with the goal of reducing the unfavorable production-volume variance.

Managers must always explore the why of a variance before concluding that the label unfavorable or favorable necessarily indicates, respectively, poor or good management performance. Understanding the reasons for a variance also helps managers decide on future courses of action. Should Webb's managers try to reduce capacity, increase sales, or do nothing? Based on their analysis of the situation, Webb's managers decided to reduce some capacity but continued to maintain some excess capacity to accommodate unexpected surges in demand. The Concepts in Action feature highlights another example of managers using variances, and the reasons behind them, to help guide their decisions.

Next we describe the journal entries Webb would make to record fixed overhead costs using standard costing.

Journal Entries for Fixed Overhead Costs and Variances

We illustrate journal entries for fixed overhead costs for April 2011 using Fixed Overhead Control and the contra account Fixed Overhead Allocated (data from Exhibit 2).

1. Fixed Overhead Control 285,000
       Salaries Payable, Accumulated Depreciation, and various other accounts 285,000
       To record actual fixed overhead costs incurred.
2. Work-in-Process Control 230,000
       Fixed Overhead Allocated 230,000
       To record fixed overhead costs allocated
       (0.40 machine-hour/unit $\times$ 10,000 units $\times$ $57.50/machine-hour). (The
       costs accumulated in Work-in-Process Control are transferred to
       Finished Goods Control when production is completed and to Cost of
       Goods Sold when the products are sold.)
3. Fixed Overhead Allocated 230,000
       Fixed Overhead Spending Variance 9,000
       Fixed Overhead Production-Volume Variance 46,000
           Fixed Overhead Control 285,000
       To record variances for the accounting period.

Overall, $285,000 of fixed overhead costs were incurred during April, but only $230,000 were allocated to jackets. The difference of $55,000 is precisely the underallocated fixed overhead costs that we introduced when studying normal costing. The third entry illustrates how the fixed overhead spending variance of $9,000 and the fixed overhead production-volume variance of $46,000 together record this amount in a standard costing system.

At the end of the fiscal year, the fixed overhead spending variance is written off to cost of goods sold if it is immaterial in amount, or prorated among Work-in-Process Control, Finished Goods Control, and Cost of Goods Sold on the basis of the fixed overhead allocated to these accounts. Some companies combine the write-off and proration methods—that is, they write off the portion of the variance that is due to inefficiency and could have been avoided and prorate the portion of the variance that is unavoidable. Assume that the balance in the Fixed Overhead Spending Variance account as of April 2011 is also the balance at the end of 2011 and is immaterial in amount. The following journal entry records the write-off to Cost of Goods Sold.

Cost of Goods Sold	9,000	
Fixed Overhead Spending Variance		9,000

We now consider the production-volume variance. Assume that the balance in Fixed Overhead Production-Volume Variance as of April 2011 is also the balance at the end of 2011. Also assume that some of the jackets manufactured during 2011 are in work-in-process and finished goods inventory at the end of the year. Many management accountants make a strong argument for writing off to Cost of Goods Sold and not prorating an unfavorable production-volume variance. Proponents of this argument contend that the unfavorable production-volume variance of $46,000 measures the cost of resources expended for 2,000 jackets that were not produced ($23 per jacket × 2,000 jackets = $46,000). Prorating these costs would inappropriately allocate fixed overhead costs incurred for the 2,000 jackets that were not produced to the jackets that were produced. The jackets produced already bear their representative share of fixed overhead costs of $23 per jacket. Therefore, this argument favors charging the unfavorable production-volume variance against the year's revenues so that fixed costs of unused capacity are not carried in work-in-process inventory and finished goods inventory.

There is, however, an alternative view. This view regards the denominator level chosen as a "soft" rather than a "hard" measure of the fixed resources required and needed to produce each jacket. Suppose that either because of the design of the jacket or the functioning of the machines, it took more machine-hours than previously thought to manufacture each jacket. Consequently, Webb could make only 10,000 jackets rather than the planned 12,000 in April. In this case, the $276,000 of budgeted fixed overhead costs support the production of the 10,000 jackets manufactured. Under this reasoning, prorating the fixed overhead production-volume variance would appropriately spread fixed overhead costs among Work-in-Process Control, Finished Goods Control, and Cost of Goods Sold.

What about a favorable production-volume variance? Suppose Webb manufactured 13,800 jackets in April 2011.

$$\text{Production-volume variance} = \begin{array}{c}\text{Budgeted}\\\text{fixed}\\\text{overhead}\end{array} - \begin{array}{c}\text{Fixed overhead allocated using}\\\text{budgeted cost per output unit overhead}\\\text{allowed for actual output produced}\end{array}$$

$$= \$276,000 - (\$23 \text{ per jacket} \times 13,800 \text{ jackets})$$

$$= \$276,000 - \$317,400 = \$41,400 \text{ F}$$

Because actual production exceeded the planned capacity level, clearly the fixed overhead costs of $276,000 supported production of, and so should be allocated to, all 13,800 jackets. Prorating the favorable production-volume variance achieves this outcome and reduces the amounts in Work-in-Process Control, Finished Goods Control, and Cost of Goods Sold. Proration is also the more conservative approach in the sense that it results in a lower operating income than if the entire favorable production-volume variance were credited to Cost of Goods Sold.

One more point is relevant to the discussion of whether to prorate the production-volume variance or to write it off to cost of goods sold. If variances are always written off to cost of goods sold, a company could set its standards to either increase (for financial reporting purposes) or decrease (for tax purposes) operating income. In other words, always writing off variances invites gaming behavior. For example, Webb could generate a favorable (unfavorable) production-volume variance by setting the denominator level used to allocate fixed overhead costs low (high) and thereby increase (decrease) operating income. The proration method has the effect of approximating the allocation of fixed costs based on actual costs and actual output so it is not susceptible to the manipulation of operating income via the choice of the denominator level.

There is no clear-cut or preferred approach for closing out the production-volume variance. The appropriate accounting procedure is a matter of judgment and depends on the circumstances of each case. Variations of the proration method may be desirable. For example, a company may choose to write off a portion of the production-volume variance and prorate the rest. The goal is to write off that part of the production-volume variance that represents the cost of capacity not used to support the production of output during the period. The rest of the production-volume variance is prorated to Work-in-Process Control, Finished Goods Control, and Cost of Goods Sold.

If Webb were to write off the production-volume variance to cost of goods sold, it would make the following journal entry.

Cost of Goods Sold	46,000	
Fixed Overhead Production-Volume Variance		46,000

Integrated Analysis of Overhead Cost Variances

As our discussion indicates, the variance calculations for variable overhead and fixed overhead differ:

- Variable overhead has no production-volume variance.
- Fixed overhead has no efficiency variance.

Exhibit 4 presents an integrated summary of the variable overhead variances and the fixed overhead variances computed using standard costs for April 2011. Panel A shows the variances for variable overhead, while Panel B contains the fixed overhead variances. As you study Exhibit 4, note how the columns in Panels A and B are aligned to measure the different variances. In both Panels A and B,

- the difference between columns 1 and 2 measures the spending variance.
- the difference between columns 2 and 3 measures the efficiency variance (if applicable).
- the difference between columns 3 and 4 measures the production-volume variance (if applicable).

Panel A contains an efficiency variance; Panel B has no efficiency variance for fixed overhead. As discussed earlier, a lump-sum amount of fixed costs will be unaffected by the degree of operating efficiency in a given budget period.

Panel A does not have a production-volume variance, because the amount of variable overhead allocated is always the same as the flexible-budget amount. Variable costs never have any unused capacity. When production and sales decline from 12,000 jackets to 10,000 jackets, budgeted variable overhead costs proportionately decline. Fixed costs are different. Panel B has a production-volume variance (see Exhibit 3) because Webb had to acquire the fixed manufacturing overhead resources it had committed to when it planned production of 12,000 jackets, even though it produced only 10,000 jackets and did not use some of its capacity.

Exhibit 4   Columnar Presentation of Integrated Variance Analysis: Webb Company for April 2011[a]

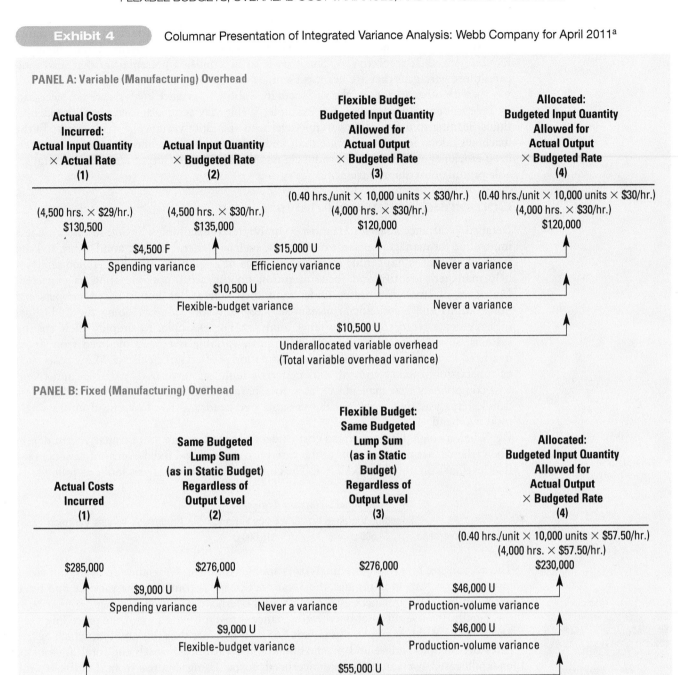

PANEL A: Variable (Manufacturing) Overhead

Actual Costs Incurred: Actual Input Quantity × Actual Rate (1)	Actual Input Quantity × Budgeted Rate (2)	Flexible Budget: Budgeted Input Quantity Allowed for Actual Output × Budgeted Rate (3)	Allocated: Budgeted Input Quantity Allowed for Actual Output × Budgeted Rate (4)
(4,500 hrs. × $29/hr.) $130,500	(4,500 hrs. × $30/hr.) $135,000	(0.40 hrs./unit × 10,000 units × $30/hr.) (4,000 hrs. × $30/hr.) $120,000	(0.40 hrs./unit × 10,000 units × $30/hr.) (4,000 hrs. × $30/hr.) $120,000

$4,500 F — Spending variance
$15,000 U — Efficiency variance
Never a variance

$10,500 U — Flexible-budget variance
Never a variance

$10,500 U — Underallocated variable overhead (Total variable overhead variance)

PANEL B: Fixed (Manufacturing) Overhead

Actual Costs Incurred (1)	Same Budgeted Lump Sum (as in Static Budget) Regardless of Output Level (2)	Flexible Budget: Same Budgeted Lump Sum (as in Static Budget) Regardless of Output Level (3)	Allocated: Budgeted Input Quantity Allowed for Actual Output × Budgeted Rate (4)
$285,000	$276,000	$276,000	(0.40 hrs./unit × 10,000 units × $57.50/hr.) (4,000 hrs. × $57.50/hr.) $230,000

$9,000 U — Spending variance
Never a variance
$46,000 U — Production-volume variance

$9,000 U — Flexible-budget variance
$46,000 U — Production-volume variance

$55,000 U — Underallocated fixed overhead (Total fixed overhead variance)

[a]F = favorable effect on operating income; U = unfavorable effect on operating income.

4-Variance Analysis

When all of the overhead variances are presented together as in Exhibit 4, we refer to it as a 4-variance analysis:

	4-Variance Analysis		
	Spending Variance	Efficiency Variance	Production-Volume Variance
Variable overhead	$4,500 F	$15,000 U	Never a variance
Fixed overhead	$9,000 U	Never a variance	$46,000 U

Note that the 4-variance analysis provides the same level of information as the variance analysis carried out earlier for variable overhead and fixed overhead separately (in Exhibits 1 and 2, respectively), but it does so in a unified presentation that also indicates those variances that are never present.

As with other variances, the variances in Webb's 4-variance analysis are not necessarily independent of each other. For example, Webb may purchase lower-quality machine fluids (leading to a favorable variable overhead spending variance), which results in the machines taking longer to operate than budgeted (causing an unfavorable variable overhead efficiency variance), and producing less than budgeted output (causing an unfavorable production-volume variance).

Combined Variance Analysis

Detailed 4-variance analyses are most common in large, complex businesses, because it is impossible for managers at large companies, such as General Electric and Disney, to keep track of all that is happening within their areas of responsibility. The detailed analyses help managers identify and focus attention on the areas not operating as expected. Managers of small businesses understand their operations better based on personal observations and nonfinancial measures. They find less value in doing the additional measurements required for 4-variance analyses. For example, to simplify their costing systems, small companies may not distinguish variable overhead incurred from fixed overhead incurred because making this distinction is often not clear-cut. Many costs such as supervision, quality control, and materials handling have both variable- and fixed-cost components that may not be easy to separate. Managers may therefore use a less detailed analysis that *combines* the variable overhead and fixed overhead into a single total overhead.

When a single total overhead cost category is used, it can still be analyzed in depth. The variances are now the sums of the variable overhead and fixed overhead variances for that level, as computed in Exhibit 4. The combined variance analysis looks as follows:

| | Combined 3-Variance Analysis | | |
	Spending Variance	Efficiency Variance	Production-Volume Variance
Total overhead	$4,500 U	$15,000 U	$46,000 U

The accounting for 3-variance analysis is simpler than for 4-variance analysis, but some information is lost. In particular, the 3-variance analysis combines the variable and fixed overhead spending variances into a single total overhead spending variance.

Finally, the overall **total-overhead variance** is given by the sum of the preceding variances. In the Webb example, this equals $65,500 U. Note that this amount, which aggregates the flexible-budget and production-volume variances, equals the total amount of underallocated (or underapplied) overhead costs. Using figures from Exhibit 4, the $65,500 U total-overhead variance is the difference between (a) the total actual overhead incurred ($130,500 + $285,000 = $415,500) and (b) the overhead allocated ($120,000 + $230,000 = $350,000) to the actual output produced. If the total-overhead variance were favorable, it would have corresponded instead to the amount of overapplied overhead costs.

> **Decision Point** ▶

What is the most detailed way for a company to reconcile actual overhead incurred with the amount allocated during a period?

Production-Volume Variance and Sales-Volume Variance

As we complete our study of variance analysis for Webb Company, it is helpful to step back to see the "big picture" and to link the accounting and performance evaluation functions of standard costing. In this chapter, we presented more detailed variances that subdivided, whenever possible, individual flexible-budget variances for selling price, direct materials, direct manufacturing labor, variable overhead, and fixed overhead. Here is a summary:

Selling price	$50,000 F
Direct materials (Price, $44,400 F + Efficiency, $66,000 U)	21,600 U
Direct manufacturing labor (Price, $18,000 U + Efficiency, $20,000 U)	38,000 U
Variable overhead (Spending, $4,500 F + Efficiency, $15,000 U)	10,500 U
Fixed overhead (Spending, $9,000 U)	9,000 U
Total flexible budget variance	$29,100 U

We also calculated one other variance in this chapter, the production-volume variance, which is not part of the flexible-budget variance. Where does the production-volume variance fit into the "big picture"? As we shall see, the production-volume variance is a component of the sales-volume variance.

Under our assumption of actual production and sales of 10,000 jackets, Webb's costing system debits to Work-in-Process Control the standard costs of the 10,000 jackets produced. These amounts are then transferred to Finished Goods and finally to Cost of Goods Sold:

Direct materials (Chapter 7, p. 240, entry 1b)	
($60 per jacket × 10,000 jackets)	$ 600,000
Direct manufacturing labor (Chapter 7, p. 240, entry 2)	
($16 per jacket × 10,000 jackets)	160,000
Variable overhead (Chapter 8, p. 270, entry 2)	
($12 per jacket × 10,000 jackets)	120,000
Fixed overhead (Chapter 8, p. 274, entry 2)	
($23 per jacket × 10,000 jackets)	230,000
Cost of goods sold at standard cost	
($111 per jacket × 10,000 jackets)	$1,110,000

Webb's costing system also records the revenues from the 10,000 jackets sold at the budgeted selling price of $120 per jacket. The net effect of these entries on Webb's budgeted operating income is as follows:

Revenues at budgeted selling price	
($120 per jacket × 10,000 jackets)	$1,200,000
Cost of goods sold at standard cost	
($111 per jacket × 10,000 jackets)	1,110,000
Operating income based on budgeted profit per jacket	
($9 per jacket × 10,000 jackets)	$ 90,000

A crucial point to keep in mind is that in standard costing, fixed overhead cost is treated as if it is a variable cost. That is, in determining the budgeted operating income of $90,000, only $230,000 ($23 per jacket × 10,000 jackets) of fixed overhead is considered, whereas the budgeted fixed overhead costs are $276,000. Webb's accountants then record the $46,000 unfavorable production-volume variance (the difference between budgeted fixed overhead costs, $276,000, and allocated fixed overhead costs, $230,000, entry 2), as well as the various flexible-budget variances (including the fixed overhead spending variance) that total $29,100 unfavorable. This results in actual operating income of $14,900 as follows:

Operating income based on budgeted profit per jacket	
($9 per jacket × 10,000 jackets)	$ 90,000
Unfavorable production-volume variance	(46,000)
Flexible-budget operating income (Exhibit 7-2)	44,000
Unfavorable flexible-budget variance for operating income (Exhibit 7-2)	(29,100)
Actual operating income (Exhibit 7-2)	$ 14,900

Concepts in Action

Variance Analysis and Standard Costing Help Sandoz Manage Its Overhead Costs

Getty Images, Inc.—Liaison

In the United States, the importance of generic pharmaceuticals is growing dramatically. In recent years, Wal-Mart has been selling hundreds of generic drugs for $4 per prescription, a price many competitors have since matched. Moreover, with recent legislation extending health insurance coverage to 32 million previously uninsured Americans, the growing use of generic drugs is certain to accelerate, a trend rooted both in demographics—the aging U.S. population takes more drugs each year—and in the push to cut health care costs.

Sandoz US, a $7.5 billion subsidiary of Swiss-based Novartis AG, is one of the largest developers of generic pharmaceutical substitutes for market-leading therapeutic drugs. Market pricing pressure means that Sandoz, Teva Pharmaceutical, and other generic manufacturers operate on razor-thin margins. As a result, along with an intricate analysis of direct-cost variances, firms like Sandoz must also tackle the challenge of accounting for overhead costs. Sandoz uses standard costing and variance analysis to manage its overhead costs.

Each year, Sandoz prepares an overhead budget based on a detailed production plan, planned overhead spending, and other factors, including inflation, efficiency initiatives, and anticipated capital expenditures and depreciation. Sandoz then uses activity-based costing techniques to assign budgeted overhead costs to different work centers (for example, mixing, blending, tableting, testing, and packaging). Finally, overhead costs are assigned to products based on the activity levels required by each product at each work center. The resulting standard product cost is used in product profitability analysis and as a basis for making pricing decisions. The two main focal points in Sandoz's performance analyses are overhead absorption analysis and manufacturing overhead variance analysis.

Each month, Sandoz uses absorption analysis to compare actual production and actual costs to the standard costs of processed inventory. The monthly analysis evaluates two key trends:

1. Are costs in line with the budget? If not, the reasons are examined and the accountable managers are notified.
2. Are production volume and product mix conforming to plan? If not, Sandoz reviews and adjusts machine capacities and the absorption trend is deemed to be permanent. Plant management uses absorption analysis as a compass to determine if it is on budget and has an appropriate capacity level to efficiently satisfy the needs of its customers.

Manufacturing overhead variances are examined at the work center level. These variances help determine when equipment is not running as expected, which leads to repair or replacement. Variances also help in identifying inefficiencies in processing and setup and cleaning times, which leads to more efficient ways to use equipment. Sometimes, manufacturing overhead variance analysis leads to the review and improvement of the standards themselves—a critical element in planning the level of plant capacity. Management reviews current and future capacity use on a monthly basis, using standard hours entered into the plan's enterprise resource planning system. The standards are a useful tool in identifying capacity constraints and future capital needs.

As the plant controller remarked, "Standard costing at Sandoz produces costs that are not only understood by management accountants and industrial engineers, but by decision makers in marketing and on the production floor. Management accountants at Sandoz achieve this by having a high degree of process understanding and involvement. The result is better pricing and product mix decisions, lower waste, process improvements, and efficient capacity choices—all contributing to overall profitability."

Source: *Booming US Generic Drug Market*. Delhi, India: RNCOS Ltd, 2010; Conversations with, and documents prepared by, Eric Evans and Erich Erchr (of Sandoz US), 2004; Day, Kathleen. 2006. Wal-Mart sets $4 price for many generic drugs. *Washington Post*, September 22; Halpern, Steven. 2010. Teva: Generic gains from health care reform. AOL Inc. "Blogging Stocks" blog, May 13. http://www.bloggingstocks.com/2010/05/13/teva-teva-generic-gains-from-healthcare-reform/

In contrast, the static-budget operating income of $108,000 is not entered in Webb's costing system, because standard costing records budgeted revenues, standard costs, and variances only for the 10,000 jackets actually produced and sold, not for the 12,000 jackets that were *planned* to be produced and sold. As a result, the sales-volume variance of $64,000 U, which is the difference between static-budget operating income,

$108,000, and flexible-budget operating income, $44,000, is never actually recorded in standard costing. Nevertheless, the sales-volume variance is useful because it helps managers understand the lost contribution margin from selling 2,000 fewer jackets (the sales-volume variance assumes fixed costs remain at the budgeted level of $276,000).

The sales-volume variance has two components. They are as follows:

1. A difference between the static-budget operating income of $108,000 for 12,000 jackets and budgeted operating income of $90,000 for 10,000 jackets. This is the **operating-income volume variance** of $18,000 U ($108,000 – $90,000), and reflects the fact that Webb produced and sold 2,000 fewer units than budgeted.

2. A difference between the budgeted operating income of $90,000 and the flexible budget operating income of $44,000 for the 10,000 actual units. This difference arises because Webb's costing system treats fixed costs as if they behave in a variable manner and so assumes fixed costs equal the allocated amount of $230,000, rather than the budgeted fixed costs of $276,000. Of course, the difference between the allocated and budgeted fixed costs is precisely the production-volume variance of $46,000 U.

In summary, we have the following:

	Operating-income volume variance	$18,000 U
(+)	Production-volume variance	46,000 U
Equals	Sales-volume variance	$64,000 U

That is, the sales-volume variance is comprised of operating-income volume and production-volume variances.

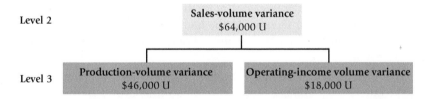

Decision Point

What is the relationship between the sales-volume variance and the production-volume variance?

Variance Analysis and Activity-Based Costing

Activity-based costing (ABC) systems focus on individual activities as the fundamental cost objects. ABC systems classify the costs of various activities into a cost hierarchy—output unit-level costs, batch-level costs, product-sustaining costs, and facility-sustaining costs. In this section, we show how a company that has an ABC system and batch-level costs can benefit from variance analysis. Batch-level costs are the costs of activities related to a group of units of products or services rather than to each individual unit of product or service. We illustrate variance analysis for variable batch-level direct costs and fixed batch-level setup overhead costs.[4]

Consider Lyco Brass Works, which manufactures many different types of faucets and brass fittings. Because of the wide range of products it produces, Lyco uses an activity-based costing system. In contrast, Webb uses a simple costing system because it makes only one type of jacket. One of Lyco's products is Elegance, a decorative brass faucet for home spas. Lyco produces Elegance in batches.

For each product Lyco makes, it uses dedicated materials-handling labor to bring materials to the production floor, transport work in process from one work center to the next, and take the finished goods to the shipping area. Therefore, materials-handling labor costs for Elegance are direct costs of Elegance. Because the materials for a batch are moved together, materials-handling labor costs vary with number of batches rather than with number of units in a batch. Materials-handling labor costs are variable direct batch-level costs.

Learning Objective 7

Calculate variances in activity-based costing

. . . compare budgeted and actual overhead costs of activities

---

[4] The techniques we demonstrate can be applied to analyze variable batch-level overhead costs as well.

To manufacture a batch of Elegance, Lyco must set up the machines and molds. Setting up the machines and molds requires highly trained skills. Hence, a separate setup department is responsible for setting up machines and molds for different batches of products. Setup costs are overhead costs of products. For simplicity, assume that setup costs are fixed with respect to the number of setup-hours. They consist of salaries paid to engineers and supervisors and costs of leasing setup equipment.

Information regarding Elegance for 2012 follows:

	Actual Result	Static-Budget Amount
1. Units of Elegance produced and sold	151,200	180,000
2. Batch size (units per batch)	140	150
3. Number of batches (Line 1 ÷ Line 2)	1,080	1,200
4. Materials-handling labor-hours per batch	5.25	5
5. Total materials-handling labor-hours (Line 3 × Line 4)	5,670	6,000
6. Cost per materials-handling labor-hour	$ 14.50	$ 14
7. Total materials-handling labor costs (Line 5 × Line 6)	$ 82,215	$ 84,000
8. Setup-hours per batch	6.25	6
9. Total setup-hours (Line 3 × Line 8)	6,750	7,200
10. Total fixed setup overhead costs	$220,000	$216,000

Flexible Budget and Variance Analysis for Direct Labor Costs

To prepare the flexible budget for materials-handling labor costs, Lyco starts with the actual units of output produced, 151,200 units, and proceeds with the following steps.

Step 1: Using Budgeted Batch Size, Calculate the Number of Batches that Should Have Been Used to Produce Actual Output. At the budgeted batch size of 150 units per batch, Lyco should have produced the 151,200 units of output in 1,008 batches (151,200 units ÷ 150 units per batch).

Step 2: Using Budgeted Materials-Handling Labor-Hours per Batch, Calculate the Number of Materials-Handling Labor-Hours that Should Have Been Used. At the budgeted quantity of 5 hours per batch, 1,008 batches should have required 5,040 materials-handling labor-hours (1,008 batches × 5 hours per batch).

Step 3: Using Budgeted Cost per Materials-Handling Labor-Hour, Calculate the Flexible-Budget Amount for Materials-Handling Labor-Hours. The flexible-budget amount is 5,040 materials-handling labor-hours × $14 budgeted cost per materials-handling labor-hour = $70,560.

Note how the flexible-budget calculations for materials-handling labor costs focus on batch-level quantities (materials-handling labor-hours per batch rather than per unit). Flexible-budget quantity computations focus at the appropriate level of the cost hierarchy. For example, because materials handling is a batch-level cost, the flexible-budget quantity calculations are made at the batch level—the quantity of materials-handling labor-hours that Lyco should have used based on the number of batches it should have used to produce the actual quantity of 151,200 units. If a cost had been a product-sustaining cost—such as product design cost—the flexible-budget quantity computations would focus at the product-sustaining level, for example, by evaluating the actual complexity of product design relative to the budget.

The flexible-budget variance for materials-handling labor costs can now be calculated as follows:

$$\text{Flexible-budget variance} = \text{Actual costs} - \text{Flexible-budget costs}$$

$$= (5,670 \text{ hours} \times \$14.50 \text{ per hour}) - (5,040 \text{ hours} \times \$14 \text{ per hour})$$

$$= \$82,215 - \$70,560$$

$$= \$11,655 \text{ U}$$

The unfavorable variance indicates that materials-handling labor costs were \$11,655 higher than the flexible-budget target. We can get some insight into the possible reasons for this unfavorable outcome by examining the price and efficiency components of the flexible-budget variance. Exhibit 5 presents the variances in columnar form.

$$\frac{\text{Price}}{\text{variance}} = \left(\frac{\text{Actual price}}{\text{of input}} - \frac{\text{Budgeted price}}{\text{of input}} \right) \times \frac{\text{Actual quantity}}{\text{of input}}$$

$$= (\$14.50 \text{ per hour} - \$14 \text{ per hour}) \times 5,670 \text{ hours}$$

$$= \$0.50 \text{ per hour} \times 5,670 \text{ hours}$$

$$= \$2,835 \text{ U}$$

The unfavorable price variance for materials-handling labor indicates that the \$14.50 actual cost per materials-handling labor-hour exceeds the \$14.00 budgeted cost per materials-handling labor-hour. This variance could be the result of Lyco's human resources manager negotiating wage rates less skillfully or of wage rates increasing unexpectedly due to scarcity of labor.

$$\frac{\text{Efficiency}}{\text{variance}} = \left(\begin{array}{c} \text{Actual} \\ \text{quantity of} \\ \text{input used} \end{array} - \begin{array}{c} \text{Budgeted quantity} \\ \text{of input allowed} \\ \text{for actual output} \end{array} \right) \times \frac{\text{Budgeted price}}{\text{of input}}$$

$$= (5,670 \text{ hours} - 5,040 \text{ hours}) \times \$14 \text{ per hour}$$

$$= 630 \text{ hours} \times \$14 \text{ per hour}$$

$$= \$8,820 \text{ U}$$

The unfavorable efficiency variance indicates that the 5,670 actual materials-handling labor-hours exceeded the 5,040 budgeted materials-handling labor-hours for actual output. Possible reasons for the unfavorable efficiency variance are as follows:

- Smaller actual batch sizes of 140 units, instead of the budgeted batch sizes of 150 units, resulting in Lyco producing the 151,200 units in 1,080 batches instead of 1,008 (151,200 ÷ 150) batches
- Higher actual materials-handling labor-hours per batch of 5.25 hours instead of budgeted materials-handling labor-hours of 5 hours

Reasons for smaller-than-budgeted batch sizes could include quality problems when batch sizes exceed 140 faucets and high costs of carrying inventory.

| Exhibit 5 | Columnar Presentation of Variance Analysis for Direct Materials-Handling Labor Costs: Lyco Brass Works for 2012[a] |

Actual Costs Incurred: Actual Input Quantity × Actual Rate (1)	Actual Input Quantity × Budgeted Rate (2)	Flexible Budget: Budgeted Input Quantity Allowed for Actual Output × Budgeted Rate (3)
(5,670 hours × \$14.50 per hour) \$82,215	(5,670 hours × \$14 per hour) \$79,380	(5,040 hours × \$14 per hour) \$70,560

Level 3 — $2,835 U Price variance — $8,820 U Efficiency variance

Level 2 — $11,655 U Flexible-budget variance

———
[a]F = favorable effect on operating income; U = unfavorable effect on operating income.

233

Possible reasons for larger actual materials-handling labor-hours per batch are as follows:

- Inefficient layout of the Elegance production line
- Materials-handling labor having to wait at work centers before picking up or delivering materials
- Unmotivated, inexperienced, and underskilled employees
- Very tight standards for materials-handling time

Identifying the reasons for the efficiency variance helps Lyco's managers develop a plan for improving materials-handling labor efficiency and to take corrective action that will be incorporated into future budgets.

We now consider fixed setup overhead costs.

Flexible Budget and Variance Analysis for Fixed Setup Overhead Costs

Exhibit 6 presents the variances for fixed setup overhead costs in columnar form.

Lyco's fixed setup overhead flexible-budget variance is calculated as follows:

$$\begin{array}{c}\text{Fixed-setup}\\\text{overhead}\\\text{flexible-budget}\\\text{variance}\end{array} = \begin{array}{c}\text{Actual costs}\\\text{incurred}\end{array} - \begin{array}{c}\text{Flexible-budget}\\\text{costs}\end{array}$$

$$= \$220,000 - \$216,000$$

$$= \$4,000 \text{ U}$$

Note that the flexible-budget amount for fixed setup overhead costs equals the static-budget amount of $216,000. That's because there is no "flexing" of fixed costs. Moreover, because fixed overhead costs have no efficiency variance, the fixed setup overhead spending variance is the same as the fixed overhead flexible-budget variance. The spending variance could be unfavorable because of higher leasing costs of new setup equipment or higher salaries paid to engineers and supervisors. Lyco may have incurred these costs to alleviate some of the difficulties it was having in setting up machines.

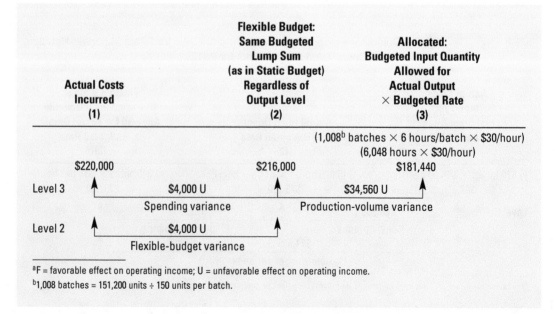

Exhibit 6 — Columnar Presentation of Fixed Setup Overhead Variance Analysis: Lyco Brass Works for 2012[a]

	Actual Costs Incurred (1)		Flexible Budget: Same Budgeted Lump Sum (as in Static Budget) Regardless of Output Level (2)		Allocated: Budgeted Input Quantity Allowed for Actual Output × Budgeted Rate (3)
					(1,008[b] batches × 6 hours/batch × $30/hour) (6,048 hours × $30/hour)
	$220,000		$216,000		$181,440
Level 3		$4,000 U		$34,560 U	
		Spending variance		Production-volume variance	
Level 2		$4,000 U			
		Flexible-budget variance			

[a]F = favorable effect on operating income; U = unfavorable effect on operating income.
[b]1,008 batches = 151,200 units ÷ 150 units per batch.

To calculate the production-volume variance, Lyco first computes the budgeted cost-allocation rate for fixed setup overhead costs using the same four-step approach described earlier in this chapter.

Step 1: Choose the Period to Use for the Budget. Lyco uses a period of 12 months (the year 2012).

Step 2: Select the Cost-Allocation Base to Use in Allocating Fixed Overhead Costs to Output Produced. Lyco uses budgeted setup-hours as the cost-allocation base for fixed setup overhead costs. Budgeted setup-hours in the static budget for 2012 are 7,200 hours.

Step 3: Identify the Fixed Overhead Costs Associated with the Cost-Allocation Base. Lyco's fixed setup overhead cost budget for 2012 is $216,000.

Step 4: Compute the Rate per Unit of the Cost-Allocation Base Used to Allocate Fixed Overhead Costs to Output Produced. Dividing the $216,000 from Step 3 by the 7,200 setup-hours from Step 2, Lyco estimates a fixed setup overhead cost rate of $30 per setup-hour:

$$\begin{array}{l}\text{Budgeted fixed} \\ \text{setup overhead} \\ \text{cost per unit of} \\ \text{cost-allocation base}\end{array} = \frac{\begin{array}{c}\text{Budgeted total costs} \\ \text{in fixed overhead cost pool}\end{array}}{\begin{array}{c}\text{Budgeted total quantity of} \\ \text{cost-allocation base}\end{array}} = \frac{\$216{,}000}{7{,}200 \text{ setup hours}}$$

$$= \$30 \text{ per setup-hour}$$

$$\begin{array}{l}\text{Production-volume} \\ \text{variance for} \\ \text{fixed setup} \\ \text{overhead costs}\end{array} = \begin{array}{c}\text{Budgeted} \\ \text{fixed setup} \\ \text{overhead} \\ \text{costs}\end{array} - \begin{array}{c}\text{Fixed setup overhead} \\ \text{allocation using budgeted} \\ \text{input allowed for actual} \\ \text{output units produced}\end{array}$$

$$= \$216{,}000 - (1{,}008 \text{ batches} \times 6 \text{ hours/batch}) \times \$30/\text{hour}$$

$$= \$216{,}000 - (6{,}048 \text{ hours} \times \$30/\text{hour})$$

$$= \$216{,}000 - \$181{,}440$$

$$= \$34{,}560 \text{ U}$$

During 2012, Lyco planned to produce 180,000 units of Elegance but actually produced 151,200 units. The unfavorable production-volume variance measures the amount of extra fixed setup costs that Lyco incurred for setup capacity it had but did not use. One interpretation is that the unfavorable $34,560 production-volume variance represents inefficient use of setup capacity. However, Lyco may have earned higher operating income by selling 151,200 units at a higher price than 180,000 units at a lower price. As a result, Lyco's managers should interpret the production-volume variance cautiously because it does not consider effects on selling prices and operating income.

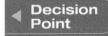

◄ Decision Point

How can variance analysis be used in an activity-based costing system?

Overhead Variances in Nonmanufacturing Settings

Our Webb Company example examines variable manufacturing overhead costs and fixed manufacturing overhead costs. Should the overhead costs of the nonmanufacturing areas of the company be examined using the variance analysis framework discussed in this chapter? Companies often use variable-cost information pertaining to nonmanufacturing, as well as manufacturing, costs in pricing and product mix decisions. Managers consider variance analysis of all variable overhead costs when making such decisions and when managing costs. For example, managers in industries in which distribution costs are high, such as automobiles, consumer durables, and cement and steel, may use standard costing to give reliable and timely information on variable distribution overhead spending variances and efficiency variances.

Consider service-sector companies such as airlines, hospitals, hotels, and railroads. The measures of output commonly used in these companies are passenger-miles flown,

Learning Objective 8

Examine the use of overhead variances in nonmanufacturing settings

. . . analyze nonmanufacturing variable overhead costs for decision making and cost management; fixed overhead variances are especially important in service settings

patient days provided, room-days occupied, and ton-miles of freight hauled, respectively. Few costs can be traced to these outputs in a cost-effective way. The majority of costs are fixed overhead costs, such as the costs of equipment, buildings, and staff. Using capacity effectively is the key to profitability, and fixed overhead variances can help managers in this task. Retail businesses, such as Kmart, also have high capacity-related fixed costs (lease and occupancy costs). In the case of Kmart, sales declines resulted in unused capacity and unfavorable fixed-cost variances. Kmart reduced fixed costs by closing some of its stores, but it also had to file for Chapter 11 bankruptcy in January 2002.

Consider the following data for the mainline operations of United Airlines for selected years from the past decade. Available seat miles (ASMs) are the actual seats in an airplane multiplied by the distance traveled.

Year	Total ASMs (Millions) (1)	Operating Revenue per ASM (2)	Operating Cost per ASM (3)	Operating Income per ASM (4) = (2) – (3)
2000	175,485	11.0 cents	10.6 cents	0.4 cents
2003	136,630	9.6 cents	10.5 cents	−0.9 cents
2006	143,095	11.5 cents	11.2 cents	0.3 cents
2008	135,861	12.6 cents	15.7 cents	−3.1 cents

After September 11, 2001, as air travel declined, United's revenues decreased but a majority of its costs comprising fixed costs of airport facilities, equipment, and personnel did not. United had a large unfavorable production-volume variance as its capacity was underutilized. As column 1 of the table indicates, United responded by reducing its capacity substantially over the next few years. Available seat miles declined from 175,485 million in 2000 to 136,630 million in 2003. Yet, United was unable to fill even the planes it had retained, so revenue per ASM declined (column 2) and cost per ASM stayed roughly the same (column 3). United filed for Chapter 11 bankruptcy in December 2002 and began seeking government guarantees to obtain the loans it needed. Subsequently, strong demand for airline travel, as well as yield improvements gained by more efficient use of resources and networks, led to increased traffic and higher average ticket prices. By maintaining a disciplined approach to capacity and tight control over growth, United saw close to a 20% increase in its revenue per ASM between 2003 and 2006. The improvement in performance allowed United to come out of bankruptcy on February 1, 2006. In the past year, however, the severe global recession and soaring jet fuel prices have had a significant negative impact on United's performance (and that of its competitor airlines), as reflected in the negative operating income for 2008.

Financial and Nonfinancial Performance Measures

The overhead variances discussed in this chapter are examples of financial performance measures. As the preceding examples illustrate, nonfinancial measures such as those related to capacity utilization and physical measures of input usage also provide useful information. Returning to the Webb example one final time, we can see that nonfinancial measures that managers of Webb would likely find helpful in planning and controlling its overhead costs include the following:

1. Quantity of actual indirect materials used per machine-hour, relative to quantity of budgeted indirect materials used per machine-hour

2. Actual energy used per machine-hour, relative to budgeted energy used per machine-hour

3. Actual machine-hours per jacket, relative to budgeted machine-hours per jacket

These performance measures, like the financial variances discussed in this chapter, can be described as signals to direct managers' attention to problems. These nonfinancial performance measures probably would be reported daily or hourly on the production floor. The overhead variances we discussed in this chapter capture the financial effects of items such as the three factors listed, which in many cases first appear as nonfinancial performance measures. An especially interesting example along these lines comes from Japan, where some companies have introduced budgeted-to-actual variance analysis and internal trading systems among group units as a means to rein in their CO_2 emissions. The goal is to raise employee awareness of emissions reduction in preparation for the anticipated future costs of greenhouse-gas reduction plans being drawn up by the new Japanese government.

Finally, both financial and nonfinancial performance measures are used to evaluate the performance of managers. Exclusive reliance on either is always too simplistic because each gives a different perspective on performance. Nonfinancial measures (such as those described previously) provide feedback on individual aspects of a manager's performance, whereas financial measures evaluate the overall effect of and the tradeoffs among different nonfinancial performance measures.

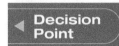

Decision Point

How are overhead variances useful in nonmanufacturing settings?

Problem for Self-Study

Nina Garcia is the newly appointed president of Laser Products. She is examining the May 2012 results for the Aerospace Products Division. This division manufactures wing parts for satellites. Garcia's current concern is with manufacturing overhead costs at the Aerospace Products Division. Both variable and fixed overhead costs are allocated to the wing parts on the basis of laser-cutting-hours. The following budget information is available:

Budgeted variable overhead rate	$200 per hour
Budgeted fixed overhead rate	$240 per hour
Budgeted laser-cutting time per wing part	1.5 hours
Budgeted production and sales for May 2012	5,000 wing parts
Budgeted fixed overhead costs for May 2012	$1,800,000

Actual results for May 2012 are as follows:

Wing parts produced and sold	4,800 units
Laser-cutting-hours used	8,400 hours
Variable overhead costs	$1,478,400
Fixed overhead costs	$1,832,200

1. Compute the spending variance and the efficiency variance for variable overhead.
2. Compute the spending variance and the production-volume variance for fixed overhead.
3. Give two explanations for each of the variances calculated in requirements 1 and 2.

Required

Solution

1 and 2. See Exhibit 7.
3. a. Variable overhead spending variance, $201,600 F. One possible reason for this variance is that the actual prices of individual items included in variable overhead (such as cutting fluids) are lower than budgeted prices. A second possible reason is that the percentage increase in the actual quantity usage of individual items in the variable overhead cost pool is less than the percentage increase in laser-cutting-hours compared to the flexible budget.
   b. Variable overhead efficiency variance, $240,000 U. One possible reason for this variance is inadequate maintenance of laser machines, causing them to take more laser-cutting time per wing part. A second possible reason is use of undermotivated, inexperienced, or underskilled workers with the laser-cutting machines, resulting in more laser-cutting time per wing part.

Exhibit 7   Columnar Presentation of Integrated Variance Analysis: Laser Products for May 2012[a]

PANEL A: Variable (Manufacturing) Overhead

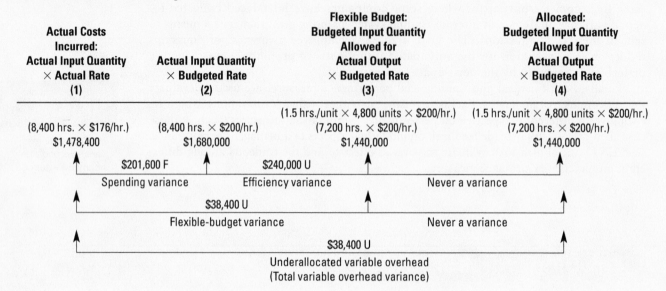

Actual Costs Incurred: Actual Input Quantity × Actual Rate (1)	Actual Input Quantity × Budgeted Rate (2)	Flexible Budget: Budgeted Input Quantity Allowed for Actual Output × Budgeted Rate (3)	Allocated: Budgeted Input Quantity Allowed for Actual Output × Budgeted Rate (4)
(8,400 hrs. × $176/hr.)	(8,400 hrs. × $200/hr.)	(1.5 hrs./unit × 4,800 units × $200/hr.) (7,200 hrs. × $200/hr.)	(1.5 hrs./unit × 4,800 units × $200/hr.) (7,200 hrs. × $200/hr.)
$1,478,400	$1,680,000	$1,440,000	$1,440,000

$201,600 F ← Spending variance → $240,000 U ← Efficiency variance → Never a variance

$38,400 U ← Flexible-budget variance → Never a variance

$38,400 U
Underallocated variable overhead
(Total variable overhead variance)

PANEL B: Fixed (Manufacturing) Overhead

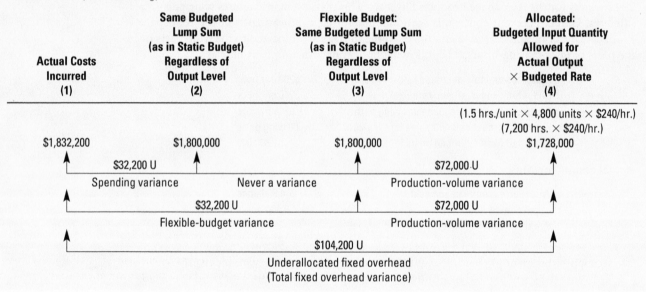

Actual Costs Incurred (1)	Same Budgeted Lump Sum (as in Static Budget) Regardless of Output Level (2)	Flexible Budget: Same Budgeted Lump Sum (as in Static Budget) Regardless of Output Level (3)	Allocated: Budgeted Input Quantity Allowed for Actual Output × Budgeted Rate (4)
			(1.5 hrs./unit × 4,800 units × $240/hr.) (7,200 hrs. × $240/hr.)
$1,832,200	$1,800,000	$1,800,000	$1,728,000

$32,200 U ← Spending variance → Never a variance → $72,000 U ← Production-volume variance

$32,200 U ← Flexible-budget variance → $72,000 U ← Production-volume variance

$104,200 U
Underallocated fixed overhead
(Total fixed overhead variance)

[a]F = favorable effect on operating income; U = unfavorable effect on operating income.

Source: Strategic finance by Paul Sherman. Copyright 2003 by INSTITUTE OF MANAGEMENT ACCOUNTANTS. Reproduced with permission of INSTITUTE OF MANAGEMENT ACCOUNTANTS in the format Other book via Copyright Clearance Center.

    c. Fixed overhead spending variance, $32,200 U. One possible reason for this variance is that the actual prices of individual items in the fixed-cost pool unexpectedly increased from the prices budgeted (such as an unexpected increase in machine leasing costs). A second possible reason is misclassification of items as fixed that are in fact variable.

    d. Production-volume variance, $72,000 U. Actual production of wing parts is 4,800 units, compared with 5,000 units budgeted. One possible reason for this variance is demand factors, such as a decline in an aerospace program that led to a decline in demand for aircraft parts. A second possible reason is supply factors, such as a production stoppage due to labor problems or machine breakdowns.

Decision Points

The following question-and-answer format summarizes the chapter's learning objectives. Each decision presents a key question related to a learning objective. The guidelines are the answer to that question.

Decision	Guidelines
1. How do managers plan variable overhead costs and fixed overhead costs?	Planning of both variable and fixed overhead costs involves undertaking only activities that add value and then being efficient in that undertaking. The key difference is that for variable-cost planning, ongoing decisions during the budget period play a much larger role; whereas for fixed-cost planning, most key decisions are made before the start of the period.
2. How are budgeted variable overhead and fixed overhead cost rates calculated?	The budgeted variable (fixed) overhead cost rate is calculated by dividing the budgeted variable (fixed) overhead costs by the denominator level of the cost-allocation base.
3. What variances can be calculated for variable overhead costs?	When the flexible budget for variable overhead is developed, an overhead efficiency variance and an overhead spending variance can be computed. The variable overhead efficiency variance focuses on the difference between the actual quantity of the cost-allocation base used relative to the budgeted quantity of the cost-allocation base. The variable overhead spending variance focuses on the difference between the actual variable overhead cost per unit of the cost-allocation base relative to the budgeted variable overhead cost per unit of the cost-allocation base.
4. What variances can be calculated for fixed overhead costs?	For fixed overhead, the static and flexible budgets coincide. The difference between the budgeted and actual amount of fixed overhead is the flexible-budget variance, also referred to as the spending variance. The production-volume variance measures the difference between budgeted fixed overhead and fixed overhead allocated on the basis of actual output produced.
5. What is the most detailed way for a company to reconcile actual overhead incurred with the amount allocated during a period?	A 4-variance analysis presents spending and efficiency variances for variable overhead costs and spending and production-volume variances for fixed overhead costs. By analyzing these four variances together, managers can reconcile the actual overhead costs with the amount of overhead allocated to output produced during a period.
6. What is the relationship between the sales-volume variance and the production-volume variance?	The production-volume variance is a component of the sales-volume variance. The production-volume and operating-income volume variances together comprise the sales-volume variance.
7. How can variance analysis be used in an activity-based costing system?	Flexible budgets in ABC systems give insight into why actual activity costs differ from budgeted activity costs. Using output and input measures for an activity, a 4-variance analysis can be conducted.
8. How are overhead variances useful in nonmanufacturing settings?	Managers consider variance analysis of all variable overhead costs, including those outside the manufacturing function, when making pricing and product mix decisions and when managing costs. Fixed overhead variances are especially important in service settings, where using capacity effectively is the key to profitability. In all cases, the information provided by variances can be supplemented by the use of suitable nonfinancial metrics.

Terms to Learn

The chapter contains definitions of the following important terms:

denominator level

denominator-level variance

fixed overhead flexible-budget
 variance

fixed overhead spending variance

operating-income volume variance

production-denominator level

production-volume variance

standard costing

total-overhead variance

variable overhead efficiency variance

variable overhead flexible-budget
 variance

variable overhead spending variance

Assignment Material

MyAccountingLab

Questions

8-1 How do managers plan for variable overhead costs?

8-2 How does the planning of fixed overhead costs differ from the planning of variable overhead costs?

8-3 How does standard costing differ from actual costing?

8-4 What are the steps in developing a budgeted variable overhead cost-allocation rate?

8-5 What are the factors that affect the spending variance for variable manufacturing overhead?

8-6 Assume variable manufacturing overhead is allocated using machine-hours. Give three possible reasons for a favorable variable overhead efficiency variance.

8-7 Describe the difference between a direct materials efficiency variance and a variable manufacturing overhead efficiency variance.

8-8 What are the steps in developing a budgeted fixed overhead rate?

8-9 Why is the flexible-budget variance the same amount as the spending variance for fixed manufacturing overhead?

8-10 Explain how the analysis of fixed manufacturing overhead costs differs for (a) planning and control and (b) inventory costing for financial reporting.

8-11 Provide one caveat that will affect whether a production-volume variance is a good measure of the economic cost of unused capacity.

8-12 "The production-volume variance should always be written off to Cost of Goods Sold." Do you agree? Explain.

8-13 What are the variances in a 4-variance analysis?

8-14 "Overhead variances should be viewed as interdependent rather than independent." Give an example.

8-15 Describe how flexible-budget variance analysis can be used in the control of costs of activity areas.

MyAccountingLab

Exercises

8-16 Variable manufacturing overhead, variance analysis. Esquire Clothing is a manufacturer of designer suits. The cost of each suit is the sum of three variable costs (direct material costs, direct manufacturing labor costs, and manufacturing overhead costs) and one fixed-cost category (manufacturing overhead costs). Variable manufacturing overhead cost is allocated to each suit on the basis of budgeted direct manufacturing labor-hours per suit. For June 2012 each suit is budgeted to take four labor-hours. Budgeted variable manufacturing overhead cost per labor-hour is $12. The budgeted number of suits to be manufactured in June 2012 is 1,040.

Actual variable manufacturing costs in June 2012 were $52,164 for 1,080 suits started and completed. There were no beginning or ending inventories of suits. Actual direct manufacturing labor-hours for June were 4,536.

Required
1. Compute the flexible-budget variance, the spending variance, and the efficiency variance for variable manufacturing overhead.
2. Comment on the results.

8-17 Fixed manufacturing overhead, variance analysis (continuation of 8-16). Esquire Clothing allocates fixed manufacturing overhead to each suit using budgeted direct manufacturing labor-hours per suit. Data pertaining to fixed manufacturing overhead costs for June 2012 are budgeted, $62,400, and actual, $63,916.

Required
1. Compute the spending variance for fixed manufacturing overhead. Comment on the results.
2. Compute the production-volume variance for June 2012. What inferences can Esquire Clothing draw from this variance?

8-18 Variable manufacturing overhead variance analysis. The French Bread Company bakes baguettes for distribution to upscale grocery stores. The company has two direct-cost categories: direct materials and direct manufacturing labor. Variable manufacturing overhead is allocated to products on the basis of standard direct manufacturing labor-hours. Following is some budget data for the French Bread Company:

Direct manufacturing labor use	0.02 hours per baguette
Variable manufacturing overhead	$10.00 per direct manufacturing labor-hour

The French Bread Company provides the following additional data for the year ended December 31, 2012:

Planned (budgeted) output	3,200,000 baguettes
Actual production	2,800,000 baguettes
Direct manufacturing labor	50,400 hours
Actual variable manufacturing overhead	$680,400

Required

1. What is the denominator level used for allocating variable manufacturing overhead? (That is, for how many direct manufacturing labor-hours is French Bread budgeting?)
2. Prepare a variance analysis of variable manufacturing overhead. Use Exhibit 4 for reference.
3. Discuss the variances you have calculated and give possible explanations for them.

8-19 Fixed manufacturing overhead variance analysis (continuation of 8-18). The French Bread Company also allocates fixed manufacturing overhead to products on the basis of standard direct manufacturing labor-hours. For 2012, fixed manufacturing overhead was budgeted at $4.00 per direct manufacturing labor-hour. Actual fixed manufacturing overhead incurred during the year was $272,000.

Required

1. Prepare a variance analysis of fixed manufacturing overhead cost. Use Exhibit 4 as a guide.
2. Is fixed overhead underallocated or overallocated? By what amount?
3. Comment on your results. Discuss the variances and explain what may be driving them.

8-20 Manufacturing overhead, variance analysis. The Solutions Corporation is a manufacturer of centrifuges. Fixed and variable manufacturing overheads are allocated to each centrifuge using budgeted assembly-hours. Budgeted assembly time is two hours per unit. The following table shows the budgeted amounts and actual results related to overhead for June 2012.

	Actual Results	Static Budget
The Solutions Corporation (June 2012)		
Number of centrifuges assembled and sold	216	200
Hours of assembly time	411	
Variable manufacturing overhead cost per hour of assembly time		$30.00
Variable manufacturing overhead costs	$12,741	
Fixed manufacturing overhead costs	$20,550	$19,200

Required

1. Prepare an analysis of all variable manufacturing overhead and fixed manufacturing overhead variances using the columnar approach in Exhibit 4.
2. Prepare journal entries for Solutions' June 2012 variable and fixed manufacturing overhead costs and variances; write off these variances to cost of goods sold for the quarter ending June 30, 2012.
3. How does the planning and control of variable manufacturing overhead costs differ from the planning and control of fixed manufacturing overhead costs?

8-21 4-variance analysis, fill in the blanks. Rozema, Inc., produces chemicals for large biotech companies. It has the following data for manufacturing overhead costs during August 2013:

	Variable	Fixed
Actual costs incurred	$31,000	$18,000
Costs allocated to products	33,000	14,600
Flexible budget	———	13,400
Actual input × budgeted rate	30,800	———

Use F for favorable and U for unfavorable:

	Variable	Fixed
(1) Spending variance	$____	$____
(2) Efficiency variance	____	____
(3) Production-volume variance	____	____
(4) Flexible-budget variance	____	____
(5) Underallocated (overallocated) manufacturing overhead	____	____

8-22 Straightforward 4-variance overhead analysis. The Lopez Company uses standard costing in its manufacturing plant for auto parts. The standard cost of a particular auto part, based on a denominator level of 4,000 output units per year, included 6 machine-hours of variable manufacturing overhead at $8 per hour and 6 machine-hours of fixed manufacturing overhead at $15 per hour. Actual output produced was 4,400 units. Variable manufacturing overhead incurred was $245,000. Fixed manufacturing overhead incurred was $373,000. Actual machine-hours were 28,400.

Required

1. Prepare an analysis of all variable manufacturing overhead and fixed manufacturing overhead variances, using the 4-variance analysis in Exhibit 4.
2. Prepare journal entries using the 4-variance analysis.
3. Describe how individual fixed manufacturing overhead items are controlled from day to day.
4. Discuss possible causes of the fixed manufacturing overhead variances.

8-23 Straightforward coverage of manufacturing overhead, standard-costing system. The Singapore division of a Canadian telecommunications company uses standard costing for its machine-paced production of telephone equipment. Data regarding production during June are as follows:

Variable manufacturing overhead costs incurred	$618,840
Variable manufacturing overhead cost rate	$8 per standard machine-hour
Fixed manufacturing overhead costs incurred	$145,790
Fixed manufacturing overhead costs budgeted	$144,000
Denominator level in machine-hours	72,000
Standard machine-hour allowed per unit of output	1.2
Units of output	65,500
Actual machine-hours used	76,400
Ending work-in-process inventory	0

Required

1. Prepare an analysis of all manufacturing overhead variances. Use the 4-variance analysis framework illustrated in Exhibit 4.
2. Prepare journal entries for manufacturing overhead costs and their variances.
3. Describe how individual variable manufacturing overhead items are controlled from day to day.
4. Discuss possible causes of the variable manufacturing overhead variances.

8-24 Overhead variances, service sector. Meals on Wheels (MOW) operates a meal home-delivery service. It has agreements with 20 restaurants to pick up and deliver meals to customers who phone or fax orders to MOW. MOW allocates variable and fixed overhead costs on the basis of delivery time. MOW's owner, Josh Carter, obtains the following information for May 2012 overhead costs:

	Home Insert Page Layout Formulas Data Review		
	A	B	C
1	**Meals on Wheels (May 2012)**	**Actual Results**	**Static Budget**
2	Output units (number of deliveries)	8,800	10,000
3	Hours per delivery		0.70
4	Hours of delivery time	5,720	
5	Variable overhead cost per hour of delivery time		$ 1.50
6	Variable overhead costs	$10,296	
7	Fixed overhead costs	$38,600	$35,000

1. Compute spending and efficiency variances for MOW's variable overhead in May 2012.
2. Compute the spending variance and production-volume variance for MOW's fixed overhead in May 2012.
3. Comment on MOW's overhead variances and suggest how Josh Carter might manage MOW's variable overhead differently from its fixed overhead costs.

8-25 Total overhead, 3-variance analysis. Furniture, Inc., specializes in the production of futons. It uses standard costing and flexible budgets to account for the production of a new line of futons. For 2011, budgeted variable overhead at a level of 3,600 standard monthly direct labor-hours was $43,200; budgeted total overhead at 4,000 standard monthly direct labor-hours was $103,400. The standard cost allocated to each output included a total overhead rate of 120% of standard direct labor costs. For October, Furniture, Inc., incurred total overhead of $120,700 and direct labor costs of $128,512. The direct labor price variance was $512 unfavorable. The direct labor flexible-budget variance was $3,512 unfavorable. The standard labor price was $25 per hour. The production-volume variance was $34,600 favorable.

1. Compute the direct labor efficiency variance and the spending and efficiency variances for overhead. Also, compute the denominator level.
2. Describe how individual variable overhead items are controlled from day to day. Also, describe how individual fixed overhead items are controlled.

8-26 Overhead variances, missing information. Dvent budgets 18,000 machine-hours for the production of computer chips in August 2011. The budgeted variable overhead rate is $6 per machine-hour. At the end of August, there is a $375 favorable spending variance for variable overhead and a $1,575 unfavorable spending variance for fixed overhead. For the computer chips produced, 14,850 machine-hours are budgeted and 15,000 machine-hours are actually used. Total actual overhead costs are $120,000.

1. Compute efficiency and flexible-budget variances for Dvent's variable overhead in August 2011. Will variable overhead be over- or underallocated? By how much?
2. Compute production-volume and flexible-budget variances for Dvent's fixed overhead in August 2011. Will fixed overhead be over- or underallocated? By how much?

8-27 Identifying favorable and unfavorable variances. Purdue, Inc., manufactures tires for large auto companies. It uses standard costing and allocates variable and fixed manufacturing overhead based on machine-hours. For each independent scenario given, indicate whether each of the manufacturing variances will be favorable or unfavorable or, in case of insufficient information, indicate "CBD" (cannot be determined).

Scenario	Variable Overhead Spending Variance	Variable Overhead Efficiency Variance	Fixed Overhead Spending Variance	Fixed Overhead Production-Volume Variance
Production output is 4% less than budgeted, and actual fixed manufacturing overhead costs are 5% more than budgeted				
Production output is 12% less than budgeted; actual machine-hours are 7% more than budgeted				
Production output is 9% more than budgeted				
Actual machine-hours are 20% less than flexible-budget machine-hours				
Relative to the flexible budget, actual machine-hours are 12% less, and actual variable manufacturing overhead costs are 20% greater				

8-28 Flexible-budget variances, review of Chapters 7 and 8. David James is a cost accountant and business analyst for Doorknob Design Company (DDC), which manufactures expensive brass doorknobs. DDC uses two direct cost categories: direct materials and direct manufacturing labor. James feels that manufacturing overhead is most closely related to material usage. Therefore, DDC allocates manufacturing overhead to production based upon pounds of materials used.

At the beginning of 2012, DDC budgeted annual production of 400,000 doorknobs and adopted the following standards for each doorknob:

	Input	Cost/Doorknob
Direct materials (brass)	0.3 lb. @ $10/lb.	$ 3.00
Direct manufacturing labor	1.2 hours @ $20/hour	24.00
Manufacturing overhead:		
Variable	$6/lb. × 0.3 lb.	1.80
Fixed	$15/lb. × 0.3 lb.	4.50
Standard cost per doorknob		$33.30

Actual results for April 2012 were as follows:

Production	35,000 doorknobs
Direct materials purchased	12,000 lb. at $11/lb.
Direct materials used	10,450 lb.
Direct manufacturing labor	38,500 hours for $808,500
Variable manufacturing overhead	$64,150
Fixed manufacturing overhead	$152,000

Required

1. For the month of April, compute the following variances, indicating whether each is favorable (F) or unfavorable (U):
   a. Direct materials price variance (based on purchases)
   b. Direct materials efficiency variance
   c. Direct manufacturing labor price variance
   d. Direct manufacturing labor efficiency variance
   e. Variable manufacturing overhead spending variance
   f. Variable manufacturing overhead efficiency variance
   g. Production-volume variance
   h. Fixed manufacturing overhead spending variance
2. Can James use any of the variances to help explain any of the other variances? Give examples.

MyAccountingLab

Problems

8-29 Comprehensive variance analysis. Kitchen Whiz manufactures premium food processors. The following is some manufacturing overhead data for Kitchen Whiz for the year ended December 31, 2012:

Manufacturing Overhead	Actual Results	Flexible Budget	Allocated Amount
Variable	$ 76,608	$ 76,800	$ 76,800
Fixed	350,208	348,096	376,320

Budgeted number of output units: 888
Planned allocation rate: 2 machine-hours per unit
Actual number of machine-hours used: 1,824
Static-budget variable manufacturing overhead costs: $71,040

Required Compute the following quantities (you should be able to do so in the prescribed order):

1. Budgeted number of machine-hours planned
2. Budgeted fixed manufacturing overhead costs per machine-hour
3. Budgeted variable manufacturing overhead costs per machine-hour
4. Budgeted number of machine-hours allowed for actual output produced
5. Actual number of output units
6. Actual number of machine-hours used per output unit

8-30 Journal entries (continuation of 8-29).

Required

1. Prepare journal entries for variable and fixed manufacturing overhead (you will need to calculate the various variances to accomplish this).
2. Overhead variances are written off to the Cost of Goods Sold (COGS) account at the end of the fiscal year. Show how COGS is adjusted through journal entries.

8-31 Graphs and overhead variances. Best Around, Inc., is a manufacturer of vacuums and uses standard costing. Manufacturing overhead (both variable and fixed) is allocated to products on the basis of budgeted machine-hours. In 2012, budgeted fixed manufacturing overhead cost was $17,000,000. Budgeted variable manufacturing overhead was $10 per machine-hour. The denominator level was 1,000,000 machine-hours.

Required

1. Prepare a graph for fixed manufacturing overhead. The graph should display how Best Around, Inc.'s fixed manufacturing overhead costs will be depicted for the purposes of (a) planning and control and (b) inventory costing.
2. Suppose that 1,125,000 machine-hours were allowed for actual output produced in 2012, but 1,150,000 actual machine-hours were used. Actual manufacturing overhead was $12,075,000, variable, and $17,100,000, fixed. Compute (a) the variable manufacturing overhead spending and efficiency variances and (b) the fixed manufacturing overhead spending and production-volume variances. Use the columnar presentation illustrated in Exhibit 4.
3. What is the amount of the under- or overallocated variable manufacturing overhead and the under- or overallocated fixed manufacturing overhead? Why are the flexible-budget variance and the under- or overallocated overhead amount always the same for variable manufacturing overhead but rarely the same for fixed manufacturing overhead?
4. Suppose the denominator level was 1,360,000 rather than 1,000,000 machine-hours. What variances in requirement 2 would be affected? Recompute them.

8-32 4-variance analysis, find the unknowns. Consider the following two situations—cases A and B—independently. Data refer to operations for April 2012. For each situation, assume standard costing. Also assume the use of a flexible budget for control of variable and fixed manufacturing overhead based on machine-hours.

	Cases	
	A	**B**
(1) Fixed manufacturing overhead incurred	$ 84,920	$23,180
(2) Variable manufacturing overhead incurred	$120,000	—
(3) Denominator level in machine-hours	—	1,000
(4) Standard machine-hours allowed for actual output achieved	6,200	—
(5) Fixed manufacturing overhead (per standard machine-hour)	—	—
Flexible-Budget Data:		
(6) Variable manufacturing overhead (per standard machine-hour)	—	$ 42.00
(7) Budgeted fixed manufacturing overhead	$ 88,200	$20,000
(8) Budgeted variable manufacturing overhead[a]	—	—
(9) Total budgeted manufacturing overhead[a]	—	—
Additional Data:		
(10) Standard variable manufacturing overhead allocated	$124,000	—
(11) Standard fixed manufacturing overhead allocated	$ 86,800	—
(12) Production-volume variance	—	$ 4,000 F
(13) Variable manufacturing overhead spending variance	$ 4,600 F	$ 2,282 F
(14) Variable manufacturing overhead efficiency variance	—	$ 2,478 F
(15) Fixed manufacturing overhead spending variance	—	—
(16) Actual machine-hours used	—	—

[a]For standard machine-hours allowed for actual output produced.

Fill in the blanks under each case. [*Hint:* Prepare a worksheet similar to that in Exhibit 4. Fill in the knowns and then solve for the unknowns.]

Required

8-33 Flexible budgets, 4-variance analysis. (CMA, adapted) Nolton Products uses standard costing. It allocates manufacturing overhead (both variable and fixed) to products on the basis of standard direct manufacturing labor-hours (DLH). Nolton develops its manufacturing overhead rate from the current annual budget. The manufacturing overhead budget for 2012 is based on budgeted output of 720,000 units, requiring 3,600,000 DLH. The company is able to schedule production uniformly throughout the year.

A total of 66,000 output units requiring 315,000 DLH was produced during May 2012. Manufacturing overhead (MOH) costs incurred for May amounted to $375,000. The actual costs, compared with the annual budget and 1/12 of the annual budget, are as follows:

Annual Manufacturing Overhead Budget 2012

	Total Amount	Per Output Unit	Per DLH Input Unit	Monthly MOH Budget May 2012	Actual MOH Costs for May 2012
Variable MOH					
Indirect manufacturing labor	$ 900,000	$1.25	$0.25	$ 75,000	$ 75,000
Supplies	1,224,000	1.70	0.34	102,000	111,000
Fixed MOH					
Supervision	648,000	0.90	0.18	54,000	51,000
Utilities	540,000	0.75	0.15	45,000	54,000
Depreciation	1,008,000	1.40	0.28	84,000	84,000
Total	$4,320,000	$6.00	$1.20	$360,000	$375,000

Required Calculate the following amounts for Nolton Products for May 2012:

1. Total manufacturing overhead costs allocated
2. Variable manufacturing overhead spending variance
3. Fixed manufacturing overhead spending variance
4. Variable manufacturing overhead efficiency variance
5. Production-volume variance

Be sure to identify each variance as favorable (F) or unfavorable (U).

8-34 Direct Manufacturing Labor and Variable Manufacturing Overhead Variances. Sarah Beth's Art Supply Company produces various types of paints. Actual direct manufacturing labor hours in the factory that produces paint have been higher than budgeted hours for the last few months and the owner, Sarah B. Jones, is concerned about the effect this has had on the company's cost overruns. Because variable manufacturing overhead is allocated to units produced using direct manufacturing labor hours, Sarah feels that the mismanagement of labor will have a twofold effect on company profitability. Following are the relevant budgeted and actual results for the second quarter of 2011.

	Budget Information	Actual Results
Paint set production	25,000	29,000
Direct manuf. labor hours per paint set	2 hours	2.3 hours
Direct manufacturing labor rate	$10/hour	$10.40/hour
Variable manufacturing overhead rate	$20/hour	$18.95/hour

Required

1. Calculate the direct manufacturing labor price and efficiency variances and indicate whether each is favorable (F) or unfavorable (U).
2. Calculate the variable manufacturing overhead spending and efficiency variances and indicate whether each is favorable (F) or unfavorable (U).
3. For both direct manufacturing labor and variable manufacturing overhead, do the price/spending variances help Sarah explain the efficiency variances?
4. Is Sarah correct in her assertion that the mismanagement of labor has a twofold effect on cost overruns? Why might the variable manufacturing overhead efficiency variance not be an accurate representation of the effect of labor overruns on variable manufacturing overhead costs?

8-35 Activity-based costing, batch-level variance analysis. Pointe's Fleet Feet, Inc., produces dance shoes for stores all over the world. While the pairs of shoes are boxed individually, they are crated and shipped in batches. The shipping department records both variable direct batch-level costs and fixed batch-level overhead costs. The following information pertains to shipping department costs for 2011.

	Static-Budget Amounts	Actual Results
Pairs of shoes shipped	250,000	175,000
Average number of pairs of shoes per crate	10	8
Packing hours per crate	1.1 hours	0.9 hour
Variable direct cost per hour	$22	$24
Fixed overhead cost	$55,000	$52,500

1. What is the static budget number of crates for 2011?
2. What is the flexible budget number of crates for 2011?
3. What is the actual number of crates shipped in 2011?
4. Assuming fixed overhead is allocated using crate-packing hours, what is the predetermined fixed overhead allocation rate?
5. For variable direct batch-level costs, compute the price and efficiency variances.
6. For fixed overhead costs, compute the spending and the production-volume variances.

8-36 Activity-based costing, batch-level variance analysis. Jo Nathan Publishing Company specializes in printing specialty textbooks for a small but profitable college market. Due to the high setup costs for each batch printed, Jo Nathan holds the book requests until demand for a book is approximately 500. At that point Jo Nathan will schedule the setup and production of the book. For rush orders, Jo Nathan will produce smaller batches for an additional charge of $400 per setup.

Budgeted and actual costs for the printing process for 2012 were as follows:

	Static-Budget Amounts	Actual Results
Number of books produced	300,000	324,000
Average number of books per setup	500	480
Hours to set up printers	8 hours	8.2 hours
Direct variable cost per setup-hour	$40	$39
Total fixed setup overhead costs	$105,600	$119,000

1. What is the static budget number of setups for 2012?
2. What is the flexible budget number of setups for 2012?
3. What is the actual number of setups in 2012?
4. Assuming fixed setup overhead costs are allocated using setup-hours, what is the predetermined fixed setup overhead allocation rate?
5. Does Jo Nathan's charge of $400 cover the budgeted direct variable cost of an order? The budgeted total cost?
6. For direct variable setup costs, compute the price and efficiency variances.
7. For fixed setup overhead costs, compute the spending and the production-volume variances.
8. What qualitative factors should Jo Nathan consider before accepting or rejecting a special order?

8-37 Production-Volume Variance Analysis and Sales Volume Variance. Dawn Floral Creations, Inc., makes jewelry in the shape of flowers. Each piece is hand-made and takes an average of 1.5 hours to produce because of the intricate design and scrollwork. Dawn uses direct labor hours to allocate the overhead cost to production. Fixed overhead costs, including rent, depreciation, supervisory salaries, and other production expenses, are budgeted at $9,000 per month. These costs are incurred for a facility large enough to produce 1,000 pieces of jewelry a month.

During the month of February, Dawn produced 600 pieces of jewelry and actual fixed costs were $9,200.

1. Calculate the fixed overhead spending variance and indicate whether it is favorable (F) or unfavorable (U).
2. If Dawn uses direct labor hours available at capacity to calculate the budgeted fixed overhead rate, what is the production-volume variance? Indicate whether it is favorable (F) or unfavorable (U).
3. An unfavorable production-volume variance is a measure of the under-allocation of fixed overhead cost caused by production levels at less than capacity. It therefore could be interpreted as the economic cost of unused capacity. Why would Dawn be willing to incur this cost? Your answer should separately consider the following two unrelated factors:
   a. Demand could vary from month to month while available capacity remains constant.
   b. Dawn would not want to produce at capacity unless it could sell all the units produced. What does Dawn need to do to raise demand and what effect would this have on profit?
4. Dawn's budgeted variable cost per unit is $25 and it expects to sell its jewelry for $55 apiece. Compute the sales-volume variance and reconcile it with the production-volume variance calculated in requirement 2. What does each concept measure?

8-38 Comprehensive review working backward from given variances. The Mancusco Company uses a flexible budget and standard costs to aid planning and control of its machining manufacturing operations. Its costing system for manufacturing has two direct-cost categories (direct materials and direct manufacturing labor—both variable) and two overhead-cost categories (variable manufacturing overhead and fixed manufacturing overhead, both allocated using direct manufacturing labor-hours).

At the 40,000 budgeted direct manufacturing labor-hour level for August, budgeted direct manufacturing labor is $800,000, budgeted variable manufacturing overhead is $480,000, and budgeted fixed manufacturing overhead is $640,000.

The following actual results are for August:

Direct materials price variance (based on purchases)	$176,000 F
Direct materials efficiency variance	69,000 U
Direct manufacturing labor costs incurred	522,750
Variable manufacturing overhead flexible-budget variance	10,350 U
Variable manufacturing overhead efficiency variance	18,000 U
Fixed manufacturing overhead incurred	597,460
Fixed manufacturing overhead spending variance	42,540 F

The standard cost per pound of direct materials is $11.50. The standard allowance is three pounds of direct materials for each unit of product. During August, 30,000 units of product were produced. There was no beginning inventory of direct materials. There was no beginning or ending work in process. In August, the direct materials price variance was $1.10 per pound.

In July, labor unrest caused a major slowdown in the pace of production, resulting in an unfavorable direct manufacturing labor efficiency variance of $45,000. There was no direct manufacturing labor price variance. Labor unrest persisted into August. Some workers quit. Their replacements had to be hired at higher wage rates, which had to be extended to all workers. The actual average wage rate in August exceeded the standard average wage rate by $0.50 per hour.

Required

1. Compute the following for August:
   a. Total pounds of direct materials purchased
   b. Total number of pounds of excess direct materials used
   c. Variable manufacturing overhead spending variance
   d. Total number of actual direct manufacturing labor-hours used
   e. Total number of standard direct manufacturing labor-hours allowed for the units produced
   f. Production-volume variance
2. Describe how Mancusco's control of variable manufacturing overhead items differs from its control of fixed manufacturing overhead items.

8-39 Review 3-variance analysis. (CPA, adapted) The Beal Manufacturing Company's costing system has two direct-cost categories: direct materials and direct manufacturing labor. Manufacturing overhead (both variable and fixed) is allocated to products on the basis of standard direct manufacturing labor-hours (DLH). At the beginning of 2012, Beal adopted the following standards for its manufacturing costs:

	Input	Cost per Output Unit
Direct materials	3 lb. at $5 per lb.	$ 15.00
Direct manufacturing labor	5 hrs. at $15 per hr.	75.00
Manufacturing overhead:		
Variable	$6 per DLH	30.00
Fixed	$8 per DLH	40.00
Standard manufacturing cost per output unit		$160.00

The denominator level for total manufacturing overhead per month in 2012 is 40,000 direct manufacturing labor-hours. Beal's flexible budget for January 2012 was based on this denominator level. The records for January indicated the following:

Direct materials purchased	25,000 lb. at $5.20 per lb.
Direct materials used	23,100 lb.
Direct manufacturing labor	40,100 hrs. at $14.60 per hr.
Total actual manufacturing overhead (variable and fixed)	$600,000
Actual production	7,800 output units

Required

1. Prepare a schedule of total standard manufacturing costs for the 7,800 output units in January 2012.
2. For the month of January 2012, compute the following variances, indicating whether each is favorable (F) or unfavorable (U):
   a. Direct materials price variance, based on purchases
   b. Direct materials efficiency variance
   c. Direct manufacturing labor price variance
   d. Direct manufacturing labor efficiency variance
   e. Total manufacturing overhead spending variance
   f. Variable manufacturing overhead efficiency variance
   g. Production-volume variance

8-40 Non-financial variances. Supreme Canine Products produces high quality dog food distributed only through veterinary offices. To ensure that the food is of the highest quality and has taste appeal, Supreme has a rigorous inspection process. For quality control purposes, Supreme has a standard based on the pounds of food inspected per hour and the number of pounds that pass or fail the inspection.

Supreme expects that for every 15,000 pounds of food produced, 1,500 pounds of food will be inspected. Inspection of 1,500 pounds of dog food should take 1 hour. Supreme also expects that 6% of the food inspected will fail the inspection. During the month of May, Supreme produced 3,000,000 pounds of food and inspected 277,500 pounds of food in 215 hours. Of the 277,500 pounds of food inspected, 15,650 pounds of food failed to pass the inspection.

1. Compute two variances that help determine whether the time spent on inspections was more or less than expected. (Follow a format similar to the one used for the variable overhead spending and efficiency variances, but without prices.) **Required**
2. Compute two variances that can be used to evaluate the percentage of the food that fails the inspection.

8-41 Overhead variances and sales volume variance. Eco-Green Company manufactures cloth shopping bags that it plans to sell for $5 each. Budgeted production and sales for these bags for 2011 is 800,000 bags, with a standard of 400,000 machine hours for the whole year. Budgeted fixed overhead costs are $470,000, and variable overhead cost is $1.60 per machine hour.

Because of increased demand, actual production and sales of the bags for 2010 are 900,000 bags using 440,000 actual machine hours. Actual variable overhead costs are $699,600 and actual fixed overhead is $501,900. Actual selling price is $6 per bag.

Direct materials and direct labor actual costs were the same as standard costs, which were $1.20 per unit and $1.80 per unit, respectively.

1. Calculate the variable overhead and fixed overhead variances (spending, efficiency, spending and volume). **Required**
2. Create a chart showing Flexible Budget Variances and Sales Volume Variances for revenues, costs, contribution margin, and operating income.
3. Calculate the operating income based on budgeted profit per shopping bag.
4. Reconcile the budgeted operating income from requirement 3 to the actual operating income from your chart in requirement 2.
5. Calculate the operating income volume variance and show how the sales volume variance is comprised of the production volume variance and the operating income volume variance.

Collaborative Learning Problem

8-42 Overhead variances, ethics. Zeller Company uses standard costing. The company has two manufacturing plants, one in Nevada and the other in Ohio. For the Nevada plant, Zeller has budgeted annual output of 4,000,000 units. Standard labor hours per unit are 0.25, and the variable overhead rate for the Nevada plant is $3.25 per direct labor hour. Fixed overhead for the Nevada plant is budgeted at $2,500,000 for the year.

For the Ohio plant, Zeller has budgeted annual output of 4,200,000 units with standard labor hours also 0.25 per unit. However, the variable overhead rate for the Ohio plant is $3 per hour, and the budgeted fixed overhead for the year is only $2,310,000.

Firm management has always used variance analysis as a performance measure for the two plants, and has compared the results of the two plants.

Jack Jones has just been hired as a new controller for Zeller. Jack is good friends with the Ohio plant manager and wants him to get a favorable review. Jack suggests allocating the firm's budgeted common fixed costs of $3,150,000 to the two plants, but on the basis of one-third to the Ohio plant and two-thirds to the Nevada plant. His explanation for this allocation base is that Nevada is a more expensive state than Ohio.

At the end of the year, the Nevada plant reported the following actual results: output of 3,900,000 using 1,014,000 labor hours in total, at a cost of $3,244,800 in variable overhead and $2,520,000 in fixed overhead. Actual results for the Ohio plant are an output of 4,350,000 units using 1,218,000 labor hours with a variable cost of $3,775,800 and fixed overhead cost of $2,400,000. The actual common fixed costs for the year were $3,126,000.

1. Compute the budgeted fixed cost per labor hour for the fixed overhead separately for each plant: **Required**
   a. Excluding allocated common fixed costs
   b. Including allocated common fixed costs
2. Compute the variable overhead spending variance and the variable overhead efficiency variance separately for each plant.
3. Compute the fixed overhead spending and volume variances for each plant:
   a. Excluding allocated common fixed costs
   b. Including allocated common fixed costs
4. Did Jack Jones's attempt to make the Ohio plant look better than the Nevada plant by allocating common fixed costs work? Why or why not?
5. Should common fixed costs be allocated in general when variances are used as performance measures? Why or why not?
6. What do you think of Jack Jones's behavior overall?

Inventory Costing and Capacity Analysis

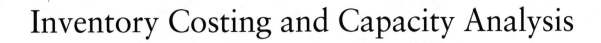

From Chapter 9 of *Cost Accounting: A Managerial Emphasis*, 14/e. Charles T. Horngren. Srikant M. Datar. Madhav Rajan.

Inventory Costing and Capacity Analysis

Few numbers capture the attention of managers and shareholders more than operating profits.

In industries that require significant upfront investments in capacity, the decisions made regarding the level of such fixed investments, and the extent to which the capacity is eventually utilized to meet customer demand, have a substantial impact on corporate profits. Unfortunately, the choice of compensation and reward systems, as well as the choice of inventory-costing methods, may induce managerial decisions that benefit short-term earnings at the expense of a firm's long-term health. It may take a substantial external shock, like a sharp economic slowdown, to motivate firms to make the right capacity and inventory choices, as the following article illustrates.

Lean Manufacturing Helps Companies Reduce Inventory and Survive the Recession[1]

Can changing the way a mattress is pieced together save a company during an economic downturn? For Sealy, the world's largest mattress manufacturer, the answer is a resounding "yes!"

Sealy is among thousands of manufacturers that have remained profitable during the recession by using lean manufacturing to become more cost-efficient. Lean manufacturing involves producing output in an uninterrupted flow, rather than as part of unfinished batches, and producing only what customers order. Driving this lean movement is an urgent need to pare inventory, which reduces inventory costs.

Before the adoption of lean practices, the company used to manufacture units at peak capacity. That is, it made as many mattresses as its resources allowed. Sealy employees were also paid based on the number of mattresses produced each day. While factories operated at peak capacity, inventory often piled up, which cost the company millions of dollars each year.

While Sealy launched its lean strategy in 2004, its efforts intensified during the recession. Old processes were reconfigured to be more efficient. As a result, each bed is now completed in 4 hours, down from 21. Median delivery times have been cut to 60 hours from 72, and plants have cut their raw-material inventories by 50%.

Additionally, the company now adheres to a precise production schedule that reflects orders from retailers such as Mattress Discounters

---
[1] *Source*: Paul Davidson. 2009. Lean manufacturing helps companies survive recession. *USA Today*, November 2; Sealy Corporation. 2009. Annual Report. Trinity, NC: Sealy Corporation, 2010. http://ccbn.10kwizard.com/xml/download.php?repo=tenk&ipage=6709696&format=PDF

and Macy's. While factories no longer run at full capacity, no mattress is made now until a customer orders it.

Sealy's manufacturing and inventory strategy has been key to its survival during the recession. While 2009 sales were 14% less than 2008 sales, earnings rose more than $16 million. Moreover, a large part of the earnings increase was due to reductions in inventory costs, which were lower by 12%, or nearly $8 million, in 2009.

Erin Siegal/Redux Pictures

Managers in industries with high fixed costs, like manufacturing, must manage capacity levels and make decisions about the use of available capacity. Managers must also decide on a production and inventory policy (as Sealy did). These decisions and the accounting choices managers make affect the operating incomes of manufacturing companies. This chapter focuses on two types of cost accounting choices:

1. *The inventory-costing choice* determines which manufacturing costs are treated as inventoriable costs. *Inventoriable costs* are all costs of a product that are regarded as assets when they are incurred and expensed as cost of goods sold when the product is sold. There are three types of inventory costing methods: absorption costing, variable costing, and throughput costing.

2. *The denominator-level capacity choice* focuses on the cost allocation base used to set budgeted fixed manufacturing cost rates. There are four possible choices of capacity levels: theoretical capacity, practical capacity, normal capacity utilization, and master-budget capacity utilization.

Variable and Absorption Costing

The two most common methods of costing inventories in manufacturing companies are *variable costing* and *absorption costing*. We describe each next and then discuss them in detail, using a hypothetical lens-manufacturing company as an example.

Variable Costing

Variable costing is a method of inventory costing in which all variable manufacturing costs (direct and indirect) are included as inventoriable costs. All fixed manufacturing costs are excluded from inventoriable costs and are instead treated as costs of the period in which they are incurred. Note that *variable costing* is a less-than-perfect term to describe this inventory-costing method, because only variable manufacturing costs are inventoried; variable nonmanufacturing costs are still treated as period costs and are expensed. Another common term used to describe this method is **direct costing**. This is also a misnomer because variable costing considers variable manufacturing overhead (an indirect cost) as inventoriable, while excluding direct marketing costs, for example.

Absorption Costing

Absorption costing is a method of inventory costing in which all variable manufacturing costs and all fixed manufacturing costs are included as inventoriable costs. That is, inventory "absorbs" all manufacturing costs.

Under both variable costing and absorption costing, all variable manufacturing costs are inventoriable costs and all nonmanufacturing costs in the value chain (such as research and development and marketing), whether variable or fixed, are period costs and are recorded as expenses when incurred.

Comparing Variable and Absoption Costing

The easiest way to understand the difference between variable costing and absorption costing is with an example. We will study Stassen Company, an optical consumer-products manufacturer, in this chapter. We focus in particular on its product line of high-end telescopes for aspiring astronomers.

Stassen uses standard costing:

- Direct costs are traced to products using standard prices and standard inputs allowed for actual outputs produced.

- Indirect (overhead) manufacturing costs are allocated using standard indirect rates times standard inputs allowed for actual outputs produced.

Stassen's management wants to prepare an income statement for 2012 (the fiscal year just ended) to evaluate the performance of the telescope product line. The operating information for the year is as follows:

	A	B
		Units
2	Beginning inventory	0
3	Production	8,000
4	Sales	6,000
5	Ending inventory	2,000

Actual price and cost data for 2012 are as follows:

	A	B
10	Selling price	$ 1,000
11	Variable manufacturing cost per unit	
12	Direct material cost per unit	$ 110
13	Direct manufacturing labor cost per unit	40
14	Manufacturing overhead cost per unit	50
15	Total variable manufacturing cost per unit	$ 200
16	Variable marketing cost per unit sold	$ 185
17	Fixed manufacturing costs (all indirect)	$1,080,000
18	Fixed marketing costs (all indirect)	$1,380,000

For simplicity and to focus on the main ideas, we assume the following about Stassen:

- Stassen incurs manufacturing and marketing costs only. The cost driver for all variable manufacturing costs is units produced; the cost driver for variable marketing costs is units sold. There are no batch-level costs and no product-sustaining costs.

- There are no price variances, efficiency variances, or spending variances. Therefore, the *budgeted* (standard) price and cost data for 2012 are the same as the *actual* price and cost data.

- Work-in-process inventory is zero.

- Stassen budgeted production of 8,000 units for 2012. This was used to calculate the budgeted fixed manufacturing cost per unit of $135 ($1,080,000/8,000 units).

- Stassen budgeted sales of 6,000 units for 2012, which is the same as the actual sales for 2012.

- The actual production for 2012 is 8,000 units. As a result, there is no production-volume variance for manufacturing costs in 2012. Later examples, based on data for 2013 and 2014, do include production-volume variances. However, even in those cases, the income statements contain no variances other than the production-volume variance.

- All variances are written off to cost of goods sold in the period (year) in which they occur.

Based on the preceding information, Stassen's inventoriable costs per unit produced in 2012 under the two inventory costing methods are as follows:

	Variable Costing		Absorption Costing	
Variable manufacturing cost per unit produced:				
Direct materials	$110		$110	
Direct manufacturing labor	40		40	
Manufacturing overhead	50	$200	50	$200
Fixed manufacturing cost per unit produced		—		135
Total inventoriable cost per unit produced		$200		$335

To summarize, the main difference between variable costing and absorption costing is the accounting for fixed manufacturing costs:

- Under variable costing, fixed manufacturing costs are not inventoried; they are treated as an expense of the period.

- Under absorption costing, fixed manufacturing costs are inventoriable costs. In our example, the standard fixed manufacturing cost is $135 per unit ($1,080,000 ÷ 8,000 units) produced.

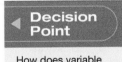

Decision Point

How does variable costing differ from absorption costing?

Variable vs. Absorption Costing: Operating Income and Income Statements

When comparing variable and absorption costing, we must also take into account whether we are looking at short- or long-term numbers. How does the data for a one-year period differ from that of a three-year period under variable and absorption costing?

Comparing Income Statements for One Year

What will Stassen's operating income be if it uses variable costing or absorption costing? The differences between these methods are apparent in Exhibit 1. Panel A shows the variable costing income statement and Panel B the absorption-costing income statement for Stassen's telescope product line for 2012. The variable-costing income statement uses the contribution-margin format. The absorption-costing income statement uses the gross-margin format. Why these differences in format? The distinction between variable costs and fixed costs is central to variable costing, and it is highlighted by the con-

255

| Exhibit 1 | Comparison of Variable Costing and Absorption Costing for Stassen Company: Telescope Product-Line Income Statements for 2012 |

	Home	Insert	Page Layout	Formulas	Data	Review	View

	A	B	C	D	E	F	G
1	Panel A: VARIABLE COSTING				Panel B: ABSORPTION COSTING		
2	Revenues: $1,000 × 6,000 units		$6,000,000		Revenues: $1,000 × 6,000 units		$6,000,000
3	Variable cost of goods sold:				Cost of goods sold:		
4	Beginning inventory	$ 0			Beginning inventory	$ 0	
5	Variable manufacturing costs: $200 × 8,000 units	1,600,000			Variable manufacturing costs: $200 × 8,000 unit	1,600,000	
6					Allocated fixed manufacturing costs: $135 × 8,000 units	1,080,000	
7	Cost of goods available for sale	1,600,000			Cost of goods available for sale	2,680,000	
8	Deduct ending inventory: $200 × 2,000 units	(400,000)			Deduct ending inventory: $335 × 2,000 units	(670,000)	
9	Variable cost of goods sold		1,200,000		Cost of goods sold		2,010,000
10	Variable marketing costs: $185 × 6,000 units sold		1,110,000				
11	Contribution margin		3,690,000		Gross Margin		3,990,000
12	Fixed manufacturing costs		1,080,000		Variable marketing costs: $185 × 6,000 units sold		1,110,000
13	Fixed marketing cost		1,380,000		Fixed marketing costs		1,380,000
14	Operating income		$1,230,000		Operating Income		$1,500,000
15							
16	Manufacturing costs expensed in Panel A:				Manufacturing costs expensed in Panel B:		
17	Variable cost of goods sold		$1,200,000				
18	Fixed manufacturing costs		1,080,000				
19	Total		$2,280,000		Cost of goods sold		$2,010,000

Learning Objective 2

Compute income under absorption costing

. . . using the gross-margin format

and variable costing,

. . . using the contribution-margin format

and explain the difference in income

. . . affected by the unit level of production and sales under absorption costing, but only the unit level of sales under variable costing

tribution-margin format. Similarly, the distinction between manufacturing and nonmanufacturing costs is central to absorption costing, and it is highlighted by the gross-margin format.

Absorption-costing income statements need not differentiate between variable and fixed costs. However, we will make this distinction between variable and fixed costs in the Stassen example to show how individual line items are classified differently under variable costing and absorption costing. In Exhibit 1, Panel B, note that inventoriable cost is $335 per unit under absorption costing: allocated fixed manufacturing costs of $135 per unit plus variable manufacturing costs of $200 per unit.

Notice how the fixed manufacturing costs of $1,080,000 are accounted for under variable costing and absorption costing in Exhibit 1. The income statement under variable costing deducts the $1,080,000 lump sum as an expense for 2012. In contrast, under absorption costing, the $1,080,000 ($135 per unit × 8,000 units) is initially treated as an inventoriable cost in 2012. Of this $1,080,000, $810,000 ($135 per unit × 6,000 units sold) subsequently becomes a part of cost of goods sold in 2012, and $270,000 ($135 per unit × 2,000 units) remains an asset—part of ending finished goods inventory on December 31, 2012.

Operating income is $270,000 higher under absorption costing compared with variable costing, because only $810,000 of fixed manufacturing costs are expensed under absorption costing, whereas all $1,080,000 of fixed manufacturing costs are expensed under variable costing. Note that the variable manufacturing cost of $200 per unit is accounted for the same way in both income statements in Exhibit 1.

These points can be summarized as follows:

	Variable Costing	**Absorption Costing**
Variable manufacturing costs: $200 per telescope produced	Inventoriable	Inventoriable
Fixed manufacturing costs: $1,080,000 per year	Deducted as an expense of the period	Inventoriable at $135 per telescope produced using budgeted denominator level of 8,000 units produced per year ($1,080,000 ÷ 8,000 units = $135 per unit)

The basis of the difference between variable costing and absorption costing is how fixed manufacturing costs are accounted for. If inventory levels change, operating income will differ between the two methods because of the difference in accounting for

INVENTORY COSTING AND CAPACITY ANALYSIS

fixed manufacturing costs. To see this difference, let's compare telescope sales of 6,000; 7,000; and 8,000 units by Stassen in 2012, when 8,000 units were produced. Of the $1,080,000 total fixed manufacturing costs, the amount expensed in the 2012 income statement under each of these scenarios would be as follows:

		Home	Insert	Page Layout	Formulas	Data	Review	View		
	A	B	C	D	E		G	H		
1			Variable Costing				Absorption Costing			
2							Fixed Manufacturing Costs			
3	Units	Ending	Fixed Manufacturing Costs				Included in Inventory	Amount Expensed		
4	Sold	Inventory	Included in Inventory	Amount Expensed			=$135 × Ending Inv.	=$135 × Units Sold		
5	6,000	2,000	$0	$1,080,000			$270,000	$ 810,000		
6	7,000	1,000	$0	$1,080,000			$135,000	$ 945,000		
7	8,000	0	$0	$1,080,000			$ 0	$1,080,000		

In the last scenario, where 8,000 units are produced and sold, both variable and absorption costing report the same net income because inventory levels are unchanged. This chapter's appendix describes how the choice of variable costing or absorption costing affects the breakeven quantity of sales when inventory levels are allowed to vary.

Comparing Income Statements for Three Years

To get a more comprehensive view of the effects of variable costing and absorption costing, Stassen's management accountants prepare income statements for three years of operations, starting with 2012. In both 2013 and 2014, Stassen has a production-volume variance, because actual telescope production differs from the budgeted level of production of 8,000 units per year used to calculate budgeted fixed manufacturing cost per unit. The actual quantities sold for 2013 and 2014 are the same as the sales quantities budgeted for these respective years, which are given in units in the following table:

	Home	Insert	Page Layout	Formulas	Data
	E	F	G	H	
1		2012	2013	2014	
2	Budgeted production	8,000	8,000	8,000	
3	Beginning inventory	0	2,000	500	
4	Actual production	8,000	5,000	10,000	
5	Sales	6,000	6,500	7,500	
6	Ending inventory	2,000	500	3,000	

All other 2012 data given earlier for Stassen also apply for 2013 and 2014.

Exhibit 2 presents the income statement under variable costing in Panel A and the income statement under absorption costing in Panel B for 2012, 2013, and 2014. As you study Exhibit 2, note that the 2012 columns in both Panels A and B show the same figures as Exhibit 1. The 2013 and 2014 columns are similar to 2012 *except for the production-volume variance line item under absorption costing in Panel B*. Keep in mind the following points about absorption costing as you study Panel B of Exhibit 2:

1. The $135 fixed manufacturing cost rate is based on the budgeted denominator capacity level of 8,000 units in 2012, 2013, and 2014 ($1,080,000 ÷ 8,000 units = $135 per unit). Whenever production (the quantity produced, not the quantity sold) deviates from the denominator level, there will be a production-volume variance. The amount of Stassen's production-volume variance is determined by multiplying $135 per unit by the difference between the actual level of production and the denominator level.

Exhibit 2 Comparison of Variable Costing and Absorption Costing for Stassen Company: Telescope Product-Line Income Statements for 2012, 2013, and 2014

| | Home | Insert | Page Layout | Formulas | Data | Review | View | | |

	A	B	C	D	E	F	G
1	**Panel A: VARIABLE COSTING**						
2			**2012**		**2013**		**2014**
3	Revenues: $1,000 × 6,000; 6,500; 7,500 units		$6,000,000		$6,500,000		$7,500,000
4	Variable cost of goods sold:						
5	Beginning inventory: $200 × 0; 2,000; 500 units	$ 0		$ 400,000		$ 100,000	
6	Variable manufacturing costs: $200 × 8,000; 5,000; 10,000 units	1,600,000		1,000,000		2,000,000	
7	Cost of goods available for sale	1,600,000		1,400,000		2,100,000	
8	Deduct ending inventory: $200 × 2,000; 500; 3,000 units	(400,000)		(100,000)		(600,000)	
9	Variable cost of goods sold		1,200,000		1,300,000		1,500,000
10	Variable marketing costs: $185 × 6,000; 6,500; 7,500 units		1,110,000		1,202,500		1,387,500
11	Contribution margin		3,690,000		3,997,500		4,612,500
12	Fixed manufacturing costs		1,080,000		1,080,000		1,080,000
13	Fixed marketing costs		1,380,000		1,380,000		1,380,000
14	Operating income		$1,230,000		$1,537,500		$2,152,500
15							
16	**Panel B: ABSORPTION COSTING**						
17			**2012**		**2013**		**2014**
18	Revenues: $1,000 × 6,000; 6,500; 7,500 units		$6,000,000		$6,500,000		$7,500,000
19	Cost of goods sold:						
20	Beginning inventory: $335 × 0; 2,000; 500 units	$ 0		$ 670,000		$ 167,500	
21	Variable manufacturing costs: $200 × 8,000; 5,000; 10,000 units	1,600,000		1,000,000		2,000,000	
22	Allocated fixed manufacturing costs: $135 × 8,000; 5,000; 10,000 units	1,080,000		675,000		1,350,000	
23	Cost of goods available for sale	2,680,000		2,345,000		3,517,500	
24	Deduct ending inventory: $335 × 2,000; 500; 3,000 units	(670,000)		(167,500)		(1,005,000)	
25	Adjustment for production-volume variance[a]	0		405,000 U		(270,000) F	
26	Cost of goods sold		2,010,000		2,582,500		2,242,500
27	Gross Margin		3,990,000		3,917,500		5,257,500
28	Variable marketing costs: $185 × 6,000; 6,500; 7,500 units		1,110,000		1,202,500		1,387,500
29	Fixed marketing costs		1,380,000		1,380,000		1,380,000
30	Operating Income		$1,500,000		$1,335,000		$2,490,000
31							
32	[a]Production-volume variance = Budgeted fixed manufacturing costs − Fixed manufacturing overhead allocated using budgeted cost per output unit allowed for actual output produced (Panel B, line 22)						
33	2012: $1,080,000 − ($135 × 8,000) = $1,080,000 − $1,080,000 = $0						
34	2013: $1,080,000 − ($135 × 5,000) = $1,080,000 − $675,000 = $405,000 U						
35	2014: $1,080,000 − ($135 × 10,000) = $1,080,000 − $1,350,000 = ($270,000) F						
36							
37	Production volume variance can also be calculated as follows:						
38	Fixed manufacturing cost per unit × (Denominator level – Actual output units produced)						
39	2012: $135 × (8,000 – 8,000) units = $135 × 0 = $0						
40	2013: $135 × (8,000 – 5,000) units = $135 × 3,000 = $405,000 U						
41	2014: $135 × (8,000 – 10,000) units = $135 × (2,000) = ($270,000) F						

In 2013, production was 5,000 units, 3,000 lower than the denominator level of 8,000 units. The result is an unfavorable production-volume variance of $405,000 ($135 per unit × 3,000 units). The year 2014 has a favorable production-volume variance of $270,000 ($135 per unit × 2,000 units), due to production of 10,000 units, which exceeds the denominator level of 8,000 units.

Recall how standard costing works under absorption costing. Each time a unit is manufactured, $135 of fixed manufacturing costs is included in the cost of goods manufactured and available for sale. In 2013, when 5,000 units are manufactured, $675,000 ($135 per unit × 5,000 units) of fixed manufacturing costs is included in the cost of goods available for sale (see Exhibit 2, Panel B, line 22). Total fixed manufacturing costs for 2013 are $1,080,000. The production-volume variance of $405,000 U equals the difference between $1,080,000 and $675,000. In Panel B, note how, for each year, the fixed manufacturing costs included in the cost of goods available for sale plus the production-volume variance always equals $1,080,000.

2. The production-volume variance, which relates only to fixed manufacturing overhead, exists under absorption costing but not under variable costing. Under variable costing, fixed manufacturing costs of $1,080,000 are always treated as an expense of the period, regardless of the level of production (and sales).

Here's a summary (using information from Exhibit 2) of the operating-income differences for Stassen Company during the 2012 to 2014 period:

	2012	2013	2014
1. Absorption-costing operating income	$1,500,000	$1,335,000	$2,490,000
2. Variable-costing operating income	$1,230,000	$1,537,500	$2,152,500
3. Difference: (1) – (2)	$ 270,000	$ (202,500)	$ 337,500

The sizeable differences in the preceding table illustrate why managers whose performance is measured by reported income are concerned about the choice between variable costing and absorption costing.

Why do variable costing and absorption costing usually report different operating income numbers? In general, if inventory increases during an accounting period, less operating income will be reported under variable costing than absorption costing. Conversely, if inventory decreases, more operating income will be reported under variable costing than absorption costing. The difference in reported operating income is due solely to (a) moving fixed manufacturing costs into inventories as inventories increase and (b) moving fixed manufacturing costs out of inventories as inventories decrease.

The difference between operating income under absorption costing and variable costing can be computed by formula 1, which focuses on fixed manufacturing costs in beginning inventory and ending inventory:

	A	B	C	D	E	F	G	H
	Home	Insert	Page Layout		Formulas	Data	Review	View
1	Formula 1							
2						Fixed manufacturing		Fixed manufacturing
3		Absorption-costing	–	Variable-costing	=	costs in ending inventory	–	costs in beginning inventory
4		operating income		operation income		under absorption costing		under absorption costing
5	2012	$1,500,000	–	$1,230,000	=	($135 × 2,000 units)	–	($135 × 0 units)
6				$ 270,000	=	$270,000		
7								
8	2013	$1,335,000	–	$1,537,500	=	($135 × 500 units)	–	($135 × 2,000 units)
9				($ 202,500)		($202,500)		
10								
11	2014	$2,490,000	–	$2,152,500	=	($135 × 3,000 units)	–	($135 × 500 units)
12				$ 337,500	=	$337,500		

Fixed manufacturing costs in ending inventory are deferred to a future period under absorption costing. For example, $270,000 of fixed manufacturing overhead is deferred to 2013 at December 31, 2012. Under variable costing, all $1,080,000 of fixed manufacturing costs are treated as an expense of 2012.

Recall that,

$$\text{Beginning inventory} + \text{Cost of goods manufactured} = \text{Cost of goods sold} + \text{Ending Inventory}$$

Therefore, instead of focusing on fixed manufacturing costs in ending and beginning inventory (as in formula 1), we could alternatively look at fixed manufacturing costs in units produced and units sold. The latter approach (see formula 2) highlights how fixed manufacturing costs move between units produced and units sold during the fiscal year.

	A	B	C	D	E	F	G	H
16	**Formula 2**							
17						**Fixed manufacturing costs**		**Fixed manufacturing costs**
18		**Absorption-costing**	–	**Variable-costing**	=	**inventoried in units produced**	–	**in cost of goods sold**
19		**operating income**		**operation income**		**under absorption costing**		**under absorption costing**
20	**2012**	$1,500,000	–	$1,230,000	=	($135 × 8,000 units)	–	($135 × 6,000 units)
21				$ 270,000	=	$270,000		
22								
23	**2013**	$1,335,000	–	$1,537,500	=	($135 × 5,000 units)	–	($135 × 6,500 units)
24				($ 202,500)	=	($202,500)		
25								
26	**2014**	$2,490,000	–	$2,152,500	=	($135 × 10,000 units)	–	($135 × 7,500 units)
27				$ 337,500	=	$337,500		

Decision Point ▶

How does income differ under variable and absorption costing?

Managers face increasing pressure to reduce inventory levels. Some companies are achieving steep reductions in inventory levels using policies such as just-in-time production—a production system under which products are manufactured only when needed. Formula 1 illustrates that, as Stassen reduces its inventory levels, operating income differences between absorption costing and variable costing become immaterial. Consider, for example, the formula for 2012. If instead of 2,000 units in ending inventory, Stassen had only 2 units in ending inventory, the difference between absorption-costing operating income and variable-costing operating income would drop from $270,000 to just $270.

Variable Costing and the Effect of Sales and Production on Operating Income

Given a constant contribution margin per unit and constant fixed costs, the period-to-period change in operating income under variable costing is *driven solely by changes in the quantity of units actually sold*. Consider the variable-costing operating income of Stassen in (a) 2013 versus 2012 and (b) 2014 versus 2013. Recall the following:

$$\frac{\text{Contribution}}{\text{margin per unit}} = \text{Selling price} - \frac{\text{Variable manufacturing}}{\text{cost per unit}} - \frac{\text{Variable marketing}}{\text{cost per unit}}$$

$$= \$1,000 \text{ per unit} - \$200 \text{ per unit} - \$185 \text{ per unit}$$

$$= \$615 \text{ per unit}$$

$$\frac{\text{Change in}}{\text{variable-costing}} = \frac{\text{Contribution}}{\text{margin}} \times \frac{\text{Change in quantity}}{\text{of units sold}}$$
$$\text{operating income} \quad \text{per unit}$$

(a) 2013 vs. 2012: $1,537,500 − $1,230,000 = $615 per unit × (6,500 unit − 6,000 units)

$$\$307,500 = \$307,500$$

(b) 2014 vs. 2013: $2,152,500 − $1,537,500 = $615 per unit × (7,500 units − 6,500 units)

$$\$615,000 = \$615,000$$

Under variable costing, Stassen managers cannot increase operating income by "producing for inventory." Why not? Because, as you can see from the preceding computations, when using variable costing, only the quantity of units sold drives operating income. We'll explain later in this chapter that absorption costing enables managers to increase operating income by increasing the unit level of sales, as well as by producing more units. Before you proceed to the next section, make sure that you examine Exhibit 3 for a detailed comparison of the differences between variable costing and absorption costing.

Exhibit 3 Comparative Income Effects of Variable Costing and Absorption Costing

Question	Variable Costing	Absorption Costing	Comment
Are fixed manufacturing costs inventoried?	No	Yes	Basic theoretical question of when these costs should be expensed
Is there a production-volume variance?	No	Yes	Choice of denominator level affects measurement of operating income under absorption costing only
Are classifications between variable and fixed costs routinely made?	Yes	Infrequently	Absorption costing can be easily modified to obtain subclassifications for variable and fixed costs, if desired (for example, see Exhibit 1, Panel B)
How do changes in unit inventory levels affect operating income?[a]			Differences are attributable to the timing of when fixed manufacturing costs are expensed
Production = sales	Equal	Equal	
Production > sales	Lower[b]	Higher[c]	
Production < sales	Higher	Lower	
What are the effects on cost-volume-profit relationship (for a given level of fixed costs and a given contribution margin per unit)?	Driven by unit level of sales	Driven by (a) unit level of sales, (b) unit level of production, and (c) chosen denominator level	Management control benefit: Effects of changes in production level on operating income are easier to understand under variable costing

[a]Assuming that all manufacturing variances are written off as period costs, that no change occurs in work-in-process inventory, and no change occurs in the budgeted fixed manufacturing cost rate between accounting periods.

[b]That is, lower operating income than under absorption costing.

[c]That is, higher operating income than under variable costing.

Absorption Costing and Performance Measurement

Absorption costing is the required inventory method for external reporting in most countries. Many companies use absorption costing for internal accounting as well. Why? Because it is cost-effective and less confusing to managers to use one common method of inventory costing for both external and internal reporting and performance evaluation. A common method of inventory costing can also help prevent managers from taking actions that make their performance measure look good but that hurt the income they report to shareholders. Another advantage of absorption costing is that it measures the cost of all manufacturing resources, whether variable or fixed, necessary to produce inventory. Many companies use inventory costing information for long-run decisions, such as pricing and choosing a product mix. For these long-run decisions, inventory costs should include both variable *and* fixed costs.

One problem with absorption costing is that it enables a manager to increase operating income in a specific period by increasing production—even if there is no customer demand for the additional production! By producing more ending inventory, the firm's margins and income can be made higher. Stassen's managers may be tempted to do this to get higher bonuses based on absorption-costing operating income. Generally, higher operating income also has a positive effect on stock price, which increases managers' stock-based compensation.

To reduce the undesirable incentives to build up inventories that absorption costing can create, a number of companies use variable costing for internal reporting. Variable costing focuses attention on distinguishing variable manufacturing costs from fixed manufacturing costs. This distinction is important for short-run decision making.

Learning Objective 3

Understand how absorption costing can provide undesirable incentives for managers to build up inventory

. . . producing more units for inventory absorbs fixed manufacturing costs and increases operating income

Companies that use both methods for internal reporting—variable costing for short-run decisions and performance evaluation and absorption costing for long-run decisions—benefit from the different advantages of both. In the next section, we explore in more detail the challenges that arise from absorption costing.

Undesirable Buildup of Inventories

Recall that one motivation for an undesirable buildup of inventories could be because a manager's bonus is based on reported absorption-costing operating income. Assume that Stassen's managers have such a bonus plan. Exhibit 4 shows how Stassen's absorption costing operating income for 2013 changes as the production level changes. This exhibit assumes that the production-volume variance is written off to cost of goods sold at the end of each year. Beginning inventory of 2,000 units and sales of 6,500 units for 2013 are unchanged from the case shown in Exhibit 2. *As you review Exhibit 4, keep in mind that the computations are basically the same as those in Exhibit 2.*

Exhibit 4 shows that production of 4,500 units meets the 2013 sales budget of 6,500 units (2,000 units from beginning inventory + 4,500 units produced). Operating income at this production level is $1,267,500. By producing more than 4,500 units, commonly referred to as *producing for inventory*, Stassen increases absorption-costing operating income. Each additional unit in 2013 ending inventory will increase operating income by $135. For example, if 9,000 units are produced (the last column in Exhibit 4), ending inventory will be 4,500 units and operating income increases to $1,875,000. This amount is $607,500 more than the operating income with zero ending inventory ($1,875,000 − $1,267,500, or 4,500 units × $135 per unit = $607,500). Under absorption costing, the company, by producing 4,500 units for inventory, includes $607,500 of fixed manufacturing costs in finished goods inventory, so those costs are not expensed in 2013.

Can top management implement checks and balances that limit managers from producing for inventory under absorption costing? While the answer is yes, as we will see in

Exhibit 4 Effect on Absorption-Costing Operating Income of Different Production Levels for Stassen Company: Telescope Product-Line Income Statement for 2013 at Sales of 6,500 Units

	A	B	C	D	E	F	G	H	I	J	K
1	**Unit Data**										
2	Beginning inventory	2,000		2,000		2,000		2,000		2,000	
3	Production	4,500		5,000		6,500		8,000		9,000	
4	Goods available for sale	6,500		7,000		8,500		10,000		11,000	
5	Sales	6,500		6,500		6,500		6,500		6,500	
6	Ending inventory	0		500		2,000		3,500		4,500	
7											
8	**Income Statement**										
9	Revenues	$6,500,000		$6,500,000		$6,500,000		$6,500,000		$6,500,000	
10	Cost of goods sold:										
11	Beginning inventory ($335 × 2,000)	670,000		670,000		670,000		670,000		670,000	
12	Variable manufacturing costs: $200 × production	900,000		1,000,000		1,300,000		1,600,000		1,800,000	
13	Allocated fixed manufacturing costs: $135 × production	607,500		675,000		877,500		1,080,000		1,215,000	
14	Cost of goods available for sale	2,177,500		2,345,000		2,847,500		3,350,000		3,685,000	
15	Deduct ending inventory: $335 × ending inventory	0		(167,500)		(670,000)		(1,172,500)		(1,507,500)	
16	Adjustment for production-volume variance[a]	472,500	U	405,000	U	202,500	U	0		(135,000)	F
17	Cost of goods sold	2,650,000		2,582,500		2,380,000		2,177,500		2,042,500	
18	Gross Margin	3,850,000		3,917,500		4,120,000		4,322,500		4,457,500	
19	Marketing costs: ($1,380,000 + $185 per unit × 6,500 units sold)	2,582,500		2,582,500		2,582,500		2,582,500		2,582,500	
20	Operating Income	$1,267,500		$1,335,000		$1,537,500		$1,740,000		$1,875,000	
21											
22	[a]Production-volume variance = Budgeted fixed manufacturing costs − Allocated fixed manufacturing costs (Income Statement, line 13)										
23	At production of 4,500 units: $1,080,000 − $607,500 = $472,500 U										
24	At production of 5,000 units: $1,080,000 − $675,000 = $405,000 U										
25	At production of 6,500 units: $1,080,000 − $877,500 = $202,500 U										
26	At production of 8,000 units: $1,080,000 − $1,080,000 = $0										
27	At production of 9,000 units: $1,080,000 − $1,215,000 = ($135,000) F										

the next section, producing for inventory cannot completely be prevented. There are many subtle ways a manager can produce for inventory that, if done to a limited extent, may not be easy to detect. For example, consider the following:

- A plant manager may switch to manufacturing products that absorb the highest amount of fixed manufacturing costs, regardless of the customer demand for these products (called "cherry picking" the production line). Production of items that absorb the least or lower fixed manufacturing costs may be delayed, resulting in failure to meet promised customer delivery dates (which, over time, can result in unhappy customers).

- A plant manager may accept a particular order to increase production, even though another plant in the same company is better suited to handle that order.

- To increase production, a manager may defer maintenance beyond the current period. Although operating income in this period may increase as a result, future operating income could decrease by a larger amount if repair costs increase and equipment becomes less efficient.

The example in Exhibit 4 focuses on only one year (2013). A Stassen manager who built up ending inventories of telescopes to 4,500 units in 2013 would have to further increase ending inventories in 2014 to increase that year's operating income by producing for inventory. There are limits to how much inventory levels can be increased over time (because of physical constraints on storage space and management supervision and controls). Such limits reduce the likelihood of incurring some of absorption costing's undesirable effects.

Proposals for Revising Performance Evaluation

Top management, with help from the controller and management accountants, can take several steps to reduce the undesirable effects of absorption costing.

- Focus on careful budgeting and inventory planning to reduce management's freedom to build up excess inventory. For example, the budgeted monthly balance sheets have estimates of the dollar amount of inventories. If actual inventories exceed these dollar amounts, top management can investigate the inventory buildups.

- Incorporate a carrying charge for inventory in the internal accounting system. For example, the company could assess an inventory carrying charge of 1% per month on the investment tied up in inventory and for spoilage and obsolescence when it evaluates a manager's performance. An increasing number of companies are beginning to adopt this inventory carrying charge.

- Change the period used to evaluate performance. Critics of absorption costing give examples in which managers take actions that maximize quarterly or annual income at the potential expense of long-run income. When their performance is evaluated over a three- to five-year period, managers will be less tempted to produce for inventory.

- Include nonfinancial as well as financial variables in the measures used to evaluate performance. Examples of nonfinancial measures that can be used to monitor the performance of Stassen's managers in 2014 are as follows:

$$\textbf{(a)}\ \frac{\text{Ending inventory in units in 2014}}{\text{Beginning inventory in units in 2014}} = \frac{3,000}{500} = 6$$

$$\textbf{(b)}\ \frac{\text{Units produced in 2014}}{\text{Units sold in 2014}} = \frac{10,000}{7,500} = 1.33$$

Top management would want to see production equal to sales and relatively stable levels of inventory. Companies that manufacture or sell several products could report these two measures for each of the products they manufacture and sell.

Decision Point

Why might managers build up finished goods inventory if they use absorption costing?

263

Comparing Inventory Costing Methods

Before we begin our discussion of capacity, we will look at *throughput costing*, a variation of variable costing, and compare the various costing methods.

Throughput Costing

Learning Objective 4

Differentiate throughput costing

... direct material costs inventoried from variable costing

... variable manufacturing costs inventoried and absorption costing

... variable and fixed manufacturing costs inventoried

Some managers maintain that even variable costing promotes an excessive amount of costs being inventoried. They argue that only direct materials are "truly variable" in output. **Throughput costing,** which also is called **super-variable costing,** is an extreme form of variable costing in which only direct material costs are included as inventoriable costs. All other costs are costs of the period in which they are incurred. In particular, variable direct manufacturing labor costs and variable manufacturing overhead costs are regarded as period costs and are deducted as expenses of the period.

Exhibit 5 is the throughput-costing income statement for Stassen Company for 2012, 2013, and 2014. *Throughput margin* equals revenues minus all direct material cost of the goods sold. Compare the operating income amounts reported in Exhibit 5 with those for absorption costing and variable costing:

	2012	2013	2014
Absorption-costing operating income	$1,500,000	$1,335,000	$2,490,000
Variable-costing operating income	$1,230,000	$1,537,500	$2,152,500
Throughput-costing operating income	$1,050,000	$1,672,500	$1,927,500

Decision Point ▶

How does throughput costing differ from variable costing and absorption costing?

Only the $110 direct material cost per unit is inventoriable under throughput costing, compared with $335 per unit for absorption costing and $200 per unit for variable costing. When the production quantity exceeds sales as in 2012 and 2014, throughput costing results in the largest amount of expenses in the current period's income statement. Advocates of throughput costing say it provides less incentive to produce for inventory than either variable costing or, especially, absorption costing. Throughput costing is a more recent phenomenon in comparison with variable costing and absorption costing and has avid supporters, but so far it has not been widely adopted.[2]

Exhibit 5

Throughput Costing for Stassen Company: Telescope Product-Line Income Statements for 2012, 2013, and 2014

	A	B	C	D
		Home Insert Page Layout Formulas Data Review View		
1		2012	2013	2014
2	Revenues: $1,000 × 6,000; 6,500; 7,500 units	$6,000,000	$6,500,000	$7,500,000
3	Direct material cost of goods sold			
4	Beginning inventory: $110 × 0; 2,000; 500 units	0	220,000	55,000
5	Direct materials: $110 × 8,000; 5,000; 10,000 units	880,000	550,000	1,100,000
6	Cost of goods available for sale	880,000	770,000	1,155,000
7	Deduct ending inventory: $110 × 2,000; 500; 3,000 units	(220,000)	(55,000)	(330,000)
8	Direct material cost of goods sold	660,000	715,000	825,000
9	Throughput margin[a]	5,340,000	5,785,000	6,675,000
10	Manufacturing costs (other than direct materials)[b]	1,800,000	1,530,000	1,980,000
11	Marketing costs[c]	2,490,000	2,582,500	2,767,500
12	Operating income	$1,050,000	$1,672,500	$1,927,500
13				
14	[a]Throughput margin equals revenues minus all direct material cost of goods sold			
15	[b]Fixed manuf. costs + [(variable manuf. labor cost per unit + variable manuf. overhead cost per unit)			
16	× units produced]; $1,080,000 + [($40 + $50) × 8,000; 5,000; 10,000 units]			
17	[c]Fixed marketing costs + (variable marketing cost per unit × units sold);			
18	$1,380,000 + ($185 × 6,000; 6,500; 7,500 units)			

[2] See E. Goldratt, *The Theory of Constraints* (New York: North River Press, 1990); E. Noreen, D. Smith, and J. Mackey, *The Theory of Constraints and Its Implications for Management Accounting* (New York: North River Press, 1995).

A Comparison of Alternative Inventory-Costing Methods

Variable costing and absorption costing (as well as throughput costing) may be combined with actual, normal, or standard costing. Exhibit 6 compares product costing under six alternative inventory-costing systems.

Variable Costing	Absorption Costing
Actual costing	Actual costing
Standard costing	Standard costing
Normal costing	Normal costing

Variable costing has been controversial among accountants, not because of disagreement about the need to delineate between variable and fixed costs for internal planning and control, but as it pertains to *external reporting*. Accountants who favor variable costing for external reporting maintain that the fixed portion of manufacturing costs is more closely related to the capacity to produce than to the actual production of specific units. Hence, fixed costs should be expensed, not inventoried.

Accountants who support absorption costing for *external reporting* maintain that inventories should carry a fixed-manufacturing-cost component. Why? Because both variable manufacturing costs and fixed manufacturing costs are necessary to produce goods. Therefore, both types of costs should be inventoried in order to match all manufacturing costs to revenues, regardless of their different behavior patterns. For external reporting to shareholders, companies around the globe tend to follow the generally accepted accounting principle that all manufacturing costs are inventoriable.

Similarly, for tax reporting in the United States, direct production costs, as well as fixed and variable indirect production costs, must be taken into account in the computation of inventoriable costs in accordance with the "full absorption" method of inventory costing. Indirect production costs include items such as rent, utilities, maintenance, repair expenses, indirect materials, and indirect labor. For other indirect cost categories (including depreciation, insurance, taxes, officers' salaries, factory administrative expenses, and strike-related costs), the portion of the cost that is "incident to and necessary for production or manufacturing operations or processes" is inventoriable for tax

Exhibit 6 Comparison of Alternative Inventory-Costing Systems

			Actual Costing	Normal Costing	Standard Costing
Absorption Costing	**Variable Costing**	**Variable Direct Manufacturing Cost**	Actual prices × Actual quantity of inputs used	Actual prices × Actual quantity of inputs used	Standard prices × Standard quantity of inputs allowed for actual output achieved
		Variable Manufacturing Overhead Costs	Actual variable overhead rates × Actual quantity of cost-allocation bases used	Budgeted variable overhead rates × Actual quantity of cost-allocation bases used	Standard variable overhead rates × Standard quantity of cost-allocation bases allowed for actual output achieved
		Fixed Direct Manufacturing Costs	Actual prices × Actual quantity of inputs used	Actual prices × Actual quantity of inputs used	Standard prices × Standard quantity of inputs allowed for actual output achieved
		Fixed Manufacturing Overhead Costs	Actual fixed overhead rates × Actual quantity of cost-allocation bases used	Budgeted fixed overhead rates × Actual quantity of cost-allocation bases used	Standard fixed overhead rates × Standard quantity of cost-allocation bases allowed for actual output achieved

265

purposes if (and only if) it is treated as inventoriable for the purposes of financial reporting. Accordingly, costs must often be allocated between those portions related to manufacturing activities and those not related to manufacturing.[3]

Denominator-Level Capacity Concepts and Fixed-Cost Capacity Analysis

Learning Objective 5

Describe the various capacity concepts that can be used in absorption costing

. . . supply-side: theoretical and practical capacity; demand-side: normal and master-budget capacity utilization

We have seen that the difference between variable and absorption costing methods arises solely from the treatment of fixed manufacturing costs. Spending on fixed manufacturing costs enables firms to obtain the scale or capacity needed to satisfy the expected demand from customers. Determining the "right" amount of spending, or the appropriate level of capacity, is one of the most strategic and most difficult decisions managers face. Having too much capacity to produce relative to that needed to meet market demand means incurring some costs of unused capacity. Having too little capacity to produce means that demand from some customers may be unfilled. These customers may go to other sources of supply and never return. Therefore, both managers and accountants should have a clear understanding of the issues that arise with capacity costs.

We start by analyzing a key question in absorption costing: Given a level of spending on fixed manufacturing costs, what capacity level should be used to compute the fixed manufacturing cost per unit produced? We then study the broader question of how a firm should decide on its level of capacity investment.

Absorption Costing and Alternative Denominator-Level Capacity Concepts

Normal costing and standard costing report costs in an ongoing timely manner throughout a fiscal year. The choice of the capacity level used to allocate budgeted fixed manufacturing costs to products can greatly affect the operating income reported under normal costing or standard costing and the product-cost information available to managers.

Consider the Stassen Company example again. Recall that the annual fixed manufacturing costs of the production facility are $1,080,000. Stassen currently uses absorption costing with standard costs for external reporting purposes, and it calculates its budgeted fixed manufacturing rate on a per unit basis. We will now examine four different capacity levels used as the denominator to compute the budgeted fixed manufacturing cost rate: theoretical capacity, practical capacity, normal capacity utilization, and master-budget capacity utilization.

Theoretical Capacity and Practical Capacity

In business and accounting, capacity ordinarily means a "constraint," an "upper limit." **Theoretical capacity** is the level of capacity based on producing at full efficiency all the time. Stassen can produce 25 units per shift when the production lines are operating at maximum speed. If we assume 360 days per year, the theoretical annual capacity for 2 shifts per day is as follows:

25 units per shift × 2 shifts per day × 360 days = 18,000 units

Theoretical capacity is theoretical in the sense that it does not allow for any plant maintenance, shutdown periods, interruptions because of downtime on the assembly lines, or any other factors. Theoretical capacity represents an ideal goal of capacity utilization. Theoretical capacity levels are unattainable in the real world but they provide a target to which a company can aspire.

---

[3] Details regarding tax rules can be found in Section 1.471-11 of the U.S. Internal Revenue Code: Inventories of Manufacturers (see http://ecfr.gpoaccess.gov). Recall that costs not related to production, such as marketing, distribution, or research expenses, are treated as period expenses for financial reporting. Under U.S. tax rules, a firm can still consider these costs as inventoriable for tax purposes provided that it does so consistently.

Practical capacity is the level of capacity that reduces theoretical capacity by considering unavoidable operating interruptions, such as scheduled maintenance time, shutdowns for holidays, and so on. Assume that practical capacity is the practical production rate of 20 units per shift (as opposed to 25 units per shift under theoretical capacity) for 2 shifts per day for 300 days a year (as distinguished from 360 days a year under theoretical capacity). The practical annual capacity is as follows:

20 units per shift $\times$ 2 shifts per day $\times$ 300 days = 12,000 units

Engineering and human resource factors are both important when estimating theoretical or practical capacity. Engineers at the Stassen facility can provide input on the technical capabilities of machines for cutting and polishing lenses. Human-safety factors, such as increased injury risk when the line operates at faster speeds, are also necessary considerations in estimating practical capacity. With difficulty, practical capacity is attainable.

Normal Capacity Utilization and Master-Budget Capacity Utilization

Both theoretical capacity and practical capacity measure capacity levels in terms of what a plant can *supply*—available capacity. In contrast, normal capacity utilization and master-budget capacity utilization measure capacity levels in terms of *demand* for the output of the plant, that is, the amount of available capacity the plant expects to use based on the demand for its products. In many cases, budgeted demand is well below production capacity available.

Normal capacity utilization is the level of capacity utilization that satisfies average customer demand over a period (say, two to three years) that includes seasonal, cyclical, and trend factors. **Master-budget capacity utilization** is the level of capacity utilization that managers expect for the current budget period, which is typically one year. These two capacity-utilization levels can differ—for example, when an industry, such as automobiles or semiconductors, has cyclical periods of high and low demand or when management believes that budgeted production for the coming period is not representative of long-run demand.

Consider Stassen's master budget for 2012, based on production of 8,000 telescopes per year. Despite using this master-budget capacity-utilization level of 8,000 telescopes for 2012, top management believes that over the next three years the normal (average) annual production level will be 10,000 telescopes. It views 2012's budgeted production level of 8,000 telescopes to be "abnormally" low because a major competitor has been sharply reducing its selling price and spending large amounts on advertising. Stassen expects that the competitor's lower price and advertising blitz will not be a long-run phenomenon and that, by 2014 and beyond, Stassen's production and sales will be higher.

Effect on Budgeted Fixed Manufacturing Cost Rate

We now illustrate how each of these four denominator levels affects the budgeted fixed manufacturing cost rate. Stassen has budgeted (standard) fixed manufacturing overhead costs of $1,080,000 for 2012. This lump-sum is incurred to provide the capacity to produce telescopes. The amount includes, among other costs, leasing costs for the facility and the compensation of the facility managers. The budgeted fixed manufacturing cost rates for 2012 for each of the four capacity-level concepts are as follows:

	A	B	C	D
		Budgeted Fixed	Budget	Budgeted Fixed
	Denominator-Level	Manufacturing	Capacity Level	Manufacturing
	Capacity Concept	Costs per Year	(in units)	Cost per Unit
	(1)	(2)	(3)	(4) = (2) / (3)
5	Theoretical capacity	$1,080,000	18,000	$ 60
6	Practical capacity	$1,080,000	12,000	$ 90
7	Normal capacity utilization	$1,080,000	10,000	$108
8	Master-budget capacity utilization	$1,080,000	8,000	$135

The significant difference in cost rates (from $60 to $135) arises because of large differences in budgeted capacity levels under the different capacity concepts.

Budgeted (standard) variable manufacturing cost is $200 per unit. The total budgeted (standard) manufacturing cost per unit for alternative capacity-level concepts is as follows:

	A	B	C	D
1		Budgeted Variable	Budgeted Fixed	Budgeted Total
2	Denominator-Level	Manufacturing	Manufacturing	Manufacturing
3	Capacity Concept	Cost per Unit	Cost per Unit	Cost per Unit
4	(1)	(2)	(3)	(4) = (2) + (3)
5	Theoretical capacity	$200	$ 60	$260
6	Practical capacity	$200	$ 90	$290
7	Normal capacity utilization	$200	$108	$308
8	Master-budget capacity utilization	$200	$135	$335

Because different denominator-level capacity concepts yield different budgeted fixed manufacturing costs per unit, Stassen must decide which capacity level to use. Stassen is not required to use the same capacity-level concept, say, for management planning and control, external reporting to shareholders, and income tax purposes.

Choosing a Capacity Level

As we just saw, at the start of each fiscal year, managers determine different denominator levels for the different capacity concepts and calculate different budgeted fixed manufacturing costs per unit. We now discuss the problems with and effects of different denominator-level choices for different purposes, including (a) product costing and capacity management, (b) pricing, (c) performance evaluation, (d) external reporting, and (e) tax requirements.

Product Costing and Capacity Management

Data from normal costing or standard costing are often used in pricing or product-mix decisions. As the Stassen example illustrates, use of theoretical capacity results in an unrealistically small fixed manufacturing cost per unit because it is based on an idealistic and unattainable level of capacity. Theoretical capacity is rarely used to calculate budgeted fixed manufacturing cost per unit because it departs significantly from the real capacity available to a company.

Many companies favor practical capacity as the denominator to calculate budgeted fixed manufacturing cost per unit. Practical capacity in the Stassen example represents the maximum number of units (12,000) that Stassen can reasonably expect to produce per year for the $1,080,000 it will spend annually on capacity. If Stassen had consistently planned to produce fewer units, say 6,000 telescopes each year, it would have built a smaller plant and incurred lower costs.

Stassen budgets $90 in fixed manufacturing cost per unit based on the $1,080,000 it costs to acquire the capacity to produce 12,000 units. This level of plant capacity is an important strategic decision that managers make well before Stassen uses the capacity and even before Stassen knows how much of the capacity it will actually use. That is, budgeted fixed manufacturing cost of $90 per unit measures the *cost per unit of supplying the capacity*.

Demand for Stassen's telescopes in 2012 is expected to be 8,000 units, which is 4,000 units lower than the practical capacity of 12,000 units. However, it costs Stassen $1,080,000 per year to acquire the capacity to make 12,000 units, so the cost of *supplying* the capacity needed to make 12,000 units is still $90 per unit. The capacity and its cost are fixed *in the short run*; unlike variable costs, the capacity supplied does not automatically reduce to match the capacity needed in 2012. As a result, not all of the capacity supplied at $90 per unit will be needed or used in 2012. Using practical capacity as the denominator level, managers can subdivide the cost of resources supplied into used and unused components. At the supply cost of $90 per unit, the manufacturing resources that Stassen will use equal $720,000 ($90 per unit × 8,000 units). Manufacturing resources that Stassen will not use are $360,000 [$90 per unit × (12,000 – 8,000) units].

Using practical capacity as the denominator level sets the cost of capacity at the cost of supplying the capacity, regardless of the demand for the capacity. Highlighting the cost of capacity acquired but not used directs managers' attention toward managing unused capacity, perhaps by designing new products to fill unused capacity, by leasing unused capacity to others, or by eliminating unused capacity. In contrast, using either of the capacity levels based on the demand for Stassen's telescopes—master-budget capacity utilization or normal capacity utilization—hides the amount of unused capacity. If Stassen had used master-budget capacity utilization as the capacity level, it would have calculated budgeted fixed manufacturing cost per unit as $135 ($1,080,000 ÷ 8,000 units). This calculation does not use data about practical capacity, so it does not separately identify the cost of unused capacity. Note, however, that the cost of $135 per unit includes a charge for unused capacity: It comprises the $90 fixed manufacturing resource that would be used to produce each unit at practical capacity plus the cost of unused capacity allocated to each unit, $45 per unit ($360,000 ÷ 8,000 units).

From the perspective of long-run product costing, which cost of capacity should Stassen use for pricing purposes or for benchmarking its product cost structure against competitors: $90 per unit based on practical capacity or $135 per unit based on master-budget capacity utilization? Probably the $90 per unit based on practical capacity. Why? Because $90 per unit represents the budgeted cost per unit of only the capacity used to produce the product, and it explicitly excludes the cost of any unused capacity. Stassen's customers will be willing to pay a price that covers the cost of the capacity actually used but will not want to pay for unused capacity that provides no other benefits to them. Customers expect Stassen to manage its unused capacity or to bear the cost of unused capacity, not pass it along to them. Moreover, if Stassen's competitors manage unused capacity more effectively, the cost of capacity in the competitors' cost structures (which guides competitors' pricing decisions) is likely to approach $90. In the next section we show how the use of normal capacity utilization or master-budget capacity utilization can result in setting selling prices that are not competitive.

Pricing Decisions and the Downward Demand Spiral

The **downward demand spiral** for a company is the continuing reduction in the demand for its products that occurs when competitor prices are not met; as demand drops further, higher and higher unit costs result in greater reluctance to meet competitors' prices.

The easiest way to understand the downward demand spiral is via an example. Assume Stassen uses master-budget capacity utilization of 8,000 units for product costing in 2012. The resulting manufacturing cost is $335 per unit ($200 variable manufacturing cost per unit + $135 fixed manufacturing cost per unit). Assume that in December 2011, a competitor offers to supply a major customer of Stassen (a customer who was expected to purchase 2,000 units in 2012) telescopes at $300 per unit. The Stassen manager, not wanting to show a loss on the account and wanting to recoup all costs in the long run, declines to match the competitor's price. The account is lost. The loss means budgeted fixed manufacturing costs of $1,080,000 will be spread over the remaining master-budget volume of 6,000 units at a rate of $180 per unit ($1,080,000 ÷ 6,000 units).

Suppose yet another Stassen customer, who also accounts for 2,000 units of budgeted volume, receives a bid from a competitor at a price of $350 per unit. The Stassen manager compares this bid with his revised unit cost of $380 ($200 + $180), declines to match the competition, and the account is lost. Planned output would shrink further to 4,000 units. Budgeted fixed manufacturing cost per unit for the remaining 4,000 telescopes would now be $270 ($1,080,000 ÷ 4,000 units). The following table shows the effect of spreading fixed manufacturing costs over a shrinking amount of master-budget capacity utilization:

	Home	Insert	Page Layout	Formulas	Data	Review	View
	A		B		C		D
1	**Master-Budget**				**Budgeted Fixed**		
2	**Capacity Utilization**		**Budgeted Variable**		**Manufacturing**		**Budgeted Total**
3	**Denominator Level**		**Manufacturing Cost**		**Cost per Unit**		**Manufacturing**
4	**(Units)**		**per Unit**		**[$1,080,000 ÷ (1)]**		**Cost per Unit**
5	**(1)**		**(2)**		**(3)**		**(4) = (2) + (3)**
6	8,000		$200		$135		$335
7	6,000		$200		$180		$380
8	4,000		$200		$270		$470
9	3,000		$200		$360		$560

Practical capacity, by contrast, is a stable measure. The use of practical capacity as the denominator to calculate budgeted fixed manufacturing cost per unit avoids the recalculation of unit costs when expected demand levels change, because the fixed cost rate is calculated based on *capacity available* rather than *capacity used to meet demand*. Managers who use reported unit costs in a mechanical way to set prices are less likely to promote a downward demand spiral when they use practical capacity than when they use normal capacity utilization or master-budget capacity utilization.

Using practical capacity as the denominator level also gives the manager a more accurate idea of the resources needed and used to produce a unit by excluding the cost of unused capacity. As discussed earlier, the cost of manufacturing resources supplied to produce a telescope is $290 ($200 variable manufacturing cost per unit plus $90 fixed manufacturing cost per unit). This cost is lower than the prices offered by Stassen's competitors and would have correctly led the manager to match the prices and retain the accounts (assuming for purposes of this discussion that Stassen has no other costs). If, however, the prices offered by competitors were lower than $290 per unit, the Stassen manager would not recover the cost of resources used to supply telescopes. This would signal to the manager that Stassen was noncompetitive even if it had no unused capacity. The only way then for Stassen to be profitable and retain customers in the long run would be to reduce its manufacturing cost per unit. The Concepts in Action feature on page 319 highlights the downward spiral currently at work in the traditional landline phone industry.

Performance Evaluation

Consider how the choice among normal capacity utilization, master-budget capacity utilization, and practical capacity affects the evaluation of a marketing manager. Normal capacity utilization is often used as a basis for long-run plans. Normal capacity utilization depends on the time span selected and the forecasts made for each year. *However, normal capacity utilization is an average that provides no meaningful feedback to the marketing manager for a particular year.* Using normal capacity utilization as a reference for judging current performance of a marketing manager is an example of misusing a long-run measure for a short-run purpose. Master-budget capacity utilization, rather than normal capacity utilization or practical capacity, should be used to evaluate a marketing manager's performance in the current year, because the master budget is the principal short-run planning and control tool. Managers feel more obligated to reach the levels specified in the master budget, which should have been carefully set in relation to the maximum opportunities for sales in the current year.

When large differences exist between practical capacity and master-budget capacity utilization, several companies (such as Texas Instruments, Polysar, and Sandoz) classify the difference as *planned unused capacity*. One reason for this approach is performance

Concepts in Action

The "Death Spiral" and the End of Landline Telephone Service

Diane Collins/Jordan Hollender/Getty Images

Can you imagine a future without traditional landline telephone service? Verizon and AT&T, the two largest telephone service providers in the United States, are already working to make that future a reality. Recently, both companies announced plans to reduce their focus on providing copper-wire telephone service to homes and businesses. According to AT&T, with the rise of mobile phones and Internet communications such as voice over Internet Protocol (VoIP), less than 20% of Americans now rely exclusively on landlines for voice service and another 25% have abandoned them altogether.

But why would telephone companies abandon landlines if 75% of Americans still use them? Continued reduced service demand is leading to higher unit costs, or a downward demand spiral. As AT&T recently told the U.S. Federal Communications Commission, "The business model for legacy phone services is in a death spiral. With an outdated product, falling revenues, and rising costs, the plain-old telephone service business is unsustainable for the long run."

Marketplace statistics support AT&T's claim. From 2000 to 2008, total long-distance access minutes fell by 42%. As a result, revenue from traditional landline phone service decreased by 27% between 2000 and 2007. In 2008 alone, AT&T lost 12% of its landline customers, while Verizon lost 10%. Industry observers estimate that customers are permanently disconnecting 700,000 landline phones every month.

As all these companies lose landline customers and revenue, the costs of maintaining the phone wires strung on poles and dug through trenches is not falling nearly as quickly. It now costs phone companies an average of $52 per year to maintain a copper phone line, up from $43 in 2003, largely because of the declining number of landlines. These costs do not include other expenses required to maintain landline phone service including local support offices, call centers, and garages.

New competitors are taking advantage of this situation. Vonage, the leading Internet phone company, offers its services for as little as $18 per month. Without relying on wires to transmit calls, its direct costs of providing telephone service come to $6.67 a month for each subscriber. And the largest part of that is not true cost, but subsidies to rural phone carriers for connecting long distance calls. As Vonage attracts more customers, its economies of scale will increase while its costs of providing service will decrease for each additional subscriber.

Hamstrung by increasing unit costs, legacy carriers like Verizon and AT&T are unable to compete with Vonage on price. As such, their traditional landline businesses are in permanent decline. So what are these companies doing about it? Verizon is reducing its landline operations by selling large parts of its copper-wire business to smaller companies at a significant discount. AT&T recently petitioned the U.S. government to waive a requirement that it and other carriers maintain their costly landline networks. As the landline phone service "death spiral" continues, the future of telecommunications will include more wireless, fiber optics, and VoIP with less of Alexander Graham Bell's original vision of telephones connected by copper wires.

Source: Comments of AT&T Inc. on the Transition from the Legacy Circuit-switched Network to Broadband. Washington, DC: AT&T Inc., December 21, 2009. http://fjallfoss.fcc.gov/ecfs/document/view?id=7020354032; Hansell, Saul. 2009. Verizon boss hangs up on landline phone business. *New York Times,* September 17; Hansell, Saul. 2009. Will the phone industry need a bailout, too? *New York Times,* May 8.

evaluation. Consider our Stassen telescope example. The managers in charge of capacity planning usually do not make pricing decisions. Top management decided to build a production facility with 12,000 units of practical capacity, focusing on demand over the next five years. But Stassen's marketing managers, who are mid-level managers, make the pricing decisions. These marketing managers believe they should be held accountable only for the manufacturing overhead costs related to their potential customer base in 2012. The master-budget capacity utilization suggests a customer base in 2012 of 8,000 units (2/3 of the 12,000 practical capacity). Using responsibility accounting principles, only 2/3 of the budgeted total fixed manufacturing costs ($1,080,000 × 2/3 = $720,000) would be attributed to the fixed capacity costs of meeting 2012 demand. The remaining 1/3 of the numerator ($1,080,000 × 1/3 = $360,000) would be separately shown as the capacity cost of meeting increases in long-run demand expected to occur beyond 2012.[4]

External Reporting

The magnitude of the favorable/unfavorable production-volume variance under absorption costing is affected by the choice of the denominator level used to calculate the budgeted fixed manufacturing cost per unit. Assume the following actual operating information for Stassen in 2012:

	A	B	C
1	Beginning inventory	0	
2	Production	8,000	units
3	Sales	6,000	units
4	Ending inventory	2,000	units
5	Selling price	$ 1,000	per unit
6	Variable manufacturing cost	$ 200	per unit
7	Fixed manufacturing costs	$ 1,080,000	
8	Variable marketing cost	$ 185	per unit sold
9	Fixed marketing costs	$ 1,380,000	

Note that this is the same data used to calculate the income under variable and absorption costing for Stassen in Exhibit 1. As before, we assume that there are no price, spending, or efficiency variances in manufacturing costs.

The equation used to calculate the production-volume variance is:

$$\text{Production-volume variance} = \left(\begin{array}{c} \text{Budgeted} \\ \text{fixed} \\ \text{manufacturing} \\ \text{overhead} \end{array} \right) - \left(\begin{array}{c} \text{Fixed manufacturing overhead allocated using} \\ \text{budgeted cost per output unit} \\ \text{allowed for actual output produced} \end{array} \right)$$

The four different capacity-level concepts result in four different budgeted fixed manufacturing overhead cost rates per unit. The different rates will result in different amounts of fixed manufacturing overhead costs allocated to the 8,000 units actually produced and different amounts of production-volume variance. Using the budgeted fixed manufacturing costs of $1,080,000 (equal to actual fixed manufacturing costs) and the rates calculated on page 315 for different denominator levels, the production-volume variance computations are as follows:

Production-volume variance (theoretical capacity) = $1,080,000 − (8,000 units × $60 per unit)

= $1,080,000 − 480,000

= 600,000 U

Production-volume variance (practical capacity) = $1,080,000 − (8,000 units × $90 per unit)

= $1,080,000 − 720,000

= 360,000 U

Production-volume variance (normal capacity utilization) = $1,080,000 − (8,000 units × $108 per unit)

= $1,080,000 − 864,000

= 216,000 U

---

[4] For further discussion, see T. Klammer, *Capacity Measurement and Improvement* (Chicago: Irwin, 1996). This research was facilitated by CAM-I, an organization promoting innovative cost management practices. CAM-I's research on capacity costs explores ways in which companies can identify types of capacity costs that can be reduced (or eliminated) without affecting the required output to meet customer demand. An example is improving processes to successfully eliminate the costs of capacity held in anticipation of handling difficulties due to imperfect coordination with suppliers and customers.

Production-volume variance (master-budget capacity utilization)

$$= \$1,080,000 - (8,000 \text{ units} \times \$135 \text{ per unit})$$

$$= \$1,080,000 - 1,080,000$$

$$= 0$$

How Stassen disposes of its production-volume variance at the end of the fiscal year will determine the effect this variance has on the company's operating income. We now discuss the three alternative approaches Stassen can use to dispose of the production-volume variance.

1. **Adjusted allocation-rate approach.** This approach restates all amounts in the general and subsidiary ledgers by using actual rather than budgeted cost rates. Given that actual fixed manufacturing costs are $1,080,000 and actual production is 8,000 units, the recalculated fixed manufacturing cost is $135 per unit ($1,080,000 ÷ 8,000 actual units). Under the adjusted allocation-rate approach, the choice of the capacity level used to calculate the budgeted fixed manufacturing cost per unit has no effect on year-end financial statements. In effect, actual costing is adopted at the end of the fiscal year.

2. **Proration approach.** The underallocated or overallocated overhead is spread among ending balances in Work-in-Process Control, Finished Goods Control, and Cost of Goods Sold. The proration restates the ending balances in these accounts to what they would have been if actual cost rates had been used rather than budgeted cost rates. The proration approach also results in the choice of the capacity level used to calculate the budgeted fixed manufacturing cost per unit having no effect on year-end financial statements.

3. **Write-off variances to cost of goods sold approach.** Exhibit 7 shows how use of this approach affects Stassen's operating income for 2012. Recall that Stassen had no beginning inventory, and it had production of 8,000 units and sales of 6,000 units. Therefore, the ending inventory on December 31, 2012, is 2,000 units. Using master-budget capacity utilization as the denominator-level results in assigning the highest amount of fixed manufacturing cost per unit to the 2,000 units in ending inventory (see the line item "deduct ending inventory" in Exhibit 7). Accordingly, operating income is highest using master-budget capacity utilization. The differences in operating income for the four denominator-level concepts in Exhibit 7 are due to different amounts of fixed manufacturing overhead being inventoried at the end of 2012:

**Fixed Manufacturing Overhead
In December 31, 2012, Inventory**

Theoretical capacity	2,000 units × $60 per unit = $120,000
Practical capacity	2,000 units × $90 per unit = $180,000
Normal capacity utilization	2,000 units × $108 per unit = $216,000
Master-budget capacity utilization	2,000 units × $135 per unit = $270,000

In Exhibit 7, for example, the $54,000 difference ($1,500,000 – $1,446,000) in operating income between master-budget capacity utilization and normal capacity utilization is due to the difference in fixed manufacturing overhead inventoried ($270,000 – $216,000).

What is the common reason and explanation for the increasing operating-income numbers in Exhibit 4 and Exhibit 7? It is the amount of fixed manufacturing costs incurred that is included in ending inventory at the end of the year. As this amount increases, so does operating income. The amount of fixed manufacturing costs inventoried depends on two factors: the number of units in ending inventory and the rate at which fixed manufacturing costs are allocated to each unit. Exhibit 4 shows the effect on operating income of increasing the number of units in ending inventory (by increasing production). Exhibit 7 shows the effect on operating income of increasing the fixed manufacturing cost allocated per unit (by decreasing the denominator level used to calculate the rate).

Exhibit 7	Income-Statement Effects of Using Alternative Capacity-Level Concepts: Stassen Company for 2012

Home   Insert   Page Layout   Formulas   Data   Review   View

	A	B	C	D	E	F	G	H	I
1		Theoretical Capacity		Practical Capacity		Normal Capacity Utilization		Master-Budget Capacity Utilization	
2	Denominator level in cases	18,000		12,000		10,000		8,000	
3	Revenues[a]	$6,000,000		$6,000,000		$6,000,000		$6,000,000	
4	Cost of goods sold								
5	Beginning inventory	0		0		0		0	
6	Variable manufacturing costs[b]	1,600,000		1,600,000		1,600,000		1,600,000	
7	Fixed manufacturing costs[c]	480,000		720,000		864,000		1,080,000	
8	Cost of goods available for sale	2,080,000		2,320,000		2,464,000		2,680,000	
9	Deduct ending inventory[d]	(520,000)		(580,000)		(616,000)		(670,000)	
10	Cost of goods sold (at standard cost)	1,560,000		1,740,000		1,848,000		2,010,000	
11	Adjustment for production-volume variance	600,000	U	360,000	U	216,000	U	0	
12	Cost of goods sold	2,160,000		2,100,000		2,064,000		2,010,000	
13	Gross margin	3,840,000		3,900,000		3,936,000		3,990,000	
14	Marketing costs[e]	2,490,000		2,490,000		2,490,000		2,490,000	
15	Operating income	$1,350,000		$1,410,000		$1,446,000		$1,500,000	
16									
17	[a]$1,000 × 6,000 units = $6,000,000			[d]Ending inventory costs:					
18	[b]$200 × 8,000 units = $1,600,000			($200 + $60) × 2,000 units = $520,000					
19	[c]Fixed manufacturing overhead costs:			($200 + $90) × 2,000 units = $580,000					
20	$60 × 8,000 units = $ 480,000			($200 + $108) × 2,000 units = $616,000					
21	$90 × 8,000 units = $ 720,000			($200 + $135) × 2,000 units = $670,000					
22	$108 × 8,000 units = $ 864,000			[e]Marketing costs:					
23	$135 × 8,000 units = $1,080,000			$1,380,000 + $185 × 6,000 units = $2,490,000					

Tax Requirements

Decision Point ▶

What are the major factors managers consider in choosing the capacity level to compute the budgeted fixed manufacturing cost rate?

For tax reporting purposes in the United States, the Internal Revenue Service (IRS) requires companies to assign inventoriable indirect production costs by a "method of allocation which fairly apportions such costs among the various items produced." Approaches that involve the use of either overhead rates (which the IRS terms the "manufacturing burden rate method") or standard costs are viewed as acceptable. Under either approach, U.S. tax reporting requires end-of-period reconciliation between actual and applied indirect costs using the adjusted allocation-rate method or the proration method.[5] More interestingly, under either approach, the IRS permits the use of practical capacity to calculate budgeted fixed manufacturing cost per unit. Further, the production-volume variance thus generated can be deducted for tax purposes in the year in which the cost is incurred. The tax benefits from this policy are evident from Exhibit 7. Note that the operating income when the

---

[5] For example, Section 1.471-11 of the U.S. Internal Revenue Code states, "The proper use of the standard cost method . . . requires that a taxpayer must reallocate to the goods in ending inventory a pro rata portion of any net negative or net positive overhead variances." Of course, if the variances are not material in amount, they can be expensed (i.e., written off to cost of goods sold), provided the same treatment is carried out in the firm's financial reports.

denominator is set to practical capacity (column D, where the production volume variance of $360,000 is written off to cost of goods sold) is lower than those under normal capacity utilization (column F) or master-budget capacity utilization (column H).

Planning and Control of Capacity Costs

In addition to the issues previously discussed, managers must take a variety of other factors into account when planning capacity levels and in deciding how best to control and assign capacity costs. These include the level of uncertainty regarding both the expected costs and the expected demand for the installed capacity, the presence of capacity-related issues in nonmanufacturing settings, and the potential use of activity-based costing techniques in allocating capacity costs.

Difficulties in Forecasting Chosen Denominator-Level Concept

Practical capacity measures the available supply of capacity. Managers can usually use engineering studies and human-resource considerations (such as worker safety) to obtain a reliable estimate of this denominator level for the budget period. It is more difficult to obtain reliable estimates of demand-side denominator-level concepts, especially longer-term normal capacity utilization figures. For example, many U.S. steel companies in the 1980s believed they were in the downturn of a demand cycle that would have an upturn within two or three years. After all, steel had been a cyclical business in which upturns followed downturns, making the notion of normal capacity utilization appear reasonable. Unfortunately, the steel cycle in the 1980s did not turn up; some companies and numerous plants closed. More recently, the global economic slowdown has made a mockery of demand projections. Consider that in 2006, the forecast for the Indian automotive market was that annual demand for cars and passenger vehicles would hit 1.92 million in the year 2009–2010. In early 2009, the forecast for the same period was revised downward to 1.37 million vehicles. Even ignoring the vagaries of economic cycles, another problem is that marketing managers of firms are often prone to overestimate their ability to regain lost sales and market share. Their estimate of "normal" demand for their product may consequently reflect an overly optimistic outlook. Master-budget capacity utilization focuses only on the expected demand for the next year. Therefore, master-budget capacity utilization can be more reliably estimated than normal capacity utilization. However, it is still just a forecast, and the true demand realization can be either higher or lower than this estimate.

It is important to understand that costing systems, such as normal costing or standard costing, do not recognize uncertainty the way managers recognize it. A single amount, rather than a range of possible amounts, is used as the denominator level when calculating the budgeted fixed manufacturing cost per unit in absorption costing. Consider Stassen's facility, which has an estimated practical capacity of 12,000 units. The estimated master-budget capacity utilization for 2012 is 8,000 units. However, there is still substantial doubt regarding the actual number of units Stassen will have to manufacture in 2012 and in future years. Managers recognize uncertainty in their capacity-planning decisions. Stassen built its current plant with a 12,000 unit practical capacity in part to provide the capability to meet possible demand surges. Even if such surges do not occur in a given period, do not conclude that capacity unused in a given period is wasted resources. The gains from meeting sudden demand surges may well require having unused capacity in some periods.

Difficulties in Forecasting Fixed Manufacturing Costs

The fixed manufacturing cost rate is based on a numerator (budgeted fixed manufacturing costs) and a denominator (some measure of capacity or capacity utilization). Our discussion so far has emphasized issues concerning the choice of the denominator. Challenging issues also arise in measuring the numerator. For example, deregulation of the U.S. electric utility industry has resulted in many electric utilities becoming unprofitable. This situation has led to write-downs in the values of the utilities' plants and equipment. The write-downs reduce the numerator because there is less depreciation expense included in the calculation of fixed capacity cost per kilowatt-hour of electricity produced. The difficulty that managers face in this situation is that the amount of write-downs is not clear-cut but, rather, a matter of judgment.

Nonmanufacturing Costs

Capacity costs also arise in nonmanufacturing parts of the value chain. Stassen may acquire a fleet of vehicles capable of distributing the practical capacity of its production facility. When actual production is below practical capacity, there will be unused-capacity cost issues with the distribution function, as well as with the manufacturing function.

Capacity cost issues are prominent in many service-sector companies, such as airlines, hospitals, and railroads—even though these companies carry no inventory and so have no inventory costing problems. For example, in calculating the fixed overhead cost per patient-day in its obstetrics and gynecology department, a hospital must decide which denominator level to use: practical capacity, normal capacity utilization, or master-budget capacity utilization. Its decision may have implications for capacity management, as well as pricing and performance evaluation.

Activity-Based Costing

Decision Point ▶

What issues must managers take into account when planning capacity levels and for assigning capacity costs?

To maintain simplicity and the focus on choosing a denominator to calculate a budgeted fixed manufacturing cost rate, our Stassen example assumed that all fixed manufacturing costs had a single cost driver: telescope units produced. Activity-based costing systems have multiple overhead cost pools at the output-unit, batch, product-sustaining, and facility-sustaining levels—each with its own cost driver. In calculating activity cost rates (for fixed costs of setups and material handling, say), management must choose a capacity level for the quantity of the cost driver (setup-hours or loads moved). Should management use practical capacity, normal capacity utilization, or master-budget capacity utilization? For all the reasons described in this chapter (such as pricing and capacity management), most proponents of activity-based costing argue that practical capacity should be used as the denominator level to calculate activity cost rates.

Problem for Self-Study

Assume Stassen Company on January 1, 2012, decides to contract with another company to preassemble a large percentage of the components of its telescopes. The revised manufacturing cost structure during the 2012–2014 period is as follows:

Variable manufacturing cost per unit produced	
Direct materials	$ 250
Direct manufacturing labor	20
Manufacturing overhead	5
Total variable manufacturing cost per unit produced	$ 275
Fixed manufacturing costs	$480,000

Under the revised cost structure, a larger percentage of Stassen's manufacturing costs are variable with respect to units produced. The denominator level of production used to calculate budgeted fixed manufacturing cost per unit in 2012, 2013, and 2014 is 8,000 units. Assume no other change from the data underlying Exhibits 1 and 2. Summary information pertaining to absorption-costing operating income and variable-costing operating income with this revised cost structure is as follows:

	2012	2013	2014
Absorption-costing operating income	$1,500,000	$1,560,000	$2,340,000
Variable-costing operating income	1,380,000	1,650,000	2,190,000
Difference	$ 120,000	$ (90,000)	$ 150,000

Required

1. Compute the budgeted fixed manufacturing cost per unit in 2012, 2013, and 2014.
2. Explain the difference between absorption-costing operating income and variable-costing operating income in 2012, 2013, and 2014, focusing on fixed manufacturing costs in beginning and ending inventory.
3. Why are these differences smaller than the differences in Exhibit 2?
4. Assume the same preceding information, except that for 2012, the master-budget capacity utilization is 10,000 units instead of 8,000. How would Stassen's absorption-costing income for 2012 differ from the $1,500,000 shown previously? Show your computations.

Solution

1. $$\text{Budgeted fixed manufacturing cost per unit} = \frac{\text{Budgeted fixed manufacturing costs}}{\text{Budgeted production units}}$$

$$= \frac{\$480,000}{8,000 \text{ units}}$$

$$= \$60 \text{ per unit}$$

2.
$$
\begin{array}{c}
\text{Absorption-costing} \\ \text{operating} \\ \text{income}
\end{array}
-
\begin{array}{c}
\text{Variable-costing} \\ \text{operating} \\ \text{income}
\end{array}
=
\begin{array}{c}
\text{Fixed manufacturing} \\ \text{costs in ending inventory} \\ \text{under absorption costing}
\end{array}
-
\begin{array}{c}
\text{Fixed manufacturing costs} \\ \text{in beginning inventory} \\ \text{under absorption costing}
\end{array}
$$

2012: $1,500,000 − $1,380,000 = ($60 per unit × 2,000 units) − ($600 per unit × 0 units)

$120,000 = $120,000

2013: $1,560,000 − $1,650,000 = ($60 per unit × 500 units) − ($60 per unit × 2,000 units)

−$90,000 = −$90,000

2014: $2,340,000 − $2,190,000 = ($60 per unit × 3,000 units) − ($60 per unit × 500 units)

$150,000 = $150,000

3. Subcontracting a large part of manufacturing has greatly reduced the magnitude of fixed manufacturing costs. This reduction, in turn, means differences between absorption costing and variable costing are much smaller than in Exhibit 2.
4. Given the higher master-budget capacity utilization level of 10,000 units, the budgeted fixed manufacturing cost rate for 2012 is now as follows:

$$\frac{\$480,000}{10,000 \text{ units}} = \$48 \text{ per unit}$$

The manufacturing cost per unit is $323 ($275 + $48). So, the production-volume variance for 2012 is

$$(10,000 \text{ units} − 8,000 \text{ units}) × \$48 \text{ per unit} = \$96,000 \text{ U}$$

The absorption-costing income statement for 2012 is as follows:

Revenues: $1,000 per unit × 6,000 units	$6,000,000
Cost of goods sold:	
Beginning inventory	0
Variable manufacturing costs: $275 per unit × 8,000 units	2,200,000
Fixed manufacturing costs: $48 per unit × 8,000 units	384,000
Cost of goods available for sale	2,584,000
Deduct ending inventory: $323 per unit × 2,000 units	(646,000)
Cost of goods sold (at standard costs)	1,938,000
Adjustment for production-volume variance	96,000 U
Cost of goods sold	2,034,000
Gross margin	3,966,000
Marketing costs: $1,380,000 fixed + ($185 per unit) × (6,000 units sold)	2,490,000
Operating income	$1,476,000

The higher denominator level used to calculate the budgeted fixed manufacturing cost per unit means that fewer fixed manufacturing costs are inventoried ($48 per unit × 2,000 units = $96,000) than when the master-budget capacity utilization was 8,000 units ($60 per unit × 2,000 units = $120,000). This difference of $24,000 ($120,000 – $96,000) results in operating income being lower by $24,000 relative to the prior calculated income level of $1,500,000.

Decision Points

The following question-and-answer format summarizes the chapter's learning objectives. Each decision presents a key question related to a learning objective. The guidelines are the answer to that question.

Decision	Guidelines
1. How does variable costing differ from absorption costing?	Variable costing and absorption costing differ in only one respect: how to account for fixed manufacturing costs. Under variable costing, fixed manufacturing costs are excluded from inventoriable costs and are a cost of the period in which they are incurred. Under absorption costing, fixed manufacturing costs are inventoriable and become a part of cost of goods sold in the period when sales occur.
2. How does income differ under variable and absorption costing?	The variable-costing income statement is based on the contribution-margin format. Under it, operating income is driven by the unit level of sales. Under absorption costing, the income statement follows the gross-margin format. Operating income is driven by the unit level of production, the unit level of sales, and the denominator level used for assigning fixed costs.
3. Why might managers build up finished goods inventory if they use absorption costing?	When absorption costing is used, managers can increase current operating income by producing more units for inventory. Producing for inventory absorbs more fixed manufacturing costs into inventory and reduces costs expensed in the period. Critics of absorption costing label this manipulation of income as the major negative consequence of treating fixed manufacturing costs as inventoriable costs.
4. How does throughput costing differ from variable costing and absorption costing?	Throughput costing treats all costs except direct materials as costs of the period in which they are incurred. Throughput costing results in a lower amount of manufacturing costs being inventoried than either variable or absorption costing.
5. What are the various capacity levels a company can use to compute the budgeted fixed manufacturing cost rate?	Capacity levels can be measured in terms of capacity supplied—theoretical capacity or practical capacity. Capacity can also be measured in terms of output demanded—normal capacity utilization or master-budget capacity utilization.
6. What are the major factors managers consider in choosing the capacity level to compute the budgeted fixed manufacturing cost rate?	The major factors managers consider in choosing the capacity level to compute the budgeted fixed manufacturing cost rate are (a) effect on product costing and capacity management, (b) effect on pricing decisions, (c) effect on performance evaluation, (d) effect on financial statements, and (e) regulatory requirements.
7. What issues must managers take into account when planning capacity levels and for assigning capacity costs?	Critical factors in this regard include the uncertainty about the expected spending on capacity costs and the demand for the installed capacity, the role of capacity-related issues in nonmanufacturing areas, and the possible use of activity-based costing techniques in allocating capacity costs.

Appendix

Breakeven Points in Variable Costing and Absorption Costing

If variable costing is used, the breakeven point (that's where operating income is $0) is computed in the usual manner. There is only one breakeven point in this case, and it depends on (1) fixed (manufacturing and operating) costs and (2) contribution margin per unit.

The formula for computing the breakeven point under variable costing is a special case of the more general target operating income formula:

Let Q = Number of units sold to earn the target operating income

$$\text{Then } Q = \frac{\text{Total fixed costs } + \text{ Target operating income}}{\text{Contribution margin per unit}}$$

Breakeven occurs when the target operating income is $0. In our Stassen illustration for 2012 (see Exhibit 1):

$$Q = \frac{(\$1,080,000 + \$1,380,000) + \$0}{(\$1,000 - (\$200 + \$185))} = \frac{\$2,460,000}{\$615}$$

$$= 4,000 \text{ units}$$

We now verify that Stassen will achieve breakeven under variable costing by selling 4,000 units:

Revenues, $1,000 × 4,000 units	$4,000,000
Variable costs, $385 × 4,000 units	1,540,000
Contribution margin, $615 × 4,000 units	2,460,000
Fixed costs	2,460,000
Operating income	$ 0

If absorption costing is used, the required number of units to be sold to earn a specific target operating income is not unique because of the number of variables involved. The following formula shows the factors that will affect the target operating income under absorption costing:

$$Q = \frac{\begin{matrix}\text{Total} \\ \text{fixed} \\ \text{costs}\end{matrix} + \begin{matrix}\text{Target} \\ \text{operating} \\ \text{income}\end{matrix} + \left[\begin{matrix}\text{Fixed} \\ \text{manufacturing} \\ \text{cost rate}\end{matrix} \times \left(\begin{matrix}\text{Breakeven} \\ \text{sales} \\ \text{in units}\end{matrix} - \begin{matrix}\text{Units} \\ \text{produced}\end{matrix} \right) \right]}{\text{Contribution margin per unit}}$$

In this formula, the numerator is the sum of three terms (from the perspective of the two "+" signs), compared with two terms in the numerator of the variable-costing formula stated earlier. The additional term in the numerator under absorption costing is as follows:

$$\left[\begin{matrix}\text{Fixed manufacturing} \\ \text{cost rate}\end{matrix} \times \left(\begin{matrix}\text{Breakeven sales} \\ \text{in units}\end{matrix} - \begin{matrix}\text{Units} \\ \text{produced}\end{matrix} \right) \right]$$

This term reduces the fixed costs that need to be recovered when units produced exceed the breakeven sales quantity. When production exceeds the breakeven sales quantity, some of the fixed manufacturing costs that are expensed under variable costing are not expensed under absorption costing; they are instead included in finished goods inventory.[6]

For Stassen Company in 2012, suppose that actual production is 5,280 units. Then, one breakeven point, Q, under absorption costing is as follows:

$$Q = \frac{(\$1,080,000 + \$1,380,000) + \$0 + [\$135 \times (Q - 5,280)]}{(\$1,000 - (\$200 + \$185))}$$

$$= \frac{(\$2,460,000 + \$135Q - \$712,800)}{\$615}$$

$$\$615Q = \$1,747,200 + \$135Q$$

$$\$480Q = \$1,747,200$$

$$Q = 3,640$$

---

[6] The reverse situation, where production is lower than the breakeven sales quantity, is not possible unless the firm has opening inventory. In that case, provided the variable manufacturing cost per unit and the fixed manufacturing cost rate are constant over time, the breakeven formula given is still valid.

We next verify that production of 5,280 units and sales of 3,640 units will lead Stassen to breakeven under absorption costing:

Revenues, $1,000 × 3,640 units		$3,640,000
Cost of goods sold:		
Cost of goods sold at standard cost, $335 × 3,640 units	$1,219,400	
Production-volume variance, $135 × (8,000 – 5,280) units	367,200 U	1,586,600
Gross margin		2,053,400
Marketing costs:		
Variable marketing costs, $185 × 3,640 units	673,400	
Fixed marketing costs	1,380,000	2,053,400
Operating income		$ 0

The breakeven point under absorption costing depends on (1) fixed manufacturing costs, (2) fixed operating (marketing) costs, (3) contribution margin per unit, (4) unit level of production, and (5) the capacity level chosen as the denominator to set the fixed manufacturing cost rate. For Stassen in 2012, a combination of 3,640 units sold, fixed manufacturing costs of $1,080,000, fixed marketing costs of $1,380,000, contribution margin per unit of $615, an 8,000-unit denominator level, and production of 5,280 units would result in an operating income of $0. *Note, however, that there are many combinations of these five factors that would give an operating income of $0.* For example, holding all other factors constant, a combination of 6,240 units produced and 3,370 units sold also results in an operating income of $0 under absorption costing. We provide verification of this alternative breakeven point next:

Revenues, $1,000 × 3,370 units		$3,370,000
Cost of goods sold:		
Cost of goods sold at standard cost, $335 × 3,370 units	$1,128,950	
Production-volume variance, $135 × (8,000 – 6,240) units	237,600 U	1,366,550
Gross margin		2,003,450
Marketing costs:		
Variable marketing costs, $185 × 3,370 units	623,450	
Fixed marketing costs	1,380,000	2,003,450
Operating income		$ 0

Suppose actual production in 2012 was equal to the denominator level, 8,000 units, and there were no units sold and no fixed marketing costs. All the units produced would be placed in inventory, so all the fixed manufacturing costs would be included in inventory. There would be no production-volume variance. Under these conditions, the company could break even under absorption costing with no sales whatsoever! In contrast, under variable costing, the operating loss would be equal to the fixed manufacturing costs of $1,080,000.

Terms to Learn

This chapter contains definitions of the following important terms:

absorption costing	master-budget capacity utilization	super-variable costing
direct costing	normal capacity utilization	theoretical capacity
downward demand spiral	practical capacity	throughput costing
		variable costing

Assignment Material

Questions

9-1 Differences in operating income between variable costing and absorption costing are due solely to accounting for fixed costs. Do you agree? Explain.

9-2 Why is the term *direct costing* a misnomer?

9-3 Do companies in either the service sector or the merchandising sector make choices about absorption costing versus variable costing?

9-4 Explain the main conceptual issue under variable costing and absorption costing regarding the timing for the release of fixed manufacturing overhead as expense.

9-5 "Companies that make no variable-cost/fixed-cost distinctions must use absorption costing, and those that do make variable-cost/fixed-cost distinctions must use variable costing." Do you agree? Explain.

9-6 The main trouble with variable costing is that it ignores the increasing importance of fixed costs in manufacturing companies. Do you agree? Why?

9-7 Give an example of how, under absorption costing, operating income could fall even though the unit sales level rises.

9-8 What are the factors that affect the breakeven point under (a) variable costing and (b) absorption costing?

9-9 Critics of absorption costing have increasingly emphasized its potential for leading to undesirable incentives for managers. Give an example.

9-10 What are two ways of reducing the negative aspects associated with using absorption costing to evaluate the performance of a plant manager?

9-11 What denominator-level capacity concepts emphasize the output a plant can supply? What denominator-level capacity concepts emphasize the output customers demand for products produced by a plant?

9-12 Describe the downward demand spiral and its implications for pricing decisions.

9-13 Will the financial statements of a company always differ when different choices at the start of the accounting period are made regarding the denominator-level capacity concept?

9-14 What is the IRS's requirement for tax reporting regarding the choice of a denominator-level capacity concept?

9-15 "The difference between practical capacity and master-budget capacity utilization is the best measure of management's ability to balance the costs of having too much capacity and having too little capacity." Do you agree? Explain.

Exercises

MyAccountingLab

9-16 Variable and absorption costing, explaining operating-income differences. Nascar Motors assembles and sells motor vehicles and uses standard costing. Actual data relating to April and May 2011 are as follows:

A	B	C	D
	April		**May**
2 Unit data			
3 Beginning inventory	0		150
4 Production	500		400
5 Sales	350		520
6 Variable costs			
7 Manufacturing cost per unit produced	$ 10,000		$ 10,000
8 Operating (marketing) cost per unit sold	3,000		3,000
9 Fixed costs			
10 Manufacturing costs	$2,000,000		$2,000,000
11 Operating (marketing) costs	600,000		600,000

The selling price per vehicle is $24,000. The budgeted level of production used to calculate the budgeted fixed manufacturing cost per unit is 500 units. There are no price, efficiency, or spending variances. Any production-volume variance is written off to cost of goods sold in the month in which it occurs.

Required

1. Prepare April and May 2011 income statements for Nascar Motors under (a) variable costing and (b) absorption costing.
2. Prepare a numerical reconciliation and explanation of the difference between operating income for each month under variable costing and absorption costing.

9-17 Throughput costing (continuation of 9-16). The variable manufacturing costs per unit of Nascar Motors are as follows:

A	B	C
1	**April**	**May**
7 Direct material cost per unit	$6,700	$6,700
8 Direct manufacturing labor cost per unit	1,500	1,500
9 Manufacturing overhead cost per unit	1,800	1,800

Required

1. Prepare income statements for Nascar Motors in April and May of 2011 under throughput costing.
2. Contrast the results in requirement 1 with those in requirement 1 of Exercise 9-16.
3. Give one motivation for Nascar Motors to adopt throughput costing.

9-18 Variable and absorption costing, explaining operating-income differences. BigScreen Corporation manufactures and sells 50-inch television sets and uses standard costing. Actual data relating to January, February, and March of 2012 are as follows:

	January	February	March
Unit data			
Beginning inventory	0	300	300
Production	1,000	800	1,250
Sales	700	800	1,500
Variable costs			
Manufacturing cost per unit produced	$ 900	$ 900	$ 900
Operating (marketing) cost per unit sold	$ 600	$ 600	$ 600
Fixed costs			
Manufacturing costs	$400,000	$400,000	$400,000
Operating (marketing) costs	$140,000	$140,000	$140,000

The selling price per unit is $2,500. The budgeted level of production used to calculate the budgeted fixed manufacturing cost per unit is 1,000 units. There are no price, efficiency, or spending variances. Any production-volume variance is written off to cost of goods sold in the month in which it occurs.

Required

1. Prepare income statements for BigScreen in January, February, and March of 2012 under (a) variable costing and (b) absorption costing.
2. Explain the difference in operating income for January, February, and March under variable costing and absorption costing.

9-19 Throughput costing (continuation of 9-18). The variable manufacturing costs per unit of BigScreen Corporation are as follows:

	January	February	March
Direct material cost per unit	$500	$500	$500
Direct manufacturing labor cost per unit	100	100	100
Manufacturing overhead cost per unit	300	300	300
	$900	$900	$900

Required

1. Prepare income statements for BigScreen in January, February, and March of 2012 under throughput costing.
2. Contrast the results in requirement 1 with those in requirement 1 of Exercise 9-18.
3. Give one motivation for BigScreen to adopt throughput costing.

9-20 Variable versus absorption costing. The Zwatch Company manufactures trendy, high-quality moderately priced watches. As Zwatch's senior financial analyst, you are asked to recommend a method of inventory costing. The CFO will use your recommendation to prepare Zwatch's 2012 income statement. The following data are for the year ended December 31, 2012:

Beginning inventory, January 1, 2012	85,000 units
Ending inventory, December 31, 2012	34,500 units
2012 sales	345,400 units
Selling price (to distributor)	$22.00 per unit
Variable manufacturing cost per unit, including direct materials	$5.10 per unit
Variable operating (marketing) cost per unit sold	$1.10 per unit sold
Fixed manufacturing costs	$1,440,000
Denominator-level machine-hours	6,000
Standard production rate	50 units per machine-hour
Fixed operating (marketing) costs	$1,080,000

Assume standard costs per unit are the same for units in beginning inventory and units produced during the year. Also, assume no price, spending, or efficiency variances. Any production-volume variance is written off to cost of goods sold in the month in which it occurs.

Required

1. Prepare income statements under variable and absorption costing for the year ended December 31, 2012.
2. What is Zwatch's operating income as percentage of revenues under each costing method?
3. Explain the difference in operating income between the two methods.
4. Which costing method would you recommend to the CFO? Why?

9-21 Absorption and variable costing. (CMA) Osawa, Inc., planned and actually manufactured 200,000 units of its single product in 2012, its first year of operation. Variable manufacturing cost was $20 per unit produced. Variable operating (nonmanufacturing) cost was $10 per unit sold. Planned and actual fixed manufacturing costs were $600,000. Planned and actual fixed operating (nonmanufacturing) costs totaled $400,000. Osawa sold 120,000 units of product at $40 per unit.

Required

1. Osawa's 2012 operating income using absorption costing is (a) $440,000, (b) $200,000, (c) $600,000, (d) $840,000, or (e) none of these. Show supporting calculations.
2. Osawa's 2012 operating income using variable costing is (a) $800,000, (b) $440,000, (c) $200,000, (d) $600,000, or (e) none of these. Show supporting calculations.

9-22 Absorption versus variable costing. Grunewald Company manufacturers a professional grade vacuum cleaner and began operations in 2011. For 2011, Grunewald budgeted to produce and sell 20,000 units. The company had no price, spending, or efficiency variances, and writes off production-volume variance to cost of goods sold. Actual data for 2011 are given as follows:

	Home Insert Page Layout Formulas Data	
	A	B
1	Units produced	18,000
2	Units sold	17,500
3	Selling price	$ 425
4	Variable costs:	
5	Manufacturing cost per unit produced	
6	Direct materials	$ 30
7	Direct manufacturing labor	25
8	Manufacturing overhead	60
9	Marketing cost per unit sold	45
10	Fixed costs:	
11	Manufacturing costs	$1,100,000
12	Administrative costs	965,450
13	Marketing	1,366,400

Required

1. Prepare a 2011 income statement for Grunewald Company using variable costing.
2. Prepare a 2011 income statement for Grunewald Company using absorption costing.
3. Explain the differences in operating incomes obtained in requirement 1 and requirement 2.
4. Grunewald's management is considering implementing a bonus for the supervisors based on gross margin under absorption costing. What incentives will this create for the supervisors? What modifications could Grunewald management make to improve such a plan? Explain briefly.

9-23 Comparison of actual-costing methods. The Rehe Company sells its razors at $3 per unit. The company uses a first-in, first-out actual costing system. A fixed manufacturing cost rate is computed at the end of each year by dividing the actual fixed manufacturing costs by the actual production units. The following data are related to its first two years of operation:

	2011	2012
Sales	1,000 units	1,200 units
Production	1,400 units	1,000 units
Costs:		
Variable manufacturing	$ 700	$ 500
Fixed manufacturing	700	700
Variable operating (marketing)	1,000	1,200
Fixed operating (marketing)	400	400

Required

1. Prepare income statements based on variable costing for each of the two years.
2. Prepare income statements based on absorption costing for each of the two years.
3. Prepare a numerical reconciliation and explanation of the difference between operating income for each year under absorption costing and variable costing.
4. Critics have claimed that a widely used accounting system has led to undesirable buildups of inventory levels. (a) Is variable costing or absorption costing more likely to lead to such buildups? Why? (b) What can be done to counteract undesirable inventory buildups?

9-24 Variable and absorption costing, sales, and operating-income changes. Helmetsmart, a three-year-old company, has been producing and selling a single type of bicycle helmet. Helmetsmart uses standard costing. After reviewing the income statements for the first three years, Stuart Weil, president of Helmetsmart, commented, "I was told by our accountants—and in fact, I have memorized—that our breakeven volume is 49,000 units. I was happy that we reached that sales goal in each of our first two years. But, here's the strange thing: In our first year, we sold 49,000 units and indeed we broke even. Then, in our second year we sold the same volume and had a positive operating income. I didn't complain, of course . . . but here's the bad part. In our third year, we *sold 20% more* helmets, but our *operating income fell by more than 80%* relative to the second year! We didn't change our selling price or cost structure over the past three years and have no price, efficiency, or spending variances . . . so what's going on?!"

	Home	Insert	Page Layout	Formulas	Data	Review	View
	A				B	C	D
1	**Absorption Costing**						
2					2011	2012	2013
3	Sales (units)				49,000	49,000	58,800
4	Revenues				$1,960,000	$1,960,000	$2,352,000
5	Cost of goods sold						
6	Beginning inventory				0	0	352,800
7	Production				1,764,000	2,116,800	1,764,000
8	Available for sale				1,764,000	2,116,800	2,116,800
9	Deduct ending inventory				0	(352,800)	0
10	Adjustment for production-volume variance				0	(215,600)	0
11	Cost of goods sold				1,764,000	1,548,400	2,116,800
12	Gross margin				196,000	411,600	235,200
13	Selling and administrative expenses (all fixed)				196,000	196,000	196,000
14	Operating income				$ 0	$ 215,600	$ 39,200
15							
16	Beginning inventory				0	0	9,800
17	Production (units)				49,000	58,800	49,000
18	Sales (units)				49,000	49,000	58,800
19	Ending inventory				0	9,800	0
20	Variable manufacturing cost per unit				$ 14	$ 14	$ 14
21	Fixed manufacturing overhead costs				$1,078,000	$1,078,000	$1,078,000
22	Fixed manuf. costs allocated per unit produced				$ 22	$ 22	$ 22

Required

1. What denominator level is Helmetsmart using to allocate fixed manufacturing costs to the bicycle helmets? How is Helmetsmart disposing of any favorable or unfavorable production-volume variance at the end of the year? Explain your answer briefly.
2. How did Helmetsmart's accountants arrive at the breakeven volume of 49,000 units?
3. Prepare a variable costing-based income statement for each year. Explain the variation in variable costing operating income for each year based on contribution margin per unit and sales volume.
4. Reconcile the operating incomes under variable costing and absorption costing for each year, and use this information to explain to Stuart Weil the positive operating income in 2012 and the drop in operating income in 2013.

9-25 Capacity management, denominator-level capacity concepts. Match each of the following items with one or more of the denominator-level capacity concepts by putting the appropriate letter(s) by each item:

a. Theoretical capacity
b. Practical capacity
c. Normal capacity utilization
d. Master-budget capacity utilization

1. Measures the denominator level in terms of what a plant can supply
2. Is based on producing at full efficiency all the time
3. Represents the expected level of capacity utilization for the next budget period
4. Measures the denominator level in terms of demand for the output of the plant
5. Takes into account seasonal, cyclical, and trend factors
6. Should be used for performance evaluation in the current year
7. Represents an ideal benchmark
8. Highlights the cost of capacity acquired but not used
9. Should be used for long-term pricing purposes
10. Hides the cost of capacity acquired but not used
11. If used as the denominator-level concept, would avoid the restatement of unit costs when expected demand levels change

9-26 Denominator-level problem. Thunder Bolt, Inc., is a manufacturer of the very popular G36 motorcycles. The management at Thunder Bolt has recently adopted absorption costing and is debating which denominator-level concept to use. The G36 motorcycles sell for an average price of $8,200. Budgeted fixed manufacturing overhead costs for 2012 are estimated at $6,480,000. Thunder Bolt, Inc., uses subassembly operators that provide component parts. The following are the denominator-level options that management has been considering:

a. Theoretical capacity—based on three shifts, completion of five motorcycles per shift, and a 360-day year—$3 \times 5 \times 360 = 5,400$.
b. Practical capacity—theoretical capacity adjusted for unavoidable interruptions, breakdowns, and so forth—$3 \times 4 \times 320 = 3,840$.
c. Normal capacity utilization—estimated at 3,240 units.
d. Master-budget capacity utilization—the strengthening stock market and the growing popularity of motorcycles have prompted the marketing department to issue an estimate for 2012 of 3,600 units.

1. Calculate the budgeted fixed manufacturing overhead cost rates under the four denominator-level concepts.
2. What are the benefits to Thunder Bolt, Inc., of using either theoretical capacity or practical capacity?
3. Under a cost-based pricing system, what are the negative aspects of a master-budget denominator level? What are the positive aspects?

Required

9-27 Variable and absorption costing and breakeven points. Mega-Air, Inc., manufactures a specialized snowboard made for the advanced snowboarder. Mega-Air began 2011 with an inventory of 240 snowboards. During the year, it produced 900 boards and sold 995 for $750 each. Fixed production costs were $280,000 and variable production costs were $335 per unit. Fixed advertising, marketing, and other general and administrative expenses were $112,000 and variable shipping costs were $15 per board. Assume that the cost of each unit in beginning inventory is equal to 2011 inventory cost.

1. Prepare an income statement assuming Mega-Air uses variable costing.
2. Prepare an income statement assuming Mega-Air uses absorption costing. Mega-Air uses a denominator level of 1,000 units. Production-volume variances are written off to cost of goods sold.
3. Compute the breakeven point in units sold assuming Mega-Air uses the following:
   a. Variable costing
   b. Absorption costing (Production = 900 boards)
4. Provide proof of your preceding breakeven calculations.
5. Assume that $20,000 of fixed administrative costs were reclassified as fixed production costs. Would this change affect breakeven point using variable costing? What if absorption costing were used? Explain.
6. The company that supplies Mega-Air with its specialized impact-resistant material has announced a price increase of $25 for each board. What effect would this have on the breakeven points previously calculated?

Required

Problems

9-28 Variable costing versus absorption costing. The Mavis Company uses an absorption-costing system based on standard costs. Total variable manufacturing cost, including direct material cost, is $3 per unit; the standard production rate is 10 units per machine-hour. Total budgeted and actual fixed manufacturing overhead costs are $420,000. Fixed manufacturing overhead is allocated at $7 per machine-hour ($420,000 ÷ 60,000 machine-hours of denominator level). Selling price is $5 per unit. Variable operating (nonmanufacturing) cost, which is driven by units sold, is $1 per unit. Fixed operating (nonmanufacturing) costs are $120,000. Beginning inventory in 2012 is 30,000 units; ending inventory is 40,000 units. Sales in 2012 are 540,000 units. The same standard unit costs persisted throughout 2011 and 2012. For simplicity, assume that there are no price, spending, or efficiency variances.

Required

1. Prepare an income statement for 2012 assuming that the production-volume variance is written off at year-end as an adjustment to cost of goods sold.
2. The president has heard about variable costing. She asks you to recast the 2012 statement as it would appear under variable costing.
3. Explain the difference in operating income as calculated in requirements 1 and 2.
4. Graph how fixed manufacturing overhead is accounted for under absorption costing. That is, there will be two lines: one for the budgeted fixed manufacturing overhead (which is equal to the actual fixed manufacturing overhead in this case) and one for the fixed manufacturing overhead allocated. Show how the production-volume variance might be indicated in the graph.
5. Critics have claimed that a widely used accounting system has led to undesirable buildups of inventory levels. (a) Is variable costing or absorption costing more likely to lead to such buildups? Why? (b) What can be done to counteract undesirable inventory buildups?

9-29 Variable costing and absorption costing, the All-Fixed Company. (R. Marple, adapted) It is the end of 2011. The All-Fixed Company began operations in January 2010. The company is so named because it has no variable costs. All its costs are fixed; they do not vary with output.

The All-Fixed Company is located on the bank of a river and has its own hydroelectric plant to supply power, light, and heat. The company manufactures a synthetic fertilizer from air and river water and sells its product at a price that is not expected to change. It has a small staff of employees, all paid fixed annual salaries. The output of the plant can be increased or decreased by adjusting a few dials on a control panel.

The following budgeted and actual data are for the operations of the All-Fixed Company. All-Fixed uses budgeted production as the denominator level and writes off any production-volume variance to cost of goods sold.

	2010	2011[a]
Sales	20,000 tons	20,000 tons
Production	40,000 tons	0 tons
Selling price	$ 20 per ton	$ 20 per ton
Costs (all fixed):		
Manufacturing	$320,000	$320,000
Operating (nonmanufacturing)	$ 60,000	$ 60,000

[a] Management adopted the policy, effective January 1, 2011, of producing only as much product as needed to fill sales orders. During 2011, sales were the same as for 2010 and were filled entirely from inventory at the start of 2011.

Required

1. Prepare income statements with one column for 2010, one column for 2011, and one column for the two years together, using (a) variable costing and (b) absorption costing.
2. What is the breakeven point under (a) variable costing and (b) absorption costing?
3. What inventory costs would be carried in the balance sheet on December 31, 2010 and 2011, under each method?
4. Assume that the performance of the top manager of the company is evaluated and rewarded largely on the basis of reported operating income. Which costing method would the manager prefer? Why?

9-30 Comparison of variable costing and absorption costing. Hinkle Company uses standard costing. Tim Bartina, the new president of Hinkle Company, is presented with the following data for 2012:

	A	B	C
		Variable	**Absorption**
		Costing	**Costing**
1	**Hinkle Company**		
2	**Income Statements for the Year Ended December 31, 2012**		
3		**Variable**	**Absorption**
4		**Costing**	**Costing**
5	Revenues	$9,000,000	$9,000,000
6	Cost of goods sold (at standard costs)	4,680,000	5,860,000
7	Fixed manufacturing overhead (budgeted)	1,200,000	-
8	Fixed manufacturing overhead variances (all unfavorable):		
9	Spending	100,000	100,000
10	Production volume	-	400,000
11	Total marketing and administrative costs (all fixed)	1,500,000	1,500,000
12	Total costs	7,480,000	7,860,000
13	Operating income	$1,520,000	$1,140,000
14			
15	Inventories (at standard costs)		
16	December 31, 2011	$1,200,000	$1,720,000
17	December 31, 2012	66,000	206,000

Required

1. At what percentage of denominator level was the plant operating during 2012?
2. How much fixed manufacturing overhead was included in the 2011 and the 2012 ending inventory under absorption costing?
3. Reconcile and explain the difference in 2012 operating incomes under variable and absorption costing.
4. Tim Bartina is concerned: He notes that despite an increase in sales over 2011, 2012 operating income has actually declined under absorption costing. Explain how this occurred.

9-31 Effects of differing production levels on absorption costing income: Metrics to minimize inventory buildups. University Press produces textbooks for college courses. The company recently hired a new editor, Leslie White, to handle production and sales of books for an introduction to accounting course. Leslie's compensation depends on the gross margin associated with sales of this book. Leslie needs to decide how many copies of the book to produce. The following information is available for the fall semester 2011:

Estimated sales	20,000 books
Beginning inventory	0 books
Average selling price	$80 per book
Variable production costs	$50 per book
Fixed production costs	$400,000 per semester

The fixed cost allocation rate is based on expected sales and is therefore equal to $400,000/20,000 books = $20 per book

Leslie has decided to produce either 20,000, 24,000, or 30,000 books.

Required

1. Calculate expected gross margin if Leslie produces 20,000, 24,000, or 30,000 books. (Make sure you include the production-volume variance as part of cost of goods sold.)
2. Calculate ending inventory in units and in dollars for each production level.

3. Managers who are paid a bonus that is a function of gross margin may be inspired to produce a product in excess of demand to maximize their own bonus. The chapter suggested metrics to discourage managers from producing products in excess of demand. Do you think the following metrics will accomplish this objective? Show your work.

    a. Incorporate a charge of 10% of the cost of the ending inventory as an expense for evaluating the manager.

    b. Include nonfinancial measures when evaluating management and rewarding performance.

9-32 Alternative denominator-level capacity concepts, effect on operating income. Lucky Lager has just purchased the Austin Brewery. The brewery is two years old and uses absorption costing. It will "sell" its product to Lucky Lager at $45 per barrel. Paul Brandon, Lucky Lager's controller, obtains the following information about Austin Brewery's capacity and budgeted fixed manufacturing costs for 2012:

	Home Insert Page Layout Formulas Data Review View				
	A	B	C	D	E
1		**Budgeted Fixed**	**Days of**	**Hours of**	
2	**Denominator-Level**	**Manufacturing**	**Production**	**Production**	**Barrels**
3	**Capacity Concept**	**Overhead per Period**	**per Period**	**per Day**	**per Hour**
4	Theoretical capacity	$28,000,000	360	24	540
5	Practical capacity	$28,000,000	350	20	500
6	Normal capacity utilization	$28,000,000	350	20	400
7	Master-budget capacity for each half year				
8	(a) January–June 2012	$14,000,000	175	20	320
9	(b) July–December 2012	$14,000,000	175	20	480

1. Compute the budgeted fixed manufacturing overhead rate per barrel for each of the denominator-level capacity concepts. Explain why they are different.
2. In 2012, the Austin Brewery reported these production results:

	Home Insert Page Layout Formulas Data	
	A	B
12	Beginning inventory in barrels, 1-1-2012	0
13	Production in barrels	2,600,000
14	Ending inventory in barrels, 12-31-2012	200,000
15	Actual variable manufacturing costs	$78,520,000
16	Actual fixed manufacturing overhead costs	$27,088,000

There are no variable cost variances. Fixed manufacturing overhead cost variances are written off to cost of goods sold in the period in which they occur. Compute the Austin Brewery's operating income when the denominator-level capacity is (a) theoretical capacity, (b) practical capacity, and (c) normal capacity utilization.

9-33 Motivational considerations in denominator-level capacity selection (continuation of 9-32).

1. If the plant manager of the Austin Brewery gets a bonus based on operating income, which denominator-level capacity concept would he prefer to use? Explain.
2. What denominator-level capacity concept would Lucky Lager prefer to use for U.S. income-tax reporting? Explain.
3. How might the IRS limit the flexibility of an absorption-costing company like Lucky Lager attempting to minimize its taxable income?

9-34 Denominator-level choices, changes in inventory levels, effect on operating income. Koshu Corporation is a manufacturer of computer accessories. It uses absorption costing based on standard costs and reports the following data for 2011:

	A	B	C
1	Theoretical capacity	280,000	units
2	Practical capacity	224,000	units
3	Normal capacity utilization	200,000	units
4	Selling price	$ 40	per unit
5	Beginning inventory	20,000	units
6	Production	220,000	units
7	Sales volume	230,000	units
8	Variable budgeted manufacturing cost	$ 5	per unit
9	Total budgeted fixed manufacturing costs	$2,800,000	
10	Total budgeted operating (nonmanuf.) costs (all fixed)	$ 900,000	

There are no price, spending, or efficiency variances. Actual operating costs equal budgeted operating costs. The production-volume variance is written off to cost of goods sold. For each choice of denominator level, the budgeted production cost per unit is also the cost per unit of beginning inventory.

Required

1. What is the production-volume variance in 2011 when the denominator level is (a) theoretical capacity, (b) practical capacity, and (c) normal capacity utilization?
2. Prepare absorption costing–based income statements for Koshu Corporation using theoretical capacity, practical capacity, and normal capacity utilization as the denominator levels.
3. Why is the operating income under normal capacity utilization lower than the other two scenarios?
4. Reconcile the difference in operating income based on theoretical capacity and practical capacity with the difference in fixed manufacturing overhead included in inventory.

9-35 Effects of denominator-level choice. Carlisle Company is a manufacturer of precision surgical tools. It initiated standard costing and a flexible budget on January 1, 2011. The company president, Monica Carlisle, has been pondering how fixed manufacturing overhead should be allocated to products. Machine-hours have been chosen as the allocation base. Her remaining uncertainty is the denominator level for machine-hours. She decides to wait for the first month's results before making a final choice of what denominator level should be used from that day forward.

During January 2011, the actual units of output had a standard of 37,680 machine-hours allowed. The fixed manufacturing overhead spending variance was $6,000, favorable. If the company used practical capacity as the denominator level, the production-volume variance would be $12,200, unfavorable. If the company used normal capacity utilization as the denominator level, the production-volume variance would be $2,400, unfavorable. Budgeted fixed manufacturing overhead was $96,600 for the month.

Required

1. Compute the denominator level, assuming that the normal-capacity-utilization concept is chosen.
2. Compute the denominator level, assuming that the practical-capacity concept is chosen.
3. Suppose you are the executive vice president. You want to maximize your 2011 bonus, which depends on 2011 operating income. Assume that the production-volume variance is written off to cost of goods sold at year-end, and assume that the company expects inventories to increase during the year. Which denominator level would you favor? Why?

9-36 Downward demand spiral. Spirelli Company is about to enter the highly competitive personal electronics market with a new optical reader. In anticipation of future growth, the company has leased a large manufacturing facility, and has purchased several expensive pieces of equipment. In 2011, the company's first year, Spirelli budgets for production and sales of 25,000 units, compared with its practical capacity of 50,000. The company's cost data follow:

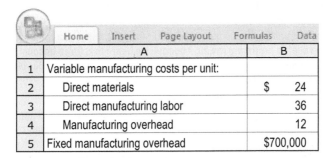

	A	B
1	Variable manufacturing costs per unit:	
2	Direct materials	$ 24
3	Direct manufacturing labor	36
4	Manufacturing overhead	12
5	Fixed manufacturing overhead	$700,000

1. Assume that Spirelli uses absorption costing, and uses budgeted units produced as the denominator for calculating its fixed manufacturing overhead rate. Selling price is set at 120% of manufacturing cost. Compute Spirelli's selling price.

2. Spirelli enters the market with the selling price computed previously. However, despite growth in the overall market, sales are not as robust as had been expected, and a competitor has priced its product $15 lower than Spirelli's. Enrico Spirelli, the company's president, insists that the competitor must be pricing its product at a loss, and that the competitor will be unable to sustain that. In response, Spirelli makes no price adjustments, but budgets production and sales for 2012 at 22,000 units. Variable and fixed costs are not expected to change. Compute Spirelli's new selling price. Comment on how Spirelli's choice of budgeted production affected its selling price and competitive position.

3. Recompute the selling price using practical capacity as the denominator level of activity. How would this choice have affected Spirelli's position in the marketplace? Generally, how would this choice affect the production-volume variance?

9-37 Absorption costing and production-volume variance—alternative capacity bases. Earth's Best Light (EBL), a producer of energy-efficient light bulbs, expects that demand will increase markedly over the next decade. Due to the high fixed costs involved in the business, EBL has decided to evaluate its financial performance using absorption costing income. The production-volume variance is written off to cost of goods sold. The variable cost of production is $2.70 per bulb. Fixed manufacturing costs are $1,015,000 per year. Variable and fixed selling and administrative expenses are $0.40 per bulb sold and $200,000, respectively. Because its light bulbs are currently popular with environmentally-conscious customers, EBL can sell the bulbs for $9.60 each.

EBL is deciding among various concepts of capacity for calculating the cost of each unit produced. Its choices are as follows:

Theoretical capacity	725,000 bulbs
Practical capacity	406,000 bulbs
Normal capacity	290,000 bulbs (average expected output for the next three years)
Master budget capacity	175,000 bulbs expected production this year

1. Calculate the inventoriable cost per unit using each level of capacity to compute fixed manufacturing cost per unit.

2. Suppose EBL actually produces 250,000 bulbs. Calculate the production-volume variance using each level of capacity to compute the fixed manufacturing overhead allocation rate.

3. Assume EBL has no beginning inventory. If this year's actual sales are 175,000 bulbs, calculate operating income for EBL using each type of capacity to compute fixed manufacturing cost per unit.

9-38 Operating income effects of denominator-level choice and disposal of production-volume variance (continuation of 9-37).

1. If EBL sells all 250,000 bulbs produced, what would be the effect on operating income of using each type of capacity as a basis for calculating manufacturing cost per unit?

2. Compare the results of operating income at different capacity levels when 175,000 bulbs are sold and when 250,000 bulbs are sold. What conclusion can you draw from the comparison?

3. Using the original data (that is, 250,000 units produced and 175,000 units sold) if EBL had used the pro-ration approach to allocate the production-volume variance, what would operating income have been under each level of capacity? (Assume that there is no ending work in process.)

9-39 Cost allocation, downward demand spiral. Cayzer Associates operates a chain of 10 hospitals in the Los Angeles area. Its central food-catering facility, Mealman, prepares and delivers meals to the hospitals. It has the capacity to deliver up to 1,300,000 meals a year. In 2012, based on estimates from each hospital controller, Mealman budgeted for 975,000 meals a year. Budgeted fixed costs in 2012 were $1,521,000. Each hospital was charged $6.46 per meal—$4.90 variable costs plus $1.56 allocated budgeted fixed cost.

Recently, the hospitals have been complaining about the quality of Mealman's meals and their rising costs. In mid-2012, Cayzer's president announces that all Cayzer hospitals and support facilities will be run as profit centers. Hospitals will be free to purchase quality-certified services from outside the system. Ron Smith, Mealman's controller, is preparing the 2013 budget. He hears that three hospitals have decided to use outside suppliers for their meals; this will reduce the 2013 estimated demand to 780,000 meals. No change in variable cost per meal or total fixed costs is expected in 2013.

1. How did Smith calculate the budgeted fixed cost per meal of $1.56 in 2012?

2. Using the same approach to calculating budgeted fixed cost per meal and pricing as in 2012, how much would hospitals be charged for each Mealman meal in 2013? What would their reaction be?

3. Suggest an alternative cost-based price per meal that Smith might propose and that might be more acceptable to the hospitals. What can Mealman and Smith do to make this price profitable in the long run?

9-40 Cost allocation, responsibility accounting, ethics (continuation of 9-39). In 2013, only 760,500 Mealman meals were produced and sold to the hospitals. Smith suspects that hospital controllers had systematically inflated their 2013 meal estimates.

Required

1. Recall that Mealman uses the master-budget capacity utilization to allocate fixed costs and to price meals. What was the effect of production-volume variance on Mealman's operating income in 2013?
2. Why might hospital controllers deliberately overestimate their future meal counts?
3. What other evidence should Cayzer's president seek to investigate Smith's concerns?
4. Suggest two specific steps that Smith might take to reduce hospital controllers' incentives to inflate their estimated meal counts.

Collaborative Learning Problem

9-41 Absorption, variable, and throughput costing; performance evaluation. Mile-High Foods, Inc., was formed in March 2011 to provide prepackaged snack boxes for a new low cost regional airline beginning on April 1. The company has just leased warehouse space central to the two airports to store materials.

To move packaged materials from the warehouses to the airports, where final assembly will take place, Mile-High must choose whether to lease a delivery truck and pay a full-time driver at a fixed cost of $5,000 per month, or pay a delivery service a rate equivalent to $0.40 per box. This cost will be included in either fixed manufacturing overhead or variable manufacturing overhead, depending on which option is chosen. The company is hoping for rapid growth, as sales forecasts for the new airline are promising. However, it is essential that Mile-High managers carefully control costs in order to be compliant with their sales contract and remain profitable.

Ron Spencer, the company's president, is trying to determine whether to use absorption, variable, or throughput costing to evaluate the performance of company managers. For absorption costing, he intends to use the practical-capacity level of the facility, which is 20,000 boxes per month. Production-volume variances will be written off to cost of goods sold.

Costs for the three months are expected to remain unchanged. The costs and revenues for April, May, and June are expected to be as follows:

Sales revenue	$6.00 per box
Direct material cost	$1.20 per box
Direct manufacturing labor cost	$0.35 per box
Variable manufacturing overhead cost	$0.15 per box
Variable delivery cost (if this option is chosen)	$0.40 per box
Fixed delivery cost (if this option is chosen)	$5,000 per month
Fixed manufacturing overhead costs	$15,000 per month
Fixed administrative costs	$28,000 per month

Projected production and sales for each month follow. High production in May is the result of an anticipated surge in June employee vacations.

	Sales (in units)	Production
April	12,000	12,200
May	12,500	18,000
June	13,000	9,000
Total	37,500	39,200

Required

1. Compute operating income for April, May, and June under absorption costing, assuming that Mile-High opts to use
   a. the leased truck and salaried driver.
   b. the variable delivery service.
2. Compute operating income for April, May, and June under variable costing, assuming that Mile-High opts to use
   a. the leased truck and salaried driver.
   b. the variable delivery service.
3. Compute operating income for April, May, and June under throughput costing, assuming that Mile-High opts to use
   a. the leased truck and salaried driver.
   b. the variable delivery service.
4. Should Mile-High choose absorption, variable, or throughput costing for evaluating the performance of managers? Why? What advantages and disadvantages might there be in adopting throughput costing?
5. Should Mile-High opt for the leased truck and salaried driver or the variable delivery service? Explain briefly.

Determining How Costs Behave

From Chapter 10 of *Cost Accounting: A Managerial Emphasis*, 14/e. Charles T. Horngren. Srikant M. Datar. Madhav Rajan.

Determining How Costs Behave

What is the value of looking at the past?

Perhaps it is to recall fond memories you've had or help you understand historical events. Maybe your return to the past enables you to better understand and predict the future. When an organization looks at the past, it typically does so to analyze its results, so that the best decisions can be made for the company's future. This activity requires gathering information about costs and how they behave so that managers can predict what they will be "down the road." Gaining a deeper understanding of cost behavior can also spur a firm to reorganize its operations in innovative ways and tackle important challenges, as the following article shows.

Management Accountants at Cisco Embrace Opportunities, Enhance Sustainability[1]

Understanding how costs behave is a valuable technical skill. Managers look to management accountants to help them identify cost drivers, estimate cost relationships, and determine the fixed and variable components of costs. To be effective, management accountants must have a clear understanding of the business's strategy and operations to identify new opportunities to reduce costs and increase profitability. At Cisco Systems, management accountants' in-depth understanding of the company's costs and operations led to reduced costs, while also helping the environment.

Cisco, makers of computer networking equipment including routers and wireless switches, traditionally regarded the used equipment it received back from its business customers as scrap and recycled it at a cost of about $8 million a year. As managers looked at the accumulated costs and realized that they may literally be "throwing away money," they decided to reassess their treatment of scrap material. In 2005, managers at Cisco began trying to find uses for the equipment, mainly because 80% of the returns were in working condition. A value recovery team at Cisco identified groups within the company that could use the returned equipment. These included its customer service group, which supports warranty claims and service

---

[1] *Source:* Nidumolu, R., C. Prahalad, and M. Rangaswami. 2009. Why sustainability is now the key driver of innovation. *Harvard Business Review,* September 2009; Cisco Systems, Inc. 2009. *2009 corporate social responsibility report.* San Jose, CA: Cisco Systems, Inc.

contracts, and the labs that provide technical support, training, and product demonstrations.

Based on the initial success of the value recovery team, in 2005, Cisco designated its recycling group as a company business unit, set clear objectives for it, and assigned the group its own income statement. As a result, the reuse of equipment rose from 5% in 2004 to 45% in 2008, and Cisco's recycling costs fell by 40%. The unit has become a profit center that contributed $153 million to Cisco's bottom line in 2008.

With product returns reducing corporate profitability by an average of about 4% a year, companies like Cisco can leverage management accountants' insight to reduce the cost of these returns while decreasing its environmental footprint. Not only can this turn a cost center into a profitable business, but sustainability efforts like these signals that the company is concerned about preventing environmental damage by reducing waste.

As the Cisco example illustrates, managers must understand how costs behave to make strategic and operating decisions that have a positive environmental impact. Consider several other examples. Managers at FedEx decided to replace old planes with new Boeing 757s that reduced fuel consumption by 36%, while increasing capacity by 20%. At Clorox, managers decided to create a new line of non-synthetic cleaning products that were better for the environment and helped create a new category of 'green' cleaning products worth about $200 million annually.

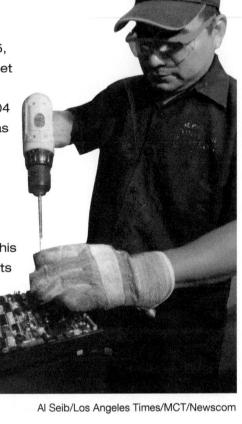

Al Seib/Los Angeles Times/MCT/Newscom

In each situation, knowledge of cost behavior was needed to answer key questions. This chapter will focus on how managers determine cost-behavior patterns—that is, how costs change in relation to changes in activity levels, in the quantity of products produced, and so on.

Basic Assumptions and Examples of Cost Functions

Learning Objective 1

Describe linear cost functions

. . . graph of cost function is a straight line

and three common ways in which they behave

. . . variable, fixed, and mixed

Managers are able to understand cost behavior through cost functions. A **cost function** is a mathematical description of how a cost changes with changes in the level of an activity relating to that cost. Cost functions can be plotted on a graph by measuring the level of an activity, such as number of batches produced or number of machine-hours used, on the horizontal axis (called the x-axis) and the amount of total costs corresponding to—or, preferably, dependent on—the levels of that activity on the vertical axis (called the y-axis).

Basic Assumptions

Managers often estimate cost functions based on two assumptions:

1. Variations in the level of a single activity (the cost driver) explain the variations in the related total costs.

2. Cost behavior is approximated by a linear cost function within the relevant range. Recall that a relevant range is the range of the activity in which there is a relationship between total cost and the level of activity. For a **linear cost function** represented graphically, total cost versus the level of a single activity related to that cost is a straight line within the relevant range.

We use these two assumptions throughout most, but not all, of this chapter. Not all cost functions are linear and can be explained by a single activity. Later sections will discuss cost functions that do not rely on these assumptions.

Linear Cost Functions

To understand three basic types of linear cost functions and to see the role of cost functions in business decisions, consider the negotiations between Cannon Services and World Wide Communications (WWC) for exclusive use of a videoconferencing line between New York and Paris.

- **Alternative 1:** $5 per minute used. Total cost to Cannon changes in proportion to the number of minutes used. The number of minutes used is the only factor whose change causes a change in total cost.

  Panel A in Exhibit 1 presents this *variable cost* for Cannon Services. Under alternative 1, there is no fixed cost. We write the cost function in Panel A of Exhibit 1 as

$$y = \$5X$$

  where X measures the number of minutes used (on the x-axis), and y measures the total cost of the minutes used (on the y-axis) calculated using the cost function. Panel A illustrates the $5 **slope coefficient,** the amount by which total cost changes when a one-unit change occurs in the level of activity (one minute of usage in the Cannon example). *Throughout the chapter, uppercase letters, such as X, refer to the actual observations, and lowercase letters, such as y, represent estimates or calculations made using a cost function.*

- **Alternative 2:** Total cost will be fixed at $10,000 per month, regardless of the number of minutes used. (We use the same activity measure, number of minutes used, to compare cost-behavior patterns under the three alternatives.)

  Panel B in Exhibit 1 presents this *fixed cost* for Cannon Services. We write the cost function in Panel B as

$$y = \$10,000$$

Exhibit 1 Examples of Linear Cost Functions

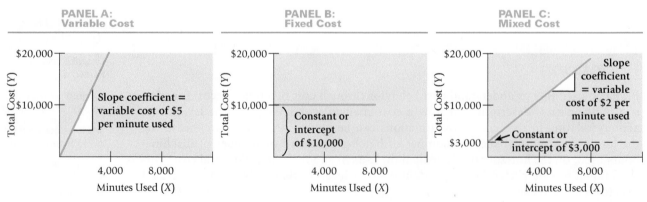

The fixed cost of $10,000 is called a **constant**; it is the component of total cost that does not vary with changes in the level of the activity. Under alternative 2, the constant accounts for all the cost because there is no variable cost. Graphically, the slope coefficient of the cost function is zero; this cost function intersects the y-axis at the constant value, and therefore the *constant* is also called the **intercept**.

■ **Alternative 3:** $3,000 per month plus $2 per minute used. This is an example of a mixed cost. A **mixed cost**—also called a **semivariable cost**—is a cost that has both fixed and variable elements.

Panel C in Exhibit 1 presents this *mixed cost* for Cannon Services. We write the cost function in Panel C of Exhibit 1 as

$$y = \$3{,}000 + \$2X$$

Unlike the graphs for alternatives 1 and 2, Panel C has both a constant, or intercept, value of $3,000 and a slope coefficient of $2. In the case of a mixed cost, total cost in the relevant range increases as the number of minutes used increases. Note that total cost does not vary strictly in proportion to the number of minutes used within the relevant range. For example, with 4,000 minutes of usage, the total cost equals $11,000 [$3,000 + ($2 per minute × 4,000 minutes)], but when 8,000 minutes are used, total cost equals $19,000 [$3,000 + ($2 per minute × 8,000 minutes)]. Although the usage in terms of minutes has doubled, total cost has increased by only about 73% [($19,000 – $11,000) ÷ $11,000].

Cannon's managers must understand the cost-behavior patterns in the three alternatives to choose the best deal with WWC. Suppose Cannon expects to do at least 4,000 minutes of videoconferencing per month. Its cost for 4,000 minutes under the three alternatives would be as follows:

■ **Alternative 1:** $20,000 ($5 per minute × 4,000 minutes)
■ **Alternative 2:** $10,000
■ **Alternative 3:** $11,000 [$3,000 + ($2 per minute × 4,000 minutes)]

Alternative 2 is the least costly. Moreover, if Cannon were to use more than 4,000 minutes, as is likely to be the case, alternatives 1 and 3 would be even more costly. Cannon's managers, therefore, should choose alternative 2.

Note that the graphs in Exhibit 1 are linear. That is, they appear as straight lines. We simply need to know the constant, or intercept, amount (commonly designated *a*) and the slope coefficient (commonly designated *b*). For any linear cost function based on a single activity (recall our two assumptions discussed at the start of the chapter), knowing *a* and *b* is sufficient to describe and graphically plot all the values within the relevant range of number of minutes used. We write a general form of this linear cost function as

$$y = a + bX$$

Under alternative 1, a = $0 and b = $5 per minute used; under alternative 2, a = $10,000 and b = $0 per minute used; and under alternative 3, a = $3,000 and b = $2 per minute used. To plot the mixed-cost function in Panel C, we draw a line starting from the point marked $3,000 on the y-axis and increasing at a rate of $2 per minute used, so that at 1,000 minutes, total costs increase by $2,000 ($2 per minute × 1,000 minutes) to $5,000 ($3,000 + $2,000) and at 2,000 minutes, total costs increase by $4,000 ($2 per minute × 2,000 minutes) to $7,000 ($3,000 + $4,000) and so on.

Review of Cost Classification

Before we discuss issues related to the estimation of cost functions, we briefly review the three criteria for classifying a cost into its variable and fixed components.

Choice of Cost Object

A particular cost item could be variable with respect to one cost object and fixed with respect to another cost object. Consider Super Shuttle, an airport transportation company. If the fleet of vans it owns is the cost object, then the annual van registration and license costs would be variable costs with respect to the number of vans owned. But if a particular van is the cost object, then the registration and license costs for that van are fixed costs with respect to the miles driven during a year.

Time Horizon

Whether a cost is variable or fixed with respect to a particular activity depends on the time horizon being considered in the decision situation. The longer the time horizon, all other things being equal, the more likely that the cost will be variable. For example, inspection costs at Boeing Company are typically fixed in the short run with respect to inspection-hours used because inspectors earn a fixed salary in a given year regardless of the number of inspection-hours of work done. But, in the long run, Boeing's total inspection costs will vary with the inspection-hours required: More inspectors will be hired if more inspection-hours are needed, and some inspectors will be reassigned to other tasks or laid off if fewer inspection-hours are needed.

Relevant Range

Managers should never forget that variable and fixed cost-behavior patterns are valid for linear cost functions only within a given relevant range. Outside the relevant range, variable and fixed cost-behavior patterns change, causing costs to become nonlinear (nonlinear means the plot of the relationship on a graph is not a straight line). For example, Exhibit 2 plots the relationship (over several years) between total direct manufacturing labor costs and the number of snowboards produced each year by Ski Authority at its Vermont plant. In this case, the nonlinearities outside the relevant range occur because of labor and other inefficiencies (first because workers are learning to produce snowboards and later because capacity limits are being stretched). Knowing the relevant range is essential to properly classify costs.

Identifying Cost Drivers

The Cannon Services/WWC example illustrates variable-, fixed-, and mixed-cost functions using information about *future* cost structures proposed to Cannon by WWC. Often, however, cost functions are estimated from *past* cost data. Managers use **cost estimation** to measure a relationship based on data from past costs and the related level of an activity. For example, marketing managers at Volkswagen could use cost estimation to understand what causes their marketing costs to change from year to year (for example, the number of new car models introduced or a competitor's sudden recall) and the fixed and variable components of these costs. Managers are interested in estimating past cost-behavior functions primarily because these estimates can help them make more-accurate **cost predictions**, or forecasts, of future costs. Better cost predictions help managers make more-informed planning and control decisions, such as preparing next year's marketing budget. But better management decisions, cost predictions, and estimation of cost functions can be achieved only if managers correctly identify the factors that affect costs.

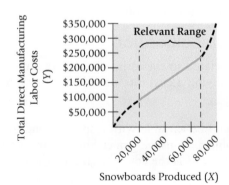

The Cause-and-Effect Criterion

The most important issue in estimating a cost function is determining whether a cause-and-effect relationship exists between the level of an activity and the costs related to that level of activity. Without a cause-and-effect relationship, managers will be less confident about their ability to estimate or predict costs. When a cause-and-effect relationship exists between a change in the level of an activity and a change in the level of total costs, we refer to the activity measure as a *cost driver*. We use the terms *level of activity* and *level of cost driver* interchangeably when estimating cost functions. Understanding the drivers of costs is crucially important for managing costs. The cause-and-effect relationship might arise as a result of the following:

- **A physical relationship between the level of activity and costs.** An example is when units of production are used as the activity that affects direct material costs. Producing more units requires more direct materials, which results in higher total direct material costs.
- **A contractual arrangement.** In alternative 1 of the Cannon Services example described earlier, number of minutes used is specified in the contract as the level of activity that affects the telephone line costs.
- **Knowledge of operations.** An example is when number of parts is used as the activity measure of ordering costs. A product with many parts will incur higher ordering costs than a product with few parts.

Managers must be careful not to interpret a high correlation, or connection, in the relationship between two variables to mean that either variable causes the other. Consider direct material costs and labor costs. For a given product mix, producing more units generally results in higher material costs and higher labor costs. Material costs and labor costs are highly correlated, but neither causes the other. Using labor costs to predict material costs is problematic. Some products require more labor costs relative to material costs, while other products require more material costs relative to labor costs. If the product mix changes toward more labor-intensive products, then labor costs will increase while material costs will decrease. Labor costs are a poor predictor of material costs. By contrast, factors that drive material costs such as product mix, product designs, and manufacturing processes, would have more accurately predicted the changes in material costs.

Only a cause-and-effect relationship—not merely correlation—establishes an economically plausible relationship between the level of an activity and its costs. Economic plausibility is critical because it gives analysts and managers confidence that the estimated relationship will appear again and again in other sets of data from the same situation. Identifying cost drivers also gives managers insights into ways to reduce costs and the confidence that reducing the quantity of the cost drivers will lead to a decrease in costs.

To identify cost drivers on the basis of data gathered over time, always use a long time horizon. Why? Because costs may be fixed in the short run (during which time they have no cost driver), but they are usually variable and have a cost driver in the long run.

Cost Drivers and the Decision-Making Process

Consider Elegant Rugs, which uses state-of-the-art automated weaving machines to produce carpets for homes and offices. Management has made many changes in manufacturing processes and wants to introduce new styles of carpets. It would like to evaluate how these changes have affected costs and what styles of carpets it should introduce. It follows the five-step decision-making process.

Step 1: Identify the problem and uncertainties. The changes in the manufacturing process were specifically targeted at reducing indirect manufacturing labor costs, and management wants to know whether costs such as supervision, maintenance, and quality control did, in fact, decrease. One option is to simply compare indirect manufacturing labor costs before and after the process change. The problem with this approach is that the volume of activity before and after the process change was very different so costs need to be compared after taking into account the change in activity volume.

Managers were fairly confident about the direct material and direct manufacturing labor costs of the new styles of carpets. They were less certain about the impact that the choice of different styles would have on indirect manufacturing costs.

Step 2: Obtain information. Managers gathered information about potential cost drivers—factors such as machine-hours or direct manufacturing labor-hours that cause indirect manufacturing labor costs to be incurred. They also began considering different techniques (discussed in the next section) such as the industrial engineering method, the conference method, the account analysis method, the high-low method, and the regression method for estimating the magnitude of the effect of the cost driver on indirect manufacturing labor costs. Their goal was to identify the best possible single cost driver.

Step 3: Make predictions about the future. Managers used past data to estimate the relationship between cost drivers and costs and used this relationship to predict future costs.

Step 4: Make decisions by choosing among alternatives. As we will describe later, Elegant Rugs chose machine-hours as the cost driver of indirect manufacturing labor costs. Using the regression analysis estimate of indirect manufacturing labor cost per machine-hour, managers estimated the costs of alternative styles of carpets and chose to introduce the most profitable styles.

Step 5: Implement the decision, evaluate performance, and learn. After the managers at Elegant Rugs introduced the new carpet styles, they focused on evaluating the results of their decision. Comparing predicted to actual costs helped managers to learn how accurate the estimates were, to set targets for continuous improvement, and to constantly seek ways to improve efficiency and effectiveness.

Decision Point ▶

What is the most important issue in estimating a cost function?

Cost Estimation Methods

Learning Objective 3

Understand various methods of cost estimation

. . . for example, the regression analysis method determines the line that best fits past data

As we mentioned in Step 2, four methods of cost estimation are the industrial engineering method, the conference method, the account analysis method, and the quantitative analysis method (which takes different forms). These methods differ with respect to how expensive they are to implement, the assumptions they make, and the information they provide about the accuracy of the estimated cost function. They are not mutually exclusive, and many organizations use a combination of these methods.

Industrial Engineering Method

The **industrial engineering method**, also called the **work-measurement method**, estimates cost functions by analyzing the relationship between inputs and outputs in physical terms. Consider Elegant Rugs. It uses inputs of cotton, wool, dyes, direct manufacturing labor, machine time, and power. Production output is square yards of carpet. Time-and-motion studies analyze the time required to perform the various operations to produce the carpet. For example, a time-and-motion study may conclude that to produce 10 square yards of carpet requires one hour of direct manufacturing labor. Standards and budgets transform these physical input measures into costs. The result is an estimated cost function relating direct manufacturing labor costs to the cost driver, square yards of carpet produced.

The industrial engineering method is a very thorough and detailed way to estimate a cost function when there is a physical relationship between inputs and outputs, but it can be very time consuming. Some government contracts mandate its use. Many organizations, such as Bose and Nokia, use it to estimate direct manufacturing costs but find it too costly or impractical for analyzing their entire cost structure. For example, physical relationships between inputs and outputs are difficult to specify for some items, such as indirect manufacturing costs, R&D costs, and advertising costs.

Conference Method

The **conference method** estimates cost functions on the basis of analysis and opinions about costs and their drivers gathered from various departments of a company (purchasing, process engineering, manufacturing, employee relations, etc.). The Cooperative Bank in the United Kingdom has a cost-estimating department that develops cost functions for its retail banking products (checking accounts, VISA cards, mortgages, and so on) based on the consensus of estimates from personnel of the particular departments. Elegant Rugs gathers opinions from supervisors and production engineers about how indirect manufacturing labor costs vary with machine-hours and direct manufacturing labor-hours.

The conference method encourages interdepartmental cooperation. The pooling of expert knowledge from different business functions of the value chain gives the conference method credibility. Because the conference method does not require detailed analysis of data, cost functions and cost estimates can be developed quickly. However, the emphasis on opinions rather than systematic estimation means that the accuracy of the cost estimates depends largely on the care and skill of the people providing the inputs.

Account Analysis Method

The **account analysis method** estimates cost functions by classifying various cost accounts as variable, fixed, or mixed with respect to the identified level of activity. Typically, managers use qualitative rather than quantitative analysis when making these cost-classification decisions. The account analysis approach is widely used because it is reasonably accurate, cost-effective, and easy to use.

Consider indirect manufacturing labor costs for a small production area (or cell) at Elegant Rugs. Indirect manufacturing labor costs include wages paid for supervision, maintenance, quality control, and setups. During the most recent 12-week period, Elegant Rugs ran the machines in the cell for a total of 862 hours and incurred total indirect manufacturing labor costs of $12,501. Using qualitative analysis, the manager and the cost analyst determine that over this 12-week period indirect manufacturing labor costs are mixed costs with only one cost driver—machine-hours. As machine-hours vary, one component of the cost (such as supervision cost) is fixed, whereas another component (such as maintenance cost) is variable. The goal is to use account analysis to estimate a linear cost function for indirect manufacturing labor costs with number of machine-hours as the cost driver. The cost analyst uses experience and judgment to separate total indirect manufacturing labor costs ($12,501) into costs that are fixed ($2,157, based on 950 hours of machine capacity for the cell over a 12-week period) and costs that are variable ($10,344) with respect to the number of machine-hours used. Variable cost per machine-hour is $10,344 ÷ 862 machine-hours = $12 per machine-hour. The linear cost equation, $y = a + bX$, in this example is as follows:

$$\text{Indirect manufacturing labor costs} = \$2,157 +$$
$$(\$12 \text{ per machine-hour} \times \text{Number of machine-hours})$$

Management at Elegant Rugs can use the cost function to estimate the indirect manufacturing labor costs of using, say, 950 machine-hours to produce carpet in the next 12-week period. Estimated costs equal $2,157 + (950 machine-hours × $12 per machine-hour) = $13,557.

To obtain reliable estimates of the fixed and variable components of cost, organizations must take care to ensure that individuals thoroughly knowledgeable about the operations make the cost-classification decisions. Supplementing the account analysis method with the conference method improves credibility.

Quantitative Analysis Method

Quantitative analysis uses a formal mathematical method to fit cost functions to past data observations. Excel is a useful tool for performing quantitative analysis. Columns B and C of Exhibit 3 show the breakdown of Elegant Rugs' total machine-hours (862) and total indirect manufacturing labor costs ($12,501) into weekly data for the most recent 12-week period. Note that the data are paired; for each week, there is data for the number of machine-hours and corresponding indirect manufacturing labor costs. For example, week 12 shows 48 machine-hours and indirect manufacturing labor costs of $963. The next section uses the data in Exhibit 3 to illustrate how to estimate a cost

Decision Point

What are the different methods that can be used to estimate a cost function?

	Home	Insert	Page Layout	Formulas
	A	B	C

	Week	Cost Driver: Machine-Hours	Indirect Manufacturing Labor Costs
1	Week	(X)	(Y)
2		(X)	(Y)
3	1	68	$ 1,190
4	2	88	1,211
5	3	62	1,004
6	4	72	917
7	5	60	770
8	6	96	1,456
9	7	78	1,180
10	8	46	710
11	9	82	1,316
12	10	94	1,032
13	11	68	752
14	12	48	963
15	Total	862	$12,501
16			

function using quantitative analysis. We examine two techniques—the relatively simple high-low method as well as the more common quantitative tool used to examine and understand data, regression analysis.

Steps in Estimating a Cost Function Using Quantitative Analysis

There are six steps in estimating a cost function using quantitative analysis of a past cost relationship. We illustrate the steps as follows using the Elegant Rugs example.

Step 1: Choose the dependent variable. Choice of the **dependent variable** (the cost to be predicted and managed) will depend on the cost function being estimated. In the Elegant Rugs example, the dependent variable is indirect manufacturing labor costs.

Step 2: Identify the independent variable, or cost driver. The **independent variable** (level of activity or cost driver) is the factor used to predict the dependent variable (costs). When the cost is an indirect cost, as it is with Elegant Rugs, the independent variable is also called a cost-allocation base. Although these terms are sometimes used interchangeably, we use the term *cost driver* to describe the independent variable. Frequently, the cost analyst, working with the management team, will cycle through the six steps several times, trying alternative economically plausible cost drivers to identify a cost driver that best fits the data.

A cost driver should be measurable and have an *economically plausible* relationship with the dependent variable. Economic plausibility means that the relationship (describing how changes in the cost driver lead to changes in the costs being considered) is based on a physical relationship, a contract, or knowledge of operations and makes economic sense to the operating manager and the management accountant. All the individual items of costs included in the dependent variable should have the same cost driver, that is, the cost pool should be homogenous. When all items of costs in the dependent variable do not have the same cost driver, the cost analyst should investigate the possibility of creating homogenous cost pools and estimating more than one cost function, one for each cost item/cost driver pair.

As an example, consider several types of fringe benefits paid to employees and the cost drivers of the benefits:

Fringe Benefit	Cost Driver
Health benefits	Number of employees
Cafeteria meals	Number of employees
Pension benefits	Salaries of employees
Life insurance	Salaries of employees

The costs of health benefits and cafeteria meals can be combined into one homogenous cost pool because they have the same cost driver—the number of employees. Pension benefits and life insurance costs have a different cost driver—the salaries of employees—and, therefore, should not be combined with health benefits and cafeteria meals. Instead, pension benefits and life insurance costs should be combined into a separate homogenous cost pool. The cost pool comprising pension benefits and life insurance costs can be estimated using salaries of employees receiving these benefits as the cost driver.

Step 3: Collect data on the dependent variable and the cost driver. This is usually the most difficult step in cost analysis. Cost analysts obtain data from company documents, from interviews with managers, and through special studies. These data may be time-series data or cross-sectional data.

Time-series data pertain to the same entity (organization, plant, activity, and so on) over successive past periods. Weekly observations of indirect manufacturing labor costs and number of machine-hours at Elegant Rugs are examples of time-series data. The ideal time-series database would contain numerous observations for a company whose operations have not been affected by economic or technological change. A stable economy and technology ensure that data collected during the estimation period represent the same underlying relationship between the cost driver and the dependent variable. Moreover, the periods used to measure the dependent variable and the cost driver should be consistent throughout the observations.

Cross-sectional data pertain to different entities during the same period. For example, studies of loans processed and the related personnel costs at 50 individual, yet similar, branches of a bank during March 2012 would produce cross-sectional data for that month. The cross-sectional data should be drawn from entities that, within each entity, have a similar relationship between the cost driver and costs. Later in this chapter, we describe the problems that arise in data collection.

Step 4: Plot the data. The general relationship between the cost driver and costs can be readily observed in a graphical representation of the data, which is commonly called a plot of the data. The plot provides insight into the relevant range of the cost function, and reveals whether the relationship between the driver and costs is approximately linear. Moreover, the plot highlights extreme observations (observations outside the general pattern) that analysts should check. Was there an error in recording the data or an unusual event, such as a work stoppage, that makes these observations unrepresentative of the normal relationship between the cost driver and the costs?

Exhibit 4 is a plot of the weekly data from columns B and C of the Excel spreadsheet in Exhibit 3. This graph provides strong visual evidence of a positive linear relationship between number of machine-hours and indirect manufacturing labor costs (that is, when machine-hours go up, so do indirect manufacturing labor costs). There do not appear to be any extreme observations in Exhibit 4. The relevant range is from 46 to 96 machine-hours per week (weeks 8 and 6, respectively).

Step 5: Estimate the cost function. We will show two ways to estimate the cost function for our Elegant Rugs data. One uses the high-low method, and the other uses regression analysis, the two most frequently described forms of quantitative analysis. The widespread availability of computer packages such as Excel makes regression analysis much more easy to use. Still, we describe the high-low method to provide some basic intuition for the idea of drawing a line to "fit" a number of data points. We present these methods after Step 6.

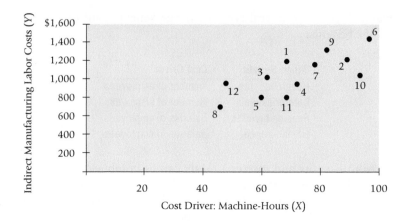

Exhibit 4

Plot of Weekly Indirect Manufacturing Labor Costs and Machine-Hours for Elegant Rugs

Step 6: Evaluate the cost driver of the estimated cost function. In this step, we describe criteria for evaluating the cost driver of the estimated cost function. We do this after illustrating the high-low method and regression analysis.

High-Low Method

The simplest form of quantitative analysis to "fit" a line to data points is the **high-low method**. It uses only the highest and lowest observed values of the cost driver within the relevant range and their respective costs to estimate the slope coefficient and the constant of the cost function. It provides a first cut at understanding the relationship between a cost driver and costs. We illustrate the high-low method using data from Exhibit 3.

	Cost Driver: Machine-Hours (X)	Indirect Manufacturing Labor Costs (Y)
Highest observation of cost driver (week 6)	96	$1,456
Lowest observation of cost driver (week 8)	46	710
Difference	50	$ 746

The slope coefficient, b, is calculated as follows:

$$\text{Slope coefficient} = \frac{\text{Difference between costs associated with highest and lowest observations of the cost driver}}{\text{Difference between highest and lowest observations of the cost driver}}$$

$$= \$746 \div 50 \text{ machine-hours} = \$14.92 \text{ per machine-hour}$$

To compute the constant, we can use either the highest or the lowest observation of the cost driver. Both calculations yield the same answer because the solution technique solves two linear equations with two unknowns, the slope coefficient and the constant. Because

$$y = a + bX$$
$$a = y - bX$$

At the highest observation of the cost driver, the constant, a, is calculated as follows:

$$\text{Constant} = \$1,456 - (\$14.92 \text{ per machine-hour} \times 96 \text{ machine-hours}) = \$23.68$$

And at the lowest observation of the cost driver,

$$\text{Constant} = \$710 - (\$14.92 \text{ per machine-hour} \times 46 \text{ machine-hours}) = \$23.68$$

Thus, the high-low estimate of the cost function is as follows:

$$y = a + bX$$
$$y = \$23.68 + (\$14.92 \text{ per machine-hour} \times \text{Number of machine-hours})$$

The purple line in Exhibit 5 shows the estimated cost function using the high-low method (based on the data in Exhibit 3). The estimated cost function is a straight line joining the observations with the highest and lowest values of the cost driver (number of machine-hours). Note how this simple high-low line falls "in-between" the data points with three observations on the line, four above it and five below it. The intercept (a = $23.68), the point where the dashed extension of the purple line meets the y-axis, is the constant component of the equation that provides the best linear approximation of how a cost behaves *within the relevant range* of 46 to 96 machine-hours. The intercept should *not* be interpreted as an estimate of the fixed costs of Elegant Rugs if no machines were run. That's because running no machines and shutting down the plant—that is, using zero machine-hours—is *outside the relevant range.*

Suppose indirect manufacturing labor costs in week 6 were $1,280, instead of $1,456, while 96 machine-hours were used. In this case, the highest observation of the cost driver (96 machine-hours in week 6) will not coincide with the newer highest observation of the costs ($1,316 in week 9). How would this change affect our high-low calculation? Given that the cause-and-effect relationship runs *from* the cost driver *to* the costs in a cost function, we choose the highest and lowest observations of the cost driver (the factor that causes the costs to change). The high-low method would still estimate the new cost function using data from weeks 6 (high) and 8 (low).

There is a danger of relying on only two observations to estimate a cost function. Suppose that because a labor contract guarantees certain minimum payments in week 8, indirect manufacturing labor costs in week 8 were $1,000, instead of $710, when only 46 machine-hours were used. The blue line in Exhibit 5 shows the cost function that would be estimated by the high-low method using this revised cost. Other than the two points used to draw the line, all other data lie on or below the line! In this case, choosing the highest and lowest observations for machine-hours would result in an estimated cost function that poorly describes the underlying linear cost relationship between number of machine-hours and indirect manufacturing labor costs. In such situations, the high-low method can be modified so that the two observations chosen to estimate the cost function are a *representative high* and a *representative low*. By using this adjustment, managers can avoid having extreme observations, which arise from abnormal events, influence the estimate of the cost function. The modification allows managers to estimate a cost function that is representative of the relationship between the cost driver and costs and, therefore, is more useful for making decisions (such as pricing and performance evaluation).

The advantage of the high-low method is that it is simple to compute and easy to understand; it gives a quick, initial insight into how the cost driver—number of machine-hours—affects indirect manufacturing labor costs. The disadvantage is that it ignores information from all but two observations when estimating the cost function. We next describe the regression analysis method of quantitative analysis that uses all available data to estimate the cost function.

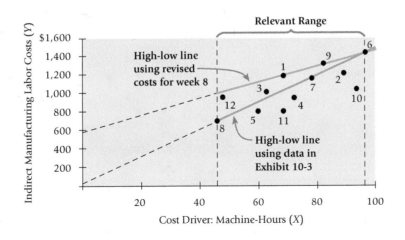

Relevant Range

Indirect Manufacturing Labor Costs (Y)

High-low line using revised costs for week 8

High-low line using data in Exhibit 10-3

Cost Driver: Machine-Hours (X)

Exhibit 5

High-Low Method for Weekly Indirect Manufacturing Labor Costs and Machine-Hours for Elegant Rugs

Regression Analysis Method

Regression analysis is a statistical method that measures the average amount of change in the dependent variable associated with a unit change in one or more independent variables. In the Elegant Rugs example, the dependent variable is total indirect manufacturing labor costs. The independent variable, or cost driver, is number of machine-hours. **Simple regression** analysis estimates the relationship between the dependent variable and *one* independent variable. **Multiple regression** analysis estimates the relationship between the dependent variable and *two or more* independent variables. Multiple regression analysis for Elegant Rugs might use as the independent variables, or cost drivers, number of machine-hours and number of batches. The appendix to this chapter will explore simple regression and multiple regression in more detail.

In later sections, we will illustrate how Excel performs the calculations associated with regression analysis. The following discussion emphasizes how managers interpret and use the output from Excel to make critical strategic decisions. Exhibit 6 shows the line developed using regression analysis that best fits the data in columns B and C of Exhibit 3. Excel estimates the cost function to be

$$y = \$300.98 + \$10.31X$$

The regression line in Exhibit 6 is derived using the least-squares technique. The least-squares technique determines the regression line by minimizing the sum of the squared vertical differences from the data points (the various points in the graph) to the regression line. The vertical difference, called the **residual term**, measures the distance between actual cost and estimated cost for each observation of the cost driver. Exhibit 6 shows the residual term for the week 1 data. The line from the observation to the regression line is drawn perpendicular to the horizontal axis, or *x*-axis. The smaller the residual terms, the better the fit between actual cost observations and estimated costs. *Goodness of fit* indicates the strength of the relationship between the cost driver and costs. The regression line in Exhibit 6 rises from left to right. The positive slope of this line and small residual terms indicate that, on average, indirect manufacturing labor costs increase as the number of machine-hours increases. The vertical dashed lines in Exhibit 6 indicate the relevant range, the range within which the cost function applies.

Instructors and students who want to explore the technical details of estimating the least-squares regression line, can go to the appendix to this chapter and return to this point without any loss of continuity.

The estimate of the slope coefficient, *b*, indicates that indirect manufacturing labor costs vary at the average amount of $10.31 for every machine-hour used within the relevant range. Management can use the regression equation when budgeting for future indirect manufacturing labor costs. For instance, if 90 machine-hours are budgeted for the upcoming week, the predicted indirect manufacturing labor costs would be

$$y = \$300.98 + (\$10.31 \text{ per machine-hour} \times 90 \text{ machine-hours}) = \$1,228.88$$

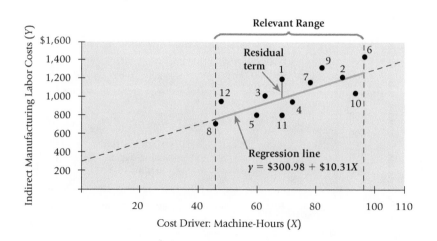

Exhibit 6

Regression Model for Weekly Indirect Manufacturing Labor Costs and Machine-Hours for Elegant Rugs

306

As we have already mentioned, the regression method is more accurate than the high-low method because the regression equation estimates costs using information from all observations, whereas the high-low equation uses information from only two observations. The inaccuracies of the high-low method can mislead managers. Consider the high-low method equation in the preceding section, y = \$23.68 + \$14.92 per machine-hour × Number of machine-hours. For 90 machine-hours, the predicted weekly cost based on the high-low method equation is \$23.68 + (\$14.92 per machine-hour × 90 machine-hours) = \$1,366.48. Suppose that for 7 weeks over the next 12-week period, Elegant Rugs runs its machines for 90 hours each week. Assume average indirect manufacturing labor costs for those 7 weeks are \$1,300. Based on the high-low method prediction of \$1,366.48, Elegant Rugs would conclude it has performed well because actual costs are less than predicted costs. But comparing the \$1,300 performance with the more-accurate \$1,228.88 prediction of the regression model tells a much different story and would probably prompt Elegant Rugs to search for ways to improve its cost performance.

Accurate cost estimation helps managers predict future costs and evaluate the success of cost-reduction initiatives. Suppose the manager at Elegant Rugs is interested in evaluating whether recent strategic decisions that led to changes in the production process and resulted in the data in Exhibit 3 have reduced indirect manufacturing labor costs, such as supervision, maintenance, and quality control. Using data on number of machine-hours used and indirect manufacturing labor costs of the previous process (not shown here), the manager estimates the regression equation,

$$y = \$546.26 + (\$15.86 \text{ per machine-hour} \times \text{Number of machine-hours})$$

The constant (\$300.98 versus \$545.26) and the slope coefficient (\$10.31 versus \$15.86) are both smaller for the new process relative to the old process. It appears that the new process has decreased indirect manufacturing labor costs.

Evaluating Cost Drivers of the Estimated Cost Function

How does a company determine the best cost driver when estimating a cost function? In many cases, the choice of a cost driver is aided substantially by understanding both operations and cost accounting.

To see why the understanding of operations is needed, consider the costs to maintain and repair metal-cutting machines at Helix Corporation, a manufacturer of treadmills. Helix schedules repairs and maintenance at a time when production is at a low level to avoid having to take machines out of service when they are needed most. An analysis of the monthly data will then show high repair costs in months of low production and low repair costs in months of high production. Someone unfamiliar with operations might conclude that there is an inverse relationship between production and repair costs. The engineering link between units produced and repair costs, however, is usually clear-cut. Over time, there is a cause-and-effect relationship: the higher the level of production, the higher the repair costs. To estimate the relationship correctly, operating managers and analysts will recognize that repair costs will tend to lag behind periods of high production, and hence, they will use production of prior periods as the cost driver.

In other cases, choosing a cost driver is more subtle and difficult. Consider again indirect manufacturing labor costs at Elegant Rugs. Management believes that both the number of machine-hours and the number of direct manufacturing labor-hours are plausible cost drivers of indirect manufacturing labor costs. However, management is not sure which is the better cost driver. Exhibit 7 presents weekly data (in Excel) on indirect manufacturing labor costs and number of machine-hours for the most recent 12-week period from Exhibit 3, together with data on the number of direct manufacturing labor-hours for the same period.

Decision Point

What are the steps to estimate a cost function using quantitative analysis?

Learning Objective 5

Describe three criteria used to evaluate and choose cost drivers

. . . economically plausible relationships, goodness of fit, and significant effect of the cost driver on costs

	Home	Insert	Page Layout	Formulas	Data	Review
	A	B	C	D		
1	Week	Original Cost Driver: Machine-Hours	Alternate Cost Driver: Direct Manufacturing Labor-Hours (X)	Indirect Manufacturing Labor Costs (Y)		
2	1	68	30	$ 1,190		
3	2	88	35	1,211		
4	3	62	36	1,004		
5	4	72	20	917		
6	5	60	47	770		
7	6	96	45	1,456		
8	7	78	44	1,180		
9	8	46	38	710		
10	9	82	70	1,316		
11	10	94	30	1,032		
12	11	68	29	752		
13	12	48	38	963		
14	Total	862	462	$12,501		
15						

Choosing Among Cost Drivers

What guidance do the different cost-estimation methods provide for choosing among cost drivers? The industrial engineering method relies on analyzing physical relationships between cost drivers and costs, relationships that are difficult to specify in this case. The conference method and the account analysis method use subjective assessments to choose a cost driver and to estimate the fixed and variable components of the cost function. In these cases, managers must rely on their best judgment. Managers cannot use these methods to test and try alternative cost drivers. The major advantages of quantitative methods are that they are objective—a given data set and estimation method result in a unique estimated cost function—and managers can use them to evaluate different cost drivers. We use the regression analysis approach to illustrate how to evaluate different cost drivers.

First, the cost analyst at Elegant Rugs enters data in columns C and D of Exhibit 7 in Excel and estimates the following regression equation of indirect manufacturing labor costs based on number of direct manufacturing labor-hours:

$$y = \$744.67 + \$7.72X$$

Exhibit 8 shows the plot of the data points for number of direct manufacturing labor-hours and indirect manufacturing labor costs, and the regression line that best fits the data. Recall that Exhibit 6 shows the corresponding graph when number of machine-hours is the cost driver. To decide which of the two cost drivers Elegant Rugs should choose, the analyst compares the machine-hour regression equation and the direct manufacturing labor-hour regression equation. There are three criteria used to make this evaluation.

1. **Economic plausibility.** Both cost drivers are economically plausible. However, in the state-of-the-art, highly automated production environment at Elegant Rugs, managers familiar with the operations believe that costs such as machine maintenance are likely to be more closely related to number of machine-hours used than to number of direct manufacturing labor-hours used.

2. **Goodness of fit.** Compare Exhibits 6 and 8. The vertical differences between actual costs and predicted costs are much smaller for the machine-hours regression than for the direct manufacturing labor-hours regression. Number of machine-hours used, therefore, has a stronger relationship—or goodness of fit—with indirect manufacturing labor costs.

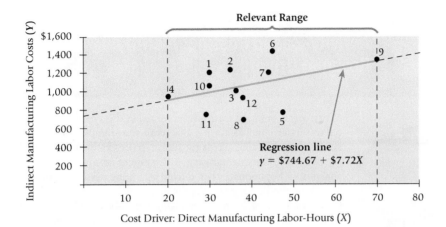

Exhibit 8

Regression Model for
Weekly Indirect
Manufacturing Labor
Costs and Direct
Manufacturing Labor-
Hours for Elegant Rugs

3. **Significance of independent variable.** Again compare Exhibits 6 and 8 (both of which have been drawn to roughly the same scale). The machine-hours regression line has a steep slope relative to the slope of the direct manufacturing labor-hours regression line. *For the same (or more) scatter of observations about the line (goodness of fit), a flat, or slightly sloped regression line indicates a weak relationship between the cost driver and costs.* In our example, changes in direct manufacturing labor-hours appear to have a small influence or effect on indirect manufacturing labor costs.

Based on this evaluation, managers at Elegant Rugs select number of machine-hours as the cost driver and use the cost function y = $300.98 + ($10.31 per machine-hour × Number of machine-hours) to predict future indirect manufacturing labor costs.

Instructors and students who want to explore how regression analysis techniques can be used to choose among different cost drivers can go to the appendix to this chapter and return to this point without any loss of continuity.

Why is choosing the correct cost driver to estimate indirect manufacturing labor costs important? Because identifying the wrong drivers or misestimating cost functions can lead management to incorrect (and costly) decisions along a variety of dimensions. Consider the following strategic decision that management at Elegant Rugs must make. The company is thinking of introducing a new style of carpet that, from a manufacturing standpoint, is similar to the carpets it has manufactured in the past. Prices are set by the market and sales of 650 square yards of this carpet are expected each week. Management estimates 72 machine-hours and 21 direct manufacturing labor-hours would be required per week to produce the 650 square yards of carpet needed. Using the machine-hour regression equation, Elegant Rugs would predict indirect manufacturing labor costs of y = $300.98 + ($10.31 per machine-hour × 72 machine-hours) = $1,043.30. If it used direct manufacturing labor-hours as the cost driver, it would incorrectly predict costs of $744.67 + ($7.72 per labor-hour × 21 labor-hours) = $906.79. If Elegant Rugs chose similarly incorrect cost drivers for other indirect costs as well and systematically underestimated costs, it would conclude that the costs of manufacturing the new style of carpet would be low and basically fixed (fixed because the regression line is nearly flat). But the actual costs driven by number of machine-hours used and other correct cost drivers would be higher. By failing to identify the proper cost drivers, management would be misled into believing the new style of carpet would be more profitable than it actually is. It might decide to introduce the new style of carpet, whereas if Elegant identifies the correct cost driver it might decide not to introduce the new carpet.

Incorrectly estimating the cost function would also have repercussions for cost management and cost control. Suppose number of direct manufacturing labor-hours were used as the cost driver, and actual indirect manufacturing labor costs for the new carpet were $970. Actual costs would then be higher than the predicted costs of $906.79. Management would feel compelled to find ways to cut costs. In fact, on the basis of the preferred machine-hour cost driver, the plant would have actual costs lower than the $1,043.30 predicted costs—a performance that management should seek to replicate, not change!

Concepts in Action

Activity-Based Costing: Identifying Cost and Revenue Drivers

Kristoffer Tripplaar/Alamy Images

Many cost estimation methods presented in this chapter are essential to service, manufacturing, and retail-sector implementations of activity-based costing across the globe. To determine the cost of an activity in the banking industry, ABC systems often rely on expert analyses and opinions gathered from operating personnel (the conference method). For example, the loan department staff at the Co-operative Bank in the United Kingdom subjectively estimate the costs of the loan processing activity and the quantity of the related cost driver—the number of loans processed, a batch-level cost driver, as distinguished from the amount of the loans, an output unit-level cost driver—to derive the cost of processing a loan.

Elsewhere in the United Kingdom, the City of London police force uses input-output relationships (the industrial engineering method) to identify cost drivers and the cost of an activity. Using a surveying methodology, officials can determine the total costs associated with responding to house robberies, dealing with burglaries, and filling out police reports. In the United States, the Boeing Commercial Airplane Group's Wichita Division used detailed analyses of its commercial airplane-manufacturing methods to support make/buy decisions for complex parts required in airplane assembly. The industrial engineering method is also used by U.S. government agencies such as the U.S. Postal Service to determine the cost of each post office transaction and the U.S. Patent and Trademark Office to identify the costs of each patent examination.

Regression analysis is another helpful tool for determining the cost drivers of activities. Consider how fuel service retailers (that is, gas stations with convenience stores) identify the principal cost driver for labor within their operations. Two possible cost drivers are gasoline sales and convenience store sales. Gasoline sales are batch-level activities because payment transactions occur only once for each gasoline purchase, regardless of the volume of gasoline purchased; whereas convenience store sales are output unit-level activities that vary based on the amount of food, drink, and other products sold. Fuel service retailers generally use convenience store sales as the basis for assigning labor costs because multiple regression analyses confirm that convenience store sales, not gasoline sales, are the major cost driver of labor within their operations.

While popular, these are not the only methods used to evaluate cost drivers. If you recall from chapter five, Charles Schwab is one of the growing number of companies using time-driven activity based costing, which uses time as the cost driver. At Citigroup, the company's internal technology infrastructure group uses time to better manage the labor capacity required to provide reliable, secure, and cost effective technology services to about 60 Citigroup business units around the world.

The trend of using activity-based costing to identify cost and revenue drivers also extends into emerging areas. For example, the U.S. government allocated $19 billion in 2009 to support the adoption of electronic health records. Using the input-output method, many health clinics and doctor's offices are leveraging activity-based costing to identify the cost of adopting this new health information technology tool.

Sources: Barton, T., and J. MacArthur. 2003. Activity-based costing and predatory pricing: The case of the retail industry. *Management Accounting Quarterly* (Spring); Carter, T., A. Sedaghat, and T. Williams. 1998. How ABC changed the post office. *Management Accounting,* (February); The Cooperative Bank. Harvard Business School. Case No. N9-195-196; Federowicz, M., M. Grossman, B. Hayes, and J. Riggs. 2010. A tutorial on activity-based costing of electronic health records. *Quality Management in Health Care* (January–March); Kaplan, Robert, and Steven Anderson. 2008. *Time-driven activity-based costing: A simpler and more powerful path to higher profits.* Boston: Harvard Business School Publishing; Leapman, B. 2006. Police spend £500m filling in forms. *The Daily Telegraph,* January 22; Paduano, Rocco, and Joel Cutcher-Gershenfeld. 2001. Boeing Commercial Airplane Group Wichita Division (Boeing Co.). MIT Labor Aerospace Research Agenda Case Study. Cambridge, MA: MIT; Peckenpaugh, J. 2002. Teaching the ABCs. *Government Executive,* April 1; The United Kingdom Home Office. 2007. *The police service national ABC model: Manual of guidance.* London: Her Majesty's Stationary Office.

Cost Drivers and Activity-Based Costing

Activity-based costing (ABC) systems focus on individual activities—such as product design, machine setup, materials handling, distribution, and customer service—as the fundamental cost objects. To implement ABC systems, managers must identify a cost driver for each activity. For example, using methods described in this chapter, the manager must decide whether the number of loads moved or the weight of loads moved is the cost driver of materials-handling costs.

To choose the cost driver and use it to estimate the cost function in our materials-handling example, the manager collects data on materials-handling costs and the quantities of the two competing cost drivers over a reasonably long period. Why a long period? Because in the short run, materials-handling costs may be fixed and, therefore, will not vary with changes in the level of the cost driver. In the long run, however, there is a clear cause-and-effect relationship between materials-handling costs and the cost driver. Suppose number of loads moved is the cost driver of materials-handling costs. Increases in the number of loads moved will require more materials-handling labor and equipment; decreases will result in equipment being sold and labor being reassigned to other tasks.

ABC systems have a great number and variety of cost drivers and cost pools. That means ABC systems require many cost relationships to be estimated. In estimating the cost function for each cost pool, the manager must pay careful attention to the cost hierarchy. For example, if a cost is a batch-level cost such as setup cost, the manager must only consider batch-level cost drivers like number of setup-hours. In some cases, the costs in a cost pool may have more than one cost driver from different levels of the cost hierarchy. In the Elegant Rugs example, the cost drivers for indirect manufacturing labor costs could be machine-hours and number of production batches of carpet manufactured. Furthermore, it may be difficult to subdivide the indirect manufacturing labor costs into two cost pools and to measure the costs associated with each cost driver. In these cases, companies use multiple regression to estimate costs based on more than one independent variable. The appendix to this chapter discusses multiple regression in more detail.

As the Concepts in Action feature illustrates, managers implementing ABC systems use a variety of methods—industrial engineering, conference, and regression analysis—to estimate slope coefficients. In making these choices, managers trade off level of detail, accuracy, feasibility, and costs of estimating cost functions.

Decision Point

How should a company evaluate and choose cost drivers?

Nonlinear Cost Functions

In practice, cost functions are not always linear. A **nonlinear cost function** is a cost function for which the graph of total costs (based on the level of a single activity) is not a straight line within the relevant range. To see what a nonlinear cost function looks like, return to Exhibit 2. The relevant range is currently set at 20,000 to 65,000 snowboards. But if we extend the relevant range to encompass the region from 0 to 80,000 snowboards produced, it is evident that the cost function over this expanded range is graphically represented by a line that is not straight.

Consider another example. Economies of scale in advertising may enable an advertising agency to produce double the number of advertisements for less than double the costs. Even direct material costs are not always linear variable costs because of quantity discounts on direct material purchases. As shown in Exhibit 9, Panel A, total direct material costs rise as the units of direct materials purchased increase. But, because of quantity discounts, these costs rise more slowly (as indicated by the slope coefficient) as the units of direct materials purchased increase. This cost function has $b = \$25$ per unit for 1–1,000 units purchased, $b = \$15$ per unit for 1,001–2,000 units purchased, and $b = \$10$ per unit for 2,001–3,000 units purchased. The direct material cost per unit falls at each price break—that is, the cost per unit decreases with larger purchase orders. If managers are interested in understanding cost behavior over the relevant range from 1 to 3,000 units, the cost function is nonlinear—not a straight line. If, however, managers are only interested in understanding cost behavior over a more narrow relevant range (for example, from 1 to 1,000 units), the cost function is linear.

Step cost functions are also examples of nonlinear cost functions. A **step cost function** is a cost function in which the cost remains the same over various ranges of the level of activity, but the cost increases by discrete amounts—that is, increases in steps—as the level of activity increases from one range to the next. Panel B in Exhibit 9 shows a *step variable-cost function*, a step cost function in which cost remains the same over *narrow* ranges of the level of activity in each relevant range. Panel B presents the relationship between units of production and setup costs. The pattern is a step cost function because setup costs are

Learning Objective 6

Explain nonlinear cost functions

. . . graph of cost function is not a straight line, for example, because of quantity discounts or costs changing in steps

in particular those arising from learning curve effects

. . . either cumulative average-time learning, where cumulative average time per unit declines by a constant percentage, as units produced double

. . . or incremental unit-time learning, in which incremental time to produce last unit declines by constant percentage, as units produced double

Exhibit 9   Examples of Nonlinear Cost Functions

PANEL A:
Effects of Quantity
Discounts on Slope
Coefficient of Direct
Material Cost Function

PANEL B:
Step Variable-Cost
Function

PANEL C:
Step Fixed-Cost
Function

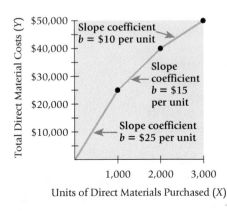

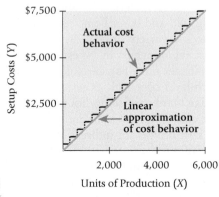

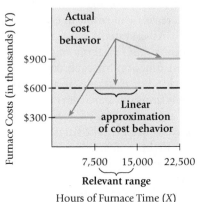

related to each production batch started. If the relevant range is considered to be from 0 to 6,000 production units, the cost function is nonlinear. However, as shown by the blue line in Panel B, managers often approximate step variable costs with a continuously-variable cost function. This type of step cost pattern also occurs when production inputs such as materials-handling labor, supervision, and process engineering labor are acquired in discrete quantities but used in fractional quantities.

Panel C in Exhibit 9 shows a *step fixed-cost function* for Crofton Steel, a company that operates large heat-treatment furnaces to harden steel parts. Looking at Panel C and Panel B, you can see that the main difference between a step variable-cost function and a step fixed-cost function is that the cost in a step fixed-cost function remains the same over *wide* ranges of the activity in each relevant range. The ranges indicate the number of furnaces being used (each furnace costs $300,000). The cost increases from one range to the next higher range when the hours of furnace time needed require the use of another furnace. The relevant range of 7,500 to 15,000 hours of furnace time indicates that the company expects to operate with two furnaces at a cost of $600,000. Management considers the cost of operating furnaces as a fixed cost within this relevant range of operation. However, if the relevant range is considered to be from 0 to 22,500 hours, the cost function is nonlinear: The graph in Panel C is not a single straight line; it is three broken lines.

Learning Curves

Nonlinear cost functions also result from learning curves. A **learning curve** is a function that measures how labor-hours per unit decline as units of production increase because workers are learning and becoming better at their jobs. Managers use learning curves to predict how labor-hours, or labor costs, will increase as more units are produced.

The aircraft-assembly industry first documented the effect that learning has on efficiency. In general, as workers become more familiar with their tasks, their efficiency improves. Managers learn how to improve the scheduling of work shifts and how to operate the plant more efficiently. As a result of improved efficiency, unit costs decrease as productivity increases, and the unit-cost function behaves nonlinearly. These nonlinearities must be considered when estimating and predicting unit costs.

Managers have extended the learning-curve notion to other business functions in the value chain, such as marketing, distribution, and customer service, and to costs other than labor costs. The term *experience curve* describes this broader application of the learning curve. An **experience curve** is a function that measures the decline in cost per unit in various business functions of the value chain—marketing, distribution, and so on—as the amount of these activities increases. For companies such as Dell Computer, Wal-Mart, and McDonald's, learning curves and experience curves are key elements of their strategies. These companies use learning curves and experience curves to reduce costs and increase customer satisfaction, market share, and profitability.

We now describe two learning-curve models: the cumulative average-time learning model and the incremental unit-time learning model.

Cumulative Average-Time Learning Model

In the **cumulative average-time learning model**, cumulative average time per unit declines by a constant percentage each time the cumulative quantity of units produced doubles. Consider Rayburn Corporation, a radar systems manufacturer. Rayburn has an 80% learning curve. The 80% means that when the quantity of units produced is doubled from X to 2X, cumulative average time *per unit* for 2X units is 80% of cumulative average time *per unit* for X units. Average time per unit has dropped by 20% (100% − 80%). Exhibit 10 is an Excel spreadsheet showing the calculations for the cumulative average-time learning model for Rayburn Corporation. Note that as the number of units produced doubles from 1 to 2 in column A, cumulative average time per unit declines from 100 hours to 80% of 100 hours (0.80 × 100 hours = 80 hours) in column B. As the number of units doubles from 2 to 4, cumulative average time per unit declines to 80% of 80 hours = 64 hours, and so on. To obtain the cumulative total time in column D, multiply cumulative average time per unit by the cumulative number of units produced. For example, to produce 4 cumulative units would require 256 labor-hours (4 units × 64 cumulative average labor-hours per unit).

Exhibit 10   Cumulative Average-Time Learning Model for Rayburn Corporation

Incremental Unit-Time Learning Model

In the **incremental unit-time learning model,** incremental time needed to produce the last unit declines by a constant percentage each time the cumulative quantity of units produced doubles. Again, consider Rayburn Corporation and an 80% learning curve. The 80% here means that when the quantity of units produced is doubled from X to $2X$, the time needed to produce the last unit when $2X$ total units are produced is 80% of the time needed to produce the last unit when X total units are produced. Exhibit 11 is an Excel spreadsheet showing the calculations for the incremental unit-time learning model for Rayburn Corporation based on an 80% learning curve. Note how when units produced double from 2 to 4 in column A, the time to produce unit 4 (the last unit when 4 units are produced) is 64 hours in column B, which is 80% of the 80 hours needed to produce unit 2 (the last unit when 2 units are produced). We obtain the cumulative total time in column D by summing individual unit times in column B. For example, to produce 4 cumulative units would require 314.21 labor-hours (100.00 + 80.00 + 70.21 + 64.00).

Exhibit 12 presents graphs using Excel for the cumulative average-time learning model (using data from Exhibit 10) and the incremental unit-time learning model (using data from Exhibit 11). Panel A graphically illustrates cumulative average time per unit as a function of cumulative units produced for each model (column A in Exhibit 10 or 11). The curve for the cumulative average-time learning model is plotted using the data from Exhibit 10, column B, while the curve for the incremental unit-time learning model is plotted using the data from Exhibit 11, column E. Panel B graphically illustrates cumulative total labor-hours, again as a function of cumulative units produced for each model. The curve for the cumulative average-time learning model is plotted using the data from Exhibit 10, column D, while that for the incremental unit-time learning model is plotted using the data from Exhibit 11, column D.

Exhibit 11	Incremental Unit-Time Learning Model for Rayburn Corporation

	A	B	C	D	E
1	Incremental Unit-Time Learning Model for Rayburn Corporation				
3		80% Learning Curve			
5	Cumulative	Individual Unit Time		Cumulative	Cumulative
6	Number	for Xth Unit (y)*:		Total Time:	Average Time
7	of Units (X)	Labor-Hours		Labor-Hours	per Unit:
8					Labor-Hours
10					E = Col D ÷ Col A
12	1	100.00		100.00	100.00
13	2	80.00	= (100 × 0.8)	180.00	90.00
14	3	70.21		250.21	83.40
15	4	64.00	= (80 × 0.8)	314.21	78.55
16	5	59.56		373.77	74.75
17	6	56.17		429.94	71.66
18	7	53.45		483.39	69.06
19	8	51.20	= (64 × 0.8)	534.59	66.82
20	9	49.29		583.89	64.88
21	10	47.65		631.54	63.15
22	11	46.21		677.75	61.61
23	12	44.93		722.68	60.22
24	13	43.79		766.47	58.96
25	14	42.76		809.23	57.80
26	15	41.82		851.05	56.74
27	16	40.96	= (51.2 × 0.8)	892.01	55.75

D14 = D13 + B14
= 180.00 + 70.21

*The mathematical relationship underlying the incremental unit-time learning model is as follows:
$$y = aX^b$$
where y = Time (labor-hours) taken to produce the last single unit
X = Cumulative number of units produced
a = Time (labor-hours) required to produce the first unit
b = Factor used to calculate incremental unit time to produce units
$$= \frac{\ln (\text{learning-curve \% in decimal form})}{\ln 2}$$
For an 80% learning curve, $b = \ln 0.8 \div \ln 2 = -0.2231 \div 0.6931 = -0.3219$
For example, when $X = 3$, $a = 100$, $b = -0.3219$,
$$y = 100 \times 3^{-0.3219} = 70.21 \text{ labor-hours}$$
The cumulative total time when $X = 3$ is $100 + 80 + 70.21 = 250.21$ labor-hours. Numbers in the table may not be exact because of rounding.

Exhibit 12   Plots for Cumulative Average-Time Learning Model and Incremental Unit-Time Learning Model for Rayburn Corporation

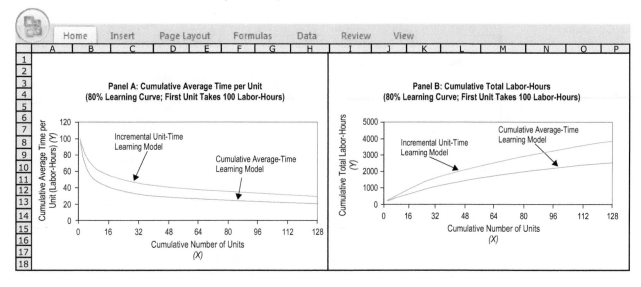

The incremental unit-time learning model predicts a higher cumulative total time to produce 2 or more units than the cumulative average-time learning model, assuming the same learning rate for both models. That is, in Exhibit 12, Panel B, the graph for the 80% incremental unit-time learning model lies above the graph for the 80% cumulative average-time learning model. If we compare the results in Exhibit 10 (column D) with the results in Exhibit 11 (column D), to produce 4 cumulative units, the 80% incremental unit-time learning model predicts 314.21 labor-hours versus 256.00 labor-hours predicted by the 80% cumulative average-time learning model. That's because under the cumulative average-time learning model *average labor-hours needed to produce all 4 units* is 64 hours; the labor-hour amount needed to produce unit 4 is much less than 64 hours—it is 45.37 hours (see Exhibit 10). Under the incremental unit-time learning model, the labor-hour amount needed to produce unit 4 is 64 hours, and the labor-hours needed to produce the first 3 units are more than 64 hours, so average time needed to produce all 4 units is more than 64 hours.

How do managers choose which model and what percent learning curve to use? It is important to recognize that managers make their choices on a case-by-case basis. For example, if the behavior of manufacturing labor-hour usage as production levels increase follows a pattern like the one predicted by the 80% learning curve cumulative average-time learning model, then the 80% learning curve cumulative average-time learning model should be used. Engineers, plant managers, and workers are good sources of information on the amount and type of learning actually occurring as production increases. Plotting this information and estimating the model that best fits the data is helpful in selecting the appropriate model.[2]

Incorporating Learning-Curve Effects into Prices and Standards

How do companies use learning curves? Consider the data in Exhibit 10 for the cumulative average-time learning model at Rayburn Corporation. Suppose variable costs subject to learning effects consist of direct manufacturing labor, at $20 per hour, and related overhead, at $30 per direct manufacturing labor-hour. Managers should predict the costs shown in Exhibit 13.

These data show that the effects of the learning curve could have a major influence on decisions. For example, managers at Rayburn Corporation might set an extremely low selling price on its radar systems to generate high demand. As its production increases to meet this growing demand, cost per unit drops. Rayburn "rides the product down the

---

[2] For details, see C. Bailey, "Learning Curve Estimation of Production Costs and Labor-Hours Using a Free Excel Add-In," *Management Accounting Quarterly*, (Summer 2000: 25–31). Free software for estimating learning curves is available at Dr. Bailey's Web site, www.profbailey.com.

	Home	Insert	Page Layout	Formulas	Data	Review	View	
	A	B	C	D	E		F
1		**Cumulative**					
2	**Cumulative**	**Average Time**	**Cumulative**	**Cumulative Costs**			**Additions to**
3	**Number of**	**per Unit:**	**Total Time:**	**at $50 per**			**Cumulative**
4	**Units**	**Labor-Hours**[a]	**Labor-Hours**[a]	**Labor-Hour**			**Costs**
5	1	100.00	100.00	$ 5,000	(100.00 × $50)		$ 5,000
6	2	80.00	160.00	8,000	(160.00 × $50)		3,000
7	4	64.00	256.00	12,800	(256.00 × $50)		4,800
8	8	51.20	409.60	20,480	(409.60 × $50)		7,680
9	16	40.96	655.36	32,768	(655.36 × $50)		12,288
10							
11	[a]Based on the cumulative average-time learning model. See Exhibit 10-10 for the computations						
12	of these amounts.						

learning curve" as it establishes a larger market share. Although it may have earned little operating income on its first unit sold—it may actually have lost money on that unit—Rayburn earns more operating income per unit as output increases.

Alternatively, subject to legal and other considerations, Rayburn's managers might set a low price on just the final 8 units. After all, the total labor and related overhead costs per unit for these final 8 units are predicted to be only $12,288 ($32,768 – $20,480). On these final 8 units, the $1,536 cost per unit ($12,288 ÷ 8 units) is much lower than the $5,000 cost per unit of the first unit produced.

Many companies, such as Pizza Hut and Home Depot, incorporate learning-curve effects when evaluating performance. The Nissan Motor Company expects its workers to learn and improve on the job and evaluates performance accordingly. It sets assembly-labor efficiency standards for new models of cars after taking into account the learning that will occur as more units are produced.

The learning-curve models examined in Exhibits 10 to 13 assume that learning is driven by a single variable (production output). Other models of learning have been developed (by companies such as Analog Devices and Hewlett-Packard) that focus on how quality—rather than manufacturing labor-hours—will change over time, regardless of whether more units are produced. Studies indicate that factors other than production output, such as job rotation and organizing workers into teams, contribute to learning that improves quality.

Data Collection and Adjustment Issues

The ideal database for estimating cost functions quantitatively has two characteristics:

1. **The database should contain numerous reliably measured observations of the cost driver (the independent variable) and the related costs (the dependent variable).** Errors in measuring the costs and the cost driver are serious. They result in inaccurate estimates of the effect of the cost driver on costs.

2. **The database should consider many values spanning a wide range for the cost driver.** Using only a few values of the cost driver that are grouped closely considers too small a segment of the relevant range and reduces the confidence in the estimates obtained.

Unfortunately, cost analysts typically do not have the advantage of working with a database having both characteristics. This section outlines some frequently encountered data problems and steps the cost analyst can take to overcome these problems.

1. The time period for measuring the dependent variable (for example, machine-lubricant costs) does not properly match the period for measuring the cost driver. This problem often arises when accounting records are not kept on the accrual basis. Consider a cost function with machine-lubricant costs as the dependent variable and number of machine-hours as the cost driver. Assume that the lubricant is purchased sporadically

and stored for later use. Records maintained on the basis of lubricants purchased will indicate little lubricant costs in many months and large lubricant costs in other months. These records present an obviously inaccurate picture of what is actually taking place. The analyst should use accrual accounting to measure cost of lubricants consumed to better match costs with the machine-hours cost driver in this example.

2. Fixed costs are allocated as if they are variable. For example, costs such as depreciation, insurance, or rent may be allocated to products to calculate cost per unit of output. *The danger is to regard these costs as variable rather than as fixed. They seem to be variable because of the allocation methods used.* To avoid this problem, the analyst should carefully distinguish fixed costs from variable costs and not treat allocated fixed cost per unit as a variable cost.

3. Data are either not available for all observations or are not uniformly reliable. Missing cost observations often arise from a failure to record a cost or from classifying a cost incorrectly. For example, marketing costs may be understated because costs of sales visits to customers may be incorrectly recorded as customer-service costs. Recording data manually rather than electronically tends to result in a higher percentage of missing observations and erroneously entered observations. Errors also arise when data on cost drivers originate outside the internal accounting system. For example, the accounting department may obtain data on testing-hours for medical instruments from the company's manufacturing department and data on number of items shipped to customers from the distribution department. One or both of these departments might not keep accurate records. To minimize these problems, the cost analyst should design data collection reports that regularly and routinely obtain the required data and should follow up immediately whenever data are missing.

4. Extreme values of observations occur from errors in recording costs (for example, a misplaced decimal point), from nonrepresentative periods (for example, from a period in which a major machine breakdown occurred or from a period in which a delay in delivery of materials from an international supplier curtailed production), or from observations outside the relevant range. Analysts should adjust or eliminate unusual observations before estimating a cost relationship.

5. There is no homogeneous relationship between the cost driver and the individual cost items in the dependent variable-cost pool. A homogeneous relationship exists when each activity whose costs are included in the dependent variable has the same cost driver. In this case, a single cost function can be estimated. As discussed in Step 2 for estimating a cost function using quantitative analysis, when the cost driver for each activity is different, separate cost functions (each with its own cost driver) should be estimated for each activity. Alternatively, the cost function should be estimated with more than one independent variable using multiple regression.

6. The relationship between the cost driver and the cost is not stationary. That is, the underlying process that generated the observations has not remained stable over time. For example, the relationship between number of machine-hours and manufacturing overhead costs is unlikely to be stationary when the data cover a period in which new technology was introduced. One way to see if the relationship is stationary is to split the sample into two parts and estimate separate cost relationships—one for the period before the technology was introduced and one for the period after the technology was introduced. Then, if the estimated coefficients for the two periods are similar, the analyst can pool the data to estimate a single cost relationship. When feasible, pooling data provides a larger data set for the estimation, which increases confidence in the cost predictions being made.

7. Inflation has affected costs, the cost driver, or both. For example, inflation may cause costs to change even when there is no change in the level of the cost driver. To study the underlying cause-and-effect relationship between the level of the cost driver and costs, the analyst should remove purely inflationary price effects from the data by dividing each cost by the price index on the date the cost was incurred.

In many cases, a cost analyst must expend considerable effort to reduce the effect of these problems before estimating a cost function on the basis of past data.

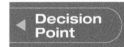

Decision Point

What are the common data problems a company must watch for when estimating costs?

Problem for Self-Study

The Helicopter Division of GLD, Inc., is examining helicopter assembly costs at its Indiana plant. It has received an initial order for eight of its new land-surveying helicopters. GLD can adopt one of two methods of assembling the helicopters:

	A	B	C	D	E
	Home Insert Page Layout Formulas Data Review View				
	A	B	C	D	E
1		Labor-Intensive Assembly Method		Machine-Intensive Assembly Method	
2	Direct material cost per helicopter	$ 40,000		$36,000	
3	Direct-assembly labor time for first helicopter	2,000	labor-hours	800	labor-hours
4	Learning curve for assembly labor time per helicopter	85%	cumulative average time*	90%	incremental unit time**
5	Direct-assembly labor cost	$ 30	per hour	$ 30	per hour
6	Equipment-related indirect manufacturing cost	$ 12	per direct-assembly labor-hour	$ 45	per direct-assembly labor-hour
7	Material-handling-related indirect manufacturing cost	50%	of direct material cost	50%	of direct material cost
8					
9					
10	*Using the formula (p. 359), for an 85% learning curve, $b = \dfrac{\ln 0.85}{\ln 2} = \dfrac{-0.162519}{0.693147} = -0.234465$				
11					
12					
13					
14					
15	**Using the formula (p. 360), for a 90% learning curve, $b = \dfrac{\ln 0.90}{\ln 2} = \dfrac{-0.105361}{0.693147} = -0.152004$				
16					
17					

Required

1. How many direct-assembly labor-hours are required to assemble the first eight helicopters under (a) the labor-intensive method and (b) the machine-intensive method?
2. What is the total cost of assembling the first eight helicopters under (a) the labor-intensive method and (b) the machine-intensive method?

Solution

1. a. The following calculations show the labor-intensive assembly method based on an 85% cumulative average-time learning model (using Excel):

	G	H	I	J	K
	Home Insert Page Layout Formulas Data Review View				
	G	H	I	J	K
1	Cumulative	Cumulative		Cumulative	Individual
2	Number	Average Time		Total Time:	time for
3	of Units	per Unit (y):		Labor-Hours	Xth unit:
4		Labor-Hours			Labor-Hours
5				Col J = Col G × Col H	
6	1	2,000		2,000	2,000
7	2	1,700	(2,000 × 0.85)	3,400	1,400
8	3	1,546		4,637	1,237
9	4	1,445	(1,700 × 0.85)	5,780	1,143
10	5	1,371		6,857	1,077
11	6	1,314		7,884	1,027
12	7	1,267		8,871	987
13	8	1,228.25	(1,445 × 0.85)	9,826	955
14					

Cumulative average-time per unit for the Xth unit in column H is calculated as $y = aX^b$; see Exhibit 10. For example, when $X = 3$, $y = 2{,}000 \times 3^{-0.234465} = 1{,}546$ labor-hours.

b. The following calculations show the machine-intensive assembly method based on a 90% incremental unit-time learning model:

	G	H	I	J	K
	Cumulative	Individual		Cumulative	Cumulative
1					
2	Number	Unit Time		Total Time:	Average Time
3	of Units	for Xth Unit (y):		Labor-Hours	Per Unit:
4		Labor-Hours			Labor-Hours
5					Col K = Col J ÷ Col G
6	1	800		800	800
7	2	720	(800 × 0.9)	1,520	760
8	3	677		2,197	732
9	4	648	(720 × 0.9)	2,845	711
10	5	626		3,471	694
11	6	609		4,081	680
12	7	595		4,676	668
13	8	583	(648 × 0.9)	5,258	657

Individual unit time for the Xth unit in column H is calculated as $y = aX^b$; see Exhibit 11. For example, when $X = 3$, $y = 800 \times 3^{-0.152004} = 677$ labor-hours.

2. Total costs of assembling the first eight helicopters are as follows:

	O	P	Q
1		Labor-Intensive	Machine-Intensive
2		Assembly Method	Assembly Method
3		(using data from part 1a)	(using data from part 1b)
4	Direct materials:		
5	8 helicopters × $40,000; $36,000 per helicopter	$320,000	$288,000
6	Direct-assembly labor:		
7	9,826 hrs.; 5,258 hrs. × $30/hr.	294,780	157,740
8	Indirect manufacturing costs		
9	Equipment related		
10	9,826 hrs. × $12/hr.; 5,258 hrs. × $45/hr.	117,912	236,610
11	Materials-handling related		
12	0.50 × $320,000; $288,000	160,000	144,000
13	Total assembly costs	$892,692	$826,350

The machine-intensive method's assembly costs are $66,342 lower than the labor-intensive method ($892,692 − $826,350).

Decision Points

The following question-and-answer format summarizes the chapter's learning objectives. Each decision presents a key question related to a learning objective. The guidelines are the answer to that question.

Decision	Guidelines
1. What is a linear cost function and what types of cost behavior can it represent?	A linear cost function is a cost function in which, within the relevant range, the graph of total costs based on the level of a single activity is a straight line. Linear cost functions can be described by a constant, a, which represents the estimate of the total cost component that, within the relevant range, does not vary with changes in the level of the activity; and a slope coefficient, b, which represents the estimate of the amount by which total costs change for each unit change in the level of the activity within the relevant range. Three types of linear cost functions are variable, fixed, and mixed (or semivariable).
2. What is the most important issue in estimating a cost function?	The most important issue in estimating a cost function is determining whether a cause-and-effect relationship exists between the level of an activity and the costs related to that level of activity. Only a cause-and-effect relationship—not merely correlation—establishes an economically plausible relationship between the level of an activity and its costs.
3. What are the different methods that can be used to estimate a cost function?	Four methods for estimating cost functions are the industrial engineering method, the conference method, the account analysis method, and the quantitative analysis method (which includes the high-low method and the regression analysis method). If possible, the cost analyst should apply more than one method. Each method is a check on the others.
4. What are the steps to estimate a cost function using quantitative analysis?	There are six steps to estimate a cost function using quantitative analysis: (a) Choose the dependent variable; (b) identify the cost driver; (c) collect data on the dependent variable and the cost driver; (d) plot the data; (e) estimate the cost function; and (f) evaluate the cost driver of the estimated cost function. In most situations, working closely with operations managers, the cost analyst will cycle through these steps several times before identifying an acceptable cost function.
5. How should a company evaluate and choose cost drivers?	Three criteria for evaluating and choosing cost drivers are (a) economic plausibility, (b) goodness of fit, and (c) significance of independent variable.
6. What is a nonlinear cost function and in what ways do learning curves give rise to nonlinearities?	A nonlinear cost function is one in which the graph of total costs based on the level of a single activity is not a straight line within the relevant range. Nonlinear costs can arise because of quantity discounts, step cost functions, and learning-curve effects. With learning curves, labor-hours per unit decline as units of production increase. In the cumulative average-time learning model, cumulative average-time per unit declines by a constant percentage each time the cumulative quantity of units produced doubles. In the incremental unit-time learning model, the time needed to produce the last unit declines by a constant percentage each time the cumulative quantity of units produced doubles.
7. What are the common data problems a company must watch for when estimating costs?	The most difficult task in cost estimation is collecting high-quality, reliably measured data on the costs and the cost driver. Common problems include missing data, extreme values of observations, changes in technology, and distortions resulting from inflation.

Appendix

Regression Analysis

This appendix describes estimation of the regression equation, several commonly used regression statistics, and how to choose among cost functions that have been estimated by regression analysis. We use the data for Elegant Rugs presented in Exhibit 3 and displayed here again for easy reference.

Week	Cost Driver: Machine-Hours (X)	Indirect Manufacturing Labor Costs (Y)
1	68	$ 1,190
2	88	1,211
3	62	1,004
4	72	917
5	60	770
6	96	1,456
7	78	1,180
8	46	710
9	82	1,316
10	94	1,032
11	68	752
12	48	963
Total	862	$12,501

Estimating the Regression Line

The least-squares technique for estimating the regression line minimizes the sum of the squares of the vertical deviations from the data points to the estimated regression line (also called *residual term* in Exhibit 6). The objective is to find the values of *a* and *b* in the linear cost function $y = a + bX$, where *y* is the *predicted* cost value as distinguished from the *observed* cost value, which we denote by Y. We wish to find the numerical values of *a* and *b* that minimize $\Sigma(Y - y)^2$, the sum of the squares of the vertical deviations between Y and y. Generally, these computations are done using software packages such as Excel. For the data in our example,[3] $a = \$300.98$ and $b = \$10.31$, so that the equation of the regression line is $y = \$300.98 + \$10.31X$.

Goodness of Fit

Goodness of fit measures how well the predicted values, y, based on the cost driver, X, match actual cost observations, Y. The regression analysis method computes a measure of goodness of fit, called the **coefficient of determination**. The coefficient of determination (r^2) measures the percentage of variation in Y explained by X (the independent variable).

---

[3] The formulae for *a* and *b* are as follows:

$$a = \frac{(\Sigma Y)(\Sigma X^2) - (\Sigma X)(\Sigma XY)}{n(\Sigma X^2) - (\Sigma X)(\Sigma X)} \text{ and } b = \frac{n(\Sigma XY) - (\Sigma X)(\Sigma Y)}{n(\Sigma X^2) - (\Sigma X)(\Sigma X)}$$

where for the Elegant Rugs data in Exhibit 3,

n = number of data points = 12
ΣX = sum of the given X values = 68 + 88 + ... + 48 = 862
ΣX^2 = sum of squares of the X values = $(68)^2 + (88)^2 + ... + (48)^2 + 4,624 + 7,744 + ... + 2,304 = 64,900$
ΣY = sum of given Y values = 1,190 + 1,211 + ... + 963 = 12,501
ΣXY = sum of the amounts obtained by multiplying each of the given X values by the associated observed
Y value = (68)(1,190) + (88)(1,211) + ... + (48)(963)
= 80,920 + 106,568 + ... + 46,224 = 928,716

$$a = \frac{(12,501)(64,900) - (862)(928,716)}{12(64,900) - (862)(862)} = \$300.98$$

$$b = \frac{12(928,716) - (862)(12,501)}{12(64,900) - (862)(862)} = \$10.31$$

It is more convenient to express the coefficient of determination as 1 minus the proportion of total variance that is *not* explained by the independent variable—that is, 1 minus the ratio of unexplained variation to total variation. The unexplained variance arises because of differences between the actual values, Y, and the predicted values, y, which in the Elegant Rugs example is given by[4]

$$r^2 = 1 - \frac{\text{Unexplained variation}}{\text{Total variation}} = 1 - \frac{\Sigma(Y - y)^2}{\Sigma(Y - \bar{Y})^2} = 1 - \frac{290{,}824}{607{,}699} = 0.52$$

The calculations indicate that r^2 increases as the predicted values, y, more closely approximate the actual observations, Y. The range of r^2 is from 0 (implying no explanatory power) to 1 (implying perfect explanatory power). Generally, an r^2 of 0.30 or higher passes the goodness-of-fit test. However, do not rely exclusively on goodness of fit. It can lead to the indiscriminate inclusion of independent variables that increase r^2 but have no economic plausibility as cost drivers. *Goodness of fit has meaning only if the relationship between the cost drivers and costs is economically plausible.*

An alternative and related way to evaluate goodness of fit is to calculate the *standard error of the regression*. The **standard error of the regression** is the variance of the residuals. It is equal to

$$S = \sqrt{\frac{\Sigma(Y - y)^2}{\text{Degrees of freedom}}} = \sqrt{\frac{\Sigma(Y - y)^2}{n - 2}} = \sqrt{\frac{290{,}824}{12 - 2}} = \$170.54$$

Degrees of freedom equal the number of observations, 12, *minus* the number of coefficients estimated in the regression (in this case two, a and b). On average, actual Y and the predicted value, y, differ by \$170.54. For comparison, $\bar{Y}$, the average value of Y, is \$1,041.75. The smaller the standard error of the regression, the better the fit and the better the predictions for different values of X.

Significance of Independent Variables

Do changes in the economically plausible independent variable result in significant changes in the dependent variable? Or alternatively stated, is the slope coefficient, $b = \$10.31$, of the regression line statistically significant (that is, different from \$0)? Recall, for example, that in the regression of number of machine-hours and indirect manufacturing labor costs in the Elegant Rugs illustration, b is estimated from a sample of 12 weekly observations. The estimate, b, is subject to random factors, as are all sample statistics. That is, a different sample of 12 data points would undoubtedly give a different estimate of b. The **standard error of the estimated coefficient** indicates how much the estimated value, b, is likely to be affected by random factors. The t-value of the b coefficient measures how large the value of the estimated coefficient is relative to its standard error.

The cutoff t-value for making inferences about the b coefficient is a function of the number of degrees of freedom, the significance level, and whether it is a one-sided or two-sided test. A 5% level of significance indicates that there is less than a 5% probability that random factors could have affected the coefficient b. A two-sided test assumes that random factors could have caused the coefficient to be either greater than \$10.31 or less than \$10.31 with equal probability. At a 5% level of significance, this means that there is less than a 2.5% (5% ÷ 2) probability that random factors could have caused the coefficient to be greater than \$10.31 and less than 2.5% probability that random factors could have caused the coefficient to be less than \$10.31. Under the expectation that the coefficient of b is positive, a one-sided test at the 5% level of significance assumes that there is less than 5% probability that random factors would have caused the coefficient to be less than \$10.31. The cutoff t-value at the 5% significance level and 10 degrees of freedom for a two-sided test is 2.228. If there were more observations and 60 degrees of freedom, the cutoff t-value would be 2.00 at a 5% significance level for a two-sided test.

The t-value (called t Stat in the Excel output) for the slope coefficient b is the value of the estimated coefficient, \$10.31 ÷ the standard error of the estimated coefficient \$3.12 = 3.30, which exceeds the cutoff t-value of 2.228. In other words, a relationship exists between the independent variable, machine-hours, and the dependent variable that cannot be attributed to random chance alone. Exhibit 14 shows a convenient format (in Excel) for summarizing the regression results for number of machine-hours and indirect manufacturing labor costs.

---

[4] From footnote 3, $\Sigma Y = 12{,}501$ and $\bar{Y} = 12{,}501 \div 12 = 1{,}041.75$.

$$\Sigma(Y - \bar{Y})^2 = (1{,}190 - 1{,}041.75)^2 + (1{,}211 - 1{,}041.75)^2 + \ldots + (963 - 1{,}041.75)^2 = 607{,}699$$

Each value of X generates a predicted value of y. For example, in week 1, $y = \$300.98 + (\$10.31 \times 68) = \$1002.06$; in week 2, $y = \$300.98 + (\$10.31 \times 88) = \$1{,}208.26$; and in week 12, $y = \$300.98 + (\$10.31 \times 48) = \$795.86$. Comparing the predicted and actual values,

$$\Sigma(Y - y)^2 = (1{,}190 - 1{,}002.06)^2 + (1{,}211 - 1208.26)^2 + \ldots + (963 - 795.86)^2 = 290{,}824.$$

Exhibit 14 Simple Regression Results with Indirect Manufacturing Labor Costs as Dependent Variable and Machine-Hours as Independent Variable (Cost Driver) for Elegant Rugs

	A	B	C	D	E	F
		Coefficients	**Standard Error**	**t Stat**		= Coefficient/Standard Error
1						
2		(1)	(2)	(3) = (1) ÷ (2)		= B3/C3
3	Intercept	$300.98	$229.75	1.31 ———→		= 300.98/229.75
4	Independent Variable: Machine-Hours (X)	$ 10.31	$ 3.12	3.30		
5						
6	**Regression Statistics**					
7	R Square	0.52				
8	Durbin-Watson Statistic	2.05				

An alternative way to test that the coefficient b is significantly different from zero is in terms of a *confidence interval*: There is less than a 5% chance that the true value of the machine-hours coefficient lies outside the range $10.31 \pm (2.228 \times \$3.12)$, or $10.31 \pm \$6.95$, or from $3.36 to $17.26. Because 0 does not appear in the confidence interval, we can conclude that changes in the number of machine-hours do affect indirect manufacturing labor costs. Similarly, using data from Exhibit 14, the t-value for the constant term a is $300.98 \div \$229.75 = 1.31$, which is less than 2.228. This t-value indicates that, within the relevant range, the constant term is *not* significantly different from zero. The Durbin-Watson statistic in Exhibit 14 will be discussed in the following section.

Specification Analysis of Estimation Assumptions

Specification analysis is the testing of the assumptions of regression analysis. If the assumptions of (1) linearity within the relevant range, (2) constant variance of residuals, (3) independence of residuals, and (4) normality of residuals all hold, then the simple regression procedures give reliable estimates of coefficient values. This section provides a brief overview of specification analysis. When these assumptions are not satisfied, more-complex regression procedures are necessary to obtain the best estimates.[5]

1. **Linearity within the relevant range.** A common assumption—and one that appears to be reasonable in many business applications—is that a linear relationship exists between the independent variable X and the dependent variable Y within the relevant range. If a linear regression model is used to estimate a nonlinear relationship, however, the coefficient estimates obtained will be inaccurate.

   When there is only one independent variable, the easiest way to check for linearity is to study the data plotted in a scatter diagram, a step that often is unwisely skipped. Exhibit 6 presents a scatter diagram for the indirect manufacturing labor costs and machine-hours variables of Elegant Rugs shown in Exhibit 3. The scatter diagram reveals that linearity appears to be a reasonable assumption for these data.

   The learning-curve models discussed in this chapter are examples of nonlinear cost functions. Costs increase when the level of production increases, but by lesser amounts than would occur with a linear cost function. In this case, the analyst should estimate a nonlinear cost function that incorporates learning effects.

2. **Constant variance of residuals.** The vertical deviation of the observed value Y from the regression line estimate y is called the *residual term, disturbance term,* or *error term, u = Y − y.* The assumption of constant variance implies that the residual terms are unaffected by the level of the cost driver. The assumption also implies that there is a uniform scatter, or dispersion, of the data points about the regression line as in Exhibit 15, Panel A. This assumption is likely to be violated, for example, in cross-sectional estimation of costs in operations of different sizes. For example, suppose Elegant Rugs has production areas of varying sizes. The company collects data from these different production areas to estimate the relationship between machine-hours and indirect manufacturing labor costs. It is very possible that the residual terms in this regression will be larger for the larger production

---

[5] For details see, for example, W. H. Greene, *Econometric Analysis*, 6th ed. (Upper Saddle River, NJ: Prentice Hall, 2007).

Exhibit 15   Constant Variance of Residuals Assumption

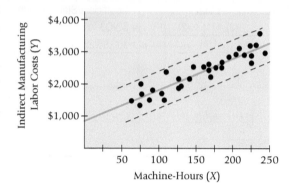

PANEL A:
Constant Variance
(Uniform Scatter of Data
Points Around Regression Line)

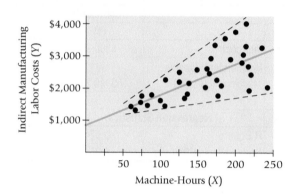

PANEL B:
Nonconstant Variance
(Higher Outputs Have
Larger Residuals)

areas that have higher machine-hours and higher indirect manufacturing labor costs. There would not be a uniform scatter of data points about the regression line (see Exhibit 15, Panel B). Constant variance is also known as *homoscedasticity*. Violation of this assumption is called *heteroscedasticity*.

   Heteroscedasticity does not affect the accuracy of the regression estimates a and b. It does, however, reduce the reliability of the estimates of the standard errors and thus affects the precision with which inferences about the population parameters can be drawn from the regression estimates.

3. **Independence of residuals.** The assumption of independence of residuals is that the residual term for any one observation is not related to the residual term for any other observation. The problem of *serial correlation* (also called *autocorrelation*) in the residuals arises when there is a systematic pattern in the sequence of residuals such that the residual in observation n conveys information about the residuals in observations $n + 1$, $n + 2$, and so on. Consider another production cell at Elegant Rugs that has, over a 20-week period, seen an increase in production and hence machine-hours. Exhibit 16 Panel B is a scatter diagram of machine-hours and indirect manufacturing labor costs. Observe the systematic pattern of the residuals in Panel B—positive residuals for extreme (high and low) quantities of machine-hours and negative residuals for moderate quantities of machine-hours. One reason for this observed pattern at low values of the cost driver is the "stickiness" of costs. When machine-hours are below 50 hours, indirect manufacturing labor costs do not decline. When machine-hours increase over time as production is ramped up, indirect manufacturing labor costs increase more as managers at Elegant Rugs struggle

Exhibit 16   Independence of Residuals Assumption

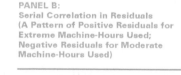

PANEL B:
Serial Correlation in Residuals
(A Pattern of Positive Residuals for
Extreme Machine-Hours Used;
Negative Residuals for Moderate
Machine-Hours Used)

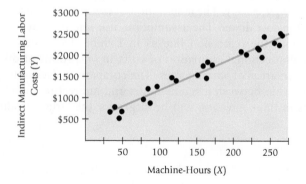

PANEL A:
Independence of Residuals
(No Pattern in Residuals)

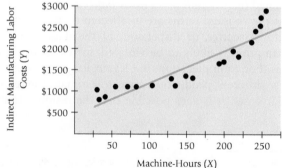

to manage the higher volume. How would the plot of residuals look if there were no auto-correlation? Like the plot in Exhibit 16, Panel A that shows no pattern in the residuals.

Like nonconstant variance of residuals, serial correlation does not affect the accuracy of the regression estimates a and b. It does, however, affect the standard errors of the coefficients, which in turn affect the precision with which inferences about the population parameters can be drawn from the regression estimates.

The Durbin-Watson statistic is one measure of serial correlation in the estimated residuals. For samples of 10 to 20 observations, a Durbin-Watson statistic in the 1.10–2.90 range indicates that the residuals are independent. The Durbin-Watson statistic for the regression results of Elegant Rugs in Exhibit 14 is 2.05. Therefore, an assumption of independence in the estimated residuals is reasonable for this regression model.

4. **Normality of residuals.** The normality of residuals assumption means that the residuals are distributed normally around the regression line. The normality of residuals assumption is frequently satisfied when using regression analysis on real cost data. Even when the assumption does not hold, accountants can still generate accurate estimates based on the regression equation, but the resulting confidence interval around these estimates is likely to be inaccurate.

Using Regression Output to Choose Cost Drivers of Cost Functions

Consider the two choices of cost drivers we described earlier in this chapter for indirect manufacturing labor costs (y):

$$y = a + (b \times \text{Number of machine-hours})$$

$$y = a + (b \times \text{Number of direct manufacturing labor-hours})$$

Exhibits 6 and 8 show plots of the data for the two regressions. Exhibit 14 reports regression results for the cost function using number of machine-hours as the independent variable. Exhibit 17 presents comparable regression results (in Excel) for the cost function using number of direct manufacturing labor-hours as the independent variable.

On the basis of the material presented in this appendix, which regression is better? Exhibit 18 compares these two cost functions in a systematic way. For several criteria, the cost function based on machine-hours is preferable to the cost function based on direct manufacturing labor-hours. The economic plausibility criterion is especially important.

Do not always assume that any one cost function will perfectly satisfy all the criteria in Exhibit 18. A cost analyst must often make a choice among "imperfect" cost functions, in the sense that the data of any particular cost function will not perfectly meet one or more of the assumptions underlying regression analysis. For example, both of the cost functions in Exhibit 18 are imperfect because, as stated in the section on specification analysis of estimation assumptions, inferences drawn from only 12 observations are not reliable.

Exhibit 17 Simple Regression Results with Indirect Manufacturing Labor Costs as Dependent Variable and Direct Manufacturing Labor-Hours as Independent Variable (Cost Driver) for Elegant Rugs

	A	B	C	D	E	F	G	H
1		**Coefficients**	**Standard Error**	*t* Stat				
2		(1)	(2)	(3) = (1) ÷ (2)				
3	Intercept	$744.67	$217.61	3.42				
4	Independent Variable: Direct Manufacturing Labor-Hours (*X*)	$ 7.72	$ 5.40	1.43		= Coefficient/Standard Error = B4/C4 = 7.72/5.40		
5								
6	**Regression Statistics**							
7	R Square	0.17						
8	Durbin-Watson Statistic	2.26						

Exhibit 18 Comparison of Alternative Cost Functions for Indirect Manufacturing Labor Costs Estimated with Simple Regression for Elegant Rugs

Criterion	Cost Function 1: Machine-Hours as Independent Variable	Cost Function 2: Direct Manufacturing Labor-Hours as Independent Variable
Economic plausibility	A positive relationship between indirect manufacturing labor costs (technical support labor) and machine-hours is economically plausible in Elegant Rugs' highly automated plant	A positive relationship between indirect manufacturing labor costs and direct manufacturing labor-hours is economically plausible, but less so than machine-hours in Elegant Rugs' highly automated plant on a week-to-week basis.
Goodness of fit[a]	$r^2 = 0.52$; standard error of regression = $170.50. Excellent goodness of fit.	$r^2 = 0.17$; standard error of regression = $224.60. Poor goodness of fit.
Significance of independent variable(s)	The t-value of 3.30 is significant at the 0.05 level.	The t-value of 1.43 is not significant at the 0.05 level.
Specification analysis of estimation assumptions	Plot of the data indicates that assumptions of linearity, constant variance, independence of residuals (Durbin-Watson statistic = 2.05), and normality of residuals hold, but inferences drawn from only 12 observations are not reliable.	Plot of the data indicates that assumptions of linearity, constant variance, independence of residuals (Durbin-Watson statistic = 2.26), and normality of residuals hold, but inferences drawn from only 12 observations are not reliable.

[a]If the number of observations available to estimate the machine-hours regression differs from the number of observations available to estimate the direct manufacturing labor-hours regression, an *adjusted* r^2 can be calculated to take this difference (in degrees of freedom) into account. Programs such as Excel calculate and present *adjusted* r^2.

Multiple Regression and Cost Hierarchies

In some cases, a satisfactory estimation of a cost function may be based on only one independent variable, such as number of machine-hours. In many cases, however, basing the estimation on more than one independent variable (that is, *multiple regression*) is more economically plausible and improves accuracy. The most widely used equations to express relationships between two or more independent variables and a dependent variable are linear in the form

$$y = a + b_1X_1 + b_2X_2 + \dots + u$$

where,

y = Cost to be predicted

$X_1, X_2, \dots$ = Independent variables on which the prediction is to be based

$a, b_1, b_2, \dots$ = Estimated coefficients of the regression model

u = Residual term that includes the net effect of other factors not in the model as well as measurement errors in the dependent and independent variables

Example: Consider the Elegant Rugs data in Exhibit 19. The company's ABC analysis indicates that indirect manufacturing labor costs include large amounts incurred for setup and changeover costs when a new batch of carpets is started. Management believes that in addition to number of machine-hours (an output unit-level cost driver), indirect manufacturing labor costs are also affected by the number of batches of carpet produced during each week (a batch-level driver). Elegant Rugs estimates the relationship between two independent variables, number of machine-hours and number of production batches of carpet manufactured during the week, and indirect manufacturing labor costs.

Exhibit 19

Weekly Indirect
Manufacturing Labor
Costs, Machine-Hours,
Direct Manufacturing
Labor-Hours, and
Number of Production
Batches for
Elegant Rugs

	A	B	C	D	E
	Week	Machine-Hours (X_1)	Number of Production Batches (X_2)	Direct Manufacturing Labor-Hours	Indirect Manufacturing Labor Costs (Y)
1					
2	1	68	12	30	$ 1,190
3	2	88	15	35	1,211
4	3	62	13	36	1,004
5	4	72	11	20	917
6	5	60	10	47	770
7	6	96	12	45	1,456
8	7	78	17	44	1,180
9	8	46	7	38	710
10	9	82	14	70	1,316
11	10	94	12	30	1,032
12	11	68	7	29	752
13	12	48	14	38	963
14	Total	862	144	462	$12,501
15					

Exhibit 20 presents results (in Excel) for the following multiple regression model, using data in columns B, C, and E of Exhibit 19:

$$y = \$42.58 + \$7.60X_1 + \$37.77X_2$$

where X_1 is the number of machine-hours and X_2 is the number of production batches. It is economically plausible that both number of machine-hours and number of production batches would help explain variations in indirect manufacturing labor costs at Elegant Rugs. The r^2 of 0.52 for the simple regression using number of machine-hours (Exhibit 14) increases to 0.72 with the multiple regression in Exhibit 20. The t-values suggest that the independent variable coefficients of both number of machine-hours ($\$7.60$) and number of production batches ($\$37.77$) are significantly different from zero ($t = 2.74$ is the t-value for number of machine-hours, and $t = 2.48$ is the t-value for number of production batches compared to the cut-off t-value of 2.26). The multiple regression model in Exhibit 20 satisfies both economic plausibility and statistical criteria, and it explains much greater variation (that

Exhibit 20   Multiple Regression Results with Indirect Manufacturing Labor Costs and Two Independent Variables of Cost Drivers (Machine-Hours and Production Batches) for Elegant Rugs

	A	B	C	D	E	F
1		Coefficients	Standard Error	t Stat		
2		(1)	(2)	(3) = (1) ÷ (2)		
3	Intercept	$42.58	$213.91	0.20		
4	Independent Variable 1: Machine-Hours ($X1$)	$ 7.60	$ 2.77	2.74		= Coefficient/Standard Error = B4/C4 = 7.60/2.77
5	Independent Variable 2: Number of Production Batches ($X2$)	$37.77	$ 15.25	2.48		
6						
7	**Regression Statistics**					
8	R Square	0.72				
9	Durbin-Watson Statistic	2.49				

is, r^2 of 0.72 versus r^2 of 0.52) in indirect manufacturing labor costs than the simple regression model using only number of machine-hours as the independent variable.[6] The standard error of the regression equation that includes number of batches as an independent variable is

$$\sqrt{\frac{\Sigma(Y - y)^2}{n - 3}} = \sqrt{\frac{170{,}156}{9}} = \$137.50$$

which is lower than the standard error of the regression with only machine-hours as the independent variable, $170.50. That is, even though adding a variable reduces the degrees of freedom in the denominator, it substantially improves fit so that the numerator, $\Sigma(Y - y)^2$, decreases even more. Number of machine-hours and number of production batches are both important cost drivers of indirect manufacturing labor costs at Elegant Rugs.

In Exhibit 20, the slope coefficients—$7.60 for number of machine-hours and $37.77 for number of production batches—measure the change in indirect manufacturing labor costs associated with a unit change in an independent variable (assuming that the other independent variable is held constant). For example, indirect manufacturing labor costs increase by $37.77 when one more production batch is added, assuming that the number of machine-hours is held constant.

An alternative approach would create two separate cost pools for indirect manufacturing labor costs: one for costs related to number of machine-hours and another for costs related to number of production batches. Elegant Rugs would then estimate the relationship between the cost driver and the costs in each cost pool. The difficult task under this approach is to properly subdivide the indirect manufacturing labor costs into the two cost pools.

Multicollinearity

A major concern that arises with multiple regression is multicollinearity. **Multicollinearity** exists when two or more independent variables are highly correlated with each other. Generally, users of regression analysis believe that a *coefficient of correlation* between independent variables greater than 0.70 indicates multicollinearity. Multicollinearity increases the standard errors of the coefficients of the individual variables. That is, variables that are economically and statistically significant will appear not to be significantly different from zero.

The matrix of correlation coefficients of the different variables described in Exhibit 19 are as follows:

	Indirect Manufacturing Labor Costs	Machine-Hours	Number of Production Batches	Direct Manufacturing Labor-Hours
Indirect manufacturing labor costs	1			
Machine-hours	0.72	1		
Number of production batches	0.69	0.4	1	
Direct manufacturing labor-hours	0.41	0.12	0.31	1

These results indicate that multiple regressions using any pair of the independent variables in Exhibit 19 are not likely to encounter multicollinearity problems.

When multicollinearity exists, try to obtain new data that do not suffer from multicollinearity problems. Do not drop an independent variable (cost driver) that should be included in a model because it is correlated with another independent variable. Omitting such a variable will cause the estimated coefficient of the independent variable included in the model to be biased away from its true value.

---

[6] Adding another variable always increases r^2. The question is whether adding another variable increases r^2 sufficiently. One way to get insight into this question is to calculate an adjusted r^2 as follows:

Adjusted $r^2 = 1 - (1 - r^2)\dfrac{n - 1}{n - p - 1}$, where n is the number of observations and p is the number of coefficients estimated. In the model with only machine-hours as the independent variable, adjusted $r^2 = 1 - (1 - 0.52)\dfrac{12 - 1}{12 - 2 - 1} = 0.41$. In the model with both machine-hours and number of batches as independent variables, adjusted $r^2 = 1 - (1 - 0.72)\dfrac{12 - 1}{12 - 3 - 1} = 0.62$. Adjusted r^2 does not have the same interpretation as r^2 but the increase in adjusted r^2 when number of batches is added as an independent variable suggests that adding this variable significantly improves the fit of the model in a way that more than compensates for the degree of freedom lost by estimating another coefficient.

Terms to Learn

This chapter contains definitions of the following important terms:

account analysis method

coefficient of determination (r^2)

conference method

constant

cost estimation

cost function

cost predictions

cumulative average-time learning
  model

dependent variable

experience curve

high-low method

incremental unit-time learning model

independent variable

industrial engineering method

intercept

learning curve

linear cost function

mixed cost

multicollinearity

multiple regression

nonlinear cost function

regression analysis

residual term

semivariable cost

simple regression

slope coefficient

specification analysis

standard error of the estimated
  coefficient

standard error of the regression

step cost function

work-measurement method

Assignment Material

Questions

10-1 What two assumptions are frequently made when estimating a cost function?

10-2 Describe three alternative linear cost functions.

10-3 What is the difference between a linear and a nonlinear cost function? Give an example of each type of cost function.

10-4 "High correlation between two variables means that one is the cause and the other is the effect." Do you agree? Explain.

10-5 Name four approaches to estimating a cost function.

10-6 Describe the conference method for estimating a cost function. What are two advantages of this method?

10-7 Describe the account analysis method for estimating a cost function.

10-8 List the six steps in estimating a cost function on the basis of an analysis of a past cost relationship. Which step is typically the most difficult for the cost analyst?

10-9 When using the high-low method, should you base the high and low observations on the dependent variable or on the cost driver?

10-10 Describe three criteria for evaluating cost functions and choosing cost drivers.

10-11 Define learning curve. Outline two models that can be used when incorporating learning into the estimation of cost functions.

10-12 Discuss four frequently encountered problems when collecting cost data on variables included in a cost function.

10-13 What are the four key assumptions examined in specification analysis in the case of simple regression?

10-14 "All the independent variables in a cost function estimated with regression analysis are cost drivers." Do you agree? Explain.

10-15 "Multicollinearity exists when the dependent variable and the independent variable are highly correlated." Do you agree? Explain.

Exercises

10-16 Estimating a cost function. The controller of the Ijiri Company wants you to estimate a cost function from the following two observations in a general ledger account called Maintenance:

Month	Machine-Hours	Maintenance Costs Incurred
January	6,000	$4,000
February	10,000	5,400

Required

1. Estimate the cost function for maintenance.
2. Can the constant in the cost function be used as an estimate of fixed maintenance cost per month? Explain.

10-17 Identifying variable-, fixed-, and mixed-cost functions. The Pacific Corporation operates car rental agencies at more than 20 airports. Customers can choose from one of three contracts for car rentals of one day or less:

- Contract 1: $50 for the day
- Contract 2: $30 for the day plus $0.20 per mile traveled
- Contract 3: $1 per mile traveled

Required

1. Plot separate graphs for each of the three contracts, with costs on the vertical axis and miles traveled on the horizontal axis.
2. Express each contract as a linear cost function of the form $y = a + bX$.
3. Identify each contract as a variable-, fixed-, or mixed-cost function.

10-18 Various cost-behavior patterns. (CPA, adapted) Select the graph that matches the numbered manufacturing cost data (requirements 1–9). Indicate by letter which graph best fits the situation or item described.

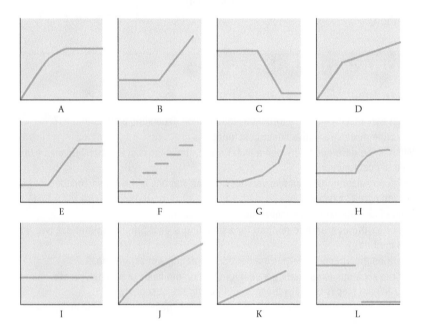

The vertical axes of the graphs represent total cost, and the horizontal axes represent units produced during a calendar year. In each case, the zero point of dollars and production is at the intersection of the two axes. The graphs may be used more than once.

Required

1. Annual depreciation of equipment, where the amount of depreciation charged is computed by the machine-hours method.
2. Electricity bill—a flat fixed charge, plus a variable cost after a certain number of kilowatt-hours are used, in which the quantity of kilowatt-hours used varies proportionately with quantity of units produced.
3. City water bill, which is computed as follows:

First 1,000,000 gallons or less	$1,000 flat fee
Next 10,000 gallons	$0.003 per gallon used
Next 10,000 gallons	$0.006 per gallon used
Next 10,000 gallons	$0.009 per gallon used
and so on	and so on

The gallons of water used vary proportionately with the quantity of production output.

4. Cost of direct materials, where direct material cost per unit produced decreases with each pound of material used (for example, if 1 pound is used, the cost is $10; if 2 pounds are used, the cost is $19.98; if 3 pounds are used, the cost is $29.94), with a minimum cost per unit of $9.20.

5. Annual depreciation of equipment, where the amount is computed by the straight-line method. When the depreciation schedule was prepared, it was anticipated that the obsolescence factor would be greater than the wear-and-tear factor.

6. Rent on a manufacturing plant donated by the city, where the agreement calls for a fixed-fee payment unless 200,000 labor-hours are worked, in which case no rent is paid.

7. Salaries of repair personnel, where one person is needed for every 1,000 machine-hours or less (that is, 0 to 1,000 hours requires one person, 1,001 to 2,000 hours requires two people, and so on).

8. Cost of direct materials used (assume no quantity discounts).

9. Rent on a manufacturing plant donated by the county, where the agreement calls for rent of $100,000 to be reduced by $1 for each direct manufacturing labor-hour worked in excess of 200,000 hours, but a minimum rental fee of $20,000 must be paid.

10-19 Matching graphs with descriptions of cost and revenue behavior. (D. Green, adapted) Given here are a number of graphs.

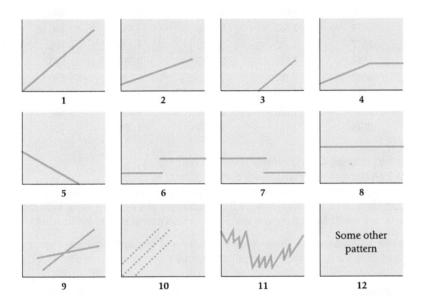

The horizontal axis represents the units produced over the year and the vertical axis represents total cost or revenues. Indicate by number which graph best fits the situation or item described (a–h). Some graphs may be used more than once; some may not apply to any of the situations.

a. Direct material costs
b. Supervisors' salaries for one shift and two shifts
c. A cost-volume-profit graph
d. Mixed costs—for example, car rental fixed charge plus a rate per mile driven
e. Depreciation of plant, computed on a straight-line basis
f. Data supporting the use of a variable-cost rate, such as manufacturing labor cost of $14 per unit produced
g. Incentive bonus plan that pays managers $0.10 for every unit produced above some level of production
h. Interest expense on $2 million borrowed at a fixed rate of interest

10-20 Account analysis method. Lorenzo operates a car wash. Incoming cars are put on an automatic conveyor belt. Cars are washed as the conveyor belt carries them from the start station to the finish station. After a car moves off the conveyor belt, it is dried manually. Workers then clean and vacuum the inside of the car. Lorenzo serviced 80,000 cars in 2012. Lorenzo reports the following costs for 2012:

Account Description	Costs
Car wash labor	$260,000
Soap, cloth, and supplies	42,000
Water	38,000
Electric power to move conveyor belt	72,000
Depreciation	64,000
Salaries	46,000

Required

1. Classify each account as variable or fixed with respect to the number of cars washed. Explain.
2. Suppose Lorenzo washed 90,000 cars in 2012. Use the cost classification you developed in requirement 1 to estimate Lorenzo's total costs in 2012. Depreciation is computed on a straight-line basis.

10-21 Account analysis, high-low. Java Joe Coffees wants to find an equation to estimate monthly utility costs. Java Joe's has been in business for one year and has collected the following cost data for utilities:

Month	Electricity Bill	Kilowatt Hours Used	Telephone Bill	Telephone Minutes Used	Water Bill	Gallons of Water Used
January	$360	1,200	$92.00	1,100	$60	30,560
February	$420	1,400	$91.20	1,060	$60	26,800
March	$549	1,830	$94.80	1,240	$60	31,450
April	$405	1,350	$89.60	980	$60	29,965
May	$588	1,960	$98.00	1,400	$60	30,568
June	$624	2,080	$98.80	1,440	$60	25,540
July	$522	1,740	$93.40	1,170	$60	32,690
August	$597	1,990	$96.20	1,310	$60	31,222
September	$630	2,100	$95.60	1,280	$60	33,540
October	$615	2,050	$93.80	1,190	$60	31,970
November	$594	1,980	$91.00	1,050	$60	28,600
December	$633	2,110	$97.00	1,350	$60	34,100

Required

1. Which of the preceding costs is variable? Fixed? Mixed? Explain.
2. Using the high-low method, determine the cost function for each cost.
3. Combine the preceding information to get a monthly utility cost function for Java Joe's.
4. Next month, Java Joe's expects to use 2,200 kilowatt hours of electricity, make 1,500 minutes of telephone calls, and use 32,000 gallons of water. Estimate total cost of utilities for the month.

10-22 Account analysis method. Gower, Inc., a manufacturer of plastic products, reports the following manufacturing costs and account analysis classification for the year ended December 31, 2012.

Account	Classification	Amount
Direct materials	All variable	$300,000
Direct manufacturing labor	All variable	225,000
Power	All variable	37,500
Supervision labor	20% variable	56,250
Materials-handling labor	50% variable	60,000
Maintenance labor	40% variable	75,000
Depreciation	0% variable	95,000
Rent, property taxes, and administration	0% variable	100,000

Gower, Inc., produced 75,000 units of product in 2012. Gower's management is estimating costs for 2013 on the basis of 2012 numbers. The following additional information is available for 2013.

a. Direct materials prices in 2013 are expected to increase by 5% compared with 2012.
b. Under the terms of the labor contract, direct manufacturing labor wage rates are expected to increase by 10% in 2013 compared with 2012.
c. Power rates and wage rates for supervision, materials handling, and maintenance are not expected to change from 2012 to 2013.
d. Depreciation costs are expected to increase by 5%, and rent, property taxes, and administration costs are expected to increase by 7%.
e. Gower expects to manufacture and sell 80,000 units in 2013.

Required

1. Prepare a schedule of variable, fixed, and total manufacturing costs for each account category in 2013. Estimate total manufacturing costs for 2013.
2. Calculate Gower's total manufacturing cost per unit in 2012, and estimate total manufacturing cost per unit in 2013.
3. How can you obtain better estimates of fixed and variable costs? Why would these better estimates be useful to Gower?

10-23 Estimating a cost function, high-low method. Reisen Travel offers helicopter service from suburban towns to John F. Kennedy International Airport in New York City. Each of its 10 helicopters makes between 1,000 and 2,000 round-trips per year. The records indicate that a helicopter that has made 1,000 round-trips in the year incurs an average operating cost of $350 per round-trip, and one that has made 2,000 round-trips in the year incurs an average operating cost of $300 per round-trip.

1. Using the high-low method, estimate the linear relationship $y = a + bX$, where y is the total annual operating cost of a helicopter and X is the number of round-trips it makes to JFK airport during the year. **Required**
2. Give examples of costs that would be included in a and in b.
3. If Reisen Travel expects each helicopter to make, on average, 1,200 round-trips in the coming year, what should its estimated operating budget for the helicopter fleet be?

10-24 Estimating a cost function, high-low method. Laurie Daley is examining customer-service costs in the southern region of Capitol Products. Capitol Products has more than 200 separate electrical products that are sold with a six-month guarantee of full repair or replacement with a new product. When a product is returned by a customer, a service report is prepared. This service report includes details of the problem and the time and cost of resolving the problem. Weekly data for the most recent 8-week period are as follows:

Week	Customer-Service Department Costs	Number of Service Reports
1	$13,700	190
2	20,900	275
3	13,000	115
4	18,800	395
5	14,000	265
6	21,500	455
7	16,900	340
8	21,000	305

1. Plot the relationship between customer-service costs and number of service reports. Is the relationship economically plausible? **Required**
2. Use the high-low method to compute the cost function, relating customer-service costs to the number of service reports.
3. What variables, in addition to number of service reports, might be cost drivers of weekly customer-service costs of Capitol Products?

10-25 Linear cost approximation. Terry Lawler, managing director of the Chicago Reviewers Group, is examining how overhead costs behave with changes in monthly professional labor-hours billed to clients. Assume the following historical data:

Total Overhead Costs	Professional Labor-Hours Billed to Clients
$335,000	2,000
400,000	3,000
430,000	4,000
472,000	5,000
533,000	6,500
582,000	7,500

1. Compute the linear cost function, relating total overhead costs to professional labor-hours, using the representative observations of 3,000 and 6,500 hours. Plot the linear cost function. Does the constant component of the cost function represent the fixed overhead costs of the Chicago Reviewers Group? Why? **Required**
2. What would be the predicted total overhead costs for (a) 4,000 hours and (b) 7,500 hours using the cost function estimated in requirement 1? Plot the predicted costs and actual costs for 4,000 and 7,500 hours.
3. Lawler had a chance to accept a special job that would have boosted professional labor-hours from 3,000 to 4,000 hours. Suppose Lawler, guided by the linear cost function, rejected this job because it would have brought a total increase in contribution margin of $35,000, before deducting the predicted increase in total overhead cost, $38,000. What is the total contribution margin actually forgone?

10-26 Cost-volume-profit and regression analysis. Goldstein Corporation manufactures a children's bicycle, model CT8. Goldstein currently manufactures the bicycle frame. During 2012, Goldstein made 32,000 frames at a total cost of $1,056,000. Ryan Corporation has offered to supply as many frames as Goldstein wants at a cost of $32.50 per frame. Goldstein anticipates needing 35,000 frames each year for the next few years.

Required

1. **a.** What is the average cost of manufacturing a bicycle frame in 2012? How does it compare to Ryan's offer?
   b. Can Goldstein use the answer in requirement 1a to determine the cost of manufacturing 35,000 bicycle frames? Explain.
2. Goldstein's cost analyst uses annual data from past years to estimate the following regression equation with total manufacturing costs of the bicycle frame as the dependent variable and bicycle frames produced as the independent variable:

$$y = \$435,000 + \$19X$$

During the years used to estimate the regression equation, the production of bicycle frames varied from 31,000 to 35,000. Using this equation, estimate how much it would cost Goldstein to manufacture 35,000 bicycle frames. How much more or less costly is it to manufacture the frames rather than to acquire them from Ryan?
3. What other information would you need to be confident that the equation in requirement 2 accurately predicts the cost of manufacturing bicycle frames?

10-27 Regression analysis, service company. (CMA, adapted) Bob Jones owns a catering company that prepares food and beverages for banquets and parties. For a standard party the cost on a per-person basis is as follows:

Food and beverages	$15
Labor (0.5 hour × $10 per hour)	5
Overhead (0.5 hour × $14 per hour)	7
Total cost per person	$27

Jones is quite certain about his estimates of the food, beverages, and labor costs but is not as comfortable with the overhead estimate. The overhead estimate was based on the actual data for the past 12 months, which are presented here. These data indicate that overhead costs vary with the direct labor-hours used. The $14 estimate was determined by dividing total overhead costs for the 12 months by total labor-hours.

Month	Labor-Hours	Overhead Costs
January	2,500	$ 55,000
February	2,700	59,000
March	3,000	60,000
April	4,200	64,000
May	7,500	77,000
June	5,500	71,000
July	6,500	74,000
August	4,500	67,000
September	7,000	75,000
October	4,500	68,000
November	3,100	62,000
December	6,500	73,000
Total	57,500	$805,000

Jones has recently become aware of regression analysis. He estimated the following regression equation with overhead costs as the dependent variable and labor-hours as the independent variable:

$$y = \$48,271 + \$3.93X$$

Required

1. Plot the relationship between overhead costs and labor-hours. Draw the regression line and evaluate it using the criteria of economic plausibility, goodness of fit, and slope of the regression line.
2. Using data from the regression analysis, what is the variable cost per person for a standard party?
3. Bob Jones has been asked to prepare a bid for a 200-person standard party to be given next month. Determine the minimum bid price that Jones would be willing to submit to recoup variable costs.

10-28 High-low, regression. Melissa Crupp is the new manager of the materials storeroom for Canton Manufacturing. Melissa has been asked to estimate future monthly purchase costs for part #4599, used in two of Canton's products. Melissa has purchase cost and quantity data for the past nine months as follows:

Month	Cost of Purchase	Quantity Purchased
January	$10,390	2,250 parts
February	10,550	2,350
March	14,400↑	3,390↑
April	13,180	3,120
May	10,970	2,490
June	11,580	2,680
July	12,690	3,030
August	8,560↓	1,930↓
September	12,450	2,960

Estimated monthly purchases for this part based on expected demand of the two products for the rest of the year are as follows:

Month	Purchase Quantity Expected
October	2,800 parts
November	3,100
December	2,500

Required

1. The computer in Melissa's office is down and Melissa has been asked to immediately provide an equation to estimate the future purchase cost for part # 4599. Melissa grabs a calculator and uses the high-low method to estimate a cost equation. What equation does she get?
2. Using the equation from requirement 1, calculate the future expected purchase costs for each of the last three months of the year.
3. After a few hours Melissa's computer is fixed. Melissa uses the first nine months of data and regression analysis to estimate the relationship between the quantity purchased and purchase costs of part #4599. The regression line Melissa obtains is as follows:

$$y = \$1,779.6 + 3.67X$$

Evaluate the regression line using the criteria of economic plausibility, goodness of fit, and significance of the independent variable. Compare the regression equation to the equation based on the high-low method. Which is a better fit? Why?
4. Use the regression results to calculate the expected purchase costs for October, November, and December. Compare the expected purchase costs to the expected purchase costs calculated using the high-low method in requirement 2. Comment on your results.

10-29 Learning curve, cumulative average-time learning model. Global Defense manufactures radar systems. It has just completed the manufacture of its first newly designed system, RS-32. Manufacturing data for the RS-32 follow:

	Home	Insert	Page Layout	Formulas	Data	Review	View

	A	B	C
1	Direct material cost	$160,000	per unit of RS-32
2	Direct manufacturing labor time for first unit	6,000	direct manufacturing labor-hours
3	Learning curve for manufacturing labor time per radar system	85%	cumulative average time[a]
4	Direct manufacturing labor cost	$ 30	per direct manufacturing labor-hour
5	Variable manufacturing overhead cost	$ 20	per direct manufacturing labor-hour
6			
7	[a]Using the formula, for a 85% learning curve, $b = \dfrac{\ln 0.85}{\ln 2} = \dfrac{-0.162519}{0.693147} = -0.234465$		
8			

Required Calculate the total variable costs of producing 2, 4, and 8 units.

10-30 Learning curve, incremental unit-time learning model. Assume the same information for Global Defense as in Exercise 10-29, except that Global Defense uses an 85% incremental unit-time learning model as a basis for predicting direct manufacturing labor-hours. (An 85% learning curve means $b = -0.234465$.)

Required
1. Calculate the total variable costs of producing 2, 3, and 4 units.
2. If you solved Exercise 10-29, compare your cost predictions in the two exercises for 2 and 4 units. Why are the predictions different? How should Global Defense decide which model it should use?

MyAccountingLab

Problems

10-31 High-low method. Ken Howard, financial analyst at KMW Corporation, is examining the behavior of quarterly maintenance costs for budgeting purposes. Howard collects the following data on machine-hours worked and maintenance costs for the past 12 quarters:

Quarter	Machine-Hours	Maintenance Costs
1	100,000	$205,000
2	120,000	240,000
3	110,000	220,000
4	130,000	260,000
5	95,000	190,000
6	115,000	235,000
7	105,000	215,000
8	125,000	255,000
9	105,000	210,000
10	125,000	245,000
11	115,000	200,000
12	140,000	280,000

Required
1. Estimate the cost function for the quarterly data using the high-low method.
2. Plot and comment on the estimated cost function.
3. Howard anticipates that KMW will operate machines for 100,000 hours in quarter 13. Calculate the predicted maintenance costs in quarter 13 using the cost function estimated in requirement 1.

10-32 High-low method and regression analysis. Local Harvest, a cooperative of organic family-owned farms outside of Columbus, Ohio, has recently started a fresh produce club to provide support to the group's member farms, and to promote the benefits of eating organic, locally-produced food to the nearby suburban community. Families pay a seasonal membership fee of $50, and place their orders a week in advance for a price of $40 per week. In turn, Local Harvest delivers fresh-picked seasonal local produce to several neighborhood distribution points. Eight hundred families joined the club for the first season, but the number of orders varied from week to week.

Harvey Hendricks has run the produce club for the first 10-week season. Before becoming a farmer, Harvey had been a business major in college, and he remembers a few things about cost analysis. In planning for next year, he wants to know how many orders will be needed each week for the club to break even, but first he must estimate the club's fixed and variable costs. He has collected the following data over the club's first 10 weeks of operation:

Week	Number of Orders per Week	Weekly Total Costs
1	351	$18,795
2	385	21,597
3	410	22,800
4	453	22,600
5	425	21,900
6	486	24,600
7	455	23,900
8	467	22,900
9	525	25,305
10	510	24,500

Required

1. Plot the relationship between number of orders per week and weekly total costs.
2. Estimate the cost equation using the high-low method, and draw this line on your graph.
3. Harvey uses his computer to calculate the following regression formula:

$$\text{Total weekly costs} = \$8,631 + (\$31.92 \times \text{Number of weekly orders})$$

Draw the regression line on your graph. Use your graph to evaluate the regression line using the criteria of economic plausibility, goodness of fit, and significance of the independent variable. Is the cost function estimated using the high-low method a close approximation of the cost function estimated using the regression method? Explain briefly.
4. Did Fresh Harvest break even this season? Remember that each of the families paid a seasonal membership fee of $50.
5. Assume that 900 families join the club next year, and that prices and costs do not change. How many orders, on average, must Fresh Harvest receive each week to break even?

10-33 High-low method; regression analysis. (CIMA, adapted) Anna Martinez, the financial manager at the Casa Real restaurant, is checking to see if there is any relationship between newspaper advertising and sales revenues at the restaurant. She obtains the following data for the past 10 months:

Month	Revenues	Advertising Costs
March	$50,000	$2,000
April	70,000	3,000
May	55,000	1,500
June	65,000	3,500
July	55,000	1,000
August	65,000	2,000
September	45,000	1,500
October	80,000	4,000
November	55,000	2,500
December	60,000	2,500

She estimates the following regression equation:

$$\text{Monthly revenues} = \$39,502 + (\$8.723 \times \text{Advertising costs})$$

Required

1. Plot the relationship between advertising costs and revenues.
2. Draw the regression line and evaluate it using the criteria of economic plausibility, goodness of fit, and slope of the regression line.
3. Use the high-low method to compute the function, relating advertising costs and revenues.
4. Using (a) the regression equation and (b) the high-low equation, what is the increase in revenues for each $1,000 spent on advertising within the relevant range? Which method should Martinez use to predict the effect of advertising costs on revenues? Explain briefly.

10-34 Regression, activity-based costing, choosing cost drivers. Fitzgerald Manufacturing has been using activity-based costing to determine the cost of product X-678. One of the activities, "Inspection," occurs just before the product is finished. Fitzgerald inspects every 10th unit, and has been using "number of units inspected" as the cost driver for inspection costs. A significant component of inspection costs is the cost of the test-kit used in each inspection.

Neela McFeen, the line manager, is wondering if inspection labor-hours might be a better cost driver for inspection costs. Neela gathers information for weekly inspection costs, units inspected, and inspection labor-hours as follows:

Week	Units Inspected	Inspection Labor-Hours	Inspection Costs
1	1,400	190	$3,700
2	400	70	1,800
3	1,700	230	4,500
4	2,400	240	5,900
5	2,100	210	5,300
6	700	90	2,400
7	900	110	2,900

Neela runs regressions on each of the possible cost drivers and estimates these cost functions:

$$\text{Inspection Costs} = \$977 + (\$2.05 \times \text{Number of units inspected})$$
$$\text{Inspection Costs} = \$478 + (\$20.31 \times \text{Inspection labor-hours})$$

Required

1. Explain why number of units inspected and inspection labor-hours are plausible cost drivers of inspection costs.
2. Plot the data and regression line for units inspected and inspection costs. Plot the data and regression line for inspection labor-hours and inspection costs. Which cost driver of inspection costs would you choose? Explain.
3. Neela expects inspectors to work 140 hours next period and to inspect 1,100 units. Using the cost driver you chose in requirement 2, what amount of inspection costs should Neela budget? Explain any implications of Neela choosing the cost driver you did not choose in requirement 2 to budget inspection costs.

10-35 Interpreting regression results, matching time periods. Brickman Apparel produces equipment for the extreme-sports market. It has four peak periods, each lasting two months, for manufacturing the merchandise suited for spring, summer, fall, and winter. In the off-peak periods, Brickman schedules equipment maintenance. Brickman's controller, Sascha Green, wants to understand the drivers of equipment maintenance costs. The data collected is shown in the table as follows:

Month	Machine-Hours	Maintenance Costs
January	5,000	$ 1,300
February	5,600	2,200
March	1,500	12,850
April	6,500	1,665
May	5,820	2,770
June	1,730	15,250
July	7,230	1,880
August	5,990	2,740
September	2,040	15,350
October	6,170	1,620
November	5,900	2,770
December	1,500	14,700

A regression analysis of one year of monthly data yields the following relationships:

$$\text{Maintenance costs} = \$18,552 - (\$2.683 \times \text{Number of machine-hours})$$

Upon examining the results, Green comments, "So, all I have to do to reduce maintenance costs is run my machines longer?! This is hard to believe, but numbers don't lie! I would have guessed just the opposite."

Required

1. Explain why Green made this comment. What is wrong with her analysis?
2. Upon further reflection, Sascha Green reanalyzes the data, this time comparing quarterly machine-hours with quarterly maintenance expenditures. This time, the results are very different. The regression yields the following formula:

$$\text{Maintenance costs} = \$2,622.80 + (\$1.175 \times \text{Number of machine-hours})$$

What caused the formula to change, in light of the fact that the data was the same?

10-36 Cost estimation, cumulative average-time learning curve. The Nautilus Company, which is under contract to the U.S. Navy, assembles troop deployment boats. As part of its research program, it completes the assembly of the first of a new model (PT109) of deployment boats. The Navy is impressed with the PT109. It requests that Nautilus submit a proposal on the cost of producing another six PT109s.

Nautilus reports the following cost information for the first PT109 assembled and uses a 90% cumulative average-time learning model as a basis for forecasting direct manufacturing labor-hours for the next six PT109s. (A 90% learning curve means $b = -0.152004$.)

	A	B	C
1	Direct material	$200,000	
2	Direct manufacturing labor time for first boat	15,000	labor-hours
3	Direct manufacturing labor rate	$ 40	per direct manufacturing labor-hour
4	Variable manufacturing overhead cost	$ 25	per direct manufacturing labor-hour
5	Other manufacturing overhead	20%	of direct manufacturing labor costs
6	Tooling costs[a]	$280,000	
7	Learning curve for manufacturing labor time per boat	90%	cumulative average time[b]
8			
9	[a]Tooling can be reused at no extra cost because all of its cost has been assigned to the first deployment boat.		
10			
11	[b]Using the formula, for a 90% learning curve, $b = \frac{\ln 0.9}{\ln 2} = \frac{-0.105361}{0.693147} = -0.152004$		
12			

Required

1. Calculate predicted total costs of producing the six PT109s for the Navy. (Nautilus will keep the first deployment boat assembled, costed at $1,575,000, as a demonstration model for potential customers.)
2. What is the dollar amount of the difference between (a) the predicted total costs for producing the six PT109s in requirement 1, and (b) the predicted total costs for producing the six PT109s, assuming that there is no learning curve for direct manufacturing labor? That is, for (b) assume a linear function for units produced and direct manufacturing labor-hours.

10-37 Cost estimation, incremental unit-time learning model. Assume the same information for the Nautilus Company as in Problem 10-36 with one exception. This exception is that Nautilus uses a 90% incremental unit-time learning model as a basis for predicting direct manufacturing labor-hours in its assembling operations. (A 90% learning curve means $b = -0.152004$.)

Required

1. Prepare a prediction of the total costs for producing the six PT109s for the Navy.
2. If you solved requirement 1 of Problem 10-36, compare your cost prediction there with the one you made here. Why are the predictions different? How should Nautilus decide which model it should use?

10-38 Regression; choosing among models. Tilbert Toys (TT) makes the popular Floppin' Freddy Frog and Jumpin' Jill Junebug dolls in batches. TT has recently adopted activity-based costing. TT incurs setup costs for each batch of dolls that it produces. TT uses "number of setups" as the cost driver for setup costs.

TT has just hired Bebe Williams, an accountant. Bebe thinks that "number of setup-hours" might be a better cost driver because the setup time for each product is different. Bebe collects the following data.

	A	B	C	D
1	Month	Number of Setups	Number of Setup Hours	Setup Costs
2	1	300	1,840	$104,600
3	2	410	2,680	126,700
4	3	150	1,160	57,480
5	4	480	3,800	236,840
6	5	310	3,680	178,880
7	6	460	3,900	213,760
8	7	420	2,980	209,620
9	8	300	1,200	90,080
10	9	270	3,280	221,040

1. Estimate the regression equation for (a) setup costs and number of setups and (b) setup costs and number of setup-hours. You should obtain the following results:

Regression 1: Setup costs = $a + (b \times$ Number of setups)

Variable	Coefficient	Standard Error	t-Value
Constant	$12,890	$61,365	0.21
Independent variable 1: No. of setups	$ 426.77	$ 171	2.49

$r^2 = 0.47$; Durbin-Watson statistic = 1.65

Regression 2: Setup costs = $a + (b \times$ Number of setup-hours)

Variable	Coefficient	Standard Error	t-Value
Constant	$6,573	$ 25,908	0.25
Independent variable 1: No. of setup-hours	$ 56.27	$ 8.90	6.32

$r^2 = 0.85$; Durbin-Watson statistic = 1.50

2. On two different graphs plot the data and the regression lines for each of the following cost functions:
   a. Setup costs = $a + (b \times$ Number of setups)
   b. Setup costs = $a + (b \times$ Number of setup-hours)
3. Evaluate the regression models for "Number of setups" and "Number of setup-hours" as the cost driver according to the format of Exhibit 18.
4. Based on your analysis, which cost driver should Tilbert Toys use for setup costs, and why?

10-39 Multiple regression (continuation of 10-38). Bebe Williams wonders if she should run a multiple regression with both number of setups and number of setup-hours, as cost drivers.

1. Run a multiple regression to estimate the regression equation for setup costs using both number of setups and number of setup-hours as independent variables. You should obtain the following result:

Regression 3: Setup costs = $a (b_1 \times$ No. of setups) $+ (b_2 \times$ No. of setup-hours)

Variable	Coefficient	Standard Error	t-Value
Constant	−$2,807	$34,850	−0.08
Independent variable 1: No. of setups	$ 58.62	$ 133.42	0.44
Independent variable 2: No. of setup-hours	$ 52.31	$ 13.08	4.00

$r^2 = 0.86$; Durbin-Watson statistic = 1.38

2. Evaluate the multiple regression output using the criteria of economic plausibility goodness of fit, significance of independent variables, and specification of estimation assumptions. (Assume linearity, constant variance, and normality of residuals.)
3. What difficulties do not arise in simple regression analysis that may arise in multiple regression analysis? Is there evidence of such difficulties in the multiple regression presented in this problem? Explain.
4. Which of the regression models from Problems 10-38 and 10-39 would you recommend Bebe Williams use? Explain.

10-40 Purchasing department cost drivers, activity-based costing, simple regression analysis. Fashion Bling operates a chain of 10 retail department stores. Each department store makes its own purchasing decisions. Barry Lee, assistant to the president of Fashion Bling, is interested in better understanding the drivers of purchasing department costs. For many years, Fashion Bling has allocated purchasing department costs to products on the basis of the dollar value of merchandise purchased. A $100 item is allocated 10 times as many overhead costs associated with the purchasing department as a $10 item.

Lee recently attended a seminar titled "Cost Drivers in the Retail Industry." In a presentation at the seminar, Couture Fabrics, a leading competitor that has implemented activity-based costing, reported number of purchase orders and number of suppliers to be the two most important cost drivers of purchasing department costs. The dollar value of merchandise purchased in each purchase order was not found to be a significant cost driver. Lee interviewed several members of the purchasing department at the Fashion Bling store in Miami. They believed that Couture Fabrics' conclusions also applied to their purchasing department.

Lee collects the following data for the most recent year for Fashion Bling's 10 retail department stores:

	Home Insert Page Layout Formulas Data Review View			
A	B	C	D	E
1 Department Store	Purchasing Department Costs (PDC)	Dollar Value of Merchandise Purchased (MP$)	Number of Purchase Orders (No. of POs)	Number of Suppliers (No. of Ss)
2 Baltimore	$1,522,000	$ 68,307,000	4,345	125
3 Chicago	1,095,000	33,463,000	2,548	230
4 Los Angeles	542,000	121,800,000	1,420	8
5 Miami	2,053,000	119,450,000	5,935	188
6 New York	1,068,000	33,575,000	2,786	21
7 Phoenix	517,000	29,836,000	1,334	29
8 Seattle	1,544,000	102,840,000	7,581	101
9 St. Louis	1,761,000	38,725,000	3,623	127
10 Toronto	1,605,000	139,300,000	1,712	202
11 Vancouver	1,263,000	130,110,000	4,736	196

Lee decides to use simple regression analysis to examine whether one or more of three variables (the last three columns in the table) are cost drivers of purchasing department costs. Summary results for these regressions are as follows:

Regression 1: PDC = $a + (b \times$ MP$)$

Variable	Coefficient	Standard Error	t-Value
Constant	$1,041,421	$346,709	3.00
Independent variable 1: MP$	0.0031	0.0038	0.83

$r^2 = 0.08$; Durbin-Watson statistic = 2.41

Regression 2: PDC = $a (b \times$ No. of POs$)$

Variable	Coefficient	Standard Error	t-Value
Constant	$722,538	$265,835	2.72
Independent variable 1: No. of POs	$ 159.48	$ 64.84	2.46

$r^2 = 0.43$; Durbin-Watson statistic = 1.97

Regression 3: PDC = $a + (b \times$ No. of Ss$)$

Variable	Coefficient	Standard Error	t-Value
Constant	$828,814	$246,570	3.36
Independent variable 1: No. of Ss	$ 3,816	$ 1,698	2.25

$r^2 = 0.39$; Durbin-Watson statistic = 2.01

1. Compare and evaluate the three simple regression models estimated by Lee. Graph each one. Also, use the format employed in Exhibit 18 to evaluate the information.   **Required**
2. Do the regression results support the Couture Fabrics' presentation about the purchasing department's cost drivers? Which of these cost drivers would you recommend in designing an ABC system?
3. How might Lee gain additional evidence on drivers of purchasing department costs at each of Fashion Bling's stores?

10-41 **Purchasing department cost drivers, multiple regression analysis (continuation of 10-40).** Barry Lee decides that the simple regression analysis used in Problem 10-40 could be extended to a multiple regression analysis. He finds the following results for two multiple regression analyses:

Regression 4: PDC = $a + (b_1 \times$ No. of POs$) + (b_2 \times$ No. of Ss$)$

Variable	Coefficient	Standard Error	t-Value
Constant	$484,522	$256,684	1.89
Independent variable 1: No. of POs	$ 126.66	$ 57.80	2.19
Independent variable 2: No. of Ss	$ 2,903	$ 1,459	1.99

$r^2 = 0.64$; Durbin-Watson statistic = 1.91

Regression 5: PDC = $a + (b_1 \times$ No. of POs$) + (b_2 \times$ No. of Ss$) + (b_3 \times$ MP$)$

Variable	Coefficient	Standard Error	t-Value
Constant	$483,560	$312,554	1.55
Independent variable 1: No. of POs	$ 126.58	$ 63.75	1.99
Independent variable 2: No. of Ss	$ 2,901	$ 1,622	1.79
Independent variable 3: MP$	0.00002	0.0029	0.01

$r^2 = 0.64$; Durbin-Watson statistic = 1.91

The coefficients of correlation between combinations of pairs of the variables are as follows:

	PDC	MP$	No. of POs
MP$	0.28		
No. of POs	0.66	0.27	
No. of Ss	0.62	0.30	0.29

Required

1. Evaluate regression 4 using the criteria of economic plausibility, goodness of fit, significance of independent variables and specification analysis. Compare regression 4 with regressions 2 and 3 in Problem 10-40. Which one of these models would you recommend that Lee use? Why?
2. Compare regression 5 with regression 4. Which one of these models would you recommend that Lee use? Why?
3. Lee estimates the following data for the Baltimore store for next year: dollar value of merchandise purchased, $78,000,000; number of purchase orders, 4,000; number of suppliers, 95. How much should Lee budget for purchasing department costs for the Baltimore store for next year?
4. What difficulties do not arise in simple regression analysis that may arise in multiple regression analysis? Is there evidence of such difficulties in either of the multiple regressions presented in this problem? Explain.
5. Give two examples of decisions in which the regression results reported here (and in Problem 10-40) could be informative.

Collaborative Learning Problem

10-42 **Interpreting regression results, matching time periods, ethics.** Jayne Barbour is working as a summer intern at Mode, a trendy store specializing in clothing for twenty-somethings. Jayne has been working closely with her cousin, Gail Hubbard, who plans promotions for Mode. The store has only been in business for 10 months, and Valerie Parker, the store's owner, has been unsure of the effectiveness of the store's advertising. Wanting to impress Valerie with the regression analysis skills she acquired in a cost accounting course the previous semester, Jayne decides to prepare an analysis of the effect of advertising on revenues. She collects the following data:

	A	B	C
	Home	Insert	Page Layout	Formulas
1	Month	Advertising Expense	Revenue
2	October	4,560	$35,400
3	November	3,285	44,255
4	December	1,200	56,300
5	January	4,099	28,764
6	February	3,452	49,532
7	March	1,075	43,200
8	April	4,768	30,600
9	May	4,775	52,137
10	June	1,845	49,640
11	July	1,430	29,542

Jayne performs a regression analysis, comparing each month's advertising expense with that month's revenue, and obtains the following formula:

$$\text{Revenue} = \$47,801 - (1.92 \times \text{Advertising expense})$$

Variable	Coefficient	Standard Error	t-Value
Constant	$47,801.72	7,628.39	6.27
Independent variable: Advertising expense	−1.92	2.26	−0.85

$r^2 = 0.43$; Standard error = 10,340.18

1. Plot the preceding data on a graph and draw the regression line. What does the cost formula indicate about the relationship between monthly advertising expense and monthly revenues? Is the relationship economically plausible?

Required

2. Jayne worries that if she makes her presentation to the owner as planned, it will reflect poorly on her cousin Gail's performance. Is she ethically obligated to make the presentation?
3. Jayne thinks further about her analysis, and discovers a significant flaw in her approach. She realizes that advertising done in a given month should be expected to influence the following month's sales, not necessarily the current month's. She modifies her analysis by comparing, for example, October advertising expense with November sales revenue. The modified regression yields the following:

$$\text{Revenue} = \$23,538 + (5.92 \times \text{Advertising expense})$$

Variable	Coefficient	Standard Error	t-Value
Constant	$23,538.45	4,996.60	4.71
Independent variable: Previous month's advertising expense	5.92	1.42	4.18

$r^2 = 0.71$; Standard error = 6,015.67

What does the revised cost formula indicate? Plot the revised data on a graph. (You will need to discard October revenue and July advertising expense from the data set.) Is this relationship economically plausible?

4. Can Jayne conclude that there is a cause and effect relationship between advertising expense and sales revenue? Why or why not?

Strategy, Balanced Scorecard, and Strategic Profitability Analysis

From Chapter 13 of *Cost Accounting: A Managerial Emphasis*, 14/e. Charles T. Horngren. Srikant M. Datar. Madhav Rajan.
Copyright © 2012 by Pearson Education. Published by Prentice Hall. All rights reserved.

Strategy, Balanced Scorecard, and Strategic Profitability Analysis

Olive Garden wants to know.

So do Barnes and Noble, PepsiCo, and L.L.Bean. Even your local car dealer and transit authority are curious. They all want to know how well they are doing and how they score against the measures they strive to meet. The balanced scorecard can help them answer this question by evaluating key performance measures. Many companies have successfully used the balanced scorecard approach. Infosys Technologies, one of India's leading information technology companies, is one of them.

Balanced Scorecard Helps Infosys Transform into a Leading Consultancy[1]

In the early 2000s, Infosys Technologies was a company in transition. The Bangalore-based company was a market leader in information technology outsourcing, but needed to expand to meet increased client demand. Infosys invested in many new areas including business process outsourcing, project management, and management consulting. This put Infosys in direct competition with established consulting firms, such as IBM and Accenture.

Led by CEO Kris Gopalakrishnan, the company developed an integrated management structure that would help align these new, diverse initiatives. Infosys turned to the balanced scorecard to provide a framework the company could use to formulate and monitor its strategy. The balanced scorecard measures corporate performance along four dimensions—financial, customer, internal business process, and learning and growth.

The balanced scorecard immediately played a role in the transformation of Infosys. The executive team used the scorecard to guide discussion during its meetings. The continual process of adaptation, execution, and management that the scorecard fostered helped the team respond to, and even anticipate, its clients' evolving needs. Eventually, use of the scorecard for performance measurement spread to the rest of the organization, with monetary incentives linked to the company's performance along the different dimensions.

Over time, the balanced scorecard became part of the Infosys culture. In recent years, Infosys has begun using the balanced

---

[1] *Source*: Asis Martinez-Jerez, F., Robert S. Kaplan, and Katherine Miller. 2011. Infosys's relationship scorecard: Measuring transformational partnerships. Harvard Business School Case No. 9-109-006. Boston: Harvard Business School Publishing.

scorecard concept to create "relationship scorecards" for many of its largest clients. Using the scorecard framework, Infosys began measuring its performance for key clients not only on project management and client satisfaction, but also on repeat business and anticipating clients' future strategic needs.

The balanced scorecard helped successfully steer the transformation of Infosys from a technology outsourcer to a leading business consultancy. From 1999 to 2007, the company had a compound annual growth rate of 50%, with sales growing from $120 million in 1999 to more than $3 billion in 2007. Infosys was recognized for its achievements by making the *Wired* 40, *BusinessWeek* IT 100, and *BusinessWeek* Most Innovative Companies lists.

This chapter focuses on how management accounting information helps companies such as Infosys, Merck, Verizon, and Volkswagen implement and evaluate their strategies. Strategy drives the operations of a company and guides managers' short-run and long-run decisions. We describe the balanced scorecard approach to implementing strategy and methods to analyze operating income to evaluate the success of a strategy. We also show how management accounting information helps strategic initiatives, such as productivity improvement, reengineering, and downsizing.

Namas Bhojani/Getty Images, Inc.—Bloomberg News

What Is Strategy?

Strategy specifies how an organization matches its own capabilities with the opportunities in the marketplace to accomplish its objectives. In other words, strategy describes how an organization can create value for its customers while differentiating itself from its competitors. For example, Wal-Mart, the retail giant, creates value for its customers by locating stores in suburban and rural areas, and by offering low prices, a wide range of product categories, and few choices within each product category. Consistent with its strategy, Wal-Mart has developed the capability to keep costs down by aggressively negotiating low prices with its suppliers in exchange for high volumes and by maintaining a no-frills, cost-conscious environment.

In formulating its strategy, an organization must first thoroughly understand its industry. Industry analysis focuses on five forces: (1) competitors, (2) potential entrants into the market, (3) equivalent products, (4) bargaining power of customers, and (5) bargaining power of input suppliers.[2] The collective effect of these forces shapes an organization's profit potential. In general, profit potential decreases with greater competition, stronger potential entrants, products that are similar, and more-demanding customers and suppliers. We illustrate these five forces for Chipset, Inc., maker of linear integrated circuit

---

[2] M. Porter, *Competitive Strategy* (New York: Free Press, 1980); M. Porter, *Competitive Advantage* (New York: Free Press, 1985); and M. Porter, "What Is Strategy?" *Harvard Business Review* (November–December 1996): 61–78.

devices (LICDs) used in modems and communication networks. Chipset produces a single specialized product, CX1, a standard, high-performance microchip, which can be used in multiple applications. Chipset designed CX1 with extensive input from customers.

1. **Competitors.** The CX1 model faces severe competition with respect to price, timely delivery, and quality. Companies in the industry have high fixed costs, and persistent pressures to reduce selling prices and utilize capacity fully. Price reductions spur growth because it makes LICDs a cost-effective option in new applications such as digital subscriber lines (DSLs).

2. **Potential entrants into the market.** The small profit margins and high capital costs discourage new entrants. Moreover, incumbent companies such as Chipset are further down the learning curve with respect to lowering costs and building close relationships with customers and suppliers.

3. **Equivalent products.** Chipset tailors CX1 to customer needs and lowers prices by continuously improving CX1's design and processes to reduce production costs. This reduces the risk of equivalent products or new technologies replacing CX1.

4. **Bargaining power of customers.** Customers, such as EarthLink and Verizon, negotiate aggressively with Chipset and its competitors to keep prices down because they buy large quantities of product.

5. **Bargaining power of input suppliers.** To produce CX1, Chipset requires high-quality materials (such as silicon wafers, pins for connectivity, and plastic or ceramic packaging) and skilled engineers, technicians, and manufacturing labor. The skill-sets suppliers and employees bring gives them bargaining power to demand higher prices and wages.

In summary, strong competition and the bargaining powers of customers and suppliers put significant pressure on Chipset's selling prices. To respond to these challenges, Chipset must choose one of two basic strategies: *differentiating its product* or *achieving cost leadership*.

Product differentiation is an organization's ability to offer products or services perceived by its customers to be superior and unique relative to the products or services of its competitors. Apple Inc. has successfully differentiated its products in the consumer electronics industry, as have Johnson & Johnson in the pharmaceutical industry and Coca-Cola in the soft drink industry. These companies have achieved differentiation through innovative product R&D, careful development and promotion of their brands, and the rapid push of products to market. Differentiation increases brand loyalty and the willingness of customers to pay higher prices.

Cost leadership is an organization's ability to achieve lower costs relative to competitors through productivity and efficiency improvements, elimination of waste, and tight cost control. Cost leaders in their respective industries include Wal-Mart (consumer retailing), Home Depot and Lowe's (building products), Texas Instruments (consumer electronics), and Emerson Electric (electric motors). These companies provide products and services that are similar to—not differentiated from—their competitors, but at a lower cost to the customer. Lower selling prices, rather than unique products or services, provide a competitive advantage for these cost leaders.

What strategy should Chipset follow? To help it decide, Chipset develops the customer preference map shown in Exhibit 1. The *y*-axis describes various attributes of the product desired by customers. The *x*-axis describes how well Chipset and Visilog, a competitor of Chipset that follows a product-differentiation strategy, do along the various attributes desired by customers from 1 (poor) to 5 (very good). The map highlights the trade-offs in any strategy. It shows the advantages CX1 enjoys in terms of price, scalability (the CX1 technology allows Chispet's customer to achieve different performance levels by simply altering the number of CX1 units in their product), and customer service. Visilog's chips, however, are faster and more powerful, and are customized for various applications such as different types of modems and communication networks.

CX1 is somewhat differentiated from competing products. Differentiating CX1 further would be costly, but Chipset may be able to charge a higher price. Conversely, reducing the cost of manufacturing CX1 would allow Chipset to lower price, spur growth, and increase market share. The scalability of CX1 makes it an effective solution for meeting

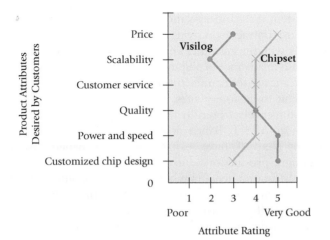

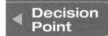

Exhibit 1

Customer Preference Map for LICDs

varying customer needs. Also, Chipset's current engineering staff is more skilled at making product and process improvements than at creatively designing new products and technologies. Chipset decides to follow a cost-leadership strategy.

To achieve its cost-leadership strategy, Chipset must improve its own internal capabilities. It must enhance quality and reengineer processes to downsize and eliminate excess capacity. At the same time, Chipset's management team does not want to make cuts in personnel that would hurt company morale and hinder future growth.

Building Internal Capabilities: Quality Improvement and Reengineering at Chipset

To improve product quality—that is, to reduce defect rates and improve yields in its manufacturing process—Chipset must maintain process parameters within tight ranges based on real-time data about manufacturing-process parameters, such as temperature and pressure. Chipset must also train its workers in quality-management techniques to help them identify the root causes of defects and ways to prevent them and empower them to take actions to improve quality.

A second element of Chipset's strategy is reengineering its order-delivery process. Some of Chipset's customers have complained about the lengthening time span between ordering products and receiving them. **Reengineering** is the fundamental rethinking and redesign of business processes to achieve improvements in critical measures of performance, such as cost, quality, service, speed, and customer satisfaction.[3] To illustrate reengineering, consider the order-delivery system at Chipset in 2010. When Chipset received an order from a customer, a copy was sent to manufacturing, where a production scheduler began planning the manufacturing of the ordered products. Frequently, a considerable amount of time elapsed before production began on the ordered product. After manufacturing was complete, CX1 chips moved to the shipping department, which matched the quantities of CX1 to be shipped against customer orders. Often, completed CX1 chips stayed in inventory until a truck became available for shipment. If the quantity to be shipped was less than the number of chips requested by the customer, a special shipment was made for the balance of the chips. Shipping documents moved to the billing department for issuing invoices. Special staff in the accounting department followed up with customers for payments.

The many transfers of CX1 chips and information across departments (sales, manufacturing, shipping, billing, and accounting) to satisfy a customer's order created delays. Furthermore, no single individual was responsible for fulfilling a customer order. To respond to these challenges, Chipset formed a cross-functional team in late 2010 and implemented a reengineered order-delivery process in 2011.

Decision Point

What are two generic strategies a company can use?

Learning Objective 2

Understand what comprises reengineering

. . . redesigning business processes to improve performance by reducing cost and improving quality

---

[3] See M. Hammer and J. Champy, *Reengineering the Corporation: A Manifesto for Business Revolution* (New York: Harper, 1993); E. Ruhli, C. Treichler, and S. Schmidt, "From Business Reengineering to Management Reengineering—A European Study," *Management International Review* (1995): 361–371; and K. Sandberg, "Reengineering Tries a Comeback—This Time for Growth, Not Just for Cost Savings," *Harvard Management Update* (November 2001).

Under the new system, a customer-relationship manager is responsible for each customer and negotiates long-term contracts specifying quantities and prices. The customer-relationship manager works closely with the customer and with manufacturing to specify delivery schedules for CX1 one month in advance of shipment. The schedule of customer orders and delivery dates is sent electronically to manufacturing. Completed chips are shipped directly from the manufacturing plant to customer sites. Each shipment automatically triggers an electronic invoice and customers electronically transfer funds to Chipset's bank.

Companies, such as AT&T, Banca di America e di Italia, Cigna Insurance, Cisco, PepsiCo, and Siemens Nixdorf, have realized significant benefits by reengineering their processes across design, production, and marketing (just as in the Chipset example). Reengineering has only limited benefits when reengineering efforts focus on only a single activity such as shipping or invoicing rather than the entire order-delivery process. To be successful, reengineering efforts must focus on changing roles and responsibilities, eliminating unnecessary activities and tasks, using information technology, and developing employee skills.

Take another look at Exhibit 1 and note the interrelatedness and consistency in Chipset's strategy. To help meet customer preferences for price, quality, and customer service, Chipset decides on a cost-leadership strategy. And to achieve cost leadership, Chipset builds internal capabilities by reengineering its processes. Chipset's next challenge is to effectively implement its strategy

Decision Point

What is reengineering?

Strategy Implementation and the Balanced Scorecard

Many organizations, such as Allstate Insurance, Bank of Montreal, BP, and Dow Chemical, have introduced a *balanced scorecard* approach to track progress and manage the implementation of their strategies.

Learning Objective 3

Understand the four perspectives of the balanced scorecard

. . . financial, customer, internal business process, and learning and growth

The Balanced Scorecard

The **balanced scorecard** translates an organization's mission and strategy into a set of performance measures that provides the framework for implementing its strategy.[4] The balanced scorecard does not focus solely on achieving short-run financial objectives. It also highlights the nonfinancial objectives that an organization must achieve to meet and sustain its financial objectives. The scorecard measures an organization's performance from four perspectives: (1) financial, the profits and value created for shareholders; (2) customer, the success of the company in its target market; (3) internal business processes, the internal operations that create value for customers; and (4) learning and growth, the people and system capabilities that support operations. A company's strategy influences the measures it uses to track performance in each of these perspectives.

Why is this tool called a balanced scorecard? Because it balances the use of financial and nonfinancial performance measures to evaluate short-run and long-run performance in a single report. The balanced scorecard reduces managers' emphasis on short-run financial performance, such as quarterly earnings, because the key strategic nonfinancial and operational indicators, such as product quality and customer satisfaction, measure changes that a company is making for the long run. The financial benefits of these long-run changes may not show up immediately in short-run earnings; however, strong improvement in nonfinancial measures usually indicates the creation of future economic value. For example, an increase in customer satisfaction, as measured by customer surveys and repeat purchases, signals a strong likelihood of higher sales and income in the future. By balancing the mix of financial and nonfinancial measures, the balanced scorecard

---

[4] See R. S. Kaplan and D. P. Norton, *The Balanced Scorecard* (Boston: Harvard Business School Press, 1996); R. S. Kaplan and D. P. Norton, *The Strategy-Focused Organization: How Balanced Scorecard Companies Thrive in the New Business Environment* (Boston: Harvard Business School Press, 2001); R. S. Kaplan and D. P. Norton, *Strategy Maps: Converting Intangible Assets into Tangible Outcomes* (Boston: Harvard Business School Press, 2004); and R. S. Kaplan and D. P. Norton, *Alignment: Using the Balanced Scorecard to Create Corporate Synergies* (Boston: Harvard Business School Press, 2006).

For simplicity, this chapter, and much of the literature, emphasizes long-run financial objectives as the primary goal of for-profit companies. For-profit companies interested in long-run financial, environmental, and social objectives adapt the balanced scorecard to implement all three objectives.

broadens management's attention to short-run *and* long-run performance. *Never lose sight of the key point. In for-profit companies, the primary goal of the balanced scorecard is to sustain long-run financial performance. Nonfinancial measures simply serve as leading indicators for the hard-to-measure long-run financial performance.*

Strategy Maps and the Balanced Scorecard

We use the Chipset example to develop strategy maps and the four perspectives of the balanced scorecard. The objectives and measures Chipset's managers choose for each perspective relates to the action plans for furthering Chipset's cost leadership strategy: *improving quality* and *reengineering processes.*

Strategy Maps

A useful first step in designing a balanced scorecard is a *strategy map*. A **strategy map** is a diagram that describes how an organization creates value by connecting strategic objectives in explicit cause-and-effect relationships with each other in the financial, customer, internal business process, and learning and growth perspectives. Exhibit 2 presents Chipset's strategy map. Follow the arrows to see how a strategic objective affects other strategic objectives. For example, empowering the workforce helps align employee and organization goals and improves processes. Employee and organizational alignment also helps improve processes that improve manufacturing quality and productivity, reduce customer delivery time, meet specified delivery dates, and improve post-sales service, all of which increase customer satisfaction. Improving manufacturing quality and productivity

Exhibit 2   Strategy Map for Chipset, Inc., for 2011

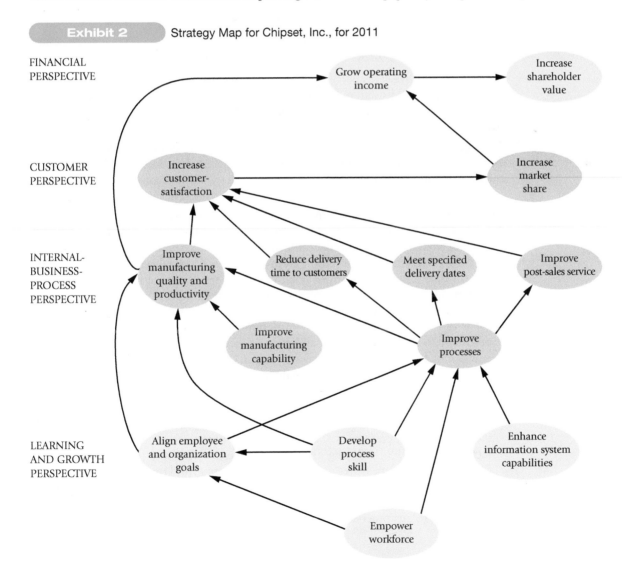

grows operating income and increases customer satisfaction that, in turn, increases market share, operating income, and shareholder value.

Chipset operates in a knowledge-intensive business. To compete successfully, Chipset invests in its employees, implements new technology and process controls, improves quality, and reengineers processes. Doing these activities well enables Chipset to build capabilities and intangible assets, which are not recorded as assets in its financial books. The strategy map helps Chipset evaluate whether these intangible assets are generating financial returns.

Chipset could include many other cause-and-effect relationships in the strategy map in Exhibit 2. But, Chipset, like other companies implementing the balanced scorecard, focuses on only those relationships that it believes to be the most significant.

Chipset uses the strategy map from Exhibit 2 to build the balanced scorecard presented in Exhibit 3. The scorecard highlights the four perspectives of performance: financial, customer, internal business process, and learning and growth. The first column presents the strategic objectives from the strategy map in Exhibit 2. At the beginning of 2011, the company's managers specify the strategic objectives, measures, initiatives (the actions necessary to achieve the objectives), and target performance (the first four columns of Exhibit 3).

Chipset wants to use the balanced scorecard targets to drive the organization to higher levels of performance. Managers therefore set targets at a level of performance that is achievable, yet distinctly better than competitors. Chipset's managers complete the fifth column, reporting actual performance at the end of 2011. This column compares Chipset's performance relative to target.

Four Perspectives of the Balanced Scorecard

We next describe the perspectives in general terms and illustrate each perspective using the measures chosen by Chipset in the context of its strategy.

1. **Financial perspective.** This perspective evaluates the profitability of the strategy and the creation of shareholder value. Because Chipset's key strategic initiatives are cost reduction relative to competitors' costs and sales growth, the financial perspective focuses on how much operating income results from reducing costs and selling more units of CX1.

2. **Customer perspective.** This perspective identifies targeted customer and market segments and measures the company's success in these segments. To monitor its customer objectives, Chipset uses measures such as market share in the communication-networks segment, number of new customers, and customer-satisfaction ratings.

3. **Internal-business-process perspective.** This perspective focuses on internal operations that create value for customers that, in turn, help achieve financial performance. Chipset determines internal-business-process improvement targets after benchmarking against its main competitors using information from published financial statements, prevailing prices, customers, suppliers, former employees, industry experts, and financial analysts. The internal-business-process perspective comprises three subprocesses:

   ■ **Innovation process:** Creating products, services, and processes that will meet the needs of customers. This is a very important process for companies that follow a product-differentiation strategy and must constantly design and develop innovative new products to remain competitive in the marketplace. Chipset's innovation focuses on improving its manufacturing capability and process controls to lower costs and improve quality. Chipset measures innovation by the number of improvements in manufacturing processes and percentage of processes with advanced controls.

   ■ **Operations process:** Producing and delivering existing products and services that will meet the needs of customers. Chipset's strategic initiatives are (a) improving manufacturing quality, (b) reducing delivery time to customers, and (c) meeting specified delivery dates so it measures yield, order-delivery time, and on-time deliveries.

   ■ **Postsales-service process:** Providing service and support to the customer after the sale of a product or service. Chipset monitors how quickly and accurately it is responding to customer-service requests.

Exhibit 3   The Balanced Scorecard for Chipset, Inc., for 2011

Strategic Objectives	Measures	Initiatives	Target Performance	Actual Performance
Financial Perspective				
Grow operating income	Operating income from productivity gain	Manage costs and unused capacity	$1,850,000	$1,912,500
Increase shareholder value	Operating income from growth	Build strong customer relationships	$2,500,000	$2,820,000
	Revenue growth		9%	10%[a]
Customer Perspective				
Increase market share	Market share in communication-networks segment	Identify future needs of customers	6%	7%
Increase customer satisfaction	Number of new customers	Identify new target-customer segments	1	1[b]
	Customer-satisfaction ratings	Increase customer focus of sales organization	90% of customers give top two ratings	87% of customers give top two ratings
Internal-Business-Process Perspective				
Improve postsales service	Service response time	Improve customer-service process	Within 4 hours	Within 3 hours
Improve manufacturing quality and productivity	Yield	Identify root causes of problems and improve quality	78%	79.3%
Reduce delivery time to customers	Order-delivery time	Reengineer order-delivery process	30 days	30 days
Meet specified delivery dates	On-time delivery	Reengineer order-delivery process	92%	90%
Improve processes	Number of major improvements in manufacturing and business processes	Organize teams from manufacturing and sales to modify processes	5	5
Improve manufacturing capability	Percentage of processes with advanced controls	Organize R&D/manufacturing teams to implement advanced controls	75%	75%
Learning-and-Growth Perspective				
Align employee and organization goals	Employee-satisfaction ratings	Employee participation and suggestions program to build teamwork	80% of employees give top two ratings	88% of employees give top two ratings
Empower workforce	Percentage of line workers empowered to manage processes	Have supervisors act as coaches rather than decision makers	85%	90%
Develop process skill	Percentage of employees trained in process and quality management	Employee training programs	90%	92%
Enhance information-system capabilities	Percentage of manufacturing processes with real-time feedback	Improve online and offline data gathering	80%	80%

[a](Revenues in 2011 − Revenues in 2010) ÷ Revenues in 2010 = ($25,300,000 − $23,000,000) ÷ $23,000,000 = 10%.

[b]Number of customers increased from seven to eight in 2011.

4. **Learning-and-growth perspective.** This perspective identifies the capabilities the organization must excel at to achieve superior internal processes that in turn create value for customers and shareholders. Chipset's learning and growth perspective emphasizes three capabilities: (1) information-system capabilities, measured by the percentage of manufacturing processes with real-time feedback; (2) employee capabilities, measured by the percentage of employees trained in process and quality management; and (3) motivation, measured by employee satisfaction and the percentage of manufacturing and sales employees (line employees) empowered to manage processes.

The arrows in Exhibit 3 indicate the *broad* cause-and-effect linkages: how gains in the learning-and-growth perspective lead to improvements in internal business processes, which lead to higher customer satisfaction and market share, and finally lead to superior financial performance. Note how the scorecard describes elements of Chipset's strategy implementation. Worker training and empowerment improve employee satisfaction and lead to manufacturing and business-process improvements that improve quality and reduce delivery time. The result is increased customer satisfaction and higher market share. These initiatives have been successful from a financial perspective. Chipset has earned significant operating income from its cost leadership strategy, and that strategy has also led to growth.

A major benefit of the balanced scorecard is that it promotes causal thinking. Think of the balanced scorecard as a *linked scorecard* or a *causal scorecard*. Managers must search for empirical evidence (rather than rely on faith alone) to test the validity and strength of the various connections. A causal scorecard enables a company to focus on the key drivers that steer the implementation of the strategy. Without convincing links, the scorecard loses much of its value.

Implementing a Balanced Scorecard

To successfully implement a balanced scorecard requires commitment and leadership from top management. At Chipset, the team building the balanced scorecard (headed by the vice president of strategic planning) conducted interviews with senior managers, probed executives about customers, competitors, and technological developments, and sought proposals for balanced scorecard objectives across the four perspectives. The team then met to discuss the responses and to build a prioritized list of objectives.

In a meeting with all senior managers, the team sought to achieve consensus on the scorecard objectives. Senior management was then divided into four groups, with each group responsible for one of the perspectives. In addition, each group broadened the base of inputs by including representatives from the next-lower levels of management and key functional managers. The groups identified measures for each objective and the sources of information for each measure. The groups then met to finalize scorecard objectives, measures, targets, and the initiatives to achieve the targets. Management accountants played an important role in the design and implementation of the balanced scorecard, particularly in determining measures to represent the realities of the business. This required management accountants to understand the economic environment of the industry, Chipset's customers and competitors, and internal business issues such as human resources, operations, and distribution.

Managers made sure that employees understood the scorecard and the scorecard process. The final balanced scorecard was communicated to all employees. Sharing the scorecard allowed engineers and operating personnel, for example, to understand the reasons for customer satisfaction and dissatisfaction and to make suggestions for improving internal processes directly aimed at satisfying customers and implementing Chipset's strategy. Too often, scorecards are seen by only a select group of managers. By limiting the scorecard's exposure, an organization loses the opportunity for widespread organization engagement and alignment.

Chipset (like Cigna Property, Casualty Insurance, and Wells Fargo) also encourages each department to develop its own scorecard that ties into Chipset's main scorecard described in Exhibit 3. For example, the quality control department's scorecard has measures that its department managers use to improve yield—number of quality circles, statistical process control charts, Pareto diagrams, and root-cause analyses.

Department scorecards help align the actions of each department to implement Chipset's strategy.

Companies frequently use balanced scorecards to evaluate and reward managerial performance and to influence managerial behavior. Using the balanced scorecard for performance evaluation widens the performance management lens and motivates managers to give greater attention to nonfinancial drivers of performance. Surveys indicate, however, that companies continue to assign more weight to the financial perspective (55%) than to the other perspectives—customer (19%), internal business process (12%), and learning and growth (14%). Companies cite several reasons for the relatively smaller weight on nonfinancial measures: difficulty evaluating the relative importance of nonfinancial measures; challenges in measuring and quantifying qualitative, nonfinancial data; and difficulty in compensating managers despite poor financial performance. Many companies, however, are giving greater weight to nonfinancial measures in promotion decisions because they believe that nonfinancial measures (such as customer satisfaction, process improvements, and employee motivation) better assess a manager's potential to succeed at senior levels of management. For the balanced scorecard to be effective, managers must view it as fairly assessing and rewarding all important aspects of a manager's performance and promotion prospects.

Aligning the Balanced Scorecard to Strategy

Different strategies call for different scorecards. Recall Chipset's competitor Visilog, which follows a product-differentiation strategy by designing custom chips for modems and communication networks. Visilog designs its balanced scorecard to fit its strategy. For example, in the financial perspective, Visilog evaluates how much of its operating income comes from charging premium prices for its products. In the customer perspective, Visilog measures the percentage of its revenues from new products and new customers. In the internal-business-process perspective, Visilog measures the number of new products introduced and new product development time. In the learning-and-growth perspective, Visilog measures the development of advanced manufacturing capabilities to produce custom chips. Visilog also uses some of the measures described in Chipset's balanced scorecard in Exhibit 3. For example, revenue growth, customer satisfaction ratings, order-delivery time, on-time delivery, percentage of frontline workers empowered to manage processes, and employee-satisfaction ratings are also important measures under the product-differentiation strategy. The goal is to align the balanced scorecard with company strategy.[5] Exhibit 4 presents some common measures found on company scorecards in the service, retail, and manufacturing sectors.

Features of a Good Balanced Scorecard

A well-designed balanced scorecard has several features:

1. It tells the story of a company's strategy, articulating a sequence of cause-and-effect relationships—the links among the various perspectives that align implementation of the strategy. In for-profit companies, each measure in the scorecard is part of a cause-and-effect chain leading to financial outcomes. Not-for-profit organizations design the cause-and-effect chain to achieve their strategic service objectives—for example, number of people no longer in poverty, or number of children still in school.

2. The balanced scorecard helps to communicate the strategy to all members of the organization by translating the strategy into a coherent and linked set of understandable and measurable operational targets. Guided by the scorecard, managers and employees take actions and make decisions to achieve the company's strategy. Companies that have distinct strategic business units (SBUs)—such as consumer

---

[5] For simplicity, we have presented the balanced scorecard in the context of companies that have followed either a cost-leadership or a product-differentiation strategy. Of course, a company may have some products for which cost leadership is critical and other products for which product differentiation is important. The company will then develop separate scorecards to implement the different product strategies. In still other contexts, product differentiation may be of primary importance, but some cost leadership must also be achieved. The balanced scorecard measures would then be linked in a cause-and-effect way to this strategy.

Financial Perspective
Income measures: Operating income, gross margin percentage
Revenue and cost measures: Revenue growth, revenues from new products, cost reductions in key areas
Income and investment measures: Economic value added (EVA®), return on investment
Customer Perspective
Market share, customer satisfaction, customer-retention percentage, time taken to fulfill customers' requests, number of customer complaints
Internal-Business-Process Perspective
Innovation Process: Operating capabilities, number of new products or services, new-product development times, and number of new patents
Operations Process: Yield, defect rates, time taken to deliver product to customers, percentage of on-time deliveries, average time taken to respond to orders, setup time, manufacturing downtime
Postsales Service Process: Time taken to replace or repair defective products, hours of customer training for using the product
Learning-and-Growth Perspective
Employee measures: Employee education and skill levels, employee-satisfaction ratings, employee turnover rates, percentage of employee suggestions implemented, percentage of compensation based on individual and team incentives
Technology measures: Information system availability, percentage of processes with advanced controls

products and pharmaceuticals at Johnson & Johnson—develop their balanced scorecards at the SBU level. Each SBU has its own unique strategy and implementation goals; building separate scorecards allows each SBU to choose measures that help implement its distinctive strategy.

3. In for-profit companies, the balanced scorecard must motivate managers to take actions that eventually result in improvements in financial performance. Managers sometimes tend to focus too much on innovation, quality, and customer satisfaction as ends in themselves. For example, Xerox spent heavily to increase customer satisfaction without a resulting financial payoff because higher levels of satisfaction did not increase customer loyalty. Some companies use statistical methods, such as regression analysis, to test the anticipated cause-and-effect relationships among nonfinancial measures and financial performance. The data for this analysis can come from either time series data (collected over time) or cross-sectional data (collected, for example, across multiple stores of a retail chain). In the Chipset example, improvements in non-financial factors have, in fact, already led to improvements in financial factors.

4. The balanced scorecard limits the number of measures, identifying only the most critical ones. Chipset's scorecard, for example, has 16 measures, between 3 and 6 measures for each perspective. Limiting the number of measures focuses managers' attention on those that most affect strategy implementation. Using too many measures makes it difficult for managers to process relevant information.

5. The balanced scorecard highlights less-than-optimal trade-offs that managers may make when they fail to consider operational and financial measures together. For example, a company whose strategy is innovation and product differentiation could achieve superior short-run financial performance by reducing spending on R&D. A good balanced scorecard would signal that the short-run financial performance might have been achieved by taking actions that hurt future financial performance because a leading indicator of that performance, R&D spending and R&D output, has declined.

Pitfalls in Implementing a Balanced Scorecard

Pitfalls to avoid in implementing a balanced scorecard include the following:

1. Managers should not assume the cause-and-effect linkages are precise. They are merely hypotheses. Over time, a company must gather evidence of the strength and timing of the linkages among the nonfinancial and financial measures. With experience,

organizations should alter their scorecards to include those nonfinancial strategic objectives and measures that are the best leading indicators (the causes) of financial performance (a lagging indicator or the effect). Understanding that the scorecard evolves over time helps managers avoid unproductively spending time and money trying to design the "perfect" scorecard at the outset. Furthermore, as the business environment and strategy change over time, the measures in the scorecard also need to change.

2. Managers should not seek improvements across all of the measures all of the time. For example, strive for quality and on-time performance but not beyond the point at which further improvement in these objectives is so costly that it is inconsistent with long-run profit maximization. Cost-benefit considerations should always be central when designing a balanced scorecard.

3. Managers should not use only objective measures in the balanced scorecard. Chipset's balanced scorecard includes both objective measures (such as operating income from cost leadership, market share, and manufacturing yield) and subjective measures (such as customer- and employee-satisfaction ratings). When using subjective measures, though, managers must be careful that the benefits of this potentially rich information are not lost by using measures that are inaccurate or that can be easily manipulated.

4. Despite challenges of measurement, top management should not ignore nonfinancial measures when evaluating managers and other employees. Managers tend to focus on the measures used to reward their performance. Excluding nonfinancial measures when evaluating performance will reduce the significance and importance that managers give to nonfinancial measures.

Evaluating the Success of Strategy and Implementation

Decision Point

How can an organization translate its strategy into a set of performance measures?

To evaluate how successful Chipset's strategy and its implementation have been, its management compares the target- and actual-performance columns in the balanced scorecard (Exhibit 3). Chipset met most targets set on the basis of competitor benchmarks in 2011 itself. That's because, in the Chipset context, improvements in the learning and growth perspective quickly ripple through to the financial perspective. Chipset will continue to seek improvements on the targets it did not achieve, but meeting most targets suggests that the strategic initiatives that Chipset identified and measured for learning and growth resulted in improvements in internal business processes, customer measures, and financial performance.

How would Chipset know if it had problems in strategy implementation? If it did not meet its targets on the two perspectives that are more internally focused: learning and growth and internal business processes.

What if Chipset performed well on learning and growth and internal business processes, but customer measures and financial performance in this year and the next did not improve? Chipset's managers would then conclude that Chipset did a good job of implementation (the various internal nonfinancial measures it targeted improved) but that its strategy was faulty (there was no effect on customers or on long-run financial performance and value creation). Management failed to identify the correct causal links. It implemented the wrong strategy well! Management would then reevaluate the strategy and the factors that drive it.

Now what if Chipset performed well on its various nonfinancial measures, and operating income over this year and the next also increased? Chipset's managers might be tempted to declare the strategy a success because operating income increased. Unfortunately, management still cannot conclude with any confidence that Chipset successfully formulated and implemented its strategy. Why? Because operating income can increase simply because entire markets are expanding, not because a company's strategy has been successful. Also, changes in operating income might occur because of factors outside the strategy. For example, a company such as Chipset that has chosen a cost-leadership strategy may find that its operating-income increase actually resulted from, say, some degree of product differentiation. *To evaluate the success of a strategy, managers and management accountants need to link strategy to the sources of operating-income increases.*

For Chipset to conclude that it was successful in implementing its strategy, it must demonstrate that improvements in its financial performance and operating income over time resulted from achieving targeted cost savings and growth in market share. Fortunately, the top two rows of Chipset's balanced scorecard in Exhibit 3 show that operating-income gains from productivity ($1,912,500) and growth ($2,820,000) exceeded targets. The next section of this chapter describes how these numbers were calculated. Because its strategy has been successful, Chipset's management can be more confident that the gains will be sustained in subsequent years.

Chipset's management accountants subdivide changes in operating income into components that can be identified with product differentiation, cost leadership, and growth. Why growth? Because successful product differentiation or cost leadership generally increases market share and helps a company to grow. Subdividing the change in operating income to evaluate the success of a strategy is conceptually similar to variance analysis. One difference, however, is that management accountants compare actual operating performance over two different periods, not actual to budgeted numbers in the same time period as in variance analysis.[6]

Strategic Analysis of Operating Income

Learning Objective 4

Analyze changes in operating income to evaluate strategy

. . . growth, price recovery, and productivity

The following illustration explains how to subdivide the change in operating income from one period to *any* future period. The individual components describe company performance with regard to product differentiation, cost leadership, and growth.[7] We illustrate the analysis using data from 2010 and 2011 because Chipset implemented key elements of its strategy in late 2010 and early 2011 and expects the financial consequences of these strategies to occur in 2011. Suppose the financial consequences of these strategies had been expected to affect operating income in only 2012. Then we could just as easily have compared 2010 to 2012. If necessary, we could also have compared 2010 to 2011 and 2012 taken together.

Chipset's data for 2010 and 2011 follow:

	2010	2011
1. Units of CX1 produced and sold	1,000,000	1,150,000
2. Selling price	$23	$22
3. Direct materials (square centimeters of silicon wafers)	3,000,000	2,900,000
4. Direct material cost per square centimeter	$1.40	$1.50
5. Manufacturing processing capacity (in square centimeters of silicon wafer)	3,750,000	3,500,000
6. Conversion costs (all manufacturing costs other than direct material costs)	$16,050,000	$15,225,000
7. Conversion cost per unit of capacity (row 6 ÷ row 5)	$4.28	$4.35

Chipset provides the following additional information:

1. Conversion costs (labor and overhead costs) for each year depend on production processing capacity defined in terms of the quantity of square centimeters of silicon wafers that Chipset can process. These costs do not vary with the actual quantity of silicon wafers processed.

2. Chipset incurs no R&D costs. Its marketing, sales, and customer-service costs are small relative to the other costs. Chipset has fewer than 10 customers, each purchasing roughly the same quantities of CX1. Because of the highly technical nature of the product, Chipset uses a cross-functional team for its marketing, sales, and customer-service activities. This cross-functional approach ensures that, although marketing, sales, and customer-service costs are small, the entire Chipset organization, including manufacturing engineers, remains focused on increasing customer satisfaction and

---

[6] Other examples of focusing on actual performance over two periods rather than comparisons of actuals with budgets can be found in J. Hope and R. Fraser, *Beyond Budgeting* (Boston, MA: Harvard Business School Press, 2003).

[7] For other details, see R. Banker, S. Datar, and R. Kaplan, "Productivity Measurement and Management Accounting," *Journal of Accounting, Auditing and Finance* (1989): 528–554; and A. Hayzen and J. Reeve, "Examining the Relationships in Productivity Accounting," *Management Accounting Quarterly* (2000): 32–39.

market share. (The Problem for Self-Study at the end of this chapter describes a situation in which marketing, sales, and customer-service costs are significant.)

3. Chipset's asset structure is very similar in 2010 and 2011.

4. Operating income for each year is as follows:

	2010	2011
Revenues		
($23 per unit × 1,000,000 units; $22 per unit × 1,150,000 units)	$23,000,000	$25,300,000
Costs		
Direct material costs		
($1.40/sq. cm. × 3,000,000 sq. cm.; $1.50/sq. cm. × 2,900,000 sq. cm.)	4,200,000	4,350,000
Conversion costs		
($4.28/sq. cm. × 3,750,000 sq. cm.; $4.35/sq. cm. × 3,500,000 sq. cm.)	16,050,000	15,225,000
Total costs	20,250,000	19,575,000
Operating income	$ 2,750,000	$ 5,725,000
Change in operating income	$2,975,000 F	

The goal of Chipset's managers is to evaluate how much of the $2,975,000 increase in operating income was caused by the successful implementation of the company's cost-leadership strategy. To do this, management accountants start by analyzing three main factors: growth, price recovery, and productivity.

The **growth component** measures the change in operating income attributable solely to the change in the quantity of output sold between 2010 and 2011.

The **price-recovery component** measures the change in operating income attributable solely to changes in Chipset's prices of inputs and outputs between 2010 and 2011. The price-recovery component measures change in output price compared with changes in input prices. A company that has successfully pursued a strategy of product differentiation will be able to increase its output price faster than the increase in its input prices, boosting profit margins and operating income: It will show a large positive price-recovery component.

The **productivity component** measures the change in costs attributable to a change in the quantity of inputs used in 2011 relative to the quantity of inputs that would have been used in 2010 to produce the 2011 output. The productivity component measures the amount by which operating income increases by using inputs efficiently to lower costs. A company that has successfully pursued a strategy of cost leadership will be able to produce a given quantity of output with a lower cost of inputs: It will show a large positive productivity component. Given Chipset's strategy of cost leadership, we expect the increase in operating income to be attributable to the productivity and growth components, not to price recovery. We now examine these three components in detail.

Growth Component of Change in Operating Income

The growth component of the change in operating income measures the increase in revenues minus the increase in costs from selling more units of CX1 in 2011 (1,150,000 units) than in 2010 (1,000,000 units), *assuming nothing else has changed.*

Revenue Effect of Growth

$$\text{Revenue effect of growth} = \left(\begin{array}{c} \text{Actual units of} \\ \text{output sold} \\ \text{in 2011} \end{array} - \begin{array}{c} \text{Actual units of} \\ \text{output sold} \\ \text{in 2010} \end{array} \right) \times \begin{array}{c} \text{Selling} \\ \text{price} \\ \text{in 2010} \end{array}$$

$$= (1{,}150{,}000 \text{ units} - 1{,}000{,}000 \text{ units}) \times \$23 \text{ per unit}$$

$$= \$3{,}450{,}000 \text{ F}$$

This component is favorable (F) because the increase in output sold in 2011 increases operating income. Components that decrease operating income are unfavorable (U).

Note that Chipset uses the 2010 price of CX1 and focuses only on the increase in units sold between 2010 and 2011, because the revenue effect of growth component measures how much revenues would have changed in 2010 if Chipset had sold 1,150,000 units instead of 1,000,000 units.

Cost Effect of Growth

The cost effect of growth measures how much costs would have changed in 2010 if Chipset had produced 1,150,000 units of CX1 instead of 1,000,000 units. To measure the cost effect of growth, Chipset's managers distinguish variable costs such as direct material costs from fixed costs such as conversion costs, because as units produced (and sold) increase, variable costs increase proportionately but fixed costs, generally, do not change.

$$\begin{pmatrix} \text{Cost effect of} \\ \text{growth for} \\ \text{variable costs} \end{pmatrix} = \begin{pmatrix} \text{Units of input} & \text{Actual units of} \\ \text{required to} & \text{input used} \\ \text{produce 2011} & - \text{to produce} \\ \text{output in 2010} & \text{2010 output} \end{pmatrix} \times \begin{matrix} \text{Input} \\ \text{price} \\ \text{in 2010} \end{matrix}$$

$$\begin{matrix} \text{Cost effect of} \\ \text{growth for} \\ \text{direct materials} \end{matrix} = \left(3{,}000{,}000 \text{ sq. cm.} \times \frac{1{,}150{,}000 \text{ units}}{1{,}000{,}000 \text{ units}} - 3{,}000{,}000 \text{ sq. cm.} \right) \times \$1.40 \text{ per sq. cm.}$$

$$= (3{,}450{,}000 \text{ sq. cm.} - 3{,}000{,}000 \text{ sq. cm.}) \times \$1.40 \text{ per sq. cm.} = \$630{,}000 \text{ U}$$

The units of input required to produce 2011 output in 2010 can also be calculated as follows:

$$\text{Units of input per unit of output in 2010} = \frac{3{,}000{,}000 \text{ sq. cm.}}{1{,}000{,}000 \text{ units}} = 3 \text{ sq. cm./unit}$$

Units of input required to produce 2011 output of 1,150,000 units in 2010 = 3 sq. cm. per unit × 1,150,000 units = 3,450,000 sq. cm.

$$\begin{matrix} \text{Cost effect of} \\ \text{growth for} \\ \text{fixed costs} \end{matrix} = \begin{pmatrix} \text{Actual units of capacity in} & \text{Actual units} \\ \text{2010 because adequate capacity} & - \text{of capacity} \\ \text{exists to produce 2011 output in 2010} & \text{in 2010} \end{pmatrix} \times \begin{matrix} \text{Price per} \\ \text{unit of} \\ \text{capacity} \\ \text{in 2010} \end{matrix}$$

$$\begin{matrix} \text{Cost effect of} \\ \text{growth for} \\ \text{conversion costs} \end{matrix} = (3{,}750{,}000 \text{ sq. cm.} - 3{,}750{,}000 \text{ sq. cm.}) \times \$4.28 \text{ per sq. cm.} = \$0$$

Conversion costs are fixed costs at a given level of capacity. Chipset has manufacturing capacity to process 3,750,000 square centimeters of silicon wafers in 2010 at a cost of $4.28 per square centimeter. To produce 1,150,000 units of output in 2010, Chipset needs to process 3,450,000 square centimeters of direct materials, which is less than the available capacity of 3,750,000 sq. cm. Throughout this chapter, we assume adequate capacity exists in the current year (2010) to produce next year's (2011) output. Under this assumption, the cost effect of growth for capacity-related fixed costs is, by definition, $0. Had 2010 capacity been inadequate to produce 2011 output in 2010, we would need to calculate the additional capacity required to produce 2011 output in 2010. These calculations are beyond the scope of the text.

In summary, the net increase in operating income attributable to growth equals the following:

Revenue effect of growth		$3,450,000 F
Cost effect of growth		
Direct material costs	$630,000 U	
Conversion costs	0	630,000 U
Change in operating income due to growth		$2,820,000 F

Price-Recovery Component of Change in Operating Income

Assuming that the 2010 relationship between inputs and outputs continued in 2011, the price-recovery component of the change in operating income measures solely the effect of price changes on revenues and costs to produce and sell the 1,150,000 units of CX1 in 2011.

Revenue Effect of Price Recovery

$$\begin{pmatrix} \text{Revenue effect of} \\ \text{price recovery} \end{pmatrix} = \begin{pmatrix} \text{Selling price} \\ \text{in 2011} \end{pmatrix} - \begin{pmatrix} \text{Selling price} \\ \text{in 2010} \end{pmatrix} \times \begin{pmatrix} \text{Actual units} \\ \text{of output} \\ \text{sold in 2011} \end{pmatrix}$$

$$= (\$22 \text{ per unit} - \$23 \text{ per unit}) \times 1{,}150{,}000 \text{ units}$$

$$= \$1{,}150{,}000 \text{ U}$$

Note that the calculation focuses on revenue changes caused by changes in the selling price of CX1 between 2010 and 2011.

Cost Effect of Price Recovery

Chipset's management accountants calculate the cost effects of price recovery separately for variable costs and for fixed costs, just as they did when calculating the cost effect of growth.

$$\begin{pmatrix} \text{Cost effect of} \\ \text{price recovery for} \\ \text{variable costs} \end{pmatrix} = \begin{pmatrix} \text{Input price} \\ \text{in 2011} \end{pmatrix} - \begin{pmatrix} \text{Input price} \\ \text{in 2010} \end{pmatrix} \times \begin{pmatrix} \text{Units of input} \\ \text{required to} \\ \text{produce 2011} \\ \text{output in 2010} \end{pmatrix}$$

$$\begin{pmatrix} \text{Cost effect of} \\ \text{price recovery for} \\ \text{direct materials} \end{pmatrix} = (\$1.50 \text{ per sq.cm.} - \$1.40 \text{ per sq.cm.}) \times 3{,}450{,}000 \text{ sq.} = \$345{,}000 \text{ U}$$

Recall that the direct materials of 3,450,000 square centimeters required to produce 2011 output in 2010 had already been calculated when computing the cost effect of growth.

$$\begin{pmatrix} \text{Cost effect of} \\ \text{price recovery for} \\ \text{fixed costs} \end{pmatrix} = \begin{pmatrix} \text{Price per} \\ \text{unit of} \\ \text{capacity} \\ \text{in 2011} \end{pmatrix} - \begin{pmatrix} \text{Price per} \\ \text{unit of} \\ \text{capacity} \\ \text{in 2010} \end{pmatrix} \times \begin{pmatrix} \text{Actual units of capacity in} \\ \text{2010 (because adequate} \\ \text{capacity exists to produce} \\ \text{2011 output in 2010)} \end{pmatrix}$$

Cost effect of price recovery for fixed costs is as follows:

Conversion costs: ($4.35 per sq. cm. – $4.28 per sq. cm.) × 3,750,000 sq. cm. = $262,500 U

Note that the detailed analyses of capacities were presented when computing the cost effect of growth.

In summary, the net decrease in operating income attributable to price recovery equals the following:

Revenue effect of price recovery		$1,150,000 U
Cost effect of price recovery		
Direct material costs	$345,000 U	
Conversion costs	262,500 U	607,500 U
Change in operating income due to price recovery		$1,757,500 U

The price-recovery analysis indicates that, even as the prices of its inputs increased, the selling prices of CX1 decreased and Chipset could not pass on input-price increases to its customers.

Productivity Component of Change in Operating Income

The productivity component of the change in operating income uses 2011 input prices to measure how costs have decreased as a result of using fewer inputs, a better mix of inputs, and/or less capacity to produce 2011 output, compared with the inputs and capacity that would have been used to produce this output in 2010.

The productivity-component calculations use 2011 prices and output. That's because the productivity component isolates the change in costs between 2010 and 2011 caused solely by the change in the quantities, mix, and/or capacities of inputs.[8]

$$\text{Cost effect of productivity for variable costs} = \left(\begin{array}{c}\text{Actual units of input used to produce 2011 output} - \text{Units of input required to produce 2011 output in 2010}\end{array}\right) \times \begin{array}{c}\text{Input price in 2011}\end{array}$$

Using the 2011 data given on page 478 and the calculation of units of input required to produce 2011 output in 2010 when discussing the cost effects of growth,

$$\text{Cost effect of productivity for direct materials} = (2{,}900{,}000 \text{ sq. cm.} - 3{,}450{,}000 \text{ sq. cm.}) \times \$1.50 \text{ per sq. cm}$$

$$= 550{,}000 \text{ sq. cm.} \times \$1.50 \text{ per sq. cm.} = \$825{,}000 \text{ F}$$

Chipset's quality and yield improvements reduced the quantity of direct materials needed to produce output in 2011 relative to 2010.

$$\text{Cost effect of productivity for fixed costs} = \left(\begin{array}{c}\text{Actual units of capacity in 2011} - \begin{array}{c}\text{Actual units of capacity in 2010 because adequate capacity exists to produce 2011 output in 2010}\end{array}\end{array}\right) \times \begin{array}{c}\text{Price per unit of capacity in 2011}\end{array}$$

To calculate the cost effect of productivity for fixed costs, we use the 2011 data and the analyses of capacity required to produce 2011 output in 2010 when discussing the cost effect of growth.

Cost effects of productivity for fixed costs are

$$\text{Conversion costs: } (3{,}500{,}000 \text{ sq. cm} - 3{,}750{,}000 \text{ sq. cm.}) \times \$4.35 \text{ per sq. cm.} = \$1{,}087{,}500 \text{ F}$$

Chipset's managers decreased manufacturing capacity in 2011 to 3,500,000 square centimeters by selling off old equipment and laying off workers.

In summary, the net increase in operating income attributable to productivity equals,

Cost effect of productivity	
Direct material costs	$ 825,000 F
Conversion costs	1,087,500 F
Change in operating income due to productivity	1,912,500 F

The productivity component indicates that Chipset was able to increase operating income by improving quality and productivity and eliminating capacity to reduce costs. The appendix to this chapter examines partial and total factor productivity changes between 2010 and 2011 and describes how the management accountant can obtain a deeper understanding of Chipset's cost-leadership strategy. Note that the productivity component focuses exclusively on costs, so there is no revenue effect for this component.

Exhibit 5 summarizes the growth, price-recovery, and productivity components of the changes in operating income. Generally, companies that have been successful at cost leadership will show favorable productivity and growth components. Companies that

---

[8] Note that the productivity-component calculation uses actual 2011 input prices, whereas its counterpart, the efficiency variance, uses budgeted prices. (In effect, the budgeted prices correspond to 2010 prices). Year 2011 prices are used in the productivity calculation because Chipset wants its managers to choose input quantities to minimize costs in 2011 based on currently prevailing prices. If 2010 prices had been used in the productivity calculation, managers would choose input quantities based on irrelevant input prices that prevailed a year ago! Why does using budgeted prices not pose a similar problem? Because, unlike 2010 prices that describe what happened a year ago, budgeted prices represent prices that are expected to prevail in the current period. Moreover, budgeted prices can be changed, if necessary, to bring them in line with actual current-period prices.

| Exhibit 5 | Strategic Analysis of Profitability |

	Income Statement Amounts in 2010 (1)	Revenue and Cost Effects of Growth Component in 2011 (2)	Revenue and Cost Effects of Price-Recovery Component in 2011 (3)	Cost Effect of Productivity Component in 2011 (4)	Income Statement Amounts in 2011 (5) = (1) + (2) + (3) + (4)
Revenues	$23,000,000	$3,450,000 F	$1,150,000 U	—	$25,300,000
Costs	20,250,000	630,000 U	607,500 U	$1,912,000 F	19,575,000
Operating income	$ 2,750,000	$2,820,000 F	$1,757,500 U	$1,912,500 F	$ 5,725,000
			$2,975,000 F		

Change in operating income

have successfully differentiated their products will show favorable price-recovery and growth components. In Chipset's case, consistent with its strategy and its implementation, productivity contributed $1,912,500 to the increase in operating income, and growth contributed $2,820,000. Price-recovery contributed a $1,757,500 decrease in operating income, however, because, even as input prices increased, the selling price of CX1 decreased. Had Chipset been able to differentiate its product and charge a higher price, the price-recovery effects might have been less unfavorable or perhaps even favorable. As a result, Chipset's managers plan to evaluate some modest changes in product features that might help differentiate CX1 somewhat more from competing products.

Further Analysis of Growth, Price-Recovery, and Productivity Components

As in all variance and profit analysis, Chipset's managers want to more closely analyze the change in operating income. Chipset's growth might have been helped, for example, by an increase in industry market size. Therefore, at least part of the increase in operating income may be attributable to favorable economic conditions in the industry rather than to any successful implementation of strategy. Some of the growth might relate to the management decision to decrease selling price, made possible by the productivity gains. In this case, the increase in operating income from cost leadership must include operating income from productivity-related growth in market share in addition to the productivity gain.

We illustrate these ideas, using the Chipset example and the following additional information. *Instructors who do not wish to cover these detailed calculations can go to the next section on "Applying the Five-Step Decision-Making Framework to Strategy" without any loss of continuity.*

- The market growth rate in the industry is 8% in 2011. Of the 150,000 (1,150,000 – 1,000,000) units of increased sales of CX1 between 2010 and 2011, 80,000 (0.08 × 1,000,000) units are due to an increase in industry market size (which Chipset should have benefited from regardless of its productivity gains), and the remaining 70,000 units are due to an increase in market share.

- During 2011, Chipset could have maintained the price of CX1 at the 2010 price of $23 per unit. But management decided to take advantage of the productivity gains to reduce the price of CX1 by $1 to grow market share leading to the 70,000-unit increase in sales.

The effect of the industry-market-size factor on operating income (not any specific strategic action) is as follows:

Change in operating income due to growth in industry market size

$$\$2,820,000 \text{ (Exhibit 5, column 2)} \times \frac{80,000 \text{ units}}{150,000 \text{ units}} = \$1,504,000 \text{ F}$$

Concepts in Action

The Growth Versus Profitability Choice at Facebook

Facebook, Inc.

Competitive advantage comes from product differentiation or cost leadership. Successful implementation of these strategies helps a company to be profitable and to grow. Many Internet start-ups pursue a strategy of short-run growth to build a customer base, with the goal of later benefiting from such growth by either charging user fees or sustaining a free service for users supported by advertisers. However, during the 1990s dot-com boom (and subsequent bust), the most spectacular failures occurred in dot-com companies that followed the "get big fast" model but then failed to differentiate their products or reduce their costs.

Today, many social networking companies (Web-based communities that connect friends, colleagues, and groups with shared interests) face this same challenge. At Facebook, the most notable of the social networking sites, users can create personal profiles that allow them to interact with friends through messaging, chat, sharing Web site links, video clips, and more. Additionally, Facebook encourages other companies to build third-party programs, including games and surveys, for its Web site and mobile applications on the iPhone and BlackBerry devices. From 2007 to 2010, Facebook grew from 12 million users to more than 400 million users uploading photos, sharing updates, planning events, and playing games in the Facebook ecosystem.

During this phenomenal growth, the company wrestled with one key question: How could Facebook become profitable? In 2009, experts estimate that Facebook had revenues of $635 million, mostly through advertising and the sale of virtual gifts (as a private company, Facebook does not publicly disclose its financial information). But the company still did not turn a profit. Why not? To keep its global Web site and mobile applications operating, Facebook requires a massive amount of electricity, Internet bandwidth, and storage servers for digital files. In 2009, the company earmarked $100 million to buy 50,000 new servers, along with a new $2 million network storage system per week.

The cost structure of Facebook means that the company must generate tens of millions a month in revenue to sustain its operations over the long term. But how? Facebook has implemented the following popular methods of online revenue generation:

- Additional advertising: To grow its already significant advertising revenue, Facebook recently introduced "Fan Pages" for brands and companies seeking to communicate directly with its users. The company is also working on a tool that will let users share information about their physical whereabouts via the site, which will allow Facebook to sell targeted advertisements for nearby businesses.

- Transactions: Facebook is also testing a feature that would expand Facebook Credits, its transactions platform that allows users to purchase games and gifts, into an Internet-wide "virtual currency," that could be accepted by any Web site integrating the Facebook Connect online identity management platform. Facebook currently gets a 30% cut of all transactions conducted through Facebook Credits.

Despite rampant rumors, Facebook has rejected the idea of charging monthly subscription fees for access to its Web site or for advanced features and premium content.

With increased growth around the world, Facebook anticipates 2010 revenues to exceed $1 billion. Despite the opportunity to become the "world's richest twenty-something," Facebook's 25-year-old CEO Mark Zuckerberg has thus far resisted taking the company public through an initial public offering (IPO). "A lot of companies can go off course because of corporate pressures," says Mr. Zuckerberg. "I don't know what we are going to be building five years from now." With his company's focus on facilitating people's ability to share almost any- and everything with anyone, at any time, via the Internet, mobile phones, and even videogames, Facebook expects to offer users a highly personal and differentiated online experience in the years ahead and expects that this product differentiation will drive its future growth and profitability.

Sources: Vascellaro, Jessica E. 2010. Facebook CEO in no rush to 'friend' wall street. *Wall Street Journal*, March 3. http://online.wsj.com/article/SB10001424052748703787304575075942803630712.html; Eldon, Eric. 2010. Facebook revenues up to $700 million in 2009, on track towards $1.1 billion in 2010. *Inside Facebook*. Blog, March 2. http://www.insidefacebook.com/2010/03/02/facebook-made-up-to-700-million-in-2009-on-track-towards-1-1-billion-in-2010/; Arrington, Michael. 2010. Facebook may be growing too fast. And hitting the capital markets again. *Tech Crunch*. Blog, October 31. http://techcrunch.com/2010/10/31/facebooks-growing-problem/

Lacking a differentiated product, Chipset could have maintained the price of CX1 at $23 per unit even while the prices of its inputs increased.

The effect of product differentiation on operating income is as follows:

Change in prices of inputs (cost effect of price recovery)	607,500 U
Change in operating income due to product differentiation	$607,500 U

To exercise cost and price leadership, Chipset made the strategic decision to cut the price of CX1 by $1. This decision resulted in an increase in market share and 70,000 units of additional sales.

The effect of cost leadership on operating income is as follows:

Productivity component	$1,912,500 F
Effect of strategic decision to reduce price ($1/unit $\times$ 1,150,000 units)	1,150,000 U
Growth in market share due to productivity improvement and strategic decision to reduce prices	
$2,820,000$ (Exhibit 5, column 2) $\times \dfrac{70,000 \text{ units}}{150,000 \text{ units}}$	1,316,000 F
Change in operating income due to cost leadership	$2,078,500 F

A summary of the change in operating income between 2010 and 2011 follows.

Change due to industry market size	$1,504,000 F
Change due to product differentiation	607,500 U
Change due to cost leadership	2,078,500 F
Change in operating income	$2,975,000 F

Consistent with its cost-leadership strategy, the productivity gains of $1,912,500 in 2011 were a big part of the increase in operating income from 2010 to 2011. Chipset took advantage of these productivity gains to decrease price by $1 per unit at a cost of $1,150,000 to gain $1,316,000 in operating income by selling 70,000 additional units. The Problem for Self-Study describes the analysis of the growth, price-recovery, and productivity components for a company following a product-differentiation strategy. The Concepts in Action feature describes the unique challenges that dot-com companies face in choosing a profitable strategy.

Under different assumptions about the change in selling price, the analysis will attribute different amounts to the different strategies.

Decision Point

How can a company analyze changes in operating income to evaluate the success of its strategy?

Applying the Five-Step Decision-Making Framework to Strategy

We next briefly describe how the five-step decision-making framework is also useful in making decisions about strategy.

1. *Identify the problem and uncertainties.* Chipset's strategy choice depends on resolving two uncertainties—whether Chipset can add value to its customers that its competitors cannot emulate, and whether Chipset can develop the necessary internal capabilities to add this value.

2. *Obtain information.* Chipset's managers develop customer preference maps to identify various product attributes desired by customers and the competitive advantage or disadvantage it has on each attribute relative to competitors. The managers also gather data on Chipset's internal capabilities. How good is Chipset in designing and developing innovative new products? How good are its process and marketing capabilities?

3. *Make predictions about the future.* Chipset's managers conclude that they will not be able to develop innovative new products in a cost-effective way. They believe that Chipset's strength lies in improving quality, reengineering processes, reducing costs, and delivering products faster to customers.

4. *Make decisions by choosing among alternatives.* Chipset's management decides to follow a cost leadership rather than a product differentiation strategy. It decides to introduce a balanced scorecard to align and measure its quality improvement and process reengineering efforts.

5. *Implement the decision, evaluate performance, and learn.* On its balanced scorecard, Chipset's managers compare actual and targeted performance and evaluate possible cause-and-effect relationships. They learn, for example, that increasing the percentage of processes with advanced controls improves yield. As a result, just as they had anticipated, productivity and growth initiatives result in increases in operating income in 2011. The one change Chipset's managers plan for 2012 is to make modest changes in product features that might help differentiate CX1 somewhat from competing products. In this way, feedback and learning help in the development of future strategies and implementation plans.

Downsizing and the Management of Processing Capacity

Learning Objective 5

Identify unused capacity

. . . capacity available minus capacity used for engineered costs but difficult to determine for discretionary costs

and how to manage it

. . . downsize to reduce capacity

As we saw in our discussion of the productivity component, fixed costs are tied to capacity. Unlike variable costs, fixed costs do not change automatically with changes in activity level (for example, fixed conversion costs do not change with changes in the quantity of silicon wafers started into production). How then can managers reduce capacity-based fixed costs? By measuring and managing unused capacity. **Unused capacity** is the amount of productive capacity available over and above the productive capacity employed to meet consumer demand in the current period. To understand unused capacity, it is necessary to distinguish *engineered costs* from *discretionary costs*.

Engineered and Discretionary Costs

Engineered costs result from a cause-and-effect relationship between the cost driver—output—and the (direct or indirect) resources used to produce that output. Engineered costs have a detailed, physically observable, and repetitive relationship with output. In the Chipset example, direct material costs are *direct engineered costs*. Conversion costs are an example of *indirect engineered costs*. Consider 2011. The output of 1,150,000 units of CX1 and the efficiency with which inputs are converted into outputs result in 2,900,000 square centimeters of silicon wafers being started into production. Manufacturing-conversion-cost resources used equal $12,615,000 ($4.35 per sq. cm. × 2,900,000 sq. cm.), but actual conversion costs ($15,225,000) are higher because Chipset has manufacturing capacity to process 3,500,000 square centimeters of silicon wafer ($4.35 per sq. cm. × 3,500,000 sq. cm. = $15,225,000). Although these costs are fixed in the short run, over the long run there is a cause-and-effect relationship between output and manufacturing capacity required (and conversion costs needed). In the long run, Chipset will try to match its capacity to its needs.

Discretionary costs have two important features: (1) They arise from periodic (usually annual) decisions regarding the maximum amount to be incurred, and (2) they have no measurable cause-and-effect relationship between output and resources used. There is often a delay between when a resource is acquired and when it is used. Examples of discretionary costs include advertising, executive training, R&D, and corporate-staff department costs such as legal, human resources, and public relations. Unlike engineered costs, the relationship between discretionary costs and output is a blackbox because it is nonrepetitive and nonroutine. A noteworthy aspect of discretionary costs is that managers are seldom confident that the "correct" amounts are being spent. The founder of Lever Brothers, an international consumer-products company, once noted, "Half the money I spend on advertising is wasted; the trouble is, I don't know which half!"[9]

Identifying Unused Capacity for Engineered and Discretionary Overhead Costs

Identifying unused capacity is very different for engineered costs compared to discretionary costs. Consider engineered conversion costs.

At the start of 2011, Chipset had capacity to process 3,750,000 square centimeters of silicon wafers. Quality and productivity improvements made during 2011 enabled Chipset to produce 1,150,000 units of CX1 by processing 2,900,000 square centimeters of silicon wafers. Unused manufacturing capacity is 850,000 (3,750,000 − 2,900,000) square centimeters of silicon-wafer processing capacity at the beginning of 2011. At the 2011 conversion cost of $4.35 per square centimeter,

$$\begin{array}{ll}
\text{Cost of} \\
\text{unused capacity}
\end{array} = \begin{array}{l}
\text{Cost of capacity} \\
\text{at the beginning} \\
\text{of the year}
\end{array} - \begin{array}{l}
\text{Manufacturing resources} \\
\text{used during the year}
\end{array}$$

$$= (3{,}750{,}000 \text{ sq. cm.} \times \$4.35 \text{ per sq. cm.}) - (2{,}900{,}000 \text{ sq. cm.} \times \$4.35 \text{ per sq. cm.})$$

$$= \$16{,}312{,}500 - \$12{,}615{,}000 = \$3{,}697{,}500$$

The absence of a cause-and-effect relationship makes identifying unused capacity for discretionary costs difficult. For example, management cannot determine the R&D resources used for the actual output produced. And without a measure of capacity used, it is not possible to compute unused capacity.

Managing Unused Capacity

What actions can Chipset management take when it identifies unused capacity? In general, it has two alternatives: eliminate unused capacity, or grow output to utilize the unused capacity.

In recent years, many companies have *downsized* in an attempt to eliminate unused capacity. **Downsizing** (also called **rightsizing**) is an integrated approach of configuring processes, products, and people to match costs to the activities that need to be performed to operate effectively and efficiently in the present and future. Companies such as AT&T, Delta Airlines, Ford Motor Company, and IBM have downsized to focus on their core businesses and have instituted organization changes to increase efficiency, reduce costs, and improve quality. However, downsizing often means eliminating jobs, which can adversely affect employee morale and the culture of a company.

Consider Chipset's alternatives with respect to its unused manufacturing capacity. Because it needed to process 2,900,000 square centimeters of silicon wafers in 2011, it could have reduced capacity to 3,000,000 square centimeters (Chipset can add or reduce manufacturing capacity in increments of 250,000 sq. cm.), resulting in cost savings of $3,262,500 [(3,750,000 sq. cm. − 3,000,000 sq. cm.) × $4.35 per sq. cm.]. Chipset's strategy, however, is not just to reduce costs but also to grow its business. So early in 2011, Chipset reduces its manufacturing capacity by only 250,000 square centimeters—from 3,750,000 square centimeters to 3,500,000 square centimeters—saving

---

[9] Managers also describe some costs as infrastructure costs—costs that arise from having property, plant, and equipment and a functioning organization. Examples are depreciation, long-run lease rental, and the acquisition of long-run technical capabilities. These costs are generally fixed costs because they are committed to and acquired before they are used. Infrastructure costs can be engineered or discretionary. For instance, manufacturing-overhead cost incurred at Chipset to acquire manufacturing capacity is an infrastructure cost that is an example of an engineered cost. In the long run, there is a cause-and-effect relationship between output and manufacturing-overhead costs needed to produce that output. R&D cost incurred to acquire technical capability is an infrastructure cost that is an example of a discretionary cost. There is no measurable cause-and-effect relationship between output and R&D cost incurred.

$1,087,500 ($4.35 per sq. cm. × 250,000 sq. cm.). It retains some extra capacity for future growth. By avoiding greater reductions in capacity, it also maintains the morale of its skilled and capable workforce. The success of this strategy will depend on Chipset achieving the future growth it has projected.

Because identifying unused capacity for discretionary costs, such as R&D costs, is difficult, downsizing or otherwise managing this unused capacity is also difficult. Management must exercise considerable judgment in deciding the level of R&D costs that would generate the needed product and process improvements. Unlike engineered costs, there is no clear-cut way to know whether management is spending too much (or too little) on R&D.

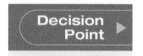

Decision Point

How can a company identify and manage unused capacity?

Problem for Self-Study

Following a strategy of product differentiation, Westwood Corporation makes a high-end kitchen range hood, KE8. Westwood's data for 2010 and 2011 follow:

		2010	2011
1.	Units of KE8 produced and sold	40,000	42,000
2.	Selling price	$100	$110
3.	Direct materials (square feet)	120,000	123,000
4.	Direct material cost per square foot	$10	$11
5.	Manufacturing capacity for KE8	50,000 units	50,000 units
6.	Conversion costs	$1,000,000	$1,100,000
7.	Conversion cost per unit of capacity (row 6 ÷ row 5)	$20	$22
8.	Selling and customer-service capacity	30 customers	29 customers
9.	Selling and customer-service costs	$720,000	$725,000
10.	Cost per customer of selling and customer-service capacity (row 9 ÷ row 8)	$24,000	$25,000

In 2011, Westwood produced no defective units and reduced direct material usage per unit of KE8. Conversion costs in each year are tied to manufacturing capacity. Selling and customer service costs are related to the number of customers that the selling and service functions are designed to support. Westwood has 23 customers (wholesalers) in 2010 and 25 customers in 2011.

Required

1. Describe briefly the elements you would include in Westwood's balanced scorecard.
2. Calculate the growth, price-recovery, and productivity components that explain the change in operating income from 2010 to 2011.
3. Suppose during 2011, the market size for high-end kitchen range hoods grew 3% in terms of number of units and all increases in market share (that is, increases in the number of units sold greater than 3%) are due to Westwood's product-differentiation strategy. Calculate how much of the change in operating income from 2010 to 2011 is due to the industry-market-size factor, cost leadership, and product differentiation.
4. How successful has Westwood been in implementing its strategy? Explain.

Solution

1. The balanced scorecard should describe Westwood's product-differentiation strategy. Elements that should be included in its balanced scorecard are as follows:
   - **Financial perspective.** Increase in operating income from higher margins on KE8 and from growth
   - **Customer perspective.** Customer satisfaction and market share in the high-end market
   - **Internal business process perspective.** New product features, development time for new products, improvements in manufacturing processes, manufacturing quality, order-delivery time, and on-time delivery
   - **Learning-and-growth perspective.** Percentage of employees trained in process and quality management and employee satisfaction ratings

2. Operating income for each year is as follows:

	2010	2011
Revenues		
($100 per unit × 40,000 units; $110 per unit × 42,000 units)	$4,000,000	$4,620,000
Costs		
Direct material costs		
($10 per sq. ft. × 120,000 sq. ft.; $11 per sq. ft. × 123,000 sq. ft.)	1,200,000	1,353,000
Conversion costs		
($20 per unit × 50,000 units; $22 per unit × 50,000 units)	1,000,000	1,100,000
Selling and customer-service cost		
($24,000 per customer × 30 customers;		
$25,000 per customer × 29 customers)	720,000	725,000
Total costs	2,920,000	3,178,000
Operating income	$1,080,000	$1,442,000
Change in operating income		$362,000 F

Growth Component of Operating Income Change

$$\text{Revenue effect of growth} = \left(\begin{array}{c} \text{Actual units of} \\ \text{output sold} \\ \text{in 2011} \end{array} - \begin{array}{c} \text{Actual units of} \\ \text{output sold} \\ \text{in 2010} \end{array} \right) \times \begin{array}{c} \text{Selling} \\ \text{price} \\ \text{in 2010} \end{array}$$

$$= (42{,}000 \text{ units} - 40{,}000 \text{ units}) \times \$100 \text{ per unit} = \$200{,}000 \text{ F}$$

$$\text{Cost effect of growth for variable costs} = \left(\begin{array}{c} \text{Units of input} \\ \text{required to produce} \\ \text{2011 output in 2010} \end{array} - \begin{array}{c} \text{Actual units of input} \\ \text{used to produce} \\ \text{2010 output} \end{array} \right) \times \begin{array}{c} \text{Input} \\ \text{price} \\ \text{in 2010} \end{array}$$

$$\text{Cost effect of growth for direct materials} = \left(120{,}000 \text{ sq. ft.} \times \frac{42{,}000 \text{ units}}{40{,}000 \text{ units}} - 120{,}000 \text{ sq. ft.} \right) \times \$10 \text{ per sq. ft.}$$

$$= (126{,}000 \text{ sq. ft.} - 120{,}000 \text{ sq. ft.}) \times \$10 \text{ per sq. ft.} = \$60{,}000 \text{ U}$$

$$\text{Cost effect of growth for fixed costs} = \left(\begin{array}{c} \text{Actual units of capacity in} \\ \text{2010, because adequate capacity} \\ \text{exists to produce 2011 output in 2010} \end{array} - \begin{array}{c} \text{Actual units} \\ \text{of capacity} \\ \text{in 2010} \end{array} \right) \times \begin{array}{c} \text{Price per} \\ \text{unit of} \\ \text{capacity} \\ \text{in 2010} \end{array}$$

Cost effects of growth for fixed costs are as follows:

$$\text{Conversion costs: } (50{,}000 \text{ units} - 50{,}000 \text{ units}) \times \$20 \text{ per unit} = \$0$$

$$\text{Selling and customer-service costs: } (30 \text{ customers} - 30 \text{ customers}) \times \$24{,}000 \text{ per customer} = \$0$$

In summary, the net increase in operating income attributable to growth equals the following:

Revenue effect of growth		$200,000 F
Cost effect of growth		
Direct material costs	$60,000 U	
Conversion costs	0	
Selling and customer-service costs	0	60,000 U
Change in operating income due to growth		$140,000 F

Price-Recovery Component of Operating-Income Change

$$\begin{array}{c} \text{Revenue effect of} \\ \text{price recovery} \end{array} = \left(\begin{array}{c} \text{Selling price} \\ \text{in 2011} \end{array} - \begin{array}{c} \text{Selling price} \\ \text{in 2010} \end{array} \right) \times \begin{array}{c} \text{Actual units} \\ \text{of output} \\ \text{sold in 2011} \end{array}$$

$$= (\$110 \text{ per unit} - \$100 \text{ per unit}) \times 42{,}000 \text{ units} = \$420{,}000 \text{ F}$$

$$\begin{array}{c} \text{Cost effect of} \\ \text{price recovery} \\ \text{for variable costs} \end{array} = \left(\begin{array}{c} \text{Input} \\ \text{price} \\ \text{in 2011} \end{array} - \begin{array}{c} \text{Input} \\ \text{price} \\ \text{in 2010} \end{array} \right) \times \begin{array}{c} \text{Units of input} \\ \text{required to produce} \\ \text{2011 output in 2010} \end{array}$$

Direct material costs: ($11 per sq. ft. − $10 per sq. ft.) × 126,000 sq. ft. = $126,000 U

$$\begin{array}{c} \text{Cost effect of} \\ \text{price recovery} \\ \text{for fixed costs} \end{array} = \left(\begin{array}{c} \text{Price per} \\ \text{unit of} \\ \text{capacity} \\ \text{in 2011} \end{array} - \begin{array}{c} \text{Price per} \\ \text{unit of} \\ \text{capacity} \\ \text{in 2010} \end{array} \right) \times \begin{array}{c} \text{Actual units of capacity in} \\ \text{2010, because adequate capacity} \\ \text{exists to produce 2011 output in 2010} \end{array}$$

Cost effects of price recovery for fixed costs are as follows:

Conversion costs: ($22 per unit − 20 per unit) × 50,000 units = $100,000 U

Selling and cust.-service costs: ($25,000 per cust. − $24,000 per cust.) × 30 customers = $30,000 U

In summary, the net increase in operating income attributable to price recovery equals the following:

Revenue effect of price recovery		$420,000 F
Cost effect of price recovery		
Direct material costs	$126,000 U	
Conversion costs	100,000 U	
Selling and customer-service costs	30,000 U	256,000 U
Change in operating income due to price recovery		$164,000 F

Productivity Component of Operating-Income Change

$$\begin{array}{c} \text{Cost effect of} \\ \text{productivity for} \\ \text{variable costs} \end{array} = \left(\begin{array}{c} \text{Actual units of} \\ \text{input used to produce} \\ \text{2011 output} \end{array} - \begin{array}{c} \text{Units of input} \\ \text{required to produce} \\ \text{2011 output in 2010} \end{array} \right) \times \begin{array}{c} \text{Input} \\ \text{price in} \\ \text{2011} \end{array}$$

$$\begin{array}{c} \text{Cost effect of} \\ \text{productivity for} \\ \text{direct materials} \end{array} = (123{,}000 \text{ sq. ft.} - 126{,}000 \text{ sq. ft.}) \times \$11 \text{ per sq. ft.} = \$33{,}000 \text{ F}$$

$$\begin{array}{c} \text{Cost effect of} \\ \text{productivity for} \\ \text{fixed costs} \end{array} = \left(\begin{array}{c} \text{Actual units} \\ \text{of capacity} \\ \text{in 2011} \end{array} - \begin{array}{c} \text{Actual units of capacity in} \\ \text{2010, because adequate} \\ \text{capacity exists to produce} \\ \text{2011 output in 2010} \end{array} \right) \times \begin{array}{c} \text{Price per} \\ \text{unit of} \\ \text{capacity} \\ \text{in 2011} \end{array}$$

Cost effects of productivity for fixed costs are as follows:

Conversion costs: (50,000 units − 50,000 units) × $22 per unit = $0

Selling and customer-service costs: (29 customers − 30 customers) × $25,000/customer = $25,000 F

In summary, the net increase in operating income attributable to productivity equals the following:

Cost effect of productivity:

Direct material costs	$33,000 F
Conversion costs	0
Selling and customer-service costs	25,000 F
Change in operating income due to productivity	$58,000 F

A summary of the change in operating income between 2010 and 2011 follows:

	Income Statement Amounts in 2010 (1)	Revenue and Cost Effects of Growth Component in 2011 (2)	Revenue and Cost Effects of Price-Recovery Component in 2011 (3)	Cost Effect of Productivity Component in 2011 (4)	Income Statement Amounts in 2011 (5) = (1) + (2) + (3) + (4)
Revenue	$4,000,000	$200,000 F	$420,000 F	—	$4,620,000
Costs	2,920,000	60,000 U	256,000 U	$58,000 F	3,178,000
Operating income	$1,080,000	$140,000 F	$164,000 F	$58,000 F	$1,442,000
			362,000 F		

Change in operating income

3. Effect of the Industry-Market-Size Factor on Operating Income

Of the increase in sales from 40,000 to 42,000 units, 3%, or 1,200 units (0.03 × 40,000), is due to growth in market size, and 800 units (2,000 – 1,200) are due to an increase in market share. The change in Westwood's operating income from the industry-market-size factor rather than specific strategic actions is as follows:

$$\$140,000 \text{ (column 2 of preceding table)} \times \frac{1,200 \text{ units}}{2,000 \text{ units}} \qquad \underline{\$84,000} \text{ F}$$

Effect of Product Differentiation on Operating Income

Increase in the selling price of KE8 (revenue effect of the price-recovery component)	$420,000 F
Increase in prices of inputs (cost effect of the price-recovery component)	256,000 U
Growth in market share due to product differentiation	
$\$140,000 \text{ (column 2 of preceding table)} \times \dfrac{800 \text{ units}}{2,000 \text{ units}}$	56,000 F
Change in operating income due to product differentiation	$220,000 F

Effect of Cost Leadership on Operating Income

Productivity component	$ 58,000 F

A summary of the net increase in operating income from 2010 to 2011 follows:

Change due to the industry-market-size factor	$ 84,000 F
Change due to product differentiation	220,000 F
Change due to cost leadership	58,000 F
Change in operating income	$362,000 F

4. The analysis of operating income indicates that a significant amount of the increase in operating income resulted from Westwood's successful implementation of its product-differentiation strategy. The company was able to continue to charge a premium price for KE8 while increasing market share. Westwood was also able to earn additional operating income from improving its productivity.

Decision Points

The following question-and-answer format summarizes the chapter's learning objectives. Each decision presents a key question related to a learning objective. The guidelines are the answer to that question.

Decision	Guidelines
1. What are two generic strategies a company can use?	Two generic strategies are product differentiation and cost leadership. Product differentiation is offering products and services that are perceived by customers as being superior and unique. Cost leadership is achieving low costs relative to competitors. A company chooses its strategy based on an understanding of customer preferences and its own internal capabilities, while differentiating itself from its competitors.
2. What is reengineering?	Reengineering is the rethinking of business processes, such as the order-delivery process, to improve critical performance measures such as cost, quality, and customer satisfaction.
3. How can an organization translate its strategy into a set of performance measures?	An organization can develop a balanced scorecard that provides the framework for a strategic measurement and management system. The balanced scorecard measures performance from four perspectives: (1) financial, (2) customer, (3) internal business processes, and (4) learning and growth. To build their balanced scorecards, organizations often create strategy maps to represent the cause-and-effect relationships across various strategic objectives.
4. How can a company analyze changes in operating income to evaluate the success of its strategy?	To evaluate the success of its strategy, a company can subdivide the change in operating income into growth, price-recovery, and productivity components. The growth component measures the change in revenues and costs from selling more or less units, assuming nothing else has changed. The price-recovery component measures changes in revenues and costs solely as a result of changes in the prices of outputs and inputs. The productivity component measures the decrease in costs from using fewer inputs, a better mix of inputs, and reducing capacity. If a company is successful in implementing its strategy, changes in components of operating income align closely with strategy.
5. How can a company identify and manage unused capacity?	A company must first distinguish engineered costs from discretionary costs. Engineered costs result from a cause-and-effect relationship between output and the resources needed to produce that output. Discretionary costs arise from periodic (usually annual) management decisions regarding the amount of cost to be incurred. Discretionary costs are not tied to a cause-and-effect relationship between inputs and outputs. Identifying unused capacity is easier for engineered costs and more difficult for discretionary costs. Downsizing is an approach to managing unused capacity that matches costs to the activities that need to be performed to operate effectively.

Appendix

Productivity Measurement

Productivity measures the relationship between actual inputs used (both quantities and costs) and actual outputs produced. The lower the inputs for a given quantity of outputs or the higher the outputs for a given quantity of inputs, the higher the productivity. Measuring productivity improvements over time highlights the specific input-output relationships that contribute to cost leadership.

Partial Productivity Measures

Partial productivity, the most frequently used productivity measure, compares the quantity of output produced with the quantity of an individual input used. In its most common form, partial productivity is expressed as a ratio:

$$\text{Partial productivity} = \frac{\text{Quantity of output produced}}{\text{Quantity of input used}}$$

The higher the ratio, the greater the productivity.

Consider direct materials productivity at Chipset in 2011.

$$\frac{\text{Direct materials}}{\text{partial productivity}} = \frac{\text{Quantity of CX1 units produced during 2011}}{\text{Quantity of direct materials used to produce CX1 in 2011}}$$

$$= \frac{1,150,000 \text{ units of CX1}}{2,900,000 \text{ sq. cm. of direct materials}}$$

$$= 0.397 \text{ units of CX1 per sq. cm. of direct materials}$$

Note direct materials partial productivity ignores Chipset's other input, manufacturing conversion capacity. Partial-productivity measures become more meaningful when comparisons are made that examine productivity changes over time, either across different facilities or relative to a benchmark. Exhibit 6 presents partial-productivity measures for Chipset's inputs for 2011 and the comparable 2010 inputs that would have been used to produce 2011 output, using information from the productivity-component calculations on page 482. These measures compare actual inputs used in 2011 to produce 1,150,000 units of CX1 with inputs that would have been used in 2011 had the input–output relationship from 2010 continued in 2011.

Evaluating Changes in Partial Productivities

Note how the partial-productivity measures differ for variable-cost and fixed-cost components. For variable-cost elements, such as direct materials, productivity improvements measure the reduction in input resources used to produce output (3,450,000 square centimeters of silicon wafers to 2,900,000 square centimeters). For fixed-cost elements such as manufacturing conversion capacity, partial productivity measures the reduction in overall capacity from 2010 to 2011 (3,750,000 square centimeters of silicon wafers to 3,500,000 square centimeters) regardless of the amount of capacity actually used in each period.

An advantage of partial-productivity measures is that they focus on a single input. As a result, they are simple to calculate and easily understood by operations personnel. Managers and operators examine these numbers and try to understand the reasons for the productivity changes—such as, better training of workers, lower labor turnover, better incentives, improved methods, or substitution of materials for labor. Isolating the relevant factors helps Chipset implement and sustain these practices in the future.

For all their advantages, partial-productivity measures also have serious drawbacks. Because partial productivity focuses on only one input at a time rather than on all inputs simultaneously, managers cannot evaluate the effect on overall productivity, if (say) manufacturing-conversion-capacity partial productivity increases while direct materials partial productivity decreases. Total factor productivity (TFP), or total productivity, is a measure of productivity that considers all inputs simultaneously.

Exhibit 6 Comparing Chipset's Partial Productivities in 2010 and 2011

Input (1)	Partial Productivity in 2011 (2)	Comparable Partial Productivity Based on 2010 Input– Output Relationships (3)	Percentage Change from 2010 to 2011 (4)
Direct materials	$\frac{1,150,000}{2,900,000} = 0.397$	$\frac{1,150,000}{3,450,000} = 0.333$	$\frac{0.397 - 0.333}{0.333} = 19.2\%$
Manufacturing conversion capacity	$\frac{1,150,000}{3,500,000} = 0.329$	$\frac{1,150,000}{3,750,000} = 0.307$	$\frac{0.329 - 0.307}{0.307} = 7.2\%$

Total Factor Productivity

Total factor productivity (TFP) is the ratio of the quantity of output produced to the costs of all inputs used based on current-period prices.

$$\text{Total factor productivity} = \frac{\text{Quantity of output produced}}{\text{Costs of all inputs used}}$$

TFP considers all inputs simultaneously and the trade-offs across inputs based on current input prices. Do not think of all productivity measures as physical measures lacking financial content—how many units of output are produced per unit of input. TFP is intricately tied to minimizing total cost—a financial objective.

Calculating and Comparing Total Factor Productivity

We first calculate Chipset's TFP in 2011, using 2011 prices and 1,150,000 units of output produced (based on information from the first part of the productivity-component calculations).

$$\frac{\text{Total factor productivity}}{\text{for 2011 using 2011 prices}} = \frac{\text{Quantity of output produced in 2011}}{\text{Costs of inputs used in 2011 based on 2011 prices}}$$

$$= \frac{1,150,000}{(2,900,000 \times \$1.50) + (3,500,000 \times \$4.35)}$$

$$= \frac{1,150,000}{\$19,575,000}$$

$$= 0.058748 \text{ units of output per dollar of input cost}$$

By itself, the 2011 TFP of 0.058748 units of CX1 per dollar of input costs is not particularly helpful. We need something to compare the 2011 TFP against. One alternative is to compare TFPs of other similar companies in 2011. However, finding similar companies and obtaining accurate comparable data are often difficult. Companies, therefore, usually compare their own TFPs over time. In the Chipset example, we use as a benchmark TFP calculated using the inputs that Chipset would have used in 2010 to produce 1,150,000 units of CX1 at 2011 prices (that is, we use the costs calculated from the second part of the productivity-component calculations). Why do we use 2011 prices? Because using the current year's prices in both calculations controls for input-price differences and focuses the analysis on adjustments the manager made in quantities of inputs in response to changes in prices.

$$\frac{\text{Benchmark}}{\text{TFP}} = \frac{\text{Quantity of output produced in 2011}}{\substack{\text{Costs of inputs at 2011 prices that would have been used in 2010} \\ \text{to produce 2011 output}}}$$

$$= \frac{1,150,000}{(3,450,000 \times \$1.50) + (3,750,000 \times \$4.35)}$$

$$= \frac{1,150,000}{\$21,487,500}$$

$$= 0.053519 \text{ units of output per dollar of input cost}$$

Using 2011 prices, TFP increased 9.8% [(058748 – 0.053519) ÷ 0.053519 = 0.098, or 9.8%] from 2010 to 2011. Note that the 9.8% increase in TFP also equals the $1,912,500 gain (Exhibit 5, column 4) divided by the $19,575,000 of actual costs incurred in 2011 (Exhibit 5, column 5). Total factor productivity increased because Chipset produced more output per dollar of input cost in 2011 relative to 2010, measured in both years using 2011 prices. The gain in TFP occurs because Chipset increases the partial productivities of individual inputs and, consistent with its strategy, combines inputs to lower costs. Note that increases in TFP cannot be due to differences in input prices because we used 2011 prices to evaluate both the inputs that Chipset would have used in 2010 to produce 1,150,000 units of CX1 and the inputs actually used in 2011.

Using Partial and Total Factor Productivity Measures

A major advantage of TFP is that it measures the combined productivity of all inputs used to produce output and explicitly considers gains from using fewer physical inputs as well as substitution among inputs. Managers can analyze these numbers to understand the reasons for changes in TFP—for example, better human resource management practices, higher quality of materials, or improved manufacturing methods.

Although TFP measures are comprehensive, operations personnel find financial TFP measures more difficult to understand and less useful than physical partial-productivity measures. For example, companies that are more labor intensive than Chipset use manufacturing-labor partial-productivity measures. However, if productivity-based bonuses depend on gains in manufacturing-labor partial productivity alone, workers have incentives to substitute materials (and capital) for labor. This substitution improves their own productivity measure, while possibly decreasing the overall productivity of the company as measured by TFP. To overcome these incentive problems, some companies—for example, TRW, Eaton, and Whirlpool—explicitly adjust bonuses based on manufacturing-labor partial productivity for the effects of other factors such as investments in new equipment and higher levels of scrap. That is, they combine partial productivity with TFP-like measures.

Many companies such as Behlen Manufacturing, a steel fabricator, and Dell Computers use both partial productivity and total factor productivity to evaluate performance. *Partial productivity and TFP measures work best together because the strengths of one offset the weaknesses of the other.*

Terms to Learn

This chapter contains definitions of the following important terms:

balanced scorecard	partial productivity	reengineering
cost leadership	price-recovery component	rightsizing
discretionary costs	product differentiation	strategy map
downsizing	productivity	total factor productivity (TFP)
engineered costs	productivity component	unused capacity
growth component		

Assignment Material

Questions

MyAccountingLab

13-1 Define strategy.

13-2 Describe the five key forces to consider when analyzing an industry.

13-3 Describe two generic strategies.

13-4 What is a customer preference map and why is it useful?

13-5 What is reengineering?

13-6 What are four key perspectives in the balanced scorecard?

13-7 What is a strategy map?

13-8 Describe three features of a good balanced scorecard.

13-9 What are three important pitfalls to avoid when implementing a balanced scorecard?

13-10 Describe three key components in doing a strategic analysis of operating income.

13-11 Why might an analyst incorporate the industry-market-size factor and the interrelationships among the growth, price-recovery, and productivity components into a strategic analysis of operating income?

13-12 How does an engineered cost differ from a discretionary cost?

13-13 What is downsizing?

13-14 What is a partial-productivity measure?

13-15 "We are already measuring total factor productivity. Measuring partial productivities would be of no value." Do you agree? Comment briefly.

Exercises

MyAccountingLab

13-16 **Balanced scorecard.** Ridgecrest Corporation manufactures corrugated cardboard boxes. It competes and plans to grow by selling high-quality boxes at a low price and by delivering them to customers quickly after receiving customers' orders. There are many other manufacturers who produce similar boxes. Ridgecrest believes that continuously improving its manufacturing processes and having satisfied employees are critical to implementing its strategy in 2012.

1. Is Ridgecrest's 2012 strategy one of product differentiation or cost leadership? Explain briefly.

   Required

2. Kearney Corporation, a competitor of Ridgecrest, manufactures corrugated boxes with more designs and color combinations than Ridgecrest at a higher price. Kearney's boxes are of high quality but require more time to produce and so have longer delivery times. Draw a simple customer preference map as in Exhibit 1 for Ridgecrest and Kearney using the attributes of price, delivery time, quality, and design.

3. Draw a strategy map as in Exhibit 2 with two strategic objectives you would expect to see under each balanced scorecard perspective.
4. For each strategic objective indicate a measure you would expect to see in Ridgecrest's balanced scorecard for 2012.

13-17 Analysis of growth, price-recovery, and productivity components (continuation of 13-16). An analysis of Ridgecrest's operating-income changes between 2011 and 2012 shows the following:

Operating income for 2011	$1,850,000
Add growth component	85,000
Deduct price-recovery component	(72,000)
Add productivity component	150,000
Operating income for 2011	$2,013,000

The industry market size for corrugated cardboard boxes did not grow in 2012, input prices did not change, and Ridgecrest reduced the prices of its boxes.

Required

1. Was Ridgecrest's gain in operating income in 2012 consistent with the strategy you identified in requirement 1 of Exercise 13-16?
2. Explain the productivity component. In general, does it represent savings in only variable costs, only fixed costs, or both variable and fixed costs?

13-18 Strategy, balanced scorecard, merchandising operation. Roberto & Sons buys T-shirts in bulk, applies its own trendsetting silk-screen designs, and then sells the T-shirts to a number of retailers. Roberto wants to be known for its trendsetting designs, and it wants every teenager to be seen in a distinctive Roberto T-shirt. Roberto presents the following data for its first two years of operations, 2010 and 2011.

		2010	2011
1	Number of T-shirts purchased	200,000	250,000
2	Number of T-shirts discarded	2,000	3,300
3	Number of T-shirts sold (row 1 – row 2)	198,000	246,700
4	Average selling price	$25.00	$26.00
5	Average cost per T-shirt	$10.00	$8.50
6	Administrative capacity (number of customers)	4,000	3,750
7	Administrative costs	$1,200,000	$1,162,500
8	Administrative cost per customer (row 8 ÷ row 7)	$300	$310

Administrative costs depend on the number of customers that Roberto has created capacity to support, not on the actual number of customers served. Roberto had 3,600 customers in 2010 and 3,500 customers in 2011.

Required

1. Is Roberto 's strategy one of product differentiation or cost leadership? Explain briefly.
2. Describe briefly the key measures Roberto should include in its balanced scorecard and the reasons it should do so.

13-19 Strategic analysis of operating income (continuation of 13-18). Refer to Exercise 13-18.

Required

1. Calculate Roberto's operating income in both 2010 and 2011.
2. Calculate the growth, price-recovery, and productivity components that explain the change in operating income from 2010 to 2011.
3. Comment on your answers in requirement 2. What does each of these components indicate?

13-20 Analysis of growth, price-recovery, and productivity components (continuation of 13-19). Refer to Exercise 13-19. Suppose that the market for silk-screened T-shirts grew by 10% during 2011. All increases in sales greater than 10% are the result of Roberto's strategic actions.

Required Calculate the change in operating income from 2010 to 2011 due to growth in market size, product differentiation, and cost leadership. How successful has Roberto been in implementing its strategy? Explain.

13-21 Identifying and managing unused capacity (continuation of 13-18). Refer to Exercise 13-18.

Required

1. Calculate the amount and cost of unused administrative capacity at the beginning of 2011, based on the actual number of customers Roberto served in 2011.
2. Suppose Roberto can only add or reduce administrative capacity in increments of 250 customers. What is the maximum amount of costs that Roberto can save in 2011 by downsizing administrative capacity?
3. What factors, other than cost, should Roberto consider before it downsizes administrative capacity?

13-22 Strategy, balanced scorecard. Stanmore Corporation makes a special-purpose machine, D4H, used in the textile industry. Stanmore has designed the D4H machine for 2011 to be distinct from its competitors. It has been generally regarded as a superior machine. Stanmore presents the following data for 2010 and 2011.

	2010	2011
1. Units of D4H produced and sold	200	210
2. Selling price	$40,000	$42,000
3. Direct materials (kilograms)	300,000	310,000
4. Direct material cost per kilogram	$8	$8.50
5. Manufacturing capacity in units of D4H	250	250
6. Total conversion costs	$2,000,000	$2,025,000
7. Conversion cost per unit of capacity (row 6 ÷ row 5)	$8,000	$8,100
8. Selling and customer-service capacity	100 customers	95 customers
9. Total selling and customer-service costs	$1,000,000	$940,500
10. Selling and customer-service capacity cost per customer (row 9 ÷ row 8)	$10,000	$9,900

Stanmore produces no defective machines, but it wants to reduce direct materials usage per D4H machine in 2011. Conversion costs in each year depend on production capacity defined in terms of D4H units that can be produced, not the actual units produced. Selling and customer-service costs depend on the number of customers that Stanmore can support, not the actual number of customers it serves. Stanmore has 75 customers in 2010 and 80 customers in 2011.

1. Is Stanmore's strategy one of product differentiation or cost leadership? Explain briefly. **Required**
2. Describe briefly key measures that you would include in Stanmore's balanced scorecard and the reasons for doing so.

13-23 Strategic analysis of operating income (continuation of 13-22). Refer to Exercise 13-22.

1. Calculate the operating income of Stanmore Corporation in 2010 and 2011. **Required**
2. Calculate the growth, price-recovery, and productivity components that explain the change in operating income from 2010 to 2011.
3. Comment on your answer in requirement 2. What do these components indicate?

13-24 Analysis of growth, price-recovery, and productivity components (continuation of 13-23). Suppose that during 2011, the market for Stanmore's special-purpose machines grew by 3%. All increases in market share (that is, sales increases greater than 3%) are the result of Stanmore's strategic actions.

Calculate how much of the change in operating income from 2010 to 2011 is due to the industry-market-size **Required** factor, product differentiation, and cost leadership. How successful has Stanmore been in implementing its strategy? Explain.

13-25 Identifying and managing unused capacity (continuation of 13-22). Refer to Exercise 13-22.

1. Calculate the amount and cost of (a) unused manufacturing capacity and (b) unused selling and **Required** customer-service capacity at the beginning of 2011 based on actual production and actual number of customers served in 2011.
2. Suppose Stanmore can add or reduce its manufacturing capacity in increments of 30 units. What is the maximum amount of costs that Stanmore could save in 2011 by downsizing manufacturing capacity?
3. Stanmore, in fact, does not eliminate any of its unused manufacturing capacity. Why might Stanmore not downsize?

13-26 Strategy, balanced scorecard, service company. Westlake Corporation is a small information-systems consulting firm that specializes in helping companies implement standard sales-management software. The market for Westlake's services is very competitive. To compete successfully, Westlake must deliver quality service at a low cost. Westlake presents the following data for 2010 and 2011.

	2010	2011
1. Number of jobs billed	60	70
2. Selling price per job	$50,000	$48,000
3. Software-implementation labor-hours	30,000	32,000
4. Cost per software-implementation labor-hour	$60	$63
5. Software-implementation support capacity (number of jobs it can do)	90	90
6. Total cost of software-implementation support	$360,000	$369,000
7. Software-implementation support-capacity cost per job (row 6 ÷ row 5)	$4,000	$4,100

Software-implementation labor-hour costs are variable costs. Software-implementation support costs for each year depend on the software-implementation support capacity Westlake chooses to maintain each year (that is the number of jobs it can do each year). It does not vary with the actual number of jobs done that year.

Required

1. Is Westlake Corporation's strategy one of product differentiation or cost leadership? Explain briefly.
2. Describe key measures you would include in Westlake's balanced scorecard and your reasons for doing so.

13-27 Strategic analysis of operating income (continuation of 13-26). Refer to Exercise 13-26.

Required

1. Calculate the operating income of Westlake Corporation in 2010 and 2011.
2. Calculate the growth, price-recovery, and productivity components that explain the change in operating income from 2010 to 2011.
3. Comment on your answer in requirement 2. What do these components indicate?

13-28 Analysis of growth, price-recovery, and productivity components (continuation of 13-27). Suppose that during 2011 the market for implementing sales-management software increases by 5%. Assume that any decrease in selling price and any increase in market share more than 5% are the result of strategic choices by Westlake's management to implement its strategy.

Required

Calculate how much of the change in operating income from 2010 to 2011 is due to the industry-market-size factor, product differentiation, and cost leadership. How successful has Westlake been in implementing its strategy? Explain.

13-29 Identifying and managing unused capacity (continuation of 13-26). Refer to Exercise 13-26.

Required

1. Calculate the amount and cost of unused software-implementation support capacity at the beginning of 2011, based on the number of jobs actually done in 2011.
2. Suppose Westlake can add or reduce its software-implementation support capacity in increments of 15 units. What is the maximum amount of costs that Westlake could save in 2011 by downsizing software-implementation support capacity?
3. Westlake, in fact, does not eliminate any of its unused software-implementation support capacity. Why might Westlake not downsize?

MyAccountingLab

Problems

13-30 Balanced scorecard and strategy. Music Master Company manufactures an MP3 player called the Mini. The company sells the player to discount stores throughout the country. This player is significantly less expensive than similar products sold by Music Master's competitors, but the Mini offers just four giga-bytes of space, compared with eight offered by competitor Vantage Manufacturing. Furthermore, the Mini has experienced production problems that have resulted in significant rework costs. Vantage's model has an excellent reputation for quality, but is considerably more expensive.

Required

1. Draw a simple customer preference map for Music Master and Vantage using the attributes of price, quality, and storage capacity. Use the format of Exhibit 1.
2. Is Music Master's current strategy that of product differentiation or cost leadership?
3. Music Master would like to improve quality and decrease costs by improving processes and training workers to reduce rework. Music Master's managers believe the increased quality will increase sales. Draw a strategy map as in Exhibit 2 describing the cause-and-effect relationships among the strategic objectives you would expect to see in Music Master's balanced scorecard.
4. For each strategic objective suggest a measure you would recommend in Music Master's balanced scorecard.

13-31 Strategic analysis of operating income (continuation of 13-30). Refer to Problem 13-30. As a result of the actions taken, quality has significantly improved in 2011 while rework and unit costs of the Mini have decreased. Music Master has reduced manufacturing capacity because capacity is no longer needed to support rework. Music Master has also lowered the Mini's selling price to gain market share and unit sales have increased. Information about the current period (2011) and last period (2010) follows:

	2010	2011
1. Units of Mini produced and sold	8,000	9,000
2. Selling price	$45	$43
3. Ounces of direct materials used	32,000	33,000
4. Direct material cost per ounce	$3.50	$3.50
5. Manufacturing capacity in units	12,000	11,000
6. Total conversion costs	$156,000	$143,000
7. Conversion cost per unit of capacity (row 6 ÷ row 5)	$13	$13
8. Selling and customer-service capacity	90 customers	90 customers
9. Total selling and customer-service costs	$45,000	$49,500
10. Selling and customer-service capacity cost per customer (row 9 ÷ row 8)	$500	$550

Conversion costs in each year depend on production capacity defined in terms of units of Mini that can be produced, not the actual units produced. Selling and customer-service costs depend on the number of customers that Music Master can support, not the actual number of customers it serves. Music Master has 70 customers in 2010 and 80 customers in 2011.

Required

1. Calculate operating income of Music Master Company for 2010 and 2011.
2. Calculate the growth, price-recovery, and productivity components that explain the change in operating income from 2010 to 2011.
3. Comment on your answer in requirement 2. What do these components indicate?

13-32 Analysis of growth, price-recovery, and productivity components (continuation of 13-31). Suppose that during 2011, the market for MP3 players grew 3%. All decreases in the selling price of the Mini and increases in market share (that is, sales increases greater than 3%) are the result of Music Master's strategic actions.

Required

Calculate how much of the change in operating income from 2010 to 2011 is due to the industry-market-size factor, product differentiation, and cost leadership. How does this relate to Music Master's strategy and its success in implementation? Explain.

13-33 Identifying and managing unused capacity (continuation of 13-31) Refer to the information for Music Master Company in 13-31.

Required

1. Calculate the amount and cost of (a) unused manufacturing capacity and (b) unused selling and customer-service capacity at the beginning of 2011 based on actual production and actual number of customers served in 2011.
2. Suppose Music Master can add or reduce its selling and customer-service capacity in increments of five customers. What is the maximum amount of costs that Music Master could save in 2011 by downsizing selling and customer-service capacity?
3. Music Master, in fact, does not eliminate any of its unused selling and customer-service capacity. Why might Music Master not downsize?

13-34 Balanced scorecard. Following is a random-order listing of perspectives, strategic objectives, and performance measures for the balanced scorecard.

Perspectives	Performance Measures
Internal business process	Percentage of defective-product units
Customer	Return on assets
Learning and growth	Number of patents
Financial	Employee turnover rate
Strategic Objectives	Net income
Acquire new customers	Customer profitability
Increase shareholder value	Percentage of processes with real-time feedback
Retain customers	Return on sales
Improve manufacturing quality	Average job-related training-hours per employee
Develop profitable customers	Return on equity
Increase proprietary products	Percentage of on-time deliveries by suppliers
Increase information-system capabilities	Product cost per unit
Enhance employee skills	Profit per salesperson
On-time delivery by suppliers	Percentage of error-free invoices
Increase profit generated by each salesperson	Customer cost per unit
Introduce new products	Earnings per share
Minimize invoice-error rate	Number of new customers
	Percentage of customers retained

Required

For each perspective, select those strategic objectives from the list that best relate to it. For each strategic objective, select the most appropriate performance measure(s) from the list.

13-35 Balanced scorecard. (R. Kaplan, adapted) Caltex, Inc., refines gasoline and sells it through its own Caltex Gas Stations. On the basis of market research, Caltex determines that 60% of the overall gasoline market consists of "service-oriented customers," medium- to high-income individuals who are willing to pay a higher price for gas if the gas stations can provide excellent customer service, such as a clean facility, a convenience store, friendly employees, a quick turnaround, the ability to pay by credit card, and high-octane premium gasoline. The remaining 40% of the overall market are "price shoppers" who look to buy the cheapest gasoline available. Caltex's strategy is to focus on the 60% of service-oriented customers. Caltex's balanced scorecard for 2011 follows. For brevity, the initiatives taken under each objective are omitted.

Objectives	Measures	Target Performance	Actual Performance
Financial Perspective			
Increase shareholder value	Operating-income changes from price recovery	$90,000,000	$95,000,000
	Operating-income changes from growth	$65,000,000	$67,000,000
Customer Perspective			
Increase market share	Market share of overall gasoline market	10%	9.8%
Internal-Business-Process Perspective			
Improve gasoline quality	Quality index	94 points	95 points
Improve refinery performance	Refinery-reliability index (%)	91%	91%
Ensure gasoline availability	Product-availability index (%)	99%	100%
Learning-and-Growth Perspective			
Increase refinery process capability	Percentage of refinery processes with advanced controls	88%	90%

Required

1. Was Caltex successful in implementing its strategy in 2011? Explain your answer.
2. Would you have included some measure of employee satisfaction and employee training in the learning-and-growth perspective? Are these objectives critical to Caltex for implementing its strategy? Why or why not? Explain briefly.
3. Explain how Caltex did not achieve its target market share in the total gasoline market but still exceeded its financial targets. Is "market share of overall gasoline market" the correct measure of market share? Explain briefly.
4. Is there a cause-and-effect linkage between improvements in the measures in the internal business-process perspective and the measure in the customer perspective? That is, would you add other measures to the internal-business-process perspective or the customer perspective? Why or why not? Explain briefly.
5. Do you agree with Caltex's decision not to include measures of changes in operating income from productivity improvements under the financial perspective of the balanced scorecard? Explain briefly.

13-36 Balanced scorecard. Lee Corporation manufactures various types of color laser printers in a highly automated facility with high fixed costs. The market for laser printers is competitive. The various color laser printers on the market are comparable in terms of features and price. Lee believes that satisfying customers with products of high quality at low costs is key to achieving its target profitability. For 2011, Lee plans to achieve higher quality and lower costs by improving yields and reducing defects in its manufacturing operations. Lee will train workers and encourage and empower them to take the necessary actions. Currently, a significant amount of Lee's capacity is used to produce products that are defective and cannot be sold. Lee expects that higher yields will reduce the capacity that Lee needs to manufacture products. Lee does not anticipate that improving manufacturing will automatically lead to lower costs because Lee has high fixed costs. To reduce fixed costs per unit, Lee could lay off employees and sell equipment, or it could use the capacity to produce and sell more of its current products or improved models of its current products.

Lee's balanced scorecard (initiatives omitted) for the just-completed fiscal year 2011 follows:

Objectives	Measures	Target Performance	Actual Performance
Financial Perspective			
Increase shareholder value	Operating-income changes from productivity improvements	$1,000,000	$400,000
	Operating-income changes from growth	$1,500,000	$600,000
Customer Perspective			
Increase market share	Market share in color laser printers	5%	4.6%
Internal-Business-Process Perspective			
Improve manufacturing quality	Yield	82%	85%
Reduce delivery time to customers	Order-delivery time	25 days	22 days
Learning-and-Growth Perspective			
Develop process skills	Percentage of employees trained in process and quality management	90%	92%
Enhance information-system capabilities	Percentage of manufacturing processes with real-time feedback	85%	87%

Required

1. Was Lee successful in implementing its strategy in 2011? Explain.
2. Is Lee's balanced scorecard useful in helping the company understand why it did not reach its target market share in 2011? If it is, explain why. If it is not, explain what other measures you might want to add under the customer perspective and why.
3. Would you have included some measure of employee satisfaction in the learning-and-growth perspective and new-product development in the internal-business-process perspective? That is, do you think employee satisfaction and development of new products are critical for Lee to implement its strategy? Why or why not? Explain briefly.
4. What problems, if any, do you see in Lee improving quality and significantly downsizing to eliminate unused capacity?

13-37 Partial productivity measurement. Gerhart Company manufactures wallets from fabric. In 2011, Gerhart made 2,520,000 wallets using 2,000,000 yards of fabric. In 2011, Gerhart has capacity to make 3,307,500 wallets and incurs a cost of $9,922,500 for this capacity. In 2012, Gerhart plans to make 2,646,000 wallets, make fabric use more efficient, and reduce capacity.

Suppose that in 2012 Gerhart makes 2,646,000 wallets, uses 1,764,000 yards of fabric, and reduces capacity to 2,700,000 wallets, incurring a cost of $8,370,000 for this capacity.

Required

1. Calculate the partial-productivity ratios for materials and conversion (capacity costs) for 2012, and compare them to a benchmark for 2011 calculated based on 2012 output.
2. How can Gerhart Company use the information from the partial-productivity calculations?

13-38 Total factor productivity (continuation of 13-37). Refer to the data for Problem 13-37. Assume the fabric costs $3.70 per yard in 2012 and $3.85 per yard in 2011.

Required

1. Compute Gerhart Company's total factor productivity (TFP) for 2012.
2. Compare TFP for 2012 with a benchmark TFP for 2011 inputs based on 2012 prices and output.
3. What additional information does TFP provide that partial productivity measures do not?

Collaborative Learning Problem

13-39 Strategic analysis of operating income. Halsey Company sells women's clothing. Halsey's strategy is to offer a wide selection of clothes and excellent customer service and to charge a premium price. Halsey presents the following data for 2010 and 2011. For simplicity, assume that each customer purchases one piece of clothing.

	2010	2011
1. Pieces of clothing purchased and sold	40,000	40,000
2. Average selling price	$60	$59
3. Average cost per piece of clothing	$40	$41
4. Selling and customer-service capacity	51,000 customers	43,000 customers
5. Selling and customer-service costs	$357,000	$296,700
6. Selling and customer-service capacity cost per customer (row 5 ÷ row 4)	$7 per customer	$6.90 per customer
7. Purchasing and administrative capacity	980 designs	850 designs
8. Purchasing and administrative costs	$245,000	$204,000
9. Purchasing and administrative capacity cost per distinct design (row 8 ÷ row 7)	$250 per design	$240 per design

Total selling and customer-service costs depend on the number of customers that Halsey has created capacity to support, not the actual number of customers that Halsey serves. Total purchasing and administrative costs depend on purchasing and administrative capacity that Halsey has created (defined in terms of the number of distinct clothing designs that Halsey can purchase and administer). Purchasing and administrative costs do not depend on the actual number of distinct clothing designs purchased. Halsey purchased 930 distinct designs in 2010 and 820 distinct designs in 2011.

At the start of 2010, Halsey planned to increase operating income by 10% over operating income in 2011.

Required

1. Is Halsey's strategy one of product differentiation or cost leadership? Explain.
2. Calculate Halsey's operating income in 2010 and 2011.
3. Calculate the growth, price-recovery, and productivity components of changes in operating income between 2010 and 2011.
4. Does the strategic analysis of operating income indicate Halsey was successful in implementing its strategy in 2011? Explain.

Cost Allocation, Customer-Profitability Analysis, and Sales-Variance Analysis

From Chapter 14 of *Cost Accounting: A Managerial Emphasis*, 14/e. Charles T. Horngren. Srikant M. Datar. Madhav Rajan.

Cost Allocation, Customer-Profitability Analysis, and Sales-Variance Analysis

Companies desperately want to make their customers happy.

But how far should they go to please them, and at what price? At what point are you better off not doing business with some customers at all? The following article explains why it's so important for managers to be able to figure out how profitable each of their customers is.

Minding the Store: Analyzing Customers, Best Buy Decides Not All Are Welcome[1]

As the former CEO of Best Buy, Brad Anderson decided to implement a rather unorthodox approach to retail: to separate his 1.5 million daily customers into "angels" and "devils."

The angels, customers who increase profits by purchasing high-definition televisions, portable electronics, and newly released DVDs without waiting for markdowns or rebates, are favored over the devils, who buy products, apply for rebates, return the purchases, and then buy them back at returned-merchandise discounts. These devils focus their spending on "loss leaders," discounted merchandise designed to encourage store traffic, but then flip the goods at a profit on sites like eBay.com.

Best Buy found that its most desirable customers fell into five distinct groups: upper-income men, suburban mothers, small-business owners, young family men, and technology enthusiasts. Male technology enthusiasts, nicknamed Buzzes, are early adopters, interested in buying and showing off the latest gadgets. Each store analyzes the demographics of its local market, and then focuses on two of these groups. For example, at stores popular with Buzzes, Best Buy sets up videogame areas with leather chairs and game players hooked to mammoth, plasma-screen televisions.

Best Buy also began working on ways to deter customers who drove profits down. It couldn't bar them from its stores. Starting in 2004, however, it began taking steps to put a stop to their most damaging practices by enforcing a restocking fee of 15% of the purchase price on returned merchandise. To discourage customers who return items with the intention of repurchasing them at an "open-box" discount, Best Buy started reselling the returned items

---

[1] *Sources*: Bustillo, Miguel. 2009. Best Buy confronts newer nemesis. *Wall Street Journal*, March 16; McWilliams, Gary. 2004. Minding the store: Analyzing customers, Best Buy decides not all are welcome. *Wall Street Journal*, November 8.

over the Internet, so the goods didn't reappear in the store where they were originally purchased.

This strategy stimulated growth for several years at Best Buy and helped the company survive the economic downturn while Circuit City, its leading competitor, went bankrupt. But Best Buy's angels and devils strategy now must confront a new competitor, Walmart. With Walmart's focus on consumers seeking no-frills bargains, Best Buy intends to match its new competitor's prices while leveraging its tech-savvy sales force to help consumers navigate increasingly complicated technology.

To determine which product, customer, program, or department is profitable, organizations must decide how to allocate costs. Best Buy analyzed its operations and chose to allocate costs towards serving its most profitable customers. In this chapter, we provide insight into cost allocation. The emphasis in this chapter is on macro issues in cost allocation: allocation of costs into divisions, plants, and customers.

Purposes of Cost Allocation

Recall that *indirect costs* of a particular cost object are costs that are related to that cost object but cannot be traced to it in an economically feasible (cost-effective) way. These costs often comprise a large percentage of the overall costs assigned to such cost objects as products, customers, and distribution channels. Why do managers allocate indirect costs to these cost objects? Exhibit 1 illustrates four purposes of cost allocation.

Different sets of costs are appropriate for different purposes described in Exhibit 1. Consider costs in different business functions of the value chain illustrated as follows:

Learning Objective 1

Identify four purposes for allocating costs to cost objects

. . . to provide information for decisions, motivate managers, justify costs, and measure income

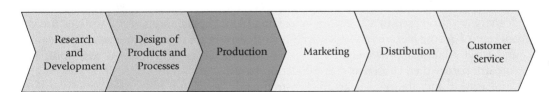

For some decisions related to the economic-decision purpose (for example, long-run product pricing), the costs in all six functions are relevant. For other decisions, particularly short-run economic decisions (for example, make or buy decisions), costs from only one or two functions, such as design and manufacturing, might be relevant.

Exhibit 1

Purposes of Cost
Allocation

Purpose	Examples
1. To provide information for economic decisions	To decide whether to add a new airline flight To decide whether to manufacture a component part of a television set or to purchase it from another manufacturer To decide on the selling price for a customized product or service To evaluate the cost of available capacity used to support different products
2. To motivate managers and other employees	To encourage the design of products that are simpler to manufacture or less costly to service To encourage sales representatives to emphasize high-margin products or services
3. To justify costs or compute reimbursement amounts	To cost products at a "fair" price, often required by law and government defense contracts To compute reimbursement for a consulting firm based on a percentage of the cost savings resulting from the implementation of its recommendations
4. To measure income and assets	To cost inventories for reporting to external parties To cost inventories for reporting to tax authorities

For the motivation purpose, costs from more than one but not all business functions are often included to emphasize to decision makers how costs in different functions are related to one another. For example, to estimate product costs, product designers at companies such as Hitachi and Toshiba include costs of production, distribution, and customer service. The goal is to focus designers' attention on how different product-design alternatives affect total costs.

For the cost-reimbursement purpose, a particular contract will often stipulate what costs will be reimbursed. For instance, cost-reimbursement rules for U.S. government contracts explicitly exclude marketing costs.

For the purpose of income and asset measurement for reporting to external parties under GAAP, only manufacturing costs, and in some cases product-design costs, are inventoriable and allocated to products. In the United States, R&D costs in most industries, marketing, distribution, and customer-service costs are period costs that are expensed as they are incurred. Under International Financial Reporting Standards (IFRS), research costs must be expensed as incurred but development costs must be capitalized if a product/process has reached technical feasibility and the firm has the intention and ability to use or sell the future asset.

Criteria to Guide Cost-Allocation Decisions

After identifying the purposes of cost allocation, managers and management accountants must decide how to allocate costs.

Exhibit 2 presents four criteria used to guide cost-allocation decisions. These decisions affect both the number of indirect-cost pools and the cost-allocation base for each indirect-cost pool. We emphasize the superiority of the cause-and-effect and the benefits-received criteria, especially when the purpose of cost allocation is to provide information for economic decisions or to motivate managers and employees.[2] Cause and effect is the primary criterion used in activity-based costing (ABC) applications. ABC systems use the concept of a cost hierarchy to identify the cost drivers that best demonstrate the cause-and-effect relationship between each activity and the costs in the related cost pool. The cost drivers are then chosen as cost-allocation bases.

Fairness and ability-to-bear are less-frequently-used and more problematic criteria than cause-and-effect or benefits-received. Fairness is a difficult criterion on which to

---

[2] The Federal Accounting Standards Advisory Board (which sets standards for management accounting for U.S. government departments and agencies) recommends the following: "Cost assignments should be performed by: (a) directly tracing costs whenever feasible and economically practicable, (b) assigning costs on a cause-and-effect basis, and (c) allocating costs on a reasonable and consistent basis" (*FASAB*, 1995, p. 12).

Exhibit 2

Criteria for Cost-
Allocation Decisions

1. Cause and Effect. Using this criterion, managers identify the variables that cause resources to be consumed. For example, managers may use hours of testing as the variable when allocating the costs of a quality-testing area to products. Cost allocations based on the cause-and-effect criterion are likely to be the most credible to operating personnel.

2. Benefits Received. Using this criterion, managers identify the beneficiaries of the outputs of the cost object. The costs of the cost object are allocated among the beneficiaries in proportion to the benefits each receives. Consider a corporatewide advertising program that promotes the general image of the corporation rather than any individual product. The costs of this program may be allocated on the basis of division revenues; the higher the revenues, the higher the division's allocated cost of the advertising program. The rationale behind this allocation is that divisions with higher revenues apparently benefited from the advertising more than divisions with lower revenues and, therefore, ought to be allocated more of the advertising costs.

3. Fairness or Equity. This criterion is often cited in government contracts when cost allocations are the basis for establishing a price satisfactory to the government and its suppliers. Cost allocation here is viewed as a "reasonable" or "fair" means of establishing a selling price in the minds of the contracting parties. For most allocation decisions, fairness is a matter of judgment rather than an operational criterion.

4. Ability to Bear. This criterion advocates allocating costs in proportion to the cost object's ability to bear costs allocated to it. An example is the allocation of corporate executive salaries on the basis of division operating income. The presumption is that the more-profitable divisions have a greater ability to absorb corporate headquarters' costs.

obtain agreement. What one party views as fair, another party may view as unfair.[3] For example, a university may view allocating a share of general administrative costs to government contracts as fair because general administrative costs are incurred to support all activities of the university. The government may view the allocation of such costs as unfair because the general administrative costs would have been incurred by the university regardless of whether the government contract existed. Perhaps the fairest way to resolve this issue is to understand, as well as possible, the cause-and-effect relationship between the government contract activity and general administrative costs. In other words, fairness is more a matter of judgment than an easily implementable choice criterion.

To get a sense of the issues that arise when using the ability-to-bear criterion, consider a product that consumes a large amount of indirect costs and currently sells for a price below its direct costs. This product has no ability to bear any of the indirect costs it uses. However, if the indirect costs it consumes are allocated to other products, these other products are subsidizing the product that is losing money. An integrated airline, for example, might allocate fewer costs to its activities in a highly contested market such as freight transportation, thereby subsidizing it via passenger transport. Some airports cross-subsidize costs associated with serving airline passengers through sales of duty-free goods. Such practices provide a distorted view of relative product and service profitability, and have the potential to invite both regulatory scrutiny as well as competitors attempting to undercut artificially higher-priced services.

Most importantly, companies must weigh the costs and benefits when designing and implementing their cost allocations. Companies incur costs not only in collecting data but also in taking the time to educate managers about cost allocations. In general, the more complex the cost allocations, the higher these education costs.

The costs of designing and implementing complex cost allocations are highly visible. Unfortunately, the benefits from using well-designed cost allocations, such as enabling managers to make better-informed sourcing decisions, pricing decisions, cost-control decisions, and so on, are difficult to measure. Nevertheless, when making cost allocations, managers should consider the benefits as well as the costs. As costs of collecting and processing information decrease, companies are building more-detailed cost allocations.

Decision Point

What criteria should managers use to guide cost-allocation decisions?

---

[3] Kaplow and Shavell, in a review of the legal literature, note that "notions of fairness are many and varied. They are analyzed and rationalized by different writers in different way, and they also typically depend upon the circumstances under consideration. Accordingly, it is not possible to identify and consensus view on these notions..." See L. Kaplow and S. Shavell, "Fairness Versus Welfare," *Harvard Law Review* (February 2001); and L. Kaplow and S. Shavell, *Fairness Versus Welfare* (Boston: Harvard University Press, 2002).

Cost Allocation Decisions

In this section, we focus on the first purpose of cost allocation: to provide information for economic decisions, such as pricing, by measuring the full costs of delivering products based on an ABC system.

ABC systems define indirect-cost pools for different activities and use cost drivers as allocation bases to assign costs of indirect-cost pools to products (the second stage of cost allocation). In this section, we focus on the first stage of cost allocation, the assignment of costs to indirect-cost pools.

We will use Consumer Appliances, Inc. (CAI), to illustrate how costs incurred in different parts of a company can be assigned, and then reassigned, for costing products, services, customers, or contracts. CAI has two divisions; each has its own manufacturing plant. The refrigerator division has a plant in Minneapolis, and the clothes dryer division has a plant in St. Paul. CAI's headquarters is in a separate location in Minneapolis. Each division manufactures and sells multiple products that differ in size and complexity.

CAI's management team collects costs at the following levels:

- **Corporate costs**—There are three major categories of corporate costs:
  1. **Treasury costs**—$900,000 of costs incurred for financing the construction of new assembly equipment in the two divisions. The cost of new assembly equipment is $5,200,000 in the refrigerator division and $3,800,000 in the clothes dryer division.
  2. **Human resource management costs**—recruitment and ongoing employee training and development, $1,600,000.
  3. **Corporate administration costs**—executive salaries, rent, and general administration costs, $5,400,000.

- **Division costs**—Each division has two direct-cost categories (direct materials and direct manufacturing labor) and seven indirect-cost pools—one cost pool each for the five activities (design, setup, manufacturing, distribution, and administration), one cost pool to accumulate facility costs, and one cost pool for the allocated corporate treasury costs. Exhibit 3 presents data for six of the division indirect-cost pools and cost-allocation bases. (In a later section, we describe how corporate treasury

Exhibit 3 — Division Indirect-Cost Pools and Cost-Allocation Bases, CAI, for Refrigerator Division (R) and Clothes Dryer Division (CD)

Division Indirect-Cost Pools	Example of Costs		Total Indirect Costs	Cost Hierarchy Category	Cost-Allocation Base	Cause-and-Effect Relationship That Motivates Management's Choice of Allocation Base
Design	Design engineering salaries	(R) (CD)	$6,000,000 4,250,000	Product sustaining	Parts times cubic feet	Complex products (more parts and larger size) require greater design resources.
Setup of machines	Setup labor and equipment cost	(R) (CD)	$3,000,000 2,400,000	Batch level	Setup-hours	Overhead costs of the setup activity increase as setup-hours increase.
Manufacturing operations	Plant and equipment, energy	(R) (CD)	$25,000,000 18,750,000	Output unit level	Machine-hours	Manufacturing-operations overhead costs support machines and, hence, increase with machine usage.
Distribution	Shipping labor and equipment	(R) (CD)	$8,000,000 5,500,000	Output unit level	Cubic feet	Distribution-overhead costs increase with cubic feet of product shipped.
Administration	Division executive salaries	(R) (CD)	$1,000,000 800,000	Facility sustaining	Revenues	Weak relationship between division executive salaries and revenues, but justified by CAI on a benefits-received basis.
Facility	Annual building and space costs	(R) (CD)	$4,500,000 3,500,000	All	Square feet	Facility costs increase with square feet of space.

costs are allocated to each division to create the seventh division indirect-cost pool.) CAI identifies the cost hierarchy category for each cost pool: output-unit level, batch level, product sustaining level, and facility-sustaining level.

Exhibit 4 presents an overview diagram of the allocation of corporate and division indirect costs to products of the refrigerator division. Note: The clothes dryer division has its own seven indirect-cost pools used to allocate costs to products. These cost pools and cost-allocation bases parallel the indirect-cost pools and allocation bases for the refrigerator division.

Look first at the middle row of the exhibit, where you see "Division Indirect-Cost Pools," and scan the lower half.

Exhibit 4 Overview Diagram of Allocation of Corporate and Division Indirect Costs to Products of the Refrigerator Division, CAI

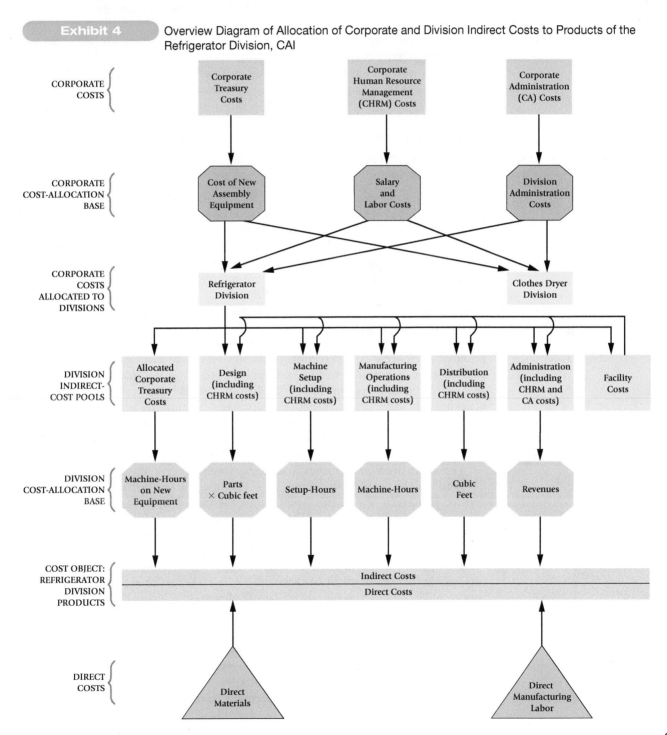

In the lower half of Exhibit 4 is the cost pool called Facility Costs (far right, middle row), which accumulates all annual costs of buildings and furnishings (such as depreciation) incurred in the division. The arrows in Exhibit 4 indicate that CAI allocates facility costs to the five activity-cost pools. Recall from Exhibit 3 that CAI uses square feet area required for various activities (design, setup, manufacturing, distribution, and administration) to allocate these facility costs. These activity-cost pools then include the costs of the building and facilities needed to perform the various activities.

The costs in the six remaining indirect-cost pools (that is, after costs of the facility cost pool have been allocated to other cost pools) are allocated to products on the basis of cost drivers described in Exhibit 3. These cost drivers are chosen as the cost-allocation bases because there is a cause-and-effect relationship between the cost drivers and the costs in the indirect-cost pool. A cost rate per unit is calculated for each cost-allocation base. Indirect costs are allocated to products on the basis of the total quantity of the cost allocation base for each activity used by the product.

Next focus on the upper half of Exhibit 4: how corporate costs are allocated to divisions and then to indirect-cost pools.

Before getting into the details of the allocations, let's first consider some broader choices that CAI faces regarding the allocation of corporate costs.

Allocating Corporate Costs to Divisions and Products

CAI's management team has several choices to make when accumulating and allocating corporate costs to divisions.

1. Which corporate-cost categories should CAI allocate as indirect costs of the divisions? Should CAI allocate all corporate costs or only some of them?
   - Some companies allocate all corporate costs to divisions because corporate costs are incurred to support division activities. Allocating all corporate costs motivates division managers to examine how corporate costs are planned and controlled. Also, companies that want to calculate the full cost of products must allocate all corporate costs to indirect-cost pools of divisions.
   - Other companies do not allocate corporate costs to divisions because these costs are not controllable by division managers.
   - Still other companies allocate only those corporate costs, such as corporate human resources, that are widely perceived as causally related to division activities or that provide explicit benefits to divisions. These companies exclude corporate costs such as corporate donations to charitable foundations because division managers often have no say in making these decisions and because the benefits to the divisions are less evident or too remote. If a company decides not to allocate some or all corporate costs, this results in total company profitability being less than the sum of individual division or product profitabilities.

     For some decision purposes, allocating some but not all corporate costs to divisions may be the preferred alternative. Consider the performance evaluation of division managers. The controllability notion is frequently used to justify excluding some corporate costs from division reports. For example, salaries of the top management at corporate headquarters are often excluded from responsibility accounting reports of division managers. Although divisions tend to benefit from these corporate costs, division managers argue they have no say in ("are not responsible for") how much of these corporate resources they use or how much they cost. The contrary argument is that full allocation is justified because the divisions receive benefits from all corporate costs.

2. When allocating corporate costs to divisions, should CAI allocate only costs that vary with division activity or should the company assign fixed costs as well? Companies allocate both variable and fixed costs to divisions and then to products, because the resulting product costs are useful for making long-run strategic decisions, such as which products to sell and at what price. To make good long-run decisions, managers

need to know the cost of all resources (whether variable or fixed) required to produce products. Why? Because in the long run, firms can manage the levels of virtually all of their costs; very few costs are truly fixed. Moreover, to survive and prosper in the long run, firms must ensure that the prices charged for products exceed the total resources consumed to produce them, regardless of whether these costs are variable or fixed in the short run.

Companies that allocate corporate costs to divisions must carefully identify relevant costs for specific decisions. Suppose a division is profitable before any corporate costs are allocated but "unprofitable" after allocation of corporate costs. Should the division be closed down? The relevant corporate costs in this case are not the allocated corporate costs but those corporate costs that will be saved if the division is closed. If division profits exceed the relevant corporate costs, the division should not be closed.

3. If CAI allocates corporate costs to divisions, how many cost pools should it use? One extreme is to aggregate all corporate costs into a single cost pool. The other extreme is to have numerous individual corporate cost pools. A major consideration is to construct **homogeneous cost pools** so that all of the costs in the cost pool have the same or a similar cause-and-effect or benefits-received relationship with the cost-allocation base.

For example, when allocating corporate costs to divisions, CAI can combine corporate administration costs and corporate human-resource-management costs into a single cost pool if both cost categories have the same or similar cause-and-effect relationship with the same cost-allocation base (such as the number of employees in each division). If, however, each cost category has a cause-and-effect relationship with a different cost-allocation base (for example, number of employees in each division affects corporate human-resource-management costs, whereas revenues of each division affect corporate administration costs), CAI will prefer to maintain separate cost pools for each of these costs. Determining homogeneous cost pools requires judgment and should be revisited on a regular basis.

The benefit of using a multiple cost-pool system must be balanced against the costs of implementing it. Advances in information-gathering technology make it more likely that multiple cost-pool systems will pass the cost-benefit test.

Implementing Corporate Cost Allocations

After much discussion and debate, CAI's management team chooses to allocate all corporate costs to divisions. We now illustrate the allocation of corporate costs to divisions in CAI's ABC system.

The demands for corporate resources by the refrigerator division and the clothes dryer division depend on the demands that each division's products place on these resources. The top half of Exhibit 4 graphically represents the allocations.

1. CAI allocates treasury costs to each division on the basis of the cost of new assembly equipment installed in each division (the cost driver of treasury costs). It allocates the $900,000 of treasury costs as follows (using information from p. 506):

$$\text{Refrigerator Division: } \$900,000 \times \frac{\$5,200,000}{\$5,200,000 + \$3,800,000} = \$520,000$$

$$\text{Clothes Dryer Division: } \$900,000 \times \frac{\$3,800,000}{\$5,200,000 + \$3,800,000} = \$380,000$$

Each division then creates a *separate cost pool* consisting of the allocated corporate treasury costs and reallocates these costs to products on the basis of machine-hours used on the new equipment. Treasury costs are an output unit-level cost because they represent resources used on activities performed on each individual unit of a product.

2. CAI's analysis indicates that the demand for corporate human resource management (CHRM) costs for recruitment and training varies with total salary and labor costs in

each division. Suppose salary and labor costs are \$44,000,000 in the refrigerator division and \$36,000,000 in the clothes dryer division. Then CHRM costs are allocated to the divisions as follows:

$$\text{Refrigerator Division: } \$1,600,000 \times \frac{\$44,000,000}{\$44,000,000 + \$36,000,000} = \$880,000$$

$$\text{Clothes Dryer Division: } \$1,600,000 \times \frac{\$36,000,000}{\$44,000,000 + \$36,000,000} = \$720,000$$

Each division reallocates the CHRM costs allocated to it to the indirect-cost pools—design, machine setup, manufacturing operations, distribution, and division administration (the allocated-corporate-treasury cost pool and the facility costs pool have no salary and labor costs, so no CHRM costs are allocated to them)—on the basis of total salary and labor costs of each indirect-cost pool. CHRM costs that are added to division indirect-cost pools are then allocated to products using the cost driver for the respective cost pool. Therefore, CHRM costs are product-sustaining costs (for the portion of CHRM costs allocated to the design cost pool), batch-level costs (for the portion of CHRM costs allocated to the machine-setup cost pool), output unit-level costs (for the portions of CHRM costs allocated to the manufacturing-operations and distribution cost pools), and facility-sustaining costs (for the portion of CHRM costs allocated to the division-administration cost pool).

3. CAI allocates corporate administration costs to each division on the basis of division-administration costs (Exhibit 3 shows the amounts of division-administration costs) because corporate administration's main role is to support division administration.

$$\text{Refrigerator Division: } \$5,400,000 \times \frac{\$1,000,000}{\$1,000,000 + \$800,000} = \$3,000,000$$

$$\text{Clothes Dryer Division: } \$5,400,000 \times \frac{\$800,000}{\$1,000,000 + \$800,000} = \$2,400,000$$

Each division adds the allocated corporate-administration costs to the division-administration cost pool. The costs in this cost pool are facility-sustaining costs and do not have a cause-and-effect relationship with individual products produced and sold by each division. CAI's policy, however, is to allocate all costs to products so that CAI's division managers become aware of all costs incurred at CAI in their pricing and other decisions. It allocates the division-administration costs (including allocated corporate-administration costs) to products on the basis of product revenues (a benefits-received criterion).

The issues discussed in this section regarding divisions and products apply nearly identically to customers, as we shall show next.

Decision Point ▶

What are two key decisions managers must make when collecting costs in indirect-cost pools?

Learning Objective 4

Discuss why a company's revenues and costs can differ across customers

... revenues can differ because of differences in the quantity purchased and the price discounts given, while costs can differ because different customers place different demands on a company's resources

Customer-Profitability Analysis

Customer-profitability analysis is the reporting and assessment of revenues earned from customers and the costs incurred to earn those revenues. An analysis of customer differences in revenues and costs can provide insight into why differences exist in the operating income earned from different customers. Managers use this information to ensure that customers making large contributions to the operating income of a company receive a high level of attention from the company.

Consider Spring Distribution Company, which sells bottled water. It has two distribution channels: (1) a wholesale distribution channel, in which the wholesaler sells to supermarkets, drugstores, and other stores, and (2) a retail distribution channel for a small number of business customers. We focus mainly on customer-profitability analysis in Spring's retail distribution channel. The list selling price in this channel is \$14.40 per case

(24 bottles). The full cost to Spring is $12 per case. If every case is sold at list price in this distribution channel, Spring would earn a gross margin of $2.40 per case.

Customer-Revenue Analysis

Consider revenues from 4 of Spring's 10 retail customers in June 2012:

	Home	Insert	Page Layout	Formulas	Data	Review	View

	A	B	C	D	E
1		**CUSTOMER**			
2		**A**	**B**	**G**	**J**
3	Cases sold	42,000	33,000	2,900	2,500
4	List selling price	$ 14.40	$ 14.40	$ 14.40	$ 14.40
5	Price discount	$ 0.96	$ 0.24	$ 1.20	$ 0.00
6	Invoice price	$ 13.44	$ 14.16	$ 13.20	$ 14.40
7	Revenues (Row 3 × Row 6)	$564,480	$467,280	$38,280	$36,000

Two variables explain revenue differences across these four customers: (1) the number of cases they purchased and (2) the magnitude of price discounting. A **price discount** is the reduction in selling price below list selling price to encourage customers to purchase more. Companies that record only the final invoice price in their information system cannot readily track the magnitude of their price discounting.[4]

Price discounts are a function of multiple factors, including the volume of product purchased (higher-volume customers receive higher discounts) and the desire to sell to a customer who might help promote sales to other customers. Discounts could also be because of poor negotiating by a salesperson or the unwanted effect of an incentive plan based only on revenues. At no time should price discounts run afoul of the law by way of price discrimination, predatory pricing, or collusive pricing.

Tracking price discounts by customer and by salesperson helps improve customer profitability. For example, Spring Distribution may decide to strictly enforce its volume-based price discounting policy. It may also require its salespeople to obtain approval for giving large discounts to customers who do not normally qualify for such discounts. In addition, the company could track the future sales of customers who its salespeople have given sizable price discounts to because of their "high growth potential." For example, Spring should track future sales to customer G to see if the $1.20-per-case discount translates into higher future sales.

Customer revenues are one element of customer profitability. The other element that is equally important to understand is the cost of acquiring, serving, and retaining customers. We study this topic next.

Customer-Cost Analysis

A **customer-cost hierarchy** categorizes costs related to customers into different cost pools on the basis of different types of cost drivers, or cost-allocation bases, or different degrees of difficulty in determining cause-and-effect or benefits-received relationships. Spring's ABC system focuses on customers rather than products. It has one direct cost, the cost of bottled water, and multiple indirect-cost pools. Spring identifies five categories of indirect costs in its customer-cost hierarchy:

1. **Customer output unit-level costs**—costs of activities to sell each unit (case) to a customer. An example is product-handling costs of each case sold.

---

[4] Further analysis of customer revenues could distinguish gross revenues from net revenues. This approach highlights differences across customers in sales returns. Additional discussion of ways to analyze revenue differences across customers is in R. S. Kaplan and R. Cooper, *Cost and Effect* (Boston, MA: Harvard Business School Press, 1998, Chapter 10); and G. Cokins, *Activity-Based Cost Management: An Executive's Guide* (New York: John Wiley & Sons, 2001, Chapter 3).

2. **Customer batch-level costs**—costs of activities related to a group of units (cases) sold to a customer. Examples are costs incurred to process orders or to make deliveries.

3. **Customer-sustaining costs**—costs of activities to support individual customers, regardless of the number of units or batches of product delivered to the customer. Examples are costs of visits to customers or costs of displays at customer sites.

4. **Distribution-channel costs**—costs of activities related to a particular distribution channel rather than to each unit of product, each batch of product, or specific customers. An example is the salary of the manager of Spring's retail distribution channel.

5. **Corporate-sustaining costs**—costs of activities that cannot be traced to individual customers or distribution channels. Examples are top-management and general-administration costs.

Spring has one additional cost hierarchy category, distribution-channel costs, for the costs it incurs to support its wholesale and retail distribution channels.

Customer-Level Costs

Spring is particularly interested in analyzing *customer-level indirect costs*—costs incurred in the first three categories of the customer-cost hierarchy: customer output-unit-level costs, customer batch-level costs, and customer-sustaining costs. Spring wants to work with customers to reduce these costs. It believes customer actions will have less impact on distribution-channel and corporate-sustaining costs. The following table shows five activities (in addition to cost of goods sold) that Spring identifies as resulting in customer-level costs. The table indicates the cost drivers and cost-driver rates for each activity, as well as the cost-hierarchy category for each activity.

	Home	Insert	Page Layout	Formulas	Data	Review	View
	G	H	I			J	
1	**Activity Area**	**Cost Driver and Rate**			**Cost-Hierarchy Category**		
2	Product handling	$0.50	per case sold		Customer output-unit-level costs		
3	Order taking	$ 100	per purchase order		Customer batch-level costs		
4	Delivery vehicles	$ 2	per delivery mile traveled		Customer batch-level costs		
5	Rush deliveries	$ 300	per expedited delivery		Customer batch-level costs		
6	Visits to customers	$ 80	per sales visit		Customer-sustaining costs		

Information on the quantity of cost drivers used by each of four customers is as follows:

	Home	Insert	Page Layout	Formulas	Data	Review
	A	B	C	D	E	
10		**CUSTOMER**				
11		**A**	**B**	**G**	**J**	
12	Number of purchase orders	30	25	15	10	
13	Number of deliveries	60	30	20	15	
14	Miles traveled per delivery	5	12	20	6	
15	Number of rush deliveries	1	0	2	0	
16	Number of visits to customers	6	5	4	3	

Exhibit 5 shows a customer-profitability analysis for the four retail customers using information on customer revenues previously presented and customer-level costs from the ABC system.

Spring Distribution can use the information in Exhibit 5 to work with customers to reduce the quantity of activities needed to support them. Consider a comparison of customer G and customer A. Customer G purchases only 7% of the cases that customer A purchases (2,900 versus 42,000). Yet, compared with customer A, customer G uses one-half as many purchase orders, two-thirds as many visits to customers, one-third as many deliveries, and twice as many rush deliveries. By implementing charges for each of these services, Spring might be able to induce customer G to make fewer but larger purchase orders, and require fewer customer visits, deliveries, and rush deliveries while looking to increase sales in the future.

Consider Owens and Minor, a distributor of medical supplies to hospitals. It strategically prices each of its services separately. For example, if a hospital wants a rush delivery or special packaging, Owens and Minor charges the hospital an additional price for each particular service. How have Owens and Minor's customers reacted? Hospitals that value these services continue to demand and pay for them while hospitals that do not value these services stop asking for them, saving Owens and Minor some costs. Owens and Minor's pricing strategy influences customer behavior in a way that increases its revenues or decreases its costs.

The ABC system also highlights a second opportunity for cost reduction. Spring can seek to reduce the costs of each activity. For example, improving the efficiency of the ordering process (such as by having customers order electronically) can reduce costs even if customers place the same number of orders.

Exhibit 6 shows a monthly operating income statement for Spring Distribution. The customer-level operating income of customers A and B in Exhibit 5 are shown in columns 8 and 9 of Exhibit 6. The format of Exhibit 6 is based on Spring's cost hierarchy. All costs incurred to serve customers are not included in customer-level costs and therefore are not allocated to customers in Exhibit 6. For example, distribution-channel costs such as the salary of the manager of the retail distribution channel are not included in customer-level costs and are not allocated to customers. Instead, these costs are identified as costs of the retail channel as a whole, because Spring's management believes that changes in customer behavior will not affect distribution-channel costs. These costs will be affected only by decisions pertaining to the whole channel, such as a decision to discontinue retail distribution. Another reason Spring does not allocate distribution-channel costs to customers is motivation. Spring's managers contend that

Exhibit 5 Customer-Profitability Analysis for Four Retail Channel Customers of Spring Distribution for June 2012

	Home Insert Page Layout Formulas Data Review View				
	A	B	C	D	E
1		CUSTOMER			
2		A	B	G	J
3	Revenues at list price: $14.40 × 42,000; 33,000; 2,900; 2,500	$604,800	$475,200	$41,760	$36,000
4	Price discount: $0.96 x 42,000; $0.24 × 33,000; $1.20 × 2,900; $0 × 2,500	40,320	7,920	3,480	0
5	Revenues (at actual price)	564,480	467,280	38,280	36,000
6	Cost of goods sold: $12 × 42,000; 33,000; 2,900; 2,500	504,000	396,000	34,800	30,000
7	Gross margin	60,480	71,280	3,480	6,000
8	Customer-level operating costs				
9	Product handling $0.50 × 42,000; 33,000; 2,900; 2,500	21,000	16,500	1,450	1,250
10	Order taking $100 × 30; 25; 15; 10	3,000	2,500	1,500	1,000
11	Delivery vehicles $2 × (5 × 60); (12 × 30); (20 × 20); (6 × 15)	600	720	800	180
12	Rush deliveries $300 × 1; 0; 2; 0	300	0	600	0
13	Visits to customers $80 × 6; 5; 4; 3	480	400	320	240
14	Total customer-level operating costs	25,380	20,120	4,670	2,670
15	Customer-level operating income	$ 35,100	$ 51,160	$ (1,190)	$ 3,330

Exhibit 6   Income Statement of Spring Distribution for June 2012

	A	B	C	D	E	F	G	H	I	J	K	L	M
									CUSTOMER DISTRIBUTION CHANNELS				
1													
2				**Wholesale Customers**						**Retail Customers**			
3		Total	Total	A1	A2	A3	▪		Total	A[a]	B[a]	C	▪
4		(1) = (2) + (7)	(2)	(3)	(4)	(5)	(6)		(7)	(8)	(9)	(10)	(11)
5	Revenues (at actual prices)	$12,138,120	$10,107,720	$1,946,000	$1,476,000	▪	▪		$2,030,400	$564,480	$467,280	▪	▪
6	Customer-level costs	11,633,760	9,737,280	1,868,000	1,416,000	▪	▪		1,896,480	529,380[b]	416,120[b]	▪	▪
7	Customer-level operating income	504,360	370,440	$ 78,000	$ 60,000	▪	▪		133,920	$ 35,100	$ 51,160	▪	▪
8	Distribution-channel costs	160,500	102,500						58,000				
9	Distribution-channel-level operating income	343,860	$ 267,940						$ 75,920				
10	Corporate-sustaining costs	263,000											
11	Operating income	$ 80,860											
12													
13	[a]Full details are presented in Exhibit 14-5.												
14	[b]Cost of goods sold + Total customer-level operating costs from Exhibit 14-5.												

salespersons responsible for managing individual customer accounts would lose motivation if their bonuses were affected by the allocation to customers of distribution-channel costs over which they had minimal influence.

Next, consider corporate-sustaining costs such as top-management and general-administration costs. Spring's managers have concluded that there is no cause-and-effect or benefits-received relationship between any cost-allocation base and corporate-sustaining costs. Consequently, allocation of corporate-sustaining costs serves no useful purpose in decision making, performance evaluation, or motivation. For example, suppose Spring allocated the $263,000 of corporate-sustaining costs to its distribution channels: $173,000 to the wholesale channel and $90,000 to the retail channel. Using information from Exhibit 6, the retail channel would then show a loss of $14,080 ($75,920 – $90,000).

If this same situation persisted in subsequent months, should Spring shut down the retail distribution channel? No, because if retail distribution were discontinued, corporate-sustaining costs would be unaffected. Allocating corporate-sustaining costs to distribution channels could give the misleading impression that the potential cost savings from discontinuing a distribution channel would be greater than the likely amount.

Some managers and management accountants advocate fully allocating all costs to customers and distribution channels so that (1) the sum of operating incomes of all customers in a distribution channel (segment) equals the operating income of the distribution channel and (2) the sum of the distribution-channel operating incomes equals company-wide operating income. These managers and management accountants argue that customers and products must eventually be profitable on a full-cost basis. In the previous example, CAI allocated all corporate and division-level costs to its refrigerator and clothes dryer products. For some decisions, such as pricing, allocating all costs ensures that long-run prices are set at a level to cover the cost of all resources used to produce and sell products. Nevertheless, the value of the hierarchical format in Exhibit 6 is that it distinguishes among various degrees of objectivity when allocating costs, and it dovetails with the different levels at which decisions are made and performance is evaluated. The issue of when and what costs to allocate is another example of the "different costs for different purposes" theme emphasized throughout this text.

> **Decision Point ▶**
>
> How can a company's revenues and costs differ across customers?

Customer-Profitability Profiles

> **Learning Objective 5**
>
> Identify the importance of customer-profitability profiles
>
> . . . highlight that a small percentage of customers contributes a large percentage of operating income.

Customer-profitability profiles provide a useful tool for managers. Exhibit 7 ranks Spring's 10 retail customers based on customer-level operating income. (Four of these customers are analyzed in Exhibit 5.)

Column 4, computed by adding the individual amounts in column 1, shows the cumulative customer-level operating income. For example, customer C has a cumulative

Exhibit 7   Customer-Profitability Analysis for Retail Channel Customers: Spring Distribution, June 2012

	A	B	C	D	E	F
1	**Customers Ranked on Customer-Level Operating Income**					
2						**Cumulative**
3						**Customer-Level**
4						**Operating Income**
5				**Customer-Level**	**Cumulative**	**as a % of Total**
6	**Retail**	**Customer-Level**	**Customer**	**Operating Income**	**Customer-Level**	**Customer-Level**
7	**Customer**	**Operating Income**	**Revenue**	**Divided by Revenue**	**Operating Income**	**Operating Income**
8	**Code**	**(1)**	**(2)**	**(3) = (1) ÷ (2)**	**(4)**	**(5) = (4) ÷ $133,920**
9	B	$ 51,160	$ 467,280	10.9%	$ 51,160	38%
10	A	35,100	564,480	6.2%	86,260	64%
11	C	27,070	295,640	9.2%	113,330	85%
12	D	20,580	277,000	7.4%	133,910	100%
13	F	12,504	143,500	8.7%	146,414	109%
14	J	3,330	41,000	8.1%	149,744	112%
15	E	176	123,000	0.1%	149,920	112%
16	G	–1,190	38,280	–3.1%	148,730	111%
17	H	–5,690	38,220	–14.9%	143,040	107%
18	I	–9,120	42,000	–21.7%	133,920	100%
19		$133,920	$2,030,400			
20						

income of $113,330 in column 4. This $113,330 is the sum of $51,160 for customer B, $35,100 for customer A, and $27,070 for customer C.

Column 5 shows what percentage the $113,330 *cumulative* total for customers B, A, and C is of the total customer-level operating income of $133,920 earned in the retail distribution channel from all 10 customers. The three most profitable customers contribute 85% of total customer-level operating income. These customers deserve the highest service and priority. Companies try to keep their best customers happy in a number of ways: special phone numbers and upgrade privileges for elite-level frequent flyers, free usage of luxury hotel suites and big credit limits for high-rollers at casinos, and so on. In many companies, it is common for a small number of customers to contribute a high percentage of operating income. Microsoft uses the phrase "not all revenue dollars are endowed equally in profitability" to stress this point.

Column 3 shows the profitability per dollar of revenue by customer. This measure of customer profitability indicates that, although customer A contributes the second-highest operating income, the profitability per dollar of revenue is lower because of high price discounts. Spring's goal is to increase profit margins for customer A by decreasing the price discounts or saving customer-level costs while maintaining or increasing sales. Customer J has a higher profit margin but has lower total sales. Spring's challenge with customer J is to maintain margins while increasing sales.

Presenting Profitability Analysis

There are two common ways of presenting the results of customer-profitability analysis. Managers often find the bar chart presentation in Exhibit 8, Panel A, to be an intuitive way to visualize customer profitability. The highly profitable customers clearly stand out. Moreover, the number of "unprofitable" customers and the magnitude of their losses are apparent. A popular alternative way to express customer profitability is

Exhibit 8

Panel A: Bar Chart of Customer-Level Operating Income for Spring Distribution's Retail Channel Customers in June 2012

Panel B: The Whale Curve of Cumulative Profitability for Spring Distribution's Retail Channel Customers in June 2012

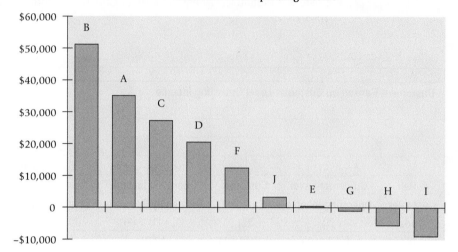

Customer-Level Operating Income

Retail Channel Customers

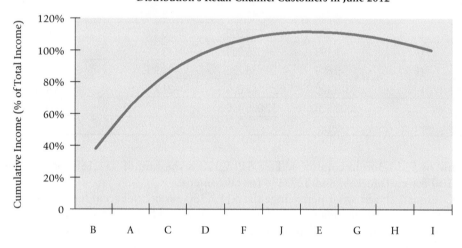

The Whale Curve of Cumulative Profitability for Spring Distribution's Retail Channel Customers in June 2012

by plotting the contents of column 5 of Exhibit 7. This chart is called the **whale curve** since it is backward bending at the point where customers start to become unprofitable, and thus resembles a humpback whale.[5]

Spring's managers must explore ways to make unprofitable customers profitable. Exhibits 5 to 8 emphasize short-run customer profitability. Other factors managers should consider in deciding how to allocate resources among customers include the following:

- **Likelihood of customer retention.** The more likely a customer will continue to do business with a company, the more valuable the customer. Customers differ in their loyalty and their willingness to frequently "shop their business."

- **Potential for sales growth.** The higher the likely growth of the customer's industry and the customer's sales, the more valuable the customer. Customers to whom a company can cross-sell other products are more desirable.

- **Long-run customer profitability.** This factor will be influenced by the first two factors specified and the cost of customer-support staff and special services required to retain customer accounts.

---

[5] In practice, the curve of the chart can be quite steep. The whale curve for cumulative profitability usually reveals that the most profitable 20% of customers generate between 150% and 300% of total profits, the middle 70% of customers break even, and the least profitable 10% of customers lose from 50% to 200% of total profits (see Robert Kaplan and V.G. Narayanan, Measuring and Managing Customer Profitability, Journal of Cost Management, Sept/Oct 2001, pp. 1–11).

- **Increases in overall demand from having well-known customers.** Customers with established reputations help generate sales from other customers through product endorsements.

- **Ability to learn from customers.** Customers who provide ideas about new products or ways to improve existing products are especially valuable.

Managers should be cautious when deciding to discontinue customers. In Exhibit 7, the current unprofitability of customer G, for example, may provide misleading signals about G's profitability in the long-run. Moreover, as in any ABC-based system, the costs assigned to customer G are not all variable. In the short run, it may well have been efficient for Spring to use its spare capacity to serve G on a contribution-margin basis. Discontinuing customer G will not eliminate all the costs assigned to that customer, and will leave the firm worse off than before.

Of course, particular customers might be chronically unprofitable and hold limited future prospects. Or they might fall outside a firm's target market or require unsustainably high levels of service relative to the firm's strategies and capabilities. In such cases, organizations are becoming increasingly aggressive in severing customer relationships. For example, ING Direct, the largest direct lender and fastest growing financial services organization in the United States, asks 10,000 "high maintenance" customers to close their accounts each month.[6] The Concepts in Action feature on the next page provides an example of a company that is struggling with the question of how to manage its resources and profitability without affecting the satisfaction of its customers.

Using the Five-Step Decision-Making Process to Manage Customer Profitability

The different types of customer analyses that we have just covered provide companies with key information to guide the allocation of resources across customers. Use the five-step decision-making process to think about how managers use these analyses to make customer-management decisions.

1. *Identify the problem and uncertainties.* The problem is how to manage and allocate resources across customers.

2. *Obtain information.* Managers identify past revenues generated by each customer and customer-level costs incurred in the past to support each customer.

3. *Make predictions about the future.* Managers estimate the revenues they expect from each customer and the customer-level costs they will incur in the future. In making these predictions, managers consider the effects that future price discounts will have on revenues, the effect that pricing for different services (such as rush deliveries) will have on the demand for these services by customers, and ways to reduce the cost of providing services. For example, Deluxe, Corp., a leading check printer, initiated process reductions to rein in its cost to serve customers by opening an electronic channel to shift customers from paper to automated ordering.

4. *Make decisions by choosing among alternatives.* Managers use the customer-profitability profiles to identify the small set of customers who deserve the highest service and priority. They also identify ways to make less-profitable customers (such as Spring's customer G) more profitable. Banks, for example, often impose minimum balance requirements on customers. Distribution firms may require minimum order quantities or levy a surcharge for smaller or customized orders. In making resource-allocation decisions, managers also consider long-term effects, such as the potential for future sales growth and the opportunity to leverage a particular customer account to make sales to other customers.

5. *Implement the decision, evaluate performance, and learn.* After the decision is implemented, managers compare actual results to predicted outcomes to evaluate the decision they made, its implementation, and ways in which they might improve profitability.

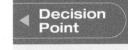

Decision Point

How do customer-profitability profiles help managers?

---

[6] See, for example, "The New Math of Customer Relationships" at http://hbswk.hbs.edu/item/5884.html.

Concepts in Action — iPhone "Apps" Challenge Customer Profitability at AT&T

Rich Schulz/AP Wide World Photos

AT&T is the second largest wireless provider in the United States. The company provides mobile telephone and data access to more than 85 million individuals, businesses, and government agencies. AT&T uses cost accounting to price its various wireless service plans and calculate overall profitability for its customers, including more than 10 million owners of Apple's iPhone. AT&T is the exclusive wireless provider for the popular iPhone smart phone.

Traditionally, the cost of serving different wireless customers varied. Most business customers, for example, required reliable service during business hours and large amounts of data bandwidth for e-mail and Internet access. In contrast, many individuals use their wireless devices extensively on nights and weekends and use features such as text messages and music ringtones. Accordingly, wireless providers considered the costs for these services when developing pricing plans and calculating customer profitability. Therefore, individuals using their phone service sparingly could select a less-expensive plan with fewer minutes, for use mostly at night and on weekends, whereas more-demanding individuals and lucrative business customers chose plans with more telephone minutes, large amounts of wireless data bandwidth, and guaranteed reliability . . . for a higher price.

When AT&T began selling the iPhone in mid-2007, cost accountants projected the profitability for its new customers, and new plans were designed accordingly. Similar to traditional wireless plans, iPhone buyers were offered subscription options with different amounts of telephone minutes at different price points. For example, 450 telephone minutes cost $59.99, while 1,350 minutes were $99.99. However, to showcase the iPhone's wireless and Internet capabilities, Apple insisted that AT&T offer only one data package, an unlimited plan.

While the unlimited data package proved initially lucrative, technology developments added significant costs to AT&T. When Apple introduced the iPhone 3G in 2008, the third-generation data capabilities encouraged software developers to build new programs for the iPhone platform. Within two years, nearly 140,000 applications, ranging from Pandora's mobile music player to Mint's on-the-go budgeting program, were downloaded more than 3 billion times by iPhone users. Each of the applications, however, uses a lot of data bandwidth.

Recall that AT&T does not charge iPhone subscribers for marginal bandwidth use. As a result, subscribers who download and use many iPhone applications quickly became unprofitable for the company. With each 100MB of bandwidth costing AT&T $1, the company is currently considering cost-reducing options, such as limiting data access and changing its all-you-can-eat data subscription plan, but it is very concerned about alienating its customers.

iPhone application usage has also created a bigger cost problem for the company. With data bandwidth on the AT&T wireless network increasing by 5,000% between 2006 and 2009, the company's network is showing signs of strain and poor performance. To act on these concerns, AT&T will spend $18–19 billion making improvements to its data network in 2010, and more in the years to come. As a result, AT&T will need to balance customer satisfaction with ensuring that its iPhone customers remain profitable for the carrier.

Sources: AT&T Inc. and Apple Inc. 2007. AT&T and Apple announce simple, affordable service plans for iPhone. AT&T Inc. and Apple Inc. Press Release, June 26. http://www.apple.com/pr/library/2007/06/26plans.html; Fazard, Roben. 2010. AT&T's iPhone mess. *Business Week*, February 3; Sheth, Niraj. 2010. AT&T, boosted and stressed by iPhone, lays out network plans. *Wall Street Journal*, January 29; Sheth, Niraj. 2010. For wireless carriers, iPad signals further loss of clout. *Wall Street Journal*, January 28.

Sales Variances

The customer-profitability analysis in the previous section focused on the actual profitability of individual customers within a distribution channel (retail, for example) and their effect on Spring Distribution's profitability for June 2012. At a more-strategic level, however, recall that Spring operates in two different markets: wholesale and retail. The operating margins in the retail market are much higher than the operating margins in the wholesale market. In June 2012, Spring had budgeted to sell 80% of its cases to wholesalers and 20% to retailers. It sold more cases in total than it had budgeted, but its actual sales mix (in cases) was 84% to wholesalers and 16% to retailers. Regardless of the profitability of sales to individual customers within each of the retail and wholesale channels, Spring's actual operating income, relative to the master budget, is likely to be positively affected by the higher sales of cases and negatively affected by the shift in mix away from the more-profitable retail customers. Sales-quantity and sales-mix variances can identify the effect of each of these factors on Spring's profitability. Companies such as Cisco, GE, and Hewlett-Packard perform similar analyses because they sell their products through multiple distribution channels like the Internet, over the telephone, and retail stores.

Spring classifies all customer-level costs as variable costs and distribution-channel and corporate-sustaining costs as fixed costs. To simplify the sales-variances analysis and calculations, we assume that all of the variable costs are variable with respect to units (cases) sold. (This means that average batch sizes remain the same as the total cases sold vary.) Without this assumption, the analysis would become more complex and would have to be done using the ABC-variance analysis approach. The basic insights, however, would not change.

Budgeted and actual operating data for June 2012 are as follows:

Learning Objective 6

Subdivide the sales-volume variance into the sales-mix variance

... the variance arises because actual sales mix differs from budgeted sales mix

and the sales-quantity variance

... this variance arises because actual total unit sales differ from budgeted total unit sales

Budget Data for June 2012

	Selling Price (1)	Variable Cost per Unit (2)	Contribution Margin per Unit (3) = (1) − (2)	Sales Volume in Units (4)	Sales Mix (Based on Units) (5)	Contribution Margin (6) = (3) × (4)
Wholesale channel	$13.37	$12.88	$0.49	712,000	80%[a]	$348,880
Retail channel	14.10	13.12	0.98	178,000	20%	174,440
Total				890,000	100%	$523,320

[a] Percentage of unit sales to wholesale channel = 712,000 units ÷ 890,000 total unit = 80%.

Actual Results for June 2012

	Selling Price (1)	Variable Cost per Unit (2)	Contribution Margin per Unit (3) = (1) − (2)	Sales Volume in Units (4)	Sales Mix (Based on Units) (5)	Contribution Margin (6) = (3) × (4)
Wholesale channel	$13.37	$12.88	$0.49	756,000	84%[a]	$370,440
Retail channel	14.10	13.17	0.93	144,000	16%	133,920
Total				900,000	100%	$504,360

[a] Percentage of unit sales to wholesale channel = 756,000 units ÷ 900,000 total unit = 84%.

The budgeted and actual fixed distribution-channel costs and corporate-sustaining costs are $160,500 and $263,000, respectively (see Exhibit 6).

Recall that the levels of detail included the static-budget variance (level 1), the flexible-budget variance (level 2), and the sales-volume variance (level 2). The sales-quantity and sales-mix variances are level 3 variances that subdivide the sales-volume variance.[7]

---

[7] The presentation of the variances in this chapter and the appendix draws on teaching notes prepared by J. K. Harris.

Static-Budget Variance

The *static-budget variance* is the difference between an actual result and the corresponding budgeted amount in the static budget. Our analysis focuses on the difference between actual and budgeted contribution margins (column 6 in the preceding tables). The total static-budget variance is $18,960 U (actual contribution margin of $504,360 – budgeted contribution margin of $523,320). Exhibit 9 (columns 1 and 3) uses the columnar format to show detailed calculations of the static-budget variance. Managers can gain more insight about the static-budget variance by subdividing it into the flexible-budget variance and the sales-volume variance.

Flexible-Budget Variance and Sales-Volume Variance

The *flexible-budget variance* is the difference between an actual result and the corresponding flexible-budget amount based on actual output level in the budget period. The flexible budget contribution margin is equal to budgeted contribution margin per unit times actual units sold of each product. Exhibit 9, column 2, shows the flexible-budget calculations. The flexible budget measures the contribution margin that Spring would have budgeted for the actual quantities of cases sold. The flexible-budget variance is the difference between columns 1 and 2 in Exhibit 9. The only difference between columns 1 and 2 is that actual units sold of each product is multiplied by actual contribution margin per unit in column 1 and budgeted contribution margin per unit in column 2. The $7,200 U flexible-budget variance arises because actual contribution margin on retail sales of $0.93 per case is lower than the budgeted amount of $0.98 per case. Spring's management is aware that this difference of $0.05 per case resulted from excessive price discounts, and it has put in place action plans to reduce discounts in the future.

The *sales-volume variance* is the difference between a flexible-budget amount and the corresponding static-budget amount. In Exhibit 9, the sales-volume variance shows the effect on budgeted contribution margin of the difference between actual quantity of units sold and budgeted quantity of units sold. The sales-volume variance of $11,760 U is the difference between columns 2 and 3 in Exhibit 9. In this case, it is unfavorable overall because while wholesale unit sales were higher than budgeted, retail sales, which are expected to be twice as profitable on a per unit basis, were below budget. Spring's

| **Exhibit 9** | Flexible-Budget and Sales-Volume Variance Analysis of Spring Distribution for June 2012 |

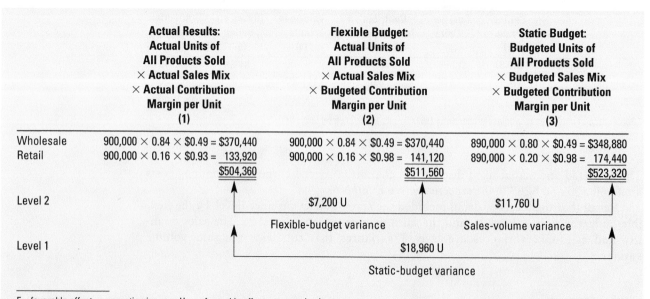

F = favorable effect on operating income; U = unfavorable effect on operating income.

managers can gain substantial insight into the sales-volume variance by subdividing it into the sales-mix variance and the sales-quantity variance.

Sales-Mix Variance

The **sales-mix variance** is the difference between (1) budgeted contribution margin for the *actual sales mix* and (2) budgeted contribution margin for the *budgeted sales mix*. The formula and computations are as follows:

	Actual Units of All Products Sold	×	Actual Sales - Mix Percentage − Budgeted Sales - Mix Percentage	×	Budgeted Contribution Margin per Unit	=	Sales-Mix Variance
Wholesale	900,000 units	×	(0.84 − 0.80)	×	$0.49 per unit	=	$17,640 F
Retail	900,000 units	×	(0.16 − 0.20)	×	$0.98 per unit	=	35,280 U
Total sales-mix variance							$17,640 U

A favorable sales-mix variance arises for the wholesale channel because the 84% actual sales-mix percentage exceeds the 80% budgeted sales-mix percentage. In contrast, the retail channel has an unfavorable variance because the 16% actual sales-mix percentage is less than the 20% budgeted sales-mix percentage. The sales-mix variance is unfavorable because actual sales mix shifted toward the less-profitable wholesale channel relative to budgeted sales mix.

The concept underlying the sales-mix variance is best explained in terms of composite units. A **composite unit** is a hypothetical unit with weights based on the mix of individual units. Given the budgeted sales for June 2012, the composite unit consists of 0.80 units of sales to the wholesale channel and 0.20 units of sales to the retail channel. Therefore, the budgeted contribution margin per composite unit for the budgeted sales mix is as follows:

$$(0.80) \times (\$0.49) + (0.20) \times (\$0.98) = \$0.5880. [8]$$

Similarly, for the actual sales mix, the composite unit consists of 0.84 units of sales to the wholesale channel and 0.16 units of sales to the retail channel. The budgeted contribution margin per composite unit for the actual sales mix is therefore as follows:

$$(0.84) \times (\$0.49) + (0.16) \times (\$0.98) = \$0.5684.$$

The impact of the shift in sales mix is now evident. Spring obtains a lower budgeted contribution margin per composite unit of $0.0196 ($0.5880 – $0.5684). For the 900,000 units actually sold, this decrease translates to a $17,640 U sales-mix variance ($0.0196 per unit × 900,000 units).

Managers should probe why the $17,640 U sales-mix variance occurred in June 2012. Is the shift in sales mix because, as the analysis in the previous section showed, profitable retail customers proved to be more difficult to find? Is it because of a competitor in the retail channel providing better service at a lower price? Or is it because the initial sales-volume estimates were made without adequate analysis of the potential market?

Exhibit 10 uses the columnar format to calculate the sales-mix variance and the sales-quantity variances.

Sales-Quantity Variance

The **sales-quantity variance** is the difference between (1) budgeted contribution margin based on *actual units sold of all products* at the budgeted mix and (2) contribution margin in the static budget (which is based on *budgeted units of all products to*

---

[8] Budgeted contribution margin per composite unit can be computed in another way by dividing total budgeted contribution margin of $523,320 by total budgeted units of 890,000: $523,320 ÷ 890,000 units = $0.5880 per unit.

Exhibit 10   Sales-Mix and Sales-Quantity Variance Analysis of Spring Distribution for June 2012

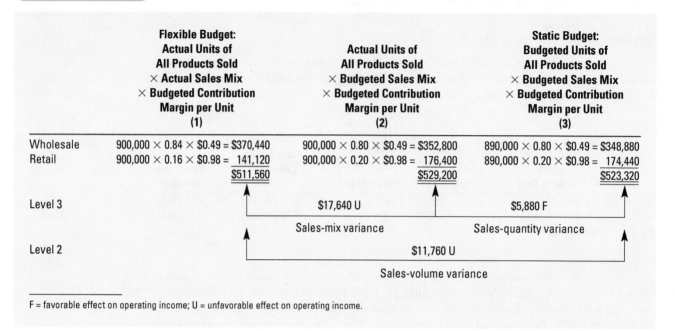

	Flexible Budget: Actual Units of All Products Sold × Actual Sales Mix × Budgeted Contribution Margin per Unit (1)	Actual Units of All Products Sold × Budgeted Sales Mix × Budgeted Contribution Margin per Unit (2)	Static Budget: Budgeted Units of All Products Sold × Budgeted Sales Mix × Budgeted Contribution Margin per Unit (3)
Wholesale	900,000 × 0.84 × $0.49 = $370,440	900,000 × 0.80 × $0.49 = $352,800	890,000 × 0.80 × $0.49 = $348,880
Retail	900,000 × 0.16 × $0.98 = 141,120	900,000 × 0.20 × $0.98 = 176,400	890,000 × 0.20 × $0.98 = 174,440
	$511,560	$529,200	$523,320

Level 3 $17,640 U $5,880 F

                    Sales-mix variance   Sales-quantity variance

Level 2 $11,760 U

                              Sales-volume variance

F = favorable effect on operating income; U = unfavorable effect on operating income.

be sold at budgeted mix). The formula and computations are as follows:

		×	Budgeted Sales-Mix Percentages	×	Budgeted Contribution Margin per Unit	=	Sales-Quantity Variance
Wholesale	(900,000 units – 890,000 units)	×	0.80	×	$0.49 per unit	=	$3,920 F
Retail	(900,000 units – 890,000 units)	×	0.20	×	$0.98 per unit	=	1,960 F
Total sales-quantity variance							$5,880 F

This variance is favorable when actual units of all products sold exceed budgeted units of all products sold. Spring sold 10,000 more cases than were budgeted, resulting in a $5,880 F sales-quantity variance (also equal to budgeted contribution margin per composite unit for the budgeted sales mix times additional cases sold, $0.5880 × 10,000). Managers would want to probe the reasons for the increase in sales. Did higher sales come as a result of a competitor's distribution problems? Better customer service? Or growth in the overall market? Additional insight into the causes of the sales-quantity variance can be gained by analyzing changes in Spring's share of the total industry market and in the size of that market. The sales-quantity variance can be decomposed into market-share and market-size variances.[9]

Exhibit 11 presents an overview of the sales-mix and sales-quantity variances for the Spring example. The sales-mix variance and sales-quantity variance can also be calculated in a multiproduct company, in which each individual product has a different contribution margin per unit. The Problem for Self-Study takes you through such a setting, and also demonstrates the link between these sales variances and the market-share and market-size variances studied earlier. The appendix to this chapter describes mix and quantity variances for production inputs.

Decision Point ▶

What are the two components of the sales-volume variance?

[9] Recall that the market-share and market-size variances were computed for Webb Company, which sold a single product (jackets) using a single distribution channel. The calculation of these variances is virtually unaffected when multiple distribution channels exist, as in the Spring example. The only change required is to replace the phrase "Budgeted Contribution Margin per Unit" in the market-share and market-size variance formulas with "Budgeted Contribution Margin per Composite Unit for Budgeted Sales Mix" (which equals $0.5880 in the Spring example). For additional details and an illustration, see the Problem for Self-Study for this chapter.

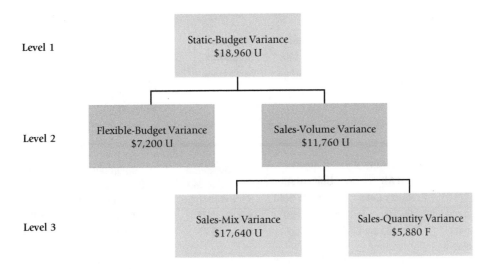

Exhibit 11

Overview of Variances
for Spring Distribution
for June 2012

F = favorable effect on operating income; U = unfavorable effect on operating income

Problem for Self-Study

The Payne Company manufactures two types of vinyl flooring. Budgeted and actual operating data for 2012 are as follows:

	Static Budget			Actual Results		
	Commercial	Residential	Total	Commercial	Residential	Total
Unit sales in rolls	20,000	60,000	80,000	25,200	58,800	84,000
Contribution margin	$10,000,000	$24,000,000	$34,000,000	$11,970,000	$24,696,000	$36,666,000

In late 2011, a marketing research firm estimated industry volume for commercial and residential vinyl flooring for 2012 at 800,000 rolls. Actual industry volume for 2012 was 700,000 rolls.

1. Compute the sales-mix variance and the sales-quantity variance by type of vinyl **Required** flooring and in total. (Compute all variances in terms of contribution margins.)
2. Compute the market-share variance and the market-size variance.
3. What insights do the variances calculated in requirements 1 and 2 provide about Payne Company's performance in 2012?

Solution

1. Actual sales-mix percentage:

$$\text{Commercial} = 25,200 \div 84,000 = 0.30, \text{ or } 30\%$$

$$\text{Residential} = 58,800 \div 84,000 = 0.70, \text{ or } 70\%$$

Budgeted sales-mix percentage:

$$\text{Commercial} = 20,000 \div 80,000 = 0.25, \text{ or } 25\%$$

$$\text{Residential} = 60,000 \div 80,000 = 0.75, \text{ or } 75\%$$

Budgeted contribution margin per unit:

$$\text{Commercial} = \$10,000,000 \div 20,000 \text{ units} = \$500 \text{ per unit}$$

$$\text{Residential} = \$24,000,000 \div 60,000 \text{ units} = \$400 \text{ per unit}$$

	Actual Units of All Products Sold	×	(Actual Sales-Mix Percentage − Budgeted Sales-Mix Percentage)	×	Budgeted Contribution Margin per Unit	=	Sales-Mix Variance
Commercial	84,000 units	×	(0.30 − 0.25)	×	$500 per unit	=	$2,100,000 F
Residential	84,000 units	×	(0.70 − 0.75)	×	$400 per unit	=	1,680,000 U
Total sales-mix variance							$ 420,000 F

	(Actual Units of All Products Sold − Budgeted Units of All Products Sold)	×	Budgeted Sales-Mix Percentage	×	Budgeted Contribution Margin per Unit	=	Sales-Quantity Variance
Commercial	(84,000 units − 80,000 units)	×	0.25	×	$500 per unit	=	$ 500,000 F
Residential	(84,000 units − 80,000 units)	×	0.75	×	$400 per unit	=	1,200,000 F
Total sales-quantity variance							$1,700,000 F

2. Actual market share = 84,000 ÷ 700,000 = 0.12, or 12%
   Budgeted market share = 80,000 ÷ 800,000 units = 0.10, or 10%

$$\text{Budgeted contribution margin per composite unit of budgeted mix} = \$34,000,000 \div 80,000 \text{ units} = \$425 \text{ per unit}$$

Budgeted contribution margin per composite unit of budgeted mix can also be calculated as follows:

Commercial: $500 per unit × 0.25   = $125
Residential: $400 per unit × 0.75   = 300
Budgeted contribution margin per composite unit   = $425

$$\text{Market-share variance} = \text{Actual market size in units} \times (\text{Actual market share} - \text{Budgeted market share}) \times \text{Budgeted contribution margin per composite unit for budgeted mix}$$

$$= 700,000 \text{ units} \times (0.12 - 0.10) \times \$425 \text{ per unit}$$

$$= \$5,950,000 \text{ F}$$

$$\text{Market-size variance} = (\text{Actual market size in units} - \text{Budgeted market size in units}) \times \text{Budgeted market share} \times \text{Budgeted contribution margin per composite unit for budgeted mix}$$

$$= (700,000 \text{ units} - 800,000 \text{ units}) \times 0.10 \times \$425 \text{ per unit}$$

$$= \$4,250,000 \text{ U}$$

Note that the algebraic sum of the market-share variance and the market-size variance is equal to the sales-quantity variance: $5,950,000 F + $4,250,000 U = $1,700,000 F.

3. Both the total sales-mix variance and the total sales-quantity variance are favorable. The favorable sales-mix variance occurred because the actual mix comprised more of the higher-margin commercial vinyl flooring. The favorable total sales-quantity variance occurred because the actual total quantity of rolls sold exceeded the budgeted amount.

The company's large favorable market-share variance is due to a 12% actual market share compared with a 10% budgeted market share. The market-size variance is unfavorable because the actual market size was 100,000 rolls less than the budgeted market size. Payne's performance in 2012 appears to be very good. Although overall market size declined, the company sold more units than budgeted and gained market share.

Decision Points

The following question-and-answer format summarizes the chapter's learning objectives. Each decision presents a key question related to a learning objective. The guidelines are the answer to that question.

Decision	Guidelines
1. What are four purposes for allocating costs to cost objects?	Four purposes of cost allocation are (a) to provide information for economic decisions, (b) to motivate managers and other employees, (c) to justify costs or compute reimbursement amounts, and (d) to measure income and assets for reporting to external parties. Different cost allocations are appropriate for different purposes.
2. What criteria should managers use to guide cost-allocation decisions?	Managers should use the cause-and-effect and the benefits-received criteria to guide most cost-allocation decisions. Other criteria are fairness or equity and ability to bear.
3. What are two key decisions managers must make when collecting costs in indirect-cost pools?	Two key decisions related to indirect-cost pools are the number of indirect-cost pools to form and the individual cost items to be included in each cost pool to make homogeneous cost pools.
4. How can a company's revenues and costs differ across customers?	Revenues can differ because of differences in the quantity purchased and price discounts given from the list selling price. Costs can differ as different customers place different demands on a company's resources in terms of processing purchase orders, making deliveries, and customer support.
5. How do customer-profitability profiles help managers?	Companies should be aware of and devote sufficient resources to maintaining and expanding relationships with customers who contribute significantly to profitability. Customer-profitability profiles often highlight that a small percentage of customers contributes a large percentage of operating income.
6. What are the two components of the sales-volume variance?	The two components of sales-volume variance are (a) the difference between actual sales mix and budgeted sales mix (the sales-mix variance) and (b) the difference between actual unit sales and budgeted unit sales (the sales-quantity variance).

Appendix

Mix and Yield Variances for Substitutable Inputs

The framework for calculating the sales-mix variance and the sales-quantity variance can also be used to analyze production-input variances in cases in which managers have some leeway in combining and substituting inputs. For example, Del Monte can combine material inputs (such as pineapples, cherries, and grapes) in varying proportions for its cans of fruit cocktail. Within limits, these individual fruits are *substitutable inputs* in making the fruit cocktail.

We illustrate how the efficiency variance can be subdivided into variances that highlight the financial impact of input mix and input yield when inputs are substitutable. Consider Delpino Corporation, which makes tomato ketchup. Our example focuses on direct material inputs and substitution among three of these inputs. The same approach can also be used to examine substitutable direct manufacturing labor inputs.

To produce ketchup of a specified consistency, color, and taste, Delpino mixes three types of tomatoes grown in different regions: Latin American tomatoes (Latoms), California tomatoes (Caltoms), and Florida tomatoes

(Flotoms). Delpino's production standards require 1.60 tons of tomatoes to produce 1 ton of ketchup; 50% of the tomatoes are budgeted to be Latoms, 30% Caltoms, and 20% Flotoms. The direct material inputs budgeted to produce 1 ton of ketchup are as follows:

0.80 (50% of 1.6) ton of Latoms at $70 per ton	$ 56.00
0.48 (30% of 1.6) ton of Caltoms at $80 per ton	38.40
0.32 (20% of 1.6) ton of Flotoms at $90 per ton	28.80
Total budgeted cost of 1.6 tons of tomatoes	$123.20

Budgeted average cost per ton of tomatoes is $123.20 ÷ 1.60 tons = $77 per ton.

Because Delpino uses fresh tomatoes to make ketchup, no inventories of tomatoes are kept. Purchases are made as needed, so all price variances relate to tomatoes purchased and used. Actual results for June 2012 show that a total of 6,500 tons of tomatoes were used to produce 4,000 tons of ketchup:

3,250 tons of Latoms at actual cost of $70 per ton	$227,500
2,275 tons of Caltoms at actual cost of $82 per ton	186,550
975 tons of Flotoms at actual cost of $96 per ton	93,600
6,500 tons of tomatoes	507,650
Budgeted cost of 4,000 tons of ketchup at $123.20 per ton	492,800
Flexible-budget variance for direct materials	$ 14,850 U

Given the standard ratio of 1.60 tons of tomatoes to 1 ton of ketchup, 6,400 tons of tomatoes should be used to produce 4,000 tons of ketchup. At standard mix, quantities of each type of tomato required are as follows:

Latoms:	0.50 × 6,400 = 3,200 tons
Caltoms:	0.30 × 6,400 = 1,920 tons
Flotoms:	0.20 × 6,400 = 1,280 tons

Direct Materials Price and Efficiency Variances

Exhibit 12 presents in columnar format the analysis of the flexible-budget variance for direct materials. The materials price and efficiency variances are calculated separately for each input material and then added together. The variance analysis prompts Delpino to investigate the unfavorable price and efficiency variances. Why did it pay more for tomatoes and use greater quantities than it had budgeted? Were actual market prices of tomatoes higher, in general, or could the purchasing department have negotiated lower prices? Did the inefficiencies result from inferior tomatoes or from problems in processing?

Exhibit 12   Direct Materials Price and Efficiency Variances for the Delpino Corporation June 2012

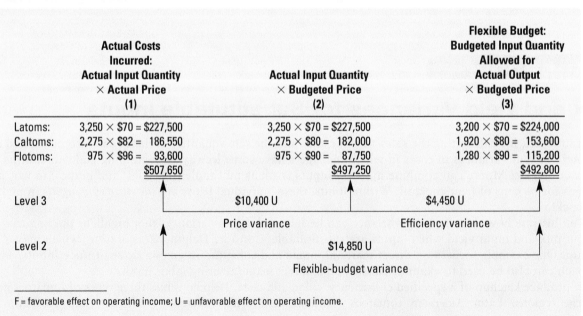

	Actual Costs Incurred: Actual Input Quantity × Actual Price (1)	Actual Input Quantity × Budgeted Price (2)	Flexible Budget: Budgeted Input Quantity Allowed for Actual Output × Budgeted Price (3)
Latoms:	3,250 × $70 = $227,500	3,250 × $70 = $227,500	3,200 × $70 = $224,000
Caltoms:	2,275 × $82 = 186,550	2,275 × $80 = 182,000	1,920 × $80 = 153,600
Flotoms:	975 × $96 = 93,600	975 × $90 = 87,750	1,280 × $90 = 115,200
	$507,650	$497,250	$492,800

Level 3 $10,400 U $4,450 U

     Price variance   Efficiency variance

Level 2 $14,850 U

     Flexible-budget variance

F = favorable effect on operating income; U = unfavorable effect on operating income.

Direct Materials Mix and Direct Materials Yield Variances

Managers sometimes have discretion to substitute one material for another. The manager of Delpino's ketchup plant has some leeway in combining Latoms, Caltoms, and Flotoms without affecting the ketchup's quality. We will assume that to maintain quality, mix percentages of each type of tomato can only vary up to 5% from standard mix. For example, the percentage of Caltoms in the mix can vary between 25% and 35% (30% ± 5%). When inputs are substitutable, direct materials efficiency improvement relative to budgeted costs can come from two sources: (1) using a cheaper mix to produce a given quantity of output, measured by the direct materials mix variance, and (2) using less input to achieve a given quantity of output, measured by the direct materials yield variance.

Holding actual total quantity of all direct materials inputs used constant, the total **direct materials mix variance** is the difference between (1) budgeted cost for actual mix of actual total quantity of direct materials used and (2) budgeted cost of budgeted mix of actual total quantity of direct materials used. Holding budgeted input mix constant, the **direct materials yield variance** is the difference between (1) budgeted cost of direct materials based on actual total quantity of direct materials used and (2) flexible-budget cost of direct materials based on budgeted total quantity of direct materials allowed for actual output produced. Exhibit 13 presents the direct materials mix and yield variances for the Delpino Corporation.

Direct Materials Mix Variance

The total direct materials mix variance is the sum of the direct materials mix variances for each input:

$$
\begin{pmatrix} \text{Direct} \\ \text{materials} \\ \text{mix variance} \\ \text{for each input} \end{pmatrix} = \begin{pmatrix} \text{Actual total} \\ \text{quantity of all} \\ \text{direct materials} \\ \text{inputs used} \end{pmatrix} \times \begin{pmatrix} \text{Actual} \\ \text{direct materials} \\ \text{input mix} \\ \text{percentage} \end{pmatrix} - \begin{pmatrix} \text{Budgeted} \\ \text{direct materials} \\ \text{input mix} \\ \text{percentage} \end{pmatrix} \times \begin{pmatrix} \text{Budgeted} \\ \text{price of} \\ \text{direct materials} \\ \text{input} \end{pmatrix}
$$

The direct materials mix variances are as follows:

Latoms:	6,500 tons × (0.50 – 0.50) × $70 per ton = 6,500 × 0.00 × $70	= $ 0
Caltoms:	6,500 tons × (0.35 – 0.30) × $80 per ton = 6,500 × 0.05 × $80	= 26,000 U
Flotoms:	6,500 tons × (0.15 – 0.20) × $90 per ton = 6,500 × –0.05 × $90	= 29,250 F
	Total direct materials mix variance	$ 3,250 F

The total direct materials mix variance is favorable because relative to the budgeted mix, Delpino substitutes 5% of the cheaper Caltoms for 5% of the more-expensive Flotoms.

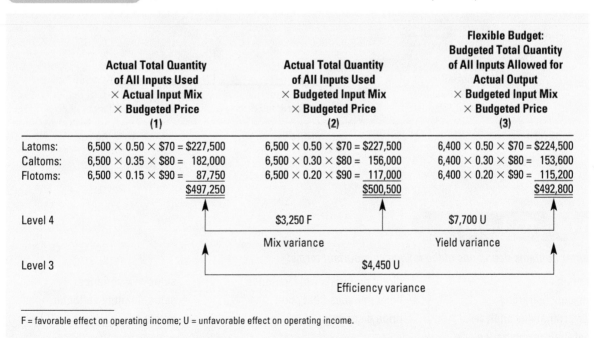

Exhibit 13 Total Direct Materials Yield and Mix Variances for the Delpino Corporation for June 2012

	Actual Total Quantity of All Inputs Used × Actual Input Mix × Budgeted Price (1)	Actual Total Quantity of All Inputs Used × Budgeted Input Mix × Budgeted Price (2)	Flexible Budget: Budgeted Total Quantity of All Inputs Allowed for Actual Output × Budgeted Input Mix × Budgeted Price (3)
Latoms:	6,500 × 0.50 × $70 = $227,500	6,500 × 0.50 × $70 = $227,500	6,400 × 0.50 × $70 = $224,500
Caltoms:	6,500 × 0.35 × $80 = 182,000	6,500 × 0.30 × $80 = 156,000	6,400 × 0.30 × $80 = 153,600
Flotoms:	6,500 × 0.15 × $90 = 87,750	6,500 × 0.20 × $90 = 117,000	6,400 × 0.20 × $90 = 115,200
	$497,250	$500,500	$492,800

Level 4 $3,250 F $7,700 U

Mix variance   Yield variance

Level 3 $4,450 U

Efficiency variance

F = favorable effect on operating income; U = unfavorable effect on operating income.

Direct Materials Yield Variance

The direct materials yield variance is the sum of the direct materials yield variances for each input:

$$
\begin{pmatrix}
\text{Direct} \\
\text{materials} \\
\text{yield variance} \\
\text{for each input}
\end{pmatrix}
=
\left(
\begin{array}{l}
\text{Actual total} \\
\text{quantity of} \\
\text{all direct} \\
\text{materials} \\
\text{inputs used}
\end{array}
-
\begin{array}{l}
\text{Budgeted total} \\
\text{quantity of all} \\
\text{direct materials} \\
\text{inputs allowed} \\
\text{for actual output}
\end{array}
\right)
\times
\begin{array}{l}
\text{Budgeted} \\
\text{direct materials} \\
\text{input mix} \\
\text{percentage}
\end{array}
\times
\begin{array}{l}
\text{Budgeted} \\
\text{price of} \\
\text{direct materials} \\
\text{input}
\end{array}
$$

The direct materials yield variances are as follows:

Latoms: (6,500 – 6,400) tons × 0.50 × $70 per ton = 100 × 0.50 × $70 = $3,500 U
Caltoms: (6,500 – 6,400) tons × 0.30 × $80 per ton = 100 × 0.30 × $80 = 2,400 U
Flotoms: (6,500 – 6,400) tons × 0.20 × $90 per ton = 100 × 0.20 × $90 = 1,800 U
Total direct materials yield variance $7,700 U

The total direct materials yield variance is unfavorable because Delpino used 6,500 tons of tomatoes rather than the 6,400 tons that it should have used to produce 4,000 tons of ketchup. Holding the budgeted mix and budgeted prices of tomatoes constant, the budgeted cost per ton of tomatoes in the budgeted mix is $77 per ton. The unfavorable yield variance represents the budgeted cost of using 100 more tons of tomatoes, (6,500 – 6,400) tons × $77 per ton = $7,700 U. Delpino would want to investigate reasons for this unfavorable yield variance. For example, did the substitution of the cheaper Caltoms for Flotoms that resulted in the favorable mix variance also cause the unfavorable yield variance?

The direct materials variances computed in Exhibits 12 and 13 can be summarized as follows:

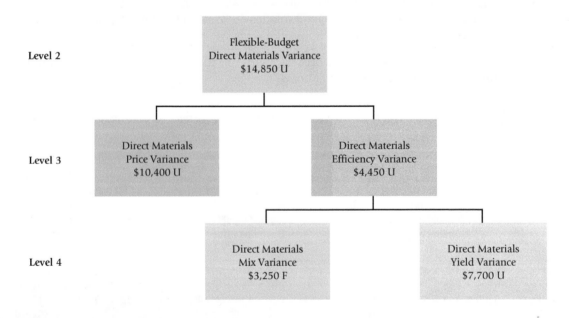

Terms to Learn

This chapter contains definitions of the following important terms:

composite unit
customer-cost hierarchy
customer-profitability analysis
direct materials mix variance

direct materials yield variance
homogeneous cost pool
price discount

sales-mix variance
sales-quantity variance
whale curve

Assignment Material

Questions

14-1 "I am going to focus on the customers of my business and leave cost-allocation issues to my accountant." Do you agree with this comment by a division president? Why?

14-2 A given cost may be allocated for one or more purposes. List four purposes.

14-3 What criteria might be used to guide cost-allocation decisions? Which are the dominant criteria?

14-4 "A company should not allocate all of its corporate costs to its divisions." Do you agree? Explain.

14-5 "Once a company allocates corporate costs to divisions, these costs should not be reallocated to the indirect-cost pools of the division." Do you agree? Explain.

14-6 Why is customer-profitability analysis a vitally important topic to managers?

14-7 How can the extent of price discounting be tracked on a customer-by-customer basis?

14-8 "A customer-profitability profile highlights those customers who should be dropped to improve profitability." Do you agree? Explain.

14-9 Give examples of three different levels of costs in a customer-cost hierarchy.

14-10 What information does the whale curve provide?

14-11 Show how managers can gain insight into the causes of a sales-volume variance by subdividing the components of this variance.

14-12 How can the concept of a composite unit be used to explain why an unfavorable total sales-mix variance of contribution margin occurs?

14-13 Explain why a favorable sales-quantity variance occurs.

14-14 How can the sales-quantity variance be decomposed further?

14-15 Explain how the direct materials mix and yield variances provide additional information about the direct materials efficiency variance.

Exercises

14-16 Cost allocation in hospitals, alternative allocation criteria. Dave Meltzer vacationed at Lake Tahoe last winter. Unfortunately, he broke his ankle while skiing and spent two days at the Sierra University Hospital. Meltzer's insurance company received a $4,800 bill for his two-day stay. One item that caught Meltzer's attention was an $11.52 charge for a roll of cotton. Meltzer is a salesman for Johnson & Johnson and knows that the cost to the hospital of the roll of cotton is in the $2.20 to $3.00 range. He asked for a breakdown of the $11.52 charge. The accounting office of the hospital sent him the following information:

a.	Invoiced cost of cotton roll	$ 2.40
b.	Cost of processing of paperwork for purchase	0.60
c.	Supplies-room management fee	0.70
d.	Operating-room and patient-room handling costs	1.60
e.	Administrative hospital costs	1.10
f.	University teaching-related costs	0.60
g.	Malpractice insurance costs	1.20
h.	Cost of treating uninsured patients	2.72
i.	Profit component	0.60
	Total	$11.52

Meltzer believes the overhead charge is obscene. He comments, "There was nothing I could do about it. When they come in and dab your stitches, it's not as if you can say, 'Keep your cotton roll. I brought my own.'"

Required

1. Compute the overhead rate Sierra University Hospital charged on the cotton roll.
2. What criteria might Sierra use to justify allocation of the overhead items **b–i** in the preceding list? Examine each item separately and use the allocation criteria listed in Exhibit 2 in your answer.
3. What should Meltzer do about the $11.52 charge for the cotton roll?

14-17 Cost allocation and decision making. Greenbold Manufacturing has four divisions named after its locations: Arizona, Colorado, Delaware, and Florida. Corporate headquarters is in Minnesota. Greenbold corporate headquarters incurs $5,600,000 per period, which is an indirect cost of the divisions. Corporate headquarters currently allocates this cost to the divisions based on the revenues of each division. The CEO has asked each division manager to suggest an allocation base for the indirect headquarters costs from among revenues, segment margin, direct costs, and number of employees. The following is relevant information about each division:

	Arizona	Colorado	Delaware	Florida
Revenues	$7,800,000	$8,500,000	$6,200,000	$5,500,000
Direct costs	5,300,000	4,100,000	4,300,000	4,600,000
Segment margin	$2,500,000	$4,400,000	$1,900,000	$ 900,000
Number of employees	2,000	4,000	1,500	500

Required

1. Allocate the indirect headquarters costs of Greenbold Manufacturing to each of the four divisions using revenues, direct costs, segment margin, and number of employees as the allocation bases. Calculate operating margins for each division after allocating headquarters costs.
2. Which allocation base do you think the manager of the Florida division would prefer? Explain.
3. What factors would you consider in deciding which allocation base Greenbold should use?
4. Suppose the Greenbold CEO decides to use direct costs as the allocation base. Should the Florida division be closed? Why or why not?

14-18 Cost allocation to divisions. Rembrandt Hotel & Casino is situated on beautiful Lake Tahoe in Nevada. The complex includes a 300-room hotel, a casino, and a restaurant. As Rembrandt's new controller, you are asked to recommend the basis to be used for allocating fixed overhead costs to the three divisions in 2012. You are presented with the following income statement information for 2011:

	Hotel	Restaurant	Casino
Revenues	$16,425,000	$5,256,000	$12,340,000
Direct costs	9,819,260	3,749,172	4,248,768
Segment margin	$ 6,605,740	$1,506,828	$ 8,091,232

You are also given the following data on the three divisions:

	Hotel	Restaurant	Casino
Floor space (square feet)	80,000	16,000	64,000
Number of employees	200	50	250

You are told that you may choose to allocate indirect costs based on one of the following: direct costs, floor space, or the number of employees. Total fixed overhead costs for 2011 was $14,550,000.

Required

1. Calculate division margins in percentage terms prior to allocating fixed overhead costs.
2. Allocate indirect costs to the three divisions using each of the three allocation bases suggested. For each allocation base, calculate division operating margins after allocations in dollars and as a percentage of revenues.
3. Discuss the results. How would you decide how to allocate indirect costs to the divisions? Why?
4. Would you recommend closing any of the three divisions (and possibly reallocating resources to other divisions) as a result of your analysis? If so, which division would you close and why?

14-19 Cost allocation to divisions. Lenzig Corporation has three divisions: pulp, paper, and fibers. Lenzig's new controller, Ari Bardem, is reviewing the allocation of fixed corporate-overhead costs to the three divisions. He is presented with the following information for each division for 2012:

	A	B	C	D
		Pulp	Paper	Fibers
2	Revenues	$8,500,000	$17,500,000	$24,000,000
3	Direct manufacturing costs	4,100,000	8,600,000	11,300,000
4	Division administrative costs	2,000,000	1,800,000	3,200,000
5	Division margin	$2,400,000	$ 7,100,000	$ 9,500,000
6				
7	Number of employees	350	250	400
8	Floor space (square feet)	35,000	24,000	66,000

Until now, Lenzig Corporation has allocated fixed corporate-overhead costs to the divisions on the basis of division margins. Bardem asks for a list of costs that comprise fixed corporate overhead and suggests the following new allocation bases:

	Fixed Corporate Overhead Costs		Suggested Allocation Bases
	F	G	H
1	**Fixed Corporate Overhead Costs**		**Suggested Allocation Bases**
2	Human resource management	$1,800,000	Number of employees
3	Facility	2,700,000	Floor space (square feet)
4	Corporate Administration	4,500,000	Division administrative costs
5	Total	$9,000,000	

Required

1. Allocate 2012 fixed corporate-overhead costs to the three divisions using division margin as the allocation base. What is each division's operating margin percentage (division margin minus allocated fixed corporate-overhead costs as a percentage of revenues)?
2. Allocate 2012 fixed costs using the allocation bases suggested by Bardem. What is each division's operating margin percentage under the new allocation scheme?
3. Compare and discuss the results of requirements 1 and 2. If division performance is linked to operating margin percentage, which division would be most receptive to the new allocation scheme? Which division would be the least receptive? Why?
4. Which allocation scheme should Lenzig Corporation use? Why? How might Bardem overcome any objections that may arise from the divisions?

14-20 Customer profitability, customer-cost hierarchy. Orsack Electronics has only two retail and two wholesale customers. Information relating to each customer for 2012 follows (in thousands):

	A	B	C	D	E
1		**Wholesale Customers**		**Retail Customers**	
2		**North America Wholesaler**	**South America Wholesaler**	**Big Sam Stereo**	**World Market**
3	Revenues at list price	$435,000	$550,000	$150,000	$115,000
4	Discounts from list prices	30,000	44,000	7,200	520
5	Cost of goods sold	330,000	475,000	123,000	84,000
6	Delivery costs	475	690	220	130
7	Order processing costs	750	1,020	175	120
8	Costs of sales visits	5,400	2,500	2,500	1,400

Orsack's annual distribution-channel costs are $34 million for wholesale customers and $5 million for retail customers. Its annual corporate-sustaining costs, such as salary for top management and general-administration costs, are $61 million. There is no cause-and-effect or benefits-received relationship between any cost-allocation base and corporate-sustaining costs. That is, corporate-sustaining costs could be saved only if Orsack Electronics were to completely shut down.

Required

1. Calculate customer-level operating income using the format in Exhibit 5.
2. Prepare a customer-cost hierarchy report, using the format in Exhibit 6.
3. Orsack's management decides to allocate all corporate-sustaining costs to distribution channels: $48 million to the wholesale channel and $13 million to the retail channel. As a result, distribution channel costs are now $82 million ($34 million + $48 million) for the wholesale channel and $18 million ($5 million + $13 million) for the retail channel. Calculate the distribution-channel-level operating income. On the basis of these calculations, what actions, if any, should Orsack's managers take? Explain.

14-21 Customer profitability, service company. Instant Service (IS) repairs printers and photocopiers for five multisite companies in a tristate area. IS's costs consist of the cost of technicians and equipment that are directly traceable to the customer site and a pool of office overhead. Until recently, IS estimated customer profitability by allocating the office overhead to each customer based on share of revenues. For 2012, IS reported the following results:

	A	B	C	D	E	F	G
		Avery	**Okie**	**Wizard**	**Grainger**	**Duran**	**Total**
2	Revenues	$260,000	$200,000	$322,000	$122,000	$212,000	$1,116,000
3	Technician and equipment cost	182,000	175,000	225,000	107,000	178,000	867,000
4	Office overhead allocated	31,859	24,507	39,457	14,949	25,978	136,750
5	Operating income	$ 46,141	$ 493	$ 57,543	$ 51	$ 8,022	$ 112,250

Tina Sherman, IS's new controller, notes that office overhead is more than 10% of total costs, so she spends a couple of weeks analyzing the consumption of office overhead resources by customers. She collects the following information:

	I	J	K
1	**Activity Area**		**Cost Driver Rate**
2	Service call handling	$75	per service call
3	Parts ordering	$80	per Web-base parts order
4	Billing and collection	$50	per bill (or reminder)
5	Customer database maintenance	$10	per service call

	A	B	C	D	E	F
8		**Avery**	**Okie**	**Wizard**	**Grainger**	**Duran**
9	Number of service calls	150	240	40	120	180
10	Number of Web-based parts orders	120	210	60	150	150
11	Number of bills (or reminders)	30	90	90	60	120

Required

1. Compute customer-level operating income using the new information that Sherman has gathered.
2. Prepare exhibits for IS similar to Exhibits 7 and 8. Comment on the results.
3. What options should IS consider, with regard to individual customers, in light of the new data and analysis of office overhead?

14-22 Customer profitability, distribution. Figure Four is a distributor of pharmaceutical products. Its ABC system has five activities:

Activity Area	Cost Driver Rate in 2012
1. Order processing	$40 per order
2. Line-item ordering	$3 per line item
3. Store deliveries	$50 per store delivery
4. Carton deliveries	$1 per carton
5. Shelf-stocking	$16 per stocking-hour

Rick Flair, the controller of Figure Four, wants to use this ABC system to examine individual customer profitability within each distribution market. He focuses first on the Ma and Pa single-store distribution market. Two customers are used to exemplify the insights available with the ABC approach. Data pertaining to these two customers in August 2012 are as follows:

	Charleston Pharmacy	Chapel Hill Pharmacy
Total orders	13	10
Average line items per order	9	18
Total store deliveries	7	10
Average cartons shipped per store delivery	22	20
Average hours of shelf-stocking per store delivery	0	0.5
Average revenue per delivery	$2,400	$1,800
Average cost of goods sold per delivery	$2,100	$1,650

Required

1. Use the ABC information to compute the operating income of each customer in August 2012. Comment on the results and what, if anything, Flair should do.
2. Flair ranks the individual customers in the Ma and Pa single-store distribution market on the basis of monthly operating income. The cumulative operating income of the top 20% of customers is $55,680. Figure Four reports operating losses of $21,247 for the bottom 40% of its customers. Make four recommendations that you think Figure Four should consider in light of this new customer-profitability information.

14-23 Variance analysis, multiple products. The Detroit Penguins play in the American Ice Hockey League. The Penguins play in the Downtown Arena (owned and managed by the City of Detroit), which has a capacity of 15,000 seats (5,000 lower-tier seats and 10,000 upper-tier seats). The Downtown Arena charges the Penguins a per-ticket charge for use of its facility. All tickets are sold by the Reservation Network, which charges the Penguins a reservation fee per ticket. The Penguins' budgeted contribution margin for each type of ticket in 2012 is computed as follows:

	Lower-Tier Tickets	Upper-Tier Tickets
Selling price	$35	$14
Downtown Arena fee	10	6
Reservation Network fee	5	3
Contribution margin per ticket	$20	$ 5

The budgeted and actual average attendance figures per game in the 2012 season are as follows:

	Budgeted Seats Sold	Actual Seats Sold
Lower tier	4,000	3,300
Upper tier	6,000	7,700
Total	10,000	11,000

There was no difference between the budgeted and actual contribution margin for lower-tier or upper-tier seats.

The manager of the Penguins was delighted that actual attendance was 10% above budgeted attendance per game, especially given the depressed state of the local economy in the past six months.

Required

1. Compute the sales-volume variance for each type of ticket and in total for the Detroit Penguins in 2012. (Calculate all variances in terms of contribution margins.)
2. Compute the sales-quantity and sales-mix variances for each type of ticket and in total in 2012.
3. Present a summary of the variances in requirements 1 and 2. Comment on the results.

14-24 Variance analysis, working backward. The Jinwa Corporation sells two brands of wine glasses: Plain and Chic. Jinwa provides the following information for sales in the month of June 2011:

Static-budget total contribution margin	$11,000
Budgeted units to be sold of all glasses	2,000 units
Budgeted contribution margin per unit of Plain	$4 per unit
Budgeted contribution margin per unit of Chic	$10 per unit
Total sales-quantity variance	$2,200 U
Actual sales-mix percentage of Plain	60%

All variances are to be computed in contribution-margin terms.

Required

1. Calculate the sales-quantity variances for each product for June 2011.
2. Calculate the individual-product and total sales-mix variances for June 2011. Calculate the individual-product and total sales-volume variances for June 2011.
3. Briefly describe the conclusions you can draw from the variances.

14-25 Variance analysis, multiple products. Soda-King manufactures and sells three soft drinks: Kola, Limor, and Orlem. Budgeted and actual results for 2011 are as follows:

	Budget for 2011			Actual for 2011		
Product	Selling Price	Variable Cost per Carton	Cartons Sold	Selling Price	Variable Cost per Carton	Cartons Sold
Kola	$8.00	$5.00	480,000	$8.20	$5.50	467,500
Limor	$6.00	$3.80	720,000	$5.75	$3.75	852,500
Orlem	$7.50	$5.50	1,200,000	$7.80	$5.60	1,430,000

Required

1. Compute the total sales-volume variance, the total sales-mix variance, and the total sales-quantity variance. (Calculate all variances in terms of contribution margin.) Show results for each product in your computations.
2. What inferences can you draw from the variances computed in requirement 1?

14-26 Market-share and market-size variances (continuation of 14-25). Soda-King prepared the budget for 2011 assuming a 12% market share based on total sales in the western region of the United States. The total soft drinks market was estimated to reach sales of 20 million cartons in the region. However, actual total sales volume in the western region was 27.5 million cartons.

Required Calculate the market-share and market-size variances for Soda-King in 2011. (Calculate all variances in terms of contribution margin.) Comment on the results.

MyAccountingLab | Problems

14-27 Allocation of corporate costs to divisions. Dusty Rhodes, controller of Richfield Oil Company, is preparing a presentation to senior executives about the performance of its four divisions. Summary data (dollar amounts in millions) related to the four divisions for the most recent year are as follows:

	Home	Insert	Page Layout	Formulas	Data	Review	View
	A	B	C	D	E	F	
1				DIVISIONS			
2		Oil & Gas Upstream	Oil & Gas Downstream	Chemical Products	Copper Mining	Total	
3	Revenues	$ 8,000	$16,000	$4,800	$3,200	$32,000	
4	Operating Costs	3,000	15,000	3,800	3,500	25,300	
5	Operating Income	$ 5,000	$ 1,000	$1,000	$ (300)	$ 6,700	
6							
7	Identifiable assets	$14,000	$ 6,000	$3,000	$2,000	$25,000	
8	Number of employees	9,000	12,000	6,000	3,000	30,000	

Under the existing accounting system, costs incurred at corporate headquarters are collected in a single cost pool ($3,228 million in the most recent year) and allocated to each division on the basis of its actual revenues. The top managers in each division share in a division-income bonus pool. Division income is defined as operating income less allocated corporate costs.

Rhodes has analyzed the components of corporate costs and proposes that corporate costs be collected in four cost pools. The components of corporate costs for the most recent year (dollar amounts in millions) and Rhodes' suggested cost pools and allocation bases are as follows:

	Home	Insert	Page Layout	Formulas	Data	Review	View	
	A		B	C	D		E	F
11	**Corporate Cost Category**		**Amount**	**Suggested Cost Pool**	**Suggested Allocation Base**			
12	Interest on debt		$2,000	Cost Pool 1	Identifiable assets			
13	Corporate salaries		150	Cost Pool 2				
14	Accounting and control		110	Cost Pool 2				
15	General marketing		200	Cost Pool 2	Division revenues			
16	Legal		140	Cost Pool 2				
17	Research and development		200	Cost Pool 2				
18	Public affairs		203	Cost Pool 3	Positive operating income*			
19	Personnel and payroll		225	Cost Pool 4	Number of employees			
20	Total		$3,228					
21								
22	*Since public affairs cost includes the cost of public relations staff, lobbyists, and donations to							
23	environmental charities, Rhodes proposes that this cost be allocated using operating income (if positive)							
24	of divisions, with only divisions with positive operating income included in the allocation base.							

Required

1. Discuss two reasons why Richfield Oil should allocate corporate costs to each division.
2. Calculate the operating income of each division when all corporate costs are allocated based on revenues of each division.
3. Calculate the operating income of each division when all corporate costs are allocated using the four cost pools.
4. How do you think the new proposal will be received by the division managers? What are the strengths and weaknesses of Rhodes' proposal relative to the existing single-cost-pool method?

14-28 Cost allocation to divisions. Forber Bakery makes baked goods for grocery stores, and has three divisions: bread, cake, and doughnuts. Each division is run and evaluated separately, but the main headquarters incurs costs that are indirect costs for the divisions. Costs incurred in the main headquarters are as follows:

Human resources (HR) costs	$1,900,000
Accounting department costs	1,400,000
Rent and depreciation	1,200,000
Other	600,000
Total costs	$5,100,000

The Forber upper management currently allocates this cost to the divisions equally. One of the division managers has done some research on activity-based costing and proposes the use of different allocation bases for the different indirect costs—number of employees for HR costs, total revenues for accounting department costs, square feet of space for rent and depreciation costs, and equal allocation among the divisions of "other" costs. Information about the three divisions follows:

	Bread	Cake	Doughnuts
Total revenues	$20,900,000	$4,500,000	$13,400,000
Direct costs	14,500,000	3,200,000	7,250,000
Segment margin	$ 6,400,000	$1,300,000	$ 6,150,000
Number of employees	400	100	300
Square feet of space	10,000	4,000	6,000

Required

1. Allocate the indirect costs of Forber to each division equally. Calculate division operating income after allocation of headquarter costs.

2. Allocate headquarter costs to the individual divisions using the proposed allocation bases. Calculate the division operating income after allocation. Comment on the allocation bases used to allocate headquarter costs.

3. Which division manager do you think suggested this new allocation. Explain briefly. Which allocation do you think is "better?"

14-29 Customer profitability. Ring Delights is a new company that manufactures custom jewelry. Ring Delights currently has six customers referenced by customer number: 01, 02, 03, 04, 05, and 06. Besides the costs of making the jewelry, the company has the following activities:

1. Customer orders. The salespeople, designers, and jewelry makers spend time with the customer. The cost driver rate is $40 per hour spent with a customer.

2. Customer fittings. Before the jewelry piece is completed the customer may come in to make sure it looks right and fits properly. Cost driver rate is $25 per hour.

3. Rush orders. Some customers want their jewelry quickly. The cost driver rate is $100 per rush order.

4. Number of customer return visits. Customers may return jewelry up to 30 days after the pickup of the jewelry to have something refitted or repaired at no charge. The cost driver rate is $30 per return visit.

Information about the six customers follows. Some customers purchased multiple items. The cost of the jewelry is 70% of the selling price.

Customer number	01	02	03	04	05	06
Sales revenue	$600	$4,200	$300	$2,500	$4,900	$700
Cost of item(s)	$420	$2,940	$210	$1,750	$3,430	$490
Hours spent on customer order	2	7	1	5	20	3
Hours on fittings	1	2	0	0	4	1
Number of rush orders	0	0	1	1	3	0
Number of returns visits	0	1	0	1	5	1

Required

1. Calculate the customer-level operating income for each customer. Rank the customers in order of most to least profitable and prepare a customer-profitability analysis, as in Exhibit 7.

2. Are any customers unprofitable? What is causing this? What should Ring Delights do with respect to these customers?

14-30 Customer profitability, distribution. Spring Distribution has decided to analyze the profitability of five new customers. It buys bottled water at $12 per case and sells to retail customers at a list price of $14.40 per case. Data pertaining to the five customers are as follows:

	Customer				
	P	Q	R	S	T
Cases sold	2,080	8,750	60,800	31,800	3,900
List selling price	$14.40	$14.40	$14.40	$14.40	$14.40
Actual selling price	$14.40	$14.16	$13.20	$13.92	$12.96
Number of purchase orders	15	25	30	25	30
Number of customer visits	2	3	6	2	3
Number of deliveries	10	30	60	40	20
Miles traveled per delivery	14	4	3	8	40
Number of expedited deliveries	0	0	0	0	1

Its five activities and their cost drivers are as follows:

Activity	Cost Driver Rate
Order taking	$100 per purchase order
Customer visits	$80 per customer visit
Deliveries	$2 per delivery mile traveled
Product handling	$0.50 per case sold
Expedited deliveries	$300 per expedited delivery

Required

1. Compute the customer-level operating income of each of the five retail customers now being examined (P, Q, R, S, and T). Comment on the results.

2. What insights are gained by reporting both the list selling price and the actual selling price for each customer?

3. What factors should Spring Distribution consider in deciding whether to drop one or more of the five customers?

14-31 Customer profitability in a manufacturing firm. Bizzan Manufacturing makes a component called P14-31. This component is manufactured only when ordered by a customer, so Bizzan keeps no inventory of P14-31. The list price is $100 per unit, but customers who place "large" orders receive a 10% discount on price. Currently, the salespeople decide whether an order is large enough to qualify for the discount. When the product is finished, it is packed in cases of 10. When a customer order is not a multiple of 10, Bizzan uses a full case to pack the partial amount left over (e.g., if customer C orders 25 units, three cases will be required). Customers pick up the order so Bizzan incurs costs of holding the product in the warehouse until customer pick up. The customers are manufacturing firms; if the component needs to be exchanged or repaired, customers can come back within 10 days for free exchange or repair.

The full cost of manufacturing a unit of P14-31 is $80. In addition, Bizzan incurs customer-level costs. Customer-level cost-driver rates are as follows:

Order taking	$390 per order
Product handling	$10 per case
Warehousing (holding finished product)	$55 per day
Rush order processing	$540 per rush order
Exchange and repair costs	$45 per unit

Information about Bizzan's five biggest customers follows:

	A	B	C	D	E
Number of units purchased	6,000	2,500	1,300	4,200	7,800
Discounts given	10%	0	10%	0	10% on half the units
Number of orders	10	12	52	18	12
Number of cases	600	250	120	420	780
Days in warehouse (total for all orders)	14	18	0	12	140
Number of rush orders	0	3	0	0	6
Number of units exchanged/repaired	0	25	4	25	80

The salesperson gave customer C a price discount because, although customer C ordered only 1,300 units in total, 52 orders (one per week) were placed. The salesperson wanted to reward customer C for repeat business. All customers except E ordered units in the same order size. Customer E's order quantity varied, so E got a discount part of the time but not all the time.

1. Calculate the customer-level operating income for these five customers. Use the format in Exhibit 5. Prepare a customer-profitability analysis by ranking the customers from most to least profitable, as in Exhibit 7

2. Discuss the results of your customer-profitability analysis. Does Bizzan have unprofitable customers? Is there anything Bizzan should do differently with its five customers?

Required

14-32 Variance analysis, sales-mix and sales-quantity variances. Chicago Infonautics, Inc., produces handheld Windows CE™-compatible organizers. Chicago Infonautics markets three different handheld models: PalmPro is a souped-up version for the executive on the go, PalmCE is a consumer-oriented version, and PalmKid is a stripped-down version for the young adult market. You are Chicago Infonautics' senior vice president of marketing. The CEO has discovered that the total contribution margin came in lower than budgeted, and it is your responsibility to explain to him why actual results are different from the budget. Budgeted and actual operating data for the company's third quarter of 2012 are as follows:

Budgeted Operating Data, Third Quarter 2012

	Selling Price	Variable Cost per Unit	Contribution Margin per Unit	Sales Volume in Units
PalmPro	$374	$185	$189	13,580
PalmCE	272	96	176	35,890
PalmKid	144	66	78	47,530
				97,000

Actual Operating Data, Third Quarter 2012

	Selling Price	Variable Cost per Unit	Contribution Margin per Unit	Sales Volume in Units
PalmPro	$365	$175	$190	10,120
PalmCE	288	94	194	32,200
PalmKid	110	75	35	49,680
				92,000

Required

1. Compute the actual and budgeted contribution margins in dollars for each product and in total for the third quarter of 2012.
2. Calculate the actual and budgeted sales mixes for the three products for the third quarter of 2012.
3. Calculate total sales-volume, sales-mix, and sales-quantity variances for the third quarter of 2012. (Calculate all variances in terms of contribution margins.)
4. Given that your CEO is known to have temper tantrums, you want to be well prepared for this meeting. In order to prepare, write a paragraph or two comparing actual results to budgeted amounts.

14-33 Market-share and market-size variances (continuation of 14-32). Chicago Infonautics' senior vice president of marketing prepared his budget at the beginning of the third quarter assuming a 25% market share based on total sales. The total handheld-organizer market was estimated by Foolinstead Research to reach sales of 388,000 units worldwide in the third quarter. However, actual sales in the third quarter were 400,000 units.

Required

1. Calculate the market-share and market-size variances for Chicago Infonautics in the third quarter of 2012 (calculate all variances in terms of contribution margins).
2. Explain what happened based on the market-share and market-size variances.
3. Calculate the actual market size, in units, that would have led to no market-size variance (again using budgeted contribution margin per unit). Use this market-size figure to calculate the actual market share that would have led to a zero market-share variance.

14-34 Variance analysis, multiple products. The Split Banana, Inc., operates a chain of Italian gelato stores. Although the Split Banana charges customers the same price for all flavors, production costs vary, depending on the type of ingredients. Budgeted and actual operating data of its three Washington, DC, stores for August 2011 are as follows:

Budget for August 2011

	Selling Price per Pint	Variable Cost per Pint	Contribution Margin per Pints	Sales Volume in Pints
Mint chocolate chip	$9.00	$4.80	$4.20	25,000
Vanilla	9.00	3.20	5.80	35,000
Rum Raisin	9.00	5.00	4.00	5,000
Peach	9.00	5.40	3.60	15,000
Coffee	9.00	3.90	5.10	20,000
				100,000

Actual for August 2011

	Selling Price per Pint	Variable Cost per Pound	Contribution Margin per Pound	Sales Volume in Pounds
Mint chocolate chip	$9.00	$4.60	$4.40	30,800
Vanilla	9.00	3.25	5.75	27,500
Rum Raisin	9.00	5.15	3.85	8,800
Peach	9.00	5.40	3.60	14,300
Coffee	9.00	4.00	5.00	28,600
				110,000

The Split Banana focuses on contribution margin in its variance analysis.

Required

1. Compute the total sales-volume variance for August 2011.
2. Compute the total sales-mix variance for August 2011.
3. Compute the total sales-quantity variance for August 2011.
4. Comment on your results in requirements 1, 2, and 3.

14-35 Direct materials efficiency, mix, and yield variances. Nature's Best Nuts produces specialty nut products for the gourmet and natural foods market. Its most popular product is Zesty Zingers, a mixture of roasted nuts that are seasoned with a secret spice mixture, and sold in one-pound tins. The direct materials used in Zesty Zingers are almonds, cashews, pistachios, and seasoning. For each batch of 100 tins, the budgeted quantities and budgeted prices of direct materials are as follows:

	Quantity for One Batch	Price of Input
Almonds	180 cups	$1 per cup
Cashews	300 cups	$2 per cup
Pistachios	90 cups	$3 per cup
Seasoning	30 cups	$6 per cup

Changing the standard mix of direct material quantities slightly does not significantly affect the overall end product, particularly for the nuts. In addition, not all nuts added to production end up in the finished product, as some are rejected during inspection.

In the current period, Nature's Best made 2,500 tins of Zesty Zingers in 25 batches with the following actual quantity, cost and mix of inputs:

	Actual Quantity	Actual Cost	Actual Mix
Almonds	5,280 cups	$ 5,280	33%
Cashews	7,520 cups	15,040	47%
Pistachios	2,720 cups	8,160	17%
Seasoning	480 cups	2,880	3%
Total actual	16,000 cups	$31,360	100%

Required

1. What is the budgeted cost of direct materials for the 2,500 tins?
2. Calculate the total direct materials efficiency variance.
3. Why is the total direct materials price variance zero?
4. Calculate the total direct materials mix and yield variances. What are these variances telling you about the 2,500 tins produced this period? Are the variances large enough to investigate?

14-36 Direct labor variances: price, efficiency, mix, and yield. Trevor Joseph employs two workers in his guitar-making business. The first worker, George, has been making guitars for 20 years and is paid $30 per hour. The second worker, Earl, is less experienced, and is paid $20 per hour. One guitar requires, on average, 10 hours of labor. The budgeted direct labor quantities and prices for one guitar are as follows:

	Quantity	Price per Hour of Labor	Cost for One Guitar
George	6 hours	$30 per hour	$180
Earl	4 hours	$20 per hour	80

That is, each guitar is budgeted to require 10 hours of direct labor, comprised of 60% of George's labor and 40% of Earl's, although sometimes Earl works more hours on a particular guitar and George less, or vice versa, with no obvious change in the quality or function of the guitar.

During the month of August, Joseph manufactures 25 guitars. Actual direct labor costs are as follows:

George (145 hours)	$4,350
Earl (108 hours)	2,160
Total actual direct labor cost	$6,510

Required

1. What is the budgeted cost of direct labor for 25 guitars?
2. Calculate the total direct labor price and efficiency variances.
3. For the 25 guitars, what is the total actual amount of direct labor used? What is the actual direct labor input mix percentage? What is the budgeted amount of George's and Earl's labor that should have been used for the 25 guitars?
4. Calculate the total direct labor mix and yield variances. How do these numbers relate to the total direct labor efficiency variance? What do these variances tell you?

14-37 Purposes of cost allocation. Sarah Reynolds recently started a job as an administrative assistant in the cost accounting department of Mize Manufacturing. New to the area of cost accounting, Sarah is puzzled by the fact that one of Mize's manufactured products, SR460, seem to have a different cost, depending on who asks for it. When the marketing department requested the cost of SR460 in order to determine pricing for the new catalog, Sarah was told to report one amount, but when a request came in the very next day from the financial reporting department, the cost of SR460, she was told the cost was very different. Sarah runs a report using Mize's cost accounting system, which produces the following cost elements for one unit of SR460:

Direct materials	$28.50
Direct manufacturing labor	16.35
Variable manufacturing overhead	8.76
Allocated fixed manufacturing overhead	32.84
Research and development costs specific to SR460[a]	6.20
Marketing costs[a]	5.95
Sales commissions[a]	11.40
Allocated administrative costs of production department	5.38
Allocated administrative costs of corporate headquarters	18.60
Customer service costs[a]	3.05
Distribution costs[a]	8.80

[a]These costs are specific to SR460, but would not be eliminated if SR460 were purchased from an outside supplier.

Required

1. Explain to Sarah why the cost given to the marketing and financial reporting departments would be different.
2. Calculate the cost of one unit of SR460 to determine the following:
   a. The selling price of SR460
   b. The cost of inventory for financial reporting
   c. Whether to continue manufacturing SR460, or to purchase it from an outside source (Assume that SR460 is used as a component in one of Mize's other products.)
   d. The ability of Mize's production manager to control costs

14-38 Customer-cost hierarchy, customer profitability. Denise Nelson operates Interiors by Denise, an interior design consulting and window treatment fabrication business. Her business is made up of two different distribution channels, a consulting business in which Denise serves two architecture firms (Attractive Abodes and Better Buildings), and a commercial window treatment business in which Denise designs and constructs window treatments for three commercial clients (Cheery Curtains, Delightful Drapes, and Elegant Extras). Denise would like to evaluate the profitability of her two architecture firm clients and three commercial window treatment clients, as well as evaluate the profitability of each of the two divisions, and the business as a whole. Information about her most recent quarter follow:

Gross revenue from Attractive Abodes (AA)	$58,500
Gross revenue from Better Buildings (BB)	47,200
Gross revenue from Cheery Curtains (CC)	89,345
Gross revenue from Delightful Drapes (DD)	36,960
Gross revenue from Elegant Extras (EE)	18,300
Costs specific to AA	36,750
Costs specific to BB	29,300
Costs specific to CC	54,645
Costs specific to DD	28,930
Costs specific to EE	14,260
Overhead costs[a]	85,100

[a]Denise has determined that 25% of her overhead costs relate directly to her architectural business, 40% relate directly to her window treatment business, and the remainder is general in nature.

Denise gave a 10% discount to Attractive Abodes in order to lure it away from a competitor, and gave a 5% discount to Elegant Extras for advance payment in cash.

Required

1. Prepare a customer-cost hierarchy report for Interiors by Denise, using the format in Exhibit 6.
2. Prepare a customer-profitability analysis for the five customers, using the format in Exhibit 7.
3. Comment on the results of the preceding reports. What recommendations would you give Denise?

Collaborative Learning Problem

14-39 Customer profitability and ethics. Snark Corporation manufactures a product called the snark, which it sells to merchandising firms such as Snark Republic (SR), Snarks-R-Us (SRU), Neiman Snark-us (NS), Snark Buy (SB), Snark-Mart (SM), and Wal-Snark (WS). The list price of a snark is $50, and the full manufacturing costs are $35. Salespeople receive a commission on sales, but the commission is based on number of orders taken, not on sales revenue generated or number of units sold. Salespeople receive a commission of $25 per order (in addition to regular salary).

Snark Corporation makes products based on anticipated demand. Snark Corporation carries an inventory of snarks so rush orders do not result in any extra manufacturing costs over and above the $35 per snark. Snark Corporation ships finished product to the customer at no additional charge to the customer for either regular or expedited delivery. Snark incurs significantly higher costs for expedited deliveries than for regular deliveries. Customers occasionally return shipments to Snark, and these returns are subtracted from gross revenue. The customers are not charged a restocking fee for returns

Budgeted (expected) customer-level cost driver rates are as follows:

Order taking (excluding sales commission)	$30 per order
Product handling	$2 per unit
Delivery	$0.50 per mile driven
Expedited (rush) delivery	$325 per shipment
Restocking	$100 per returned shipment
Visits to customers	$150 per customer

Because salespeople are paid $25 per order, they often break up large orders into multiple smaller orders. This practice reduces the actual order taking cost by $16 per smaller order (from $30 per order to $14 per order) because the smaller orders are all written at the same time. This lower cost rate is not included in budgeted rates because salespeople create smaller orders without telling management or the accounting department. All other actual costs are the same as budgeted costs.

Information about Snark's clients follows:

	SR	SRU	NS	SB	SM	WS
Total number of units purchased	250	550	320	130	450	1,200
Number of actual orders	3	15	3	4	5	15
Number of written orders	6	15*	8	7	20	30
Total number of miles driven to deliver all products	420	620	470	280	806	900
Total number of units returned	20	35	0	0	40	60
Number of returned shipments	2	1	0	0	2	6
Number of expedited deliveries	0	6	0	0	2	5

*Because SRU places 15 separate orders, its order costs are $30 per order. All other orders are multiple smaller orders and so have actual order costs of $14 each.

Required

1. Classify each of the customer-level operating costs as a customer output-unit-level, customer batch-level, or customer-sustaining cost.
2. Using the preceding information, calculate the expected customer-level operating income for the six customers of Snark Corporation. Use the number of written orders at $30 each to calculate expected order costs.
3. Recalculate the customer-level operating income using the number of written orders but at their actual $14 cost per order instead of $30 (except for SRU, whose actual cost is $30 per order). How will Snark Corporation evaluate customer-level operating cost performance this period?
4. Recalculate the customer-level operating income if salespeople had not broken up actual orders into multiple smaller orders. Don't forget to also adjust sales commissions.
5. How is the behavior of the salespeople affecting the profit of Snark Corporation? Is their behavior ethical? What could Snark Corporation do to change the behavior of the salespeople?

Allocation of Support-Department Costs, Common Costs, and Revenues

From Chapter 15 of *Cost Accounting: A Managerial Emphasis*, 14/e. Charles T. Horngren. Srikant M. Datar. Madhav Rajan.

Allocation of Support-Department Costs, Common Costs, and Revenues

How a company allocates its overhead and internal support costs—costs related to marketing, advertising, and other internal services—among its various production departments or projects, can have a big impact on how profitable those departments or projects are.

While the allocation won't affect the firm's profit as a whole, if the allocation isn't done properly, it can make some departments and projects (and their managers) look better or worse than they should profit-wise. As the following article shows, the method of allocating costs for a project affects not just the firm but also the consumer. Based on the method used, consumers may spend more, or less, for the same service.

Cost Allocation and the Future of "Smart Grid" Energy Infrastructure[1]

Across the globe, countries are adopting alternative methods of generating and distributing energy. In the United States, government leaders and companies ranging from GE to Google are advocating the movement towards a "Smart Grid"—that is, making transmission and power lines operate and communicate in a more effective and efficient manner using technology, computers, and software. This proposed system would also integrate with emerging clean energy sources, such as solar farms and geothermal systems, to help create a more sustainable electricity supply that reduces carbon emissions.

According to the Electric Power Resource Institute, the cost of developing the "Smart Grid" is $165 billion over the next two decades. These costs include new infrastructure and technology improvements—mostly to power lines—as well as traditional indirect costs for the organizations upgrading the power system, which include traditional support-department costs and common costs. Private utilities and the U.S. government will pay for the upfront costs of "Smart Grid" development, but those costs will be recouped over time by charging energy consumers. But one question remains: How should those costs be allocated for reimbursement?

A controversy has emerged as two cost allocation methods are being debated by the U.S. government. One method is

---

[1] *Sources*: Garthwaite, Josie. 2009. The $160B question: Who should foot the bill for transmission buildout?" Salon.com, March 12; Jaffe, Mark. 2010. Cost of Smart-Grid projects shocks consumer advocates. *The Denver Post*, February 14.

interconnection-wide cost allocation. Under this system, everybody in the region where a new technology is deployed would have to help pay for it. For example, if new power lines and "smart" energy meters are deployed in Denver, everybody in Colorado would help pay for them. Supporters argue that this method would help lessen the costs consumers would be charged by utilities for the significant investments in new technology.

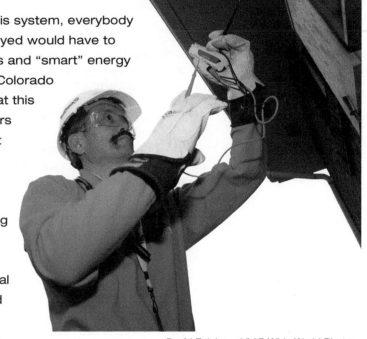

David Zalubowski\AP Wide World Photos

Another competing proposal would only allocate costs to utility ratepayers that actually benefit from the new "Smart Grid" system. Using the previous example, only utility customers in Denver would be charged for the new power lines and energy meters (likely through additional monthly utility costs). Supporters of this method believe that customers with new "Smart Grid" systems should not be subsidized by those not receiving any of the benefits.

Regardless of the method selected, cost allocation is going to play a key role in the future of the U.S. energy generation and distribution system. The same allocation dilemmas apply to the costs of corporate support departments and the apportionment of revenues when products are sold in bundles. These concerns are common to managers at manufacturing companies such as Nestle, service companies such as Comcast, merchandising companies such as Trader Joe's, and academic institutions such as Auburn University. This chapter focuses on several challenges that arise with regard to cost and revenue allocations.

Allocating Support Department Costs Using the Single-Rate and Dual-Rate Methods

Learning Objective 1

Distinguish the single-rate method

. . . one rate for allocating costs in a cost pool

from the dual-rate method

. . . two rates for allocating costs in a cost pool—one for variable costs and one for fixed costs

Companies distinguish operating departments (and operating divisions) from support departments. An **operating department,** also called a **production department,** directly adds value to a product or service. A **support department,** also called a **service department,** provides the services that assist other internal departments (operating departments and other support departments) in the company. Examples of support departments are information systems and plant maintenance. Managers face two questions when allocating the costs of a support department to operating departments or divisions: (1) Should fixed costs of support departments be allocated to operating divisions? (2) If fixed costs are allocated, should variable and fixed costs be allocated in the same way? With regard to the first question, most companies believe that fixed costs of support departments should be allocated because the support department needs to incur fixed costs to provide operating divisions with the services they require. Depending on the answer to the second question, there are two approaches to allocating support-department costs: the *single-rate cost-allocation method* and the *dual-rate cost-allocation method*.

Single-Rate and Dual-Rate Methods

The **single-rate method** makes no distinction between fixed and variable costs. It allocates costs in each cost pool (support department in this section) to cost objects (operating divisions in this section) using the same rate per unit of a single allocation base. By contrast, the **dual-rate method** partitions the cost of each support department into two pools, a variable-cost pool and a fixed-cost pool, and allocates each pool using a different cost-allocation base. When using either the single-rate method or the dual-rate method, managers can allocate support-department costs to operating divisions based on either a *budgeted* rate or the eventual *actual* cost rate. The latter approach is neither conceptually preferred nor widely used in practice (we explain why in the next section). Accordingly, we illustrate the single-rate and dual-rate methods next based on the use of *budgeted* rates.

Consider the central computer department of Sand Hill Company (SHC). This support department has two users, both operating divisions: the microcomputer division and the peripheral equipment division. The following data relate to the 2012 budget:

Practical capacity	18,750 hours
Fixed costs of operating the computer facility in the 6,000-hour to 18,750-hour relevant range	$3,000,000
Budgeted long-run usage (quantity) in hours:	
Microcomputer division	8,000 hours
Peripheral equipment division	4,000 hours
Total	12,000 hours
Budgeted variable cost per hour in the 6,000-hour to 18,750-hour relevant range	$200 per hour used
Actual usage in 2012 in hours:	
Microcomputer division	9,000 hours
Peripheral equipment division	3,000 hours
Total	12,000 hours

The budgeted rates for central computer department costs can be computed based on either the demand for computer services or the supply of computer services. We consider the allocation of central computer department costs based first on the demand for (or usage of) computer services and then on the supply of computer services.

Allocation Based on the Demand for (or Usage of) Computer Services

We present the single-rate method followed by the dual-rate method.

Single-Rate Method

In this method, a combined budgeted rate is used for fixed and variable costs. The rate is calculated as follows:

Budgeted usage	12,000 hours
Budgeted total cost pool: $3,000,000 + (12,000 hours × $200/hour)	$5,400,000
Budgeted total rate per hour: $5,400,000 ÷ 12,000 hours	$450 per hour used
Allocation rate for microcomputer division	$450 per hour used
Allocation rate for peripheral equipment division	$450 per hour used

Note that the budgeted rate of $450 per hour is substantially higher than the $200 budgeted *variable* cost per hour. That's because the $450 rate includes an allocated amount of $250 per hour (budgeted fixed costs, $3,000,000, ÷ budgeted usage, 12,000 hours) for the *fixed* costs of operating the facility.

Under the single-rate method, divisions are charged the budgeted rate for each hour of *actual* use of the central facility. Applying this to our example, SHC allocates central computer department costs based on the $450 per hour budgeted rate and actual hours used by the operating divisions. The support costs allocated to the two divisions under this method are as follows:

Microcomputer division: 9,000 hours × $450 per hour	$4,050,000
Peripheral equipment division: 3,000 hours × $450 per hour	$1,350,000

Dual-Rate Method

When the dual-rate method is used, allocation bases must be chosen for both the variable and fixed cost pools of the central computer department. As in the single-rate method, variable costs are assigned based on the *budgeted* variable cost per hour of $200 for *actual* hours used by each division. However, fixed costs are assigned based on *budgeted* fixed costs per hour and the *budgeted* number of hours for each division. Given the budgeted usage of 8,000 hours for the microcomputer division and 4,000 hours for the peripheral equipment division, the budgeted fixed-cost rate is $250 per hour ($3,000,000 ÷ 12,000 hours), as before. Since this rate is charged on the basis of the *budgeted* usage, however, the fixed costs are effectively allocated in advance as a lump-sum based on the relative proportions of the central computing facilities expected to be used by the operating divisions.

The costs allocated to the microcomputer division in 2012 under the dual-rate method would be as follows:

Fixed costs: $250 per hour × 8,000 (budgeted) hours	$2,000,000
Variable costs: $200 per hour × 9,000 (actual) hours	1,800,000
Total costs	$3,800,000

The costs allocated to the peripheral equipment division in 2012 would be as follows:

Fixed costs: $250 per hour × 4,000 (budgeted) hours	$1,000,000
Variable costs: $200 per hour × 3,000 (actual) hours	600,000
Total costs	$1,600,000

Note that each operating division is charged the same amount for variable costs under the single-rate and dual-rate methods ($200 per hour multiplied by the actual hours of use). However, the overall assignment of costs differs under the two methods because the single-rate method allocates fixed costs of the support department based on actual usage of computer resources by the operating divisions, whereas the dual-rate method allocates fixed costs based on budgeted usage.

We next consider the alternative approach of allocating central computer department costs based on the capacity of computer services supplied.

Allocation Based on the Supply of Capacity

We illustrate this approach using the 18,750 hours of practical capacity of the central computer department. The budgeted rate is then determined as follows:

Budgeted fixed-cost rate per hour, $3,000,000 ÷ 18,750 hours	$160 per hour
Budgeted variable-cost rate per hour	200 per hour
Budgeted total-cost rate per hour	$360 per hour

Using the same procedures for the single-rate and dual-rate methods as in the previous section, the support cost allocations to the operating divisions are as follows:

Single-Rate Method

Microcomputer division: $360 per hour × 9,000 (actual) hours	$3,240,000
Peripheral equipment division: $360 per hour × 3,000 (actual) hours	1,080,000
Fixed costs of unused computer capacity:	
$160 per hour × 6,750 hours[a]	1,080,000

[a]6,750 hours = Practical capacity of 18,750 – (9,000 hours used by microcomputer division + 3,000 hours used by peripheral equipment division).

Dual-Rate Method

Microcomputer division

Fixed costs: $160 per hour × 8,000 (budgeted) hours	$1,280,000
Variable costs: $200 per hour × 9,000 (actual) hours	1,800,000
Total costs	$3,080,000

Peripheral equipment division

Fixed costs: $160 per hour × 4,000 (budgeted) hours	$ 640,000
Variable costs: $200 per hour × 3,000 (actual) hours	600,000
Total costs	$1,240,000

Fixed costs of unused computer capacity:

$160 per hour × 6,750 hours[b]	$1,080,000

[b]6,750 hours = Practical capacity of 18,750 hours − (8,000 hours budgeted to be used by microcomputer division + 4,000 hours budgeted to be used by peripheral equipment division).

When practical capacity is used to allocate costs, the single-rate method allocates only the actual fixed-cost resources used by the microcomputer and peripheral equipment divisions, while the dual-rate method allocates the budgeted fixed-cost resources to be used by the operating divisions. Unused central computer department resources are highlighted but usually not allocated to the divisions.[2]

The advantage of using practical capacity to allocate costs is that it focuses management's attention on managing unused capacity. Using practical capacity also avoids burdening the user divisions with the cost of unused capacity of the central computer department. In contrast, when costs are allocated on the basis of the demand for computer services, all $3,000,000 of budgeted fixed costs, including the cost of unused capacity, are allocated to user divisions. If costs are used as a basis for pricing, then charging user divisions for unused capacity could result in the downward demand spiral.

Single-Rate Versus Dual-Rate Method

There are benefits and costs of both the single-rate and dual-rate methods. One benefit of the single-rate method is the low cost to implement it. The single-rate method avoids the often-expensive analysis necessary to classify the individual cost items of a department into fixed and variable categories. Also, by conditioning the final allocations on the actual usage of central facilities, rather than basing them solely on uncertain forecasts of expected demand, it offers the user divisions some operational control over the charges they bear.

A problem with the single-rate method is that it makes the allocated fixed costs of the support department appear as variable costs to the operating divisions. Consequently, the single-rate method may lead division managers to make outsourcing decisions that are in their own best interest but that may be inefficient from the standpoint of the organization as a whole. Consider the setting where allocations are made on the basis of the demand for computer services. In this case, each user division is charged $450 per hour under the single-rate method (recall that $250 of this charge relates to the allocated fixed costs of the central computer department). Suppose an external vendor offers the microcomputer division computer services at a rate of $340 per hour, at a time when the central computer department has unused capacity. The microcomputer division's managers would be tempted to use this vendor because it would lower the division's costs ($340 per hour instead of the $450 per hour internal charge for computer services). In the short run, however, the fixed costs of the central computer department remain unchanged in the relevant range (between 6,000 hours of usage and the practical capacity of 18,750 hours). SHC will therefore incur an additional cost of $140 per hour if the managers were to take this offer—the difference between the $340 external purchase price and the true internal variable cost of $200 of using the central computer department.

---

[2] In our example, the cost of unused capacity under the single-rate and the dual-rate methods coincide (each equals $1,080,000). This occurs because the total actual usage of the facility matches the total expected usage of 12,000 hours. The budgeted cost of unused capacity (in the dual-rate method) can be either greater or lower than the actual cost (in the single-rate method), depending on whether the total actual usage is lower or higher than the budgeted usage.

The divergence created under the single-rate method between SHC's interests and those of its division managers is lessened when allocation is done on the basis of practical capacity. The variable cost per hour perceived by the operating division managers is now $360 (rather than the $450 rate when allocation is based on budgeted usage). However, any external offer above $200 (SHC's true variable cost) and below $360 (the single-rate charge per hour) will still result in the user manager preferring to outsource the service at the expense of SHC's overall profits.

A benefit of the dual-rate method is that it signals to division managers how variable costs and fixed costs behave differently. This information guides division managers to make decisions that benefit the organization as a whole, as well as each division. For example, using a third-party computer provider that charges more than $200 per hour would result in SHC's being worse off than if its own central computer department were used, because the latter has a variable cost of $200 per hour. Under the dual-rate method, neither division manager has an incentive to pay more than $200 per hour for an external provider because the internal charge for computer services is precisely that amount. By charging the fixed costs of resources budgeted to be used by the divisions as a lump-sum, the dual-rate method succeeds in removing fixed costs from the division managers' consideration when making marginal decisions regarding the outsourcing of services. It thus avoids the potential conflict of interest that can arise under the single-rate method.

Recently, the dual-rate method has been receiving more attention. Resource Consumption Accounting (RCA), an emerging management accounting system, employs an allocation procedure akin to a dual-rate system. For each cost/resource pool, cost assignment rates for fixed costs are based on practical capacity supplied, while rates for proportional costs (i.e., costs that vary with regard to the output of the resource pool) are based on planned quantities.[3]

Decision Point

When should managers use the dual-rate method over the single-rate method?

Budgeted Versus Actual Costs, and the Choice of Allocaton Base

The allocation methods previously outlined follow specific procedures in terms of the support department costs that are considered as well as the manner in which costs are assigned to the operating departments. In this section, we examine these choices in greater detail and consider the impact of alternative approaches. We show that the decision whether to use actual or budgeted costs, as well as the choice between actual and budgeted usage as allocation base, has a significant impact on the cost allocated to each division and the incentives of the division managers.

Budgeted Versus Actual Rates

In both the single-rate and dual-rate methods, we use budgeted rates to assign support department costs (fixed as well as variable costs). An alternative approach would involve using the actual rates based on the support costs realized during the period. This method is much less common because of the level of uncertainty it imposes on user divisions. When allocations are made using budgeted rates, managers of divisions to which costs are allocated know with certainty the rates to be used in that budget period. Users can then determine the amount of the service to request and—if company policy allows—whether to use the internal source or an external vendor. In contrast, when actual rates are used for cost allocation, user divisions are kept unaware of their charges until the end of the budget period.

Budgeted rates also help motivate the manager of the support (or supplier) department (for example, the central computer department) to improve efficiency. During the

Learning Objective 2

Understand how divisional incentives are affected by the choice between allocation based on budgeted and actual rates,

. . . budgeted rates provide certainty to users about charges and motivate the support division to engage in cost control

and budgeted and actual usage

. . . budgeted usage helps in planning and efficient utilization of fixed resources, actual usage controls consumption of variable resources

---

[3] Other salient features of Resource Consumption Accounting (RCA) include the selective use of activity-based costing, the nonassignment of fixed costs when causal relationships cannot be established, and the depreciation of assets based on their replacement cost. RCA has its roots in the nearly fifty-year-old German cost accounting system called Grenzplankostenrechnung (GPK), which is used by organizations such as Mercedes-Benz, Porsche, and Stihl. For further details, as well as illustrations of the use of RCA and GPK in organizations, see S. Webber and B. Clinton, "Resource Consumption Accounting Applied: The Clopay Case," *Management Accounting Quarterly* (Fall 2004) and B. Mackie, "Merging GPK and ABC on the Road to RCA," *Strategic Finance* (November 2006).

budget period, the support department, not the user divisions, bears the risk of any unfavorable cost variances. That's because user divisions do not pay for any costs or inefficiencies of the supplier department that cause actual rates to exceed budgeted rates.

The manager of the supplier department would likely view the budgeted rates negatively if unfavorable cost variances occur due to price increases outside of his or her control. Some organizations try to identify these uncontrollable factors and relieve the support department manager of responsibility for these variances. In other organizations, the supplier department and the user division agree to share the risk (through an explicit formula) of a large, uncontrollable increase in the prices of inputs used by the supplier department. This procedure avoids imposing the risk completely on either the supplier department (as when budgeted rates are used) or the user division (as in the case of actual rates).

For the rest of this chapter, we will continue to consider only allocation methods that are based on the budgeted cost of support services.

Budgeted Versus Actual Usage

In both the single-rate and dual-rate methods, the variable costs are assigned on the basis of budgeted rates and actual usage. Since the variable costs are directly and causally linked to usage, charging them as a function of the actual usage is appropriate. Moreover, allocating variable costs on the basis of budgeted usage would provide the user departments with no incentive to control their consumption of support services.

What about the fixed costs? Consider the budget of $3,000,000 fixed costs at the central computer department of SHC. Recall that budgeted usage is 8,000 hours for the microcomputer division and 4,000 hours for the peripheral equipment division. Assume that actual usage by the microcomputer division is always equal to budgeted usage. We consider three cases: when actual usage by the peripheral equipment division equals (Case 1), is greater than (Case 2), and is less than (Case 3) budgeted usage.

Fixed Cost Allocation Based on Budgeted Rates and Budgeted Usage

This is the dual-rate procedure outlined in the previous section. When budgeted usage is the allocation base, regardless of the actual usage of facilities (i.e., whether Case 1, 2, or 3 occurs), user divisions receive a preset lump-sum fixed cost charge. If rates are based on expected demand ($250 per hour), the microcomputer division is assigned $2,000,000 and the peripheral equipment division, $1,000,000. If rates are set using practical capacity ($160 per hour), the microcomputer division is charged $1,280,000, the peripheral equipment division is allocated $640,000, and the remaining $1,080,000 is the unallocated cost of excess capacity.

The advantage of knowing the allocations in advance is that it helps the user divisions with both short-run and long-run planning. Companies commit to infrastructure costs (such as the fixed costs of a support department) on the basis of a long-run planning horizon; budgeted usage measures the long-run demands of the user divisions for support-department services.

Allocating fixed costs on the basis of budgeted long-run usage may tempt some managers to underestimate their planned usage. Underestimating will result in their divisions bearing a lower percentage of fixed costs (assuming all other managers do not similarly underestimate their usage). To discourage such underestimates, some companies offer bonuses or other rewards—the "carrot" approach—to managers who make accurate forecasts of long-run usage. Other companies impose cost penalties—the "stick" approach—for underestimating long-run usage. For instance, a higher cost rate is charged after a division exceeds its budgeted usage.

Fixed Cost Allocation Based on Budgeted Rates and Actual Usage

Column 2 of Exhibit 1 provides the allocations when the budgeted rate is based on expected demand ($250 per hour), while column 3 shows the allocations when practical capacity is used to derive the rate ($160 per hour). Note that each operating division's

Exhibit 1   Effect of Variations in Actual Usage on Fixed Cost Allocation to Operating Divisions

	(1) Actual Usage		(2) Budgeted Rate Based on Expected Demand[a]		(3) Budgeted Rate Based on Practical Capacity[b]		(4) Allocation of Budgeted Total Fixed Cost	
Case	Micro. Div.	Periph. Div.	Micro. Div.	Periph. Div.	Micro. Div.	Periph. Div.	Micro. Div.	Periph. Div.
1	8,000 hours	4,000 hours	$2,000,000	$1,000,000	$1,280,000	$ 640,000	$2,000,000[c]	$1,000,000[d]
2	8,000 hours	7,000 hours	$2,000,000	$1,750,000	$1,280,000	$1,120,000	$1,600,000[e]	$1,400,000[f]
3	8,000 hours	2,000 hours	$2,000,000	$ 500,000	$1,280,000	$ 320,000	$2,400,000[g]	$ 600,000[h]

$$a \quad \frac{\$3,000,000}{(8,000 + 4,000) \text{ hours}} = \$250 \text{ per hour} \qquad b \quad \frac{\$3,000,000}{18,750 \text{ hours}} = \$160 \text{ per hour} \qquad c \quad \frac{8,000}{(8,000 + 4,000)} \times \$3,000,000 \qquad d \quad \frac{4,000}{(8,000 + 4,000)} \times \$3,000,000$$

$$e \quad \frac{8,000}{(8,000 + 7,000)} \times \$3,000,000 \qquad f \quad \frac{7,000}{(8,000 + 7,000)} \times \$3,000,000 \qquad g \quad \frac{8,000}{(8,000 + 2,000)} \times \$3,000,000 \qquad h \quad \frac{2,000}{(8,000 + 2,000)} \times \$3,000,000$$

fixed cost allocation varies based on its actual usage of support facilities. However, variations in actual usage in one division do not affect the costs allocated to the other division. The microcomputer division is allocated either $2,000,000 or $1,280,000, depending on the budgeted rate chosen, independent of the peripheral equipment division's actual usage. Therefore, combining actual usage as the allocation base with budgeted rates provides user divisions with advanced knowledge of rates, as well as control over the costs charged to them.[4]

Note, however, that this allocation procedure for fixed costs is exactly the same as that under the single-rate method. As such, the procedure shares the disadvantages of the single-rate method discussed in the previous section, such as charging excessively high costs, including the cost of unused capacity, when rates are based on expected usage. Moreover, even when rates are based on practical capacity, recall that allocating fixed cost rates based on actual usage induces conflicts of interest between the user divisions and the firm when evaluating outsourcing possibilities.

Allocating Budgeted Fixed Costs Based on Actual Usage

Finally, consider the impact of having actual usage as the allocation base when the firm assigns total budgeted fixed costs to operating divisions (rather than specifying budgeted fixed cost rates, as we have thus far). If the budgeted fixed costs of $3,000,000 are allocated using budgeted usage, we are back in the familiar dual-rate setting. On the other hand, if the actual usage of the facility is the basis for allocation, the charges would equal the amounts in Exhibit 1, column 4. In Case 1, the fixed-cost allocation equals the budgeted amount (which is also the same as the charge under the dual-rate method). In Case 2, the fixed-cost allocation is $400,000 less to the microcomputer division than the amount based on budgeted usage ($1,600,000 versus $2,000,000). In Case 3, the fixed-cost allocation is $400,000 more to the microcomputer division than the amount based on budgeted usage ($2,400,000 versus $2,000,000). Why does the microcomputer division receive $400,000 more in costs in Case 3, even though its actual usage equals its budgeted usage? Because the total fixed costs of $3,000,000 are now spread over 2,000 fewer hours of actual total usage. In other words, the lower usage by the peripheral equipment division leads to an increase in the fixed costs allocated to the microcomputer division. When budgeted fixed costs are allocated based on actual usage, user divisions will not know their fixed cost allocations until the end of the budget period. This method therefore shares the same flaw as those that rely on the use of actual cost realizations rather than budgeted cost rates.

To summarize, there are excellent economic and motivational reasons to justify the precise forms of the single-rate and dual-rate methods considered in the previous section, and in particular, to recommend the dual-rate allocation procedure.

◀ **Decision Point**

What factors should managers consider when deciding between allocation based on budgeted and actual rates, and budgeted and actual usage?

---

[4] The total amount of fixed costs allocated to divisions will in general not equal the actual realized costs.

Allocating Costs of Multiple Support Departments

Learning Objective 3

Allocate multiple support-department costs using the direct method,

. . . allocates support-department costs directly to operating departments

the step-down method,

. . . partially allocates support-department costs to other support departments

and the reciprocal method

. . . fully allocates support-department costs to other support departments

We just examined general issues that arise when allocating costs from one support department to operating divisions. In this section, we examine the special cost-allocation problems that arise when two or more of the support departments whose costs are being allocated provide reciprocal support to each other as well as to operating departments. An example of reciprocal support is a firm's human resource department providing recruiting, training, and performance management services to all employees of a firm, including those who work in the legal department, while also utilizing the services of the legal department for compliance activities, drafting of contracts, checking stock option plan documents, etc. More accurate support-department cost allocations result in more accurate product, service, and customer costs.

Consider Castleford Engineering, which operates at practical capacity to manufacture engines used in electric-power generating plants. Castleford has two support departments and two operating departments in its manufacturing facility:

Support Departments	Operating Departments
Plant (and equipment) maintenance	Machining
Information systems	Assembly

The two support departments at Castleford provide reciprocal support to each other as well as support to the two operating departments. Costs are accumulated in each department for planning and control purposes. Exhibit 2 displays the data for this example. To understand the percentages in this exhibit, consider the plant maintenance department. This support department provides a total of 20,000 hours of support work: 20% (4,000 ÷ 20,000 = 0.20) for the information systems department, 30% (6,000 ÷ 20,000 = 0.30) for the machining department, and 50% (10,000 ÷ 20,000 = 0.50) for the assembly department.

We now examine three methods of allocating the costs of reciprocal support departments: *direct*, *step-down*, and *reciprocal*. To simplify the explanation and to focus on concepts, we use the single-rate method to allocate the costs of each support department using budgeted rates and budgeted hours used by the other departments. (The Problem for Self-Study illustrates the dual-rate method for allocating reciprocal support-department costs.)

Direct Method

The **direct method** allocates each support department's costs to operating departments only. The direct method does not allocate support-department costs to other support departments. Exhibit 3 illustrates this method using the data in Exhibit 2. The

Exhibit 2   Data for Allocating Support-Department Costs at Castleford Engineering for 2012

	A	B	C	D	E	F	G
		SUPPORT DEPARTMENTS			**OPERATING DEPARTMENTS**		
		Plant Maintenance	**Information Systems**		**Machining**	**Assembly**	**Total**
3	Budgeted overhead costs						
4	before any interdepartment cost allocations	$6,300,000	$1,452,150		$4,000,000	$2,000,000	$13,752,150
5	Support work furnished:						
6	By plant maintenance						
7	Budgeted labor-hours	—	4,000		6,000	10,000	20,000
8	Percentage	—	20%		30%	50%	100%
9	By information systems						
10	Budgeted computer hours	500	—		4,000	500	5,000
11	Percentage	10%	—		80%	10%	100%

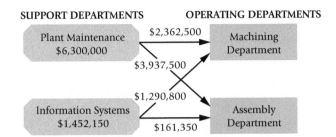

Exhibit 3

Direct Method of
Allocating Support-
Department Costs at
Castleford Engineering
for 2012

	A	B	C	D	E	F	G
		SUPPORT DEPARTMENTS			OPERATING DEPARTMENTS		
2		Plant Maintenance	Information Systems		Machining	Assembly	Total
3	Budgeted overhead costs						
4	before any interdepartment cost allocations	$6,300,000	$1,452,150		$4,000,000	$2,000,000	$13,752,150
5	Allocation of plant maintenance (3/8, 5/8)[a]	(6,300,000)			2,362,500	3,937,500	
6	Allocation of information systems (8/9, 1/9)[b]		(1,452,150)		1,290,800	161,350	
7							
8	Total budgeted overhead of operating departments	$ 0	$ 0		$7,653,300	$6,098,850	$13,752,150
9							
10	[a] Base is (6,000 + 10,000), or 16,000 hours; 6,000 ÷ 16,000 = 3/8; 10,000 ÷ 16,000 = 5/8.						
11	[b] Base is (4,000 + 500), or 4,500 hours; 4,000 ÷ 4,500 = 8/9; 500 ÷ 4,500 = 1/9.						

base used to allocate plant maintenance costs to the operating departments is the budgeted total maintenance labor-hours worked in the operating departments: 6,000 + 10,000 = 16,000 hours. This amount excludes the 4,000 hours of budgeted support time provided by plant maintenance to information systems. Similarly, the base used for allocation of information systems costs to the operating departments is 4,000 + 500 = 4,500 budgeted hours of computer time, which excludes the 500 hours of budgeted support time provided by information systems to plant maintenance.

An equivalent approach to implementing the direct method involves calculating a budgeted rate for each support department's costs. For example, the rate for plant maintenance department costs is $6,300,000 ÷ 16,000 hours, or $393.75 per hour. The machining department is then allocated $2,362,500 ($393.75 per hour × 6,000 hours) while the assembly department is assigned $3,937,500 ($393.75 per hour × 10,000 hours). For ease of explanation throughout this section, we will use the fraction of the support-department services used by other departments, rather than calculate budgeted rates, to allocate support-department costs.

The direct method is widely practiced because of its ease of use. The benefit of the direct method is simplicity. There is no need to predict the usage of support-department services by other support departments. A disadvantage of the direct method is that it ignores information about reciprocal services provided among support departments and can therefore lead to inaccurate estimates of the cost of operating departments. We now examine a second approach, which partially recognizes the services provided among support departments.

Step-Down Method

Some organizations use the **step-down method**, also called the **sequential allocation method,** which allocates support-department costs to other support departments and to operating departments in a sequential manner that partially recognizes the mutual services provided among all support departments.

Exhibit 4 shows the step-down method. The plant maintenance costs of $6,300,000 are allocated first. Exhibit 2 shows that plant maintenance provides 20% of its services

Exhibit 4

Step-Down Method of
Allocating Support-
Department Costs at
Castleford Engineering
for 2012

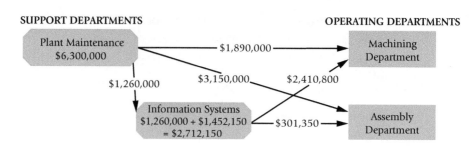

	SUPPORT DEPARTMENTS			OPERATING DEPARTMENTS		
	A	B	C	D	E	F	G

	A	Plant Maintenance	Information Systems		Machining	Assembly	Total
1		**SUPPORT DEPARTMENTS**			**OPERATING DEPARTMENTS**		
2		**Plant Maintenance**	**Information Systems**		**Machining**	**Assembly**	**Total**
3	Budgeted overhead costs before any						
4	interdepartment cost allocations	$6,300,000	$1,452,150		$4,000,000	$2,000,000	$13,752,150
5	Allocation of plant maintenance (2/10, 3/10, 5/10)[a]	(6,300,000)	1,260,000		1,890,000	3,150,000	
6			2,712,150				
7	Allocation of information systems (8/9, 1/9)[b]		(2,712,150)		2,410,800	301,350	
8							
9	Total budgeted overhead of operating departments	$ 0	$ 0		$8,300,800	$5,451,350	$13,752,150
10							
11	[a] Base is (4,000 + 6,000 + 10,000), or 20,000 hours; 4,000 ÷ 20,000 = 2/10; 6,000 ÷ 20,000 = 3/10; 10,000 ÷ 20,000 = 5/10.						
12	[b] Base is (4,000 + 500), or 4,500 hours; 4,000 ÷ 4,500 = 8/9; 500 ÷ 4,500 = 1/9.						

to information systems, 30% to machining, and 50% to assembly. Therefore, $1,260,000 is allocated to information systems (20% of $6,300,000), $1,890,000 to machining (30% of $6,300,000), and $3,150,000 to assembly (50% of $6,300,000). The information systems costs now total $2,712,150: budgeted costs of the information systems department before any interdepartmental cost allocations, $1,452,150, plus $1,260,000 from the allocation of plant maintenance costs to the information systems department. The $2,712,150 is then only allocated between the two operating departments based on the proportion of the information systems department services provided to machining and assembly. From Exhibit 2, the information systems department provides 80% of its services to machining and 10% to assembly, so $2,410,800 (8/9 × $2,712,150) is allocated to machining and $301,350 (1/9 × $2,712,150) is allocated to assembly.

Note that this method requires the support departments to be ranked (sequenced) in the order that the step-down allocation is to proceed. In our example, the costs of the plant maintenance department were allocated first to all other departments, including the information systems department. The costs of the information systems support department were allocated second, but only to the two operating departments. If the information systems department costs had been allocated first and the plant maintenance department costs second, the resulting allocations of support-department costs to operating departments would have been different. A popular step-down sequence begins with the support department that renders the highest percentage of its total services to *other support departments*. The sequence continues with the department that renders the next-highest percentage, and so on, ending with the support department that renders the lowest percentage.[5] In our example, costs of the plant maintenance department were allocated first because it provides 20% of its services to the information systems department, whereas the information systems department provides only 10% of its services to the plant maintenance department (see Exhibit 2).

---

[5] An alternative approach to selecting the sequence of allocations is to begin with the support department that renders the highest dollar amount of services to other support departments. The sequence ends with the allocation of the costs of the department that renders the lowest dollar amount of services to other support departments.

Under the step-down method, once a support department's costs have been allocated, no subsequent support-department costs are allocated back to it. Once the plant maintenance department costs are allocated, it receives no further allocation from other (lower-ranked) support departments. The result is that the step-down method does not recognize the total services that support departments provide to one another. The reciprocal method fully recognizes all such services, as you will see next.

Reciprocal Method

The **reciprocal method** allocates support-department costs to operating departments by fully recognizing the mutual services provided among all support departments. For example, the plant maintenance department maintains all the computer equipment in the information systems department. Similarly, information systems provide database support for plant maintenance. The reciprocal method fully incorporates interdepartmental relationships into the support-department cost allocations.

One way to understand the reciprocal method is as an extension of the step-down method. This approach is illustrated in Exhibit 5. As in the step-down procedure, plant maintenance costs are first allocated to all other departments, including the information systems support department: information systems, 20%; machining, 30%; assembly, 50%. The costs in the information systems department then total $2,712,150 ($1,452,150 + $1,260,000 from the first-round allocation), as in Exhibit 4. Under the step-down method, these costs are allocated directly to the operating departments alone. But the reciprocal method recognizes that a portion of the information systems department costs arises

Exhibit 5   Reciprocal Method of Allocating Support-Department Costs Using Repeated Iterations at Castleford Engineering for 2012

	Home	Insert	Page Layout	Formulas	Data	Review	View				

	A	B	C	D	E	F	G
1		SUPPORT DEPARTMENTS			OPERATING DEPARTMENTS		
2		Plant Maintenance	Information Systems		Machining	Assembly	Total
3	Budgeted overhead costs before any						
4	interdepartment cost allocations	$6,300,000	$1,452,150		$4,000,000	$2,000,000	$13,752,150
5	First allocation of plant maintenance (2/10, 3/10, 5/10)[a]	(6,300,000)	1,260,000		1,890,000	3,150,000	
6			2,712,150				
7	First allocation of information systems (1/10, 8/10, 1/10)[b]	271,215	(2,712,150)		2,169,720	271,215	
8	Second allocation of plant maintenance (2/10, 3/10, 5/10)[a]	(271,215)	54,243		81,364	135,608	
9	Second allocation of information systems (1/10, 8/10, 1/10)[b]	5,424	(54,243)		43,395	5,424	
10	Third allocation of plant maintenance (2/10, 3/10, 5/10)[a]	(5,424)	1,085		1,627	2,712	
11	Third allocation of information systems (1/10, 8/10, 1/10)[b]	109	(1,085)		867	109	
12	Fourth allocation of plant maintenance (2/10, 3/10, 5/10)[a]	(109)	22		33	54	
13	Fourth allocation of information systems (1/10, 8/10, 1/10)[b]	2	(22)		18	2	
14	Fourth allocation of plant maintenance (2/10, 3/10, 5/10)[a]	(2)	0		1	1	
15							
16	Total budgeted overhead of operating departments	$ 0	$ 0		$8,187,025	$5,565,125	$13,752,150
17							
18	Total support department amounts allocated and reallocated (the numbers in parentheses in the first two columns):						
19	Plant Maintenance: $6,300,000 + $271,215 + $5,424 + $109 + $2 = $6,576,750						
20	Information Systems: $2,712,150 + $54,243 + $1,085 + $22 = $2,767,500						
21							
22	[a] Base is (4,000 + 6,000 + 10,000), or 20,000 hours; 4,000 ÷ 20,000 = 2/10; 6,000 ÷ 20,000 = 3/10; 10,000 ÷ 20,000 = 5/10.						
23	[b] Base is (500 + 4,000 + 500), or 5,000 hours; 500 ÷ 5,000 = 1/10; 4,000 ÷ 5,000 = 8/10; 500 ÷ 5,000 = 1/10.						

because of the support it provides to plant maintenance. Accordingly, the $2,712,150 is allocated to all departments supported by the information systems department, including the plant maintenance department: plant maintenance, 10%; machining, 80%; and assembly, 10% (see Exhibit 2). The plant maintenance costs that had been brought down to $0 now have $271,215 from the information systems department allocation. In the next step, these costs are again reallocated to all other departments, including information systems, in the same ratio that the plant maintenance costs were previously assigned. Now the information systems department costs that had been brought down to $0 have $54,243 from the plant maintenance department allocations. These costs are again allocated in the same ratio that the information systems department costs were previously assigned. Successive rounds result in smaller and smaller amounts being allocated to and reallocated from the support departments until eventually all support-department costs are allocated to the operating departments. The final budgeted overhead costs for the operating departments under the reciprocal method are given by the amounts in line 16 of Exhibit 5.

An alternative way to implement the reciprocal method is to formulate and solve linear equations. This process requires three steps.

Step 1: **Express Support Department Costs and Reciprocal Relationships in the Form of Linear Equations.** We will use the term **complete reciprocated costs** or **artificial costs** to mean the support department's own costs plus any interdepartmental cost allocations. Let *PM* be the *complete reciprocated costs* of plant maintenance and *IS* be the *complete reciprocated costs* of information systems. We can then express the data in Exhibit 2 as follows:

$$PM = \$6,300,000 + 0.1IS \quad (1)$$
$$IS = \$1,452,150 + 0.2PM \quad (2)$$

The $0.1IS$ term in equation 1 is the percentage of the information systems services *used by* plant maintenance. The $0.2PM$ term in equation 2 is the percentage of plant maintenance services *used by* information systems.

Step 2: **Solve the Set of Linear Equations to Obtain the Complete Reciprocated Costs of Each Support Department.** Substituting equation 1 into 2,

$$IS = \$1,452,150 + [0.2(\$6,300,000 + 0.1IS)]$$
$$IS = \$1,452,150 + \$1,260,000 + 0.02IS$$
$$0.98IS = \$2,712,150$$
$$IS = \$2,767,500$$

Substituting this into equation 1,

$$PM = \$6,300,000 + 0.1(\$2,767,500)$$
$$PM = \$6,300,000 + \$276,750 = \$6,576,750$$

The complete reciprocated costs or artificial costs for plant maintenance and information systems are $6,576,750 and $2,767,500, respectively. Note that these are the same amounts that appear at the bottom of Exhibit 5 (lines 19 and 20) as the total support department costs allocated and reallocated during the iterative process. By setting up the system of simultaneous equations, we are able to solve for these amounts directly. When there are more than two support departments with reciprocal relationships, software such as Excel or Matlab is required to compute the complete reciprocated costs of each support department. Since the calculations involve finding the inverse of a matrix, the reciprocal method is also sometimes referred to as the **matrix method.**[6]

Step 3: **Allocate the Complete Reciprocated Costs of Each Support Department to All Other Departments (Both Support Departments and Operating Departments) on the Basis of the Usage Percentages (Based on Total Units of Service Provided to All Departments).**

---

[6] If there are *n* support-departments, then Step 1 will yield *n* linear equations. Solving the equations to calculate the complete reciprocated costs then requires finding the inverse of an *n*-by-*n* matrix.

Consider the information systems department. The complete reciprocated costs of $2,767,500 are allocated as follows:

To plant maintenance (1/10) $\times$ $2,767,500	=$ 276,750
To machining (8/10) $\times$ $2,767,500	= 2,214,000
To assembly (1/10) $\times$ $2,767,500	= 276,750
Total	$2,767,500

Exhibit 6 presents summary data pertaining to the reciprocal method.

Castleford's $9,344,250 complete reciprocated costs of the support departments exceed the budgeted amount of $7,752,150.

Support Department	Complete Reciprocated Costs	Budgeted Costs	Difference
Plant maintenance	$6,576,750	$6,300,000	$ 276,750
Information systems	2,767,500	1,452,150	1,315,350
Total	$9,344,250	$7,752,150	$1,592,100

Each support department's complete reciprocated cost is greater than the budgeted amount to take into account that the support costs will be allocated to all departments using its services and not just to operating departments. This step ensures that the reciprocal method fully recognizes all interrelationships among support departments, as well as relationships between support and operating departments. The difference between complete

Exhibit 6 Reciprocal Method of Allocating Support-Department Costs Using Linear Equations at Castleford Engineering for 2012

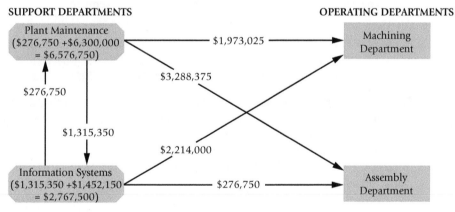

	A	B	C	D	E	F	G
1		SUPPORT DEPARTMENTS			OPERATING DEPARTMENTS		
2		Plant Maintenance	Information Systems		Machining	Assembly	Total
3	Budgeted overhead costs before any						
4	interdepartment cost allocations	$6,300,000	$1,452,150		$4,000,000	$2,000,000	$13,752,150
5	Allocation of plant maintenance (2/10, 3/10, 5/10)[a]	(6,576,750)	1,315,350		1,973,025	3,288,375	
6	Allocation of information systems (1/10, 8/10, 1/10)[b]	276,750	(2,767,500)		2,214,000	276,750	
7							
8	Total budgeted overhead of operating departments	$ 0	$ 0		$8,187,025	$5,565,125	$13,752,150
9							
10	[a] Base is (4,000 + 6,000 + 10,000), or 20,000 hours; 4,000 ÷ 20,000 = 2/10; 6,000 ÷ 20,000 = 3/10; 10,000 ÷ 20,000 = 5/10.						
11	[b] Base is (500 + 4,000 + 500), or 5,000 hours; 500 ÷ 5,000 = 1/10; 4,000 ÷ 5,000 = 8/10; 500 ÷ 5,000 = 1/10.						

reciprocated costs and budgeted costs for each support department reflects the costs allocated among support departments. The total costs allocated to the operating departments under the reciprocal method are still only $7,752,150.

Overview of Methods

Assume that Castleford reallocates the total budgeted overhead costs of each operating department in Exhibits 3 through 6 to individual products on the basis of budgeted machine-hours for the machining department (18,000 hours) and budgeted direct labor-hours for the assembly department (25,000 hours). The budgeted overhead allocation rates (to the nearest dollar) for each operating department by allocation method are as follows:

Support Department Cost-Allocation Method	Total Budgeted Overhead Costs After Allocation of All Support-Department Costs		Budgeted Overhead Rate per Hour for Product-Costing Purposes	
	Machining	Assembly	Machining (18,000 machine-hours)	Assembly (25,000 labor-hours)
Direct	$7,653,300	$6,098,850	$425	$244
Step-down	8,300,800	5,451,350	461	218
Reciprocal	8,187,025	5,565,125	455	223

These differences in budgeted overhead rates under the three support-department cost-allocation methods can, for example, affect the amount of costs Castleford is reimbursed for engines it manufactures under cost-reimbursement contracts. Consider a cost-reimbursement contract for a project that uses 200 machine-hours in the machining department and 50 direct labor-hours in the assembly department. The overhead costs allocated to this contract under the three methods would be as follows:

Direct:	$97,200 ($425 per hour × 200 hours + $244 per hour × 50 hours)
Step-down:	103,100 ($461 per hour × 200 hours + $218 per hour × 50 hours)
Reciprocal:	102,150 ($455 per hour × 200 hours + $223 per hour × 50 hours)

The amount of cost reimbursed to Castleford will differ depending on the method used to allocate support-department costs to the contract. Differences among the three methods' allocations increase (1) as the magnitude of the reciprocal allocations increases and (2) as the differences across operating departments' usage of each support department's services increase. Note that while the final allocations under the reciprocal method are in between those under the direct and step-down methods in our example, this is not true in general. To avoid disputes in cost-reimbursement contracts that require allocation of support-department costs, managers should always clarify the method to be used for allocation. For example, Medicare reimbursements and federal contracts with universities that pay for the recovery of indirect costs typically mandate use of the step-down method, with explicit requirements about the costs that can be included in the indirect cost pools.

The reciprocal method is conceptually the most precise method because it considers the mutual services provided among all support departments. The advantage of the direct and step-down methods is that they are simple to compute and understand relative to the reciprocal method. However, as computing power to perform repeated iterations (as in Exhibit 5) or to solve sets of simultaneous equations increases, more companies find the reciprocal method easier to implement.

Another advantage of the reciprocal method is that it highlights the complete reciprocated costs of support departments and how these costs differ from budgeted or actual costs of the departments. Knowing the complete reciprocated costs of a support department is a key input for decisions about whether to outsource all the services that the support department provides.

Suppose all of Castleford's support-department costs are variable over the period of a possible outsourcing contract. Consider a third party's bid to provide, say, all the information systems services currently provided by Castleford's information systems department. Do not compare the bid to the $1,452,150 costs reported for the information systems department. The complete reciprocated costs of the information systems department, which include the services the plant maintenance department provides the information systems department, are $2,767,500 to deliver 5,000 hours of computer time to all other departments at Castleford. The complete reciprocated costs for computer time are $553.50 per hour ($2,767,500 ÷ 5,000 hours). Other things being equal, a third party's bid to provide the same information services as Castleford's internal department at less than $2,767,500, or $553.50 per hour (even if much greater than $1,452,150) would improve Castleford's operating income.

To see this point, note that the relevant savings from shutting down the information systems department are $1,452,150 of information systems department costs *plus* $1,315,350 of plant maintenance department costs. By closing down the information systems department, Castleford will no longer incur the 20% of reciprocated plant maintenance department costs (equal to $1,315,350) that were incurred to support the information systems department. Therefore, the total cost savings are $2,767,500 ($1,452,150 + $1,315,350).[7] Neither the direct nor the step-down methods can provide this relevant information for outsourcing decisions.

We now consider common costs, another special class of costs for which management accountants have developed specific allocation methods.

Decision Point

What methods can managers use to allocate costs of multiple support departments to operating departments?

Allocating Common Costs

A **common cost** is a cost of operating a facility, activity, or like cost object that is shared by two or more users. Common costs exist because each user obtains a lower cost by sharing than the separate cost that would result if such a user were an independent entity.

The goal is to allocate common costs to each user in a reasonable way. Consider Jason Stevens, a graduating senior in Seattle who has been invited to a job interview with an employer in Albany. The round-trip Seattle–Albany airfare costs $1,200. A week later, Stevens is also invited to an interview with an employer in Chicago. The Seattle–Chicago round-trip airfare costs $800. Stevens decides to combine the two recruiting trips into a Seattle–Albany–Chicago–Seattle trip that will cost $1,500 in airfare. The $1,500 is a common cost that benefits both prospective employers. Two methods of allocating this common cost between the two prospective employers are the stand-alone method and the incremental method.

Learning Objective 4

Allocate common costs using the stand-alone method

. . . uses cost information of each user as a separate entity to allocate common costs

and the incremental method

. . . allocates common costs primarily to one user and the remainder to other users

Stand-Alone Cost-Allocation Method

The **stand-alone cost-allocation method** determines the weights for cost allocation by considering each user of the cost as a separate entity. For the common-cost airfare of $1,500, information about the separate (stand-alone) round-trip airfares ($1,200 and $800) is used to determine the allocation weights:

$$\text{Albany employer:} \quad \frac{\$1,200}{\$1,200 + \$800} \times \$1,500 = 0.60 \times \$1,500 = \$900$$

$$\text{Chicago employer:} \quad \frac{\$800}{\$800 + \$1,200} \times \$1,500 = 0.40 \times \$1,500 = \$600$$

Advocates of this method often emphasize the fairness or equity criterion described in Exhibit 2. The method is viewed as reasonable because each employer bears a proportionate share of total costs in relation to the individual stand-alone costs.

Incremental Cost-Allocation Method

The **incremental cost-allocation method** ranks the individual users of a cost object in the order of users most responsible for the common cost and then uses this ranking to allocate cost among those users. The first-ranked user of the cost object is the *primary user* (also called the *primary party*) and is allocated costs up to the costs of the primary user as a stand-alone user. The second-ranked user is the *first-incremental user* (*first-incremental party*) and

---

[7] Technical issues when using the reciprocal method in outsourcing decisions are discussed in R. S. Kaplan and A. A. Atkinson, *Advanced Management Accounting*, 3rd ed. (Upper Saddle River, NJ: Prentice Hall, 1998), 73–81.

is allocated the additional cost that arises from two users instead of only the primary user. The third-ranked user is the *second-incremental user* (*second-incremental party*) and is allocated the additional cost that arises from three users instead of two users, and so on.

To see how this method works, consider again Jason Stevens and his $1,500 airfare cost. Assume the Albany employer is viewed as the primary party. Stevens' rationale is that he had already committed to go to Albany before accepting the invitation to interview in Chicago. The cost allocations would be as follows:

Party	Costs Allocated	Cumulative Costs Allocated
Albany (primary)	$1,200	$1,200
Chicago (incremental)	300 ($1,500 – $1,200)	$1,500
Total	$1,500	

The Albany employer is allocated the full Seattle–Albany airfare. The unallocated part of the total airfare is then allocated to the Chicago employer. If the Chicago employer had been chosen as the primary party, the cost allocations would have been Chicago $800 (the stand-alone round-trip Seattle–Chicago airfare) and Albany $700 ($1,500 – $800). When there are more than two parties, this method requires them to be ranked from first to last (such as by the date on which each employer invited the candidate to interview).

Under the incremental method, the primary party typically receives the highest allocation of the common costs. If the incremental users are newly formed companies or subunits, such as a new product line or a new sales territory, the incremental method may enhance their chances for short-run survival by assigning them a low allocation of the common costs. The difficulty with the method is that, particularly if a large common cost is involved, every user would prefer to be viewed as the incremental party!

One approach to sidestep disputes in such situations is to use the stand-alone cost-allocation method. Another approach is to use the *Shapley value*, which considers each party as first the primary party and then the incremental party. From the calculations shown earlier, the Albany employer is allocated $1,200 as the primary party and $700 as the incremental party, for an average of $950 [($1,200 + $700) ÷ 2]. The Chicago employer is allocated $800 as the primary party and $300 as the incremental party, for an average of $550 [($800 + 300) ÷ 2]. The Shapley value method allocates, to each employer, the average of the costs allocated as the primary party and as the incremental party: $950 to the Albany employer and $550 to the Chicago employer.[8]

As our discussion suggests, allocating common costs is not clear-cut and can generate disputes. Whenever feasible, the rules for such allocations should be agreed on in advance. If this is not done, then, rather than blindly follow one method or another, managers should exercise judgment when allocating common costs. For instance, Stevens must choose an allocation method for his airfare cost that is acceptable to each prospective employer. He cannot, for example, exceed the maximum reimbursable amount of airfare for either firm. The next section discusses the role of cost data in various types of contracts, another area where disputes about cost allocation frequently arise.

Decision Point ▶

What methods can managers use to allocate common costs to two or more users?

Learning Objective 5

Explain the importance of explicit agreement between contracting parties when the reimbursement amount is based on costs incurred

. . . to avoid disputes regarding allowable cost items and how indirect costs should be allocated

Cost Allocations and Contract Disputes

Many commercial contracts include clauses based on cost accounting information. Examples include the following:

- A contract between the Department of Defense and a company designing and assembling a new fighter plane specifies that the price paid for the plane is to be based on the contractor's direct and overhead costs plus a fixed fee.

- A contract between an energy-consulting firm and a hospital specifies that the consulting firm receive a fixed fee plus a share of the energy-cost savings that arise from implementing the consulting firm's recommendations.

---

[8] For further discussion of the Shapley value, see J. Demski, "Cost Allocation Games," in *Joint Cost Allocations*, ed. S. Moriarity (University of Oklahoma Center for Economic and Management Research, 1981); L. Kruz and P. Bronisz, "Cooperative Game Solution Concepts to a Cost Allocation Problem," *European Journal of Operations Research* 122 (2000): 258–271.

Contract disputes often arise with respect to cost allocation. The areas of dispute between the contracting parties can be reduced by making the "rules of the game" explicit and in writing at the time the contract is signed. Such rules of the game include the definition of allowable cost items; the definitions of terms used, such as what constitutes direct labor; the permissible cost-allocation bases; and how to account for differences between budgeted and actual costs.

Contracting with the U.S. Government

The U.S. government reimburses most contractors in one of two main ways:

1. **The contractor is paid a set price without analysis of actual contract cost data.** This approach is used, for example, when there is competitive bidding, when there is adequate price competition, or when there is an established catalog with prices quoted for items sold in substantial quantities to the general public.

2. **The contractor is paid after analysis of actual contract cost data.** In some cases, the contract will explicitly state that the reimbursement amount is based on actual allowable costs plus a fixed fee.[9] This arrangement is called a *cost-plus contract*.

All contracts with U.S. government agencies must comply with cost accounting standards issued by the **Cost Accounting Standards Board (CASB).** For government contracts, the CASB has the exclusive authority to make, put into effect, amend, and rescind cost accounting standards and interpretations. The standards are designed to achieve *uniformity and consistency* in regard to measurement, assignment, and allocation of costs to government contracts within the United States.[10]

In government contracting, there is a complex interplay of political considerations and accounting principles. Terms such as "fairness" and "equity," as well as cause and effect and benefits received, are often used in government contracts.

Fairness of Pricing

In many defense contracts, there is great uncertainty about the final cost to produce a new weapon or equipment. Such contracts are rarely subject to competitive bidding. The reason is that no contractor is willing to assume all the risk of receiving a fixed price for the contract and subsequently incurring high costs to fulfill it. Hence, setting a market-based fixed price for the contract fails to attract contractors, or requires a contract price that is too high from the government's standpoint. To address this issue, the government typically assumes a major share of the risk of the potentially high costs of completing the contract. Rather than relying on selling prices as ordinarily set by suppliers in the marketplace, the government negotiates contracts on the basis of *costs plus a fixed fee*. In costs-plus-fixed-fee contracts, which often involve billions of dollars, the allocation of a specific cost may be difficult to defend on the basis of any cause-and-effect reasoning. Nonetheless, the contracting parties may still view it as a "reasonable" or "fair" means to help establish a contract amount.

Some costs are "allowable;" others are "unallowable." An **allowable cost** is a cost that the contract parties agree to include in the costs to be reimbursed. Some contracts specify how allowable costs are to be determined. For example, only economy-class airfares are allowable in many U.S. government contracts. Other contracts identify cost categories that are unallowable. For example, the costs of lobbying activities and alcoholic beverages are not allowable costs in U.S. government contracts. However, the set of allowable costs is not always clear-cut. Contract disputes and allegations about overcharging the government arise from time to time (see Concepts in Action).

Decision Point

How can contract disputes over reimbursement amounts based on costs be reduced?

---

[9] The Federal Acquisition Regulation (FAR), issued in March 2005 (see https://www.acquisition.gov/far/current/pdf/FAR.pdf) includes the following definition of "allocability" (in FAR 31.201-4): "A cost is allocable if it is assignable or chargeable to one or more cost objectives on the basis of relative benefits received or other equitable relationship. Subject to the foregoing, a cost is allocable to a Government contract if it:
  (a) Is incurred specifically for the contract;
  (b) Benefits both the contract and other work, and can be distributed to them in reasonable proportion to the benefits received; or
  (c) Is necessary to the overall operation of the business, although a direct relationship to any particular cost objective cannot be shown."

[10] Details on the Cost Accounting Standards Board are available at www.whitehouse.gov/omb/procurement/casb.html. The CASB is part of the Office of Federal Procurement Policy, U.S. Office of Management and Budget.

Contract Disputes over Reimbursable Costs for the U.S. Department of Defense

Erik S. Lesser\AP Wide World Photos

For 2011, United States combat activities in Afghanistan are budgeted to cost $159 billion. As in prior years, a portion of this money is allocated to private companies to carry out specific contracted services for the U.S. Department of Defense. In recent years, the U.S. government has pursued cases against several contractors for overcharging for services provided in the combat zone. The following four examples are from cases pursued by the U.S. Department of Justice's Civil Division, who did so on behalf of the federal government. These recent examples illustrate several types of cost disputes that arise in practice.

1. Eagle Global Logistics agreed to pay $4 million to settle allegations of allegedly inflating invoices for military cargo shipments to Iraq. The complaint alleged that a company executive added an extra 50 cents per kilogram "war risk surcharge" to invoices for flights between Dubai and Iraq. This bogus surcharge, which was not part of Eagle's U.S. Department of Defense contract, was applied 379 times between 2003 and 2004.

2. In another shipping case, APL Limited paid the federal government $26.3 million to resolve claims of knowingly overcharging and double-billing the U.S. Department of Defense to transport thousands of containers to destinations in Afghanistan and Iraq. APL was accused of inflating invoices in several ways: marking up electricity costs for containers with perishable cargo, billing in excess of the contractual rate to maintain the operation of refrigerated containers in the port of Karachi, Pakistan, and billing for non-reimbursable services performed by an APL subcontractor at a Kuwaiti port.

3. L-3 communications, a leading defense contractor, paid $4 million to settle a complaint that it overbilled for hours worked by the firm's employees on a contract supporting military operations by the United States in Iraq. The company allegedly submitted false time records and inflated claims for personnel hours as part of an ongoing contract with the U.S. Army to provide helicopter maintenance services at Camp Taji, Iraq.

4. In late 2009, Public Warehousing Company—a principal food supplier for the U.S. military in Iraq, Kuwait, and Jordan since 2003—was sued by the U.S. government for presenting false claims for payment under the company's multibillion dollar contract with the Defense Logistics Agency. The complaint alleged that the company overcharged the U.S. for locally available fresh fruits and vegetables and failed to disclose pass through rebates and discounts it obtained from U.S.-based suppliers, as required by its contracts.

Source: Press releases from the United States Department of Justice, Civil Division (2006–2009).

Bundled Products and Revenue Allocation Methods

Learning Objective 6

Understand how bundling of products

. . . two or more products sold for a single-price

gives rise to revenue allocation issues

. . . allocating revenues to each product in the bundle to evaluate managers of individual products

and the methods for doing so

. . . using the stand-alone method or the incremental method

Allocation issues can also arise when revenues from multiple products (for example, different software programs or cable and internet packages) are bundled together and sold at a single price. The methods for revenue allocation parallel those described for common-cost allocations.

Bundling and Revenue Allocation

Revenues are inflows of assets (almost always cash or accounts receivable) received for products or services provided to customers. Similar to cost allocation, **revenue allocation** occurs when revenues are related to a particular *revenue object* but cannot be traced to it in an economically feasible (cost-effective) way. A **revenue object** is anything for which a separate measurement of revenue is desired. Examples of revenue objects include products, customers, and divisions. We illustrate revenue-allocation issues for Dynamic Software Corporation, which develops, sells, and supports three software programs:

1. WordMaster, a word-processing program, released 36 months ago
2. DataMaster, a spreadsheet program, released 18 months ago
3. FinanceMaster, a budgeting and cash-management program, released six months ago with a lot of favorable media attention

Dynamic Software sells these three products individually as well as together as bundled products.

A **bundled product** is a package of two or more products (or services) that is sold for a single price but whose individual components may be sold as separate items at their own "stand-alone" prices. The price of a bundled product is typically less than the sum of the prices of the individual products sold separately. For example, banks often provide individual customers with a bundle of services from different departments (checking, safety-deposit box, and investment advisory) for a single fee. A resort hotel may offer, for a single amount per customer, a weekend package that includes services from its lodging (the room), food (the restaurant), and recreational (golf and tennis) departments. When department managers have revenue or profit responsibilities for individual products, the bundled revenue must be allocated among the individual products in the bundle.

Dynamic Software allocates revenues from its bundled product sales (called "suite sales") to individual products. Individual-product profitability is used to compensate software engineers, outside developers, and product managers responsible for developing and managing each product.

How should Dynamic Software allocate suite revenues to individual products? Consider information pertaining to the three "stand-alone" and "suite" products in 2012:

	Selling Price	Manufacturing Cost per Unit
Stand-alone		
WordMaster	$125	$18
DataMaster	150	20
FinanceMaster	225	25
Suite		
Word + Data	$220	
Word + Finance	280	
Finance + Data	305	
Word + Finance + Data	380	

Just as we saw in the section on common-cost allocations, the two main revenue-allocation methods are the stand-alone method and the incremental method.

Stand-Alone Revenue-Allocation Method

The **stand-alone revenue-allocation method** uses product-specific information on the products in the bundle as weights for allocating the bundled revenues to the individual products. The term *stand-alone* refers to the product as a separate (nonsuite) item. Consider the Word + Finance suite, which sells for $280. Three types of weights for the stand-alone method are as follows:

1. **Selling prices.** Using the individual selling prices of $125 for WordMaster and $225 for FinanceMaster, the weights for allocating the $280 suite revenues between the products are as follows:

$$\text{WordMaster:} \quad \frac{\$125}{\$125 + \$225} \times \$280 = 0.357 \times \$280 = \$100$$

$$\text{FinanceMaster:} \quad \frac{\$225}{\$125 + \$225} \times \$280 = 0.643 \times \$280 = \$180$$

2. **Unit costs.** This method uses the costs of the individual products (in this case, manufacturing cost per unit) to determine the weights for the revenue allocations.

$$\text{WordMaster:} \quad \frac{\$18}{\$18 + \$25} \times \$280 = 0.419 \times \$280 = \$117$$

$$\text{FinanceMaster:} \quad \frac{\$25}{\$18 + \$25} \times \$280 = 0.581 \times \$280 = \$163$$

3. **Physical units.** This method gives each product unit in the suite the same weight when allocating suite revenue to individual products. Therefore, with two products in the Word + Finance suite, each product is allocated 50% of the suite revenues.

$$\text{WordMaster: } \frac{1}{1+1} \times \$280 = 0.50 \times \$280 = \$140$$

$$\text{FinanceMaster: } \frac{1}{1+1} \times \$280 = 0.50 \times \$280 = \$140$$

These three approaches to determining weights for the stand-alone method result in very different revenue allocations to the individual products:

Revenue-Allocation Weights	WordMaster	FinanceMaster
Selling prices	$100	$180
Unit costs	117	163
Physical units	140	140

Which method is preferred? The selling prices method is best, because the weights explicitly consider the prices customers are willing to pay for the individual products. Weighting approaches that use revenue information better capture "benefits received" by customers than unit costs or physical units.[11] The physical-units revenue-allocation method is used when any of the other methods cannot be used (such as when selling prices are unstable or unit costs are difficult to calculate for individual products).

Incremental Revenue-Allocation Method

The **incremental revenue-allocation method** ranks individual products in a bundle according to criteria determined by management—such as the product in the bundle with the most sales—and then uses this ranking to allocate bundled revenues to individual products. The first-ranked product is the *primary product* in the bundle. The second-ranked product is the *first-incremental product*, the third-ranked product is the *second-incremental product*, and so on.

How do companies decide on product rankings under the incremental revenue-allocation method? Some organizations survey customers about the importance of each of the individual products to their purchase decision. Others use data on the recent stand-alone sales performance of the individual products in the bundle. A third approach is for top managers to use their knowledge or intuition to decide the rankings.

Consider again the Word + Finance suite. Assume WordMaster is designated as the primary product. If the suite selling price exceeds the stand-alone price of the primary product, the primary product is allocated 100% of its *stand-alone* revenue. Because the suite price of $280 exceeds the stand-alone price of $125 for WordMaster, WordMaster is allocated revenues of $125, with the remaining revenue of $155 ($280 – $125) allocated to FinanceMaster:

Product	Revenue Allocated	Cumulative Revenue Allocated
WordMaster	$125	$125
FinanceMaster	155 ($280 – $125)	$280
Total	$280	

If the suite price is less than or equal to the stand-alone price of the primary product, the primary product is allocated 100% of the *suite* revenue. All other products in the suite receive no allocation of revenue.

---

[11] Revenue-allocation issues also arise in external reporting. The AICPA's Statement of Position 97-2 (Software Revenue Recognition) states that with bundled products, revenue allocation "based on vendor-specific objective evidence (VSOE) of fair value" is required. The "price charged when the element is sold separately" is said to be "objective evidence of fair value" (see "Statement of Position 97-2," Jersey City, NJ: AICPA, 1998). In September 2009, the FASB ratified Emerging Issues Task Force (EITF) Issue 08-1, specifying that with no VSOE or third-party evidence of selling price for all units of accounting in an arrangement, the consideration received for the arrangement should be allocated to the separate units based upon their relative selling prices.

Now suppose FinanceMaster is designated as the primary product and WordMaster as the first-incremental product. Then, the incremental revenue-allocation method allocates revenues of the Word + Finance suite as follows:

Product	Revenue Allocated	Cumulative Revenue Allocated
FinanceMaster	$225	$225
WordMaster	55 ($280 – $225)	$280
Total	$280	

If Dynamic Software sells equal quantities of WordMaster and FinanceMaster, then the Shapley value method allocates to each product the average of the revenues allocated as the primary and first-incremental products:

WordMaster: ($125 + $ 55) ÷ 2 = $180 ÷ 2 = $ 90
FinanceMaster: ($225 + $155) ÷ 2 = $380 ÷ 2 = 190
Total $280

But what if, in the most recent quarter, the firm sells 80,000 units of WordMaster and 20,000 units of FinanceMaster. Because Dynamic Software sells four times as many units of WordMaster, its managers believe that the sales of the Word + Finance suite are four times more likely to be driven by WordMaster as the primary product. The *weighted Shapley value method* takes this fact into account. It assigns four times as much weight to the revenue allocations when WordMaster is the primary product as when FinanceMaster is the primary product, resulting in the following allocations:

WordMaster: ($125 × 4 + $ 55 × 1) ÷ (4 + 1) = $555 ÷ 5 = $111
FinanceMaster: ($225 × 1 + $155 × 4) ÷ (4 + 1) = $845 ÷ 5 = 169
Total $280

When there are more than two products in the suite, the incremental revenue-allocation method allocates suite revenues sequentially. Assume WordMaster is the primary product in Dynamic Software's three-product suite (Word + Finance + Data). FinanceMaster is the first-incremental product, and DataMaster is the second-incremental product. This suite sells for $380. The allocation of the $380 suite revenues proceeds as follows:

Product	Revenue Allocated	Cumulative Revenue Allocated
WordMaster	$125	$125
FinanceMaster	155 ($280 – $125)	$280 (price of Word + Finance suite)
DataMaster	100 ($380 – $280)	$380 (price of Word + Finance + Data suite)
Total	$380	

Now suppose WordMaster is the primary product, DataMaster is the first-incremental product, and FinanceMaster is the second-incremental product.

Product	Revenue Allocated	Cumulative Revenue Allocated
WordMaster	$125	$125
DataMaster	95 ($220 – $125)	$220 (price of Word + Data suite)
FinanceMaster	160 ($380 – $220)	$380 (price of Word + Data + Finance suite)
Total	$380	

The ranking of the individual products in the suite determines the revenues allocated to them. Product managers at Dynamic Software likely would differ on how they believe their individual products contribute to sales of the suite products. In fact, each product manager would claim to be responsible for the primary product in the Word + Finance + Data suite![12]

Decision Point

What is product bundling and how can managers allocate revenues of a bundled product to individual products in the package?

---

[12]Calculating the Shapley value mitigates this problem because each product is considered as a primary, first-incremental, and second-incremental product. Assuming equal weights on all products, the revenue allocated to each product is an average of the revenues calculated for the product under these different assumptions. In the preceding example, the interested reader can verify that this will result in the following revenue assignments: FinanceMaster, $180; WordMaster, $87.50; and DataMaster, $112.50.

Because the stand-alone revenue-allocation method does not require rankings of individual products in the suite, this method is less likely to cause debates among product managers.

Problem for Self-Study

This problem illustrates how costs of two corporate support departments are allocated to operating divisions using the dual-rate method. Fixed costs are allocated using budgeted costs and budgeted hours used by other departments. Variable costs are allocated using actual costs and actual hours used by other departments.

Computer Horizons budgets the following amounts for its two central corporate support departments (legal and personnel) in supporting each other and the two manufacturing divisions, the laptop division (LTD) and the work station division (WSD):

	A	B	C	D	E	F	G
		SUPPORT			OPERATING		
		Legal Department	Personnel Department		LTD	WSD	Total
3	**BUDGETED USAGE**						
4	Legal (hours)	—	250		1,500	750	2,500
5	(Percentages)	—	10%		60%	30%	100%
6	Personnel (hours)	2,500	—		22,500	25,000	50,000
7	(Percentages)	5%	—		45%	50%	100%
8							
9	**ACTUAL USAGE**						
10	Legal (hours)	—	400		400	1,200	2,000
11	(Percentages)	—	20%		20%	60%	100%
12	Personnel (hours)	2,000	—		26,600	11,400	40,000
13	(Percentages)	5%	—		66.50%	28.5%	100%
14	Budgeted fixed overhead costs before any						
15	interdepartment cost allocations	$360,000	$475,000		—	—	$835,000
16	Actual variable overhead costs before any						
17	interdepartment cost allocations	$200,000	$600,000		—	—	$800,000

Required What amount of support-department costs for legal and personnel will be allocated to LTD and WSD using (a) the direct method, (b) the step-down method (allocating the legal department costs first), and (c) the reciprocal method using linear equations?

Solution

Exhibit 7 presents the computations for allocating the fixed and variable support-department costs. A summary of these costs follows:

	Laptop Division (LTD)	Work Station Division (WSD)
(a) Direct Method		
Fixed costs	$465,000	$370,000
Variable costs	470,000	330,000
	$935,000	$700,000
(b) Step-Down Method		
Fixed costs	$458,053	$376,947
Variable costs	488,000	312,000
	$946,053	$688,947
(c) Reciprocal Method		
Fixed costs	$462,513	$372,487
Variable costs	476,364	323,636
	$938,877	$696,123

Exhibit 7 Alternative Methods of Allocating Corporate Support-Department Costs to Operating Divisions of Computer Horizons: Dual-Rate Method

| | Home | Insert | Page Layout | Formulas | Data | Review | View | | | | |

	A	B	C	D	E	F	G
		CORPORATE SUPPORT DEPARTMENTS			OPERATING DIVISIONS		
20							
21	**Allocation Method**	**Legal Department**	**Personnel Department**		**LTD**	**WSD**	**Total**
22	**A. DIRECT METHOD**						
23	Fixed costs	$360,000	$475,000				
24	Legal (1,500 ÷ 2,250; 750 ÷ 2,250)	(360,000)			$240,000	$120,000	
25	Personnel (22,500 ÷ 47,500; 25,000 ÷ 47,500)		(475,000)		225,000	250,000	
26	Fixed support dept. cost allocated to operating divisions	$ 0	0		$465,000	$370,000	$835,000
27	Variable costs	$200,000	$600,000				
28	Legal (400 ÷ 1,600; 1,200 ÷ 1,600)	(200,000)			$ 50,000	$150,000	
29	Personnel (26,600 ÷ 38,000; 11,400 ÷ 38,000)		(600,000)		420,000	180,000	
30	Variable support dept. cost allocated to operating divisions	$ 0	0		$470,000	$330,000	$800,000
31	**B. STEP-DOWN METHOD**						
32	(Legal department first)						
33	Fixed costs	$360,000	$475,000				
34	Legal (250 ÷ 2,500; 1,500 ÷ 2,500; 750 ÷ 2,500)	(360,000)	36,000		$216,000	$108,000	
35	Personnel (22,500 ÷ 47,500; 25,000 ÷ 47,500)		(511,000)		242,053	268,947	
36	Fixed support dept. cost allocated to operating divisions	$ 0	0		$458,053	$376,947	$835,000
37	Variable costs	$200,000	$600,000				
38	Legal (400 ÷ 2,000; 400 ÷ 2,000; 1,200 ÷ 2,000)	(200,000)	40,000		$ 40,000	$120,000	
39	Personnel (26,600 ÷ 38,000; 11,400 ÷ 38,000)		(640,000)		448,000	192,000	
40	Variable support dept. cost allocated to operating divisions	$ 0	0		$488,000	$312,000	$800,000
41	**C. RECIPROCAL METHOD**						
42	Fixed costs	$360,000	$475,000				
43	Legal (250 ÷ 2,500; 1,500 ÷ 2,500; 750 ÷ 2,500)	(385,678)[a]	38,568		$231,407	$115,703	
44	Personnel (2,500 ÷ 50,000; 22,500 ÷ 50,000; 25,000 ÷ 50,000)	25,678	(513,568)[a]		231,106	256,784	
45	Fixed support dept. cost allocated to operating divisions	$ 0	$ 0		$462,513	$372,487	$835,000
46	Variable costs	$200,000	$600,000				
47	Legal (400 ÷ 2,000; 400 ÷ 2,000; 1,200 ÷ 2,000)	(232,323)[b]	46,465		$ 46,465	$139,393	
48	Personnel (2,000 ÷ 40,000; 26,600 ÷ 40,000; 11,400 ÷ 40,000)	32,323	(646,465)[b]		429,899	184,243	
49	Variable support dept. cost allocated to operating divisions	$ 0	$ 0		$476,364	$323,636	$800,000
50							
51	[a] FIXED COSTS	[b] VARIABLE COSTS					
52	Letting LF = Legal department fixed costs, and PF = Personnel department fixed costs, the simultaneous equations for the reciprocal method for fixed costs are	Letting LF = Legal department variable costs, and PV = Personnel department variable costs, the simultaneous equations for the reciprocal method for variable costs are					
53	$LF = \$360,000 + 0.05\ PF$	$LV = \$200,000 + 0.05\ PV$					
54	$PF = \$475,000 + 0.10\ LF$	$PV = \$600,000 + 0.20\ LV$					
55	$LF = \$360,000 + 0.05\ (\$475,000 + 0.10\ LF)$	$LV = \$200,000 + 0.05\ (\$600,000 + 0.20\ LV)$					
56	$LF = \$385,678$	$LV = \$232,323$					
57	$PF = \$475,000 + 0.10\ (\$385,678) = \$513,568$	$PV = \$600,000 + 0.20\ (\$232,323) = \$646,465$					

Decision Points

The following question-and-answer format summarizes the chapter's learning objectives. Each decision presents a key question related to a learning objective. The guidelines are the answer to that question.

Decision	Guidelines
1. When should managers use the dual-rate method over the single-rate method?	The single-rate method aggregates fixed and variable costs and allocates them to objects using a single allocation base and rate. Under the dual-rate method, costs are grouped into separate variable cost and fixed cost pools; each pool uses a different cost-allocation base and rate. If costs can be easily separated into variable and fixed costs, the dual-rate method should be used because it provides better information for making decisions.
2. What factors should managers consider when deciding between allocation based on budgeted and actual rates, and budgeted and actual usage?	The use of budgeted rates enables managers of user departments to have certainty about the costs allocated to them, and insulates users from inefficiencies in the supplier department. Charging budgeted variable cost rates to users based on actual usage is causally appropriate and promotes control of resource consumption. Charging fixed cost rates on the basis of budgeted usage helps user divisions with planning, and leads to goal congruence when considering outsourcing decisions.
3. What methods can managers use to allocate costs of multiple support departments to operating departments?	The three methods managers can use are the direct, the step-down, and the reciprocal methods. The direct method allocates each support department's costs to operating departments without allocating a support department's costs to other support departments. The step-down method allocates support-department costs to other support departments and to operating departments in a sequential manner that partially recognizes the mutual services provided among all support departments. The reciprocal method fully recognizes mutual services provided among all support departments.
4. What methods can managers use to allocate common costs to two or more users?	Common costs are the costs of a cost object (such as operating a facility or performing an activity) that are shared by two or more users. The stand-alone cost-allocation method uses information pertaining to each user of the cost object to determine cost-allocation weights. The incremental cost-allocation method ranks individual users of the cost object and allocates common costs first to the primary user and then to the other incremental users. The Shapley value method considers each user, in turn, as the primary and the incremental user.
5. How can contract disputes over reimbursement amounts based on costs be reduced?	Disputes can be reduced by making the cost-allocation rules as explicit as possible and in writing at the time the contract is signed. These rules should include details such as the allowable cost items, the acceptable cost-allocation bases, and how differences between budgeted and actual costs are to be accounted for.
6. What is product bundling and how can managers allocate revenues of a bundled product to individual products in the package?	Bundling occurs when a package of two or more products (or services) is sold for a single price. Revenue allocation of the bundled price is required when managers of the individual products in the bundle are evaluated on product revenue or product operating income. Revenues can be allocated for a bundled product using the stand-alone method, the incremental method, or the Shapley value method.

Terms to Learn

This chapter contains definitions of the following important terms:

allowable cost

artificial costs

bundled product

common cost

complete reciprocated costs

Cost Accounting Standards Board (CASB)

direct method

dual-rate method	production department	stand-alone cost-allocation method
incremental cost-allocation method	reciprocal method	stand-alone revenue-allocation
incremental revenue-allocation	revenue allocation	method
method	revenue object	step-down method
matrix method	service department	support department
operating department	single-rate method	
	sequential allocation method	

Assignment Material

Questions

15-1 Distinguish between the single-rate and the dual-rate methods.

15-2 Describe how the dual-rate method is useful to division managers in decision making.

15-3 How do budgeted cost rates motivate the support-department manager to improve efficiency?

15-4 Give examples of allocation bases used to allocate support-department cost pools to operating departments.

15-5 Why might a manager prefer that budgeted rather than actual cost-allocation rates be used for costs being allocated to his or her department from another department?

15-6 "To ensure unbiased cost allocations, fixed costs should be allocated on the basis of estimated long-run use by user-department managers." Do you agree? Why?

15-7 Distinguish among the three methods of allocating the costs of support departments to operating departments.

15-8 What is conceptually the most defensible method for allocating support-department costs? Why?

15-9 Distinguish between two methods of allocating common costs.

15-10 What role does the Cost Accounting Standards Board play when companies contract with the U.S. government?

15-11 What is one key way to reduce cost-allocation disputes that arise with government contracts?

15-12 Describe how companies are increasingly facing revenue-allocation decisions.

15-13 Distinguish between the stand-alone and the incremental revenue-allocation methods.

15-14 Identify and discuss arguments that individual product managers may put forward to support their preferred revenue-allocation method.

15-15 How might a dispute over the allocation of revenues of a bundled product be resolved?

Exercises

15-16 **Single-rate versus dual-rate methods, support department.** The Chicago power plant that services all manufacturing departments of MidWest Engineering has a budget for the coming year. This budget has been expressed in the following monthly terms:

Manufacturing Department	Needed at Practical Capacity Production Level (Kilowatt-Hours)	Average Expected Monthly Usage (Kilowatt-Hours)
Rockford	10,000	8,000
Peoria	20,000	9,000
Hammond	12,000	7,000
Kankakee	8,000	6,000
Total	50,000	30,000

The expected monthly costs for operating the power plant during the budget year are $15,000: $6,000 variable and $9,000 fixed.

Required

1. Assume that a single cost pool is used for the power plant costs. What budgeted amounts will be allocated to each manufacturing department if (a) the rate is calculated based on practical capacity and costs are allocated based on practical capacity, and (b) the rate is calculated based on expected monthly usage and costs are allocated based on expected monthly usage?

2. Assume the dual-rate method is used with separate cost pools for the variable and fixed costs. Variable costs are allocated on the basis of expected monthly usage. Fixed costs are allocated on the basis of practical capacity. What budgeted amounts will be allocated to each manufacturing department? Why might you prefer the dual-rate method?

15-17 Single-rate method, budgeted versus actual costs and quantities. Chocolat Inc. is a producer of premium chocolate based in Palo Alto. The company has a separate division for each of its two products: dark chocolate and milk chocolate. Chocolat purchases ingredients from Wisconsin for its dark chocolate division and from Louisiana for its milk chocolate division. Both locations are the same distance from Chocolat's Palo Alto plant.

Chocolat Inc. operates a fleet of trucks as a cost center that charges the divisions for variable costs (drivers and fuel) and fixed costs (vehicle depreciation, insurance, and registration fees) of operating the fleet. Each division is evaluated on the basis of its operating income. For 2012, the trucking fleet had a practical capacity of 50 round-trips between the Palo Alto plant and the two suppliers. It recorded the following information:

	A	B	C
		Budgeted	Actual
1			
2	Costs of truck fleet	$115,000	$96,750
3	Number of round-trips for dark chocolate division (Palo Alto plant—Wisconsin)	30	30
4	Number of round-trips for milk chocolate division (Palo Alto plant—Louisiana)	20	15

Required

1. Using the single-rate method, allocate costs to the dark chocolate division and the milk chocolate division in these three ways.
   a. Calculate the budgeted rate per round-trip and allocate costs based on round-trips budgeted for each division.
   b. Calculate the budgeted rate per round-trip and allocate costs based on actual round-trips used by each division.
   c. Calculate the actual rate per round-trip and allocate costs based on actual round-trips used by each division.
2. Describe the advantages and disadvantages of using each of the three methods in requirement 1. Would you encourage Chocolat Inc. to use one of these methods? Explain and indicate any assumptions you made.

15-18 Dual-rate method, budgeted versus actual costs and quantities (continuation of 15-17). Chocolat Inc. decides to examine the effect of using the dual-rate method for allocating truck costs to each round-trip. At the start of 2012, the budgeted costs were as follows:

Variable cost per round-trip	$ 1,350
Fixed costs	$47,500

The actual results for the 45 round-trips made in 2012 were as follows:

Variable costs	$58,500
Fixed costs	38,250
	$96,750

Assume all other information to be the same as in Exercise 15-17.

Required

1. Using the dual-rate method, what are the costs allocated to the dark chocolate division and the milk chocolate division when (a) variable costs are allocated using the budgeted rate per round-trip and actual round-trips used by each division and when (b) fixed costs are allocated based on the budgeted rate per round-trip and round-trips budgeted for each division?
2. From the viewpoint of the dark chocolate division, what are the effects of using the dual-rate method rather than the single-rate methods?

15-19 Support-department cost allocation; direct and step-down methods. Phoenix Partners provides management consulting services to government and corporate clients. Phoenix has two support departments—administrative services (AS) and information systems (IS)—and two operating departments—government consulting (GOVT) and corporate consulting (CORP). For the first quarter of 2012, Phoenix's cost records indicate the following:

A	B	C	D	E	F	G
1		SUPPORT		OPERATING		
2		AS	IS	GOVT	CORP	Total
3 Budgeted overhead costs before any						
4 interdepartment cost allocations	$600,000	$2,400,000		$8,756,000	$12,452,000	$24,208,000
5 Support work supplied by AS (budgeted head count)	—	25%		40%	35%	100%
6 Support work supplied by IS (budgeted computer time)	10%	—		30%	60%	100%

Required

1. Allocate the two support departments' costs to the two operating departments using the following methods:
   a. Direct method
   b. Step-down method (allocate AS first)
   c. Step-down method (allocate IS first)
2. Compare and explain differences in the support-department costs allocated to each operating department.
3. What approaches might be used to decide the sequence in which to allocate support departments when using the step-down method?

15-20 Support-department cost allocation, reciprocal method (continuation of 15-19). Refer to the data given in Exercise 15-19.

Required

1. Allocate the two support departments' costs to the two operating departments using the reciprocal method. Use (a) linear equations and (b) repeated iterations.
2. Compare and explain differences in requirement 1 with those in requirement 1 of Exercise 15-19. Which method do you prefer? Why?

15-21 Direct and step-down allocation. E-books, an online book retailer, has two operating departments—corporate sales and consumer sales—and two support departments—human resources and information systems. Each sales department conducts merchandising and marketing operations independently. E-books uses number of employees to allocate human resources costs and processing time to allocate information systems costs. The following data are available for September 2012:

A	B	C	D	E	F
1	SUPPORT DEPARTMENTS			OPERATING DEPARTMENTS	
2	Human Resources	Information Systems		Corporate Sales	Consumer Sales
3 Budgeted costs incurred before any					
4 interdepartment cost allocations	$72,700	$234,400		$998,270	$489,860
5 Support work supplied by human resources department					
6 Budgeted number of employees	—	21		42	28
7 Support work supplied by information systems department					
8 Budgeted processing time (in minutes)	320	—		1,920	1,600

Required

1. Allocate the support departments' costs to the operating departments using the direct method.
2. Rank the support departments based on the percentage of their services provided to other support departments. Use this ranking to allocate the support departments' costs to the operating departments based on the step-down method.
3. How could you have ranked the support departments differently?

15-22 Reciprocal cost allocation (continuation of 15-21). Consider E-books again. The controller of E-books reads a widely used textbook that states that "the reciprocal method is conceptually the most defensible." He seeks your assistance.

Required

1. Describe the key features of the reciprocal method.
2. Allocate the support departments' costs (human resources and information systems) to the two operating departments using the reciprocal method.
3. In the case presented in this exercise, which method (direct, step-down, or reciprocal) would you recommend? Why?

15-23 Allocation of common costs. Ben and Gary are students at Berkeley College. They share an apartment that is owned by Gary. Gary is considering subscribing to an Internet provider that has the following packages available:

Package	Per Month
A. Internet access	$60
B. Phone services	15
C. Internet access + phone services	65

Ben spends most of his time on the Internet ("everything can be found online now"). Gary prefers to spend his time talking on the phone rather than using the Internet ("going online is a waste of time"). They agree that the purchase of the $65 total package is a "win–win" situation.

Required

1. Allocate the $65 between Ben and Gary using (a) the stand-alone cost-allocation method, (b) the incremental cost-allocation method, and (c) the Shapley value method.
2. Which method would you recommend they use and why?

15-24 Allocation of common costs. Sunny Gunn, a self-employed consultant near Sacramento, received an invitation to visit a prospective client in Baltimore. A few days later, she received an invitation to make a presentation to a prospective client in Chicago. She decided to combine her visits, traveling from Sacramento to Baltimore, Baltimore to Chicago, and Chicago to Sacramento.

Gunn received offers for her consulting services from both companies. Upon her return, she decided to accept the engagement in Chicago. She is puzzled over how to allocate her travel costs between the two clients. She has collected the following data for regular round-trip fares with no stopovers:

Sacramento to Baltimore	$1,200
Sacramento to Chicago	$ 800

Gunn paid $1,600 for her three-leg flight (Sacramento–Baltimore, Baltimore–Chicago, Chicago–Sacramento). In addition, she paid $40 each way for limousines from her home to Sacramento Airport and back when she returned.

Required

1. How should Gunn allocate the $1,600 airfare between the clients in Baltimore and Chicago using (a) the stand-alone cost-allocation method, (b) the incremental cost-allocation method, and (c) the Shapley value method?
2. Which method would you recommend Gunn use and why?
3. How should Gunn allocate the $80 limousine charges between the clients in Baltimore and Chicago?

15-25 Revenue allocation, bundled products. Yves Parfum Company blends and sells designer fragrances. It has a Men's Fragrances Division and a Women's Fragrances Division, each with different sales strategies, distribution channels, and product offerings. Yves is now considering the sale of a bundled product consisting of a men's cologne and a women's perfume. For the most recent year, Yves reported the following:

	A	B
1	**Product**	**Retail Price**
2	Monaco (men's cologne)	$ 48
3	Innocence (women's perfume)	112
4	L'Amour (Monaco + Innocence)	130

Required

1. Allocate revenue from the sale of each unit of L'Amour to Monaco and Innocence using the following:
   a. The stand-alone revenue-allocation method based on selling price of each product
   b. The incremental revenue-allocation method, with Monaco ranked as the primary product
   c. The incremental revenue-allocation method, with Innocence ranked as the primary product
   d. The Shapley value method, assuming equal unit sales of Monaco and Innocence
2. Of the four methods in requirement 1, which one would you recommend for allocating L'Amour's revenues to Monaco and Innocence? Explain.

15-26 Allocation of common costs. Jim Dandy Auto Sales uses all types of media to advertise its products (television, radio, newspaper, etc.). At the end of 2011, the company president, Jim Dandridge, decided that all advertising costs would be incurred by corporate headquarters and allocated to each of the company's three sales locations based on number of vehicles sold. Jim was confident that his corporate purchasing manager could negotiate better advertising contracts on a corporate-wide basis than each of the sales managers could on their own. Dandridge budgeted total advertising cost for 2012 to be $1.8 million. He introduced the new plan to his sales managers just before the New Year.

The manager of the east sales location, Tony Snider, was not happy. He complained that the new allocation method was unfair and would increase his advertising costs significantly over the prior year. The east location sold high volumes of low-priced used cars and most of the corporate advertising budget was related to new car sales.

Following Tony's complaint, Jim decided to take another hard look at what each of the divisions were paying for advertising before the new allocation plan. The results were as follows:

Sales Location	Actual Number of Cars Sold in 2011	Actual Advertising Cost Incurred in 2011
East	3,150	$ 324,000
West	1,080	432,000
North	2,250	648,000
South	2,520	756,000
	9,000	$2,160,000

Required

1. Using 2011 data as the cost bases, show the amount of the 2012 advertising cost ($1,800,000) that would be allocated to each of the divisions under the following criteria:
   a. Dandridge's allocation method based on number of cars sold
   b. The stand-alone method
   c. The incremental-allocation method, with divisions ranked on the basis of dollars spent on advertising in 2011
2. Which method do you think is most equitable to the divisional sales managers? What other options might President Jim Dandridge have for allocating the advertising costs?

Problems

MyAccountingLab

15-27 Single-rate, dual-rate, and practical capacity allocation. Perfection Department Store has a new promotional program that offers a free gift-wrapping service for its customers. Perfection's customer-service department has practical capacity to wrap 7,000 gifts at a budgeted fixed cost of $6,650 each month. The budgeted variable cost to gift wrap an item is $0.40. Although the service is free to customers, a gift-wrapping service cost allocation is made to the department where the item was purchased. The customer-service department reported the following for the most recent month:

	A	B	C	D
1	Department	Actual Number of Gifts Wrapped	Budgeted Number of Gifts to Be Wrapped	Practical Capacity Available for Gift-Wrapping
2	Women's face wash	2,020	2,470	2,640
3	Men's face wash	730	825	945
4	Fragrances	1,560	1,805	1,970
5	Body wash	545	430	650
6	Hair products	1,495	1,120	795
7	Total	6,350	6,650	7,000

Required

1. Using the single-rate method, allocate gift-wrapping costs to different departments in these three ways.
   a. Calculate the budgeted rate based on the budgeted number of gifts to be wrapped and allocate costs based on the budgeted use (of gift-wrapping services).
   b. Calculate the budgeted rate based on the budgeted number of gifts to be wrapped and allocate costs based on actual usage.
   c. Calculate the budgeted rate based on the practical gift-wrapping capacity available and allocate costs based on actual usage.

2. Using the dual-rate method, compute the amount allocated to each department when (a) the fixed-cost rate is calculated using budgeted costs and the practical gift-wrapping capacity, (b) fixed costs are allocated based on budgeted usage of gift-wrapping services, and (c) variable costs are allocated using the budgeted variable-cost rate and actual usage.

3. Comment on your results in requirements 1 and 2. Discuss the advantages of the dual-rate method.

15-28 Revenue allocation. Lee Shu-yu Inc. produces and sells DVDs to business people and students who are planning extended stays in China. It has been very successful with two DVDs: Beginning Mandarin and Conversational Mandarin. It is introducing a third DVD, Reading Chinese Characters. It has decided to market its new DVD in two different packages grouping the Reading Chinese Characters DVD with each of the other two language DVDs. Information about the separate DVDs and the packages follow.

DVD	Selling Price
Beginning Mandarin (BegM)	$ 50
Conversational Mandarin (ConM)	$ 90
Reading Chinese Characters (RCC)	$ 30
BegM + RCC	$ 60
ConM + RCC	$100

Required

1. Using the selling prices, allocate revenues from the BegM + RCC package to each DVD in that package using **(a)** the stand-alone method; **(b)** the incremental method, in either order; and **(c)** the Shapley value method.

2. Using the selling prices, allocate revenues from the ConM + RCC package to each DVD in that package using **(a)** the stand-alone method; **(b)** the incremental method, in either order; and **(c)** the Shapley value method.

3. Which method is most appropriate for allocating revenues among the DVDs? Why?

15-29 Fixed cost allocation. State University completed construction of its newest administrative building at the end of 2011. The University's first employees moved into the building on January 1, 2012. The building consists of office space, common meeting rooms (including a conference center), a cafeteria and even a workout room for its exercise enthusiasts. The total 2012 building space of 125,000 square feet was utilized as follows:

Usage of Space	% of Total Building Space
Office space (occupied)	52%
Vacant office space	8%
Common meeting space	25%
Workout room	5%
Cafeteria	10%

The new building cost the university $30 million and was depreciated using the straight-line method over 20 years. At the end of 2012 three departments occupied the building: executive offices of the president, accounting, and human resources. Each department's usage of its assigned space was as follows:

Department	Actual Office Space Used (sq. ft.)	Planned Office Space Used (sq. ft.)	Practical Capacity Office Space (sq. ft.)
Executive	16,250	12,400	18,000
Accounting	26,000	26,040	33,000
Human resources	22,750	23,560	24,000

Required

1. How much of the total building cost will be allocated in 2012 to each of the departments, if allocated on the basis of the following?
   a. Actual usage
   b. Planned usage
   c. Practical capacity

2. Assume that State University allocates the total annual building cost in the following manner:
   a. All vacant office space is absorbed by the university and is not allocated to the departments.
   b. All occupied office space costs are allocated on the basis of actual square footage used.
   c. All common costs are allocated on the basis of a department's practical capacity.
   Calculate the cost allocated to each department in 2012 under this plan. Do you think the allocation method used here is appropriate? Explain.

15-30 Allocating costs of support departments; step-down and direct methods. The Central Valley Company has prepared department overhead budgets for budgeted-volume levels before allocations as follows:

Support departments:		
Building and grounds	$10,000	
Personnel	1,000	
General plant administration	26,090	
Cafeteria: operating loss	1,640	
Storeroom	2,670	$ 41,400
Operating departments:		
Machining	$34,700	
Assembly	48,900	83,600
Total for support and operating departments		$125,000

Management has decided that the most appropriate inventory costs are achieved by using individual-department overhead rates. These rates are developed after support-department costs are allocated to operating departments.

Bases for allocation are to be selected from the following:

Department	Direct Manufacturing Labor-Hours	Number of Employees	Square Feet of Floor Space Occupied	Manufacturing Labor-Hours	Number of Requisitions
Building and grounds	0	0	0	0	0
Personnel[a]	0	0	2,000	0	0
General plant administration	0	35	7,000	0	0
Cafeteria: operating loss	0	10	4,000	1,000	0
Storeroom	0	5	7,000	1,000	0
Machining	5,000	50	30,000	8,000	2,000
Assembly	15,000	100	50,000	17,000	1,000
Total	20,000	200	100,000	27,000	3,000

[a]Basis used is number of employees.

Required

1. Using the step-down method, allocate support-department costs. Develop overhead rates per direct manufacturing labor-hour for machining and assembly. Allocate the costs of the support departments in the order given in this problem. Use the allocation base for each support department you think is most appropriate.
2. Using the direct method, rework requirement 1.
3. Based on the following information about two jobs, determine the total overhead costs for each job by using rates developed in (a) requirement 1 and (b) requirement 2.

	Direct Manufacturing Labor-Hours	
	Machining	Assembly
Job 88	18	2
Job 89	3	17

4. The company evaluates the performance of the operating department managers on the basis of how well they managed their total costs, including allocated costs. As the manager of the machining department, which allocation method would you prefer from the results obtained in requirements 1 and 2? Explain.

15-31 Support-department cost allocations; single-department cost pools; direct, step-down, and reciprocal methods. The Manes Company has two products. Product 1 is manufactured entirely in department X. Product 2 is manufactured entirely in department Y. To produce these two products, the Manes Company has two support departments: A (a materials-handling department) and B (a power-generating department).

An analysis of the work done by departments A and B in a typical period follows:

	Used By			
Supplied By	A	B	X	Y
A	—	100	250	150
B	500	—	100	400

The work done in department A is measured by the direct labor-hours of materials-handling time. The work done in department B is measured by the kilowatt-hours of power. The budgeted costs of the support departments for the coming year are as follows:

	Department A (Materials Handling)	Department B (Power Generation)
Variable indirect labor and indirect materials costs	$ 70,000	$10,000
Supervision	10,000	10,000
Depreciation	20,000	20,000
	$100,000	$40,000
	+Power costs	+Materials-handling costs

The budgeted costs of the operating departments for the coming year are $1,500,000 for department X and $800,000 for department Y.

Supervision costs are salary costs. Depreciation in department B is the straight-line depreciation of power-generation equipment in its 19th year of an estimated 25-year useful life; it is old, but well-maintained, equipment.

Required

1. What are the allocations of costs of support departments A and B to operating departments X and Y using (a) the direct method, (b) the step-down method (allocate department A first), (c) the step-down method (allocate department B first), and (d) the reciprocal method?
2. An outside company has offered to supply all the power needed by the Manes Company and to provide all the services of the present power department. The cost of this service will be $40 per kilowatt-hour of power. Should Manes accept? Explain.

15-32 Common costs. Wright Inc. and Brown Inc. are two small clothing companies that are considering leasing a dyeing machine together. The companies estimated that in order to meet production, Wright needs the machine for 800 hours and Brown needs it for 200 hours. If each company rents the machine on its own, the fee will be $50 per hour of usage. If they rent the machine together, the fee will decrease to $42 per hour of usage.

Required

1. Calculate Wright's and Brown's respective share of fees under the stand-alone cost-allocation method.
2. Calculate Wright's and Brown's respective share of fees using the incremental cost-allocation method. Assume Wright to be the primary party.
3. Calculate Wright's and Brown's respective share of fees using the Shapley value method.
4. Which method would you recommend Wright and Brown use to share the fees?

15-33 Stand-alone revenue allocation. MaxSystems, Inc., sells computer hardware to end consumers. Its most popular model, the CX30 is sold as a "bundle," which includes three hardware products: a personal computer (PC) tower, a 23-inch monitor, and a color laser printer. Each of these products is made in a separate manufacturing division of MaxSystems and can be purchased individually, as well as in a bundle. The individual selling prices and per unit costs are as follows:

Computer Component	Individual Selling Price per Unit	Cost per Unit
PC tower	$ 840	$300
Monitor	$ 280	$180
Color laser printer	$ 480	$270
Computer bundle purchase price	$1,200	

Required

1. Allocate the revenue from the computer bundle purchase to each of the hardware products using the stand-alone method based on the individual selling price per unit.
2. Allocate the revenue from the computer bundle purchase to each of the hardware products using the stand-alone method based on cost per unit.
3. Allocate the revenue from the computer bundle purchase to each of the hardware products using the stand-alone method based on physical units (that is, the number of individual units of product sold per bundle).
4. Which basis of allocation makes the most sense in this situation? Explain your answer.

15-34 Support-department cost allocations; single-department cost pools; direct, step-down, and reciprocal methods. Spirit Training, Inc., manufactures athletic shoes and athletic clothing for both amateur and professional athletes. The company has two product lines (clothing and shoes), which are produced in separate manufacturing facilities; however, both manufacturing facilities share the same support services for information technology and human resources. The following shows total costs for each manufacturing facility and for each support department.

	Variable Costs	Fixed Costs	Total Costs by Department (in thousands)
Information technology (IT)	$ 500	$ 1,500	$ 2,000
Human resources (HR)	$ 100	$ 900	$ 1,000
Clothing	$3,000	$ 7,000	$10,000
Shoes	$2,500	$ 5,500	$ 8,000
Total costs	$7,100	$16,900	$24,000

The total costs of the support departments (IT and HR) are allocated to the production departments (clothing and shoes) using a single rate based on the following:

Information technology:	Number of IT labor hours worked by department
Human resources:	Number of employees supported by department

Data on the bases, by department, are given as follows:

Department	IT Hours Used	Number of Employees
Clothing	5,000	120
Shoes	3,000	40
Information technology	-	40
Human resources	2,000	-

1. What are the total costs of the production departments (clothing and shoes) **after** the support department costs of information technology and human resources have been allocated using (a) the direct method, (b) the step-down method (allocate information technology first), (c) the step-down method (allocate human resources first), and (d) the reciprocal method?

2. Assume that all of the work of the IT department could be outsourced to an independent company for $97.50 per hour. If Spirit Training no longer operated its own IT department, 30% of the fixed costs of the IT department could be eliminated. Should Spirit outsource its IT services?

Collaborative Learning Problem

15-35 Revenue allocation, bundled products. Exclusive Resorts (ER) operates a five-star hotel with a championship golf course. ER has a decentralized management structure, with three divisions:

- Lodging (rooms, conference facilities)
- Food (restaurants and in-room service)
- Recreation (golf course, tennis courts, swimming pool, etc.)

Starting next month, ER will offer a two-day, two-person "getaway package" for $1,000. This deal includes the following:

	As Priced Separately
Two nights' stay for two in an ocean-view room	$ 800 ($400 per night)
Two rounds of golf (can be used by either guest)	$ 375 ($187.50 per round)
Candlelight dinner for two at ER's finest restaurant	$ 200 ($100 per person)
Total package value	$1,375

Jenny Lee, president of the recreation division, recently asked the CEO of ER how her division would share in the $1,000 revenue from the getaway package. The golf course was operating at 100% capacity. Currently, anyone booking the package was guaranteed access to the golf course. Lee noted that every "getaway" booking would displace $375 of other golf bookings not related to the package. She emphasized that the high demand reflected the devotion of her team to keeping the golf course rated one of the "Best 10 Courses in the World" by *Golf Monthly*. As an aside, she also noted that the lodging and food divisions had to turn away customers during only "peak-season events such as the New Year's period."

1. Using selling prices, allocate the $1,000 getaway-package revenue to the three divisions using:
   a. The stand-alone revenue-allocation method
   b. The incremental revenue-allocation method (with recreation first, then lodging, and then food)
2. What are the pros and cons of the two methods in requirement 1?
3. Because the recreation division is able to book the golf course at 100% capacity, the company CEO has decided to revise the getaway package to only include the lodging and food offerings shown previously. The new package will sell for $900. Allocate the revenue to the lodging and food divisions using the following:
   a. The Shapley value method.
   b. The weighted Shapley value method, assuming that lodging is three times as likely to sell as the food.

Index

Page references followed by "f" indicate illustrated figures or photographs; followed by "t" indicates a table.